GENERAL GEORGE
WASHINGTON

GENERAL GEORGE
WASHINGTON

A MILITARY LIFE

Edward G. Lengel

 RANDOM HOUSE · NEW YORK

Copyright © 2005 by Edward Lengel
Maps copyright © 2005 by Rick Britton

Published in the United States by Random House, an imprint of the Random
House Publishing Group, a division of Random House, Inc., New York.

RANDOM HOUSE and colophon are registered trademarks of Random House, Inc.

ISBN 1-4000-6081-8

Printed in the United States of America on acid-free paper

www.atrandom.com

2 4 6 8 9 7 5 3 1

First Edition

Text design by Simon M. Sullivan

To my parents,
Alan and Shelbia Lengel

PROLOGUE

The good opinion of honest men, friends to freedom and well-wishers to mankind, where ever they may happen to be born or reside, is the only kind of reputation a wise man would ever desire.
—GEORGE WASHINGTON, JUNE 20, 1788

ON DECEMBER 18, 1799, a crowd assembled at Mount Vernon to attend the funeral of George Washington. It was a soldier's funeral. Leading the procession across the front lawn were splendidly uniformed cavalry and infantry of the Alexandria Militia. Behind them a band of musicians played a dirge. Next came four clergymen and two black-clad grooms leading Washington's horse, saddled with pistols in holsters. The body, encased in a mahogany coffin borne by four militia lieutenants and accompanied by six pallbearers, followed its former mount. Family, friends, the local Freemasons, farm overseers, and the public came last. As they walked, a schooner on the Potomac fired its guns every minute. At the vault, a clergyman gave a short speech and the Freemasons performed their rites. The infantry then fired three volleys of musketry, eleven artillery pieces discharged, and Washington, commander-in-chief of the United States Army, was laid to rest.

On the following day, President John Adams announced to the United States Army "the death of its beloved Chief, General GEORGE WASHINGTON. Sharing in the grief, which every heart must feel for so heavy and afflicting a public loss, and desirous to express his high sense of the vast debt of gratitude, which is due to the virtues, talents and ever memorable services of the illustrious deceased, he directs that funeral honors be paid to him at all the military stations, and that the officers of the army and of the several corps of volunteers wear crape on their left arm by way of mourning for six months." On the 20th, "desirous that the Navy and Marines should express, in common with every other description of American citizens, the high sense which all feel of the loss our country has sustained in the death of this good and great man," Adams decreed "that the vessels of the Navy, in our own, and foreign ports, be put in mourning for one week, by wearing their colours half-mast high." The president, Congress, and practically everybody else in the country also donned black.

Congress held its own funeral procession on the day after Christmas. Major General Henry Lee—a Revolutionary War hero and Washington's military protégé—delivered the eulogy in Philadelphia's German Lutheran church before President Adams and his wife and 4,000 spectators. "Where," he asked his listeners, "shall I begin in opening to your view a character throughout sublime? Shall I speak of his warlike achievements, all springing from obedience to his country's will—all directed to his country's good?" Lee transported them first "to the banks of the Monongahela" in 1755, "to see your youthful Washington supporting, in the dismal hour of Indian victory, the ill-fated Braddock, and saving, by his judgment and by his valor, the remains of a defeated army, pressed by the conquering savage foe." Then he swept them "to the high grounds of Boston" in 1775, "where, to an undisciplined, coura-geous, and virtuous yeomanry, [Washington's] presence gave the stability of system, and infused the invincibility of love of country." The oratorical jour-ney continued through 1776, past "the painful scenes of Long Island, [New] York Island, and New Jersey" to "the precarious fields of Trenton, where deep glooms, unnerving every arm, reigned triumphant through our thinned, worn down, unaided ranks." There "Washington, self-collected, viewed the tre-mendous scene; his country called. Unappalled by surrounding dangers, he passed to the hostile shore; he fought—he conquered!"

Lee took his audience to "the lawns of Princeton," "the vales of Brandy-wine, the fields of Germantown," and "the plains of Monmouth," building up a heroic image of Washington the soldier. "Everywhere present, wants of every kind obstructing, numerous and valiant armies encountering, himself a host, he assuaged our sufferings, limited our privations, and upheld our tot-tering republic." But his finest laurels had not been won in battle. "To the horrid din of war sweet peace succeeded; and our virtuous chief, mindful only of the public good, in a moment tempting personal aggrandizement, hushed the discontents of growing sedition, and, surrendering his power into the hands from which he had received it, converted his sword into a ploughshare, teaching an admiring world that, to be truly great, you must be truly good." As president, Washington had "laid the foundations of our na-tional policy in the unerring, immutable principles of morality, based on reli-gion; exemplifying the pre-eminence of free government by all the attributes which win the affections of its citizens or command the respect of the world." As soldier, as president, and in "the humble walks of private life," Washington had been "First in war, first in peace, and first in the hearts of his countrymen."

Eulogists elsewhere also paid tribute to Washington's virtues in peace as well as war. But in public demonstrations of grief all around the new nation, especially in ceremonial funeral processions, the military elements were foremost. As at Mount Vernon, mourners were led by formations of infantry, cavalry, and artillery in full uniform. Soldiers carried their muskets reversed and pointed to the ground, marching to "the mournful cadence of the muffled drums and the dirges played by their company musicians." Army veterans, particularly members of the Society of the Cincinnati that Washington had helped to found, typically served as pallbearers for an empty coffin. And as at Mount Vernon, civilians—including Freemasons, clergy, civil officials, and private citizens—brought up the rear. Graveside services usually were accompanied by salutes of cannon and musketry, and followed by the erection of martial monuments before which sentries were placed.

The mourning ceremonies were militaristic partly because Washington died while serving as commander-in-chief of the army during an undeclared war with France. But more than anything else they marked the passing of the nation's foremost soldier, a man who had spent much of his life at war and won American independence on the battlefield. In retrospect, it was easy for Americans at the beginning of the nineteenth century to imagine that their nation's founder had been born not a farmer, but a warrior. As a young man, his yearning for battle had led him to the frontier, where his exploits—or mishaps—as a provincial lieutenant colonel touched off the French and Indian War in 1754. His first experience of battle left him feeling that there was "something charming" in the sound of the bullets' whine. The next year he tasted defeat with a British army on the banks of the Monongahela River in western Pennsylvania. Returning to Virginia, he built America's first regular military force, the Virginia Regiment, and led it back to the frontier for a victorious campaign to the Ohio River in 1758. As the French and Indian War ended, Washington returned home to Virginia and a political career in the House of Burgesses, only to reenter military life in 1775 as commander-in-chief of the Continental Army. Then, during the nine years of the Revolutionary War, he led the army through battle and—what was often worse—the privations of camp, to victory.

Wherever his true greatness actually lay, it was to his career as a soldier that people usually turned to remember Washington for the first century and a half after his death. Washington's early biographers focused almost exclusively on his military exploits.

Parson Mason Locke Weems started the trend with the publication in 1800 of the first edition of his *Life and Memorable Actions of George Washington*. An expert storyteller, Weems did not just recount the cherry tree myth but expounded on Washington's wartime accomplishments and imagined Napoleon sighing at his military brilliance. He also popularized earlier comparisons of Washington to Cincinnatus, a legendary Roman general who had saved his country and then renounced power to become a simple citizen. Supreme Court Justice John Marshall's five-volume *The Life of George Washington* (1804–7), portrayed Washington as a brilliant tactician responsible for "a series of judicious measures adapted to circumstances, which probably saved his country." And another prominent nineteenth-century biographer, the writer Washington Irving, placed General George Washington firmly in the heroic mold.

Washington's military life continued to fascinate as America entered the twentieth century. General Henry B. Carrington's *Washington the Soldier* (1898–99) and Thomas G. Frothingham's *Washington: Commander in Chief* (1930) employed the same heroic but one-dimensional images that had prevailed in the nineteenth century: Washington standing proudly in the prow of a longboat, crossing the Delaware; Washington on horseback, leading his troops into battle; Washington kneeling in the snow at Valley Forge, praying for deliverance; Washington as Fabius, the crafty Roman general who had worn down Hannibal as he wore down the British, by avoiding battle until the moment was right.

Yet now there were also critics. Writing in 1930, Rupert Hughes decried the idea of Washington as a kind of "bland miracle-worker," claiming instead that as a soldier he was "infinitely human, incessantly guessing wrong, making innumerable false prophecies, countless mistakes, losing his temper, regaining it, being coerced into defeats and dragged away from them, driven into victories in spite of himself and driving others to heights they could not otherwise have attained." Other writers picked up on Hughes's lead and dismantled a hundred years of legend to uncover a man who was shockingly temperamental, stubborn, impatient, and even foolish. In so doing they reduced Washington from a hero to an "important scamp."

Since World War II, seeking to get away from decades of fixation on Washington the soldier, his biographers have spent most of their time studying his political and personal life. Seeking balance, they have acknowledged his failings as a general but found redemption in his moral character and deference to civil authority. In Douglas Southall Freeman's Pulitzer Prize–winning biography (published in seven volumes, from 1948 to 1957), Washington appears as a fallible but nonetheless heroic leader with several "cardinal characteristics" that had helped him to win the war despite losing most of its battles: love of country, combativeness, ambition, courage, willpower, caution, sound judgment, patience, diligence, justice, and respect for civil authority. James Thomas Flexner's colorful *George Washington in the American Revolution* (1968) paints the commander-in-chief as an "unreconstructed civilian" in uniform who had "considered force secondary in winning the war to gentleness, justice, forbearance." Don Higginbotham finds virtue in Washington the military administrator, but argues that his most important role was as a national linchpin, a mediator between civilians and the military whose strategic vision of a united America gave scope and meaning to the new country.

Other recent biographers—John Alden, Richard Brookhiser, Harrison Clark, John Ferling, Willard Sterne Randall, Richard Norton Smith, and Joe Ellis, to name a few—have likewise sought the broader view, examining Washington in the context of his life as a planter, politician, and president of the United States. And they are right to do so, for Washington was a multidimensional man. Yet although it is true, as Gordon Wood has argued, that "military glory was *not* the source"—at least not the *only* source—of his greatness, that does not justify the recent loss of interest in his life *as a soldier.* Not since Carrington in 1899 has there appeared a military life of George Washington that examines his wartime experiences from the 1750s to the 1790s and evaluates his qualities and defects as a strategist, tactician, administrator, and leader of men. Some of his most important battles have yet to be studied in depth.

There is less excuse for the omission now than ever before. Washington considered one of his most important legacies to the United States to be his public and personal papers, which he assiduously collected, copied, and preserved. After his death about half of these papers, including letters to as well as from Washington, were scattered across the globe in archives and private collections, while the rest ended up in public institutions like the Library of Congress and National Archives in Washington, D.C. No attempt was made to track down the papers and transcribe them into a single printed edition until the 1960s, when the Papers of George Washington documentary editing project in Charlottesville, Virginia, was founded. These efforts have shown that a staggering two-thirds of Washington's total correspondence, tens of thousands of documents, concern military affairs. These papers, many of which are as yet unstudied and unpublished, form the foundation of this book.

The story of Washington the soldier is one of the most fascinating in American history. It begins with a young man venting his urge for military distinction on the American frontier, and ends with that man, now an old soldier, betraying the trust of a loyal friend and comrade from his writing desk at Mount Vernon. Between those episodes appears a man of many contradictions: one who, though brave, once fled in fear of his life; who went to war out of idealism and made victory more difficult with his prejudice; who showed remarkable perseverance and patience but rushed impetuously into battle; who failed to win the respect of his soldiers in battle but won it in camp; who conquered and blundered, was vindictive and fair, kind and cruel. Taking the measure of the soldier is as difficult as understanding the man. Was he, as some have said, a better strategist than a tactician? Was he an enlisted man's general? Did his example keep the soldiers fighting through snow and starvation, or did they endure in spite of him? Were his losses his own fault, or was he betrayed by disloyal and incompetent subordinates? Were his victories won through skill or luck? Was he a dullard, as some have claimed, or James Thomas Flexner's "indispensable man"?

The following pages reveal Washington as the archetypal *American* soldier—the amateur citizen-soldier who has struggled to learn war on the job in each one of the nation's conflicts. Washington was typical in many of the attitudes, prejudices, qualities, and flaws that he shared with his countrymen. Yet he also was unique; not so much because he excelled in any particular area—there were better strategists, tacticians, administrators, and politicians among his contemporaries—but because he possessed all of the qualities his country required, and in perfect combination. To survive its difficult birth, America did not need just a courageous soldier, a savvy politician, a hard-working manager, a charismatic leader, a principled believer in democracy, or an intelligent general; it needed all of these things, *and in one man.* George Washington was that man. No one else could have taken his place.

ACKNOWLEDGMENTS

ONCE UPON A TIME, many historians thought there was nothing new to be learned about George Washington. The Papers of George Washington documentary editing project proved them wrong. Established at the University of Virginia in 1969 by the late Donald Jackson, the project began with a comprehensive search for Washington documents in public and private repositories all over the world. Since then it has amassed a collection of photographic copies of some 135,000 documents, including letters written to and from Washington; his diaries, accounts, school exercises, and miscellaneous personal papers; and reports, returns, and other administrative materials relating to his careers in the military and in politics. The search continues, and the project turns up new documents almost monthly. At the time of writing, the project has transcribed, annotated, and published fifty-two volumes of Washington's papers, with another forty yet to go.

Since 1996 it has been my privilege to work at the Papers of George Washington, first as a graduate student and now as an associate editor. The privilege comes not just from access to the project's unparalleled collection of documents and research materials, but also from working with such a group of fine scholars and good people. My list of debts at the project, both intellectual and personal, includes Ted Crackel, Frank E. Grizzard, Jr., David R. Hoth, Beverly H. Runge, Christine Sternberg Patrick, Philander D. Chase, Beverly S. Kirsch, James E. Guba, Daniel B. Smith, and Adam Jortner. I am particularly grateful to W. W. Abbot, editor emeritus, who continues to inspire as a mentor, scholar, and friend; and to J.C.A. Stagg, editor in chief of the Papers of James Madison, for his help and encouragement as I struggled to find time to finish writing this book. Thanks must also go to the Papers of George Washington project's primary sources of financial support, the National Endowment for the Humanities, the National Historical Publications and Records Commission, the Mount Vernon Ladies' Association, and the University of Virginia.

Several scholars read drafts of my book at various stages in its writing, and while none of them are responsible for its shortcomings, all of them saved me from embarrassing gaffes and helped make the book better than it was. My heartfelt thanks go to Peter Henriques, emeritus professor at George Mason University; Don Higginbotham of the University of North Carolina at Chapel Hill; Frank E. Grizzard, Jr., of the Papers of George Washington; and Guy Chet of the University of North Texas. I also appreciate the encouragement and advice on research, writing, and interpretation given by John Whiteclay Chambers II of Rutgers University, John P. Resch of the University of New Hampshire at Manchester, Gary Wheeler Stone of Monmouth Battlefield State Park, David R. Hoth of the Papers of George Washington, Patricia Brady, Mike Hill, and Ed Crews; and the folks at the Society for Military History and the Association for Documentary Editing.

I cannot adequately express my gratitude to Rick Britton, cartographer and creator of the wonderful series of maps that grace this volume. His artistry, skill, and patience have been on constant display as he balanced contradictory sources, complicated maneuvers, and squiggly colonial road systems, to make visual sense out of my sometimes opaque summaries of Washington's battles. Rick would have made a fine addition to General George Washington's military staff!

Writing well is a skill not easily acquired, particularly for one who has spent years writing only for academics. I was fortunate to polish my rough edges under the tutelage of the fine team of editors at Random House, who rapped my knuckles when I wrote astray and patiently worked to clarify my prose. I would like to offer particular thanks to my editor Will Murphy, and to Robert Loomis, Ed Cohen, Benjamin Dreyer, Dennis Ambrose, and Fleetwood Robbins. Thanks also to my indefatigable agent Peter Matson, and to Patricia Hass, who seized on the idea of a military life of George Washington and helped the book to get off the ground.

My deepest gratitude is reserved for my family: my father, Alan, who always believed I would be a writer; my mother, Shelbia, who read and edited every word of the manuscript, making it much better; my wife, Laima, who encouraged me to write and wouldn't let me give up even when I became absolutely convinced of my incompetence; my brother, Eric, who bragged about me to his friends; my brother-in-law, Julius, who took that nifty snapshot of me in Gdansk; my son Mike, who couldn't wait to show this book to his class; my daughter, Laura, and the girls on her soccer team, who welcomed me as their coach and kept me distracted from the foibles of the grown-up world; and my son Tomas, who by pushing all my buttons helped to keep me both awake and alive.

CONTENTS

LIST OF MAPS

BIOGRAPHIES

JOHN ADAMS (1753–1826)   Massachusetts delegate to the Second Continental Congress who formally introduced Washington to that assembly as a potential commander-in-chief in June 1775. His opinion of Washington's military acumen subsequently declined somewhat, although he was never a vehement critic. Adams later served as Washington's vice-president (1789–97); as president during the Quasi-War with France (1798–99) he nominated Washington commander-in-chief of the army and then quarreled with him over the ranking of the army's major generals.

WILLIAM ALEXANDER (1726–1783)   New Jersey native known as Lord Stirling because of his claim to an English title. A veteran of the French and Indian War and an acquaintance of Washington, Alexander was appointed colonel of the First New Jersey Regiment in November 1775. He rose to the rank of brigadier general in March 1776 and became a major general in February 1777. Captured at the Battle of Long Island in August 1776, he returned to service in time to see action at Brandywine (September 1777), Germantown (October 1777), and Monmouth (June 1778). Stubborn and courageous, he was one of Washington's better officers.

BENEDICT ARNOLD (1741–1801)   A well-educated, handsome, wealthy, and mercurial businessman from New Haven, Connecticut, Arnold established his military reputation by capturing the British garrison at Ticonderoga, New York, together with Ethan Allen in May 1775. Washington made his acquaintance a few months later and sent Arnold, a newly commissioned colonel, on an expedition to Canada that autumn. That expedition ended in disaster, but Washington continued to hold him in high regard and finally convinced Congress to commission Arnold a major general in the spring of 1777. Arnold subsequently played a major role in the victory at Saratoga in October 1777, an action for which Horatio Gates received all the public credit. This and other perceived slights finally drove Arnold into a treasonous correspondence with the British that ended in a failed attempt to betray the American garrison at West Point in September 1780. Arnold was subsequently commissioned a brigadier general in the British army and, an unquestionably talented commander, led raids on Connecticut and Virginia. He left Yorktown before its capitulation in October 1781—thus avoiding capture and certain execution—and moved to England, where he died in bitter obscurity. Washington never forgave Arnold's perfidy, which he considered not only a betrayal of the nation but a personal affront from a man he had considered his friend.

EDWARD BRADDOCK (c.1695–1755)   Longtime British army veteran who came to America in February 1755 as a major general in command of an expeditionary army ordered to destroy French-built Fort Duquesne at what is now Pittsburgh, Pennsylvania. Washington served as Braddock's aide-de-camp, and watched as the arrogant and ill-tempered general alienated the Americans on whom he depended for supply before blundering with his army into a French and Indian ambush on the Monongahela River in July. Braddock was killed in the battle, but Washington survived and led the remnants of the army back to Fort Cumberland.

THOMAS CONWAY (1733–1795)   Irish native who joined the French army in 1747 and served in Europe for twenty-five years before becoming a colonel in 1772. In April 1777 he sailed to America, where he won appointment as a brigadier general, serving with Washington at Brandywine (September 1777) and Germantown (October 1777). Impressed by the boastful Conway's supposed abilities, Congress appointed him inspector general with the rank of major general in December 1777, but he fell afoul of Washington after criticizing him in a letter to Major General Horatio Gates. Washington subsequently refused to work with Conway, who resigned his commission in April 1778 and later returned to France.

CHARLES CORNWALLIS (1738–1805)   Cornwallis had already enjoyed a distinguished military career with the English army in Europe before he sailed to America as a newly minted major general in February 1776. He took part in the Battle of Long Island and subsequent campaigns across Manhattan and New Jersey in August–December 1776, and was about to return to England on leave when he heard of Washington's victory at Trenton. Washington followed this up by evading Cornwallis's attempt to trap him east of the Delaware River and attacking Princeton before retreating to safety. Cornwallis got vengeance of a sort in September and October 1777 as a participant in Howe's victories at Brandywine and Germantown. He fought in the Battle of Monmouth the following summer and then sailed for England to attend to his terminally ill wife. Returning to America in August 1779, he took charge of the British campaign in the southern states, smashing Horatio Gates at Camden, South Carolina, in August 1780 before struggling to overcome Nathanael Greene in a subsequent campaign in the Carolinas. In May 1781 Cornwallis moved north to Virginia, taking post at Yorktown, where, after a siege of six weeks, Washington forced his surrender on October 19th. Paroled to England and exchanged for former president of congress Henry Laurens in May 1782, Cornwallis went on to become viceroy of Ireland and governor general of England. Aggressive, intelligent, and in many ways a much abler commander than Washington, Cornwallis was nevertheless one of Britain's least successful generals of the war.

ROBERT DINWIDDIE (1693–1770)   Born of a wealthy and prominent Scottish family, Dinwiddie left Glasgow in 1721 for the New World, serving in various administrative posts in Bermuda and British North America before taking office as lieutenant governor of Virginia in July 1751. Deeply interested in westward expansion, Dinwiddie made George Washington Virginia's emissary to the French in the Ohio Valley in October 1753, and in the following year he appointed Washington lieutenant colonel and sent him on a military expedition to the Forks of the Ohio River. This expedition culminated in armed confrontations at Jumonville's Glen and Fort Necessity, and helped to spark the French and Indian War—an outcome Dinwiddie may have anticipated when he sent Washington to the frontier. Dinwiddie resigned as governor and returned to Britain in 1758. As Washington's first important political ally, Dinwiddie played a major role in his rise to fame; nevertheless, relations between the two men were often strained.

LORD THOMAS FAIRFAX (1693–1781)   Born at Leeds Castle in England, Thomas Fairfax became the sixth Baron Fairfax of Cameron in 1710 after the death of his father. He settled permanently in Virginia in 1747, becoming one of the most powerful men in America by virtue of his control of the sprawling Northern Neck Proprietary. His influence helped to secure Washington's appointment as surveyor for Culpeper County in July 1749. Washington returned the favor during the Revolutionary War, making sure that Virginia's revolutionary government did not molest Lord Fairfax's estates despite his loyalist sympathies.

WILLIAM FAIRFAX (1691–1757)   Cousin of Lord Thomas Fairfax and agent for the Northern Neck Proprietary, William Fairfax mentored the young George Washington and helped to secure his first civil and military appointments. William's daughter, Ann (d.1761), married George Washington's half brother Lawrence; his son Bryan Fairfax, eighth Baron Fairfax of Cameron (1736–1802), became George's lifelong friend.

JOHN FORBES (1707–1759)   Scottish medical doctor who became colonel of the British Seventeenth Regiment of Foot, rising to the rank of adjutant general and eventually becoming brigadier general in command of the 1758 British expedition against Fort Duquesne. Forbes was a much better general than his predecessor, General Edward Braddock, but he sparred with Colonel George Washington over the choice of a road to Fort Duquesne. Washington nevertheless learned much about military command from Forbes, who died shortly after the victorious conclusion of his expedition.

THOMAS GAGE (c.1719–1787)   Entering the British army in the late 1730s, Gage served at the battles of Fontenoy and Culloden before being appointed lieutenant colonel of the Forty-fourth Regiment of Foot in 1751. His regiment was sent to America in 1754, and it was there, during the disastrous Braddock expedition of the following year, that he became acquainted with George Washington. The two men continued to correspond after the campaign was over, and Gage lent support to Washington's search for a royal commission. In 1761 Gage was promoted to major general, and in 1763 he became commander of the British land forces in North America. In 1770 he was promoted to lieutenant general, and in 1773, when Gage left America for a leave of absence in England, Washington attended his farewell dinner and afterward a private meal with the general and his American wife. Gage returned to America the following year and commanded the British forces at Boston in

1775 when Washington was appointed commander-in-chief, but he was re-called to England in October. He and Washington never corresponded again.

HORATIO GATES (c.1728–1806) An Englishman who served during the French and Indian War as a captain in the British army, Gates became acquainted with Washington during the campaign leading to General Edward Braddock's defeat in western Pennsylvania in July 1755. Regaining Washington's acquaintance after settling in western Virginia in 1772, he became adjutant general of the Continental Army in June 1775 and distinguished himself as a military administrator before taking command of the northern American army in New England as a major general in May 1776. His subsequent feuds for primacy in that region with Major General Philip Schuyler earned him a reputation as an intriguer, but after being given credit for the victory over General John Burgoyne at Saratoga, New York, in October 1777, he was viewed by some as an alternative to the struggling George Washington. His relations with the commander-in-chief continued to decline after Congress appointed him president of the Board of War the following year. During his tenure in that office Washington and his aides suspected him and Brigadier General Thomas Conway of being members of a "cabal" that wanted to overthrow the commander-in-chief. Gates evaded the disgrace that subsequently sent Conway packing to France, and continued working in the Continental Army administration until his return to field command culminated in disastrous defeat at the Battle of Camden, South Carolina, in August 1780, effectively ending his military career.

CHRISTOPHER GIST (c.1706–1759) An expert frontiersman from Maryland who served as Washington's guide during his journey to Fort Le Boeuf in the autumn of 1753, Gist saved Washington from drowning and an apparent assassination attempt on the way back. He accompanied Braddock's expedition as a guide in the summer of 1755, and later acted as a captain of scouts in Washington's Virginia Regiment. He died of smallpox in 1759.

NATHANAEL GREENE (1742–1786) This ex-Quaker from Rhode Island became one of Washington's most valuable and trusted officers. He was appointed a brigadier general in June 1775 and became a major general in August 1776, missing the Battle of Long Island (August 1776) because of illness but serving with distinction at Trenton (December 1776), Princeton (January 1777), Brandywine (September 1777), and Germantown (October 1777). He took over the quartermaster general's department in March 1778, and did an excellent job of reorganizing that department and revitalizing the army's logistical system. Greene returned to the field in December 1780, replacing Horatio Gates in command of the southern army. His subsequent campaign against Lord Cornwallis in the Carolinas—including the Battle of Guilford Courthouse in March 1781—is widely recognized as among the most brilliant in American military history.

ALEXANDER HAMILTON (1757–1804) Born the illegitimate son of James Hamilton and Rachel Fawcett Levine in the British island colony of Nevis in the Leeward Islands, Alexander Hamilton went to New York in 1772 to study at King's College. Two years later he dropped out of school to become a full-time patriot, writing essays in support of the colonial cause against Great Britain. He was appointed captain of a New York artillery company in March 1776, and his service during the retreat across New Jersey that autumn brought him to the attention of the commander-in-chief, who took Hamilton on in March 1777 as an aide-de-camp with the rank of lieutenant colonel. Hamilton quickly became indispensable to Washington, penning many of his most important letters and riding at the commander-in-chief's side in every major battle. He and Washington became friends, but the confident and quick-tempered Hamilton also had his abrasive side, and following a quarrel during the war the two men were no longer on speaking terms. They made up, however, and in October 1781 Washington acceded to his aide's desire for battlefield glory by putting him in command of the assault on redoubt number 10 at the Battle of Yorktown. Hamilton returned to New York after Cornwallis's surrender and entered politics, writing *The Federalist* with John Jay and James Madison in support of the Constitution that would replace the Articles of Confederation. Hamilton served as President Washington's secretary of the treasury from 1789 to 1795; and as the two-party system emerged in American politics around the turn of the century, he became known as a forceful and articulate spokesman for the Federalists. He and Washington joined forces one more time in 1798–99 during the Quasi-War with France, when the aging ex-president depended heavily on Hamilton to administer the army of which Washington had been appointed commander-in-chief. Hamilton was killed in a duel with Aaron Burr in 1804.

JOHN HANCOCK (1737–1793)   Heir to a mercantile fortune and one of the richest men in Massachusetts, Hancock was elected president of the Second Continental Congress in May 1775. Lacking military experience but extremely ambitious, Hancock angled to be appointed commander-in-chief of the Continental Army in May 1775, only to be beaten out by George Washington. Hancock bore no grudge, however, and cooperated closely with Washington until resigning as president of Congress in October 1777.

WILLIAM HOWE (1729–1814)   This British aristocrat entered the army as a cornet in 1746 and rose to the rank of lieutenant colonel in 1759, when he distinguished himself by scaling the Heights of Abraham with a battalion of light troops during Major General James Wolfe's expedition against Quebec. William Howe and his older brother Richard, who as Lord Howe became commander of the British navy during the Revolutionary War, were also active in British politics; and as Whigs they decried the Lord North government's punitive measures against the colonies in the early 1770s. Appointed a major general in 1772, William Howe, despite his Whig sympathies, accepted an offer to command troops in North America three years later, and in April 1776 he was named commander-in-chief of the British forces operating in the thirteen colonies. Howe's conduct in subsequent campaigns and battles through Germantown in October 1777 revealed him to be Washington's superior as a tactician and also showed his qualities as a military administrator; but his excessive caution in pursuit allowed the Americans to escape from situations in which they might have been annihilated. Howe was popular with his troops, but friction with the government in London led him to resign his command in the autumn of 1777. He returned to England the following spring.

DAVID HUMPHREYS (1752–1818)   This Connecticut native and Yale graduate served as an aide-de-camp to Israel Putnam from 1778 until 1780, when he joined Washington's staff. Humphreys remained with Washington until the end of the war, becoming an indispensable aide and close personal friend. In 1786 he took up residence at Mount Vernon for the purpose of writing his *Life of General Washington,* which would become the first biography of the great man. Despite being an "official" biography, it provides an unusually detailed and accurate portrait of Washington's life.

HENRY KNOX (1750–1806)   Born in Boston, Knox dropped out of school after his father died and worked in a bookstore to support his mother and younger brother. He opened his own bookstore in Boston when he was only twenty years old. An enthusiastic reader, Knox took a particular interest in military history and devoured every book he could find on the subject. It may have been because of this shared interest that he and Washington became friends after the latter's arrival at Cambridge as commander-in-chief in June 1775. Impressed by Knox's intelligence, easy nature, and good judgment, in November of that year Washington agreed to John Adams's suggestion that the young bookseller should be put in command of the fledgling Continental artillery. Washington never regretted his decision, and Knox, who was promoted to brigadier general in December 1776 and to major general in March 1782, stood by his side in every battle of the war. Knox was also responsible for transforming the Continental artillery into one of the most efficient branches of the American military service. After Washington's resignation in December 1783, Knox was rewarded with the command of the entire Continental Army, a post in which he served until June of the following year. Knox continued his association with Washington after the end of the Revolutionary War, working with him to found the Society of the Cincinnati and later serving as secretary of war during Washington's first presidential term. Tragically, their friendship foundered during the Quasi-War with France in 1798 because of Washington's preference for Alexander Hamilton over Knox as the army's highest-ranking major general. Knox died in 1806, choking one morning on a chicken bone at breakfast.

MARQUIS DE LAFAYETTE (1757–1834)   Nobleman born Marie-Joseph-Paul-Yves-Roch-Gilbert du Motier, marquis de Lafayette, at Chavaniac in Auvergne, France. Although his father had been killed at the Battle of Minden in 1759, the young Lafayette was eager to seek glory in war, and in April 1777 he outfitted a ship that carried him and several other young Frenchmen to America. Lafayette was luckier than most of his countrymen in securing a commission, for Congress promptly appointed him a major general effective July 1777. He was also lucky in securing an immediate audience with Washington, who happened to be in Philadelphia at the time and dined with him at the City Tavern. Lafayette and Washington took an immediate liking to each other, and the commander-in-chief invited the Frenchman to join his staff. Over the following years their relationship grew, with Washington assuming the role of mentor and Lafayette becoming a kind of surrogate son. Lafayette was wounded in the leg while observing the Battle of Brandywine, and a few months later he was given command of a division in the army. In the winter of 1777–78 he fiercely defended Washington against those who spoke of replacing him as commander-in-chief. In May 1778 he extricated his force from a precarious position at Barren Hill, Pennsylvania—Washington had put him there, but Lafayette held no grudge—and the following month he led his troops with distinction at the Battle of Monmouth. Lafayette returned to France in 1778–79 to canvass support for the American cause. After his return to America in 1780 he rejoined Washington's army, participating in the Yorktown campaign in 1781. Lafayette returned to France after the war, and although he and Washington never saw each other again after 1784 they remained constant correspondents and good friends. Lafayette's return to America in 1824 and his subsequent tour of the country, which included an emotional visit to Mount Vernon, became a national event.

HENRY LAURENS (1724–1792)   Prominent South Carolina patriot who served as president of Congress from October 1777 until 1779, when he was appointed minister to Holland. Captured on his way to Europe, he was imprisoned in the Tower of London until 1781. Congress then appointed him a peace commissioner to Great Britain, and he signed a preliminary peace treaty with his former captors in 1782. He was the father of Washington's aide John Laurens.

JOHN LAURENS (1754–1782)   Educated in Europe, John Laurens, son of President of Congress Henry Laurens, became one of Washington's aides-de-camp in 1777. He and Alexander Hamilton served as the commander-in-chief's French translators, and also as go-betweens for Washington and many of the foreign volunteers serving in his army. Dashing and idealistic, John Laurens pressed his father to end slavery and urged Washington to systematically enlist black troops into his army. He was killed in an insignificant skirmish at Combahee Ferry (South Carolina) in 1782, to Washington's great sorrow.

CHARLES LEE (1731–1782)   Englishman who served as a lieutenant during the French and Indian War before settling in America in 1773. An early contender for the post of commander-in-chief of the Continental Army, he settled instead for a commission as major general and became one of Washington's most trusted officers. He helped to plan the defense of New York in 1776 and served at the Battle of New York in August of that year before being captured by the British under suspicious circumstances during Washington's retreat through New Jersey. Exchanged in the spring of 1778, he returned to lead the vanguard of the Continental Army during the Battle of Monmouth (June 1778), only to be sacked for misconduct after a disastrous run-in with the commander-in-chief.

HENRY LEE (1756–1818)   Born near Dumfries, Virginia, and educated at the College of New Jersey, Henry Lee (known to later generations as "Lighthorse Harry Lee") was one of the ablest exponents and practitioners of partisan warfare in the Revolutionary War. Appointed captain of a troop of Virginia cavalry in June 1776, Lee joined Washington's army in February 1777. The commander-in-chief quickly recognized the young officer's abilities, and gave him and his horsemen practically complete freedom to do as they pleased. This Lee did with relish, raiding British outposts, capturing enemy patrols, and generally making a nuisance of himself to William Howe, who dispatched cavalry parties for the sole purpose of having Lee captured. Lee was promoted to major in April 1778 and lieutenant colonel in November 1780. His command grew, too, becoming a mixed force of cavalry and infantry that was known first as Lee's Partisan Corps and then Lee's Legionary Corps. Lee was an active and invaluable participant in Nathanael Greene's southern campaign of 1781 before he left the army in 1782, going on to serve as a delegate to the Continental Congress (1785–88), governor of Virginia (1791–94), and member of the U.S. Congress (1799–1801). He was the father of Robert E. Lee.

JAMES MCHENRY (1753–1816)   Born in Ireland and educated in Dublin, in 1771 McHenry immigrated to Maryland, where he studied medicine under Benjamin Rush. His skill and dedication as a surgeon during the Revolutionary War impressed Washington, who made him an aide shortly before the Monmouth campaign in 1778. McHenry served loyally under Washington for two years, joining Lafayette's staff in 1780 and retiring from the army in 1781. After the war he had a successful career in politics, serving as a Maryland delegate to the Continental Congress (1783–86) and as secretary of war under Washington and John Adams (1796–1800). Although he liked McHenry personally, in later years Washington seems to have decided that the gentle Irishman was a bit softheaded, and he made no secret of his belief that McHenry was an incompetent secretary of war.

WILLIAM MAXWELL (c.1733–1796)   This hard-drinking Scotsman settled in New Jersey as a teenager and served as a soldier in a British regiment during Braddock's defeat in 1755. In October 1775 he was appointed colonel of the American Second New Jersey Regiment. His dedicated service during fighting in Canada led to his promotion to brigadier general a year later. He commanded Washington's light infantry during the Philadelphia campaign of 1777, and despite allegations of drunkenness he continued in service until July 1780, when he resigned.

THOMAS MIFFLIN (1744–1800)   Philadelphia Quaker and merchant educated at the College of Pennsylvania who became one of the most radical American patriots at the beginning of the Revolutionary War. Mifflin served during the summer of 1775 as one of Washington's aides-de-camp before becoming quartermaster general of the Continental Army, a post in which he remained until the autumn of 1777. That winter, Mifflin became one of Washington's bitterest critics, and he was associated with Thomas Conway and Horatio Gates in the so-called Conway cabal. He served briefly in 1778 on the Board of War and as a division commander in the Continental Army, but allegations of misconduct led to his resigning from the army in February 1779. Mifflin's political career quickly revived, however, and he became president of the Continental Congress in 1783. Ironically, he accepted Washington's commission upon his resignation as commander-in-chief at the end of the war.

DANIEL MORGAN (c.1735–1802)   The son of a Pennsylvania ironmaster and first cousin of Daniel Boone, Morgan served as a teamster during the 1755 Braddock expedition, in the course of which he suffered five hundred lashes for striking back at a British officer who had hit him, and lost half of his teeth after taking an Indian bullet through the mouth. After the French and Indian War ended he lived as a successful farmer in Virginia's Shenandoah Valley. In June 1775 he was appointed captain of a Virginia rifle company. He led the vanguard of Benedict Arnold's march on Quebec that autumn, earning fame as an expert frontiersman and a canny and fearless fighter. Morgan joined the main American army after being commissioned colonel of the Eleventh Virginia Regiment in November 1776. Washington immediately recognized his skill as an irregular fighter, giving him, like Henry Lee, substantial freedom to operate with detachments of riflemen against the British. It was with great reluctance that the commander-in-chief agreed to detach Morgan to reinforce Horatio Gates in the autumn of 1777, but Morgan went on to play a decisive role in the Battle of Saratoga in October of that year, rejoining Washington at Valley Forge and during the Monmouth campaign in 1778. He demonstrated his mastery of irregular warfare again during the southern campaign, in 1780–81, when he commanded an elite brigade of light troops. Morgan was one of the outstanding American officers of the war.

TIMOTHY PICKERING (1745–1829)   A Massachusetts native and Harvard graduate, Pickering prospered as a lawyer until the outbreak of the Revolutionary War, when he became colonel of the Essex County Militia. Though a newcomer to the military life, Pickering proved remarkably adept at training his troops and wrote a drill manual titled *An Easy Plan of Discipline for a Militia,* which he presented to Washington. As a result, in 1777 Washington had Pickering appointed adjutant general of the Continental Army; but he served in that post for only a few months before Congress transferred him to the Board of War. Pickering subsequently served as a very efficient quartermaster general from 1780 until 1785, and during Washington's presidency he was given several important federal appointments, becoming secretary of war in 1795. Though intelligent, Pickering also had a spiteful streak and denigrated almost everyone with whom he worked, including Washington, behind their backs.

ISRAEL PUTNAM (1718–1790)   This French and Indian War veteran from Connecticut was appointed major general in June 1775 and commanded troops at the siege of Boston (1775–76) and the Battle of Long Island (August 1776). Though popular in New England, his military abilities were modest, and he left the army after suffering a stroke in 1779.

JOSEPH REED (1741–1785)   A successful New Jersey lawyer educated at the College of New Jersey and London's Inns of Court, in 1774–75 Reed became known as one of the most articulate and passionate spokesmen for the patriot cause. He met Washington at the First Continental Congress, and the two got on so well that Washington asked Reed to become his first military secretary in 1775. Reed served as adjutant general from early 1776 until January 1777, when he left the army to enter Pennsylvania politics, becoming president of the Pennsylvania Supreme Executive Council in 1778. Reed's criticism of the commander-in-chief's conduct during the campaign of 1776 and the loss of Fort Washington in the autumn of that year strained their friendship, but they later made up their differences.

COMTE DE ROCHAMBEAU (1725–1807) Born Jean-Baptiste-Donatien de Vimeur, comte de Rochambeau, at Vendôme, France, this career officer was appointed lieutenant general in 1780. In the same year he took command of a French army that landed at Rhode Island and subsequently linked up with Washington to conduct offensive operations against the British. Rochambeau treated Washington with deference and respect, going along at first with the American's wrongheaded plans for an attack on New York and then acceding to a change of plans that sent the Franco-American army marching to Virginia instead. Rochambeau and Washington continued their cooperation during the siege of Yorktown, and shared victory there in October 1781.

WILLIAM SMALLWOOD (1732–1792) A Maryland native and French and Indian War veteran who was appointed colonel of the First Maryland Regiment in January 1776, Smallwood rose to the rank of brigadier general later that year. Washington found him a useful officer during the Philadelphia campaign in 1777, frequently deferring to his local knowledge and putting him in charge of the unruly Maryland and Delaware militias. Smallwood served with distinction during the southern campaign of 1780–81 and later became a three-term governor of Maryland.

ADAM STEPHEN (c.1718–1791) Scottish doctor who settled in Virginia and became a captain in the Virginia Regiment in 1754, serving with Washington at Fort Necessity and subsequently earning promotion to lieutenant colonel before he accompanied Braddock's doomed expedition to the Monongahela River in July 1755. Stephen became Washington's second in command in the reformed Virginia Regiment later that year, and proved immensely helpful in transforming the unit into an efficient military force. Cranky and tenacious, Stephen was also a steady ally for Washington in his disputes with civilian officials and the British military hierarchy. In 1761, three years after Washington's resignation, he took command of the Virginia Regiment. War brought the two men together again in 1775, with Stephen rising from the rank of colonel in February 1776 to major general in February 1777, when he took command of one of the divisions in Washington's army. Unfortunately their close association did not last, for although Stephen performed reasonably well at Brandywine and Germantown, his heavy drinking led to his dismissal from the army after a court-martial in November 1777—a dismissal that Stephen blamed on Washington. For his part, Washington seems to have had second thoughts about Stephen's abilities as a field commander. The two men never spoke again after Stephen left the army.

LORD STIRLING *see* William Alexander.

JOHN SULLIVAN (1740–1795) New Hampshire lawyer who became a brigadier general in the Continental Army in June 1775 and a major general in August 1776, when he led troops at the Battle of Long Island. He was captured there, and after his exchange he returned to the army to participate in the battles of Trenton (December 1776), Brandywine (September 1777), and Germantown (October 1777). He led an expedition against the Iroquois Indians in 1779 before resigning from the army in November of that year.

TANACHARISON (c.1700–1754) Seneca Indian chief, also known as the Half-King, who sided—at least apparently—with Great Britain in its dispute with France over the Ohio Country in the early 1750s. Tanacharison accompanied Washington's expedition to Fort Le Boeuf in the autumn of 1753, and the following spring he guided Washington to his ambush of a French force under Jumonville, whom the chief reportedly killed. Tanacharison was subsequently disowned by his Indian allies and failed to aid Washington at Fort Necessity. He died a few months later of acute alcoholism.

JONATHAN TRUMBULL, SR. (1710–1785) Appointed governor of Connecticut in 1769, Trumbull was the only colonial governor to side with America against the British in the Revolutionary War. At first he bristled at Washington's peremptory demands for support, but the two men quickly made up their differences and cooperated closely for the duration of the war. Trumbull resigned as governor in 1784 and died the following year.

ARTEMAS WARD (1727–1800)   A native of Massachusetts, Ward contended for the post of commander-in-chief of the Continental Army before his appointment as major general and Washington's second in command at Boston in June 1775. He quarreled with Washington, and after the British evacuation of Boston in March 1776 he never again commanded troops in the field.

AUGUSTINE WASHINGTON (1694–1743)   George Washington resembled his father, Augustine, in many respects, from his tall and athletic appearance, to his love of farming and success as a land speculator, to the manner of his death. By all accounts a soft-spoken and caring father, Augustine, upon his death in 1743, left his son George bereaved but in possession of valuable property at Fredericksburg, Virginia, that would later be called Ferry Farm.

LAWRENCE WASHINGTON (c.1718–1752)   George Washington's elder half brother and role model, Lawrence tutored him in manners and deportment and taught him to love the military life. Lawrence was himself a veteran of the War of Jenkins' Ear, serving as a captain in the American Regiment during the siege of Cartagena in the spring of 1741. Lawrence's marriage in July 1743 to Ann Fairfax connected him to one of the most powerful families in Virginia, and he exploited that connection to further George's career as a surveyor. He also connived in a family plot in 1746 to send George to sea with the British navy, but his plans fortunately fell through. His death in 1752 left George the residuary heir to Mount Vernon.

MARTHA DANDRIDGE CUSTIS WASHINGTON (1731–1802)   Daughter of John and Frances Jones Dandridge of New Kent County, Virginia, Martha Dandridge married the wealthy planter Daniel Parke Custis in June 1749. She bore four children before Daniel died in July 1757, leaving her one of the richest, and therefore most desirable, widows in the colony. George Washington's marriage to her in January 1759 was a social coup comparable to his half brother Lawrence's marriage to Ann Fairfax in July 1743. But whatever it may have been at first, the union of George and Martha Washington became one of deep and enduring love, marked by mutual support and respect. Martha stayed with her husband for much of the Revolutionary War, joining him at headquarters and helping him through some of his most difficult moments. During the trying winter encampment at Valley Forge in 1777–78 she is said to have helped care for sick soldiers, and she became popular throughout the army. While Martha may not have been the key to her husband's greatness, she certainly played a very large part in it.

MARY BALL WASHINGTON (c.1708–1789)   George Washington's devoted and strong-willed mother played an important role in his development as a child and young man, overseeing the family estates after her husband Augustine's death and managing her children's education. George came to resent his mother's interference in his life, however, and after the French and Indian War their relationship gradually grew more distant.

ANTHONY WAYNE (1745–1796)   Born near Paoli in Chester County, Pennsylvania, as a child Anthony Wayne played incessantly at war, leading other boys in mock battles and building elaborate redoubts. His love of the military life continued as he became an adult, and when the Revolutionary War began he eagerly joined the Continental Army. He was commissioned colonel of the Fourth Pennsylvania Regiment in January 1776, and that spring he first saw action at the Battle of Trois Rivières in Canada. He was promoted to brigadier general in February 1777 and joined Washington's army, where he became known as a strict disciplinarian, an able tactician, and a bold and fearless leader. Wayne fought effectively at the battles of Brandywine, Germantown, and Monmouth, but on September 20, 1777, he allowed a British raiding party to surprise his camp near his home at Paoli, Pennsylvania, and massacre dozens of his soldiers. Wayne learned from this mistake but lost nothing of his aggressiveness, which eventually earned him the sobriquet "Mad Anthony." His daring and successful attack on a British bastion at Stony Point, New York, in July 1779 won him the thanks of Congress and the respect of Washington, whom Wayne had once regarded as overly cautious but eventually came to admire. Wayne went on to participate in the siege of Yorktown. After the war he dabbled in politics before President Washington called on him to lead an expedition against the Iroquois, a commission that Wayne carried out successfully in a campaign that culminated in the Battle of Fallen Timbers, Ohio, in August 1794.

CHRONOLOGY

1732	February 22	George Washington's birth (Gregorian calendar).
1739		American Regiment formed for service in War of Jenkins' Ear; Lawrence Washington, George's elder half brother, becomes captain in regiment.
1741	March–April	Defeat of British land-sea force at Cartagena.
1743	January	Lawrence Washington returns home.
	April 12	Death of George's father, Augustine Washington.
1746		George considers running away to join British navy.
1748	March–April	Washington's surveying trip to Virginia frontier.
1751	September–December	George and Lawrence in Barbados.
1752	July 26	Lawrence Washington's death.
1753	February	George becomes adjutant of Virginia's Southern District; some months later he is appointed adjutant of Northern District.
	October–January 1754	Washington serves as Virginia's emissary to French in Ohio country.
1754	March	Washington is appointed lieutenant colonel of Virginia Regiment.
	April	Washington leads regiment to frontier.
	May 28	Washington defeats French at Jumonville's Glen.

	July 4	Capitulation of Fort Necessity.
1755	March	Washington is appointed aide-de-camp to British general Edward Braddock.
	April	Braddock leads force toward frontier.
	July 9	Braddock's defeat on Monongahela River.
	August	Washington is appointed colonel and commander of Virginia Regiment; he commences training the regiment as a regular force.
1756	February–March	Washington travels to Boston to seek royal commission.
1758	March–May	General John Forbes takes command of Anglo-American expeditionary force; Second Virginia Regiment formed and placed under Washington's command.
	September 14	Major James Grant's force of British and Virginians defeated near Fort Duquesne.
	October 25–26	Treaty of Easton (Pennsylvania) concludes peace between Britain and Ohio Indians.
	November 12	Washington and his Virginians engage French raiders near Loyalhanna, Pennsylvania.
	November 23	French destroy and abandon Fort Duquesne.
	December	Washington resigns command of Virginia Regiment.
1759	January 6	Washington marries Martha Custis.
	February	Washington takes seat in Virginia House of Burgesses.
1774	July	Washington and other burgesses promulgate Fairfax Resolves; he is elected delegate to First Continental Congress.
	September–October	Washington attends First Continental Congress in Philadelphia.
1775	March	Washington is elected delegate to Second Continental Congress.

	April 19	Battles of Lexington and Concord in Massachusetts.
	May 9	Washington arrives in Philadelphia to attend Congress.
	June 15	Congress elects Washington commander-in-chief of the Continental Army.
	June 17	Battle of Bunker Hill.
	July 2	Washington arrives at Cambridge, Massachusetts, and takes command of Continental Army.
	September–December	Benedict Arnold's Canadian expedition.
1776	March 4–5	Americans occupy Dorchester Heights, overlooking Boston.
	March 17	British evacuate Boston.
	April 13	Washington arrives in New York.
	July 2	British land on Staten Island.
	July 4	Declaration of Independence.
	August 27	Battle of Long Island.
	August 29–30	American army evacuated from Brooklyn Heights to Manhattan.
	September 12–15	Washington evacuates Manhattan.
	September 15	Battle of Kip's Bay; British occupy Manhattan.
	September 16	Battle of Harlem Heights, New York.
	September 21	Manhattan fire.
	October 17	Washington retreats from Harlem Heights.
	October 28	Battle of White Plains.
	November 16	British capture Fort Washington, New York.
	November–December	Washington's retreat across New Jersey.
	December	British occupy Newport, Rhode Island.
	December 7–8	Washington's army crosses Delaware River into Pennsylvania.

	December 26	Battle of Trenton (New Jersey).
1777	January 3	Battle of Princeton (New Jersey).
	May–June	Washington and Howe maneuver in New Jersey.
	July 8–23	British army embarks fleet and leaves coast at Sandy Hook, New Jersey.
	August 25	British land at Head of Elk, Maryland.
	September 3	Battle of Cooch's Bridge (Delaware).
	September 11	Battle of Brandywine (Pennsylvania).
	September 16	"Battle of the Clouds."
	September 26	British occupy Philadelphia.
	October 4	Battle of Germantown (Pennsylvania).
	October 17	Burgoyne's surrender at Saratoga, New York.
	November 15–16	Americans evacuate Fort Mifflin, Pennsylvania, opening Delaware River to British ships.
	December 19	American army establishes winter quarters at Valley Forge, Pennsylvania.
1778	May 4	Congress ratifies alliance with France.
	June 18	British evacuate Philadelphia and begin retreat across New Jersey; Washington's army leaves Valley Forge and follows.
	June 28	Battle of Monmouth (New Jersey).
	June 29–July 5	British army evacuates from Sandy Hook, New Jersey, to New York.
	July 29–August 31	Failed Franco-American attack on British-occupied Newport, Rhode Island.
	December	British capture Savannah, Georgia.
1779	June–October	John Sullivan's expedition against the Iroquois Indians.
	July 16	Anthony Wayne's attack on Stony Point, New York.
	August 19	Attack on Paulus Hook, New Jersey.

	October	Failed Franco-American attack on Savannah, Georgia.
	December 1– June 22, 1780	Continental Army encamped at Morristown, New Jersey.
1780	May 12	British capture Charleston, South Carolina.
	May 25	American troops mutiny at Morristown, New Jersey.
	July 10	French fleet with army under Rochambeau arrives at Newport, Rhode Island.
	August	Battle of Camden (South Carolina).
	September	Benedict Arnold's treason at West Point, New York.
	October 7	Battle of King's Mountain (South Carolina).
1781	January 1	Mutiny of Pennsylvania line at Morristown, New Jersey.
	January 5–7	Benedict Arnold sacks Richmond, Virginia.
	January 17	Battle of Cowpens (South Carolina).
	March 15	Battle of Guilford Courthouse (North Carolina).
	May 20	Cornwallis arrives at Petersburg, Virginia.
	May 22	Franco-American conference at Wethersfield, Connecticut.
	July 6	American and French armies under Washington and Rochambeau link up at White Plains, New York.
	July–August	Cornwallis moves his army to Yorktown, Virginia.
	August 19	Anglo-French army leaves New York, marching south, toward Virginia.
	September 14	Washington arrives at Williamsburg, Virginia.
	September 28	Siege of Yorktown begins.
	October 14–15	Attack on redoubts 9 and 10.

	October 19	Capitulation of British army at Yorktown.
1783	March 10–15	Continental Army mutinies at Newburgh, New York.
	September 3	Treaty of Paris ends Revolutionary War.
	November 2	Washington's farewell orders to Continental Army.
	November 25	British evacuate New York.
	December 4	Washington's farewell to his officers at Fraunces Tavern (New York).
	December 23	Washington submits resignation to Congress at Annapolis, Maryland.
	December 24	Washington returns home to Mount Vernon, Virginia.
1787	May 25	Constitutional Convention convenes at Philadelphia; Washington elected president of convention.
	September 17	Constitution signed.
1789	April 30	Washington inaugurated for first term as president of the United States.
1791	November	Defeat of Arthur St. Clair's expedition by Indians.
1793	March 4	Washington inaugurated for second term as president of the United States.
1794	August 20	Anthony Wayne's victory over Indians at Fallen Timbers, Ohio.
	August–November	Washington suppresses Whiskey Rebellion in western Pennsylvania.
1797	March 4	Washington retires from presidency—and, he hopes, from public life.
1798	July 13	Washington accepts commission as commander-in-chief of U.S. Army during Quasi-War with France.
1799	December 14	Washington dies at Mount Vernon.

GENERAL GEORGE
WASHINGTON

1

YOUNG FRONTIERSMAN

May 1741 – February 1753

AT THE END OF MAY 1741, a young American officer stood sweltering on the sun-baked deck of a warship off the coast of Jamaica. Transports full of red-coated soldiers surrounded him, clogging the horizon with wooden hulls, masts, and sails that announced the presence of a British expeditionary army. As a captain in the provincial infantry, he occupied only a small corner of that army, and counted for little; but as an American he felt proud to participate in Great Britain's glorious military tradition.

Or at least he had at first. Now all reason for pride had gone. The army was dying. It had won no laurels, just a watery shroud. Most of the men had perished in the last four months, and disease stalked every survivor. As the American captain watched, daily burials at sea became feasts for frenzied sharks. He had no reason to think that he would not end the same way. Officers enjoyed no immunity to tropical disease or ignominious burial.

Like all soldiers, Captain Lawrence Washington found refuge in thoughts of home. He came from Fredericksburg, Virginia, over a thousand miles away. He had not been there in over a year. Letters took weeks to travel each way, and often never arrived at all. Still, writing to his loved ones could make them seem closer, so retreating from the sun to his cabin or a shady place on deck, he turned from the horrors surrounding him, took up a pen, and wrote a letter to his father.

Lawrence Washington wrote as a recent eyewitness to the most important battle of the War of Jenkins' Ear, and as a participant in its miserable aftermath. Named after the alleged mutilation of English sailor Robert Jenkins, the conflict had started in the summer of 1739 as a minor colonial fray between Great Britain and Spain. The bloodletting centered in the Caribbean, where the British sought to strangle Spain's communications with the gold and silver mines of South America by snatching some of her outposts. Victors of the war's early encounters, the British expected to make short work of the decrepit Spanish empire by capturing the important port of Cartagena off the northeast coast of South America. After this, with the Spanish reeling, they expected to move on to seize the even more important settlement of Havana on the island of Cuba.

As plans for its Caribbean offensive jelled in 1739, the British government announced its intention to form an American regiment to serve as part of an amphibious army of six marine regiments and other regular units. Virginia, whose governor was appointed to command the regiment, provided the largest number of volunteers when recruitment began in the spring of 1740. The common Virginians made unimpressive soldiers—a British observer called them "Blacksmiths, Tailors, Barbers, Shoemakers, and all the Banditry the colonies afford"—but their officers were privileged, cultured, and generally intelligent young men, anxious to earn good reputations in battle. Sons of the Old Dominion had besieged colonial officials with requests for commissions, and Lawrence Washington was one of the many who lobbied fiercely for the four captaincies available from his colony. Thanks to his family's influence and his own considerable personal charm, he received the highest-ranking spot.

The newly appointed Captain Washington followed the American Regiment to Jamaica near the end of 1740. At first, his soldiers showed little promise. Like the British redcoats, the American enlisted men came from the scum of society; and the Virginians stood out even in such rough company. Among them were vagrants, loafers, cutpurses, and former convicts. Soldiering did not come naturally to them, as Lawrence and his fellow officers swiftly discovered. They looked bad, too. Only about one in every six of the scrawny, ill-fed men possessed a uniform.

British Brigadier General Thomas Wentworth reviewed the Americans on Jamaica in January 1741 and shook his head at the spectacle they presented. Yet there was some innate quality in the common soldiers that he liked. Under proper leadership and discipline, he decided, they might eventually prove useful. For American officers, on the other hand, he expressed complete and unreserved contempt. Branding them naïve and stupid, and certain that they would falter in combat, he attempted to replace them with British regulars. But by then the scruffy American enlisted soldiers had bonded with their young officers, and they bluntly refused to serve under anyone else. Irritated, Wentworth relented, but he privately resolved to keep all of the Americans on shipboard during the approaching campaign. It was inconceivable to him that the redcoats might need their provincial allies' support.

Wentworth commanded the land element of the expeditionary force of 8,000 British regulars and 3,000 Americans that left Jamaica in February 1741. The fleet carrying his troops sailed under Admiral Edward Vernon, a fifty-five-year-old, ill-tempered naval commander known in the fleet as "Grog" because of his grogram cloak. Sailors also applied this nickname to the watered-down rum that he forced upon them. But the ribbing was good-natured. Vernon's capture of Porto Bello on the Panamanian isthmus in November 1739 had made him a popular hero. Capturing Cartagena would add to his reputation and clear the way for other conquests in the Caribbean.

The fleet dropped anchor off Cartagena in early March 1741, and the redcoats quickly debarked, eager to fight. Yet their enthusiasm availed little in the ensuing six weeks as the expedition foundered and disintegrated. The British easily invested the port, but instead of storming its fortifications, Vernon and Wentworth quarreled over the plan of attack. Finally, after weeks of dithering that left the troops gravely weakened by dysentery and malaria, the British launched a large-scale assault on April 9th. Their officers bungled the advance, and the well-entrenched Spanish refused to budge. Nearly 700 redcoats fell slain without penetrating the enemy entrenchments. The siege then stalled while the British returned to the ships where their American allies had spent the last month languishing in stifling heat. Though spared the horrors of battle, the colonials had not been able to avoid the equally appalling threats of heatstroke, fever, and disease.

British surgeons and their assistants—among them a young writer named Tobias Smollett—struggled to care for the sick and wounded, and as soldiers perished in increasing numbers, discipline collapsed. Officers gave up on their duties and avoided their haggard men. The living casually dumped the bodies of dead comrades overboard, strewing the waters of Cartagena with bloated corpses. The trail of bodies led all the way to Jamaica, where the fleet arrived several weeks after abandoning its siege. But that island offered little relief, and the fever epidemic continued unabated. The army's effective strength rapidly fell to fewer than 2,000 British and just over 1,000 Americans.

Captain Lawrence Washington, by some miracle still alive and apparently healthy despite the carnage surrounding him, had the Cartagena fiasco fresh in his mind as he wrote to his father from on board the British warship in May 1741. The crisis continued as he wrote, and the expeditionary force still wasted away. Total disintegration was near. Yet he knew the keen anticipation with which his news-starved family would read his letter. His father would seek war news as well as hints on the state of trade and commerce in the Caribbean. His mother would want to know about Lawrence's health, and to hear about the fates of other friends and relations. And nine-year-old George, Lawrence's half brother, would look for descriptions of the roar of the cannon or the sight of infantry boldly charging the Spanish fortifications. None of them would want to hear about a disaster.

Lawrence wrote his letter with a mixture of sulkiness and reticence, providing only the briefest summary of the terrible expedition. He did not, or could not, bear to confess that the American Regiment had succumbed to disease without firing a shot. Instead he hid the truth with gentle boasting, including some lines possibly intended for George. "Our Regiment has not recd that treatment we expected," Lawrence wrote, "but I am resolved to persivere in the undertaking. War is horrid in fact, but much more so in imagination; We there learn'd to live on ordinary diet, to watch much, & disregard the noise, or shot of Cannon." These words must have impressed themselves on the boy's memory, for he echoed them with his own pen thirteen years later.

Lawrence returned to Fredericksburg in January 1743 after Admiral Vernon discarded his government's grandiose plans for the conquest of the Caribbean and sent the exhausted troops home. No parades greeted the Americans, who had failed to garner any kind of military glory. Most of the young officers who had left Virginia so confidently in 1740 had not fallen nobly in battle but died in squalid ships' holds before being dined upon by sea creatures. Veterans discovered that society had grown used to getting on without them, and the best jobs, honors, and appointments had already been taken by the stay-at-homes. The thought that he had squandered some of the most important years of his life must have lain heavily on Lawrence's mind.

Yet a child's love can heal many wounds, as Lawrence learned from his admiring young half brother George. The two came from a large family. Their father, Augustine, born in 1694, was a soft-spoken but energetic and physically powerful man. In 1738 he had settled at Ferry Farm, which stood across the Rappahannock River from Fredericksburg, and he now owned 10,000 acres and fifty slaves. His first wife, Jane Butler, died in 1729 after bearing three children: Lawrence (born around 1717), Augustine Jr., and Jane. Augustine Sr.'s second wife, the orphan Mary Ball, who had been born around 1708, gave birth to five more children. George, born February 22, 1732, according to the new calendar adopted in 1752, was the first. He was followed by Betty, Samuel, John Augustine, and Charles.

Among all of his siblings, George developed the strongest bond with Lawrence. And who could blame him for that? People liked Lawrence. Physically plain, he earned friends with kindness, affability, and good manners. Several years of schooling in England before the war had taught him graceful deportment and elegant handwriting. He lacked practicality and business sense, but to a child this may have made him all the more appealing. Lawrence was the type of man who set his own work aside in order to answer childish questions that others dismissed as foolish or irrelevant, and George's questions—which doubtless included how an officer drilled his men, what it felt like to stand on the deck of a warship with all guns ablaze, how it looked when landing boats full of British soldiers set out for shore, and how it sounded when the rattle of musketry and cannon announced their attack—always found a friendly ear.

The siblings' relationship grew as the Washington family settled down to everyday life in the first months of 1743. Lawrence came and went as he angled to become adjutant general of the Virginia Militia. George's younger brothers and sister grew under the care of Mary Washington, servants, slaves, and tutors. George had a tutor—according to one tradition a convict servant—and he learned quickly. As a reward for his studies, or maybe just to get him out of Lawrence's hair, Augustine decided in the spring of 1743 to send the boy off to visit some cousins living in the Chotank district on the Northern Neck of the Potomac River. George enjoyed the visit, but it did not last long. In early April, his father, to all appearances healthy and vigorous, rode out in a storm and fell ill. Within a short time, his condition was grave. A messenger called George home, but when he reached Ferry Farm he learned that Augustine had passed away, on April 12th.

Augustine's sudden death at age forty-nine left George and the rest of the family shorn of a vital source of strength and stability. Adults and children alike would have to assume more responsibilities. Augustine's will gave Ferry Farm to George, but if his family told him about the inheritance he may have felt more fear than satisfaction at gaining such a valuable tract. At eleven years old he was far too young to manage it, and without careful stewardship the estate could easily fall into ruin—or out of his hands altogether—before he reached his majority.

Fortunately, two relatives took control of the farm's affairs and his own. With remarkable energy, Mary Washington managed Ferry Farm while raising George and his younger siblings. Lawrence, who had inherited a plantation on Little Hunting Creek, meanwhile took time out from his own responsibilities to supervise George's education and upbringing. Over time Lawrence rapidly took on the role of substitute father, guiding the development of George's interests and personality as he became a young man.

The teenage George Washington was neither the budding Hercules of his hagiographers nor the vain, ambitious nonentity concocted by some debunking historians. He was neither an intellectual nor a yokel, but a typical, somewhat precocious boy eager to learn about the world and distinguish himself in it. Inherently somewhat reserved, he nevertheless made several close friends, boys his own age for the most part. In their early teens, they probably shared tales of war and adventure; later on they traded boasts on their affairs of the heart. "I might perhaps form some pleasures in the conversations of an agreeable young Lady," George wrote a cousin when he was about seventeen, "as there['s] one now Lives in the same house with me but as thats only nourishment to my former Affair for by often seeing her brings the other into my remembrance."

Washington stood about six feet tall by the time he was a young adult, a height that made him tower over most of his contemporaries. A fine posture, acquired under Lawrence's careful tutelage, complemented his height. At twenty-eight a friend called him "as straight as an Indian." Large of bone but well-proportioned, he possessed a fine mop of dark brown hair over a face with regular and firm but pleasant features. His only physical defects were a slight case of amblyopia, or "wandering eye," and increasingly bad teeth. Most imposing was the athletic physique he maintained throughout his youth and early manhood. David Humphreys, his friend and early biographer, wrote that Washington often claimed that "he never met any man who could throw a stone to so great a distance as himself; and, that when standing in the valley beneath the natural bridge in Virginia, he has thrown one up to that stupendous arch"—a height of about 215 feet.

In the social graces—prerequisites for entrance into polite society in eighteenth-century Virginia—Washington also excelled. Lawrence under-stood the value of good breeding from his own experience and probably played a crucial role in educating George in what Humphreys called "the graceful accomplishments of dancing, fencing, [and] riding." He was an ex-cellent horseman, and spent days riding and hunting in the Virginia country-side. Dancing grew to become one of Washington's favorite pastimes, and his skill in the ballroom, and in pleasant conversation at the table, made him a welcome guest in the homes of politically influential neighbors. Another fac-tor in his favor was the care he took with his clothing, a quality he practiced to a degree exceptional even by contemporary standards. From the age of sixteen—when he wrote for his own reference an elaborately detailed de-scription of his next suit of clothes—to the end of his life, Washington took great pleasure in dressing well.

Some historians have interpreted Washington's emphasis on proper social bearing, appearance, and conduct as vanity. Yet at this time and place, a man had to cultivate a good public image in order to rise in society. A reputation for amiability and probity was especially important for an ambitious young-ster like Washington. Although the well-known "Rules of Civility and Decent Behaviour in Company and Conversation" that he copied when he was six-teen had originated in a sixteenth-century French work rather than from his own imagination, he tried scrupulously to follow the 110 maxims in his own personal conduct. Throughout his life, and especially as he embarked on public careers in the military and in politics, he jealously guarded his reputa-tion, taking care to allow others no excuse to question his conduct. Washing-ton's fixation eventually reached the point where he would turn savagely on any critics, especially anyone who challenged his rights and prerogatives.

As a young man, when Washington had not yet learned to harness his emotions, they militated against the image of politeness and self-control he fought so hard to maintain. Frustrated over military or business affairs, he would write hasty, overdramatic letters to friends or rivals. Washington the general and president later mastered, to some extent, the gentle art of exag-geration, calculating the occasional written display of outrage or despon-dency in order to get what he wanted; but as a young man he had not yet perfected his persuasive techniques. As a result he alienated some people, including Virginia governor Robert Dinwiddie and Brigadier General John Forbes, who had helped to foster his career as a soldier.

In person, Washington usually maintained self-control. Although anger could on rare occasions drive him to cursing—and a change of facial expression that witnesses never forgot—he never became physically threatening. On one occasion in December 1755, Washington declined to strike back when a much smaller man knocked him down with a stick during an argument. Instead he left the room, pondered his conduct, and later apologized for the hot words he had used before being hit. His assumed *gravitas,* or seriousness of demeanor, did not allow for much laughter, either. He had a sense of humor that emerged when he dropped his guard, but he usually suppressed it.

When he spoke in public, Washington became stiff and uncomfortable. Thomas Jefferson recalled in 1814 that, "when called on for a sudden opinion, he was unready, short and embarrassed." Jefferson attributed this awkwardness to a mind that "was slow in operation, being little aided by invention or imagination, but sure in conclusion." Once he had made a decision, Washington became stubborn and accepted new information only with difficulty— a trait he showed on numerous occasions in battle. At other times, however, Washington reacted quickly to new circumstances. What Jefferson saw as slowness of mind may have been simply a reflection of the diligence and care with which Washington maintained his outward image and approached every object of his study.

Some of Washington's later critics, including Jefferson, denigrated his supposed lack of education. His detractors sometimes regarded him as little better than a bumpkin who had acquired his fame by accident. In reality, though he never approached the intellectual attainments of contemporaries like Jefferson, Washington was both intelligent and reasonably learned. Had he lived, Augustine Washington would have sent George to school in England, but his father's death and the inheritance of Ferry Farm forced the boy to stay at home and master subjects essential to his future responsibilities as a landowner. He bore the burden well, with Lawrence's help. When George entered day school as a juvenile in 1743 he showed remarkable promise. But unlike many of his more fortunate contemporaries, George never enjoyed a methodical education. He remained ashamedly aware throughout his life of gaps in his knowledge. He filled many of them only after years of independent writing, reading, work, and study.

New ideas fascinated Washington, especially during his teenage years. He attacked every subject with vigor, often drawing meticulous diagrams and taking notes. Later on, he might become bored and seek distraction in another area, but only after learning the original subject to his satisfaction. His surviving school exercises demonstrate a precise and organized mind. He filled pages and pages with mathematics, geometry, spelling, grammar, and copy work. The care with which Washington tackled these subjects indicates that he genuinely enjoyed studying them.

When possible, Washington preferred to learn hands-on; but reading also provided him a lifetime of pleasure and learning that gradually compensated for his early deficiencies in spelling and grammar. He read newspapers from youth until the day he died. An enthusiastic book collector, he also opened and read most of what he purchased. Little is known about his early reading, but it certainly included some mixture of agriculture, natural history, and military history and theory. As a young man he also enjoyed the theater. Joseph Addison's 1713 play *Cato,* a tragedy about the Roman Civil War, impressed Washington so much that he quoted from it throughout his life and even had it performed during the dark Valley Forge winter in 1777–78. He modeled his own ideals on the Stoic, incorruptible republican principles of the play's hero.

Many elements of George Washington's education helped to prepare him for a career in the military, a profession in which, as Humphreys claimed, "his mental acquisitions & exterior accomplishments were calculated to give him distinction." George's own youthful fascination with the military probably had the most to do with this, although he later claimed in a note to Humphreys' biography that "it was rather the wish of my eldest brother (on whom the several concerns of the family devolved) that this should take place." In any case, Washington took to drill and other elements of his informal military training with enthusiasm. Unfortunately, his martial ardor almost came to a premature and disastrous end in a scheme that must have left Mary Washington wondering whether Lawrence was the best mentor for her eldest son.

Mary Washington was not a meek woman. At the time of her husband's death in 1743 she was only in her mid-thirties and could have expected to remarry. Instead she devoted herself to managing the Ferry Farm property and raising her children. She ran a strictly ordered household, demanding and receiving obedience from her children. George's cousin and playmate, Lawrence Washington of Chotank, remembered that on his visits to Ferry Farm "I was ten times more afraid [of Mary Washington] than I ever was of my own parents. She awed me in the midst of her kindness, for she was, indeed, truly kind. I have often been present with her sons, proper tall fellows too, and we were all as mute as mice." She had high expectations of her children, and the rapid progress of George's education gave her reason to hope that he could take his father's place as a prosperous planter. Then, she learned to her outrage in the summer of 1746 that her son was on the verge of discarding his patrimony. His half brother Lawrence had convinced him to run away from home and join the British navy.

It is impossible to say exactly what was going through Lawrence's mind as he forged this cockeyed scheme. Apparently his continuing friendship with Admiral Vernon and others in the navy led him to believe that he could secure rapid promotion for George and eventually an officer's commission. Having a brother in the navy might also boost his own ambitions in the colonial government. Whatever his reasons, he avoided tackling the daunting Mary Washington directly. Instead he asked Colonel William Fairfax, a politically powerful family friend, to convince Mrs. Washington that her son would flourish at sea. Lawrence meanwhile informed his young half brother that a British vessel anchored at Alexandria was waiting to take him on as a midshipman. George promised in return to "be steady and thankfully follow your Advice," and packed his bags.

Mary Washington humored George at first, promising to let him leave—eventually. But soon she began finding reasons to postpone his trip. When Lawrence tried to pressure her, she put him off with "several trifling objections such as fond & unthinking moth[er]s naturally suggest." Finally, when Mrs. Washington's half brother Joseph Ball wrote her from England that George would be better off becoming an "aprentice to a Tinker" than joining the British navy, where his superiors would "Cut him & Slash him and use him like a Negro, or rather, like a Dog," she put down her fist. There would, she ruled, be no going to sea. George had found a more determined force than his half brother, and he obeyed. By that time, in any case, he had found other things to distract him.

In July 1743 Lawrence Washington pulled off a social coup that connected him to one of the most powerful families in Virginia. Shortly after the death that year of his father, he had moved to the estate on Little Hunting Creek, renaming it Mount Vernon in honor of his old commander at Cartagena. He promptly worked to transform the property into a suitable family seat by constructing a new mansion house. At the same time, he began to court a young woman named Ann Fairfax, who lived at the stunningly beautiful estate of Belvoir, just four miles downstream on the Potomac River.

William Fairfax, Ann's father, served as agent for the Northern Neck Proprietary. This huge tract of land, which spanned some one and a half million acres at its inception under King Charles II in the mid-seventeenth century, stretched across some of the best land in Virginia, from the Potomac to the Rappahannock. Though much of it had since been sold to individual landholders, William's cousin, Lord Thomas Fairfax, still held nominal authority over the whole area. As Lord Fairfax's agent, William had authority to dispense and withhold grants within the territory, making him one of the most powerful men in Virginia. Lawrence Washington's marriage to Ann Fairfax in July 1743 thus cemented an alliance that promised to win political influence for his family.

The connection between the two families passed beyond the merely formal. Lawrence's personal charm made him a welcome guest at Belvoir, only a short trip by boat or carriage from Mount Vernon, and before long he began to appear there in the company of his half brother George. With its armies of servants and ostentatious wealth, Belvoir was an entirely new world; but George adapted easily. Two of William Fairfax's sons, George William and Bryan, became his lifelong friends; and he also won the affection of Lord Fairfax himself, who lived at Belvoir for a short time after his arrival in Virginia in 1747.

George Washington's warm relationship with the Fairfaxes led to the first great adventure of his life: a surveying expedition to the western reaches of the Proprietary in the Shenandoah Valley of Virginia. George had both a meticulous mind and an instinctive aptitude for judging terrain, and surveying—which involved painstaking measurements of land and topography with primitive instruments—provided an ideal outlet for his talents. He had taken notes on the subject at age thirteen and later did some experimental fieldwork at Chotank and Mount Vernon. Lawrence encouraged this interest and hired a professional to instruct George. By the autumn of 1747 the boy had learned enough to earn money by surveying for local landowners. When the offer came to accompany twenty-four-year-old George William Fairfax and a party of experienced surveyors on a month-long trip to western

Virginia, young George accepted immediately. In anticipation of this trip, which commenced in March 1748, he bought a small notebook and titled it "A Journal of my Journey over the Mountains."

The image emerging from the journal is that of a young man who loved the wilderness and tried with varying degrees of success to live like a frontiersman. In their first few days the expedition rode across the Shenandoah River and over the Blue Ridge Mountains to what is now Winchester, Virginia, a location that George would later come to know well. He appreciated natural beauty, and along the way to Winchester he commented on the "beautiful Groves of Sugar Trees" and the "richness of the Land." During breaks from surveying he joined some of his companions in hunting wild turkeys. He shot at the birds twice, missing both times.

Young Washington struggled each night to decide whether he preferred sleeping under a roof or among the trees. At first he sheltered in inns and cabins, but after tossing all night on a bed with "one Thread Bear blanket with double its Weight of Vermin such as Lice Fleas &c.," he "made a Promise" to sleep from then on "in the open Air before a fire." The next night the lure of a feather bed and clean sheets put an end to that resolution. But he did not give up, and after a few more attempts at sleeping outdoors he learned the joys of roughing it. Though not, he wryly admitted, "so good a Woodsman as the rest of my Company," he came to enjoy camping in a haystack and making use of sticks and stones for eating utensils. He did not even get upset when the wind blew away his tent.

Encounters with Indians fascinated Washington. He had never seen them before. The surveyors met friendly natives on several occasions. One day, after a rainstorm that had prevented the party from doing any work, a group of about thirty Indians appeared "coming from War with only one Scalp." The white men offered liquor to the warriors and convinced them to perform a war dance. But Washington had come to survey, and although he took notes on the Indians, he filled most of his notebook with lengthy notes and descriptions of the lots that the expedition laid out through the countryside. The job was tedious and time-consuming, but George worked with enthusiasm. The meticulous records he kept reflect his concern for detail.

When the surveyors returned home in April they reported their expedition to William Fairfax. Young Washington had acquitted himself well, so with support from the Proprietor, Fairfax sought to secure him a commission as surveyor from the president and masters of the College of William and Mary in Williamsburg, the capital of Virginia. The college officials responded to the request in July 1749 by appointing Washington surveyor of the newly formed Culpeper County. He was only seventeen, and his appointment was a blatant act of patronage. Any other young man his age could only have hoped for an assistantship, at best.

Washington laid out only one piece of property in Culpeper County during his three-year term as a professional surveyor. He had no interest in surveying among Virginia farmers and their sedate little settlements, and asked for something more exciting. When William Fairfax offered to send him wherever he wanted, George chose the frontier. There, working mainly in the beautiful rolling woodland of the northern Shenandoah Valley, he surveyed dozens of lots in the spring and fall, when mild weather and thin foliage made his job easier. Between expeditions he returned to Ferry Farm or Mount Vernon, where he neatly platted, or mapped, the surveys for submission to the Proprietor's office.

In three years Washington earned about £400 from surveying fees. More important, he took advantage of his position and connection to the Proprietor to acquire about 2,300 acres of excellent Shenandoah Valley land, enough to establish him as a landowner of the first rank. His numerous expeditions had taught him how to appreciate good land, and that skill later helped him to expand his property through Virginia and beyond. By the autumn of 1752 he had taken the best possible advantage of the chance he had been offered three years before. New opportunities, and new responsibilities, now beckoned.

When George Washington took up his surveying career in the summer of 1749 his half brother Lawrence was already gravely ill. In his earliest surviving letter, dated May 5, 1749, George wrote to Lawrence that he hoped his cough was "much mended since I saw you last, if so likewise hope you have given over the thoughts of leaving Virginia." A few days earlier Lawrence had vacated his seat in the House of Burgesses because of his deteriorating health, and shortly afterward he boarded a ship for England in search of medical treatment. George busied himself with surveying and amorous adventures at Belvoir and Chotank until Lawrence returned from England, his health unimproved.

Still seeking a cure, Lawrence invited George to accompany him to the island of Barbados in the British West Indies, where the climate was reputedly healthier. George's concern over his brother's health vied with excitement at the travel opportunity. George abandoned his surveying and the pair sailed for the Caribbean in September 1751. Seafaring intrigued him. He learned navigation and nautical terminology, and kept a record of weather and the ship's progress modeled on a captain's log. His log included mentions of rough seas and high winds—including a dangerous swell brought on by an earthquake—along with "clear & pleasant Weather."

Life on Barbados seemed to consist of an endless round of social pleasures. The climate was mild, but Lawrence, no longer the popular and easygoing young man of ten years before, grew weary. "We soon tire of the same prospect," he wrote William Fairfax. "We have no bodily diversions but dancing." George, despite a brief struggle with smallpox that scarred his face, meanwhile reveled in everything from dancing, dinners, and the theater to avocados and pineapples. He watched the soldiers of the British garrison drill, and studied their fortifications. He took notes on everything he saw, including tropical methods of agriculture and the workings of a sociopolitical system based on slavery.

Much as it probably galled him to spend Christmas at sea instead of in Barbados, George nevertheless had to return to his surveying and business responsibilities in Virginia. Leaving Lawrence behind, on December 19, 1751, he boarded the ship *Industry* and began an unpleasant journey home. The weather was worse than it had been on the trip to Barbados, and a crewman emptied George's purse while he slept. Arriving home in early 1752, George diverted himself with some surveying in Frederick before riding back to Ferry Farm on the Rappahannock. There he awaited news of his brother.

Lawrence was approaching the end of his life. Depressed and lonely in Barbados, he yearned to see his native land one last time. He struggled back to Virginia in early June 1752. After a painful journey to Mount Vernon, he spent his remaining energy on trying to save his financial affairs from what George later called "the utmost confusion." Never much of a manager, Lawrence had lived beyond his means. His debts were considerable, if not overwhelming. In the terminal stages of pulmonary tuberculosis, Lawrence signed his will on June 20th. Little more than a month later he died. He was thirty-four years old.

Lawrence's death, followed within nine years by the passing of his wife and only child, left George in control of Mount Vernon. But the material gains did not soften the emotional blow. For ten years Lawrence had guided his younger brother as a friend, mentor, and substitute father. He had bequeathed to him an affinity for military life, a love for travel and adventure, a well-balanced education and personal deportment, an appreciation for the importance of social and political connections, and the skills for making them. The gap left by Lawrence's death could never be filled. From now on, instead of seeking guidance from a mentor, George would have to rely on himself.

George Washington's military career began almost immediately after his brother's death, which left a vacancy in the Virginia adjutant general's office. The adjutant general, who held the rank of major, was responsible for raising militia volunteers upon demand from the colonial government. He then had to form the volunteers into companies and train them for service. Lawrence's illness had long prevented him from performing these duties, but by the time he died it had become evident that even a healthy adjutant could not serve the entire colony. Lieutenant Governor Robert Dinwiddie and the House of Burgesses solved the problem by dividing the office into four districts, each with its own adjutant.

Washington sought one of the appointments as soon as they were advertised in 1752. Of the four districts, he was most interested in the Northern Neck. As adjutant for that region he would operate near home, and in the wealthiest part of Virginia. Dinwiddie first offered the post to William Fitzhugh, a veteran of the old American Regiment, but when Fitzhugh hesitated, Washington rushed to take his place. "In case Colo. Fitzhugh does not [accept]," he informed Dinwiddie, "[I] should take the greatest pleasure in punctually obeying from time, to time, your Honours commands; and by a strict observance of my Duty, render myself worthy of the trust reposed in Me: I am sensible my best endeavours will not be wanting, and doubt not, but by a constant application to fit myself for the Office, could I presume Your Honour had not in view a more deserving Person I flatter myself I should meet with the approbation of the Gentlemen of the Council."

Fitzhugh nevertheless eventually accepted the Northern Neck, and Dinwiddie offered Washington the scarcely less prestigious position of adjutant for the Southern District. Both districts received the same yearly salary of £100. Washington accepted, taking the oath of office in February 1753. It was an excellent first step for an ambitious twenty-one-year-old, giving him oversight of some of the better companies of the Virginia militia. But he remained unsatisfied. Immediately after his appointment he let the Virginia Council know that he still wanted the Northern Neck. The president of the council warned him that two other men, "both strongly recommended," had also requested the post; yet the ambitious youngster's persistence paid off. When Fitzhugh resigned after just a few months in office, George Washington resigned his former position to become adjutant of the Northern Neck. Though still an insignificant provincial officer, within a few months he would approach the world stage.

2

THE OHIO

October 1753 – January 1754

IN THE AUTUMN of 1753 George Washington set out for the Ohio River valley, then one of the most sensitive boundary regions in the world. France, Great Britain, and the Indian Iroquois Confederacy all laid claim to this territory stretching through what is now southwestern Pennsylvania, and each power tried to outmaneuver its rivals in political and military intrigue. Competition for the Ohio Valley divided Americans, as well. In 1745, hoping to acquire reputedly boundless wealth in timber, furs, and potential farmland ahead of competitors from Pennsylvania, the Virginia House of Burgesses had granted 200,000 acres in the region to the Ohio Company, a group of speculators that included Lawrence and Augustine Washington. Eventually the company laid claim to 500,000 acres. By the time Lawrence Washington became president of the company, in 1751, it had set up trading posts and small forts throughout the valley in preparation for permanent settlements to follow.

Virginia governor Robert Dinwiddie assumed control of the Ohio Company in 1752. Patient and practical, Dinwiddie made no further land claims. Instead he focused on securing his company's grip on the strategic heart of the valley at the junction of the Allegheny and Ohio rivers at modern-day Pittsburgh. That place, known in the mid-eighteenth century as the Forks of the Ohio, held the key to navigation of the region. Whoever held the Forks controlled the rivers, and thus the entire valley. Dinwiddie began by sending men to scout sites for a fort. The work parties that followed would bring muskets and cannon.

American penetration of the Ohio Valley alarmed French Canada's governor-general, the Marquis de Duquesne, who saw it as a major threat to his own ambitions. He reacted in June 1752 by wrecking a large American trading post in the region. With no illusions that one raid would be enough, he next ordered the construction of a chain of four French forts, including one at the Forks of the Ohio. These forts would block further American expansion, and also link French settlements in Canada to those in the Gulf of Mexico by way of the Ohio and Mississippi rivers. If left unmolested, the forts eventually would turn the Ohio Valley into a French domain.

Duquesne's aggressive policy forced the British government to respond in kind. London instructed Dinwiddie to investigate reports that the French were trying to take control of the Ohio Valley. If the reports proved true, and forts were indeed being constructed in the region, the governor was to demand an immediate French withdrawl. If the French rejected his ultimatum, he had permission to "drive them off by Force of Arms." Dinwiddie responded to these instructions by looking for an officer who could gather a small group of frontiersmen and lead them on a reconnaissance-cum-diplomatic expedition to the Ohio Valley. He had hardly begun the search for a candidate when Major George Washington appeared at the governor's mansion in Williamsburg. Swelling with military ambition and well recommended by other influential Virginians, Washington "offered himself to go." After a short discussion, Dinwiddie and his council agreed.

Dinwiddie handed Washington a commission and a set of instructions on the last day of October 1753. The commission authorized Washington to proceed "with all convenient & possible Dispatch, to that Part, or Place, on the River Ohio, where the French have lately erected a Fort, or Forts"—assuming they had done so—"or where the Commandant of the French Forces resides." On the way there, he was to parley with the Indian "Sachems of the Six Nations" and secure a native escort in order to attach them, if possible, to Virginia's cause. Dinwiddie also directed Washington to gather information on the structure, location, and garrisons of French forts on the Ohio and "learn what gave Occasion to this Expedition of the French. How they are like to be supported, & what their Pretentions are." But the young major had to hurry. After presenting Dinwiddie's letter to the French leader and "waiting not exceeding one Week for an Answer," he was to "return immediately back" and report to Williamsburg.

Some government officials derided the governor for naïvely entrusting such responsibility to a cocky young officer. But Washington confounded their expectations by setting himself vigorously and carefully to the task of preparing the expedition. He meticulously gathered the best supplies available—including goods for Indian trade—and dallied, no doubt happily,

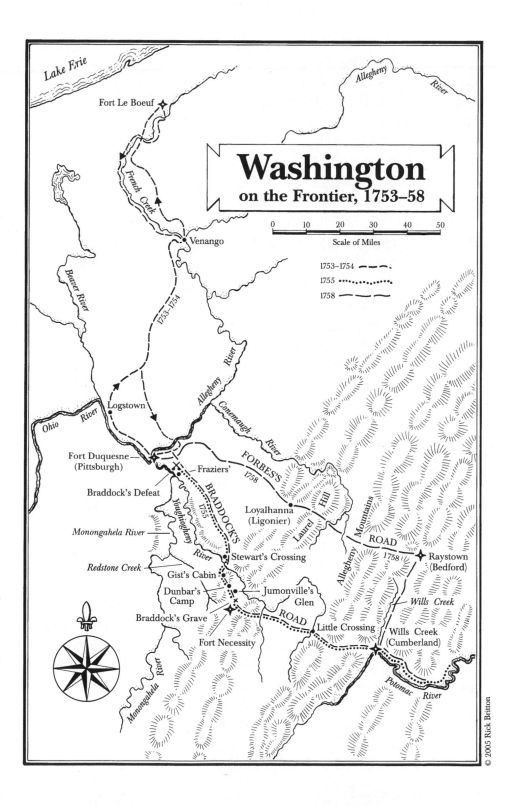

Lake Erie

Fort Le Boeuf

French Creek

Venango

Allegheny River

Beaver River

Washington
on the Frontier, 1753–58

Scale of Miles
0   10   20   30   40   50

1753–1754 — — —
1755 • • • • • • • •
1758 – – – –

Conemaugh River

Logstown

Ohio River

Fort Duquesne—
(Pittsburgh)

Braddock's Defeat

Fraziers'

FORBES'S

1758

BRADDOCK'S

1755

Youghiogheny River

Loyalhanna
(Ligonier)

Laurel Hill

Monongahela River

Stewart's Crossing

Redstone Creek

Gist's Cabin

Dunbar's
Camp

Jumonville's
Glen

Braddock's Grave

ROAD

Little Crossing

Fort Necessity

Monongahela River

Allegheny Mountains

ROAD

1758

Raystown
(Bedford)

Wills Creek

Wills Creek
(Cumberland)

Potomac River

over materials for a wilderness clothes outfit. He also took time to select good companions. His choice for a guide was a canny Maryland trader and explorer named Christopher Gist, who had led an expedition to the same place a year before. Gist knew the land as well as any Indian. Washington's French interpreter was Jacob Van Braam, a former lieutenant in the Dutch army who had arrived in America only the year before and worked as a private tutor. Four other men, all experienced Indian traders, also accompanied the expedition; and somewhere along the way Washington picked up another trader named John Davidson, who served as an Indian translator.

Major Washington and his troupe of frontiersmen began their wilderness journey from Wills Creek, a settlement on the Potomac in western Maryland, on November 15th. Their route was difficult, running eighty miles over a poorly maintained trail that traversed dense woods, numerous streams, and 3,000-foot high ridges of the Allegheny Mountains. Bad weather dogged them all the way, causing a steady drizzle of rain and wet snow to drip through leafless tree branches onto their heads as they clambered over leagues of broken ground covered by slushy snow half a foot deep. Soaked to the skin and utterly miserable after an exhausting week's march, they reached their first checkpoint at a trading post near the junction of the Monongahela and Youghiogheny rivers on the 22nd.

The owner of the trading post, one John Fraser, offered to make the men welcome for as long as they liked; but any hopes they had for drying out in front of a fire and awaiting better weather were dashed by the ever-impatient Major Washington, who ordered two men to float a canoe carrying the party's baggage ten miles downstream to the Forks of the Ohio while he rode ahead with the rest of his companions. Reaching the Forks first, he plunged his horse into the icy water and swam it all the way across the Allegheny River. Emerging from the water as if it had been a warm bath, he then calmly surveyed the ground around him. Here was where both Dinwiddie and the French intended to build forts; and even a cursory examination, he noted in satisfaction, showed that the site was "extreamly well situated" for that purpose, offering "the absolute Command of both Rivers."

After the canoe arrived and ferried Washington's less venturesome companions across the river while their horses swam behind, the group made camp. Early the next morning, the 24th, they resumed their journey, meeting along the way some Indians who agreed to accompany them to their next destination: the native village of Logstown, which lay thirteen miles northwest on the Ohio. Riding all day, the group followed the Ohio on their left for several miles before reaching a rich floodplain where the river flowed with a "majestic, easy current" some five hundred yards wide. As they rode farther, a steep ridge began rising to their right, and they splashed across a stream. Then they spotted an Indian longhouse ahead, surrounded by a cluster of several dozen log cabins and huts stretching from the bank of the river to the crest of the ridge. It was sunset. The day's journey was complete.

Washington's intentions on reaching Logstown were to meet Tanacharison— a Seneca chief and sometime British ally also known as the Half-King—and announce his mission, requesting an escort of warriors for the journey to the French outposts farther north. Tanacharison claimed to represent the Iroquois Confederacy, so his presence in the expedition would both guarantee its safety and symbolically associate the Confederacy with Virginia and Great Britain. As the Half-King had just left on a hunting trip, Washington was forced to wait, but he amused himself in the meantime by interrogating four Frenchmen who had just deserted a provisioning party bound upriver from New Orleans to the French settlements on Lake Erie. Who, he asked the bedraggled Frenchmen, were they, and where had they come from? How many French were on the Mississippi? Where were the new French forts? How many cannon, and what type, were mounted in each? Brushing aside their vaguely grumbled replies and demanding exact details, Washington eventually learned that the French had built forts farther north, Fort Presque Isle on Lake Erie and Fort Le Boeuf on a branch of French Creek. Their presence confirmed Duquesne's intention to expand southward.

The Half-King returned from his hunting trip on the 25th, just after the interrogation finished, and joined Washington in his tent. The two men got along surprisingly well, and were soon chatting like close friends. The closest French fort, Tanacharison told the attentive young major, was on French Creek only five or six nights' march away, but he warned that the Americans should not expect a friendly reception there. Several weeks earlier, Tanacharison had visited the fort in peace only to be bullied by its haughty commander, who compared Indians to "Flies or Musquito's" and scoffed at Anglo-American ambitions on the Ohio. The French officer had since met his just reward in a painful death by disease, but his insults against the Six Nations and Great Britain continued to rankle, and Tanacharison swore that he would demand an official apology or compensation. Washington assiduously took notes, and assured the chief that the French would have to be taught respect. After a few more vows of comradeship, the meeting broke up in a spirit of shared grievance.

The next day saw Washington delivering the first speech of his life to an audience of Indians that the Half-King had assembled in council. Speaking "by Order of your Brother the Governor of Virginia," he described his mission, asked for provisions and an escort of "young Men," and confirmed his words by proffering a string of wampum. The Half-King nodded his approval and then began his own harangue in Washington's favor, boasting to his fellow natives that he would accompany the expedition in hopes of defying the French in person. Turning to Washington, he then asked for a few days to consult further with the council, gather warriors, and fetch his ceremonial "French Speech Belt," which he had left at his hunting cabin somewhere in the wilderness.

Impatient as always, Washington urged haste; but when the Half-King showed signs of annoyance he quickly backed down and "consented to stay" at Logstown while the Indians completed their preparations. The wait lasted three days and ended in disappointment. Although Tanacharison had bragged of his authority over his fellow Indians, he had serious trouble persuading the leaders of the Delaware, Shawnee, Seneca, and other tribes near Logstown to support the tiny American expedition. Finally, on the evening of the 29th, the Half-King confessed to Washington that the other tribes had agreed to send only three chiefs and a hunter as an escort. "A greater Number," they claimed, "might give the French Suspicion of some bad Design, & cause them to be treated rudely." As Washington suspected, they actually were refusing to commit themselves to the British.

A frustrated Washington left Logstown on the last day of November with his original party, the Half-King, and a small group of Indian allies. The French-controlled village of Venango—located where French Creek met the Allegheny River, about sixty miles north of Logstown—was his next destination. It rained almost without letup as the men trekked north, sloshing through streams and rivulets past an Indian village forebodingly named Murdering Town, until they arrived at Venango on December 4th. The commander of the French garrison at that place, a forty-six-year-old half-breed army captain named Philippe Thomas de Joncaire, welcomed the Americans in a relaxed and easy manner. The next day, he told them, they would need to carry their message another forty miles north to the regional French commander at Fort Le Boeuf; in the meantime, why not join him and his officers for dinner before taking a night's rest? Washington, ever on the lookout for opportunities to gather information, politely agreed.

The food was good, the conversation excellent. Drinking freely, Joncaire and his officers kept up a constant chatter at the dinner table while Washington, smirking inwardly at their apparent carelessness, took mental notes. "The Wine," he wrote that night in his journal, "as they dos'd themselves pretty plentifully with it, soon banish'd the restraint which at first appear'd in their Conversation, & gave license to their Tongues to reveal their Sentiments more freely." They boasted of "their absolute Design to take Possession of the Ohio" and insisted that "by G— they wou'd do it." Washington accepted the threat amiably enough and slyly asked where they would find the necessary supplies and men. To his astonishment, they obliged by telling him the exact location of their forts and the state of their garrisons and supplies!

Washington was delighted at the apparent ease with which he had duped the French into sharing their plans. But Joncaire, a seasoned frontiersman who was acquainted with Indian ways, was craftier than he seemed. The next morning, friendly as ever but quite sober, he greeted the Americans and then turned to the Half-King and his fellow chiefs. Joncaire had ignored the Indians the night before; now it was the Virginians' turn to feel invisible. Why, the Frenchman cried with mock incredulity, had the major not told him of these distinguished guests? Ushering the Indians into his tent, he proceeded to fete them with every luxury at his command—especially liquor. Within a couple of days, Washington's stock with the Indians had fallen so far that they refused even to enter his tent. Helplessly he appealed to Gist, who struggled to convince the chiefs to remain with Washington while Joncaire urged them to stay at Venango.

Finally, at midmorning on the 7th, after "great Perswasion," Gist convinced the Indians to rejoin the expedition on its way north to Fort Le Boeuf. With them came an "escort" of four French officers, loaned by Joncaire to keep them from being mistaken for a raiding party and slaughtered by his countrymen. The next forty miles were marked by wretched weather and "many Mires & Swamps." Rain and snow fell relentlessly, swelling the creeks so much that the party had to swim their horses through the frigid water while floating their baggage across on trees. Soaked and dejected, men and animals became increasingly desperate for rest.

They encountered the first patrols from Fort Le Boeuf after sunset on December 11th. The French politely conducted the shivering Americans inside the fort to rooms where they could dry out and rest. The next day Washington presented himself to the commandant, a one-eyed Knight of St. Louis named Jacques Legardeur de Saint-Pierre who had "much the air of a Soldier," but looked like "an elderly Gentleman" despite his fifty-two years. Legardeur welcomed the Virginian politely and accepted Dinwiddie's letter demanding a French withdrawal from the Ohio. He would, he said, confer with a council of war and meet him again in a few days. In the meantime, Washington had the run of the fort.

For most of the next two days Washington ambled about with Van Braam in tow, taking careful notes on the fort's construction, armament, and garrison. He chatted occasionally with Legardeur and the other French officers, but found them more reticent than Joncaire had been. Finally, on the evening of the 14th, the French commandant called Washington to his office and presented his reply to Dinwiddie in a sealed letter. Although no doubt curious of the letter's contents, which he was not permitted to open, Washington had the satisfaction of knowing at least one thing: the first part of his mission was over. It was time to return home.

Early the next day Washington rose to find that Legardeur, still apparently "extreamly complaisant," had thoughtfully packed the expedition's canoe with liquor and provisions. But like Joncaire, his politeness masked a sinister side. Once again, the Indians refused to go. Washington discovered that the French officer had offered guns to the Indians if they would wait before leaving, "ploting every Scheme that the Devil & Man cou'd invent, to set our Indians at Variance with us, to prevent their going 'till after our Departure." Such a separation, Washington knew, would symbolize the breakup of his already tenuous Indian alliance. Angrily, he postponed the departure until the following morning. "I can't say," he wrote in his journal, "that ever in my Life I suffer'd so much Anxiety as I did in this affair."

Washington again tried to get the Indians to leave with him on the 16th but still found them recalcitrant in face of the "Power of Liquor." Unable any longer to restrain his temper, Washington confronted Tanacharison and "tax'd the King so close upon his Word that he refrain'd, & set off with us as he had engag'd." Afraid that the Indians might reconsider, he immediately drove them from the fort and pressed homeward. At all costs he must reach Williamsburg before the winter weather forced him to take shelter and give up hope of presenting Legardeur's letter to Dinwiddie before the spring. If he delayed, the whole expedition might have been for naught.

Nature continued to conspire against him. The canoe trip back to Venango took six miserable days. French Creek's swollen waters drove the canoes against rocks, and several times the men had to plunge into the deep icy water to guide their vessels over the shoals. They spent a whole night trying to hack through thick ice before giving up and carrying the canoes for a quarter-mile across a neck of land. The men's nerves did not relax until, close to their destination, they saw a passing French canoe full of trading liquor capsize in the swift current. Laughing contemptuously after "seeing the French overset, and the brandy and wine floating in the creek," they continued on and left the boatmen to "shift for themselves." A day later, the expedition reached Venango.

As the white men paused to get their gear in order for the remainder of their trip, the Half-King apologetically told them that he could go no farther. Pressed for time, Washington acquiesced. Admonishing the Indian to guard against Joncaire's "Flattery," he left the village and continued south. His horses were by now so sick that the major ordered his men to dismount and lead them on foot. Setting the example, he donned "an Indian walking Dress" and marched forward into the sodden, uninviting woods. After three days the path deteriorated as the snow became deeper, and the horses could travel no farther. Washington told Van Braam and the others to remain with them and the baggage while he and Gist continued alone.

Washington recorded the moment in his journal. "I took my necessary Papers," he wrote, "pull'd off my Cloths; tied My Self up in a Match Coat; & with my Pack at my back, with my Papers & Provisions in it, & a Gun, set out with Mr. Gist, fitted in the same manner." Gist actually tried to dissuade him, "unwilling," he himself recorded, that the young major "should undertake such a travel, who had never been used to walking before this time." But Washington ignored Gist's protests, and the two men spent the next day slogging eighteen bitter miles through the snow and ice. "That night," Gist wrote in his journal with perhaps a hint of amusement, "we lodged at an Indian cabin, and the Major was much fatigued."

Washington would not admit it, but as they left the cabin early the next morning, the 27th, he was nearing the end of his strength. Stumbling ahead, they reached Murdering Town, where a shifty-eyed Indian emerged from the village and offered to guide them to the Forks of the Ohio. Gist looked at the young warrior suspiciously, for he thought he had seen him with Joncaire at Venango, but Washington was either too tired or too impatient to care and agreed to let the Indian lead them on. Before long the Indian offered to carry his pack, and Washington, laboring under exhaustion that extinguished his pride, accepted. Even so, after a few miles he was on the verge of collapse. The warrior, who had a musket of his own, then suggested carrying Washington's gun. The major refused, but he also dismissed Gist's worry that the offer suggested treachery.

As the day wore on the trio marched through increasingly unfamiliar and isolated territory. Gist took his bearings and discovered that the Indian had led them astray from their intended route. At that moment they emerged from the woods into a snow-covered meadow. Walking several steps ahead, the Indian continued through the clearing to a stand of trees on the other side. Once there, with the white men in the open and an escape route at his back, he wheeled around, quickly aimed his gun, and fired. Washington, who apparently had been stumbling half-asleep, woke up in an instant and looked around in shock. Ahead he saw Gist sprinting toward the Indian, who was leaning against an oak tree and frantically reloading his gun. "Are you shot?" Washington blurted out; Gist—somewhat superfluously considering he was running for all he was worth—yelled back "no" and kept going as Washington staggered onward in his tracks. Reaching his quarry just in time, Gist knocked the warrior's gun aside and thrust his own musket toward his heart. Washington came panting up at that moment and gasped to Gist not to pull the trigger. Instead, at Washington's insistence, they pretended that the attempted murder had been nothing more than an accident. Taking his gun, Gist sent the Indian away. The two white men then turned and fled through the woods. Washington imagined a whole party of Indians in pursuit.

Their tracks in the snow would betray their route, but their only choice was to keep going until they reached the Allegheny River. After plodding all that night and another day without much rest or any sleep, the two men arrived at the riverside. In the bitter cold, they hacked down trees with "one poor Hatchet," and roped together a makeshift raft, which Gist guided toward a small island in the middle of the river. Halfway across, the raft became so badly mired in ice floes that Washington "expected every Moment our Raft wou'd sink, & we Perish." He tried to push them past the floes with a pole but, in a final humiliation, a chunk of ice rammed the raft with such violence that it knocked Washington into the water. Fortunately he kept a hold on the pole, and Gist, whose own fingers and toes had become frostbitten, hauled him out.

That night on the island, which he spent huddled on frozen mud among reeds and scrub, was among the worst Washington ever experienced. Thankfully no pursuers appeared, and the next day the two men crossed the now frozen river on foot and made their way to Fraser's trading post, which they reached that evening. They lingered there in relief for a few days, procured horses, and set out again on New Year's Day, 1754. On the 6th, Washington and Gist reached Wills Creek and parted, with what emotions we can only imagine.

Setting out alone, the major arrived five days later at the much-welcome refuge of Belvoir, where he "stop'd one Day to take necessary rest." At last, on January 16th, the bedraggled but triumphant young man walked into Governor Dinwiddie's mansion in Williamsburg and handed him the sealed letter from the French commandant at Fort Le Boeuf. Not even twenty-two years old, Washington had accomplished the first important public mission of his life. In doing so he set the scene for the next stage of his military career, his first experience of combat, and his first defeat.

3

FORT NECESSITY

January – October 1754

THE ULTIMATUM FROM Governor Dinwiddie that Washington had carried to Fort Le Boeuf demanded French withdrawal from the Ohio Valley, a region "notoriously known to be the Property of the Crown of Great Britain." But Legardeur was uncompromising, and in his reply to the governor he scoffed at threats of military force. "As to the summons you send me to retire," he wrote, "I do not think myself obliged to obey it." He had other instructions, and intended "to follow them with all the exactness and determination which can be expected from a good officer." These unyielding words, and Washington's report of French military activities in the region, convinced Dinwiddie that force was his only remaining option.

Washington's 7,000-word journal of his expedition to the Ohio made good propaganda, so Dinwiddie had it published. He then ordered the creation of a military force for the frontier. Washington, in his capacity as adjutant of the Northern Neck, would train and equip one hundred militiamen from Frederick and Augusta counties. These troops, along with another hundred frontiersmen under Captain William Trent, an Indian trader and land speculator, would then head for the Forks of the Ohio. There they would start building a fort and await a reinforcement of 300 soldiers and artillery that would leave Alexandria in March.

Dinwiddie's orders were more difficult to execute than they seemed. Virginia law required every free white man more than twenty-one years old to serve in his county's militia company when called, or else supply a substitute. But years of neglect had left the mechanism for raising the Virginia militia in decay. Eligible men ignored the call to enlist; and county officials, who for years had neglected elementary record-keeping, did not know who lived under their jurisdiction. Enforcing the militia law was impossible. Washington sulked for two weeks at Belvoir, waiting futilely for men to answer his call, before giving up and returning to Williamsburg in humiliation. The adjutant of the Northern Neck—the wealthiest district in Virginia—had been unable to raise a single militia soldier.

Dinwiddie forgave the young major and turned to the House of Burgesses, which granted him a £10,000 loan after fierce lobbying and debate. With this money—and despite the lack of support from Maryland and Pennsylvania—Dinwiddie decided to try again. This time he would abandon the useless militia system and resort to paid volunteers, who would be formed into a regiment with six companies of fifty men each. Washington welcomed the news and began lobbying for a commission in the regiment. Sensing his inexperience, he did not ask for the colonelcy. "The command of the whole forces is what I neither look for, expect, nor desire," he admitted, "for I must be impartial enough to confess, it is a charge too great for my youth and inexperience to be intrusted with." All he asked, with disingenuous modesty, was for an appointment as lieutenant colonel and second in command!

Dinwiddie's choice for colonel was Joshua Fry, a middle-aged mathematician and capable frontiersman who had been to Logstown. Washington was made lieutenant colonel. He had no sooner received his commission in March 1754 than he began grumbling about pay; but the prospect of action distracted him from his complaints. Reports of an imminent French military presence at the Forks persuaded Dinwiddie that further delay meant losing the Ohio Valley. The governor ordered Lieutenant Colonel Washington to march for the frontier with any volunteers he could quickly raise and all the supplies he could gather. Fry, the governor promised, would meet him along the way with the rest of the Virginia Regiment.

This time Washington found his volunteers readily enough. They joined up for their daily pay—a decent sum equivalent to fifteen pounds of tobacco—and for promised settlement land along the Ohio. Yet the regimental officers arrived only slowly, so the lieutenant colonel had to drill the men alone. He discovered that they were not only "loose, Idle Persons," but "selfwill'd" and "ungovernable" too. He did not yet have the knack for military command, and this was not the best situation in which to acquire it. The volunteers had emerged from levels of society into which Washington had never ventured. He frankly did not understand them. For their part, they did not include training and discipline in the bargain they had accepted, and showed little awe for their officious lieutenant colonel.

Procuring clothing and equipment required Washington to cudgel unco-

operative contractors with sharply worded and detailed demands for supplies, and to keep badgering them until they complied. But he handled this
part of his command well. It allowed him both to indulge his sartorial fancies
and demonstrate his professed knowledge of the frontier. "It is the nature of
Indians," he wrote to Dinwiddie, "to be struck with, and taken by show." For
that reason he suggested fitting out the troops entirely in red uniforms. With
the Indians, he declared, red "is compard to Blood and is look'd upon as the
distinguishing marks of Warriours and great Men." By contrast, "the shabby
and ragged appearance the French common soldiers make affords great matter for ridicule amongst the Indians and I really believe is the chief motive
why they hate and despise them as they do." Dinwiddie replied that "You
have not Time to get them made, unless to be sent after You."

Washington led his bedraggled regiment out of Alexandria, bound for the
frontier, on April 2nd. He had assembled a total of 186 men, including officers, in two companies of volunteer soldiers, along with twenty-five guards
for two wagons. His two captains were both Scots. The senior captain was a
middle-aged recent immigrant from Edinburgh named Peter Hog; the other,
not yet present, was an irascible thirty-year-old former physician, Adam
Stephen. Jacob Van Braam held the rank of lieutenant. James Craik, another
Scot who served as the expedition's surgeon, would attend Washington on his
deathbed forty-five years later. An assortment of noncommissioned officers, a
drummer, and a Swedish volunteer marched with the regiment too.

The expedition's route ran northwest, through Fairfax and Loudoun counties to Hillsboro, and then across the Shenandoah River at Vestal's Ferry to
Winchester. Stephen met him there with a few dozen volunteers, and after a
delay caused by a shortage of wagons Washington resumed the march for
Wills Creek on the 18th. Along the way he received bad news in letters from
Captain William Trent, who had arrived at the Forks on February 17th with
two companies of frontiersmen. The Half-King was also there with a few
warriors, helping Trent build a fort, but the chief had failed to keep his
promises of more substantial support. The frontier companies, numbering
just over forty men, were running short of provisions when the French began
closing on them with 800 soldiers. Trent needed Washington's help.

With growing concern, Washington rode ahead on April 20th to Wills
Creek. There he unexpectedly met Trent's ensign, Edward Ward. On April
17th, Ward said, a small fleet of canoes bearing one thousand French soldiers
had landed near the unfinished frontier fort. Trent had left to hunt for provi-

sions some days earlier, and Ward faced the crisis as the temporary American commander. The French—now led by Captain Claude-Pierre Pécaudy, sieur de Contrecoeur, who had replaced Legardeur as commandant of the Ohio country—gave the bewildered ensign one hour to evacuate his command. Ward complied, despite the protests of the Half-King. Contrecoeur tore down the English fort and built a replacement while Ward led his dejected men back toward Wills Creek.

Ward's report put Washington in a difficult position. Fry continued to tarry at Alexandria, and to wait for him before responding to the French move was unthinkable. But Washington did not want to bear all of the responsibility for deciding what to do, so he called his officers to a council of war. The council concluded that the Virginia Regiment was too small to face Contrecoeur alone. On the other hand, abandoning the Half-King and the Indians he supposedly represented might jeopardize future assistance from that source. He would, the officers agreed, need reassurance that the Americans did not plan to turn tail and run.

On the council's advice, Washington sent an Indian warrior to Tanacharison with a letter signed by himself as "Connotaucarious," or the "devourer of villages," an Indian name given him by the Half-King in honor of his great-grandfather John Washington, who had borne the same appellation. Washington promised that the Virginia Regiment formed only an advance party of "a great Number of our Warriors that are immediately to follow with our Great Guns, our Ammunition, and our Provision." To keep this from becoming another white man's empty promise, the council encouraged Washington to push ahead to the mouth of Red Stone Creek on the Monongahela River, over eighty miles from Wills Creek and about thirty-seven miles south of the Forks. There, the officers advised, the regiment should "raise a Fortification, clearing a Road broad enough to pass with all our Artillery and our Baggage, and there to wait for fresh Orders." The task would keep the soldiers too busy to grumble and preserve them from all other "ill Consequences of inaction."

The lieutenant colonel knew that this decision had political implications extending far beyond his little camp. He accordingly wrote to the governors of Maryland and Pennsylvania, informing them of the situation and asking for help. Washington poured all of his untested rhetorical skills into the appeals, demanding attention to "this interesting cause—that should rouse from the lethargy we have fallen into, the heroick spirit of every free-born Englishman to support the rights and privileges of our king (if we don't consult the benefit of ourselves) and resque from the invasions of a usurping enemy, our majesty's property, his dignity, and lands." In writing these letters Washington surpassed his province as a humble Virginia lieutenant colonel; but he also showed awareness of his inability to succeed without political support.

The march to Red Stone Creek was exceptionally difficult, and working parties made slow progress in widening the road. On some days the Virginians could make only two or three miles through the wilderness. Trent's men might have been some help, but Washington hesitated to use them. A few weeks before he would not have believed that any men could be more surly or disobedient than his own; but these frontiersmen were the worst he had ever seen. With salaries twice what the volunteers from Virginia received, they swaggered and boasted incessantly.

The unruly frontiersmen went home before they became insufferable, but they left Lieutenant Colonel Washington and his men seething. Their salaries, which they once considered reasonable, had now become unacceptable. The officers protested formally to the governor, demanding higher pay, and Washington covered it with a petulant diatribe. "Upon the whole," he wrote, "I find so many clogs upon the expedition, that I quite despair of success; nevertheless, I humbly beg it, as a particular favor, that your Honor will continue me in the post I now enjoy, the duty whereof I will most cheerfully execute as a volunteer, but by no means upon the present pay." Dinwiddie replied angrily to such "ill timed Complaints," but by the time Washington drafted an impertinent retort an event of much greater moment than a few shillings had taken place.

While Washington fumed, French soldiers worked steadily by the Forks of the Ohio, felling trees and stacking logs. Their completed fort, dubbed Fort Duquesne, made a mockery of the American stick-castle it replaced. Captain Contrecoeur meanwhile pondered Indian reports of the advance of the Virginia Regiment. He longed to slaughter the ragged Americans as they hacked and swore their way through the forest, but Governor Duquesne had forbidden him to attack unless provoked. Yet he could still threaten them. For that purpose Contrecoeur instructed his subordinate, Ensign Joseph Coulon de Villiers, sieur de Jumonville, to take a detachment of soldiers and order Lieutenant Colonel Washington out of French territory. The ensign left the Forks with thirty-five men on May 23rd.

By that time Washington and his men had reached a clearing known as Great Meadows, about twenty-seven miles southeast of Red Stone Creek. In the morning a courier brought him a translated message from the Half-King, which he struggled to decipher from semiliterate interpreter John Davidson's crabbed scrawl. Davidson quoted the Half-King as giving "an acct of a french armey to meat Miger Georg Wassiontton therefor my Brotheres I deisir you to be awar of them for deisind to strike the forist Englsh they see." A scout seconded this account by reporting that he had sighted the French at a crossing of the Youghiogheny River, about eighteen miles north in the general direction of Fort Duquesne.

Assuming that the French were preparing a surprise attack on his straggling, outnumbered regiment, Washington ordered his troops to dig in. They "made a good Intrenchment and by clearing the Bushes out of these Meadows prepar'd a charming field for an Encounter," he later boasted to Dinwiddie. In reality, they dug some mucky ditches in the sodden fields and flipped over a few wagons. In this modest shelter the lieutenant colonel ordered his men to spend the night under arms. After midnight the crackling of twigs seemed to announce the feared attack, and nervous sentries opened fire into the darkness. But the footsteps receded, and no French or bloodthirsty Indians came screaming into camp. The next morning Washington called roll and found six of his men missing. The phantoms of the night before had been nothing more than deserters from his own regiment.

The next two days were a period of constant anxiety for the Virginians. Small parties of mounted scouts roved the woods without seeing anything but trees and squirrels, but Washington still expected an attack. Finally, early on the morning of the 27th, Christopher Gist entered camp past trigger-happy sentries and shook hands with his old comrade. Gist owned a cabin at a new settlement thirteen miles west, on the way to Red Stone Creek. He reported that fifty French soldiers had recently stopped at his cabin, threatened to kill his cow and break "every Thing in the House," and then passed on toward Washington's camp. By now they were probably only a few miles away. Enraged at this threat to Gist's unoffending cow—or perhaps seeing an opportunity for defeating a relatively small raiding party—Washington sent Captain Hog "in pursuit" with a detachment of about seventy-five men.

Dinwiddie's original orders for the expedition had been flexible, instructing Washington to "act on the Difensive" after reaching the Forks, "but in Case any Attempts are made to obstruct the Works or interrupt our Settlemts by any Persons whatsoever, You are to restrain all such Offenders, & in Case of resistance to make Prisoners of or kill & destroy them." In all other things, the governor declared, Washington could act "as the Circumsts. of the Service shall require." But Dinwiddie never suggested that the Virginia Regiment should slaughter French scouts, and—the threat to Christopher Gist's cow notwithstanding—the approaching band of fifty men had harmed neither people nor property. They may or may not have been raiders, but Washington had no business attacking them until he was sure.

Of course, no officer worth his salt would have waited for the French to declare their intentions without making preparations for the defense of his post. In this respect Washington's decision to divide the Virginia Regiment was an act of extreme folly. If the Frenchmen were only part of a larger force, as indeed he feared, the puny pursuit party would end up fighting a superior enemy in the trackless woods while the camp at Great Meadows languished in a gravely weakened condition. If, on the other hand, the French had ventured out on their own, their defeat would only draw swift retaliation from Contrecoeur's main force at the Forks. Even the most conservative estimate made this force more than a match for the Virginia Regiment and the few hundred reinforcements that Fry and Dinwiddie had promised to send at some unspecified time in the future.

Washington *wanted* a fight, however, and as the last of Hog's men disappeared into the trees he called together some young Indians in camp. The French, he announced, had arrived at Gist's cabin in search of the Half-King, whom they intended to hunt down and kill. This lie, Washington later recalled, had "its desired Effect." Outraged, the Indians vowed to find the Frenchmen and kill them if they had so much as treated the Half-King disrespectfully. If Hog did not find the French, the Indians would.

At eight o'clock that evening an Indian runner slipped into camp and handed Washington another message from the Half-King. Hoping to link up with the Americans at Great Meadows, the chief had led a group of warriors to a place in the woods only a few miles away. But before he could reach Washington's camp, the Half-King had happened upon the tracks of French soldiers. He followed them until they took shelter in a "low obscure Place" and then sent word of their presence to the Virginia lieutenant colonel.

Ironically, Washington, who thought he had just duped a group of naïve Indians into attacking the French, reacted to the Half-King's message "that very Moment" by deciding to attack them himself. Leaving behind only three-dozen soldiers at Great Meadows as a baggage guard, he took forty men through "a Night as dark as Pitch, along a Path scarce broad enough for one Man," toward the Half-King's camp. All night the Virginians stumbled, cursing, through the darkness, blundering into trees and one another as rain pattered steadily around them. Miraculously, as the rain tapered off just after sunrise they found Tanacharison, who had made camp with twelve warriors, two of them boys, just six miles from Great Meadows.

The lieutenant colonel and his old Indian acquaintance then entered into council, assisted by an interpreter, while the weary Virginians rested from their night march. Though sodden, Washington still looked forward to a fight. The Half-King, furious at how the French had pulled down "his" fort at the Forks—and possibly feeling he had nothing to lose—was in the same frame of mind. For once the two men found themselves in complete agreement about the French, and resolved to "fall on them together." Two of the Half-King's warriors loped off into the woods to determine the French party's strength and position, and quickly returned. The enemy had camped in a rocky glen half a mile from the main road to the Forks, without taking any precaution against attack. It would be a simple matter to surround and ambush them. Forming their men into single file, Washington and the Half-King set off to do just that.

The attackers slipped into position among the rocks that surrounded the damp little French camp, where soldiers struggled to light cooking fires after the rain of the previous night. It was seven o'clock in the morning. Captain Stephen led twenty of the Virginians on one side, and Washington commanded the others. The Half-King and his warriors drifted silently from place to place around the perimeter, which progressively shrank as the Virginians crept closer to the campfires. Then Washington rose from shelter to give the order to attack. He startled an enemy soldier, who sounded the alarm; the French scrambled for their guns, and Washington ordered his men to open fire.

The battle, such as it was, took no more than fifteen minutes. Jumonville's men never had a chance. When the firing stopped, about ten or twelve Frenchmen lay dead, and two, including Jumonville, were wounded. The large proportion of dead to wounded has led some historians to claim that a massacre took place after the battle, and that Washington covered it up. In fact the Indians butchered some wounded Frenchmen while the fighting still raged. Far from trying to conceal this, Washington told Dinwiddie that six Indians who lacked muskets had "servd to knock the poor unhappy wounded in the head and beriev'd them of their Scalps." Apparently he thought such behavior was typical. Twenty-one Frenchmen survived as prisoners, and one escaped. Only one Virginian had been killed. Washington had won his first "battle."

As Washington surveyed the carnage he noticed Jumonville, who lay clutching some papers that he implored the lieutenant colonel to read. The Frenchman had been calling for a cease-fire for several minutes, but in their excitement the attackers had taken no heed. Now Jumonville insisted that Washington had made a terrible mistake. His men had not intended to attack but to parley. The Virginian accepted the papers, which offered evidence that he had just massacred a diplomatic mission. But Jumonville did not live to see Washington's reaction. An Indian, by some accounts the Half-King himself, murdered him as he lay helpless on the ground, crushing his skull with a tomahawk and then washing his hands in the Frenchman's brains. Though gory, that was probably the extent of the reputed post-battle "massacre."

Washington never recorded his response to the murder, which had taken him unawares, perhaps while he read Jumonville's papers. But he immediately wrote Dinwiddie in defense of the attack on the French expedition. If Jumonville had been on a peaceful mission, he asked, what business did he have with such a large and well-armed escort? Why did he approach the British camp secretly, camping in a "sculking place" rather than "coming up in a Publick manner" as diplomatic emissaries were supposed to do? Both were valid points, and suggested more nefarious motives than the delivery of a summons. Jumonville's instructions, Washington continued angrily, "were to reconnoitre the Country, Roads, Creeks &ca to Potomack"; all, he had no doubt, "through no other view, than to get sufficient Reinforcements to fall upon us imediately after." Even the summons that the French officer had intended to deliver to Washington was undiplomatic. "The Summon's is so insolent, & savour's so much of Gascoigny," he wrote, "that if two Men only had come openly to deliver it[,] It was too great Indulgence to have sent them back."

Washington observed no parallel between Jumonville's mission and his own expedition of the previous autumn to Fort Le Boeuf. Instead, convinced that he had been in the right, Washington preened himself in the wake of what he saw as a brilliant military victory. Writing again to Dinwiddie a week after the encounter, he boasted that "we had but 40 Men with which we killd and took 32 or 3 Men besides those who may have escap'd." The behavior of the French vindicated his long-held contempt for them. "If the whole Detachment of the French behave with no more Risolution than this chosen Party did," he crowed, "we shall have no great trouble in driving them" back to Montreal.

In a letter to his eighteen-year-old brother, John, Washington described his first experience of battle. In writing it his mind may have wandered back to the letter that Lawrence Washington had sent to his family from off the coast of Jamaica in 1741. "I fortunately escaped without a wound," he triumphantly told Jack, "tho' the right Wing where I stood was exposed to & received all the Enemy's fire and was the part where the man was killed & the rest wounded. I can with truth assure you, I heard Bulletts whistle and believe me there was something charming in the sound."

The letter eventually found its way into publication, and that summer King George II of Great Britain read it in a copy of the *London Magazine*. Turning to his companions, the king quipped, "He would not say so, if he had been used to hear many."

Only later, as news of Jumonville's death spread through the colonies and to Fort Duquesne, did Washington consider the consequences of his attack. "I shall expect every hour to be attackd and by unequal number's, which I must withstand if there is 5 to 1," he wrote. For his part, Tanacharison decided that the time for negotiation and half measures had passed. Bearing several French scalps, he left to try and persuade the Delaware, Seneca, and Shawnee Indians to join the Virginians at Great Meadows. Washington sent thirty men and horses to escort the chief, gathered his prisoners, and trekked back to Great Meadows. At the same time he sent a courier to Fry, appealing for him to come "with all imaginable dispatch."

Upon his return to Great Meadows Washington sent the prisoners back to Williamsburg with twenty soldiers and a warning for Dinwiddie to ignore the Frenchmen's "many smooth Story's." With the return of Captain Hog's party there were now just over 100 Virginians at Great Meadows. Washington set them to work felling trees and constructing "a small palisadod Fort," which they completed on June 3rd—a circular stockade made of seven-foot-high upright logs covered with bark and skins, and built around a little hut containing ammunition and provisions. Appropriately, Washington named it Fort Necessity.

Just as his men finished Fort Necessity, Washington welcomed the Half-King and his precious escort of soldiers back to camp. The chief brought no warriors, only eighty elderly Indians, with many women and children. To the Virginians' amazement, more families arrived almost every day thereafter, beseeching their protection from French retribution. But although the Half-King continued to promise, he failed to produce a single warrior. The Virginians, it seemed, would face the enemy alone.

The remainder of the Virginia Regiment finally filed into the clearing at Great Meadows on June 9th, minus Fry, who had broken his neck and died in a fall from his horse. George Muse, who had taken temporary command in Fry's place, saluted Washington as the new colonel of the Virginia Regiment. Muse was now lieutenant colonel and Stephen a major. Muse presented the new colonel with a medal, a letter from Dinwiddie expressing approval of his "highly pleasing" defeat of the French, and a quantity of rum from the governor's private supply. Until Colonel James Innes arrived at Fort Necessity with a regiment of reinforcements from North Carolina, Dinwiddie wrote, Washington would command the entire expedition.

By the middle of June, while the French gathered forces at Fort Duquesne in preparation for a counterstrike, about 400 troops had assembled at Fort Necessity. Muse had brought nearly 200 men along with nine small swivel cannon, and a few days later 100 British regulars from South Carolina marched into Great Meadows. Their thoughts on seeing the Virginians' puny and ill-sited fort can only be imagined. Declining the dubious honor of joining the provincials in Fort Necessity, the British, who were organized into an independent company under the command of James Mackay, made their own camp.

Mackay had over fifteen years' military experience and may have resented subordinating his men to the obviously inexperienced Virginian; but aside from establishing a separate camp he behaved politely. Washington resented this affront to his commission and fretted about the need for a single command. Yet his earlier fears of an immediate French attack had faded, and instead of holing up indefinitely at Fort Necessity he decided to resume the earlier advance on Red Stone Creek. He had heard that only 500 ill-supplied French soldiers now garrisoned Fort Duquesne, and discounted all evidence to the contrary. Washington led the 300 Virginians out of Great Meadows on June 16th and ordered them to widen the trail for those who would follow. They made slow progress.

Two days later, Washington sat down with the Half-King and forty Indians in a council at Gist's settlement. Their meeting lasted three days and did not go well. Tanacharison had not convinced the other chiefs to make war on the French and now seemed reluctant himself. The Indians had their people's welfare to consider. Fort Necessity was a child's toy compared to Fort Duquesne. Why should they make league with soldiers who could hardly defend themselves, much less protect Indian women and children from the French? Washington's diplomacy had little effect. Eventually the Half-King deserted him, never to return, and the families at Fort Necessity left as well.

The loss of Indian support dealt a serious blow to Virginia's ambitions on the Ohio. For a few days Washington attempted to carry on the fiction of a march to Red Stone Creek. He kept the men working on the wilderness road, but with the Indians gone his force was increasingly vulnerable to attack from the forest. No longer potential allies, the Indian chiefs who had attended the council became "treacherous Devils, who had been sent by the *French* as Spies" and could pounce on the Virginians at any moment. French deserters also brought news of a major buildup of troops at Fort Duquesne. On the 28th, after a hasty council of war, Washington ordered the retreat to Great Meadows.

He did so just in time, for on the same day 600 French and Canadians and about 100 Indians left Fort Duquesne to avenge Jumonville. Captain Louis Coulon de Villiers—the dead ensign's older brother—commanded the French force, and he hounded the Virginians, who had to abandon most of their supplies just to keep ahead of him. Washington loaded his own horse with powder and shot, and led the way on foot. His men were reduced to gnawing pocketfuls of parched corn while they trudged through the forest. On July 1st they finally staggered into Great Meadows.

Fort Necessity offered the Virginians scant haven. The provision hut in the middle of the fort was depleted, and when commissaries ransacked the supply wagons that arrived from the east that evening they discovered only a few bags of flour. Nor could the men find any shelter, other than a few tents, from the heavy rain that started falling on the evening of the 2nd. Small ponds formed around the stockade as the marshy meadow became saturated, and the shallow trenches turned into streams. Washington's "charming field for an encounter" now looked like a death trap.

In building the fort Washington had thought in terms of defending against a frontal assault. But hills dominated the surrounding fields; and the woods—at one point only sixty yards away—stood within musket range. A besieging force could surround the stockade and pick off the defenders with ease. Yet the tired men could retreat no further, so Washington had to try holding on until reinforcements arrived. His soldiers improved the defenses slightly by felling trees and piling them into makeshift breastworks next to the stockade.

As they worked, Villiers and his 600 French and Indians bore down on Fort Necessity, using the road the Virginians had built. Guided by his Indian scouts, the French captain stepped into Jumonville's glen early in the morning of July 3rd to see where his brother had died. Clambering among the rocks in the driving rain, Villiers expected to find perhaps a dozen graves. Instead, to his horror, he stumbled on several scalped French bodies, either dug up by animals from shallow graves or left unburied by Washington. He ordered the bodies to be buried and furiously drove his force toward Great Meadows.

Villiers came in sight of Fort Necessity just before eleven o'clock that morning as the Virginians were digging a trench in the viscous mud. The surprised American pickets fired their muskets and ran back toward the fort, followed by three columns of French soldiers and an irregular formation of Indians, who emerged from the woods and advanced downhill across the clearing. But Villiers had miscalculated the location of Fort Necessity. Instead of deploying immediately, he advanced with the fort to his right and then halted his troops in some confusion. The mistake gave Washington and his troops a few precious minutes to prepare.

Redeploying his troops, Villiers advanced in irregular formation and at an oblique angle to the fort. Washington and Mackay watched in puzzlement, until they noticed that the enemy movement inclined for a "Point of Woods" on a slope only sixty yards away. Once there, they quickly realized, the French and Indian forces would overlook the fort and fire unobstructed on Washington's men. Villiers, it was now apparent, had declined to waste his men in the open, opting instead for slow but certain victory. With his position rapidly becoming impossible, Washington was now forced to do exactly what he had been trying to get Villiers to do instead: attack across the open with his entire force. If successful, he might just forestall the French from occupying the point of woods and prevent them from making Fort Necessity untenable. More likely, he would only delay certain defeat.

The French were unimpressed by the American advance. At Villiers's order, his soldiers faced back toward Fort Necessity and, led by dozens of screaming Indians, charged directly at Washington's line with a "great Cry" Mackay's regulars stood firm, but a shudder ran through the Virginians. Ignoring their hesitancy, Washington shouted orders for a volley. The regulars complied, supported by two of the fort's swivel cannon, and blasted many of the Indians to the ground. But whatever satisfaction Washington felt at this sight evaporated when he turned around to discover that the Virginia Regiment was nowhere to be seen. Led by Muse, the volunteers had scrambled for shelter in the attack's first moments, vaulting over the breastworks and diving into the watery trenches. Here and there a man's head or a musket peeped out from over a parapet; otherwise, the Virginians had disappeared. Chagrined, Washington called the retreat and scurried back under cover of a British rear guard, which did its job efficiently while taking several casualties.

Having broken up Washington's rather pathetic assault, Villiers quickly took possession of the point of woods. The surrender of Fort Necessity was now only a matter of time, but Washington defiantly urged his skulking Virginians to fire on the French positions. They were bad marksmen and aimed too high, only showering the French with shredded leaves and pieces of bark. Fort Necessity's swivel cannon, poorly mounted and exposed to enemy fire, did no better. Their crews soon abandoned them.

Villiers's men were elusive targets as they spread out around the clearing in a semicircle. From the high ground in the point of woods, and "from every little rising tree—stump—stone—and bush" they kept up a heavy fire on Fort Necessity and its surrounding entrenchments. The garrison's predicament worsened when "the most tremendous rain that can be conceived" began falling that afternoon. Washington's soldiers could not keep their powder dry and had only two screws to clear the wet charges that lodged in their muskets. By evening they had only "a few (for all were not provided with them) Bayonets" with which to defend themselves after having suffered a staggering one hundred casualties. Thirty dead bodies lay scattered about the fort's perimeter—including Washington's personal servant, a slave—along with all of the garrison's horses, cattle, and other animals, "even to the very Dogs."

With the memory of the decomposed and mutilated bodies at Jumonville's glen still fresh in his mind, Villiers may well have wanted to press the siege of Fort Necessity until he wiped out the garrison in a bloody settling of accounts. But he did not know when American reinforcements would arrive, and rather than take a chance he chose to seek Washington's sword rather than his scalp. Villiers sent an officer under a white flag to parley with the man he regarded as his brother's killer.

Washington refused to allow the French emissary near his fort but sent Van Braam and another volunteer to negotiate with Villiers. The discipline of the exhausted Virginians collapsed as the negotiations began. Ignoring Washington, they broke into the fort's liquor supply and within thirty minutes half of them were drunk. The inebriated volunteers sang and caroused noisily enough to be heard halfway to Williamsburg. Villiers noted his enemy's disarray and exploited it in his negotiations with Van Braam. The purpose of the French expedition, he explained to the Dutchman, had been to avenge his brother's assassination. Surrender would settle that. Villiers now was prepared to treat the Americans and British as "friends," and allow them to leave with the honors of war. In return, they must abandon Fort Necessity along with the swivel guns and leave two officers as hostages for the safe return of the French prisoners that Washington had sent to Williamsburg. If Washington refused these terms, Villiers warned that he could not restrain his Indians, who wanted to storm Fort Necessity and scalp the entire garrison.

Van Braam went back to the fort to consult with Washington and returned a short time later to tell Villiers that the garrison was ready to capitulate. All that remained was to put the terms of surrender in writing. Villiers dictated them to an aide with atrocious handwriting, who scrawled them on a sheet of paper that the Dutchman carried with him back to Fort Necessity. It was still raining, and as Van Braam slopped across the muddy meadow the paper became as limp and soggy as its bearer. Huddled in Washington's tent, the American officers tried to read the paper by the light of a flickering candle that they could barely keep alight. No one could make any sense of it. Water had made the ink run, and even where it remained dry the handwriting was nearly illegible. Nobody except Van Braam could read French anyway, so they relied on his verbal translation. It was inaccurate and possibly dishonest.

Speaking in halting and heavily accented English, Van Braam neglected to translate certain words appearing in the articles of capitulation. These words, "venger L'assasin," and "l'assasinat du Sr de Jumonville," indicated that Ensign Jumonville had been assassinated rather than killed in battle. Had they known the complete contents of the articles, Washington and his staff would have insisted that these incriminating words be removed. Otherwise the terms seemed generous. Washington and Mackay signed them after confirming that the garrison would be allowed to keep its arms and ammunition. The next day, July 4th, Washington abandoned Fort Necessity.

Fort Necessity's garrison marched away with drums beating and flags flying. Van Braam and Captain Robert Stobo remained behind as hostages, along with Dr. Craik and some of the wounded. Villiers, however, had prepared a final humiliation for the American colonel in the form of one hundred Indians who suddenly appeared and demanded scalps. The French commander pretended to restrain the Indians from committing a massacre, but did not prevent them and some of his soldiers from plundering the garrison's baggage.

Washington, afraid of a bloodbath, did not try to stop the looting and rode stoically ahead. Only the hot-tempered Major Stephen refused to stand for the abuse. Seeing a French soldier carrying off his portmanteau, he plunged into the crowd of white men and Indians, yanked the portmanteau off the Frenchman's shoulder, and "kicked the fellows back side." Two French officers accosted him and jokingly criticized such conduct as contradictory to the terms of the convention. Stephen, whose exertions of the previous day had left him "wet, muddy half thigh up, without Stockings, face & hands besmeared with powder," furiously "damned the Capitulation, & swore they had Broke it already." The officers smilingly looked him up and down and then asked whether such a "dirty, half naked fellow" could be an officer. By way of answer Stephen ordered a servant to open the portmanteau and donned a "flaming suit of laced Regimentals" over his muddy clothing as the dumbfounded Frenchmen watched.

Short on food and supplies, Washington's men began the long march back to Wills Creek while Fort Necessity burned behind them. Well into the next day Indians continued to harass Washington's retreat, mocking and stealing from the exhausted soldiers. The Virginia Regiment started to disintegrate. Deserters fled in the night—three, four, even a dozen at a time—leaving fewer men to answer roll call each morning. Colonel Washington was helpless to stop them. His authority had evaporated.

French soldiers rummaging through the baggage seized during the withdrawal from Fort Necessity opened trunks belonging to the fort's former commander. Inside they discovered some pieces of surveying equipment, clothing, books, papers, and a small notebook. Villiers confiscated the notebook and opened it to find the diary of Colonel Washington. After satisfying his curiosity, he sent it on to Contrecoeur, who perused and then forwarded it to Governor Duquesne. "There is nothing more unworthy and lower, and even blacker, than the sentiments and the way of thinking of this Washington," Duquesne wrote Contrecoeur after reading the diary. "It would have been a pleasure to read his outrageous journal under his very nose." Two years later he had it published in Paris. The French people could thereby learn what a contemptible man their soldiers had to deal with.

George Washington's military career had reached its nadir, scarcely before it began. Young, brash, and overconfident—and complaining all the while about pay—he had led a motley assortment of untried volunteers into the wilderness, plunging them into a conflict for which they were unprepared. In ambushing Jumonville, Washington had precipitated a conflict that probably would have occurred anyway; but he had done it in a manner that gave the French cause for retaliation. Afterward, instead of withdrawing to Winchester, where he could gather reinforcements and place himself under the command of the more experienced Innes, Washington *advanced* toward the heart of French-controlled territory. Withdrawing just in time, he holed up in a tiny fort that had been sited at his amateurish instructions. He faced Villiers's attack on Great Meadows bravely, but his faulty preparations had already put the outcome beyond doubt. Worse, after the surrender of Fort Necessity, his command had completely fallen apart. His humiliation was complete.

Several factors may mitigate Washington's poor performance in the Fort Necessity campaign. Perhaps Dinwiddie should never have entrusted him with such an important mission. Sending a twenty-two-year-old lieutenant colonel to the frontier with a vague set of instructions and a ragged collection of volunteers was asking for trouble. The situation demanded either a tested soldier or, if none could be found, a young officer with explicit instructions to avoid an engagement. Also, the Virginia Regiment had no value as a fighting force. Recruited from unemployed townsmen and drifters—poorly clothed, badly supplied, and wholly untrained—it never stood a chance against even an equal number of French soldiers. The Virginians' abandonment of Washington on the field at Great Meadows and their collapse into drunkenness thereafter indicated how they would have responded to an open fight against a determined enemy. Washington had warned Dinwiddie of their weakness, but the governor's hurry to put armed men at the Forks of the Ohio outweighed his prudence, and he ordered the volunteers ahead without waiting for reinforcements. Perhaps most critically, Washington's inability to convince the Indians of the Six Nations to join the British cause left his garrison isolated in hostile country. The young colonel showed little skill as a negotiator, but Dinwiddie had given him little to bargain with.

In his later correspondence about the Fort Necessity disaster Washington pointed again and again to factors beyond his control, and never admitted making any mistakes. The attack on Jumonville's party, he insisted, had not been a blunder, or even a miscalculation, but a daring repulse of a group of raiders. Poorly chosen terrain and weak command had not doomed Fort Necessity, but inadequate supply, bad weather, and indifferent soldiers. Not so much as a confession of weakness or failure due to inexperience ever escaped his pen.

Had Washington's fellow officers been of a backbiting cast of mind, of course, he could never have exculpated himself. But to his lasting credit as a leader who commanded the loyalty of his officers—if not his enlisted men—Mackay, Stephen, and the other officers stood by his account of the campaign. Stephen published his version of the battle in Maryland and Virginia newspapers, excusing the officers of all wrongdoing and emphasizing that Villiers had been the first to ask for terms. Mackay also resisted any temptation to gripe, perhaps because he had risked his own reputation by signing the articles of capitulation at Fort Necessity. These articles constituted a potentially major public humiliation for both men, but with Stephen's support they argued that Van Braam's treachery or incompetence had misled them.

The government of Virginia proved equally loyal. When Washington delivered his report to Governor Dinwiddie in Williamsburg on July 17, 1754, less than two weeks after the surrender of Fort Necessity, he half expected a formal rebuke. Instead the House of Burgesses passed a vote of thanks to him and the other officers—with the exceptions of Muse and Van Braam—and individual burgesses stepped forward to offer their regards and condolences for a loss they agreed Washington could not have avoided. Dinwiddie mildly censured the young colonel for his attempted advance to Red Stone Creek after the skirmish with Jumonville; but otherwise he agreed with his protégé that the disaster had come about because of poor supply and the refusal of the other colonies to lend help.

Dinwiddie toyed briefly with the idea of sending a new expedition to the frontier, but by October he abandoned the idea as unworkable. Resigned to waiting for British help, he broke up the Virginia Regiment into its constituent companies and sent them on garrison duty. Washington, disgusted with the new arrangement, resigned his commission. Despite the extreme tolerance with which his failures had been received in Williamsburg, he felt unappreciated. Still, he wrote Lawrence Washington's old comrade, the burgess William Fitzhugh, "I have the consolation itself, of knowing, that I have opened the way when the smallness of our numbers exposed us to the attacks of a Superior Enemy; That I have hitherto stood the heat and brunt of the Day, and escaped untouched, in time of extreme danger; and that I have the Thanks of my Country, for the Services I have rendered it." But Washington was too young to sing his swan song. "My inclinations are strongly bent to arms," he hinted. Fate soon fulfilled his desire for another try.

4

BRADDOCK

January – July 1755

WHEN GOVERNOR DINWIDDIE reported the disaster at Fort Necessity to the Lords of Trade in London, he presented it as a "small Engagement, conducted with Judgment by the Officers, and great Bravery by our few Forces," but warned that only a major offensive could prevent the French from occupying the entire Ohio Valley. To do nothing, he said, would "be of the greatest Prejudice to the Nation and to all His Majesty's Colonies on this Continent," and amount to a strategic capitulation. Yet Virginia lacked the resources to launch a major military campaign. The mother country would have to help.

King George II's ministers agreed that the French "invasion" of the Ohio Valley required the commitment of Great Britain's military resources. The Duke of Cumberland, the king's son and captain general of the army, planned a four-pronged attack on French possessions in North America. The main expedition, consisting of two regular infantry regiments augmented by provincials and willing Indians, would follow Colonel Washington's route from Virginia to the Forks of the Ohio and destroy Fort Duquesne. The other expeditions would target Nova Scotia and forts at Niagara on Lake Ontario and Crown Point on Lake Champlain. If successful, they would break French control over the Ohio Valley and the entire Great Lakes Basin.

Cumberland appointed Major General Edward Braddock overall commander of the British forces in North America, with money and authority sufficient to persuade or coerce the colonials into providing troops and supplies. The sixty-year-old Braddock had served for four decades in the British army, but never outside Europe. Short and round but brave as a bulldog, he was a stern disciplinarian who tolerated no opposition from his inferiors. He also had a crude and overbearing manner, leading one of his detractors to call him "a very Iroquois in disposition." Sometimes Braddock's surliness overcame his military judgment.

Hard-pressed to defend the many outposts of the British Empire, George II's ministers had few resources to spare for Braddock's expedition. They gave him two inexperienced infantry regiments, the Forty-fourth and Forty-eighth Foot, which had spent several years on garrison duty in Ireland. To support them, Braddock assembled a siege train of astonishing size and weight, consisting of four twelve-pounder and six six-pounder cannon, four eight-inch howitzers, and fifteen Coehorn mortars. Although guns of that size could splinter the stoutest frontier forts, hauling them through the wilderness from Alexandria to Fort Duquesne would be extremely difficult.

The troops and guns of the British expedition left Europe at the beginning of January 1755, and sailed for six weeks through stormy seas before finally anchoring off Hampton Roads, Virginia. Braddock went ashore on February 20th, expecting to find the colonials busy mustering troops and stockpiling supplies. But the Americans had done nothing to put the spring campaign in motion. They had no prepared transport, no provisions, no soldiers, and no money. Worst of all, they had no plans. Enraged, the general rode to Williamsburg and confronted Governor Dinwiddie. Why, he demanded, were Americans so half-hearted about a campaign conducted in their interest? But his rude demands for immediate action accomplished nothing.

Mapping a route to Fort Duquesne was one of Braddock's first priorities. Captain Robert Stobo, who remained a hostage because of Dinwiddie's refusal to repatriate the prisoners from Jumonville's party, had drawn a map of the fort at great personal risk and smuggled it to Virginia. He claimed that the French garrison numbered no more than 400 men. If true, Braddock had a good chance of taking the fort. But frontiersmen warned him that getting men and supplies over the Allegheny Mountains required local knowledge and experience. Somebody proposed consulting Colonel George Washington.

Washington had written a congratulatory letter to Braddock after his safe arrival at Hampton Roads. But he balked at suggestions of serving in the new campaign. What place could he, lacking a royal commission, have in a British military force? The king's regulations stipulated that a provincial colonel ranked below a regular major, possibly even below a regular captain. That meant he might have to take orders from a junior officer—clearly impossible for a military man with any pride. He would, he said, serve under Braddock; but not in the capacity of a provincial officer.

Braddock discussed Washington's objections with Dinwiddie, who still valued the young officer. Washington, they agreed, could not be given a royal commission above the rank of captain; but if he served as an aide-de-camp he could stand apart from the ordinary chain of command, inheriting authority from Braddock and enjoying immunity from the field officers' orders. Braddock's principal aide, Captain Robert Orme, extended the proposal by letter on March 2nd. He assured Washington that the general would "be very glad of your Company in his Family," and expressed his own hopes of forming "an acquaintance with a person so universally esteem'd."

Washington accepted immediately. As he wrote his younger brother John Augustine on May 14th, "I am thereby freed from all command but [Braddock's], and give Order's to all, which must be implicitly obey'd." The new position would allow him to serve a military apprenticeship under experienced British officers and learn what it meant to run a professional military force. "I wish for nothing more earnestly, than to attain a small degree of knowledge in the Military Art," Washington wrote Orme. He saw a most "favourable oppertunity" to do so "under a Gentleman of his Excellencys known ability and experience." The connection with Braddock could also help him to acquire a royal commission later on by providing "a good oppertunity . . . of forming an acquaintance which may be serviceable hereafter, if I can find it worth while pushing my Fortune in the Military way."

On March 26th, Braddock and Dinwiddie rode into the little town of Alexandria, where the two British infantry regiments had camped after their long shipboard ordeal. A messenger brought word of their arrival to George Washington at Mount Vernon a few miles away. He had just taken control of the estate, and the business of moving furniture, hiring workers and house-keepers, and putting slaves to work on the first spring planting kept him on edge. So did his mother, Mary Ball Washington, who came to Mount Vernon to help arrange the household. She was as much against his joining Braddock as she had been against his going to sea. Although Washington joked with Orme about her alarm at "my attending your Fortunes," placating the head-strong woman must have cost him a good deal of energy and time.

Washington spent the next few weeks shuttling between Alexandria and

Mount Vernon. In his free moments he watched the infantry drill and parade, and doubtless discussed tactics with their officers. Braddock did not altogether impress him. He was, Washington later remembered, "a man, whose good & bad qualities were intimately blended. He was brave even to a fault and in regular Service would have done honor to his profession—His attachments were warm—his enmities were strong—and having no disguise about him, both appeared in full force. He was generous & disinterested—but plain and blunt in his manner even to rudeness." Captain Orme, on the other hand, was cultivated, intelligent, and polite. He also had a reputation as a young upstart. The two men quickly became friends.

Braddock ordered his troops to leave Alexandria in early April, sending them toward Wills Creek by separate routes through Virginia and Maryland. He did not accompany them. First he had to meet Dinwiddie and four other governors—Horatio Sharpe of Maryland, Robert Hunter Morris of Pennsylvania, James De Lancey of New York, and William Shirley of Massachusetts—to coordinate strategy according to Cumberland's plans. Shirley, they agreed, would attack French forts at Niagara and in Nova Scotia, De Lancey would launch an expedition against Crown Point, and the others would make similar efforts elsewhere—all with volunteers and militia. For his part, Braddock promised to link up with Shirley at Niagara after capturing Fort Duquesne and routing the French from the Ohio Valley.

Braddock left Alexandria for Wills Creek on April 20th and quickly caught up with his troops. He found them trapped in a logistical morass, with neither wagons nor supplies. Colonial suppliers had a habit of listening to requests for assistance and then quietly drifting away, never to be heard from again. Braddock's hot-tempered quartermaster, Sir John St. Clair, quickly became fed up with this game and swore "that instead of marching to the Ohio, he would in nine days march his army into Cumberland County [Pennsylvania] . . . and that if the French defeated them by the Delays of this Province he would with his Sword drawn pass through the Province and treat the Inhabitants as a parcel of Traitors to his Master." But neither Braddock's bluster nor St. Clair's threats brought any results. The Americans sullenly ignored them—and Washington watched, learning how much an army's supply depended on civilian goodwill.

Washington also learned something about the importance of moving light. The whole expedition was overloaded with useless baggage, and the huge artillery train created major problems. Hauling the big guns required hundreds of horses, which in turn needed tons of grain and dozens of teamsters. How were the horses going to negotiate the narrow, muddy, and stump-ridden trail that meandered across the Allegheny Mountains? Washington predicted serious delays. "Our march must be regulated by the slow movements of the [artillery] Train," he wrote William Fairfax, "which I am sorry to say, I think, will be tedious in advancing—very tedeous indeed—answerable to the expectation I have long conceived, tho' few believ'd." Braddock admitted that the artillery train might "retard me considerably," but refused to leave it behind.

Braddock reached the orderly little German settlement town of Frederick, Maryland, on April 21st. Supply problems forced him to remain there until the end of the month. Then he rode to Winchester, only to encounter further delay and disappointment. The Native American reinforcements that were supposed to meet him there failed to materialize. The Six Nations still saw no future in a British alliance, and did not even attempt to open negotiations. Braddock gloomily left Winchester on May 7th and pressed forward to Wills Creek. Washington, who had lost the use of every one of his four horses since leaving Alexandria, followed him on a borrowed horse.

On May 10th, Braddock and his entourage splashed across Wills Creek, climbed a hill, and emerged from the trees in front of the log palisades of the newly constructed Fort Cumberland, whose guns saluted the general with several booming shots. This was to be his base of operations for the conquest of the Forks of the Ohio. But what, St. Clair wondered incredulously, "cou'd induce People ever to think of making a fort" at such a place? Surrounded and dominated by a series of high ridges, it was both vulnerable to attack and completely isolated; and the poor roads over the mountains made it next to useless as a source of supply. Braddock's two infantry regiments and two independent companies of regulars nevertheless drilled under the flagpole as he arrived, while ten provincial companies of "languid, spiritless, and unsoldierlike" men from Virginia and Maryland milled around their tents on a nearby hillside.

There were Indians at Fort Cumberland, too. Some just wanted to barter for goods, but others represented important Ohio tribes that had come to negotiate with the British general. Although Braddock made "use of every argument to persuade them to take up the hatchet" and "behaved as kindly to them as he possibly could," he failed to secure their friendship. The Indians demanded concessions to the rights of the Six Nations in the Ohio Valley. He refused. Offended, they quietly heard him out and then discreetly left Fort Cumberland, never to return.

Braddock then confronted the problem of how to cross the mountains to Fort Duquesne. Washington's wilderness "road" to Great Meadows—already overgrown since the previous summer—was now little more than a rough trail. Braddock sent work parties to improve it, but they made slow headway as they sweated and swore their way over the rocky, heavily forested Alleghenies. At the same time, supplies of animal fodder and human food were becoming dangerously low. The soldiers, who had marched 200 miles on nothing but salted meat, hunted for fresh provisions but caught only mosquitoes and burrs. The action that Washington craved seemed farther away than ever. "I shall spend my time very agreeably this Campaigne, tho' not advantageously," he wrote despondently to his half brother Augustine, "as I conceive a little experience will be my chief reward."

If ever the expedition got going, Washington was sure that French opposition would be "trifling." Neither he nor the general believed reports that a large force of Indians and soldiers were marching from Canada to strengthen the small garrison at Fort Duquesne. They believed that Lord Cumberland's plan of coordinated attacks would prevent Governor Duquesne from concentrating his forces. But only one of the colonial expeditions to Canada set out before summer, and all of them eventually collapsed. Governor Duquesne felt so secure at Montreal, in fact, that before the British had even reached Fort Cumberland he released 1,000 soldiers and Indians to reinforce the Forks of the Ohio. Only after the march to Fort Duquesne began did Washington worry that "we shall not take possession of Fort Duquisne so quietly as was imagined."

Braddock marched his army of 2,900 men out of Fort Cumberland in detachments from May 30th to June 10th, sending them forward over trails of "perpendicular rock." Almost immediately the overstuffed wagons ground to a halt, too heavy to move. The incensed general ordered each wagon emptied and repacked, and returned some guns, supplies, and all except two female camp followers per company to Fort Cumberland. Washington gave up half his portmanteau and one horse. The army's pace improved, but only slightly. After a few days dragging wagons up mountainsides, staggering over sharp granite and loose shale, hauling at block and tackle to lower cannon over steep slopes, and slogging through swamps in the valleys, animals and men could take no more. Horses dropped dead in harness, and soldiers in full uniform collapsed beside them. Realizing that it would take months to reach the Ohio at this pace, Braddock at Washington's urging decided to plunge ahead with a picked detachment of eight hundred regulars, eight pieces of artillery, and thirty wagons while the rest of the troops and baggage followed under the command of Colonel Thomas Dunbar.

Feeling "infinite delight" at the increased pace, Washington rode forward with Braddock on June 18th. He anticipated hearing bullets whistle once more; but within a few hours he "found, that instead of pushing on with vigour, without regarding a little rough Road, [the soldiers] were halting to Level every Mold Hill, & to erect Bridges over every brook." His spirits plunged. Sick with impatience and frustration, he also sagged in his saddle with a high fever and a brutal headache. Washington tried to conceal his illness but soon had to lie down in a covered wagon, which jolted him mercilessly as it bounced over the stumpy road. On June 23rd, still ten miles east of the main crossing of the Youghiogheny River, he accepted the inevitable and asked to be left behind. Braddock gave Washington a packet of Dr. James's fever powder, which the sick young man found "the most excellent medicine in the World"; Braddock further pledged his word of honor not to fight a battle without sending for him. He then pushed on in hopes of reaching Fort Duquesne before the garrison was reinforced.

On the 24th, wet to their thighs after fording the Youghiogheny River, the troops trudged through an abandoned Indian camp, past still-smoldering campfires and almost 200 bark lean-tos. Entering the woods beyond, they paused to gaze at stripped and brightly painted trees on which the French and Indians had left graffiti, taunting them with "many threats and bravados with all kinds of scurrilous language." The provincial soldiers in Braddock's force had been brought up on atrocity stories, and joked about what their red-coated comrades could expect from native tomahawks. At daybreak the next morning, three of the English soldiers were found dead in the underbrush. They had been murdered and scalped.

Captain Contrecoeur declared Fort Duquesne, which he commanded, finished on May 24th. The garrison was at first weak and vulnerable, but reinforcements had brought it to 600 men by July 6th, when word arrived of Braddock's approach. By that time the French also could count on the support of several hundred nearby Indians. With a respectable striking force now at his disposal, Contrecoeur decided to attack the British. It would be risky, but to wait for Braddock's artillery to pound Fort Duquesne into submission would be suicidal. And hesitating might convince the Indians that the French were not worth fighting for. Contrecoeur had little hope of destroying the British expedition, but he wanted at least to check Braddock and give time for more reinforcements to arrive from Canada.

Before sunrise on the morning of July 9th, the French army at Fort Duquesne broke into a hurried but determined commotion. With half of the men looking on enviously, the other half wolfed down breakfast, snatched their muskets, and paraded in front of Captain Daniel Liénard de Beaujeu, who would lead them that day. As if in premonition, Beaujeu had taken communion in the morning, and the priests heard confessions from many otherwise irreligious men. The mood became more confident as the battle flag was unfurled some time after nine o'clock and the fort's commandant, Captain Contrecoeur, gave the order to march. Within moments, 72 French soldiers and 146 Canadian militiamen, shepherded by 36 officers, marched past the gate, through cornfields, and into the woods beyond. There, 637 Indians from at least seven French-allied tribes joined the soldiers and fanned out in loose formation, leading the way ahead. Their quarry lay struggling in the dense woods ten miles to the southeast.

On July 8th Washington, now mostly recovered from his illness, rejoined Braddock after an agonizing ride in a rattling, bouncing covered wagon. The next morning he prepared to spend his first day on horseback in over two weeks. Still weak, and now possibly suffering from hemorrhoids, he had a servant tie cushions to the saddle before he mounted. Braddock's soldiers meanwhile continued grappling with nature, felling trees and hacking underbrush, and wondering what anyone could possibly find attractive in the so-called New World. Their goal, Fort Duquesne, was no longer very far away.

Lieutenant Colonel Thomas Gage of the Forty-fourth Foot, an ardent young man much liked by Washington, led the advance party of some 300 regulars on July 9th. Gage's men broke camp before dawn and, marching cautiously with the help of several Indian scouts and strong flanking parties, scattered a group of about thirty Indians before crossing the Monongahela via two shallow fords just after seven o'clock. At the river, Gage's Indian scouts called his attention to signs of recent activity—footprints and muddied water—but when Gage sent a note back to Braddock announcing the crossing he made no mention of their warning. He pushed on, inclining gradually northward and advancing slowly with the river on his left.

Close behind Gage followed 100 men of a New York independent company under Captains Robert Cholmley and Horatio Gates, who guarded St. Clair's working party of 250 men, two six-pounder cannons, and a line of tool wagons 200 yards long. A quarter of a mile behind the working party marched 500 regulars in parallel columns, guarding an agglomeration of about thirty light horse, eleven artillery pieces, a few dozen sailors detached on land transport duty, fifty camp women, cattle, pack animals, and dozens of wagons. Captain Adam Stephen and 100 Virginia provincials, outfitted in blue coats with red facings and blue breeches, formed the rear guard.

Braddock and his staff, including Orme and Washington, rode with the main body of 500 regulars. They'd left camp at about five o'clock and reached the Monongahela three hours later. The crossing was unhurried, and the last wagon did not trundle across the river until two o'clock in the afternoon. The general then ordered the front of the column, which had halted to wait for the rear to catch up, to renew the advance. His officers, who had congratulated themselves at the absence of any French opposition during the crossing, confidently led their men forward. The worst seemed finally behind them. Some speculated that the French might already have abandoned Fort Duquesne. The light horsemen with the main body had hardly spurred their mounts, however, when they heard a rattle of musketry in the forest ahead. Gage's advance party was under attack.

Braddock halted his wagons at the sound of firing and sent half his regulars to reinforce Gage, retaining the rest as baggage guards. An aide rode ahead to reconnoiter, but when the firing increased, the general raced forward with the rest of his aides close behind. They immediately crashed into workmen, horses, and redcoats fleeing in the opposite direction. All they could gather from the fugitives was that Indians armed with muskets had enveloped Gage's and St. Clair's detachments. St. Clair then appeared, covered with blood from a musket wound but attempting to organize guards for his artillery. Gage, miraculously unwounded, turned up just beyond, trying to keep the advance party's withdrawal from turning into a rout. Most of his officers lay dead farther up the road.

Gage told Braddock that his men had blundered into a powerful force of French and Indians. The death of Captain Beaujeu in the first exchange of fire disorganized the French and made them hesitate, but the Indians raced through the woods on both sides of the road, routed the flanking parties, and fell on the British column. They attacked so furiously that the regulars scattered in panic. Gage's officers did their best to form the stouter soldiers into line, but the Indians refused to make proper targets, hiding among the trees and picking off officers and men with terrible accuracy before moving in to scalp their victims. Gage's situation worsened as he withdrew. As his men moved into areas that the workers had cleared that morning they became easier targets, even though the "road" was never more than twelve feet wide. Canadians and Indians made use of higher ground along a ridge to the right, and the rest of the Indians infested the woods to the left while the French pressed on the front. None fought in groups of more than three or four at a time.

As Gage finished his report to Braddock, the whole perimeter of the army became wreathed in smoke and fire. The regulars from the main body had become hopelessly entwined in the debris of the advance parties, and before long they, too, were driven inward among the baggage train as the enemy pushed them relentlessly back. Gunners unlimbered their artillery and tried to bring the guns into action, but there was no way to find a clear field of fire or even a target. Their shots, fired through gaps, or making new gaps in the crowd of men, women, wagons, and horses, were ineffective. The gunners soon unhitched their horses and joined the throng desperately trying to get back across the Monongahela.

Braddock tried to rally the regulars into small groups and resume the advance. He even managed to collect a hundred men of the Forty-eighth to take the ridge on the right. But the counterattack quickly broke down. Other groups of redcoats, confused by the smoke and unsure of where their enemy lay, fired into one another. Dozens fell to friendly fire. Indian war whoops echoed among the trees along with the screams of the wounded. Their discipline utterly shattered, the Forty-fourth and Forty-eighth degenerated into a mob. Soon the only ones who still tried to shoot at the enemy did so with an almost deranged randomness, aiming harmlessly above their attackers' heads. The rest simply threw their muskets away and fled. Garrison detail in Ireland had not prepared them for anything like this.

At this point Braddock could only try to preserve some remnants of his former army. One of his aides, the Massachusetts governor's son, William

Shirley, Jr., lay dead with a musket ball in his brain, and Orme nursed a severe wound. Among the general's entourage only Washington remained un hurt, although enemy fire had perforated his hat and shredded his coat. Washington was also one of the few Americans left on the field. Although Stephen's Virginians had stood their ground bravely for a time, they, too, disintegrated after being slaughtered by gunfire from some regular platoons that formed up behind them.

Four horses were shot from under Braddock before he finally fell out of the saddle with a ball through his arm and into his body. He begged to be left behind, and according to one account even asked for a pistol to commit suicide, but Washington had him placed in a wagon and moved toward what was left of the rear. The few officers and men who continued to fight then turned "by one common consent" and ran, abandoning their baggage and disabled comrades to the enemy. The Indians massacred many of the wounded and all but seven of the women, and that night they tortured and burned to death some of their captives. But they did not pursue the remnants of Braddock's army across the Monongahela. The baggage train, bursting with supplies that the quartermaster St. Clair had spent months wresting from recalcitrant American farmers, was a more attractive target.

Gage formed a rear guard on the other side of the river, near where the troops had broken camp in what must have seemed a lifetime away early that morning. Braddock's wagon had creaked to the rear almost unguarded. From his makeshift litter he ordered Washington to ride back and tell Colonel Dunbar, who was still struggling along the road from Fort Cumberland with the rest of the army, to hasten forward food and medical supplies. Washington rode all that night through the detritus of Braddock's command, which fled before him. "The shocking scenes which presented themselves in this Nights march are not to be described," he later wrote. "The dead—the dying—the groans—lamentations—and crys along the Road of the wounded for help . . . were enough to pierce the heart of an adamant." The darkness became so impenetrable that his two guides sometimes had to dismount and grope with their hands to determine whether they were on or off the road.

Washington made contact with Dunbar's troops a day later, on July 10th. Stories of the general's defeat, wildly exaggerated by rumor, had thrown them into a frenzy. Many of Dunbar's provincials and even some of the regulars had scampered back toward Fort Cumberland. Braddock's command linked up with Dunbar near Christopher Gist's plantation on the 11th, and the reunited army continued its slow retreat. The soldiers shuffled into Great Meadows two days later.

Braddock died at Great Meadows. At Washington's suggestion he was wrapped in two blankets and buried on the road in an unmarked grave a mile from the ruins of Fort Necessity. The wagons that retreated along that road in the following day obliterated all trace of his grave, which remained unknown for fifty years. Of the approximately 1,500 fighting troops that Braddock had commanded on the Monongahela, a staggering two-thirds had become casualties in about three hours of fighting, with 456 dead, 520 wounded—many of whom would eventually die from their injuries—and about a dozen taken prisoner. French and Indian casualties together numbered less than forty.

The myth of the invincibility of British regulars died on the Monongahela. "The dastardly behaviour of those they call regular's, exposd all other's that were inclind to do their duty to almost certain death," Washington wrote his mother from Fort Cumberland on July 18th, "and at last, in dispight of all the efforts of the Officer's to the Contrary, they broke, and run as Sheep pursued by dogs; and it was impossible to rally them." He repeated the words almost verbatim the next day in a letter to Dinwiddie. Attempting to rally the regulars, Washington told the governor, was like trying to stop "the wild Bears of the Mountains." The officers had fought bravely, but their "cowardly dogs of Soldiers" refused to obey them. "The Virginians," by contrast, "behaved like Men, and died like Soldiers," fighting to the death as others fled around them. Colonials, at least in Washington's public accounts of the battle, had emerged as better soldiers than their English counterparts.

Popular rumor magnified the Virginians' achievements even further. American militiamen who fought to defend their homes, it was said, had proven their superiority to British regulars, who fought for pay. A report circulated in the colonies a month after the battle that the wounded Braddock had cried out from his litter "my dear Blue's (which was the Colors the Virginians wore) give em tother Fire, you Fight like Men, & will die like Shouldiers . . . [he] could not bare the sight of a red Coat, whenever one came in his View, he raved imoderately, but when one of the blues, he said he hop'd to live to reward 'em." Another rumor had Washington begging the general for permission to take the provincials into the woods in order to fight the enemy in irregular fashion, only to be denied. Many colonials drew the lesson that regular troops should not fight in America, where irregulars—Indians, frontiersmen, and especially militiamen—must always hold sway.

This simplistic analysis obscured a much more complex reality. From the beginning, Braddock had shown little appreciation of logistics. His arrogance alienated suppliers and caused numerous delays. The massive, poorly managed artillery and baggage train further hindered the advance and at last forced him to leave it and most of his force behind just as he approached Fort Duquesne. The British did not entirely neglect the principles of irregular warfare, but marched with moderate caution under the protection of flankers and advance parties. Yet the absence of effective scouts ensured surprise; and the precipitate collapse of the flanking parties accelerated the disaster by allowing the Indians to attack the British main body before it had a chance to form properly.

In later years the story arose that excessive discipline had doomed Braddock's army in its fight with the Indians. It fit in well with the popular stereotype of the robotic, unthinking redcoat, and is repeated by many historians today. But the truth is quite the opposite. When the Indians hit Braddock's main force it dissolved almost immediately into a rabble. Many enlisted men ignored their officers and either fled or fought—to their ultimate sorrow—as individuals or small groups. Those who stood in formation like the Virginians had more success in fending off the attackers, but officers wasted their men by arraying them haphazardly and launching foolish counterattacks. Their poor fire discipline led them to inflict many more casualties on one another than they did on the enemy. As a result, Braddock's army ceased to constitute a viable force well before its commander fell mortally wounded. The redcoats' problem was not discipline, but *indiscipline*.

Washington understood this, and his experiences on the Monongahela reinforced his conviction that sound management, ample supply, efficient transport, solid training, and strict discipline were crucial to an effective military force. It is often said that he revolted against the conventional belief in tight military formations as well, but this is not in fact the case. Although he would later advocate semiflexible formations and tactics in combat with Indians, his sense of how to fight regular troops remained thoroughly orthodox. Washington shared popular faith in the superiority of American soldiers, but he believed they fought best in an army modeled on European standards. The militia, composed of civilians called to uniform temporarily in times of emergency, had its uses; but the battlefield would always belong to professional soldiers.

Washington never impugned Braddock's conduct, but others lacked his restraint. Colonial and British critics damned the fallen general as a pompous and ignorant bully who had lived to regret his disdain for the colonials. Washington's prestige rose by contrast. The well-known Virginia Presbyterian preacher Samuel Davies spoke for many when he hailed "that heroic Youth Col. Washington, who I cannot but hope Providence has hitherto preserved in so signal a Manner for some important Service to his Country." Colonial newspapers celebrated his bravery, and for the first time in his young life he began to receive flattering letters. William Fairfax wrote a letter to Washington lionizing his "Heroick Virtue"; Dinwiddie praised his "gallant Behavior"; Virginia councilor Philip Ludwell "thought he deserved every thing that his Country cou'd do for him"; and Washington's cousin Charles Lewis proclaimed from Virginia that "the People in these Parts seem very desirous of serving under the brave Colo. Washington." Aspiring young soldiers sought his recommendation in expectation that he eventually would take command of Virginia's troops.

Ironically, military disaster had transformed Colonel George Washington from a minor provincial officer into a colonial hero. But he had not yet proven to the rulers in London that he deserved a commission in the British army and the command of regular troops. He might have convinced them through political patronage, or by winning a major battle single-handed. Other men had done so before him, and would again after. But Washington, destined in so many ways to be a pioneer, was fated to make his mark in an unprecedented manner. When his superiors hesitated to let him command British troops, Washington tried to impress them by creating regulars of his own. In so doing he built the first professional American military force in history—one of his greatest military accomplishments—and set out firmly on the road to becoming general and commander-in-chief.

5

THE VIRGINIA REGIMENT

July 1755 – January 1759

WASHINGTON WAS PONDERING a return to military service within a week of his arrival at Mount Vernon in July 1755. His friends encouraged these thoughts and goaded him to ask for a royal commission and the command of regular troops. He would, he said, accept nothing less. "I am so little dispirited at what has happen'd," he wrote his half brother Augustine, "that I am always ready, and always willing to do my Country any Services that I am capable off; but never upon the Terms I have done, having suffer'd much in my private fortune beside impairing one of the best of Constitution's." Washington's mother, fearful that her impetuous son would expose his scalp to the tomahawk once again, tried to talk him out of it. He dismissed her worries. "Honoured Madam," he wrote, "if it is in my power to avoid going to the Ohio again, I shall, but if the Command is press'd upon me by the general voice of the Country, and offerd upon such terms as can't be objected against, it would reflect eternal dishonour upon me to refuse it; and that I am sure must, or ought, to give you greater cause of uneasiness than my going in an honourable Command."

Governor Dinwiddie had taken advantage of the alarm at Braddock's defeat to squeeze £40,000 from the House of Burgesses. He also won authority to raise 1,200 soldiers, arranged in a Virginia Regiment of sixteen companies. Dinwiddie offered Washington command of the regiment along with an aide-de-camp, a secretary, and a "small Military Chest" of disposable funds. The Burgesses sweetened the offer by awarding him £300 in reimbursement for past expenses. After demanding a say in the appointment of the field officers, Washington accepted command of the Virginia Regiment at the end of August. He now enjoyed almost unquestioned military authority within the colony.

Dinwiddie designated Fort Cumberland as regimental headquarters, but Washington chose to base himself at the newly constructed Fort Dinwiddie in Winchester, Virginia. Adam Stephen, now a lieutenant colonel, took command at Fort Cumberland. At Winchester, Washington began the exhausting task of recruiting and supplying his new regiment. Past experience led him to anticipate trouble raising men, and he was not mistaken. Young men ignored calls for enlistment, and those who did not were unruly or even mutinous. Washington hanged some of the miscreants, but desertions and grumbling continued.

Imposing discipline on such shiftless and cranky men would be difficult. But Washington had ideas on how it could be done. "Remember," he told his officers, "that it is the actions, and not the commission, that make the Officer—and that there is more expected from him than the *Title*." All of them, he insisted, must command by example and refrain from gaming, carousing, bickering, swearing, drinking, and all other forms of indecorous behavior. They must also strictly punish disobedience—with lashes or death, when necessary. Inhumane as such strictures now seem, they worked, and as time went on the troops became amazingly obedient.

Washington next commenced an exacting program of drill and training based on techniques taught in the British army, with the addition of lessons in target shooting and woodland tactics. But the emphasis always remained on marching and fighting like European armies on European battlefields. Washington wanted his soldiers to look European too. Believing that regular uniforms were essential to the creation of unit identity and discipline, he had regimental clothing designed and imported from England, and by the spring of 1757 both officers and men wore uniforms of provincial blue. Washington also saw to the equitable and frequent distribution of pay and provisions, a seemingly routine but nonetheless critical detail that did much for unit morale. Before long discipline and training had improved so much that he could boast, "if it shou'd be said, the Troops of Virginia are Irregulars, and cannot expect more notice than other Provincials, I must beg leave to differ, and observe in turn, that we want nothing but Commissions from His Majesty to make us as regular a Corps as any upon the Continent."

Supply shortages at first caused Washington headaches. Commissaries tested his patience just as they had tormented Braddock, making promises they knew they could not keep. On one occasion their recalcitrance forced him to seize supplies from civilians. The outraged civilians threatened, as

Washington aggrievedly told Dinwiddie, "to blow out my brains." Declining to put their words to the test, he discreetly withdrew. Chastened, from then on he tried not to cajole or threaten his suppliers—as Braddock had done to his sorrow—but soothed and persuaded them into giving help. It worked. After a time the Virginia Regiment no longer had to struggle to find adequate supplies.

Washington's success in building the Virginia Regiment helped him to grow more mature, both as a leader and as a man. Although still sensitive to personal criticism, he gradually realized that even success would not free him from political and personal detractors. He simply had to deal with them. At first he let his emotions get the better of him, threatening to resign, for example, over some oblique newspaper criticism of his management and complaining when others had questioned his conduct. Yet in time Washington learned to temper his anger, at least in public. He discovered that he could accomplish more by working through subordinates or political back channels than he could through petulance or bluster.

Washington also became more practical as well as politically savvy. As he had seen in his months under Braddock, maintaining a colonial military force was about much more than drill and discipline. There was no vast military bureaucracy or modern technology that he could use to manage the minutiae of organization, logistics, and supply. He had to handle almost everything himself—designing uniforms, securing cloth, superintending military organization, supervising barracks construction, overseeing training, appointing officers, mediating rank disputes, distributing pay, procuring transport, gathering arms and ammunition, and managing provisions, to say nothing of planning and preparation for actual conflict. Washington learned how to do all of these things, and he did them well. His capacity for hard work and detail allowed him to accomplish tasks that were beyond Braddock and other professional soldiers.

In his relations with civil and military officials Washington became more adept, too. Civilian criticism sometimes goaded him into angry, undiplomatic rants against "Chimney Corner Politicians," but he also learned how to manipulate the unwieldy and inefficient colonial system by coaxing politicians, commissaries, quartermasters, and civilian contractors to do his bidding. He navigated the halls of the governor's palace and the capitol building in Williamsburg with ease, but he could also find his way among the humbler abodes of the local officials on whom he depended for supply. As officials at all levels began to respect his authority, he in turn became a better officer and leader.

Washington's care rapidly transformed the Virginia Regiment from a scraggly, neglected collection of misfits into an efficient, well-equipped and organized little fighting machine. Surely he deserved some credit for this, like a royal commission? Other Americans had won commissions by pulling strings—a method he tried himself, but with less success. But he also thought he had merited one through actual service, including risking his life in battle. On the same grounds, he wanted all of his officers and men to be placed on the royal establishment and accepted as members of the British army. Washington's intentions were not all altruistic, of course, for commissions also meant money. He received a generous salary—thirty shillings a day, £100 per year for food expenses (later £200), and a 2 percent commission on all the regimental funds he handled—but a royal commission brought even more. Most important, Washington wanted the added authority that came with the king's seal. Without it he had no guarantee against losing command of his regiment if someone with a royal commission, even a captain, tried to usurp him.

A dispute with a captain named John Dagworthy in the autumn of 1755 seemed to justify all of Washington's fears. Dagworthy was a New Jersey storekeeper with almost no military experience, but he held a royal commission as captain dating from 1746. He also commanded a small Maryland company at Fort Cumberland, where Washington intended to concentrate the Virginia Regiment, and boasted that he outranked anyone with a colonial commission. Lieutenant Colonel Stephen warned Washington that Dagworthy—or "Dogworthy," as he called him—would "look upon himself as Commanding Officer after You have joined the Troops."

Washington refused to accept this upstart's pretension, writing angrily to the governor that he could "never submit to the command of Captain Dagworthy." In response Dinwiddie wrote to the new commander-in-chief of the British forces in North America, Governor William Shirley of Massachusetts, recommending royal commissions for Washington and Stephen. Weeks passed while Washington lobbied in Williamsburg, refused to go to Fort Cumberland, and suggested the construction of another fort for his regiment. Still no decision came. Finally, the Virginia Regiment's officers signed a petition asking to be put on the royal establishment. Washington requested permission from Dinwiddie to deliver the petition to Shirley in Boston. If Dinwiddie refused, Washington "determined to resign a Commission which You were generously pleased to offer Me . . . rather than submit to the Command of a Person who I think has not such superlative Merit to balance the inequality of Rank."

On February 3, 1756, accompanied by his aides and two servants clad in elaborate livery on horses decorated with the family coat of arms, Washington embarked on his first journey to the Northeast. He staged ostentatious arrivals and departures at Annapolis, Philadelphia, New York, and other cities with the goal of attracting notice from newspapers and society. After reaching Boston on the 27th, he formally laid his petition before Governor Shirley. He may have softened the old man with memories of his son, who was killed at Braddock's defeat. In any case, Shirley decreed that he and every other provincial officer above captain outranked Dagworthy. Washington returned home satisfied. His quest to place the Virginia Regiment on the royal establishment continued for a time, but eventually faded.

The Virginia Regiment did not participate in any serious military engagements before 1758. Indians marauded periodically along the Virginia and Maryland frontiers, but Washington could do little about them. The Virginia General Assembly ordered him to distribute his troops in a series of eighteen small frontier stockades that the Indians simply bypassed. He insisted that only a fresh offensive against Fort Duquesne could put a stop to the raids, but London seemed determined to procrastinate. In 1754 Dinwiddie had warned that French victory on the Ohio would lead to the destruction of the colonies. His prediction seemed destined to come true.

As Indian raids grew bolder in the summer of 1757, Washington began developing symptoms of dysentery. He expected to recover soon and continued his usual duties, but during the autumn he became seriously ill and quitted Winchester for Mount Vernon. Washington's robust health normally would have brought him quickly back; but after two years as colonel of the Virginia Regiment he was tired, frustrated, and bored. He also felt depressed at the death on September 3rd of his longtime mentor and friend William Fairfax, and at his deteriorating relations with Governor Dinwiddie, who resigned his office and left Virginia early in 1758. In such circumstances it is possible that Washington's persistent illness was at least partially psychosomatic.

Washington struggled with dysentery for months, leaving his sickbed one day only to return to it the next. For weeks he consumed little but hart's horn jelly and sweet wine mixed with gum arabic, and well-intentioned physicians weakened him with repeated bleedings. By March 1758, Washington thought he might never fully recover. "My Constitution I believe has receivd great Injury," he wrote to British army colonel John Stanwix on March 4th, "and as nothing can retrieve it but the greatest care, & most circumspect Conduct— As I now see no prospect of preferment in a Military Life—and as I despair of rendering that immediate Service which this Colony may require of the Person Commanding their Troops, I have some thoughts of quitting my Command & retiring from all Publick Business, leaving my Post to be filld by others more Capable of the Task."

Stanwix was a grizzled fifty-year-old regular army veteran used to commanding temperamental young officers, and he knew how to cure Washington's kind of depression better than any physician. "I am much concern'd to hear [your health] is in so bad a Condition," he replied to the Virginian on March 10th, "as to put you upon resigning your Command which I am very sure will not be so well filled for the Interest of the Country in General and for my own wishes in particular." Resigning his commission now, Stanwix wrote slyly, would especially be a shame in view of rumors that "a very large Fleet is expected & seven Thousand men," heralding a change in command of His Majesty's forces in North America and a new campaign, possibly against Fort Duquesne. The promise of action rejuvenated Washington, and on March 18th—a day or two after his first meeting with the twenty-six-year-old widow Martha Custis—he told a cousin that he was "now in a fair way of regaining my health." Two weeks later he rode back to his regiment at Winchester.

On March 21st, acting governor John Blair read to the Virginia Council a letter that had just arrived from Prime Minister William Pitt to the effect that Great Britain had resolved on a major offensive against the French and needed Virginia to raise as many men as possible. The British government's decision had followed two more humiliating defeats in the summer of 1757. While the transports were at sea for an amphibious British expedition against Louisburg, in Nova Scotia, which suffered logistical breakdowns and never even landed, a French force captured Fort William Henry on Lake George. France's Indian allies followed up the capture by massacring dozens of captives. The situation was scarcely better in Europe, where Britain, Prussia, and a few German states struggled against a coalition of France, Russia, and

Austria. In September, Lord Cumberland surrendered his German army to the French at the village of Kloster Zeven; and although Frederick the Great of Prussia scored the first in a series of stunning victories against the coalition that autumn, no one expected his tiny country to survive for long.

William Pitt's accession to the office of secretary of state in June 1757 brought a new energy and optimism to the British war effort. With Cumberland's influence gone after Braddock's defeat, Pitt could devise strategy as he pleased. In Europe, France's strength on land was overwhelming. But in North America, about 7,000 French and Canadian soldiers and a miscellaneous collection of Indian allies were spread across thousands of miles of wilderness. If the British navy severed communications between France and her American possessions, a strong land force of redcoats and provincials would stand a good chance of conquering Canada and the Ohio Valley.

Pitt decided to launch three major expeditions in North America. They would not be assigned to provincial commanders and militia troops—as had been the case in 1755—but to professional officers and soldiers. One force, commanded by Major General Jeffery Amherst, would make a fresh attempt on Louisburg (Nova Scotia). Another, commanded by Major General James Abercromby and Brigadier General George Augustus Howe, would lay siege to Fort Ticonderoga on the Hudson River. Brigadier General John Forbes would command the third expedition, targeting Fort Duquesne.

Forbes was a very different creature from Edward Braddock. Born in Scotland in 1710, he had over twenty years of military experience in Europe. Forbes had commanded the Seventeenth Foot in the abortive Louisburg expedition of 1757, and despite not seeing any fighting he impressed his superiors, who afterward appointed him adjutant general. His bravery was tempered by a caution that Washington later found infuriating, but his patience and affability made him much more capable than Braddock had been at dealing with colonial politicians and commissaries. He was a fine administrator, popular with both soldiers and civilians, and a good choice to command an expedition that required more than the usual amount of prudence.

As yet, George Washington remained only one of a "motley herd" of provincial officers chosen to lead troops under Forbes. "Mention me in favorable terms to General Forbes," Washington begged Stanwix on April 10, 1758, "not as a person who would depend upon him for further recommendation to military preferment . . . but as a person who would gladly be distinguished in some measure from the *common run* of provincial Officers." The Virginia

General Assembly added weight to his demand by passing a bill in early April for the recruitment of another 1,000 volunteers for the Second Virginia Regiment. William Byrd III, a twenty-nine-year-old Virginian with experience in Indian negotiations, took command of the new regiment, though Washington retained overall control by virtue of his seniority. He could now expect to lead a substantial force of about two thousand men into battle.

Forbes had already counted on Washington's help. On March 20th, the day before he officially took command, Forbes asked acting governor Blair to concentrate the Virginia Regiment at Winchester under its colonel, whom he characterized as "a good and knowing Officer in the Back Countries." Delighted at this endorsement, Washington wrote to Forbes "to assure you, that to merit a continuance of the good opinion you seem to entertain of me, shall be one of my Principal Studies; for I have now no ambition that is higher, and it is the greatest reward I expect for my Services in the Ensuing Campaigne." Forbes nevertheless expected little from the Virginia Regiment, and neither he nor his quartermaster, John St. Clair—who had recovered from the wounds he received on the Monongahela—expected more than a thousand ragged, ill-trained, and undisciplined troops to show up at Winchester. But Washington proved them wrong. Assembled on parade in new uniforms and Indian leggings, the Virginians exhibited fine discipline and precise drill. Even St. Clair admitted that they looked like "a fine body of men." Washington's three years of diligent management and stern discipline had paid off. The new Second Virginia Regiment, meanwhile, recruited quickly, and by the end of May, both regiments approached full strength with almost a thousand men each. Reinforced by troops from Delaware, Maryland, North Carolina, and Pennsylvania, the provincial contingent would total about 5,000 men.

Forbes's regular troops—the First Highland Battalion, Seventy-seventh Foot under Lieutenant Colonel Archibald Montgomery, and the First Battalion, Royal American Regiment under Colonel Henry Bouquet—were superior to those who had gone to the frontier in 1755. But even the best European troops would make little headway into the Ohio Valley without help from the Indians. With memories of Braddock's defeat still fresh in his mind, Washington urged Forbes to secure native allies. Indians, he lectured the general, were "the only Troops fit to Cope" with fighting Indians. Forbes agreed, and spent much of the spring and summer of 1758 trying to make friends with the Ohio Indian tribes, or at least separate them from the French. He had little luck. Negotiations with the Delawares and other tribes of the Six Nations bogged down despite the general's willingness to compromise about their rights to the Ohio Valley. By the beginning of September the Indians still refused to support the British.

Forbes's other major worry was the choice of a route to the Forks of the Ohio. Braddock's trail of 1755 was reasonably well known to Virginia frontiersmen and looked simple on paper; but it was extremely rugged, and—as Braddock had demonstrated—difficult for baggage wagons and artillery to negotiate. Forbes nevertheless considered it, but changed his mind at the behest of some influential Philadelphia politicians, who suggested he avoid Washington's ill-omened wilderness track and take a more direct route through southwestern Pennsylvania. His troops would construct a road from Shippensburg to Raystown, thirty miles north of Fort Cumberland, and then move slowly westward through the forests of western Pennsylvania until they reached Fort Duquesne, about eighty miles away. On the way they would establish small forts and supply depots. By this means, Forbes wrote Pitt, "altho' I advance but gradually, yet I shall go more Surely by Lessening the Number, and immoderate long train of provisions." In the event of enemy attack, the troops would fall back on the most recently constructed stockade, providing what Forbes regarded as a "sure retreat." Nothing, he thought, could be more prudent or simple.

For Washington, Forbes's plan "seemd to forebode our manifest Ruin." The northern route looked shorter, he admitted—though according to his calculations not by much—but appreciably more difficult than the old road from Fort Cumberland. From Raystown the army would have to advance through practically virgin forest and climb mountains just as high as those that Braddock had crossed. "Making it over such monstrous Mountains coverd with Woods and Rocks," he wrote Bouquet, "wou'd require so much time as to blast our otherwise well grounded hopes of striking the long wishd for, and Important Stroke this Season." The provincial troops would disband, and the colonies would run out of money while the Cherokees and other southern Indians fell overwhelmingly on Virginia's western frontier. Why take the risk, Washington argued, when a suitable road already existed just thirty miles to the south? Braddock's road, he insisted, although it had not been used for three years, was "a Road that has been so long opend—so well repaird—and so often, [that it] must be much firmer and better than a new one."

Forbes dismissed Washington's insistence on the southern route as mere provincial politics. A well-established frontier road to the Ohio built by British troops would be a prize for traders and land speculators, who would turn it to civilian use after the war was over. Virginia and Pennsylvania both wanted such a road, and the Washington family's interest in the Ohio Company was well known. Forbes justified his decision on the basis of standard military principles, but Washington continued to push his case. Instead of confronting Forbes directly, he complained to Henry Bouquet and Francis Halkett, the general's brigade major and acting secretary. Washington became especially intemperate in his letter to Halkett, and blamed Bouquet for influencing Forbes in favor of the northern route. "If Colo. Bouquet succeeds in this point with the General," Washington lamented, "all is lost!—All is lost by Heavens!—our Enterprize Ruind. . . . The Southern Indians turn against Us—and these Colonies become desolate. . . . These are the Consequences of a Miscarriage, and a Miscarriage the Consequence of the Attempt."

Halkett passed the letter on to Forbes, who bristled at Washington's "unguarded" criticism of Bouquet and himself. "I am now at the bottom, of their Scheme against this new road," Forbes angrily wrote Bouquet on August 9th, "a Scheme that I think was a shame for any officer to be Concerned in." Two days later, he told Abercromby that he had let the Virginians "very roundly know, that their Judging and determining of my actions and intentions . . . was so premature, and was taking the lead in so ridiculous a way that I could by no means suffer it."

Having seriously damaged his relationship with his commanding officer, Washington should have let the matter rest. But instead of backing down, Washington bypassed Forbes and Bouquet—though he continued to write impertinently to the latter—and took his case to the Virginia government. Writing to the new Virginia governor, Francis Fauquier, he appealed for a stop to Forbes's "fatal Resolution." To Speaker John Robinson, he gave his fury free rein. "All is lost," he groaned. "We seem then—to act under an evil Geni—the conduct of our Leaders . . . is temperd with something—I dont care to give a name to—indeed I will go further, and say they are d[upe]s, or something worse to [Pennsylvanian] Artifice—to whose selfish views I attribute the miscarriage of this Expedition, for nothing now but a miracle can bring this Campaigne to a happy Issue." In despair, he implored Robinson to "let a full representation of the matter go to His Majesty. Let him know how grossly his Honor and the Publick money has been prostituted." Washington even volunteered to go to London himself and represent the matter to the king.

Lieutenant Colonel Adam Stephen made relations between the Virginians and the British even worse by refusing to obey St. Clair's orders at Fort Cumberland, claiming, as St. Clair remembered, that "rather than receive any Orders from me he would brake his Sword in pieces." Eventually St. Clair had the surly Virginian arrested; but until then, "as I had not sufficient Strength to take him by the neck from amongst his own Men, I was obliged to let him have his own way, that I might not be the Occasion of Blood Shed." Stephen was released after a short cooling-off period, but Forbes, who was becoming ill with chronic dysentery, struggled to prevent the break between his officers and the Virginians from becoming permanent.

Soon he had another, more serious problem. In the first week of September, the advance guard under Bouquet had begun constructing Fort Ligonier at Loyalhanna, halfway on the northern route to Fort Duquesne. Forbes, who remained near Shippensburg and Raystown, worried that the French would launch a preemptive attack. He ordered Bouquet to proceed cautiously, avoid contact with the enemy, and watch out for Indians. Bouquet at first obeyed the general's injunction, but when his scouts reported no enemy activity after several days he decided to take the initiative. On September 11th he ordered Major James Grant of the Highlanders to lead a force of 800 men, including 150 from the First Virginia Regiment and 200 Marylanders and Pennsylvanians, toward the Forks of the Ohio. The detachment was too small to threaten Fort Duquesne and too large for reconnaissance, but it is possible that Bouquet and Grant had hoped to drive off the French-allied Indians encamped around the Forks and force the European garrison to take shelter in Fort Duquesne.

Grant reached the Forks on the evening of the 13th without having been detected by the French. He might have scouted the fort, or even launched a lightning raid on the largely unguarded camp that surrounded it before withdrawing. Instead, Grant's troops announced their presence on the morning of the 14th by burning a barn and then standing in the open to draw plans of the fort while British drummers beat reveille. The French failed to see any humor in the display and immediately sallied out with a large force of Indians. The ensuing battle was a repeat of Braddock's defeat, in miniature. The Highlanders stood firm at first, but when the French and Indians split into small parties and sniped at the British officers, they broke in disorder. The

Pennsylvanians and Marylanders also fled without firing a shot. The only organized resistance came from one hundred men of the First Virginia, who stood rearguard under Captain Thomas Bullitt while the regulars escaped. "Had it not been for the Virginians," Bouquet later told Forbes, "all would have been cut to pieces." Even so, the rout was general. The battle ended with Grant captured and 300 of his men killed, including sixty-two Virginians.

For Forbes, who had spent the last two months pondering the strategic consequences of the defeat of Abercromby's expedition to Ticonderoga in July, the shattering of Grant's "rash attempt" came as a heavy blow. "Thus the breaking in upon," he scolded Bouquet, "not to say disappointments of—our hitherto so fair and flattering hopes of sucess touches [me] most sensibly. How far we shall find the bad effects of it, I shall not pretent to say." He took out some of his frustration on Washington, who appeared with Byrd at Raystown on the very day Forbes learned of Grant's defeat. The general gave Washington credit for the good behavior of the Virginians under Bullitt, but he then rounded on the two colonels for "their weakness in their attachment to the province they belong to, by declaring so publickly in favour of one road without their knowing anything of the other." As for himself, Forbes thundered, he did not value "provincial interest, jealousys, or suspicions, one single twopence."

Forbes's anger would have withered a man less self-assured than Colonel Washington, who believed that Grant's defeat and the rapid approach of winter had proven the Pennsylvania route a mistake. "I may venture to declare," he wrote Governor Fauquier on September 25th, "that our affairs in general appear with a greater gloom than ever; and I see no probability of opening the Road this Campaign." Washington nevertheless respectfully obeyed the general's orders to move the remainder of his regiment from Fort Cumberland to Raystown. He took pride in the generally acknowledged brave performance of his troops as he paraded them before the critical eyes of Forbes and his staff. At the general's request, he also drew up meticulous plans for "a Line of March through a Country covered with Wood, & how that Line of March may be formed, in an instant, into an Order of Battle." When Forbes led his army to Fort Duquesne in November he followed, whether deliberately or not, many of Washington's suggestions.

The slowly improving relations between Washington and Forbes coincided with renewed hopes of ending the campaign before winter. Until mid-October, rain and supply problems made this possibility seem remote. On October 12th, the French even carried out a cheeky attack on Loyalhanna that the British repulsed with difficulty. Forbes was at Loyalhanna, where he had moved his headquarters, on November 7th when he learned of a treaty that changed British prospects. This was the Treaty of Easton (Pennsylvania), signed on October 25th–26th, which recognized Iroquois rights in the Ohio Valley and concluded peace between the British and the Ohio Indians. Forbes promptly sent messengers into the wilderness to spread the news to the surrounding Indian tribes. With only the French to deal with, the road to Fort Duquesne looked clear.

But news of the Treaty of Easton did not send the French packing back to Canada; instead, on November 12th a French raiding party of about two hundred men ventured within a few miles of Loyalhanna to attack British horses and livestock. Although accounts of the British response are contradictory, Forbes apparently sent Lieutenant Colonel George Mercer of the Second Virginia in pursuit with a few hundred provincial soldiers. Mercer failed to defeat the enemy force and, as the volume of firing increased, Forbes sent Washington into the woods to reinforce him with a few hundred more volunteers. When Washington's detachment neared the scene of the fighting at dusk, they and Mercer's men mistook one another for the enemy and fired volley after volley into the shadowy shapes that emerged behind muzzle flashes and drifting gray-white powder smoke. Captain Bullitt quickly realized the mistake and took off running between the opposing lines, frantically waving his hat and screaming for the Virginians to stop firing. Washington claimed that he too tried to stop the gunfire, placing himself in "imminent danger by being between two fires, [and] knocking up with his sword the presented pieces." Nevertheless, by the time the muskets fell silent fourteen men lay dead and twenty-six wounded from friendly fire. Bullitt blamed Washington for the fiasco, and became so openly angry that it "gave rise to a resentment in the mind of General Washington which never subsided."

For Forbes, the skirmish brought a prize that overshadowed any blundering on the part of his subordinates. The French had run off into the forest before the Virginians began shooting one another, but they left behind three prisoners. On interrogation, the prisoners indicated that they had left Fort Duquesne lightly garrisoned, and that their commanders were preparing to abandon it. Gambling on the accuracy of the prisoners' information, Forbes ordered a full-scale advance westward from Loyalhanna in hopes that a determined British push against the Forks might succeed.

As his men drowned their sorrows in labor, clearing three to five miles of road a day, Washington continued to urge the general to abandon his enterprise and return to "General Braddocks road—which is in the first place good, and in the next, fresh." Forbes brushed aside the colonel's objections—which were, to be honest, rather silly—and continued the advance. If his attack failed, the Forks of the Ohio would remain in French possession for at least another year, perhaps longer should the Ohio Indians return to French allegiance. The provincial troops were due to disband on November 30th. Everything, he insisted, must be thrown into this last-ditch effort to end the campaign in 1758.

On November 23rd, as provincials and redcoats toiled side by side in the woods ten miles from Fort Duquesne, they heard a distant and powerful explosion. The next day a scouting party of light infantry set out to investigate. When they arrived at the Forks of the Ohio that evening, they looked in amazement on the smoking ashes of Fort Duquesne. Isolated by the loss of their Indian allies and unwilling to face Forbes's guns alone, the French garrison of perhaps five hundred men had blown up the fort. They retreated by canoe up the Allegheny River, leaving not a man in sight. Washington's feelings when he arrived on the scene can only be imagined. He announced the event to Governor Fauquier by praising Forbes for his "great merit (which I hope will be rewarded) for the happy issue he has brought our Affairs to—infirm and worn down as he is," but refused to admit error in advocating Braddock's road to Fort Duquesne.

With the British in possession of the Ohio Valley, Virginia's part in the French and Indian War effectively came to an end. The increasingly infirm General Forbes stayed at the Forks of the Ohio only a few days. He ordered the construction of Fort Pitt and then began his painful journey back to Philadelphia, where he died on March 11th. Washington meanwhile made his own way home, arriving in Williamsburg by the end of December with news of the victory. His previous returns from the frontier in 1754 and 1755 had presaged new military ambitions, but this time he determined to quit the field of battle in favor of new challenges in political and domestic life. To everybody's surprise, he delivered his report, tendered his resignation as colonel of the First Virginia, and then mounted his horse, riding north, where he had more pleasant things to do, like get married.

In a display of loyalty, the officers of the Virginia Regiment wrote Washington in protest at the "disagreeable News" of his resignation. "The happiness we have enjoy'd and the Honor we have acquir'd," they declared, "together with the mutual Regard that has always subsisted between you and your Officers, have implanted so sensible an Affection in the Minds of us all, that we cannot be silent at this critical Occasion." They praised his tutelage "in the Practice of that Discipline which alone can constitute good Troops," his "steady adherance to impartial Justice," and his "quick Discernment and invaluable Regard to Merit, wisely intended to inculcate those genuine Sentiments, of true Honor and Passion for Glory, from which the great military Atchievements have been deriv'd." Washington replied gratefully: "your approbation of my conduct, during my command of the Virginia Troops, I must esteem an honor that will constitute the greatest happiness of my life, and afford in my latest hours the most pleasing reflections. I had nothing to boast, but a steady honesty—this I made the invariable rule of my actions; and I find my reward in it." But he would not reconsider his resignation. On January 6, 1759, he married Martha Custis at her home on White House Plantation in New Kent County, Virginia. Six weeks later, on his twenty-seventh birthday, he took his seat in the Virginia House of Burgesses.

George Washington's military career from 1754 to 1758 was in some ways not exemplary. Although his rise in rank and responsibility had been extraordinary, his battlefield performance had not. His first experience of action in Jumonville's glen had resulted in a dubious victory. A little over a month later, he suffered a humiliating and very public defeat at Fort Necessity. In 1755 Washington witnessed but played no significant role in Braddock's catastrophe on the Monongahela. In 1758 he led two regiments totaling 2,000 men in the Forbes expedition; but aside from bickering over the route to Fort Duquesne and participating in the murky friendly-fire incident of November 12th, he did not contribute to the final victory.

Some unattractive facets of Washington's personality arose during the French and Indian War, and they would continue to mark his conduct twenty years later. Highly sensitive and easily hurt, he sometimes overreacted to his military, political, or social failures by lashing out at perceived enemies, or by falling into a despondency that made him yearn for the simplicity of farm life. Washington's associates learned that a touch of carefully directed praise or even flattery often sufficed to pull him out of these moods. When that failed, only action could raise his spirits. Washington's impatience and hatred of in-activity left him with little tolerance for any kind of delay or obstruction. When frustration or boredom led him into a funk, therefore, the prospect of battle or work could throw him almost instantaneously into a more optimistic frame of mind.

Yet there was more in young George Washington than the vain, emotional man of great ambition and ordinary military ability that some debunking his-torians have portrayed. None of his failures exposed any elemental incompe-tence, and his successes revealed traits that would prove crucial to the foundation of the United States of America. His battlefield mistakes at Fort Necessity, Loyalhanna, and elsewhere earned him little merit, but were per-haps to be expected of a young, inexperienced, and headstrong officer. The British regular officers who fought under Braddock and Forbes did no better, and often much worse. Like them, Washington showed great personal brav-ery and coolness under fire, and his composure in times of crisis helped him earn the respect of the soldiers he commanded in the Revolutionary War. Al-though the common soldiers who served under Washington in the 1750s seem to have regarded him without any special admiration, his subordinate officers were almost uniformly faithful, and with the possible exception of Bullitt at Loyalhanna none of them took him publicly to task over his mis-takes. On the contrary, officers like Stephen expressed a degree of loyalty that arose from deep personal respect.

As was true with much of his education, Washington learned his military skills on the job. The British regular officers who fought beside him had learned how to handle men, guns, transport, and supply during years, some-times decades, of experience. Washington, by contrast, had no military back-ground whatsoever when he first commanded troops in battle at the age of twenty-two. He made up the difference with careful observation and inde-pendent study. He watched Braddock and Forbes run their armies, learned from the successes and mistakes of both, and supplemented the resulting firsthand knowledge with extensive reading. "Do not forget," Washington ex-horted his officers in 1756, "that there ought to be a time appropriated to at-tain [military] knowledge; as well as to indulge pleasure. As we now have no opportunities to improve from example; let us read, for this desirable end."

Washington read Caesar's *Commentaries,* a biography of the soldier-king Charles XII of Sweden, *A Panegyrick to the Memory of Frederick, Late Duke of Schomberg*—a seventeenth-century German mercenary general—and the translated works of French military masters. Among the military books he considered indispensable were: *An Essay on the Art of War* by the Comte de Turpin de Crisse, and *The Partisan: or, The Art of Making War in Detachment* by Louis de Jeney. De Crisse emphasized the importance of efficient military administration. De Jeney provided instruction on the art of interdicting enemy supply lines with light infantry—Washington would use militia—in an early form of guerrilla warfare. Humphrey Bland's *Treatise of Military Discipline* stood at the top of Washington's prescribed list of military reading. This standard British manual of field tactics, drill, and discipline appeared in several editions after its first publication in 1727 and became particularly popular among young colonial officers like Lawrence Washington, who had owned a copy during his half brother's youth. George bought his own edition after Braddock's defeat and referred to it constantly in his lifelong quest to create a trained, professional American army.

Washington's mastery of military theory bore fruit in the training of the Virginia Regiment. He exaggerated in comparing the regiment to British regulars, for provincial officers, training, and supply never reached such high standards. Nevertheless, Washington worked wonders with the Virginia troops in three years, from 1755 to 1758. By the time he finished with the regiment it had become the best-trained and equipped provincial unit in the thirteen colonies. It continued to impress observers until its disbandment in 1762. Washington had forged the unit partly by resort to a traditionally harsh code of discipline that grates on modern sensibilities—decreeing, for example, that profanity merited twenty-five lashes from a cat-o'-nine-tails—and partly through dedication and hard work. The results broke through even the most ingrained antiprovincial prejudices of British officers, and when Captain Bullitt's Virginians covered the retreat of Montgomery's Highlanders in Grant's defeat of September 1758, the regulars credited their bravery and professionalism.

Washington did not return this respect. Although he held Montgomery's Highlanders in high regard, the sight of the hapless regulars of the Forty-fourth and Forty-eighth Foot fleeing the battlefield in Braddock's defeat left a permanent impression on his mind. He was convinced that adequately trained and supplied provincial troops—especially Virginians—could stand man to man with the best of the British army, particularly in the wilderness of North America. This conviction would sometimes lead to overconfidence during the Revolutionary War, when General Washington denigrated the British regulars and overestimated the ability of his Continentals. On the other hand, Washington's confidence in American soldiery would inoculate him against the defeatism that crept among some of his generals in the dark days of 1776, and again in 1780.

Perhaps the most important element in Washington's military education during the French and Indian War was his development of a strategic sense. The struggle for the Forks of the Ohio had started as a Virginia affair, but it quickly took on international prominence. Washington became one of the men at the center of the conflict. Although he had a limited understanding of the European politics and diplomacy that helped to fuel the war, he nevertheless sensed the crucial importance of Indian affairs. He also perceived the strategic value of the different regions of North America—such as the Middle Atlantic, the Ohio, and the Hudson Valley—and learned how British ministers thought of conquering or defending the continent. Most of all, he learned how war could become a battleground for the competing ambitions and interests of the various colonies. He was partial to the interests of Virginia, but his partiality did not prevent him from seeing the importance of uniting, for example, the resources of New York, Pennsylvania, Maryland, and Virginia in any common fight, and the dangers that would result if the colonies refused to work together. They needed a cause, representatives speaking with one voice, and a man to unite them. George Washington's grasp of this fact helped him to lead and preserve the Revolution.

6

CALL TO ARMS

1759 – 1775

THE SIXTEEN YEARS of peace that followed his retirement from the Virginia Regiment in December 1758 changed Washington. His interest in military affairs subsided as the French and Indian War wound down, and by the time he entered his forties in the 1770s he had no more dreams of martial glory. He no longer lived and thought as a soldier, but as a family man, planter, and politician. Each of those roles carried heavy responsibilities. He served as legal guardian to Martha Washington's children—his stepchildren—by her deceased first husband, and conscientiously managed their property and education. At the sprawling and valuable estate of Mount Vernon, he managed crops, livestock, commercial enterprises, a mansion house, and hundreds of slaves. And he tirelessly pursued various private investments and indulged his passion for accumulating land.

Competing with Washington's domestic concerns were his activites in government and politics. His ambition helped to drive his politicking, but so did his belief in *noblesse oblige,* or the responsibility of the privileged to play an honorable and active role in public life. After being elected to the Virginia House of Burgesses and taking his seat in February 1759 he devoted himself to public affairs, including local and colony-wide politics and administration. Washington also used his connections with the Fairfaxes and other important Virginia families to angle for favor. Although he never entered the highest circles of colonial government, by the eve of the American Revolution Washington had acquired a prominent political profile and a substantial personal fortune.

As Washington rose in Virginia politics he joined the swelling ranks of those disenchanted with Great Britain. For him as for many other planters, British taxation both offended his sense of morality and threatened his commercial ventures. He denounced the 1765 Stamp Act as "ill judgd" and "unconstitutional," and predicted that popular resistance would force Parliament to repeal it. His attitude hardened further in 1767, when those he called "our lordly Masters in Great Britain" imposed the Townshend duties on tea, paper, and other items.

Although Washington regarded these new taxes as outrageous, the question of how to resist them baffled him. Every potential solution seemed too dangerous to contemplate. "Addresses to the Throne, and remonstrances to parliament" had proven ineffective, Washington told his friend and fellow politician George Mason in April 1769, and he doubted whether the nonimportation associations that some colonies had formed to boycott British trade would hold together. But if peaceful measures failed to protect "the liberty which we have derived from our Ancestors," he feared the logical next step. "That no man shou'd scruple," he wrote, "or hesitate a moment to use a[r]ms in defence of so valuable a blessing, on which all the good and evil of life depends; is clearly my opinion; Yet A[r]ms I wou'd beg leave to add, should be the last resource; the de[r]nier resort."

At first it seemed the colonies could avoid such a terrible last resort. In April 1770, at the behest of Prime Minister Lord North's new administration, Parliament repealed all of the Townshend duties except for the one on tea. To some colonials, including Washington, this was not enough; yet when the boycotting nonimportation associations collapsed, he happily resumed trading with the mother country. Then Parliament passed the 1773 Tea Act, which allowed the East India Company to bypass American middlemen and ship tea directly to the colonies. Boston, Philadelphia, and New York broke into revolt, and mobs tarred and feathered British agents. The disorder culminated in the notorious Boston Tea Party of December 1773. Six months later Parliament passed the Coercive Acts, a series of punitive measures that closed the port of Boston, quartered troops there, restricted the Massachusetts government, and prescribed deportation for offenders against the revenue laws.

The Coercive Acts radicalized colonial intellectuals and politicians, including Washington. The Virginia House of Burgesses condemned the acts even before they took effect, prompting Governor Dunmore, a loyal king's man, to order it dissolved. Washington reacted to the governor's move by becoming even more outspoken. Relieved from his responsibilities in the Burgesses, he openly decried Parliament's measures as a "Tyrannical System . . . a regular Plan at the expence of Law & justice, to overthrow our

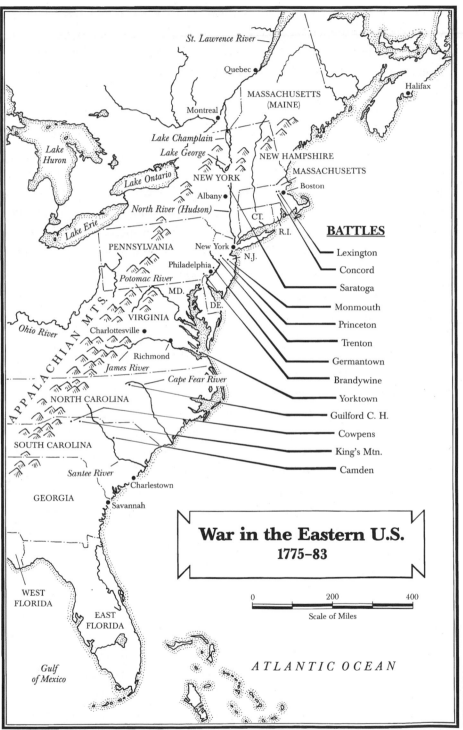

St. Lawrence River

Quebec

MASSACHUSETTS
(MAINE)

Halifax

Montreal

Lake
Huron

Lake Champlain
Lake George

NEW HAMPSHIRE

Lake Ontario

MASSACHUSETTS

NEW YORK

Boston

Albany

North River (Hudson)

CT.

Lake Erie

R.I.

PENNSYLVANIA

New York

N.J.

BATTLES

Philadelphia

Potomac River

MD.

DE.

Lexington

Concord

Saratoga

Ohio River

VIRGINIA

Charlottesville

Monmouth

Princeton

Richmond

James River

Trenton

Cape Fear River

Germantown

NORTH CAROLINA

Brandywine

Yorktown

SOUTH CAROLINA

Guilford C. H.

Cowpens

King's Mtn.

Santee River

Charlestown

Camden

GEORGIA

Savannah

War in the Eastern U.S.
1775–83

WEST
FLORIDA

EAST
FLORIDA

0   200   400

Scale of Miles

Gulf
of Mexico

ATLANTIC OCEAN

Constitutional Rights & liberties." He also helped organize and equip militia companies that formed in Fairfax and other Virginia counties, and reassured hesitant patriots that trained American soldiers could fight and even defeat British regulars. Armed rebellion, hitherto unthinkable, had become a very real prospect.

Yet independence was still "farthest of anything" from the thoughts of Washington and many other Americans. Most prominent Virginians refused even to consider it. In July 1774, Washington presided over the so-called Fairfax Resolves, in which he and other former Burgesses from the county rebuked the British government, promised that they would "use every Means which Heaven hath given Us to prevent our becoming it's Slaves," and laid out a plan for colonial resistance. All the same, they expressed their desire "to continue our Connection with, and Dependance upon the British Government." Few believed that in struggling for their liberties they were setting the stage for the birth of a new country.

Later that month in Williamsburg, the Virginia Convention adopted the Fairfax Resolves as a basis for its own platform and elected seven delegates, including Washington and Patrick Henry, to represent Virginia in the First Continental Congress. Convened in Philadelphia between September 5th and October 26th, the Congress condemned the Coercive Acts, cut off trade with Great Britain, and asked the colonies to prepare their men for war. Washington voted for these resolutions and then returned to Mount Vernon, where he spent the winter following political events and overseeing the supply of the local militia. Relations with Great Britain did not improve, and in March 1775 the Virginia Convention reconvened at Richmond to elect the same seven delegates to the Second Continental Congress. Once again, Washington dutifully packed his bags and left Mount Vernon, riding through the spring bloom toward Philadelphia. He was about to witness the beginning of the Revolutionary War.

Washington arrived in Philadelphia on May 9th, just in time to attend the opening of the Congress on the next day. He found the city animated with news of war. On April 19th, bloody skirmishes had taken place near Lexington and Concord in Massachusetts between British redcoats and American minutemen. After the skirmishes ended, express riders spread news of the fighting from Boston to Philadelphia, shouting that the British soldiers had been defeated. Those who could read snatched at the latest newspapers before the ink was dry, while those who could not jammed the streets to learn what they could from gossip or town criers. Children sensed the agitation of their parents and joined in the spirit of the times. One observer wrote of seeing "boys, who are still quite small, marching in companies with little drums and wooden flints to defend their inherited liberty." Men did the same thing, perhaps not much less naïvely, but with real guns. Mustering hurriedly in their local militia companies, they played at being soldiers, and got ready to oppose the expected British invaders. Other men, less sympathetic to the American cause, girded themselves to defend royal government.

In Philadelphia, where express riders from Boston arrived only a couple of days after Lexington and Concord, companies of city militiamen began drilling from early May. They were shabby but earnest, and their appearance delighted the civilians who gathered to watch them. The city's light infantry—sporting green coats, white breeches, and hunting caps—trained where unfinished streets and houses faded into open fields west of town. "Firing at Marks, and throwing their Tomahawks," the soldiers presented an impressive spectacle. At a single word of command they would form "on a sudden into one Line . . . break their Order, and take their posts, to hit their mark." The crowds were thrilled and cheered raucously. These were the men, they hoped, who would teach Great Britain how Americans could fight.

Washington must have paused to watch the soldiers drill as he walked to and from the Philadelphia State House, where Congress was ensconced. But he kept immune, outwardly at least, from all the popular excitement. In debate, he reinforced the reputation for prudence and moderation that he had earned in the Virginia House of Burgesses. His attitude was based on principle. Emotions, he believed, had no place in politics. A good politician stood above the passions and factions of the mob, detached but not indifferent, swayed by neither party nor self-interest. Aspiring to this ideal, Washington was neither ardent nor frenzied before Congress, even when he lambasted Lord North's "despotick Measures." Fierce oratory of the sort perfected by Samuel Adams, Patrick Henry, and James Otis had no place in his repertoire.

Washington won respect for the sober sincerity and maturity of his thought, which distinguished him from some of his fellow patriots, and he received attention at Congress without seeming to seek it. His gravity of countenance, careful modesty, and measured speech marked him out to the delegates as a judicious man who would lead them forward with a steady hand, rather than drag them like a fury over the precipice. "He seems discret & Virtuous, no harum Starum ranting Swearing fellow but Sober, steady, & Calm," wrote one Connecticut delegate. But this magisterial figure clearly was also a soldier. Most people knew of the courage he had shown in Braddock's defeat, and remembered him as a champion of the provincial soldiers. And for anyone who had forgotten, the buff-and-blue uniform of the Fairfax County Militia that Washington wore (and which he had designed himself in 1774) served as a reminder.

Congress's first priority was to determine how to employ the musket-wielding amateur soldiers who drilled outside. The decision had to be made quickly. Fighting threatened to erupt again in Massachusetts, and in colonies like Virginia royal governors spoke of forming private armies to put down any rebellion. The British troops of General Thomas Gage, reeling from their reportedly disastrous defeats at Lexington and Concord, had retired to Boston; but no one expected them to remain idle for long. If the redcoats attacked again, they might prove unstoppable. And although a vast and eager force of New England militiamen surrounded the British, it lacked guns, ammunition, training, and leadership. The Americans needed an army, and a commander-in-chief to lead it.

Foremost on Congress's list of candidates for commander-in-chief were Artemas Ward and John Hancock, both from Massachusetts, and the Englishman-turned-patriot Charles Lee. Since Massachusetts and the other New England colonies had so far carried on the struggle by themselves, many delegates favored either Ward, a longtime revolutionary who had served as a provincial colonel during the French and Indian War and now commanded the Massachusetts troops besieging the British army at Boston; or Hancock, who was both president of Congress and the richest patriot in New England. Other delegates argued that the colonies needed a professional soldier at the helm. Their choice was Lee, who had been a lieutenant in the Forty-fourth Regiment of Foot during Braddock's defeat and served in various European armies until his immigration to America in 1773. Both Lee and Hancock craved the appointment, and marshaled delegates to their support.

Yet as the delegates considered the three main candidates, one factor—the need for unity—came to dominate their thoughts. British policy, as embodied in the Coercive Acts, had singled out Boston for punishment. People living elsewhere—meaning everyone from Georgia to Canada—would need to be convinced that Boston's problem was theirs, too. To unite them, Congress had to create an army composed of soldiers from every colony, with a commander whose authority encompassed the entire continent. The New England troops would naturally prefer a general who was one of their own; but soldiers from other colonies, especially those with large loyalist populations like New Jersey, North Carolina, and Georgia, might refuse to accept his authority. The people of these colonies might react to a New England commander by remaining neutral, or even supporting the Crown.

The only man who could symbolize the kind of unity they needed was George Washington. He was from Virginia, one of the most prosperous and densely populated colonies in America, and while hardly anyone outside New England had heard of Ward and Hancock, Washington's name was familiar in every region. His partisan advocacy of Virginia's interests over those of other colonies during the Forbes campaign of 1758 had been forgotten. People now identified him not with his colony, but with the frontier, and ultimately with America. He had patriot friends in every colony, he discriminated against no one, and he often spoke of the need to unite all the colonies in one cause. In this respect, no one better fitted the role of commander-in-chief.

Another point in Washington's favor was his apparent lack of interest in the appointment, an attitude that set him apart from Hancock and Lee. Americans were deeply suspicious of military men who grasped for power, and if Washington had asked to command the army he probably would have been turned down. Instead, he quietly went about his duties and declined to ask for the post. "So far from seeking this appointment," he told Martha, "I have used every endeavour in my power to avoid it." He could not have thought of a better way to get the delegates' attention.

John Adams, an intelligent and widely respected Massachusetts delegate, focused their attention further when he rose to address Congress on June 14th. The army at Boston needed a commander-in-chief as soon as possible, he said. Starved of supplies, the troops were already showing signs of dissatisfaction and might quit the field altogether. If this happened, Congress might not be able to raise another army. The British looked forward to the moment when they might "take Advantage of our delays, march out of Boston and spread desolation as far as they could go." The only way for the Congress to stave off disaster, Adams warned, was to take charge of the army at Boston immediately and appoint a commanding general. Adams declined to make a formal nomination, but he "had no hesitation to declare that I had but one

Gentleman in my Mind for that important command, and that was a Gentleman from Virginia who was among Us and very well known to all of Us, a Gentleman whose Skill and Experience as an Officer, whose independent fortune, great Talents and excellent universal Character, would command the Approbation of all America, and unite the cordial Exertions of all the Colonies better than any other person in the Union." Everyone knew who he meant, but Washington got up from his seat in the chamber and fled to the adjoining library before Adams had a chance to speak his name.

Not expecting Washington's coyness to last, the delegates elected him the army's commander-in-chief anyway. But in his acceptance speech on June 16th, Washington spoke with such reluctance that some delegates wondered whether they had made a mistake, and one delegate questioned whether the Virginian was not being just a little bit "too modest." "I am truly sensible of the high Honour done me in this Appointment," Washington declared. "Yet I feel great distress, from a consciousness that my abilities & Military experience may not be equal to the extensive & important Trust . . . lest some unlucky event should happen unfavourable to my reputation, I beg it may be remembered by every Gentn in the room, that I this day declare with the utmost sincerity, I do not think my self equal to the Command I am honoured with." A few days later, Washington tearfully told Patrick Henry "that he was unequal to the station in which his country had placed him." "Remember, Mr. Henry, what I now tell you," he vowed. "From the day I enter upon the command of the American armies, I date my fall, and the ruin of my reputation." He wrote to Martha that he had resisted the appointment partly "from a consciousness of its being a trust too great for my Capacity and that I should enjoy more real happiness and felicity in one month with you, at home, than I have the most distant prospect of reaping abroad."

What was wrong with this man? Some of his contemporaries suspected hypocrisy; and historians usually argue that his reluctance masked hidden ambition. Washington never asked to head the army, but his service on defense committees and his uniform—although other men almost certainly wore military uniforms in the Congress—indicate that he may have wanted others to see him in the position. In the French and Indian War he had sought commissions by portraying himself as a military expert, maneuvering himself into position for promotion while he protested his lack of ambition. Was he playing the same game in the halls of Congress? Surely, it seems, the Great Man cannot have fallen victim to self-doubt and developed cold feet.

It is much easier—acclimated as we have become to insincere politicians—to forgive a little affectation, dishonesty, and hypocrisy so long as it implies hidden ambition. And ambition, almost everyone assumes, is what really made Washington tick.

No one, of course, can know Washington's conscious or unconscious mental processes; but if we must speculate—and speculation is, after all, integral to the historians' art—keeping it simple is a good rule of thumb. With imagination, countless explanations are possible; and in this case several are plausible. Washington's ambition may have been so deep, even subconscious, that he did not realize its presence. Or perhaps it *was* conscious, in which case he chose to conceal his motivations from his wife, the Congress, and others. He might also have been of two minds, with his love of military achievement struggling against uncertainty and doubt. But what about the simplest explanation? Could it be that he meant what he said and really felt unfit for command?

Washington had already seen more than enough bloodletting to sate his youthful fancy. War no longer seemed the romantic adventure he had imagined it to be as a young man; rather it loomed now as a tragic necessity. As he explained in a letter to George William Fairfax after learning of the war's first skirmishes: "Unhappy it is . . . to reflect, that a Brother's Sword has been sheathed in a Brother's breast, and that, the once happy and peaceful plains of America are either to be drenched with Blood, or Inhabited by Slaves. Sad alternative! But can a virtuous Man hesitate in his choice?" The military aggressiveness that Washington would later show did not spring from any love of battle, but from his impatience and desire for quick, decisive resolutions to every problem.

A "virtuous Man," Washington backed armed resistance against Great Britain. But he genuinely doubted his ability to lead the army to victory. Years of meditation on his youthful military experiences had brought his own limitations and shortcomings into sharper focus. The prospect of taking such a huge responsibility on his shoulders overawed him. He also realized that Congress had chosen him partly out of "political motives," he being a man who could unite the colonies, and he well knew that political appointees made notoriously poor generals. Moreover, he recognized the immense power of the mother country and knew that defeating it would not be easy. Above all, Washington prized his public reputation. Risking it on victory against the greatest military power in the world was surely a poor bet, and at times in the years that followed he would regret taking the gamble. "May God grant," he wrote to his friend Burwell Bassett, "that my acceptance . . . may be attended with some good to the common cause & without Injury (from Want of Knowledge) to my own reputation . . . as reputation derives it['s] principal support from success."

Despite his misgivings, Washington could not decline his commission. Personal honor, he told Martha, forbade him from "exposing my Character to such censures as would have reflected dishonour upon myself, and given pain to my friends." More important was his passionate, and even ideological, devotion to the American cause. He would not shirk an opportunity to serve it. Washington considered his time, wealth, life, and even his reputation to be expendable. His uniform and his service on defense committees were in that respect expressions of his sense of public duty, and so advertised his willingness to make sacrifices for the cause.

Washington also believed in his personal mission. His attitude was not messianic, however, but stoic. He felt that Providence had chosen him, and although he had no idea what the result would be, he submitted in a spirit of resignation and self-sacrifice. "As it has been a kind of destiny that has thrown me upon this Service," he wrote Martha, "I shall hope that my undertaking of it, is designed to answer some good purpose." Washington was not an overtly religious man, but he did have a strict personal moral code, and he hoped to justify Providence's call by behaving with exemplary honesty, self-abnegation, and scrupulous attention to duty. "I can answer but for three things," he told Bassett: "a firm belief of the justice of our Cause—close attention in the prosecution of it—and the strictest Integrity." If he failed, he would "have the consolation of knowing (if I act to the best of my judgment) that the blame ought to lodge on the appointers, not the appointed, as it was by no means a thing of my own seeking, or proceeding from any hint of my friends."

Washington's refusal to accept a salary for his services was emblematic of his somewhat ostentatious public virtue. He did open a public expense account, however, and some have claimed that he made money from it by over-charging Congress. In fact, the £150 per month that he requested for expenses was not just for him, but also for his entourage, which sometimes swelled to a crowd. His account books, which still exist, list charges for things like ferry fares, innkeepers' fees, candlesticks, saddle repair, meat, fruit, mounds of cabbages and beets, and (admittedly) oceans of grog, liquor, and wine. Washington even charged Congress for fifteen shillings "Cash paid a beggar by the General's order." But although he was not averse to placing his headquarters in the occasional mansion, he otherwise made do with precious few luxuries.

As Washington pondered his place in the coming war, he endured endless misgivings. "I am now to bid adieu to you, & to every kind of domestick ease, for a while," he wrote morosely to his brother John Augustine on June 20th. "I am Imbarked on a wide Ocean, boundless in its prospect & from whence, perhaps, no safe harbour is to be found." He consoled Martha with plans to "return safe to you in the fall," repeating the age-worn promises of soldiers to be home by Christmas. Yet he perceived that American prospects were bleak unless the king was forced to accept a political compromise.

Relative numbers demonstrated that a full-scale conflict would be difficult to win. Great Britain had a population of about eleven million. By contrast, Congress estimated the colonial population to be three million; and over 500,000 of them were slaves or free blacks whom the rebels were reluctant to entrust with weapons. Of the eligible population, only about 250,000 were adult men capable of bearing arms. Moreover, an unknown but probably significant proportion of them were either loyalists, who might take up arms against Congress, or pacifists, who would refuse to fight at all.

What kind of Americans *would* fight? Memories of the shambling drunks and sluggards who had accompanied him to Fort Necessity in 1754 must have haunted Washington. The same types of men—some recklessly brave, others sullen and mutinous, all clueless when it came to military discipline— inevitably would enlist in 1775. Washington could not dream of making an army out of them unless he repeated the combination of strict discipline, good example, and sound management that had built the old Virginia Regiment.

Americans feared standing armies, believing that they crushed the individuality of free citizens and reduced them to tools of oppression. This prejudice dated back through generations of English popular belief—the seventeenth-century military dictator Oliver Cromwell was still remembered and reviled on both sides of the Atlantic—and had been reinforced lately by the forcible quartering of British troops on American civilians. For Washington, it meant that if he pressed discipline too far, a deeply suspicious population might regard him as a military autocrat.

The British army, Americans believed, was like that: an instrument of unjust men who ruled through fear. With spirit and initiative drilled out of them, they followed orders blindly, and to their eventual doom. By contrast, the American way of war meant fighting as a citizen first and a soldier second. In the popular mind, a citizen-soldier was a patriotic volunteer who accepted military authority, but to a limited degree, and only so long as his life and liberty were in danger. He joined the militia, repelled the invader, and went home. Anything beyond that was unnatural and dangerous.

The militia typically assembled in response to calls from colonial governors. Regiments were organized by county, with companies from individual townships or districts. Pay was poor, and discipline worse. Military training was rudimentary. Nor was the raw human material much to boast of. Recruiters accepted almost anyone—teens and old men, the obese and the consumptive, black and white, bright lawyers and village idiots, the lithe and the lame. Terms of enlistment, which could run for weeks or months, often included provisions that a militia unit would not serve more than fifty or a hundred miles away from the place where it had been mustered. Some volunteers brought their own guns and clothing; others "borrowed" government-issue firearms and supplies when their enlistments expired. But in most places, no fixed system existed to keep the militia supplied. If food ran out, if the weather became inclement, if the troops did not like their officers—who usually came from their own communities—whole companies and regiments could pack up and leave for home.

The idea of an army made up of such troops—and in the spring of 1775 most Americans who took up arms did so as members of the militia—must have made Washington sweat. They had their uses, to be sure. Militiamen could collect and transport supplies, put down Tories, and carry out raids. They could also fill gaps in a line of battle, although they had an annoying tendency to melt away when challenged. Yet for the core of his army, Washington knew he would need soldiers who could form into lines in the open, trade fire with opposing lines of redcoats, hold fixed positions, and protect cities. He needed regular troops, or at least something like them.

The Continental Congress laid the groundwork for a regular army four days after Lexington and Concord, when it voted to raise a force of 30,000 men. The New England colonies responded by raising regiments that would join the army outside Boston. Washington's appointment as commander-in-chief symbolically transformed that army into part of an intercolonial force that represented all the colonies; and Congress sealed the transformation later that spring by requesting Virginia, Pennsylvania, and Maryland to send north regiments of their own. Together—in theory anyway—these regiments would form a Continental or national army operating under unified command.

Yet *calling* this collection of men from different colonies a regular army was one thing, and *making* it so another. Haste, politics, and the pervasive myth of the citizen-soldier meant compromise and haphazard organization. Washington and the four major generals that Congress appointed—Artemas Ward, Charles Lee, Philip Schuyler, and Israel Putnam—stood at the top of a chain of command that mimicked that of the British army. But the delegates spent little time on working out the finer details of rank and seniority in the Continental Army. They were more concerned with the danger of a Cromwellian *coup d'état* and strained to emphasize that all of the officers were ultimately responsible to civilian authority in a democratic government. The result, at least at first, was organizational chaos, with cooperation and obedience asked for but rarely enforced.

Casually organized, the Continental Army was also heterogeneous. Its soldiers came from all kinds of social, cultural, and economic backgrounds: immigrants from England, Scotland, Ireland, and Germany; farmers, shopkeepers, and rich merchants; ministers and convicts; and so on. Officers were often but by no means always better educated than their men, and sometimes they were completely illiterate. Nothing like the strict social divisions between officers and enlisted men that prevailed in the British army prevailed in the Continental Army. This was good in the sense that it made the army look more "democratic," but it also undercut the strict hierarchy of rank that Washington would demand. Quite often genteel subordinates rebelled at taking orders from illiterate superiors, however much the latter— for example, the backwoods Virginia colonel Daniel Morgan—had demonstrated their mastery of the art of war. Divisions also appeared according to colony or state. Although Congress paid their soldiers' salaries, each colony raised, clothed, and sometimes equipped its own regiments, with varying degrees of success. Reviewing what he called "the Troops of the United Provinces of North America" assembled on parade during the war, Washington would more than once walk past a regiment of plump, nattily dressed, and beautifully equipped soldiers from one state, only to discover a half-starved, ragged, and hideously accoutered regiment from another state on the other side.

Congress modified its original call for an army of 30,000 by instructing Washington that he was to have no more than two Americans for every British soldier *in Boston*. It was a ridiculous restriction that proved impossible to enforce, and in July, Congress amended it by limiting the army to no more than 22,000 men. In a spirit of egalitarianism, Congress also passed sixty-nine articles of war that strictly limited officers' ability to impose discipline and granted common soldiers extensive rights of appeal. Washington did not protest the articles at first. But after watching some military malefactors saunter free from the provost despite the spluttering protests of their accusers, he tried to impose stronger regulations, initiating a running battle with Congress over discipline that would linger for the rest of the war.

Beyond these measures, Congress did little to help Washington mold and manage the army. He had to shunt the regiments into brigades and divisions as they arrived in camp and make sure that they were trained, disciplined (as far as the articles of war allowed), and fed. If they showed up without guns or other items, he provided them with new ones. If soldiers fell sick or got wounded, he decided where to send them. If weapons and tools broke or ran short, he looked for local sources of repair and supply. If the army needed more horses or wagons—and it always did—he arranged for their procurement. Countless other duties settled upon him as well.

Washington had help from some of his subordinates. Congress allowed him to appoint two young Philadelphians, Thomas Mifflin as his aide-de-camp and Joseph Reed as his secretary. Neither had any military experience, but they were well educated, patriotic, and eager to assist the commander-in-chief by writing his letters and carrying out other mundane tasks. The army's new adjutant general, Horatio Gates, had learned administration in the British army and performed superbly in his new post. Congress also named, or directed Washington to appoint, quartermasters and commissaries for the army. With the exception of Gates and a few others, however, the new appointees took office with little idea of what they were supposed to do, and looked to Washington for guidance in almost every particular. Time and again he would have to drop whatever he was doing in order to instruct them in their jobs.

Deploying the army and preparing to oust the British army from North

America was Washington's most obvious duty. In its instructions, the Congress directed him to proceed to the American camp outside Boston at Cambridge and to "take every method in your power, consistent with prudence, to destroy or make prisoners of all persons, who now are, or who hereafter shall appear in arms against the good people of the United Colonies." Once there, he could "dispose of the said army under your command, as may be most advantageous for obtaining the end, for which these forces have been raised."

Yet Washington did not hold unlimited military authority. Congress expressed confidence in his "best circumspection," but suggested that he should act only after "advising with your council of war," a kind of military cabinet composed of major- and brigadier generals. Washington took this proviso quite seriously. On several occasions in the first year of the war, he would allow his general officers to overrule him. He also felt constrained to get Congress's approval for almost every move of consequence. As Washington would soon discover to his sorrow, politicians and other civilian officials also had ways of pressuring him to act on their behalf.

Washington held nominal authority over military forces in every colony, but in practice he could do little to control or coordinate them. Military emergencies outside the range of the main army had to be prosecuted locally or regionally, by bodies of colonial militias or detachments of regular troops. Congress never established a central strategic authority, creating only the loosest structures of regional command. Instead, it assembled *ad hoc* armies under temporary leaders who roamed under little or, in some cases, no restraint at all. As political appointees, these commanders often frittered away American military strength with their own pet projects and expeditions. Washington could do little to rein them in, and he would often squabble with them over troops and supplies.

The dangers posed by the absence of strategic coordination did not occur to many Americans in 1775. Most people, including Washington, entered the war with the sole purpose of extending congressional authority throughout the colonies and containing the enemy in Boston. "To compel them to remain there," he wrote his brother Samuel on July 20th, "is the principal object we have in view indeed the only"; and he and many others failed to appreciate the strategic importance of the capture by Benedict Arnold and Ethan Allen of the approaches to the Hudson Valley at Ticonderoga and Crown Point in May of 1775. Only in 1776, after the British evacuated Boston, did Americans begin to think more adventurously.

—

Patriotic propagandists did not worry much about how Great Britain would try to subdue America. The pudgy, goggle-eyed Prime Minister Lord North who appeared in colonial caricatures did not impress them as another William Pitt. Nor did his army of red-coated marionettes concern them much. Few redcoats would even cross the Atlantic, patriots believed, before the British people rose up and refused to pay for the oppression of America. As for the British troops already in America, a few more rebuffs of the sort delivered at Lexington and Concord would send them scurrying home. Liberty would be secure in a matter of months.

This was all fantasy, of course. The propagandists seriously underestimated the strength, skill, and resolution of their foe. Nevertheless, Great Britain did have significant problems in the summer of 1775. North and many of his ministers dreaded the coming struggle as much as did Washington. They believed that if the flame of rebellion in Massachusetts was not put out quickly, it might engulf all of the British possessions in North America. Anything less than a rapid and victorious military campaign would tax Britain's military and economic resources to an extent almost unimaginable, with possibly tragic consequences for her position among the great powers of Europe.

The ministry's decision to put down the American rebellion by military force gained widespread popular support, but no one believed that the British army should systematically conquer and occupy the colonies. The area was simply too vast. Instead, North and his ministers planned to overawe the rebels by destroying the main American army in New England—hopefully in no more than one or two battles—while a naval blockade severed colonial trade with Europe. The cowed Americans would then presumably negotiate a settlement.

But even these modest plans outstripped Britain's capacity. The country was completely unprepared for a major war in North America in 1775. In London, the venomous political climate threatened to sink Lord North's administration despite his skill as a politician. Practically the only point upon which British politicians could agree was the need to put down rebellion in the colonies. Fifteen years earlier William Pitt had navigated the shoalridden waters of Parliament with relative ease; but North and his cabinet lacked the political adroitness to repeat the feat during the Revolutionary War. North's cabinet also had little grasp of global strategy, and no inclination for military affairs, although they were directly responsible for guiding the operations of the armed forces. Lord Dartmouth, the secretary of state for the American Department at the beginning of the war, detested the war and did little to prosecute it until Lord George Germain replaced him in November 1775. Germain was an abler minister than his predecessor and tried to energize the war effort, but he never accumulated enough prestige and authority. As a result the British army, like the American, lacked firm strategic direction. The king for the most part avoided interfering in such matters, and North had neither the skills nor the desire to do so.

The British war effort suffered from administrative gridlock fueled by incompetence, infighting, and overlapping spheres of authority. The secretary at war, who administered the army, competed with the navy's First Lord of the Admiralty for funds and supplies awarded by the Treasury, the Board of Ordnance, and other departments. These departments in their turn fought for contracts with private suppliers, who charged exorbitant prices for shoddy merchandise in hopes of turning a profit at the government's expense. Unsurprisingly, the British logistical system worked only fitfully; better than the American, but still inadequate to the demands of an unprecedented war.

The British military command structure was unwieldy and inefficient. The king stood as titular head of the army, but he did not appoint a commander-in-chief for it until 1778. Until then, no one man would be responsible for the direction of land operations against the colonies. At the outset of the war, General Gage held the dual offices of governor of Massachusetts and commander-in-chief of the British forces in North America from his post in Boston; but his military authority did not stretch far outside New England. London dispatched three major generals to support him during the siege in May, and five months later one of them, William Howe, replaced Gage in command of British forces from Florida to Nova Scotia. At the same time, Major General Guy Carleton, who had been governor of Quebec since January 1775 and outranked Howe as the senior general in North America, was given a separate command in Canada, with authority to raise his own army. As one might expect, Howe and Carleton had to compete for their share of troops and supplies from Britain, where the political influence that either of them enjoyed at any given moment made all the difference in what they received. Other semi-independent commands would also crop up from time to time, like General John Burgoyne's in the autumn of 1777.

William Howe, whose elder brother Richard (Lord Howe) took control of the British North American fleet in February 1776, would be George Washington's principal military adversary for two and a half bloody years. Howe was forty-six years old when he succeeded Gage in October 1775. His military career began when he was eighteen and reached its pinnacle in September 1759, when, as a lieutenant colonel in command of a battalion of light troops, he scaled the Heights of Abraham during British major general James Wolfe's expedition against Quebec. He went on to distinguish himself in the conquest of the remainder of Canada, as well as in the capture of Havana in 1762. When Howe attained the rank of major general in 1772, he was already one of the most distinguished officers in the British army.

Both the Howe brothers sympathized with American grievances, though not to the extent of advocating separation or autonomy. William went so far as to tell his parliamentary constituents that he rejected North's policy of crushing the rebellion and would never agree to command troops in North America. But his ambitions got the better of him when the ministry asked him to replace Gage. Howe accepted the post with an alacrity that some people considered unseemly.

Howe's high living and legendary affinity for grand banquets have obscured his qualities as a military commander. Dark-complexioned and taciturn, at six feet Howe stood about the same height as Washington. Intelligent and well educated, he understood the principles of infantry tactics very well and excelled at handling troops in battle. His creative and nimble military mind allowed him to take the measure of his opponent, anticipate his reaction, and plan accordingly. He was also personally brave. The only doubts that Howe's superiors had about him arose from his reputation for slowness and excessive caution. In the eyes of some, it bordered on laziness; to others, it would eventually smack of cowardice or even treason.

Howe's army gave him his biggest advantage over Washington. Contrary to popular belief, British officers were not always better trained than their American counterparts. Military academies had yet to be established, and the common practice of purchasing commissions allowed many wealthy but ignorant aristocrats to advance to high military rank. But most British officers typically had at least a modicum of military experience. They had gained most of it in Europe, but despite the claims of the patriots this did not necessarily leave them at a disadvantage in America. In places like New Jersey and southeastern Pennsylvania, where Washington conducted some of his most important campaigns, the fighting conditions in terms of climate, settlement patterns, and topography were not all that different from Europe.

Furthermore, British officers served in a professional army with established military traditions a far cry indeed from the makeshift American army, in which traditions had yet to develop.

Common soldiers earned scant respect on either side. Americans had long reviled the redcoats as brutal, unintelligent tin soldiers. The British typically regarded Yankees as undisciplined cowards who fought well only if they were recent Irish or Scottish immigrants. Germans, who fought on both sides but especially with the British, were despised by everyone. Americans hated these mercenary soldiers, and the British laughed at their gaudy uniforms. The redcoats joked that Germans could march and plunder, but not fight. For their part, the Germans were jealous of their British allies, complained of mistreatment, and thoroughly loathed the colonials they fought. Respect grew among Americans, British, and Germans only with the shedding of blood.

Modern caricature has made eighteenth-century warfare seem like a simple, almost silly affair, with neat, colorful rows of flag-waving infantry marching slowly in rigid formation and slaughtering one another at close range with cannons and muskets. In reality, the art of land warfare had never been more complex. There were many elements to it, including fortification and siege craft, artillery and cavalry, reconnaissance and espionage. The best generals knew how to use their combined assets in all of these areas. But infantry dominated the battlefield. Good infantry soldiers were well trained, disciplined, motivated, and, of course, equipped. To use them properly, officers had to understand tactics, especially with regard to maneuver and the application of firepower. Maneuver was not just for show, but sought to apply superior force at the enemy's weak points. Infantry formations, which were not colored wooden blocks but complicated and fluid arrangements of varying densities and shapes, had the same purpose. Battles developed quickly, so an officer who could not assemble his men rapidly in the proper formation—allowing for variables such as topography and weather—had little chance of victory.

Britain and America fought the Revolutionary War with different understandings of tactics that originated in their diverging temperaments and material circumstances. Lacking skill in drill and marching, American officers and soldiers initially had trouble maneuvering in the open, and preferred to operate in small groups while making use of woods and other natural features for cover. From there they sniped at the enemy, especially targeting officers in order to demoralize their men. Carleton, speaking for many British officers, called this tactic "a cowardly and cruel manner of carrying on the war," but the French had used it effectively in the 1750s. Americans also liked fixed entrenchments, from which they used their muskets and artillery to pound an enemy moving in the open. Washington resisted his troops' instinctive preference for entrenched or irregular warfare, but it was not until the arrival of Baron von Steuben as the army's inspector general in 1778 that their tactics were brought more or less in line with European standards.

The British typically deployed and fought in two lines, advancing on opposing forces in reasonably flexible order according to the circumstances. Their object in almost every case was to close with the Americans, absorbing casualties until they could charge with bayonets. These weapons, which by 1783 had come to symbolize British ruthlessness, probably killed most of the Americans who died in combat during the war. Fixed bayonets dominated battlefields in the era before machine guns and massed artillery. The most common firearms, muskets, took an agonizingly long time to load and fired inaccurately. They inflicted relatively few casualties, even on densely formed troops marching at a deliberate pace, and rarely repulsed a determined enemy. Bayonet charges thus made good tactical sense so long as the defenders were not too well entrenched.

American soldiers found themselves facing the bayonet's business end much more frequently than they wished. Until large arms shipments from France started arriving in 1777, the American munitions industry could barely produce enough muskets, ammunition, and artillery to keep the army supplied. Bayonets came last on the forge owners' list of priorities. In addition, the long rifles that some backcountry Americans carried could not be fitted with bayonets. The result was that Continentals could not stand up to the redcoats in close combat, for the prospect of being spitted on British bayonets tempted them to break and run before coming to close quarters.

For the British, superior experience and training meant better fire discipline. It also meant weapons that were well cared for. British industry produced reliable muskets and superior ammunition, and in quantities that the Americans could not hope to equal. In the manufacture of artillery, too, Great Britain had a greater number of skilled workmen and better facilities to cast guns than did America. The king possessed skilled artillery officers who knew how to site, aim, and operate cannon. American artillerists generally learned their jobs as they went along. In artillery and engineering, the American army would have to rely on an influx of French volunteer officers and munitions to make up part of the difference.

Unlike in the Civil War, when cavalry was crucially important to both sides and changed the course of many campaigns, neither of the belligerents in the Revolutionary War understood the value of mounted troops. This is somewhat strange, as the wide spaces and sparse settlements of America seemed ideal for an army strong in cavalry. In this respect both sides suffered from a lack of vision; but there were practical difficulties as well. The British had difficulty transporting horses across the Atlantic and finding remounts in America. The Americans had less trouble procuring horses, but lacked suitable cavalry officers and struggled to pay for and manufacture equipment. (Captain Henry Lee, Jr.—"Lighthorse Harry Lee" of legend—was an exception to this rule.) Indeed, Washington's most effective practitioners of partisan warfare, such as Daniel Morgan and Allen McLane, operated mostly on foot. Although British and loyalist cavalry raiders caused the Americans fits, especially in the South, cavalry was never much of a factor in the war.

None of these characteristics of the coming conflict were evident to the leaders of Great Britain and America in the summer of 1775. Both shared the same goal of, in Washington's words, "the re establishment of Peace & Harmony between the Mother Country and the Colonies," and hoped for a short conflict that would not unduly test the resolve of soldiers and civilians in either country. Neither side made any strenuous efforts to prepare for a war of attrition. But just a few days after Washington's appointment as commander-in-chief of the American army, blood began to flow on a scale that threatened to drown all hopes of a political solution. A few battles, it became apparent, were not going to force a decision, even if one side won all of them. By 1776, the politicians in London and Philadelphia would face what they feared most: a long and terrible war.

7

BOSTON

June 1775 – March 1776

ON JUNE 18, 1775, two days after he officially accepted his appointment as commander-in-chief, Washington attended a party given in his honor at Thomas Mullen's Vauxhall Tavern on the Schuylkill River below Philadelphia. Several prominent delegates and Philadelphians were there, including Benjamin Franklin, Thomas Jefferson, and Dr. Benjamin Rush. Washington detested dramatic scenes, and as he ate he may have been thinking about how he could escape before the toast without offending anybody. But he was too late. When the last plate was cleared away, a voice bellowed, "the Commander in Chief of the American armies!"

With the dread moment upon him, Rush remembered, "General Washington rose from his seat, and with some confusion thanked the company for the honor they did him. The whole company instantly rose, and drank the toast standing. This scene, so unexpected, was a solemn one. A silence followed it, as if every heart was penetrated with the awful, but great events which were to follow the use of the sword of liberty which had just been put into General Washington's hands by the unanimous voice of his country."

Back at his lodgings that evening, George penned a letter to Martha, giving her news of his appointment and explaining how he had acquiesced in it despite his better judgment. "I shall feel no pain from the Toil, or the danger of the Campaign," he assured her. "My unhappiness will flow, from the uneasiness I know you will feel at being left alone—I therefore beg of you to summon your whole fortitude & Resolution, and pass your time as agreeably as possible." Whether she decided to move to Alexandria, or decided to move in with her friends, would be all the same to him so long as she was happy. "My earnest, & ardent desire is," he wrote, "that you would pursue any Plan that is most likely to produce content, and a tolerable degree of Tranquility as it must add greatly to my uneasy feelings to hear that you are dissatisfied, and complaining at what I really could not avoid."

On June 19th Washington returned to the State House to receive his commission from Congress, and that evening he scribbled his last diary entry until New Years' Day, 1780. He spent the following few days getting ready for his journey and writing letters of farewell to friends and relatives in Virginia. Finally, on June 22nd, Congress gave Washington his instructions to join the army at Boston. At sunrise the next morning he prepared to leave Philadelphia.

Well-wishers crowded into his room almost immediately after he finished dressing, but he fended them off long enough to write a last letter to Martha. With that of June 18th, it was among the few letters from George that Martha apparently could not bring herself to burn near the end of her life. "I go fully trusting in that Providence, which has been more bountiful to me than I deserve," he wrote. For her grief, he had just a line of consolation: "I retain an unalterable affection for you, which neither time or distance can change." Then, hastily signing himself "with the utmost truth & sincerity Yr entire Go: Washington," he put down his pen and rose to go.

Picking his way through a thicket of outstretched hands, Washington stepped out of the building where he had stayed for the last several weeks. He then mounted his horse and began his journey to Boston. Mounted beside him were Major Generals Charles Lee and Philip Schuyler; his aide-de-camp, Major Thomas Mifflin; and his secretary, Joseph Reed. A troop of Philadelphia light horse escorted the men out of the city to the accompaniment of fifes and drums, while a mixed crowd of militia officers, civilians, and delegates—including John Adams, a "poor creature, worn out with scribbling, for my Bread and my Liberty"—drifted in and out of orbit around them. Five miles outside the city, the crowd dissipated and Washington hurried on with his immediate entourage and the escort of light horse.

Washington entered New York City two days later. Men and women poured out of their churches, abandoning Sunday services to welcome the commander-in-chief. It may have been the largest crowd the city had ever seen. On the fringes of the throng, loyalists looked on in disgust at "the repeated shouts and huzzas of the seditious and rebellious multitude," who cavorted in a "tumultuous and ridiculous manner" as they serenaded Washington all the way to his lodgings on Broadway. Before he went to bed an ex-

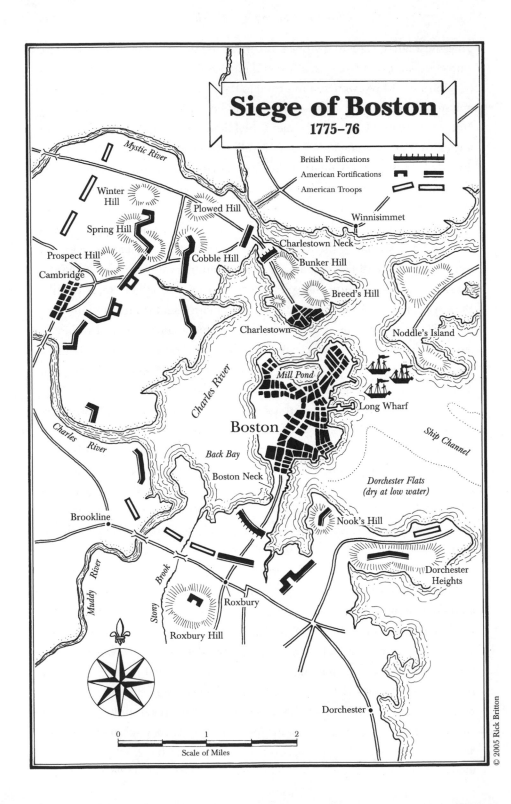

Siege of Boston
1775–76

British Fortifications
American Fortifications
American Troops

Mystic River

Winter Hill
Plowed Hill
Winnisimmet
Spring Hill
Charlestown Neck
Prospect Hill
Cobble Hill
Bunker Hill
Cambridge
Breed's Hill
Charlestown
Noddle's Island

Charles River

Mill Pond
Boston
Long Wharf

Ship Channel

Charles River
Back Bay
Boston Neck
*Dorchester Flats
(dry at low water)*

Brookline
Nook's Hill
Muddy River
Stony Brook
Dorchester Heights
Roxbury
Roxbury Hill

Dorchester

0   1   2
Scale of Miles

© 2005 Rick Britton

press rider arrived in the restless city with a letter from the Massachusetts provincial congress to the Continental Congress. Opening the letter even though it had not been addressed to him, Washington discovered that a major battle had taken place at Boston on June 17th.

Informed that the British troops in Boston intended to occupy the as yet undefended hills surrounding the city, the Committee of Safety that governed Massachusetts had decided to counter them by sending 3,000 troops to Bunker and Breed's hills on Charlestown Peninsula. Gage could have cut off and probably captured the Americans sent to those hills by seizing the peninsula at its neck; unaccountably, he instead ordered Howe to land 2,500 redcoats at its southeastern tip. Howe did so, and then launched three frontal assaults against the makeshift American entrenchments; but his adversaries were better dug-in and more determined than he had expected. The British suffered awful casualties as their first two assaults collapsed, and it was only on the third try that they finally managed to drive the Americans from their trenches with bayonets. The Americans suffered 441 casualties and abandoned Charlestown Peninsula to Howe, who had lost about 1,150 men—a staggering 40 percent of his force.

The Battle of Bunker Hill had a profound effect on American and British military thinking. Put simply, the Americans henceforward became fixated on forcing similar encounters while the British did everything to avoid them. Much of the excessive caution that characterized Howe's later conduct can be attributed to his Bunker Hill trauma. The same event boosted Washington's confidence, but also made him reckless. "Winning" another Bunker Hill and thereby bringing a quick end to the war became for him a kind of obsession.

Washington left New York on the afternoon of June 26th. Six hot and dusty days later, on July 2nd, he passed the first pickets around the American lines at Cambridge, Massachusetts. Just as he entered camp it began to rain, sending the troops that had been assembled to greet him scrambling for shelter. He had to wait until the following morning to meet his army on a muddy parade ground. The new commander-in-chief then delivered a short speech, read from the 101st Psalm, and reviewed the fidgety lines of paraded troops. "Joy was visible on every countenance," Brigadier General Nathanael Greene later wrote, "and it seemed as if the spirit of conquest breathed through the whole army." He was too optimistic. Soldiers who bothered to record the day's events in their diaries concluded that the military spectacle had amounted to "nothing remarkable," and ambled back to camp mildly disillusioned. The new commander-in-chief had failed to impress them.

Washington was disappointed, too. He had been promised an army of about 20,000 men but only 14,000 were present and fit for duty. The Continental regiments from Massachusetts, Connecticut, Rhode Island, and New Hampshire that he saw—and he had to look hard, since they dressed and carried themselves like the militias that surrounded them—were incomplete. Some of them were boys or, to his evident astonishment, free blacks. They were filthy—the Massachusetts Provincial Congress warned him too late that "the Youth in the Army are not possess'd of the absolute Necessity of Cleanliness in their Dress"—and threadbare, too. Toes poked out from fantastic footwear below a stunning array of mismatched civilian clothing. Soldiers presented their rusty or broken weapons askew, and filled their empty cartridge boxes with knickknacks.

The troops slept in weird collections of shelters made of boards, sailcloth, stone, turf, bark, and bracken; some huts were "curiously wrought with doors and windows done with wreaths and withes in the manner of a basket," while only a few managed to resemble "your proper tents and marquees." Wandering loose about this strange settlement, horses and other animals spread offal, blundered into tents, and feasted on uncollected garbage. Uncovered latrines presented pitfalls for the unwary and emitted a nauseating stench that permeated everything in camp.

The men behaved much as they looked. Washington dubbed them "a numerous army of Provencials under very little command, discipline, or order"—in other words, a rabble. Officers held only tenuous authority. Sentries drifted away from their posts or fell asleep on duty. Bands of soldiers looted and destroyed private property. The provost, or military prison, overflowed with troops accused of desertion and theft. Some Continental recruits deserted their regiments and reenlisted in others for an extra helping of bounty money. Soldiers amused themselves by randomly firing off muskets or even cannon in camp. And to top it all, a local politician solemnly warned Washington that several of his officers were "very equivocal with respect to courage."

"It requires no military Skill to judge of the Difficulty of introducing proper Discipline & Subordination into an Army while we have the Enemy in View, & are in daily Expectation of Attack," Washington wrote John Hancock, "but it is of so much Importance that every Effort will be made which Time & Circumstance will admit." Discipline was the key to his philosophy of military command, and he used it as a starting point for the army's reformation. "Be strict in your discipline," he exhorted a young colonel. "Require nothing unreasonable of your officers and men, but see that whatever is required be punctually complied with. Reward and punish every man according to his merit, without partiality or prejudice; hear his complaints; if well founded, redress them; if otherwise, discourage them, in order to prevent frivolous ones. Discourage vice in every shape, and impress upon the mind of every man, from the first to the lowest, the importance of the cause, and what it is they are contending for. . . . Be plain and precise in your orders, and keep copies of them to refer to, that no mistakes may happen. Be easy and condescending in your deportment to your officers, but not too familiar, lest you subject yourself to a want of that respect, which is necessary to support a proper command."

Washington accepted the title of "His Excellency," although Lee considered it a "bauble" that made him "spew." He expected common soldiers to address their officers by the appropriate military titles as well—that is, if they could tell the officers apart from privates. Some colonels wore humble homespun garments, while some lieutenants or even enlisted men sported fantastic uniforms that had been looted from royal storehouses or preserved as family heirlooms. Washington consequently donned a light-blue ribbon to set him apart from the others, and ordered his officers to wear ribbons of different colors according to their rank.

Washington insisted on obedience to superiors at every level of the army. "Disobedience of orders," he proclaimed in general orders, "is amongst the first and most atrocious of all military Crimes." Not everyone had viewed it that way before he arrived in camp. The Massachusetts officers in particular showed a marked reluctance to enforce their authority. They had been elected by their men, and tried to earn the soldiers' favor with "Smiles." Washington called such conduct a "kind of stupidity" and "made a pretty good Slam among such kind of officers" by cashiering some of them for cowardice or corruption. But he could not entirely root out this military egalitarianism.

A disciplined army, Washington believed, treated civilians with respect. Long before commanding his troops in battle, he understood that winning in the field would be impossible without earning the allegiance of the American people. Although plundering had already been winked at enough to make it widespread, he had no intention of putting up with it. Soldiers who roved about the countryside stealing horses, dismantling fences for firewood, and chasing farmers' chickens were special targets of his wrath. As he reminded each one of his soldiers, "it is unmanly and sully's the dignity of the great cause, in which we are all engaged, to violate that property, he is called to protect, and especially . . . it is most cruel and inconsistant, thus to add to the Distresses of those of their Countrymen, who are suffering under the Iron hand of oppression." He extended this principle even to the property of reputed loyalists, which until then had been considered fair game.

Washington's directives encompassed every conceivable aspect of military conduct. He exhorted his men to obey the articles of war, especially those relating to "profane cursing, swearing & drunkeness," and required "punctual attendance on divine service, to implore the blessings of heaven upon the means used for our safety and defence." "Toss-up, pitch & hustle," and other games of chance were prohibited. Full latrines were not to be left fermenting in the open air. Soldiers with an inclination for angling were forbidden from fishing in ponds for fear of spreading typhoid or cholera. They were also discouraged from bathing in a river at Cambridge and then "running about naked upon the Bridge, whilst Passengers, and even Ladies of the first fashion in the neighbourhood, are passing over it, as if they meant to glory in their shame." Chatting with the enemy, hitherto common, would be punished with the "utmost severity." And Washington "strictly required and commanded" his troops not to fire their weapons except in case of emergency.

This new system of discipline took only partial hold with the troops. Washington had to repeat most of his orders several times before they were obeyed. Each day accordingly became "one continued round of annoyance & fatigue." Again, the Massachusetts soldiers were especially difficult to control. They resented Washington's strictures as encroachments on their liberties and sidestepped them whenever they could. Artemas Ward, who had commanded the army until Washington arrived, shared their grievances. Ward eventually became so discontented that he could hardly bear speaking to the commander-in-chief, and the dislike grew mutual. Washington especially despised the Massachusetts officers and regarded the common soldiers of that colony as "an exceeding dirty & nasty people," an antipathy perhaps originating in the social differences between a southern planter and New England merchants and small farmers.

Washington also had problems in establishing a military bureaucracy to run the army and keep it supplied. The officers who preceded him thought they had come to Boston for fighting, not paperwork, and they had not kept track of how many men, guns, provisions, and other supplies they had on hand. They lived from hand to mouth, as it were, seeking resupply from private sources when the need arose but making little provision for the future. From the moment he arrived in camp, Washington insisted that adjutants, commissaries, quartermasters, and others face their responsibilities and learn how to carry them out.

The army could not function, Washington knew, without proper record-keeping; so he insisted on "speedy and exact" returns, or written inventories, of almost everything imaginable. On July 3rd, his first full day in Cambridge, he commanded the colonels of each regiment to provide him with two forms stating the number of men in each regiment, and the proportion of them sick, wounded, or on furlough. The next day he solicited lists of "all the Provisions, Ordnance, Ordnance stores, Powder, Lead, working tools of all kinds, Tents, Camp Kettles, and all other Stores." Similar directives followed almost every day, and Washington soon settled on a system of weekly returns for men and every item of military importance.

Requisitions for military paperwork are always unpopular, and it is not difficult to imagine the groans that greeted each one of the general's demands for fresh returns. The supply officers, "not being sufficiently acquainted with the Nature of a Return," and unwilling to work any harder than they felt necessary, submitted their paperwork carelessly. The first returns of powder, for example, indicated that the army had ten times the amount actually in their possession. Four weeks passed before Washington uncovered the mistake, and in the meantime he did not have enough powder with which to supply his troops in case of a major British attack. After that experience, he made no apologies for resorting to even the most "threatning means"—including incarceration—to obtain accurate paperwork.

Even accurate and timely returns were unsatisfactory when they revealed shortages, which haunted the army throughout its stay at Cambridge. Clothing and munitions in particular remained desperately scarce. Although wealthy compared to the rest of the colonies, New England just did not have the industrial base necessary to produce these commodities in quantity. Washington could not change this painful reality. But he could, through attention and diligence, keep a trickle of supplies flowing into camp—enough at least to keep the troops in the field.

Knowing that good civil-military relations were essential to keeping the army supplied, Washington established lines of communication with Congress and the governors and politicians of each colony. Patronage sometimes helped to strengthen his influence. He recommended one of Connecticut governor Jonathan Trumbull, Sr.'s sons for commissary general and made another his aide-de-camp. Washington also applied judicious doses of both heartfelt and calculated patriotic jargon in his appeals for material support. "The Cause," "the Salvation of the Country," and the need for "the most strenuous Exertions of every Friend of his Country" were some of his favorite themes. He was not averse to using flattery, either, when he thought it would do some good—even with Massachusetts officials, whom he regarded as stupid and corrupt.

Whether he liked them or not, Washington avoided irritating civilians with any behavior that implied military arrogance. With the New Englanders in particular, he learned, any real or perceived lack of respect for civilian authority went down rather badly. Governor Trumbull reacted so angrily to what he considered a "peremptory requisition" from the commander-in-chief in September that it took weeks for Washington to repair their relationship, despite his earlier favors to the governor's sons. Other politicians were equally touchy, and placating them became a full-time occupation. Every request to them had to be phrased respectfully and explained in detail. He sent them copies of every important military document, laid out the army's needs in each essential article, and explained exactly how he needed their assistance. When possible, he visited them to press his points in person.

Washington likewise had to tread carefully with his officers. They were a diverse and volatile lot. His three major generals at Boston, all appointed by Congress, were Artemas Ward, Charles Lee, and Israel Putnam. Ward was deeply patriotic but cranky with pain from a chronic illness and refused to warm to the new commander-in-chief. The Englishman Lee was vain and spiteful. He was also stunningly ugly, with a spindly body that featured sticklike limbs punctuated with tiny hands and feet, and a hook nose that delighted the wits, who dubbed him "Naso." Washington respected his learning and military experience, however, even if he occasionally cocked an eyebrow in irritation at Lee's omnipresent, yapping dogs. "Old Put," Israel Putnam, had become a New England folk hero through popular tales of his derring-do on the frontier. His military ability was less apparent, and although his robust physique impressed everybody, so did his illiteracy. Putnam's incomprehensible handwriting puzzled his correspondents so much that they eventually persuaded him to dictate letters to an aide.

Among Washington's brigadier generals were John Sullivan, Horatio Gates, and Nathanael Greene. Sullivan was thirty-five years old, a ruddy, dark-haired provincial lawyer from Durham, New Hampshire, who had a talent for getting into trouble. His friends considered him brave, passionate, and gregarious. His numerous enemies regarded him as arrogant, greedy, and reckless. Sullivan knew almost nothing about war or the military. But he was ambitious, and craved an opportunity to forge his reputation on the battlefield.

Gates was a bespectacled, pudgy man with a receding forehead and a nose that rivaled Lee's in prominence. A native Englishman of humble background, he had commanded an independent company of British soldiers during Braddock's defeat, and on Washington's advice, and with his assistance, he settled in 1772 in what is now West Virginia. Washington may also have had a hand in his appointment as adjutant general, with the rank of brigadier general, in June 1775. Gates rewarded him by working loyally and efficiently. He was a good administrator but did not possess Washington's tact. Although his later reputation as an intriguer (gained in part from his supposed participation in a plot to unseat Washington in the winter of 1777–78) is unjustified, his querulous, sometimes sullen temper alienated him from the commander-in-chief and other officers. Gates also had yet to prove he had any gift for a field command.

Nathanael Greene, a Rhode Islander only thirty-two years old, was the youngest and most capable of Washington's generals. Physically vigorous despite a congenitally stiff knee that made him walk with a slight limp, he had a quick mind tempered by a good education. Although he was a Quaker by upbringing, an indiscreet visit to an alehouse had resulted in his suspension from the Society of Friends in July 1773, and no pacifist scruples restrained him from supporting the patriots against Great Britain. He had marched to Lexington in April 1775 as a common soldier, but his learning and eagerness impressed Congress, which appointed him a brigadier general of the Continental Army in June of that year. Few others could boast of such rapid promotion. Greene developed an immediate liking for Washington and took to his military system with enthusiasm. "Under the Generals wise direction," he hoped, "we shall establish such excellent order and discipline as to invite Victory to attend him wherever he goes."

—

As Washington and his generals turned their attention to Boston, which the American army besieged, they detected many peculiarities in its topography. At first glance the city looked like a fortress, but on closer study it seemed more like a trap for the occupying British garrison. Boston's approximately 16,000 civilian residents and 6,000 British soldiers were confined to a small peninsula about two miles long and a mile wide. Their only link to the mainland was to the south, by way of a narrow and heavily fortified isthmus called Boston Neck. No American attack via the neck could succeed, and the floating batteries and warships that bobbed in Boston Harbor demonstrated the futility of an amphibious attack. Yet the water that surrounded Boston on the west, north, and east did not isolate it. In the first place, it froze hard in winter, offering approaches to the city for infantry and even cavalry. Second, and more important, the water did not put much distance between Boston and the hills that overlooked it on two sides. To the north, Charlestown Peninsula had fallen into British hands after the Battle of Bunker Hill, but no one, apart from animals and some farmers, held the rolling slopes of Dorchester Heights to the southeast. With enough heavy guns and ammunition, Washington could occupy Dorchester Heights and bludgeon Boston at will—that is, if he realized the importance of the position.

For now, though, all Washington could see was the "exceeding dangerous" nature of his own army's position. His officers told him that the British garrison was an intimidating 11,500 strong, almost twice the actual number. His own army was not much larger than that: 14,000 troops in two brigades of six regiments each, arranged in three divisions under Ward, Lee, and Putnam. It lay stretched in a thin arc from Winter and Prospect hills west of Charlestown Neck to Roxbury, outside Boston Neck. These exterior lines made it difficult for Washington to reinforce any one point in case of enemy attack. In addition, although the British had only two natural points of land egress, they could put troops ashore almost anywhere since the Americans had only a few whaleboats to protect the coastline.

Washington considered loosening the siege of Boston and withdrawing a few miles into the country, but his officers demurred. Retreat, they reminded him, would hardly endear a new commander-in-chief to the troops, Massachusetts patriots, or Congress. "The publick Service requires the Defence of the present Posts," they insisted, and voted unanimously to that effect in council. Acquiescing, Washington focused on improving and extending the army's entrenchments, up to now little more than ditches and rock piles. There were no trained engineers in camp, so the officers overseeing the work improvised. Within a few weeks they had built some respectable trenches and breastworks.

The summer passed as soldiers on both sides settled into the monotonous routine of siege warfare, with only occasional alarms and firefights to interrupt the tedium. One such affair occurred on August 2nd, when the British killed a Continental soldier in a skirmish and then hung his body on a gibbet in view of the American lines. Enraged, a group of Continentals approached Washington to beg for vengeance; and uncharacteristically—perhaps he was angry too, or just bored—the commander-in-chief agreed to let them "go and do as they pleased." The American soldiers spent the rest of the afternoon dodging about the front lines and sniping at redcoats, killing several before the body of their fallen comrade was taken down.

For the most part, however, the enemy stayed inactive; and Washington's defensive posture slowly relaxed. Spies reported that British morale was falling as their provisions ran short. Washington began to hope the enemy would either evacuate or seek peace, so that the war might end by Christmas after all. Yet neither peace feelers nor preparations for evacuation or attack became visible, and Washington grew increasingly frustrated with the inactivity. The British even ignored him when he tried to tempt Gage into a "general Action" by pushing his cannon to within point-blank range of the positions on Charlestown Neck.

As he cast about for an end to the deadlock, Washington's thoughts strayed away from Boston. "An Expedition," he informed Schuyler on August 20th, "has engrossed my Thoughts for several Days: It is to penetrate into Canada, by Way of Kennebeck River, and so to Quebec, by a Rout 90 Miles below Montreal." Excited by rumors of Canadian restiveness, he thought an American expedition to Quebec could throw the entire province into turmoil. The northwest Indian tribes might be encouraged to fight the British or at least be cowed into quiescence.

Congress approved the plan, and Washington sent Colonel Benedict Arnold—a thirty-five-year-old Connecticut merchant and French and Indian War veteran with aristocratic mannerisms and a rebellious streak—north with 1,000 men on September 11th. The troops came "not to plunder, but to protect you," Washington promised the Canadians; "to animate, and bring forth into Action those Sentiments of Freedom you have disclosed, and

which the Tools of Despotism would extinguish through the whole Creation." But he had badly underestimated the difficulty of Arnold's route. The
little expedition did not reach its main objective until November, after an
epic march that owed many of its hardships to Washington. It was the opening act to a prolonged campaign that culminated disastrously on New Year's
Eve in the icy wilderness outside Quebec.

With Arnold's departure, Washington turned his attention back to Cambridge and the dull, sometimes sordid routine of camp life. Each day a litany
of petty problems drained his patience. "The inactive state we lye in is exceedingly disagreeable," he wrote his brother John Augustine, "especially as
we can see no end to it, having had no advices lately from Great Britain to
form a judgment upon. . . . Unless the Ministerial Troops in Boston are waiting for reinforcements, I cannot devise what they are staying there after—
and why (as they affect to despise the Americans) they do not come forth,
& put an end to the contest at once."

Boredom was not the only cause of Washington's restlessness. He and
most other patriots had anticipated a campaign lasting only a few months,
but as summer ended, it looked as if the siege might last indefinitely. Realizing that he could not keep his promise to be home by Christmas, he invited
Martha to join him in Cambridge. The harsh New England winter loomed
ahead, and the troops still lacked food, clothes, housing, and pay. Washington initially had hoped that the expense of maintaining a useless garrison in
Boston would lead the British to make terms; he now doubted whether
America could afford to pay for the upkeep of its own army.

Even if the army held together for the present, in three months almost all
of it would disband. The terms of enlistment for the troops from Connecticut and Rhode Island expired on December 1st, and the Continental troops
from the other New England states would be free to leave on the last day
of the year. Their departure, the commander-in-chief chided his troops,
would expose "the Country to desolation, and the Cause perhaps to irretriev-
able Ruin." But these erstwhile patriots, whose smugness had already irritated Washington beyond endurance, had no ear for the preaching of their
commander-in-chief. They were not conscripts, but citizen-soldiers. They
had signed a contract to serve to the end of the year, and that they would do;
but no more. Almost every soldier was determined to go home at break of
dawn on January 1, 1776.

"These things are not unknown to the Enemy," Washington warned his officers; "perhaps it is the very ground they are building on." The enemy had only to gather reinforcements, wait until the end of the year, and then attack the remnants of the American army. If the Continentals and the militia refused to stay, then Washington either would have to replace them or capture Boston before they left. Neither option appealed to him. An assault on the city had little hope of success. Recruiting and training a new army was a thought too horrible for Washington to contemplate after the trials he had undergone in the past few months. But containing the British in the hopes of forcing a negotiated settlement, an outcome that King George III publicly foreswore in October, was no longer feasible. Pressed to use a new strategy, Washington chose the offensive.

Washington's attack plan was born of impatience and smacked of desperation. The main element was an open assault into the teeth of the British entrenchments on Boston Neck. At the same time, whaleboats and other small vessels would conduct rapid amphibious landings elsewhere on the peninsula. Heavy guns would support the attacks by "Bombarding, & Firing the Town" from Dorchester Heights. Their shells might burn Boston to the ground, but the conflagration would also consume the British army or force it to surrender. The fate of Boston's civilians did not figure in Washington's calculations.

The army had no guns heavy enough to reach the city from Dorchester Heights, though, and Washington consequently ordered the new commander of his artillery, a portly and magisterial Boston bookseller named Henry Knox, to scour New England and Canada for every cannon he could find. Washington was especially interested in the dozen or so big eighteen-pounder guns and thirteen-inch mortars reported to be at Ticonderoga, which Ethan Allen and Benedict Arnold had captured back in May. Knox went there and found the guns, but when he asked for custody of them the New York provincial congress refused. Annoyed that previous shipments of ammunition had not yet been paid for, the New York delegates would not trust Knox's promises until he had money to back them up. The attack on Boston would have to wait.

Washington needed political approval for his plan as well. On September 30th, Congress had elected Benjamin Franklin and two other men to a Camp Committee and ordered them to ride to Cambridge and confer with the commander-in-chief. They arrived on October 15th, and Washington presented them with a list of major and minor issues. Seven days of deliberations followed. The general wanted freedom to begin enlisting a new army of 20,000 men without waiting for the old one to disband, and the committee agreed. Franklin and his companions also approved most of Washington's recommendations on a host of other issues, including toughening the Articles of War and preventing blacks from enlisting in Continental regiments.

The touchiest question was saved for last. Would Congress, Washington asked, permit an attack on Boston even when it appeared that "the Town must of Consequence be destroyed"? The idea took the committee completely by surprise. What would Washington's army do if he ordered his soldiers to fire on Boston, where many of them lived? How could the rebellion survive if its very cradle, Massachusetts, disintegrated in an inferno of blood and flames? Deferring an answer, Franklin put Washington off and promised to raise the matter before Congress.

For over a month, the delegates postponed considering Washington's proposal. On December 22nd, when they finally concluded weeks of angry debate with a grudging resolve that "if General Washington and his council of war should be of opinion, that a successful attack may be made on the troops in Boston, he [may] do it in any manner he may think expedient, notwithstanding the town and the property in it may thereby be destroyed," it hardly mattered anymore. By that time, Washington not only had no heavy cannon, he also lacked the troops to defend Cambridge, let alone attack Boston.

As Washington expected, few of his troops had let idealism overcome their self-interest. The Connecticut regiments disbanded as scheduled on December 1st. A draft of 5,000 militiamen brought temporary relief on December 10th—although Washington carped that they would "destroy the little subordination I have been labouring to establish"—but they planned to leave just four weeks later. Finally, on New Years' Day, all the remaining New England troops, voicing no regrets despite Washington's admonition that they would thereby "not only fix eternal disgrace upon themselves as Soldiers, but inevitable Ruin perhaps upon their Country & families," departed in what he called a "dirty, mercenary Spirit."

Recruiting for the new army meanwhile proceeded sluggishly. By November 28, 1775, only 3,500 men had signed up for Continental duty. Civilian officials did little to expedite the new army's organization and supply, although when it came to securing profitable contracts they exploded with energy.

"Such a dearth of Publick Spirit, & want of Virtue," Washington bemoaned to Reed, who had resigned as secretary to seek more promising fields for his ambition in politics, "such stock jobbing, and fertility in all the low Arts to obtain advantages, of one kind or another, in this great change of Military arrangemt I never saw before, and pray God I may never be Witness to again."

With the old army gone and its replacement struggling to take shape in the immediate vicinity of a large, professional enemy force, Washington found his predicament unparalleled in all "the vast volumes of history. . . . [F]or more than two Months past I have scarcely immerged from one difficulty before I have plunged into another." Even Martha's arrival in camp on December 11th did not lift his mood. "I have often thought, how much happier I should have been" he wrote Reed on January 14th, "if, instead of accepting of a command under such Circumstances I had taken my Musket upon my Shoulder & enterd the Ranks, or, if I could have justified the Measure to Posterity, & my own Conscience, had retir'd to the back Country, & livd in a Wigwam."

Washington might have worried less, at least in the short term, if he had had any inkling of British intentions. The spies who had told him of an impending British evacuation in the summer of 1775 were wrong; but they had been correct about the difficulty Britain had in keeping her army supplied. A largely hostile population kept local resources unavailable, and the inefficiency of Canadian and British contractors made supply from those sources unreliable. Gage and Howe decided the city was untenable, and North's cabinet agreed. Boston would be evacuated before the end of the year in favor of New York. From there, Howe's army would await 14,000 British and German reinforcements and prepare for the conquest of the Hudson Valley in conjunction with another army from Canada.

Benedict Arnold had unwittingly put a hitch in the British plan by startling Canada with his now legendary march on Quebec. Governor Guy Carleton spent weeks in a panic before Arnold was wounded in a suicidal attack on December 31st, but the Americans maintained their "siege" of Quebec, such as it was, until the spring. Gathering reinforcements and supplies in Europe, meanwhile, proved more difficult than anticipated, and storms further complicated British strategy by scattering Howe's transports and supply ships. Howe nevertheless intended to evacuate Boston as soon as weather and the state of British shipping allowed, and for that reason he chose not to attack or otherwise harass the rebuilding American army.

Washington's new force took form slowly, but without interference from British forays. Although about 8,200 men had been recruited by January 10th, only 5,600 were present and fit for duty. A month later, Washington still claimed to have fewer than 10,000 men under his command and confessed to Reed that he had been "obliged to use art to conceal" the true number from his officers. The process of enforcing discipline, cleanliness, and a hundred other duties on officers and men began again. Progress was steadier than it had been in 1775, but he still had to supervise even the smallest details.

Henry Knox had meanwhile freed the artillery at Ticonderoga from the clutches of the New York legislature, and when a hard freeze occurred on January 6th the guns were brought across the Hudson River. It took two weeks for eighty teams of oxen to haul makeshift sledges bearing the massive guns over three hundred miles of hilly, ice-encrusted roads before Knox parked his artillery train twenty miles from Cambridge at the town of Framingham. The men assigned to man these guns stood back cautiously as the snow-covered monsters were unloaded from their sledges, and wondered how they worked. There could be no test-firing the cannon, as powder remained extremely scarce; but the gunners were not alone in their lack of training. Thousands of Continental troops had no way of learning how to use muskets: they didn't have any.

Washington nevertheless revived his plan to attack Boston. "All the Generals upon Earth should not have convinced me of the propriety of delaying an Attack upon Boston till this time," he wrote Reed on January 14th; "no oppertunity can present itself earlier than my wishes." On January 16th he convened another council of war, and lectured the officers until they accepted the "indispensible necessity of making a Bold attempt to Conquer the Ministerial Troops in Boston, before they can be reinforced in the Spring." To make the attack possible, Washington requested thirteen militia regiments from the neighboring colonies.

Washington waited for a month, gathering troops and supplies, before deciding that the critical moment had at last arrived. On February 16th, he called his general officers—all except Lee, who had taken command of New York, and Greene, who was ill—to another council of war, and presented them with an ultimatum. The attack must begin immediately, he declared, or be abandoned forever. Enough militiamen had arrived in camp to bring the army's strength to 16,000, in roughly equal numbers of Continentals and militia. The British, he claimed, had less than a third that number, 5,000, in Boston. Even better, ice covered Back Bay. It was thick enough to support troops, and would allow the army to bypass British fortifications on Boston Neck.

Because of the powder shortage no guns had been stationed on Dorchester Heights, and the artillery would not lend much support. But Washington now disingenuously claimed that he did not need the guns since his earlier idea of driving the British out of Boston by burning the town no longer looked realistic. "A Bombardment might probably destroy the Town," he told the council, but "without doing much damage to the Ministerial Troops within It, as there were Transports Wooded & Watered, with a view more than probable, to take them in upon any sudden emergency." "Small Arms," accordingly, "must be our principal reliance." But he was confident that by making use of the wider front offered by the ice, "a Stroke well aim'd at this critical juncture, might put a final end to the War, and restore peace & tranquility, so much to be wished for."

His arguments concluded, Washington "desired to know the Sentiments of the General Officers respecting a general Assault upon the Town," and sat down to await their reply. A novelist would fill the next few moments with nervous coughs and shuffling feet. The officers had already read an advance copy of Washington's speech and debated it in private. They may also have perused a note from Greene, who had put himself on record the day before as being "glad to see the attempt made," though not without artillery. The attack plan thus came well recommended. But the officers were having none of it. Standing up to speak for the council, Gates unconsciously rehearsed his later role as Washington's enemy and rival. "Perhaps a greater Question was never agitated in a Council of War, than the present," he pronounced. "Our Defeat, may risque the entire loss of the Liberties of America forever." The officers had considered the problem from every possible angle, and their conclusion was that Washington did not know what he was talking about.

Gates phrased it more delicately, of course, but that was the gist of his argument. To start with, Washington had provided inaccurate figures. The British army was larger, and the American army smaller, than he claimed. According to the council's informants, the garrison in Boston amounted to "a much larger number than 5,000—furnished with Artillery, Assisted by a Fleet and possessed of every advantage the situation of the place affords." Coming down from the previous summer's estimates, the council guessed 6,500—in fact, Howe now had about 9,000 troops. Nor, it appeared, did Washington know the size of his own army. Only 12,600 Americans were available to launch an attack, Gates claimed, far less than Washington's figure of 16,000 and "a force not more than sufficient to defend the Lines & maintain the Blockade." The "art" of concealment that Washington had privately confessed using to hide the size of his army had fallen flat.

The success of Washington's planned attack, Gates concluded, was "exceedingly doubtful." He also questioned its necessity in strategic terms. "I think there is no part of America where the Kings Troops can do so little injury to the United Colonies as the very spot they are now confin'd in," he said. Washington's duty was not to fling America's only army in headlong assault against entrenched positions, but to fight a successful *defensive* war. "If the Ministry are able to continue the War," Gates explained, "there is no doubt but The Kings Generals will be commanded to risque Battle at all Events as a defensive War must Uterly ruin their Affairs, therefore the Choice is offered Us either to attack them in their Fortifications, or leave it to them to give us the Advantage, by attacking Ours."

The officers, Gates declared, were not against taking Boston; but only if it could be done on the cheap. They were willing to try a preliminary bombardment of Boston, to "see how the Force of Artillery may effect them there." How, Washington interjected testily, could his guns bombard Boston "with the present stock of powder"? Gates replied that of course they would have to wait for a proper supply. "In the mean Time," he suggested, "preparations should be made to take possession of Dorchester Hill, with a view of drawing out the Enemy." Doing so might take days or weeks, thereby losing what Washington called a "golden opportunity" to attack over the ice. But it offered a better option than military suicide.

Washington had never before faced such a rebuke from his officers. They had rejected his judgment and questioned his grasp on reality. They were also probably right. The original attack plan was far too optimistic. "Perhaps the irksomeness of my Situation led me to undertake more than could be warranted by prudence," he later admitted to Reed. Washington had overestimated the capabilities of his troops—an odd miscalculation given his repeated difficulties in training them. Few of the militia and half-trained Continentals possessed bayonets or had ever fired a shot in anger, and without artillery support they had no chance of storming fixed positions held by well-armed regulars. An attack would have meant the destruction of the American army, as well as Washington's reputation.

Shortly after the council's decision Washington detected an intensification of enemy activity in Boston Harbor. Through his field glasses he could see Howe's troops removing heavy brass cannon and other artillery from Bunker Hill and loading them on board ships that stood "ready waterd & their Sails bent." Stacks of supplies grew ever larger on Boston's wharves, and every few days another convoy of empty transports sailed into harbor. Witnesses told of loyalists walking through the streets, muttering and wringing their hands while their wives and children wept or, less dramatically, gathering their possessions in preparation for a long voyage. Boston, it seemed, would be liberated without a struggle. The British were preparing to evacuate.

A bloodless end to the siege of Boston was more than the Americans had dared to wish for, but to Washington the event had all the bitterness of anticlimax. He felt "the Eyes of the whole Continent fixed" on him, waiting in "anxious expectation of hearing of some great event." Gates's talk of defensive war was all very well; but Washington, a man who always sensed the dramatic moment and the power of symbolism, empathized with and shared the public craving for some glorious event. The British could not be allowed to withdraw quietly. They, and everyone else in the world, had to know they had been beaten. "I am determined to do every Thing in my power" to bring on a battle, he wrote, "and that as soon as possible."

The council had already rejected the notion of a headlong attack, but in its suggestion of occupying Dorchester Heights, Washington saw a chance of forcing a military encounter by another route, enticing Howe to "be so kind as to come out to us." If the British wanted a quiet evacuation, they could not allow the Americans to control the heights that dominated the city. Yet until now Dorchester Heights had been neutral ground, left unoccupied by tacit agreement. The first side to dig earthworks would do so under artillery bombardment, and have to prepare for immediate attack. At Bunker Hill the previous summer, this problem had been solved by erecting fortifications overnight. Doing the same at Dorchester Heights would be far more difficult, however, not least because the same cold weather that had frozen Back Bay also froze the ground. Trenches that had taken hours to dig on Bunker Hill would now take days, allowing Howe plenty of time to react and scatter the Americans before they dug in.

Washington had conducted several surveys of Dorchester Heights, giving him a good grasp of its most prominent and defensible points. His companion on those surveys was a cousin of General Israel Putnam, Lieutenant Colonel Rufus Putnam, who resembled the commander-in-chief in both appearance and character. Rufus Putnam stood six feet tall, with strong facial features and a wayward eye caused by a childhood injury. A French and Indian War veteran and former surveyor, he had no formal education and a tenuous grasp of ordinary mathematics; but he had some experience in engineering and claimed to have a scheme for putting Dorchester Heights in a defensible state in less than twelve hours.

No digging was necessary, Lieutenant Colonel Putnam assured Washington. The elements of above-ground fortifications could be prepared beforehand and positioned overnight. The key to his plan was a wooden contraption called a chandelier, a heavy wooden frame commonly used in European siege warfare as a movable breastwork or parapet. Built in camp, transferred in wagons to the heights, and reinforced with bundles of sticks called fascines, bales of hay, and stone-filled wicker cylinders called gabions, chandeliers would provide quick and durable protection for the artillery. Impressed, Washington ordered work on the chandeliers to begin immediately. At the suggestion of a Boston merchant, he also directed his troops to fill dozens of barrels with earth. They would be heavy, and difficult to cart uphill; but the soldiers were promised the pleasure of rolling them back down onto the heads of any British attackers.

As the construction of these items began, Washington beseeched the colonies for powder, urging them "to throw, without delay, every ounce that can be procured, into this Camp." The response fell short of his expectations, but Governor Trumbull of Connecticut dispatched almost two tons of powder and "small parcells," and promises of more to come trickled in from elsewhere. By the beginning of March the army had just enough to keep the mortars and cannon firing for a few days. Some of the big guns from Ticonderoga then were placed outside Roxbury, ready to move along with their portable fortifications. Others, including a huge thirteen-inch brass mortar that had been captured from a British brig the previous November and dubbed the "Congress," were stationed west of Bunker Hill on Cobble Hill and Lechmere Point, and at Lamb's Dam near Roxbury. They would fire the preliminary bombardment on Boston. Two divisions, totaling 4,000 men under Major General Israel Putnam, simultaneously took up positions at the mouth of Cambridge River with sixty flatboats. If Howe exposed himself by assaulting Dorchester Heights, Putnam would cross Back Bay in a flanking attack on Boston Neck.

Men, guns, and equipment waited as darkness fell on the night of March 2nd. Workers piled wagons full of tools, barrels, and wooden chandeliers until the axles threatened to crack. Teamsters hitched massive iron and brass cannon to teams of draft horses. Surgeons and nurses, who had been told to anticipate up to 2,000 casualties over the next few days, prepared wheelbarrows to transport the wounded, and stocked lint, bandages and bone saws "for fractured limbs and other gun-shot wounds." Washington inspected these preparations and then assembled his officers in a final conference. This time there was no debate. The occupation of Dorchester Heights would begin in two days.

Sudden flashes of light in Boston's night sky heralded the first shots of the American bombardment at 11:00 P.M. on March 2nd. Piercing cracks followed almost immediately, as cannon barrels burst—inexperienced gunners had placed their mortars flat on the frozen ground, without bedding, or used too much powder. Within minutes, four priceless ten- and thirteen-inch mortars on Lechmere Point and Lamb's Dam were shattered and useless. The few shots they successfully fired landed well astray—"without hurting any Body," said a British engineer—while Howe's artillery returned the compliment "two for one," smashing the thigh of an American lieutenant and causing several other casualties. The futile American bombardment continued for forty-eight hours, persisting even after the mishandled and badly aimed "Congress" exploded. The barrage achieved little except to alert the British to an impending American movement.

Troops, teams, and wagons left camp at dusk on March 4th and headed across Dorchester Neck. As they marched the Americans could see "the Moon shining in its full lustre." The lunar light silhouetted them so starkly that it might as well have been noon, and made them prime targets for the British artillery. Washington and his officers had likely anticipated the full moon but decided to risk its glare rather than admit delay. By way of distraction, he ordered the artillery bombardment to intensify until the noise reached an "incessant roar." The result, he thought, "answer our expectation fully" as the British seemed too stunned by the guns' display to pay attention to the heights. Actually the British hardly noticed the bombardment, for it did no damage. The previous nights' gunfire had put them in the habit of scanning the American lines, however, and they detected the activity on Dorchester Heights as soon as it began.

"Perhaps there never was so much work done in so short a space of time," boasted American General William Heath. At the start of the operation, a wall, or blind, of stone, earth, and timber was erected on the marshy causeway leading to the heights in order to shield the workers from view at the most vulnerable part of their path. The British watched but for some reason—their hesitation has never been adequately explained—they did not interfere. Thus protected from the artillery on Boston Neck, 1,200 workers and 360 oxcarts bristling with equipment hurried uphill to erect fortifications and gun mounts. Coached ahead of time, they worked enthusiastically and efficiently. Hundreds of men meanwhile felled trees from nearby orchards and dragged them uphill to form abatis, or log barricades. Every hour the profile of Dorchester Heights changed as strange new growths appeared like mushrooms on its surface, while Bostonians cursed at the gunfire—now inexplicably mingled with the sound of falling trees—that had kept them awake for three nights.

British scouts observed the whole undertaking, but Howe and his officers did not consider the American activity an immediate threat and took no countermeasures. Fortifying Dorchester Heights, they were certain, would take days. What they saw in the morning startled them. A small city of wooden fortifications had sprung up overnight! Surely, the British exclaimed, Washington could only have accomplished this by putting his whole army to work. "The Materials for the whole Works must all have been carried, Chandeleers, fascines, Gabions, Trusses of hay pressed and Barrels, a most astonishing nights work [that] must have Employ'd from 15 to 20,000 men," remarked Archibald Robertson, a British officer and professional engineer. Howe, not usually given to overstatement, reputedly quipped that "the rebels have done more in one night than my whole army could do in months."

No one was more surprised than Washington at the "great activity and Industry" of his troops. The fortifications were incomplete—he intended to push them forward even farther to Nook's Hill on the northern edge of the heights—but they had progressed enough to be reasonably secure against a

British attack. Now, he thought, Howe would have to come out and fight in order to protect his army from destruction by bombardment. March 5th, Washington thought, was "a day never to be forgotten—an Ingagement was fully expected—& I never saw spirits higher, or more ardour prevailing." Another Battle of Bunker Hill, this time with himself as the hero, seemed within sight. It was the sixth anniversary of the "Boston Massacre," and the troops were ready to celebrate it with a retaliatory massacre of their own.

At first Howe seemed set to fall for the trap. "In a situation so critical," he wrote Lord Dartmouth, "I determined upon an immediate attack with all the force I could transport; the ardour of the troops encouraged me in this hazardous enterprise." The commander of the harbor fleet told him that if the Americans were not removed, he would have to withdraw his ships. Howe accordingly ordered 2,400 infantry to the city's long wharf, where they embarked on transports for an all-out attack. It was, one British officer wrote, "the most serious step ever an army of this strength in such a situation took, considering the state the Rebel's Works are in and the Number of men they Appear to have under Arms. The fate of this whole Army and the town is at stake not to say the fate of America."

The Americans watched British preparations closely, and Putnam's men waited anxiously for the signal to leap into their boats. "But," remembered Heath, "kind Heaven, which more than once saved the Americans when they would have destroyed themselves, did not allow the signals to be made." Just as the British assault was about to commence, Howe and his officers reconsidered. Bunker Hill must have entered their minds. A bloody attack against a larger, entrenched enemy force, in order to gain more time for an inevitable evacuation, seemed senseless. Instead, Howe and his officers "agreed immediately to Embark everything." A storm arrived later that night, giving Howe a convenient excuse for calling off the attack, and he made use of it in his general orders the next day and in his official explanation to London.

On March 7th, as Washington and his soldiers watched, the British rushed their artillery and supplies on board transports with "the utmost precipitation." Boston's selectmen quickly confirmed the evacuation, sending word that Howe promised not to burn the town unless the Americans interfered with the British departure. If they did, he threatened "Intire destruction." Washington had no intention of hindering the enemy's "shameful retreat," and ignored Howe's threat to burn Boston. Instead, assuming that the British would sail to New York, he detached five regiments to that city and prepared to follow them with the rest of the army as soon as the last British topmast had disappeared over the horizon. The final act in the siege of Boston came on March 17th. The last British troops paraded at 4:00 A.M., and six hours later they were all on board transports, including a rear guard that had waited until the last minute, prepared to burn the best houses in the city if the Americans intervened. On Bunker Hill the British left dummy sentinels to greet the conquerors: "Images dressed in the Soldiers Habit with Laced Hats and for a Gorget an Horse Shoe with Paper Ruffles, their Pieces Shouldered fixed Bayonets, with this Inscription wrote on their Breast (viz.) Welcome Brother Jonathan."

Worried about a reported smallpox epidemic and concerned lest his militias start digging for "hidden treasures" left behind by fleeing civilians the previous year, Washington strictly forbade any but patrols of a few hundred men to enter the city that day. He waited until March 18th to ride into Boston, and the rest of the army followed a few days later to the "joy inexpressible" of the long-suffering inhabitants. On the wharves of the city were parting gifts much more valuable than the dummies on Bunker Hill: sixty-nine salvageable cannon and a surprising quantity of other supplies, including ammunition, blankets, provisions, coal, and "Genl Gages Chariot, taken out of the Dock, broke." The Americans were still sorting through the plunder on March 27th, when the last British transports put to sea from Nantasket Road. They would never return to Boston.

As Americans celebrated the liberation of Boston they rejoiced that it had been "made with so little Effusion of human Blood." Washington had sought a far more violent denouement to the campaign. Even after the British left, he could "scarce forbear lamenting the disappointment" that Howe had not attacked the American positions on Dorchester Heights. The "great event" which he had anticipated seemed to have degenerated into anticlimax. Washington nevertheless welcomed the bloodless outcome, although it did not match his conception of a grand military victory. He even treated the seizure of Dorchester Heights as if it had been his own idea, and never mentioned that his council of war had imposed the plan over his better judgment. None of the officers ever questioned his conduct. After Boston, as after Fort Necessity, all of his potential critics remained silent.

Washington stood unchallenged as the hero of the hour. The capture of Boston, wrote his friend George Mason, was "an Event which will render

General Washington's Name immortal in the Annals of America, endear his Memory to the latest Posterity, and entitle him to those Thanks which Heaven appointed the Reward of public Virtue." President of Congress John Hancock was among the first to congratulate Washington. "This Success of our Arms naturally calls upon me to congratulate you, Sir, to whose Wisdom and Conduct, it has been owing," he declared. Congress ordered a gold medal to be struck in his honor, and Harvard College granted him the honorary degree of doctor of laws.

Such adulation was heady stuff for a man who had taken command with apparent misgivings. "To obtain the applause of deserving men, is a heart felt satisfaction—to merit them, is my highest wish," Washington confessed. "If my conduct therefore as an Instrument in the late signal interposition of Providence hath merited the approbation of the great Country I shall esteem it one of the most fortunate & happy events of my life." But the glory was fleeting. Five months later, William Howe would have his moment in the limelight and damage Washington's precious reputation almost beyond repair.

8

NEW YORK

March – August 1776

THE SPRING THAW was under way when Washington's army left Boston at the beginning of April 1776. Rain and melting snow had turned dirt roads into streams, and the soldiers' shoes and trousers became sodden with mud as they marched south. Yet they were not sorry to leave what seemed an ungrateful city. The first euphoria attending liberation had proven transitory, and as the celebrations ended the streets subsided into a silence tinged with apathy. Normally industrious Bostonians left their business untended and wandered about aimlessly, dreading the future and uncertain what to do with their lives. Awestruck at the effect that war had wrought on the city's psychology, one woman remarked that "the total stagnation of business within, and the still calm without the walls of Boston resemble that serenity which often succeeds the most violent concussion in the world of nature."

Washington avoided such moody reflections, concentrating his thoughts instead on the challenges that awaited him at his next destination, New York City. Well before Howe's evacuation, the American commander-in-chief had looked ahead to the defense of New York as a daunting problem. If the British seized the city—which they inevitably would attempt to do—the entire Hudson River valley would become vulnerable to invasion. From New York, the British could thrust upriver to Albany and isolate New England from the rest of America. In addition, a British army operating in New Jersey or Pennsylvania could use New York as a base of supply. With superior port facilities and an excellent harbor, the city was an ideal point of entry for men and equipment from Europe. British vessels operating from there could also attack American traders and privateers along the coast, or sail up the Hudson to support a land offensive in that direction. Finally, with a British army in New York, loyalists in the surrounding colonies might turn the tables on their patriot overlords and persuade fence-sitters to declare for the king.

New York also was important to America. The British blockade reduced the city's overseas trade, though it remained a significant hub of commercial activity. Its loss would cripple the struggling colonial economy and increase popular dissatisfaction with Congress. Even more important, every major road between New England and the rest of the colonies ran through New York. If the British cut these roads and occupied the Hudson Valley, north–south communications and supply might become impossible. "Should they get that town & the Command of the North River," Washington wrote, "they can Stop the intercourse between the Northern & Southern Colonies, upon which depends the Safety of America."

Considering possession of New York to be "of the last importance to us in the present Controversy," at the beginning of February 1776 Washington had ordered Charles Lee to take command of the city with whatever troops he could muster. Lee arrived on the 12th, studied the surrounding geography, and considered how to counter the expected British landing. His first impressions were all negative. "What to do with the City, I own puzzles me," he wrote Washington. "It is so encircle'd with deep navigable water, that whoever commands the Sea must command the Town." As long as the British commanded the sea, he warned, holding New York might be impossible.

New York City's 4,000 houses stood in a square mile covering the southern end of Manhattan Island, the rest of which was largely rural. To reach Manhattan by the most obvious route, British warships would have to navigate the treacherous currents between Sandy Hook and the sandbars south of Coney Island and Jamaica Bay, and then pass through the Narrows between Staten Island and the village of Brooklyn on Long Island. In theory, these bottlenecks could be closed by batteries on Sandy Hook, Staten Island, and Brooklyn, and a string of chevaux-de-frise—underwater obstacles made of logs and iron—across the Narrows. But Lee had only a few dozen cannon, most of them in poor repair and too small to reach British vessels except at close range. Even if Washington brought heavier guns from Boston they would have to be mounted in well-fortified emplacements to protect them from bombardment or assault. Building such emplacements and the chevaux-de-frise was too difficult for Lee's ill-equipped garrison of 2,000 civilians and militiamen, which included no trained engineers.

Abandoning any idea of repelling a landing, Lee concentrated his forces in a relatively small area. He did not anticipate holding Manhattan indefinitely; instead, he resolved to make the British pay a bloody toll for its possession.

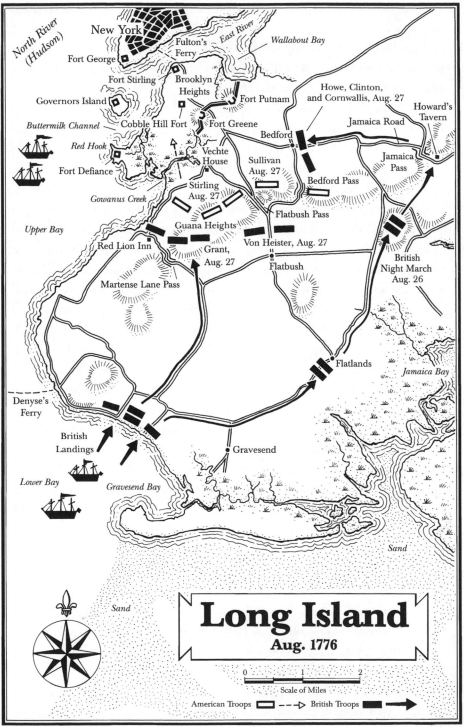

North River (Hudson)

New York

Fulton's Ferry

East River

Wallabout Bay

Fort George

Fort Stirling

Brooklyn Heights

Fort Putnam

Howe, Clinton, and Cornwallis, Aug. 27

Howard's Tavern

Governors Island

Jamaica Road

Buttermilk Channel

Cobble Hill Fort

Fort Greene

Bedford

Jamaica Pass

Red Hook

Vechte House

Sullivan Aug. 27

Fort Defiance

Bedford Pass

Gowanus Creek

Stirling Aug. 27

Upper Bay

Guana Heights

Flatbush Pass

Red Lion Inn

Grant, Aug. 27

Von Heister, Aug. 27

British Night March Aug. 26

Martense Lane Pass

Flatbush

Flatlands

Jamaica Bay

Denyse's Ferry

British Landings

Gravesend

Lower Bay

Gravesend Bay

Sand

Sand

Long Island

Aug. 1776

0   1   2

Scale of Miles

American Troops   British Troops

To that end, civilian volunteers and soldiers constructed a ramshackle chain of barricades and redoubts in and around the city proper while officers drew up plans for defending every house and street. Across the East River, Lee directed the establishment of a heavily armed bastion on Brooklyn Heights, which stood within artillery range of southern Manhattan, overlooking it from a height of a hundred feet. It would be "almost impossible," Lee believed, for the British army to hold Manhattan without assaulting this bastion. Finally, Lee planned additional batteries at Hell Gate to prevent the British from approaching via Long Island Sound.

"I am much pleas'd with your plans for the defence and Security of New York," Washington told Lee. Their straightforward character suited his tastes. Yet Lee's plans had several weaknesses. The American positions were separated by the East River, easily outflanked, and lacked secure lines of retreat. The Hudson, deep and wide, remained passable to shipping despite some weak batteries that were erected in March at Paulus Hook, New Jersey. Washington ordered underwater obstructions to be laid across the river, but they were far from complete when the battle began that summer. If British vessels sailed up the Hudson, they could land on northern Manhattan Island and cut off any American troops in the city. At the same time, the positions on Brooklyn Heights could be isolated by a successful British advance across Long Island. If that happened after the British occupied Manhattan, the entire American defending force would have no options but surrender or death.

In fact, no American defensive system was tenable without oversight by trained engineers and substantially more time, manpower, and artillery. Lacking these, abandoning the city and preserving the army, though politically difficult, would have been the wiser course. Washington nevertheless decided to defend New York. The easy success at Boston had blinded him and his officers to the dangers of a British attack. New York was not only indefensible; it was an open grave waiting for an occupant. Washington very nearly filled it with the corpse of his army.

Shortly before Washington departed Boston on April 4th, coast watchers reported that the British transports carrying Howe's army had not sailed south but north, apparently to Halifax. This eliminated the possibility of an early British attack on New York. Thus Washington took a leisurely nine days to ride south by way of Providence, Norwich, and New Haven to Manhattan. Accompanying him were 10,000 troops, Horatio Gates (who was promoted to major general in May and reassigned to upper New England), and two new aides-de-camp, William Palfrey and Stephen Moylan. Washington arrived on April 13th, and chose a town house on Broadway for his headquarters. It was too small for domestic comfort, and when Martha came to town on April 17th the couple sequestered a beautiful mansion just outside the city limits.

New York City welcomed the commander-in-chief, but the raucous optimism of the previous summer had passed. Tension, even paranoia, now gripped the city's inhabitants. Loyalists were publicly abused—"Several of them ware handeld very Roughly Being Caried trugh the Streets on Rails, there Cloaths Tore from there becks and there Bodies pritty well Mingled with the dust," one patriot crowed—but growled that they would not stay down for long. The loyalists' silence was ominous rather than submissive. Intimidated despite their swagger, patriots discovered plots "as deep as Hell" in every corner, and imagined spies drinking grog at taverns or skulking through the streets in disguise.

These threats were not all fancied. New York's former royal governor, William Tryon, boasted of his plans for a triumphal return from London, and his numerous supporters in the city promised to welcome him back. Boatloads of loyalists brazenly rowed to two British warships anchored offshore, plying trade goods and information while patriots hopped in vexation. Out in the countryside, disaffected civilians interfered with recruitment and supply to a degree unimaginable in Massachusetts, waylaying patrols and intercepting messengers. Several local militia companies openly awaited the opportunity to defect.

Washington protected loyalists from lynching and plunder, even though he despised them. When some of those who had been left behind in Boston committed suicide, he joked that "it would have been happy for Mankind if more of them had done long ago." In New York, he treated loyalism as a serious threat, looked into each conspiracy theory, and appointed a secret committee to find and apprehend loyalist agents. He probably also recruited a few spies of his own, the first of hundreds who would burrow through the city's warrens before the end of the war. The shadow war of subversion and counterespionage excited him and provided distraction from the often mind-numbing duties that glued him to headquarters.

The tiresome routine of recruiting, training, and equipping an army troubled Washington, as it had in Massachusetts. Congress had authorized him to recruit an army of up to 28,500 men, but the 19,000 troops who entered camp by the end of June were almost too much to handle. Military discipline was alien to most of them, and the most basic orders had to be repeated incessantly. The prohibition on firing weapons in camp was strictly enforced, but soldiers found another diversion by "snapping their pieces continually" and ruining the flints. The bayonets that had been gathered for a few regiments at tremendous expense were thrown away or used as knives and crowbars by careless soldiers. Muskets, which the men rarely bothered to clean, were in "the most shocking situation," rusty, dirty, or even bent. Such waste made it exceptionally difficult for commissaries and quartermasters to procure supplies.

Though eager to fight, the troops were poorly trained and shoddily clothed and equipped. "The clothing of the enemy is bad," a German officer remarked. "A few wear black, white, or violet linen, short blouses with fringes, and of a Spanish style. They also have a linen sack in which they carry their rations, and a powder horn. Others, on the other hand, have nothing but a wretched farmer's costume and a weapon. Most of their officers are no better dressed and until recently were only ordinary manual laborers." Many Americans wore red coats that made them almost indistinguishable from the British. To avoid confusion, the Continentals put sprigs of leaves in their hats.

Working with such rough material quickly became an ordeal, and the deteriorating strategic situation depressed Washington further. The American army that Benedict Arnold had led to Quebec the previous winter was now scattered, and reports said that the British had taken advantage of this to send an invasion armada toward New York City. If the expected amphibious attack coincided with an invasion of the Hudson Valley from Canada, Washington's army in Manhattan might be trapped. "We expect a very bloody Summer of it at New York & Canada, as it is there I expect the grand efforts of the Enemy will be aim'd," Washington mused. "I am sorry to say that we are not, either in Men, or Arms prepared for it."

New York's defenses, which had consisted of little more than scattered ditches and dusty holes in the ground when Washington arrived, were being constructed with "every possible dispatch." But the commander-in-chief made no serious alterations to Lee's overall plan. He considered fortifying the Narrows, but abandoned the project as "useless" when the necessary heavy artillery failed to arrive. A scheme to fill the Upper Bay with row galleys, floating batteries, and fire rafts also came to nothing when the shipwright

hired to construct them proved incompetent. He ordered the occupation of
Governor's Island at the mouth of the East River, but the move accomplished
little except to further disperse the army. Long Island remained unfortified,
and mostly unexplored, outside Brooklyn Heights. By the middle of June,
New York's defenses had been improved but not extended.

Washington had more artillery than had been available to Lee, but it remained inadequate in both quantity and quality. Henry Knox reported in
June that he had accumulated a total of 121 cannon, including fifty heavy
guns and nineteen mortars, for use against British shipping. To defend *every*
critical point, however, many more were necessary; and Knox had only
enough men—trained, more or less—to operate half of the cannon in his arsenal. The infantry that Washington drafted to complete the gun teams had
no knowledge of artillery and little time to learn. When a gun burst during
training, destroying a nearby house, it offered an unpleasant reminder of the
self-destruction of Washington's artillery at Boston and augured badly for the
future.

Yet prepared or unprepared, Washington meant to fight. The problems
posed by geography and British mastery of the sea did not worry him; he was
certain instead that the quality and quantity of guns and men would decide
the fight. Lee had provided a defensive strategy, Washington would oversee
training and supply, and Providence would take care of the rest.

Lieutenant General William Howe would have liked nothing better than
to spend spring in Manhattan. Long term, his goals were much as the Americans feared: pincers on the Hudson, with Carleton advancing from Canada
and himself occupying New York before marching north up the Hudson Valley. The two armies would meet at Albany in the summer, isolating New England and thus decapitating the colonies. Political overtures to the Americans
would coincide with these movements and perhaps even make the linkup at
Albany unnecessary. Either way, the war would end in 1776.

But the British fell behind schedule. Lacking sufficient troops and supplies, Howe left Boston for Halifax, Nova Scotia, instead of New York. Secretary of State Lord Germain meanwhile gathered 4,500 British troops and
17,000 mercenaries from Hesse and Brunswick—George III's possessions in
Germany—but could not find enough ships to carry them across the Atlantic
until April. Transporting adequate supplies proved just as difficult, and the

government economized by assuming that sympathetic American farmers would enable the troops to live off the land.

In Halifax, weeks turned into months as Howe awaited supplies and reinforcements. The first troop transports sailed from England in late April, before word arrived that Howe had gone to Halifax, and several of them anchored and were seized in Boston Harbor. Other transports left England in May and June with no idea of their destination. Lord Richard Howe tried to herd them into one armada of 150 ships, but could not get them to New York until July. As a result, on June 11th William Howe embarked 9,000 men at Halifax and prepared to begin operations off New York without waiting for reinforcements from Europe. His army lacked adequate provisions and most of its camp equipment.

Frustrated and having perhaps too much time for thought, Howe lost the aggressiveness that he cultivated after leaving Boston. In April, he had looked forward to attacking New York as soon as possible in order to force a quick decision in battle. Now, the rapidly advancing season focused his thoughts more on preserving what he had. London's remoteness freed Howe from oversight, but also left him solely responsible for Great Britain's largest single army. He could not help thinking what would happen if he lost it. With patience, he could accumulate an army that was unbeatable; why press ahead with an incomplete force just to end the campaign in 1776? If the Americans did not agree to peace terms, 1777 would do just as well.

The vanguards of William Howe's fleet reached Sandy Hook on June 25th. Less than a week later, he had all of his 130 ships in the Lower Bay. He took them through the Narrows on July 2nd, and as the transports "fell into great Confusion all dropping upon one another" in that confined area, one British officer noted in relief that "lucky for us the Rebels had no Cannon here or we must have suffered a good deal." Some Continentals on Long Island, evidently tired of snapping their firelocks with no charges in them, took potshots at the ships, to no effect. Staten Island's small American garrison fled before the redcoats tumbled ashore that evening in a driving rain. Delighted loyalists came out to welcome the British, and the island's militia switched to their side.

A few hours earlier, on July 2, 1776, Congress had approved the Declaration of Independence.

—

On July 9th, just before 6:00 P.M., New York's fields and parade grounds filled up with crowds of soldiers and civilians eager to hear the Declaration. Earlier that day, Washington had celebrated the occasion in general orders: "The General hopes this important Event will serve as a fresh incentive to every officer, and soldier, to act with Fidelity and Courage, as knowing that now the peace and safety of his Country depends (under God) solely on the success of our arms: And that he is now in the service of a State, possessed of sufficient power to reward his merit, and advance him to the highest Honors of a free Country." Now he and his aides rode gravely into the Common, where a hollow square of soldiers formed to separate them from the crowds.

At the stroke of six, one of Washington's aides spurred his horse a few paces forward, stopped, and opened a piece of paper. "In Congress, July 4, 1776," he began. "A Declaration by the Representatives of the United States of America in General Congress Assembled." He continued reading in a clear voice that carried well above the silent crowd. "And for the support of this Declaration, with a firm reliance on the protection of divine Providence," he concluded, "we mutually pledge to each other our Lives, our Fortunes and our sacred Honour." Three cheers later, the soldier and civilian spectators dispersed into the streets. Their cause had been transformed in minutes; and like all revolutionaries they sought some emblem of their break with the past.

After a riotous march down Broadway, the mob found just the thing: an equestrian statue of George III that still stood at Bowling Green despite a year of revolt. Bedecked to portray the king as the Roman emperor Marcus Aurelius, it offered an ideal target for symbolic mischief. Men and boys swarmed over the statue, tying ropes and then pulling it down with wild cheers. Some, mixing idealism with prudence, stripped it of gold leaf. Others decapitated the fallen monarch, cut off his nose, and clipped his laurel wreaths. Soldiers finished him off with their muskets, and then carted the head in a wheelbarrow to the commander-in-chief. The Declaration of Independence "seemed to have their most hearty assent," Washington informed Hancock the next day.

Washington stopped short of endorsing the Declaration. Perhaps he had concerns about its timing. "It is certain that It is not with us to determine in many Instances what consequences will flow from our Counsels," he wrote Hancock, "but yet It behoves us to adopt such, as under the smiles of a Gracious & All kind Providence will be most likely to promote our happiness; I trust the late decisive part they have taken is calculated for that end, and will secure us that freedom and those privileges which have been and are refused us." But his private concerns, if he had any, faded next to his belief in the right of Congress to legislate for the country. He would behave in strict conformity with America's new war aims.

As Howe's troops scrambled ashore on Staten Island, some talkative British deserters entered the American lines. Escorted to Washington, they gave him an accurate count of the men and ships in the British armada and of the number of reinforcements Lord Howe was expected to bring in a few days. The report was not encouraging—the British army would eventually number 25,000 men—but Washington, who had wallowed in gloom for the past several weeks, now recovered his confidence. Perhaps he was thrilled at the commitment his countrymen had just made, and the violence with which they would shortly seal their pledge. The British "will have to wade through much blood & Slaughter before they can carry any part of our Works, If they carry 'em at all, and at best be in possession of a melancholy and mournfull victory," he enthused.

Lord Howe's 150 ships appeared in the Lower Bay on July 12th. Intimidating and majestic, the sails of the combined fleet formed a white mass that clogged the horizon. Sailors swelled with pride at taking part in such a magnificent demonstration by the world's most powerful navy. "A finer Scene could not be exhibited, both of Country, Ships, and men, all heightened by one of the brightest Days that can be imagined," one of them wrote. To be certain that those on shore shared in the awe requisite to the occasion, two warships announced the fleet's arrival by brushing past the American river defenses and penetrating the Hudson. Sailing upriver, they shelled Manhattan and killed several civilians, leaving flesh-and-blood corpses next to George III's headless statue on Bowling Green.

When the firing began, many American artillerymen failed to join their batteries. They were too drunk. Others, either incompetent or inebriated, could not figure out how to work their cannon. One mishandled gun blew up, along with its entire crew. Still, the artillery managed to perforate some sails and crack some hulls, and that satisfied Knox. It "proves to me beyond doubt," he wrote complacently to his wife, "that their Ships cannot lay before our batteries." To the British, it proved the opposite. Almost all of the 196 shots that the Americans fired from Paulus Hook and Manhattan had fallen short. The Hudson was easily passable.

As New Yorkers recovered from the shelling, Lord Howe sent a boat bearing a flag of truce and a letter for Washington toward Manhattan on July 14th. The Americans stopped it a short distance from Governor's Island, and Knox and Joseph Reed, who had consulted with Washington beforehand, stepped aboard. The British emissary stood and bowed with his hat in his hand.

"I have a letter sir from Lord Howe to Mr. Washington," said the Englishman.

"We have no person in our army with that address," Reed stiffly replied.

The emissary then asked Reed if he would at least look at the address of the letter. He agreed, but refused to touch the proffered letter. "George Washington Esqr. New York," was written on the cover.

"No sir," Reed said. "I cannot Receive that Letter."

Sensing the problem, the emissary ventured another tack. "I am very sorry," he pronounced, "and so will be Lord Howe, that any Error in the superscription should prevent the Letter being received by *General Washington.*" Lord Howe, who sincerely wanted peace, had no doubt expected the use of Washington's military title to be a sticking point. But London refused to admit formally that the Virginian was anything more than a rebel chieftain. In that respect, Lord Howe's hands were tied, but he had instructed his emissary to see if a verbal acknowledgment of Washington's rank would suffice. It did not.

"Why sir," said Reed, whom Washington had coached, "I must obey orders."

"Oh Yes sir," the emissary nodded, "you must obey orders to be sure." They parted.

Further negotiations foundered on the same point of protocol, although the British politely referred to Washington—verbally—as "General" or even "His Excellency." William Howe eventually solved the problem by addressing letters to "Genl Washington &ca &ca," but too late. Patriots throughout the colonies applauded their leader's resolve and urged him to pay no heed to British flattery. Britain's peace efforts had become mere charade. The fate of America would be resolved in blood.

By the middle of August, nearly 25,000 British and German soldiers picked fruit on Staten Island, or chewed salt pork on 400 transports in the Lower Bay. Three thousand of them had just returned from a disastrous expedition to Charleston under generals Henry Clinton and Lord Charles Cornwallis;

others were long-awaited reinforcements from Europe. William Howe had an army more powerful than any Great Britain had ever fielded outside Europe and the largest it had assembled anywhere in the last several decades. Ships had finally arrived with camp equipment and other supplies necessary for the launch of a major attack.

Despite his large army and great stores of equipment, Howe did not attempt to encircle and destroy Washington's army. In keeping with his increasingly cautious mind-set, he resolved simply to expel it from New York. Later, he would dispatch a separate expedition to capture Rhode Island; but the grand pincers he had planned to use on the Hudson would have to wait. Governor Carleton was not ready to move from Canada, anyway.

The American defenses had been planned and erected with the idea that the British would attack Manhattan first, but Howe had another idea. On August 22nd, the morning after three American officers died in a horrific thunderstorm, he ferried 15,000 British and German troops with artillery from Staten Island to Long Island. Five thousand more soldiers came ashore in the next few days, and Howe took command of the entire force. His deputies were Generals Clinton and Cornwallis.

From their landing place in Gravesend Bay, the soldiers fanned out to the north and east across the Flatlands. They skirmished here and there with small parties of rebels, who torched reputed loyalist property and "left behind burned-out houses, grain standing in the fields, some of it in ashes, and the road lined with dead cattle." Fancying themselves liberators, the British turned toward Brooklyn Heights.

The week before, Washington had advised New York City's civilians to evacuate. Some of them did, but most remained. Now he exhorted his troops to prepare for battle. "Remember," he told them, "that you are Freemen, fighting for the blessings of Liberty—that slavery will be your portion, and that of your posterity, if you do not acquit yourselves like men: Remember how your Courage and Spirit have been dispised, and traduced by your cruel invaders; though they have found by dear experience at Boston, Charlestown and other places, what a few brave men contending in their own land, and in the best of causes can do, against base hirelings and mercenaries." If "every one for himself resolving to conquer, or die, and trusting to the smiles of heaven upon so just a cause, will behave with Bravery and Resolution," Washington declared he had "no doubt they will, by a glorious Victory, save their Country, and acquire to themselves immortal Honor." Just in case they did not, Washington collected all of his military papers into a wooden box, nailed it shut, and sent it to Congress. He did so secretly, lest the sight raise any "disagreable Ideas" among his men.

Washington had almost 20,000 men in total, but because of detachments and illness he could bring only about half that number to bear against Howe. On Long Island, Nathanael Greene commanded 4,000 troops, most of them garrisoning the forts at Brooklyn Heights. About 9,000 men waited in the city behind barricades and in redoubts, and a few regiments garrisoned Governor's Island, Paulus Hook, and other minor outposts. A strong brigade of 2,400 soldiers garrisoned Fort Washington on northern Manhattan Island. Another 1,800 troops guarded Kingsbridge, the northern tip of the island and its only link with the mainland, from a possible loyalist attack timed to coincide with the British landing.

Long Island's defenses were abysmal, thanks in part to Washington himself. He had delegated the responsibility for holding the island to Greene, but prevented him from positioning his regiments by constantly shuffling them elsewhere. Just as Greene finished training and familiarizing his troops with the terrain, Washington pulled them out for garrison duty at Governor's Island, Fort Washington, and other places. More often than not their replacements came from the bottom of the Continental barrel. "The most of the Troops that come over here," Greene lamented to him on August 15th, "are strangers to the Ground, undisciplined and badly furnish'd with arms"; but Washington refused to reconsider the redeployments.

Greene succumbed to a "raging Fever" on the eve of the British landing, and Washington replaced him with John Sullivan. Sullivan, now a major general, had spent little time on Long Island, and showed more pugnacity than good sense as he tried to organize his new command. The appointment proved troublesome on another count as well. The British landed two days after Sullivan's appointment. As they marched toward Brooklyn Heights, General Putnam appeared at Washington's headquarters, where he buttonholed the commander-in-chief and claimed his right to take command over Sullivan. "The brave old man was quite miserable at being kept here" in Manhattan, Joseph Reed explained to his wife. A grizzled, irritable, and mediocre general, Old Put had already lost the regard of many officers despite his achievements at Boston. But Washington empathized with Putnam's lust for action, and agreed on the 24th to let him assume control of the troops on

Long Island. Sullivan, who had spent only two days in command, spluttered furiously. Putnam was probably the only person in the army who knew less about Long Island than *he* did.

Some of Washington's miscalculations on Long Island may have been caused by his faulty intelligence service, which may have led him to underestimate the size of the British army. Yet he knew that there were 25,000 men in the British army in July, even before they all came to New York. When his scouts estimated the enemy force on Long Island at between 8,000 and 9,000 men, it reinforced his suspicion that the landing was just a feint intended to distract him from an attack on Manhattan. By the 25th, however, he expected the British "to land the Main Body of their Army on Long Island and to make their Grand push there." The "Main Body," he knew, must contain at least 20,000 troops; but even so, he only sent enough reinforcements to Long Island to bring American strength there to about 8,000 men—still less than half the British force. How he expected such a force to stop the British without itself being destroyed is unknown.

Washington stumbled in other ways, too. In his four months in New York, he had made no preparations of any sort for a land campaign on Long Island. The possibility of a British movement there should have been obvious, yet he had only the haziest conception of Long Island's terrain. Four days after the landing, he still did not know the names of many of the island's most important natural features. After August 22nd Washington took a crash course in Long Island geography, crossing the East River each day to scout inland from Brooklyn Heights, poke about the fortifications with Putnam, and point out a muddy earthwork here and a knoll there. The two generals then joined Sullivan in a reconnaissance to the southeast, where a wooded ridge known as Guana Heights blocked the most obvious route of advance. After a cursory inspection of the ridge and its passes—for nobody, including Lee and Greene, had reconnoitered it thoroughly—Washington ordered Putnam to establish his first line of defense there. "Your best men should at all hazards prevent the enemy's passing the woods," he told the general; Putnam could sort out the details himself.

Practical instructions on defending Guana Heights came almost as afterthoughts. In neglecting them, Washington was severely remiss, for a careful survey could have shown him the difficulty of holding the ridge. Although it was up to 150 feet high and too rough in most places to be scaled by infantry in formation, its passes were unfortified and hard to defend. If they were not all well protected, the entire position could be penetrated and destroyed in detail, or even wholly outflanked. Washington saw the troops on the ridge as forming an "advanced party" that could inflict losses on the British and then retire to Brooklyn Heights. But they were far from expendable, and he paid no heed to securing their line of retreat.

Thus unsupervised by the commander-in-chief, Putnam spread about 3,000 troops across Guana Heights. He dispersed them in such a way that they could neither hold off the British nor lend one another support. On the right flank, where a road snaked along the shore of Gowanus Bay, Lord Stirling commanded a brigade that was one of the Continental Army's best. Stirling, whose real name was William Alexander, had taken the noble title to support his claim to an inheritance in England. Gout-ridden and rheumatic but possessing a martial bearing that rivaled Washington's, he was a brilliant New Jersey lawyer with no military experience but a great deal of natural ability. He blocked the road with 550 New York and Pennsylvania Continentals and kept two strong regiments in reserve about half a mile to the rear.

Sullivan's headquarters was about a mile and a half from Stirling, at Flatbush Pass. Three New England regiments, totaling about 1,000 men with a few small cannon, waited there behind makeshift breastworks. A mile to their left, 800 Connecticut troops guarded Bedford Pass. Two miles farther, 400 Pennsylvanians ostensibly defended Jamaica Pass, the last passable route across the ridge. They were given leave to wander where their fancy took them, however, and found traipsing about the woods more pleasant than squatting behind logs in a desolate pass. No troops anchored the left flank; it just faded away.

Washington took the ferry from Long Island to Manhattan on the evening of the 26th. "A few days more I should think will bring matters to an Issue one way or other or else the Season for Action will leave them," he mused after returning. An immediate British attack was unlikely, but if it came he expected the positions on Guana Heights to "prevent or at least weaken them much should they effect their purpose of passing." And who knew? Maybe he had been wrong to expect the "grand push" on Long Island—was it a feint, after all? Turning these thoughts over in his mind, Washington went to bed. At about the same time, Howe mounted his horse and led his army forward through the darkness.

—

Drama is sometimes born in unlikely circumstances. The Battle of Gettysburg began as a dispute over shoes. The first shots of the battle of Long Island were fired in defense of a few humble watermelons.

Just before midnight on August 26th, Stirling's Pennsylvania riflemen drove off a couple of redcoats who were attempting to pilfer watermelons near Gowanus Bay. Satisfied that the rest of the night would pass quietly, the riflemen retired to rest while other troops, apparently militia, took up vigil over the patch. Then the redcoats returned, in greater numbers and apparently determined to take their share of the summer delicacy. To the militia's surprise, however, the British loomed ever closer in the darkness and then attacked. The Americans fled before their bayonets. These redcoats were no mere scroungers, but the vanguard of a column of 5,000 troops that was bearing down on the American right flank.

At Brooklyn Heights, Putnam lit signal lights to wake Washington at Manhattan and put his troops on alert. Then he rode south, rousing Stirling—who despite being just half a mile from the fighting had not yet been notified of it—at 3:00 A.M. Putnam ordered his sleepy general to gather every available man, and Stirling rushed to obey as the last stars faded in the lightening sky. Within hours he assembled his reserves, two regiments of crack Delaware and Maryland Continentals, and led them toward the front through a crisp dawn.

Stirling established a line by eight o'clock, on an eminence blocking the British advance. He anchored the position on Gowanus Bay and the edge of Guana Heights. "There was no ground for drawing up two armies regularly opposed to each other," an observer wrote, "the ground being woody and the fields small"; so "divided parties" of Continentals and redcoats faced off in every open space. General James Grant, who had little respect for American fighting ability, commanded the British column. He pressed close, not expecting the Continentals to last long before his superior firepower. Muskets and cannons accordingly reaped a steady harvest for the rest of the morning. But the bloody gaps were closed, and neither side flinched.

Sullivan's troops meanwhile hunkered down at Flatbush and Bedford passes, watched 5,000 German mercenaries putter about to the front, and listened to musket fire on the right. His men were eager to fight the Germans, but when they did not attack, Sullivan detached a regiment to help Stirling, who seemed to be facing the main enemy effort. Sullivan neither worried about his left nor issued any orders to the Pennsylvanians who roamed there.

Then, at 8:30 A.M., he heard shots there, and to his rear. His position was flanked!

The British had an uncomplicated plan of attack. European generals would have seen through it easily: demonstrate in the enemy's front, causing him to commit his reserves, and then turn his flank. Yet against Washington, it would work almost every time. If the American had an Achilles' heel, it was his preference for doing battle head-on. By 1777 Howe had taken Washington's measure well enough to exploit this weakness. But on this occasion he borrowed the idea from his subordinate, General Henry Clinton, a man he happened to despise.

Clinton, the son of former colonial governor George Clinton, had grown up in New York City and knew Long Island well. He knew how to fight but was unstable, having been driven nearly insane by the death of his wife in 1772. Clinton also was prone to alternating fits of moroseness—he called himself a "shy bitch"—and aggression. His arrogant self-regard persisted even in failure, and Howe grew so irritated with Clinton that he refused to speak to him. Then, on Long Island, Clinton broke the silence by suggesting a march around the American left flank. Howe at first refused to listen, but after interrogating locals and reconnoitering Long Island, he agreed that the plan made sense. The American left flank simply begged to be turned, and Howe decided to join his prickly general at the head of the flanking column.

The advance began late in the evening of August 26th. With two brigades, General James Grant marched up Gowanus Road, pressuring the Americans into committing their reserves on the right. Five thousand Germans under German general Philip von Heister demonstrated against the center, but not too vigorously lest they draw reserves in their direction. Meanwhile, Howe, Clinton, and Cornwallis followed three loyalist guides in a brilliant night march around the American left with 10,000 troops and twenty-eight cannon. Marching nine miles in less than six hours, they captured an American patrol of five men and penetrated Jamaica Pass. By 8:30 A.M. on August 27th they had positioned themselves on Sullivan's flank and rear. Howe waited half an hour and then ordered his troops to fire two cannons, signaling every detachment to begin the general attack.

Washington had been at Brooklyn Heights less than an hour when he heard firing on his left. Even then, he had no idea of the weakness of his army's position. Musketry and cannon soon crackled and boomed along the entire line, but instead of riding toward the sound he waited impatiently at Brooklyn Heights for somebody to tell him what was happening. Nobody did, because nobody knew.

When Howe fired his signal guns, Heister's Germans marched immediately on Sullivan's headquarters at Flatbush Pass. Arrogantly resplendent in elaborate uniforms, with drums beating and flags waving, their advance invited a bloody repulse. Under any other circumstances, the Americans would have delighted in giving it. Yet Sullivan had departed just before the German advance began, rambling about somewhere with a scouting detachment of 400 men and completely out of touch with his command. Left leaderless, his troops at Flatbush Pass grew alarmed. To their left and rear, shouts and the rattle of musketry drew rapidly closer. Soon the Pennsylvanians who had been posted toward Jamaica Pass began bursting like fugitives through the underbrush. The garrison at Bedford Pass followed them. The Germans' garish uniforms began to intimidate rather than amuse.

The reaction was instantaneous. Some Continentals, a German soldier remembered, "surrendered and dropped their weapons, calling out, 'Pardon!' " The rest scattered in every direction, fleeing pell-mell for Brooklyn Heights. Their pursuers shot or bayoneted many of those they caught. Some German officers seized an American flag and then squabbled over who would keep it. Sullivan's isolated detachment meanwhile stood and fought somewhere behind Flatbush Pass before surrendering just after noon. Three German fusiliers nabbed Sullivan hiding in a cornfield.

Howe and Heister cleared the entire ridge by 11:00 A.M., shattering the whole American left. That left Stirling with his two regiments increasingly isolated as Howe pressed on toward Brooklyn Heights. Attacked in front by Grant—who had been reinforced with 2,000 marines—and on the right by Heister's Germans, the Delaware and Maryland Continentals fought fiercely. Withdrawing slowly along the coast, they paused now and then to counterattack with remarkable success; but their bravery carried a heavy price. Before they had retreated half a mile, Cornwallis and a regiment of Highlanders formed a roadblock along their most direct line of retreat.

Stirling was surrounded on three sides. Now the only way back to Brooklyn Heights was across eighty yards of the shallow water and mucky salt marshes of Gowanus Creek. The troops tried to flee across it but the mud sucked at their feet and slowed them down. Others stripped, took to the water along the coast, and swam for their lives while British and German fire plunged among them. In a desperate distraction, Stirling heroically flung himself and 250 Marylanders in six headlong attacks against Cornwallis until the American detachment shattered. Only ten escaped, and Stirling was captured. The soldiers slogging across Gowanus Creek were luckier. "When they came out of the water and mud to us," one soldier remembered, "looking like water rats, it was a truly pitiful sight." Covered by fire from batteries at Brooklyn Heights, almost all of them made it back alive.

Howe's redcoats, thrilled by their easy victory over the Americans, did not want to stop. Pursuing the remnants of Sullivan's command, they reached the eastern outworks of Brooklyn Heights in the early afternoon. Only 4,000, perhaps 5,000, fit Continentals remained there. Howe still had 20,000 troops, plenty of daylight remained, and Washington himself lay within reach. The British plunged forward.

Stunned by the rapidity of the enemy advance, the Americans blanched at this sudden assault. The commander-in-chief sensed their hesitance and tried to encourage them. "I will not ask any man to go further than I do; I will fight as long as I have a leg or an arm," an old soldier remembered him saying. Putnam did his best to help. "Gentlemen, by your dress I conclude you are country-men and if so, are good marksmen," he rumbled. "Now don't fire till you see the white of their eyes." But it was no good. Washington's army trembled; within minutes it would have buckled.

Persistent good luck—all good generals have it—saved him from catastrophe. The redcoats had hardly started vaulting the entrenchments when their officers called them back; Howe wanted no more bloodshed. They returned reluctantly. Clinton, who had tried to lead the assault in person, later sullenly wrote that "if we succeeded, everything on the island must have been ours." The Americans at Brooklyn Heights could not believe their eyes. They had been saved from almost certain destruction.

Remarkably, Howe knew that by recalling his troops he was declining almost certain victory. "It is my opinion they would have carried the redoubt," he wrote Germain a week later, "but as it was apparent the lines must have been ours by a very cheap rate by regular approaches I would not risk the loss that might have been sustained in the assault and ordered them back." Perhaps Bunker Hill still haunted him. Disappointed officers, incredulous at not being allowed to storm works that "would not have stopped a foxhunter," struggled to understand what had happened. "It must be allowed that it was extremely proper in him to consider what fatal consequences might have attended any check which the Army might have received in the first action of the Campaign," one of them wrote. "He has therefore conducted every enterprize in that cautious, circumspect manner, which, altho not so brilliant and striking, is productive of certain and real advantages, at the same time that very little is set at stake." Others during and after the war were less sympathetic, and accused Howe of allowing his sympathies for the Americans to become treasonous.

For his part, Washington gave no indication of knowing how badly he had been defeated. He had watched Stirling's destruction—shouting "Good God! What brave fellows I must this day lose," according to legend—and admitted to "a pretty considerable loss." Sullivan and Stirling were prisoners, along with just over a thousand men. Two or three hundred Continentals, many of them from the brave Delaware and Maryland regiments, were dead. More lay wounded, "some with broken arms, some with broken legs, and some with broken heads." British casualties were under four hundred, with only sixty-three dead and most of the rest wounded.

Washington, who underestimated his own casualties by half and imagined that the British had been severely bloodied, could not blame the battle's outcome on shortages of arms and ammunition. Yet he refused to point fingers at his generals or admit any failures of his own. Instead, in a letter to John Hancock, Washington shifted much of the responsibility for defeat onto *his* men. "With the deepest concern I am obliged to confess my want of confidence in the Generality of the Troops," he wrote. Their shameful collapse on Long Island was evidence of "an entire disregard of that order and subordination necessary to the well doing of an Army." What more could be expected from men fighting on short enlistments? "Men who have been free and subject to no controul cannot be reduced to order in an Instant," he pointed out, but just as he finished training them, they went home. Until he had a "permanent, standing Army" of Continental troops enlisted for the war's duration, he could promise nothing. He could hold New York even now, he insisted, "if Men would do their duty, but this I despair of."

A cold rain pelted Long Island on the evening of August 27th and continued relentlessly for two days. Under its demoralizing effect, the Continentals at Brooklyn Heights glumly watched redcoats dig zigzagging trenches toward

their redoubts. Howe was proceeding with "regular approaches," in the tradition of European siegecraft. Eventually the trenches would reach a point
from where his troops could assault Brooklyn Heights without having to
march for long across the open. This tactic also gave Washington time to prepare. But if he stood and fought, both Americans and British could predict
the outcome.

The bad weather persisted, and after another gale on the 29th a pea-soup
fog descended. That night was eerie as a Victorian graveyard: misty, "still, the
water quiet, the atmosphere luminous." Patrol duty fell to an unhappy British
detachment before dawn. As they groped their way toward the American
lines, their officer noticed that there did not seem to be any pickets. Perhaps
the rebels were simply too oppressed by the night to stir. The redcoats edged
closer to the outworks and finally peered inside. They were empty!

Shortly after the British patrol made this discovery, the fog became particularly dense. Other British patrols moved through it cautiously. As they did so,
Washington stepped aboard the ferry to Manhattan. He was the last to leave.
The entire American army on Long Island had been evacuated in less than
six hours, without a hitch except for a brief period in which the rear guard
abandoned the works prematurely. Only three stragglers and five cannon too
heavy to move were left behind. Governor's Island was successfully abandoned, too. "In the history of warfare I do not recollect a more fortunate retreat," one American remembered. Washington had lost a battle, but he
conducted a splendid withdrawal.

"If a good Bleeding can bring those Bible faced Yankees to their senses,"
General James Grant wrote on September 2nd, "the fever of Independency
should soon abate." The next stage of the battle seemed obvious. The defeated American army lay concentrated in lower Manhattan, like a prize at
the bottom of a bag. If Howe reached out and tied off the bag's opening, the
war would be over. It would take much more than luck to save Washington
now.

9

RETREAT

September – December 1776

WASHINGTON KNEW THAT his problems had not ended with the successful evacuation of Brooklyn Heights. "It is now extremely obvious from all Intelligence," he reported to Hancock on September 8th, that "they mean to inclose us on the Island of New York by taking post in our Rear, while the Shipping effectually secure the Front; and thus either by cutting off our Communication with the Country oblige us to fight them on their own Terms or Surrender at discretion." Yet the danger of encirclement did not bother him as much as his fear "that all our Troops will not do their duty." Defeated, outnumbered, and lacking basic supplies, the Continental soldiers had become rebellious and cynical, their willingness to fight open to question. Sensing the increasing hopelessness of his situation, Washington decided that New York City would have to be abandoned.

Retreat presented problems of its own, not least the possibility that it might further demoralize the troops. It could also raise questions about Washington's military leadership. He justified it as part of an overall strategic plan. "On our side the War should be defensive," he explained. "It has even been called a War of posts. . . . [W]e should on all occasions avoid a general Action or put anything to the risque unless compelled by a necessity into which we ought never to be drawn."

The strategy that Washington pursued after the Battle of Long Island is sometimes called Fabian, after the Roman general Fabius, who defeated Hannibal during the Second Punic War. Admiring historians have described Washington, like Fabius, as standing patiently on the defensive, preserving his forces, and watching for the right moment to strike. Some have even drawn comparisons between Washington and twentieth-century practitioners of guerrilla warfare, who attacked only when circumstances promised a stunning victory and defended only when critical objectives were at stake. In the interim, it is said, he limited himself to interdicting and harassing the enemy with small parties of militia or other "expendable" military assets.

Yet Washington's reputation as a Fabian, and particularly as a guerrilla warrior, is unjustified. Despite what he sometimes said in writing, his instincts were always for seeking decisive engagements that would kill redcoats, demoralize the British in America and Europe, and speed the end of the war. At Boston he had proposed finishing the siege with a climactic battle by flinging his army into an attack against the entrenchments that guarded the city. In New York he stood on the defensive because he had no other choice, but instead of avoiding battle he placed his army in dangerously exposed positions in hopes of making the enemy "wade through much blood & Slaughter." He told Hancock that "the Arguments on which such a System was founded were deemed unanswerable & experience has given her sanction," implying that he had pursued a cautious strategy from the war's beginning; but in fact he had not, and he never consistently avoided major battles. He would put his army "to the risque" in attack and defense many times before the end of the war.

Washington was a fighting general. If Abraham Lincoln had been president of Congress in 1776, he might have said of Washington instead of Ulysses S. Grant that, "I can't spare this man, he fights!" Both men hated idleness and were temperamentally inclined for battle. But while Grant typically fought battles in order to pursue his broad strategy of wearing down the enemy, Washington showed no such consistency. Sometimes he confronted the enemy because he thought a major strategic prize was at stake. At other times he simply threw caution to the winds and trusted to luck and instinct. If William Howe had been even half as daring as Robert E. Lee, Washington might have ended his military career in 1776 as a British prisoner in lower Manhattan.

If left to his own judgment, Washington would have burned New York City and evacuated Manhattan by mid-September. But he did not feel authorized to make such major decisions alone. Congress vetoed any idea of torching the city; and some generals, far from agreeing to an evacuation, insisted on holding on for "a while longer." Bringing them around took time, and it was not until September 10th that Congress resolved that Washington did not have to stay in New York City "a Moment longer than he shall think it

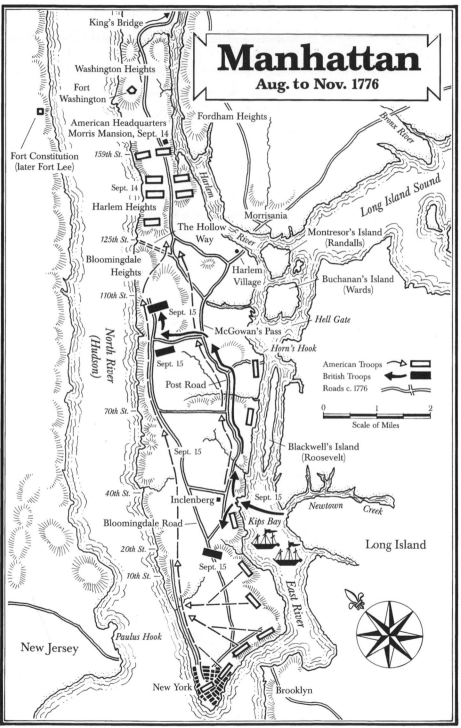

Manhattan
Aug. to Nov. 1776

King's Bridge

Washington Heights

Fort Washington

Fort Constitution (later Fort Lee)

Fordham Heights

American Headquarters Morris Mansion, Sept. 14

159th St.

Sept. 14

Harlem Heights

Morrisania

Montresor's Island (Randalls)

The Hollow Way

125th St.

Bloomingdale Heights

Harlem Village

Buchanan's Island (Wards)

110th St.

Sept. 15

McGowan's Pass

Hell Gate

Horn's Hook

Sept. 15

Post Road

Sept. 15

70th St.

Bronx River

Harlem River

Long Island Sound

North River (Hudson)

American Troops
British Troops
Roads c. 1776

0   1   2
Scale of Miles

Blackwell's Island (Roosevelt)

40th St.

Inclenberg

Sept. 15

Newtown Creek

Bloomingdale Road

Kips Bay

Long Island

20th St.

Sept. 15

10th St.

East River

New Jersey

Paulus Hook

New York

Brooklyn

© 2005 Rick Britton

proper for the publick Service." Two days later, a council of war voted to withdraw the army to upper Manhattan. The decision came almost too late.

Soldiers, civilians, horses, and wagons quickly clogged the roads north as the evacuation began. Washington had not won approval of his plan to burn New York City, but he tried to make sure that nothing useful was left behind. Buildings were looted, and supplies tossed into the Hudson or burned at the docks. At the orders of the New York Convention, teams of men removed bells from churches and public buildings in order to preserve a "necessary tho' unfortunate resource for Supplying our want of Cannon." Aside from their primary purpose of announcing services and meetings, the bells had been the city's primary alarm system in case of fire. Their removal would prove disastrous, and for some provide evidence of nefarious design.

The evacuation proceeded slowly, and by nightfall on September 14th there were 3,500 Continentals remaining in lower Manhattan. The rest of the army sprawled torpidly at roadsides or in scattered posts across the island. As the soldiers dozed, a chain of American sentries patrolled the East River at Kip's Bay, a tiny inlet at the end of what is now Thirty-fourth Street. "All is well," the sentries called out lazily to each other every thirty minutes. And all seemed well, until a sarcastic English accent came from the darkness somewhere offshore: "We will alter your tune before tomorrow night."

Washington was fortunate that Howe did not attack earlier. Dispersed and incapable of mounting effective resistance to invasion at any one point, the Continental Army was extremely vulnerable. American morale was abysmal. Desertions and resignations sloughed off dozens or even hundreds of Continentals every day, and the militia left in droves. The entire force was ripe for dissolution. But Howe, a "generous, merciful, forbearing enemy who would take no unfair advantages," did nothing for two weeks after Washington's withdrawal from Brooklyn Heights; leaving the British troops to "stand on the banks of the East River, like Moses on Mount Pisgah, looking at their promised land, little more than half a mile distant."

Howe's foot-dragging may have been due to an abortive peace conference on Staten Island that took place on September 11th. But the British peace emissaries offered nothing new, and their American counterparts, with no idea of the gravity of Washington's plight, were stubborn. When the conference dissolved after only a day, Howe acted decisively. Four British warships sailed unmolested up the East River on September 13th while Washington watched and wondered what they were about. They arrived at Kip's Bay on the evening of the 14th, and at dawn the next morning flatboats full of British and German soldiers left Long Island and formed offshore "like a large clover field in full bloom."

At 11:00 A.M., the flatboats began rowing ashore under cover of a cannonade. "It is hardly possible to conceive what a tremendous fire was kept up by those five ships for only fifty-nine minutes," a British seaman wrote. The ineffective but noisy bombardment shattered the morale of the green Continentals and Connecticut militiamen at Kip's Bay even before the landing began, and Connecticut colonel William Douglas watched his militia brigade dissolve almost instantaneously. "I Lay myself on the Right wing," he remembered, "wateing for the boats untill Capt. Printice Came to me and told if I ment to Save my Self to Leave the Lines for that was the orders on the Left and that they had Left the Lines. I then told my men to make the best of their way as I then found I had but about ten Left with me." Meanwhile, more British ships sailed up the Hudson and bombarded the city.

Scouting reports had made Washington expect the British to land farther north, so he was four miles away in Harlem when Howe's troops started coming ashore at Kip's Bay just after noon. Riding toward the fray, he encountered Brigadier General Samuel Holden Parsons with a thousand Continental reinforcements and rode with them up Murray Hill, which overlooked Kip's Bay from the northwest. A vanguard of British grenadiers was marching up the opposite slope at the same time.

A post road ran along the crest of Murray Hill, flanked by stone walls and a dense cornfield occupied by a timid brigade of Massachusetts militiamen. As soon as Washington detected the enemy advance on the road he screamed out for Parsons's men to "Take the walls!" and "Take the corn-field!" "The men ran to the walls and some into the cornfield," Parsons remembered, but "in a most confused and disordered manner." Washington, Parsons, and their aides struggled unsuccessfully to get them into formation. All the while, militiamen from the shore defenses sprinted through the cornfield, bounded over walls, and threw away their weapons in panicked flight. Their example proved infectious. The Massachusetts militia brigade shuddered and broke, followed by the three Continental regiments. Within seconds, Washington stood in "surprize and Mortification" amid a stampede of soldiers "flying in every direction."

So many stories have been told about Washington's reaction that it is difficult to know exactly what happened during the next half hour. Certainly, he lost his temper. "I used every means in my power to rally and get them into some order but my attempts were fruitless and ineffectual," he explained to Hancock. Aide Tench Tilghman, probably an eyewitness, described Washington's behavior more colorfully. "He laid his Cane over many of the Officers who shewed their men the Example of running," Tilghman wrote. Other stories, modified after circulating for days, said that the commander-in-chief drew his sword and "snapped his pistols," "caned and whipped" his men, "three times dashed his hatt on the Ground, and at last exclaimed 'Good God have I got such Troops as Those.'" Raging "within eighty yards of the enemy, so vexed at the infamous conduct of the troops, that he sought death rather than life," Washington reportedly had to be dragged from the field by his aides.

"The dastardly Behaviour of the Rebels . . . sinks below Remark," observed Lord Richard Howe's secretary. About fifty Americans were killed, and over three hundred captured. Some of the victors expressed contempt for their opponents by bayoneting the wounded and then mutilating their corpses. While rambling over the battlefield that afternoon in search of "curious trifles," a British midshipman "saw a Hessian sever a rebel's head from his body and clap it on a pole in the intrenchments." Eager for fresh victims, some Germans captured the midshipman, whose uniform was identical to that of an American officer "who lay there with his leg shot off," and beat him and his companions mercilessly until a British general intervened.

Howe had put 4,000 troops ashore at Kip's Bay in the first wave, and 9,000 more landed in the early afternoon. With Murray Hill in his hands, he easily could have pushed west to the Hudson and trapped thousands of Americans in lower Manhattan. Inexplicably, he did not. An amusing but probably spurious legend claims that Howe and his fellow officers were so seduced by the offer of wine and pastries from some Quaker women that they wasted hours "quaffing and laughing, and bantering their patriotic hostess about the ludicrous panic and discomfiture of her countrymen." More likely, he did not want to move until his landing parties had been properly organized.

Either way, he lost a priceless opportunity to hack off a quarter of the American army. Washington instantly appreciated the danger to his troops, and ordered General Putnam to evacuate them as quickly as possible. Putnam obeyed, "flying, on his horse, covered with foam, wherever his presence was most necessary" to rouse the Continentals from their camps. Leaving behind all of their cannon and heavy equipment, 3,500 Continentals started leaving New York City at 4:00 P.M. They marched up the Hudson shore and reached the safety of Harlem Heights by nightfall.

Behind them in New York City, exultant loyalists indulged in frenzied celebration and looting. Their time had come at last, and they made the most of it by exacting revenge on the persons and property of their patriot tormentors. A British naval captain who approached the city in a longboat that evening apprehensively watched a frenzied "rabble on the walls," but instead of lynching him the "mob . . . gave me three cheers, took me on their shoulders, carried me to the Governor's Fort, put me under the English colours now hoisted, and again gave me three cheers, which they frequently repeated, men, women, and children chaking me by the hand, and giving me their blessing, and crying out 'God Save the King!' " They were "like overjoyed Bedlamites," another British observer remembered. "A Woman pulled down the Rebel Standard upon the Fort, and a Woman hoisted up in its Stead His Majesty's Flat, after trampling the other under Foot with the most contemptuous Indignation." British engineer captain John Montresor recovered the head from George III's statue and sent it to England, "in order to convince them at home of the Infamous Disposition of the Ungrateful people of this distressed Country."

Washington's troops spent the night less happily at Harlem Heights. There, "excessively fatigued by the sultry march of the day, their clothes wet by a severe shower of rain that succeeded towards the evening, their blood chilled by the cold wind that produced a sudden change in the temperature of the air, and their hearts sunk within them by the loss of baggage, artillery, and works in which they had been taught to put great confidence, [they] lay upon their arms, covered only by the clouds of an uncomfortable sky." But they had survived, and would fight again sooner than they expected.

The American positions at Harlem Heights lay in a series of entrenched lines, extending north from the "Hollow Way," a little valley just south of present-day 125th Street, up to a place around what is now 160th Street. General Greene, now recovered from his fever, commanded the first line with about 3,300 troops. The exhausted remnants of Putnam's command lay half a mile to his rear, and the rest of the army was deployed farther north toward Fort Washington and Kingsbridge.

Before sunrise on September 16th, Washington detached Colonel Thomas Knowlton with 150 volunteer rangers from various New England regiments to reconnoiter the British forward positions, which lay about two miles to the south. The rangers moved stealthily through woody, broken terrain, and made contact with the enemy at sunrise near what is now 106th and Broadway. Exchanging fire with several hundred English light infantry and Highlanders from the Black Watch, Knowlton slowly withdrew.

Washington was supervising defensive preparations at the Hollow Way when he heard gunfire in front of his line. Joseph Reed, newly returned to service as the general's adjutant general, had accompanied Knowlton, and he rode back to tell Washington what was going on while the rangers broke contact and withdrew. As soon as Reed started talking, "the Enemy appeared in open view & in the most insulting manner sounded their Bugle Horns as is usual after a Fox Chase. I never felt such a sensation before," he remembered, "it seem'd to crown our Disgrace."

Within the past three weeks, Washington's army had made two humiliating withdrawals and suffered poundings on Long Island and at Kip's Bay. The British sensed that they did not need to push very hard to rout the Americans altogether, and used the hunting horns in expectation of a chase rather than a battle. But in an early glimmer of the courage and resolve that would rally the Continentals from many a tight spot later on, Washington refused to behave like the commander of a defeated army. A cautious general—or an inferior one—would have pulled Knowlton's party back to the forward entrenchments and invited the Highlanders to attack. Washington chose to advance, surround the enemy, and destroy them.

The daring plan nearly succeeded. Sending a brigade of 1,000 men to bait the British by advancing "as If to attack them in front," Washington ordered three companies of his beloved Virginia Continentals and Knowlton's rangers to work their way around the enemy's right flank and into their rear. "This took effect as I wished on the part of the Enemy," he recalled. "On the appearance of our party in front, they immediately ran down the Hill, took possession of some fences & Bushes and a Smart firing began." Unfortunately, Knowlton and the Virginians miscalculated their route and attacked the British flank instead of their rear. Thus alerted to their predicament, the Highlanders slowly withdrew, making brief stands in a buckwheat field and an orchard as both sides received reinforcements. Each side suffered about 150 casualties, and Knowlton fell mortally wounded.

Washington refused to risk his troops further and halted their advance, ordering them to break off the engagement and withdraw at about 2:00 P.M. Tilghman, who delivered the commander-in-chief's order, recalled that the troops "gave a Hurra and left the Field in good Order." This minor but victorious skirmish boosted morale even among the troops who had not been engaged. Among them, Colonel David Humphreys later wrote, "every visage was seen to brighten, and to assume, instead of the gloom of despair, the glow of animation." It was Washington's first battlefield victory of the war.

Washington had not abandoned lower Manhattan without regrets. "Had I been left to the dictates of my own judgment, New York should have been laid in Ashes before I quitted it," he wrote to a distant cousin, Lund Washington, on October 6th. "To this end I applied to Congress, but was absolutely forbid. . . . [T]his in my judgment may be set down among one of the capitol errors of Congress." Fortunately, he went on, "Providence—or some good honest Fellow, has done more for us than we were disposed to do for ourselves, as near One fourth of the City is supposed to be consumed."

He was referring to a fire that destroyed about a thousand houses west of Broadway on the morning of September 21st. Beginning near Manhattan's southern tip around midnight, the flames spread north rapidly. No mass alarms were possible because the city's bells had been taken for recasting as munitions, and the citizens were slow to respond to the fire, which soon raged out of control. Only a providential wind shift to the southeast, which blew the flames toward the river, spared the city from complete destruction.

Washington justified the destruction of New York City on elementary strategic principles. "It will be next to impossible for us to dispossess them of it again as all their Supplies come by Water, whilst ours were derived by Land," he wrote Lund. With the British in indefinite possession, the city provided "warm & comfortable Barracks, in which their whole Force may be concentred"—a force that could use the city as a secure base for operations almost anywhere in the country. He saw no fortune in the wind's fickleness, but found it lamentable that "enough of [New York] remains to answer their purposes."

Refusing to believe that the fire was accidental, many British and loyalists suspected Washington of removing the city's bells and recruiting arsonists for the "devilish purpose" of starting an unstoppable conflagration. Like Napoleon's French during the Moscow fire of 1812, the British claimed to have seen "picked incendiaries" rushing about the streets that night "with faggots dipp'd in Brimstone." Some of the suspected arsonists were lynched, including "one fanatical rebel, whose wife and five children could not persuade him to refrain from this murderous arson, [and] mortally injured his wife with a knife when she tried to extinguish the fire with buckets of water"—or so the story went. A group of British tars seized the man, stabbed him to death, and then strung him up by his feet in front of his home. Another victim was Washington's spy Nathan Hale, who was caught that evening and hanged on the 22nd. But the British never found enough evidence to convict anyone of starting the fires.

The fire may or may not have been accidental, and in any case Washington's involvement is questionable. He would have hesitated to disobey Congress's orders not to harm the city, and also realized the danger of appearing to persecute American civilians. On the other hand, deeply interested as he was, and would continue to be, in the city's intrigues, Washington just possibly might have encouraged the plots of others without giving them his explicit sanction. He could be ruthless when he wanted. The true causes of the New York fire of 1776—like the Moscow fire of 1812—will always remain mysterious.

After the Battle of Harlem Heights the Continental Army again had received a respite, thanks to General Howe, who wanted to consolidate his positions on Manhattan before driving farther inland. Howe also may have hoped for a Canadian advance on Albany, not knowing that Governor Carleton had called off his offensive after barely defeating Benedict Arnold's fleet on Lake Champlain on October 11th. The three weeks thus gained allowed Washington to reinforce his positions and mold his tattered army into some degree of order.

The Continental Army was in desperately bad condition. Recent reinforcements had brought it to almost 27,000 men, but 8,000 of them were too sick to fight and about 3,500 more were absent on detachment. The 14,759 troops stretched across Harlem Heights were only nominally "fit for duty." Their raggedness and poor equipment presented nothing unusual, but their mutinous behavior was unprecedented. Officers—those who had not resigned—could not control their men. Plunderers raided the countryside with such savagery that Washington admitted "such a Spirit has gone forth in our Army that neither publick or private Property is secure." Militia troops were particularly troublesome. They slouched, they defied, they ran—and corrupted others by their example. "Being subject to no controul themselves they introduce disorder among the Troops [I] have attempted to discipline," Washington complained. The Continentals were more amenable to discipline, but most had enlisted for only twelve months. By the time he finished training them, they would disappear; and the cycle would begin anew. Washington was like the mythical Greek Sisyphus, who endlessly pushed a boulder up a hill only to watch it roll down again.

Frustration thus deepened to despair, and Washington seriously contemplated resignation. "If I were to wish the bitterest curse to an enemy on this side of the grave, I should put him in my stead with feelings," he wrote sadly to Lund. "I see the impossibility of serving with reputation, or doing any essential service to the cause by continuing in command, and yet I am told that if I quit the command inevitable ruin will follow from the distraction that will ensue. In confidence I tell you that I never was in such an unhappy, divided state since I was born."

Washington could complain with the best. But he did not spend all his time griping. Instead, though sagging with depression and fatigue, Washington wracked his brain for solutions. Awaking well before dawn on the morning of September 25th, he borrowed "from the hours allotted to Sleep" to write a lengthy letter to Congress in his own hand, without dictating to an aide. Exhaustion made the general's hand slip, and he scattered the letter with "blots and scratchings"; but his ideas came through with remarkable forcefulness and clarity.

Congress, he said, had put too much stock in patriotism—keeping officers' salaries low, for instance, as if paying them well would turn them into mercenaries. But patriotism alone did not make good soldiers. "When Men are irritated, & the Passions inflamed, they fly hastily, and chearfully to Arms, but after the first emotions are over to expect . . . that they are influenced by any other principles than those of Interest, is to look for what never did, & I fear never will happen." "The few therefore," he continued, "who act upon Principles of disinteredness, are, comparitively speaking—no more than a drop in the Ocean."

Attacking another prejudice of the young nation, citizen-soldiery, Washington frankly told Congress that placing "any dependence upon Militia, is, assuredly, resting upon a broken staff." The legends that had been propagated since the French and Indian War were wrong. A man did *not* fight better just because he was defending his home. On the contrary, "men just dragged from the tender Scenes of domestick life—unaccustomed to the din of Arms—totally unacquainted with every kind of Military skill, which being followed by a want of Confidence in themselves when opposed to Troops regularly traind—disciplined, and appointed—superior in knowledge, & superior in Arms, makes them timid, and ready to fly from their own Shadows."

Washington wanted the delegates to overcome their prejudices and commit themselves entirely toward forming a standing army. He detailed what he needed in every particular, down to the amount of money, acres of land, and other material inducements to be offered to each new soldier. Regular troops, enlisted for the war's duration, well-paid and supplied, disciplined and obedient, were indispensable to final victory. "The Jealousies of a standing army, and the Evils to be apprehended from one, are remote; and in my judgment, situated & circumstanced as we are, not at all to be dreaded," Washington soothed. "But the consequences of wanting one . . . is certain, and inevitable Ruin."

Two days after Washington dispatched this demanding but deeply considered and insightful letter to Philadelphia, a political sinkhole—otherwise known as a Congressional committee—sucked it from view. The delegates would enact no reforms in army recruitment and administration until it was almost too late.

On October 11, 1776, William Howe shook off his increasingly habitual lethargy and decided to force Washington off Manhattan Island. That evening, eighty ships departed Kip's Bay and took advantage of a dense fog to navigate the "amazing strong tide" in Hell Gate without being seen. At nine the next morning the ships began disgorging 4,000 troops at Throg's Neck, a high-tide island now in southeast Bronx.

The landing appeared to threaten Washington's left flank, but Howe quickly discovered that he had misjudged the terrain. Marshes forced the British through two bottlenecks, a ford and a causeway, and Tench Tilghman observed that the stone fences lining the roads made them "as defensible as they can be wished." "I think," Tilghman wrote smugly, "if they are well lined with Troops we may make a considerable Slaughter if not discomfit them totally." Washington, enjoying the tonic that activity gave to his mood, easily halted the British advance with less than 2,000 men. Howe had to pause and reconsider.

Washington did some thinking, too. The enemy plan, "that of getting in our rear & cutting off our communication with the Country," was obvious, and nothing could stop them from eventually accomplishing it at some place more auspicious than Throg's Neck. On the 16th, therefore, Washington convened his general officers and convinced them that it was time for yet another withdrawal. Charles Lee, who had just returned to the army, in fact "urged the absolute necessity of the measure." The main army started marching north toward White Plains the next day. They left behind a dangerously isolated garrison of 1,200 men at Fort Washington in northwest Manhattan, "to maintain it if possible, in order to preserve the Communication with the Jerseys" and block further British naval penetration of the lower Hudson.

The retreat from Harlem Heights began just in time. On the 18th, thousands of British and German troops spilled ashore at Pell's Point, three miles north of Throg's Neck. If Washington had remained at Harlem Heights, the enemy would have cut him off. Yet when Howe noticed the Americans pulling back, he did not pursue. Instead his troops pushed slowly inland against a weak screen of Massachusetts Continentals, and waited until the 21st to occupy New Rochelle. Howe then reverted to inactivity while the Americans left Manhattan at Kingsbridge and withdrew unmolested to the village of White Plains.

The American positions at White Plains were stretched along a three-mile line, anchored on the left by a lake and on the right by Chatterton Hill. This hill, really a ridge one mile long, held the key to the whole position. It was steep and heavily wooded on its southern slope, below which ran the Bronx River—only fourteen feet wide at this point. Fields broken by stone walls and clumps of trees covered its crest. With adequate troops and artillery it could have been a formidable position. But Washington left it bare of fortifications, put several hundred militiamen there, and then promptly forgot about them. Their "Humours & intolerable Caprices" had nearly driven him out of his mind, and he was glad to be rid of their presence.

Preoccupied with logistical and strategic concerns, Washington did not explore the ground around White Plains personally until the morning of the 28th. At that time the first elements of Howe's vanguard had already appeared and, as Washington set off to reconnoiter, his skirmishers made contact with the enemy. The commander-in-chief rode to the top of Chatterton Hill. He could see several miles in every direction. Charles Lee was with him and pointed north. "Yonder," said Lee, "is the ground we ought to occupy."

"Let us then go and view it," Washington replied; but as the party rode north they were intercepted by a light horseman, who "came up in full gallop, his horse almost out of breath, and addressed Gen. Washington—'The British are on the camp, Sir.' The General observed—'Gentlemen, we have now other business than reconnoitring,' putting his horse in full gallop for the camp." There was no more time to redeploy the troops. They would have to fight where they stood.

Back at headquarters, in the center of his line, Washington "turned round to the officers, and only said, 'Gentlemen, you will repair to your respective posts, and do the best you can.' " Washington reinforced the shaky militia-men on Chatterton Hill with a few artillery pieces and just over a thousand Continentals, who positioned themselves behind stone walls on the crest while the militia shifted over to the extreme right flank. The skirmishers meanwhile retired slowly in the face of the British advance and passed through the main lines about noon.

Howe, who had left almost half of his army on Manhattan, drew up be-fore the American positions at White Plains with only 13,000 troops, most of them German. Grasping the importance of Chatterton Hill, he ordered two columns to attack it. The first consisted of a brigade of Germans under Colonel Johann Gottlieb Rall. Holding their fire and advancing on the Ameri-can right flank with fixed bayonets, Rall's Germans easily scattered the mili-tia opposing them and marched for the crest. The other column, made up largely of Germans from the Lossberg Regiment, attacked frontally but bogged down as the troops waded knee-deep across the Bronx under heavy American fire. Two British regiments that initially supported them became impatient and crossed at a shallower place. Jeering at their German allies, the redcoats moved ahead and started climbing the ridge in column. A Ger-man officer admitted that the British "withstood an even hotter fire of grapeshot" than the Germans but "were not disturbed and kept on march-ing." Eventually, the Germans extricated themselves and followed behind.

Washington now paid the price for neglecting to fortify Chatterton Hill days earlier. His Continentals fought well—the Marylanders even counter-attacked downhill and drove the enemy before them for a time—but were unable to site their guns, build strong points, or establish fields of fire. British artillery did gory work among them. "As we were on the declivity of the hill," a Connecticut soldier recalled, "a cannon ball cut down Lt. Youngs Platoon which was next to that of mine[;] the ball first took the head of Smith, a Stout heavy man & dash't it open, then it took off Chilsons arm which was ampu-tated . . . it then took Taylor across the Bowels, it then Struck Sergt. Garret of our Company on the hip [and] took off the point of the hip bone . . . now to think, oh! What a Sight that was to See within a distance of Six rods those men with their legs & arms & guns & packs all in a heap." Deserted by the militia on their right and faced by a determined force of bayonet-wielding redcoats, the Continentals gave way. Washington ceded the hill and pulled his troops back to positions just east of White Plains.

The defeat was galling for the Americans. British and German casualties had been about 276, nearly twice the number suffered by Washington's army. Many of the Continentals felt they had lost a chance at inflicting even heavier casualties and ultimately winning a significant victory. "In this affair, as in too many more of a similar nature," a Maryland lieutenant later wrote, "our Generals show'd not equal judgment to that of the Enemy." The British lost a chance, too, for Howe again did not give chase. Instead, he waited three days and leisurely disposed his army for another assault on the morn-ing of October 31st; but a heavy rain fell that evening, providing enough cover for Washington to slip away.

The Americans laid waste to homes and barns and torched the settlement of White Plains as they withdrew, leaving dozens of families homeless. As usual, their leader issued dire proclamations against such malicious cruelty; and, as usual, the country burnt anyway. After marching about five miles, Washington's troops occupied the rugged hills called Mount Castle that Lee had pointed out from Chatterton Hill. The weather had turned cold, herald-ing the approaching end of the traditional campaigning season, and camp life slowed down in pace with the deepening autumn chill. The enemy was less than three miles away, but "all matters are as quiet as if the enemy were one hundred miles distant from us," Tench Tilghman wrote on November 2nd. The commander-in-chief spent his time reconnoitering while his troops, drooping with fatigue after "enduring almost a Weeks constant Fatigue by Night and Day," retired to their tents and built "Small Chimneys in them to warm them with a Little Fire."

As the Americans suspected, Howe had no stomach for pressing farther north. He made one halfhearted attempt to draw Washington out from his mountain aerie, but when his bait was ignored Howe decided that he "did not think the driving their rearguard further back an object of the least con-sequence." On November 4th, he abandoned White Plains and marched south. He had some unfinished business to attend to in Manhattan.

Washington often deferred to his officers' advice during the war. Whether he did so in order to follow Congress's 1775 injunction that he act only after "advising with your council of war," from doubts of his own military ability, or from a combination of the two is difficult to determine. Some have regarded it as evidence of his indecisiveness, though Washington's officers sometimes prevented him from carrying out some truly harebrained ideas. But at other times his deference led to disaster. That was what happened in November 1776.

When the American army withdrew from Harlem Heights on October 18th, they left behind two garrisoned forts on the Hudson River. Fort Wash-ington stood 230 feet above the river on a northern Manhattan bluff known as Mount Washington. By mid-November, its garrison and covering force numbered nearly 3,000 troops. An additional 2,000 soldiers were stationed at Fort Lee, on the other side of the river, in New Jersey. Between the two forts, chevaux-de-frise and a group of sunken hulks blocked passage of the Hudson River. In theory, any British ships that tried to sail up the Hudson would be hung up on these underwater obstructions and blasted by the guns at Forts Washington and Lee.

Israel Putnam held nominal command of all the troops in northern Man-hattan but Washington, who had begun to lose respect for Old Put's opin-ions, ignored him; Nathanael Greene, with headquarters at Fort Lee, thus took overall responsibility for both forts. He crossed the river several times a day to give orders to Colonel Robert Magaw, a feisty Pennsylvanian who com-manded Fort Washington.

Exposed on Manhattan Island, Fort Washington would bear the first shock of any British attempt to seize the forts. Unfortunately, the place looked like a half-ruined sand castle. Amateurishly constructed as a five-sided earthwork in July 1776, it included no barracks to shelter the garrison, no internal water supply, and feeble outworks. The impenetrable granite that underlaid the whole area made it impossible to dig deep, anyway. No one could have imagined it capable of enduring a siege; it served more as gift-wrap than protection for the priceless guns and Continentals that garrisoned its four acres. Why, then, did Washington try to hold it?

One reason was that Congress had insisted he use "every art and whatever expence to obstruct effectually the navigation of the North River." That included Fort Washington. A council of war reinforced this opinion in a vote on October 16th. The Hudson River, all agreed, was so strategically important that the British must be kept out for as long as possible. Writing in 1779, Washington added that "when I considered that our policy led us to waste [that is, to spend] the campaign without coming to a general action on the one hand, or to suffer the enemy to overrun the Country on the other I conceived that every impediment that stood in their way was a mean to answer these purposes." In other words, he thought holding Fort Washington might slow the British advance without risking a major battle.

That was poor logic, for nothing justified throwing 3,000 good troops away on an indefensible position. Yet men Washington trusted believed the fort could be held. Colonel Magaw, General Putnam, and Fort Washington's original builders all thought so. More important, so did General Greene, "whose judgment & candor" Washington valued very highly. Greene supposedly knew the ground better than anyone, so Washington deferred to his opinion.

Then three British ships forced their way past the forts, and Washington became worried again. "The late passage of the 3 Vessells" up the Hudson, he wrote nervously to Greene on November 8th, "is so plain a proof of the inefficacy of all the Obstructions we have thrown into it that I cannot but think it will fully justify a Change in the Disposition which has been made. If we cannot prevent Vessells passing up, and the Enemy are possessed of the surrounding Country, what valuable purpose can it answer to attempt to hold a post from which the expected Benefit cannot be had—I am therefore inclined to think it will not be prudent to hazard the Men & Stores at Mount Washington." The commander-in-chief's tone was hesitant, almost apologetic. Greene did not have to evacuate, but Washington revoked his previous orders to defend the place "to the last."

Greene confidently brushed Washington's fears aside. He had seen an earlier attempt to force the barriers fail on October 27th, and this time the enemy vessels had been "prodigiously shatterd from the fire of our Cannon." Just let them try it again; the cannoneers were ready. "I cannot help thinking the Garrison is of advantage, and I cannot conceive the Garrison to be in any great danger," he wrote. It was not Greene's profoundest military insight.

Washington came to visit his namesake fort on November 12th. For three days, he inspected the troops and peered into every corner of the outworks and central fortifications. An engineer would have seen the futility of trying to hold such a place against the combined might of the British army and navy, but Washington was no engineer. Greene and Magaw exuded confidence strong enough to buttress even the flimsiest walls. Washington let them do as they pleased.

On the night of November 14th–15th, while Washington slept at Fort Lee, thirty British flatboats paddled gently up the Hudson. Undetected by American sentries, the boats went past the forts and entered the Harlem River by way of Spuyten Duyvil Creek. Washington awoke the next morning unaware of the British movement, and after dictating a short letter to the Board of War he mounted his horse and rode six miles west to Hackensack. From there, he probably intended to proceed to New Brunswick as part of a survey of affairs in New Jersey.

Then a courier arrived from Fort Lee with a message that Greene had just received from Magaw. "A flag of truce came out just now from Kingsbridge," Magaw blustered, "the [British] Adjutant Genl was at the head of it. . . . The Adjutant Genl would hardly give two hours for an Alternative between surrendering at discretion or every man being put to the sword. He waits for an answer—I shall send a proper one—You'll I dare say do what is best—We are determined to defend the post or die." Washington rode back to Fort Lee.

On arrival, the commander-in-chief walked to the riverbank and hopped on a boat bound for Fort Washington. Halfway across he met Greene and Putnam coming the other way, and called for a report as they passed. "The Troops were in high Spirits and would make a good Defence," they shouted. Reassured, Washington ordered his boatmen to turn about and go back to Fort Lee, where he spent the night.

The attack began at 10:00 A.M. the next day, November 16th. Over five thousand British and German troops advanced on the works from three directions, some landing from the flatboats on the Harlem River and others marching from the north and south. Washington crossed the river again as the firing began. With Greene, Putnam, and General Hugh Mercer he watched the enemy's slow advance through Magaw's outworks, which he had constructed up to a mile outside the main fort. The Americans fought stubbornly, and in some places they fired with such effect that Washington entertained "great Hopes the Enemy was intirely repulsed."

"Before us, beside, and behind us," a traumatized German soldier remembered, "we saw our unfortunate comrades lying beside and upon one another.

They lay battered and in part shattered; dead on the earth in their own blood; some whimpering, looked at us, pleading that in one way or another we would ease their suffering and unbearable pain." Another German recalled seeing "many dead and wounded; among others, a German jaeger [light infantryman] who had just been shot through the head. His brother stood over the body, complaining that he could not be buried. Another jaeger had both eyes shot out. He still lived. Farther along, the rebels lay packed together like herring." Before the end, 458 German and British soldiers would fall dead or wounded.

Stolidly, courageously, the German and British infantry forced the Americans back until they approached the walls of the fort itself. It was noon. "There we all stood in a very awkward situation," Greene later wrote. "We all urged his Excellency to come off. I offered to stay. General Putnam did the same and so did General Mercer, but his Excellency thought it best for us all to come off together, which we did about half an hour before the Enemy surrounded the fort." Shortly after they left, the last lines of defense collapsed. Magaw capitulated at 3:00 P.M.

One hour later, over 2,800 Americans stacked their arms and marched solemnly out of the fort. "The Rebel prisoners were in general but very indifferently clothed," a British witness noted with amused disgust. "Few of them appeared to have a Second shirt, nor did they appear to have washed themselves during the Campaign. A great many of them"—and these were some of Washington's best Continental regiments—"were lads under 15, and old men: and few of them had the appearance of Soldiers. Their odd figures frequently excited the laughter of our Soldiers." Aside from occasional snickering, the redcoats watched silently as the Americans presented their colors to two German regiments that had led the attack. The scene went smoothly, as if it had been choreographed.

That is, until the Germans started beating their prisoners.

"Despite the strictest orders, the prisoners received a number of blows," a lighthearted German chaplain wrote in his diary that evening. He thought one beating "especially comical . . . [O]ne of the rebels being led through looked proudly to the left and right. [A] grenadier grabbed him on the ears with both hands, and said, 'Wait a bit, and I'll show you the big city.' Another tied him with his scarf. Two others hit him on the sides of his head. A third gave him a kick in the rump, so that he flew through three ranks. . . . The poor guy never knew what hit him, or why he had been hit." Many others received like treatment. "The Hessians were roused," James Grant wrote. "They had been pretty well pelted, were angry & would not have spared the Yankeys," but their officers intervened and put a stop to a potential massacre.

If Washington watched the surrender from across the river, he might have remembered his humiliation following the capitulation of Fort Necessity. "This is a most unfortunate affair and has given me great Mortification," he wrote. "We have lost not only two thousand Men that were there, but a good deal of Artillery, & some of the best Arms we had." He had also lost some of the best troops in his army, all Continentals. The capture of Fort Washington was an unmitigated disaster for the American cause, the worst defeat in the war so far and a severe blow to the commander-in-chief's reputation.

"Oh General," Charles Lee wailed, "why wou'd you be over-perswaded by Men of inferior judgment to your own? It was a cursed affair." In a letter to the commander-in-chief's aide Joseph Reed that Washington opened and read, Lee expounded on the theme, this time more personally: "[I] lament with you that fatal indecision of mind which in war is a much greater disqualification than stupidity or even want of personal courage. Accident may put a decisive Blunderer in the right—but eternal defeat and miscarriage must attend the man of the best parts if curs'd with indecision."

Washington could guess what his friend Reed had written to Lee. It was this: "General Washington's own Judgment seconded by Representations from us, would I believe have saved the Men & their Arms but unluckily, General Greene's Judgt was contrary[.] This kept the Generals Mind in a State of Suspence till the Stroke was struck—Oh! General—an indecisive Mind is one of the greatest Misfortunes that can befall an Army—how often have I lamented it this Campaign."

Reed and Lee had reason to complain, for by November 1776 Washington had nearly lost the war several times over. His performance on the battlefield, in truth, had been practically incompetent. On Long Island and at White Plains, his attackers—strangers to the country—had known the ground better than he. This failure to reconnoiter battlefields adequately, an elementary fault, would plague his military career again and again. Washington had shown other faults, too. In planning the defense of New York City, he was overconfident when he should have been careful. At Fort Washington, he was humble when he should have been bold. Only at Harlem Heights, where he alertly and creatively responded to a rash enemy advance, did he get his timing right. It was a minor affair that demonstrated Washington's talent for quick turnarounds. He would put that talent to more effective use at Trenton in December.

As if the loss of Fort Washington were not enough, the commander-in-chief now found himself in a situation similar to the one he had experienced the year before. His army was less than six weeks away from total dissolution. The enlistments of 2,000 men expired on December 1st. All the rest were due to go home a month later.

Hoping to cover as much of the country as possible after the battle at White Plains, Washington had dispersed his 14,000 troops in contingents at Mount Castle, Peekskill, Hackensack, Haverstraw, and Fort Lee. Now, somehow, he would have to bring them together again. Unfortunately Howe, who had allowed Washington to escape from many tight situations before, now chose to pursue the defeated Americans. On November 20th, he ordered Cornwallis to cross the Hudson and take Fort Lee. Washington declared Fort Lee "of no importance" after the fall of its sister fort across the river, but he had not yet evacuated it when the British arrived. The 2,000-man garrison escaped just in time, but left behind almost all of their equipment.

Leaving a rear guard at Hackensack, Washington withdrew the rest of this portion of his army, about three thousand "broken & dispirited" men, to Newark. He then asked Lee, who commanded at Mount Castle, to bring his detachment down to New Jersey; but Lee, taking advantage of the hesitant language of Washington's request, refused to budge. Cornwallis meanwhile continued his advance, entering Newark on November 28th as Washington retreated to New Brunswick and absorbed a tiny but welcome detachment of 1,200 men.

With the retreat in full swing, panic spread throughout the region. "The people here have been horridly frightened," delegate William Hooper wrote from Philadelphia to a friend. "The [Pennsylvania] Council of Safety a set of water Gruel Sons of B——s told the people a damned Lie 'that they had certain information that 100 Ships had left Sandyhook for this City'—the people at first believed & trembled, the tories grinned." Atrocity stories of rapes and other depredations committed by enemy soldiers in New Jersey gained wide circulation and led many families to take to the roads as refugees.

Washington's friend William Gordon later recounted a conversation between Joseph Reed and the commander-in-chief that may have taken place around this time. If genuine, the conversation showed Washington in one of his darkest moods. He asked:

"Should we retreat to the back parts of Pennsylvania, will the Pennsylvanians support us?"

"If the lower counties are subdued and given up, the back counties will do the same," Reed replied.

Washington touched a hand to his throat. "My neck does not feel as though it was made for a halter," he said grimly. "We must retire to Augusta County in Virginia. Numbers will be obliged to repair to us for safety and we must try what we can do in carrying on a predatory war, and, if overpowered, we must cross the Alleghany Mountains."

More immediately, Washington wanted to put the Delaware River between himself and his pursuers—and to make sure they could not follow. He therefore ordered every available boat on the Delaware to be gathered at Trenton "for the purpose of Carrying over the Troops & Baggage in [the] most expeditious Manner." All the boats from there to seventy miles upstream were seized, burnt, or taken to the Pennsylvania shore.

Washington entered Princeton on December 2nd, and hurried on to Trenton the following day. Close behind, Cornwallis entered New Brunswick. One quick march would have brought him plunging into the American rear. Instead, Howe inexplicably called yet another halt, and Cornwallis's men spent three and a half days "standing quietly" while their opponents drifted farther out of reach. By December 7th, most of the American baggage had safely crossed the Delaware.

At Princeton, Washington had left a rear guard of 1,200 Continentals, whose situation was next to hopeless. Every day they waited bleakly for the ravenous British lion to consume them. But the lion had fallen asleep. Washington, with perhaps more valor than sense, stopped retreating, reversed direction, and went to see if he could wake it. "Nothing but necessity obliged me to retire before the Enemy, & leave so much of the Jerseys unprotected," he told Hancock. "I conceive it my duty, and," he added revealingly, "it corresponds with my Inclination to make head against them so soon as there shall be the least probability of doing it with propriety." He spurned the opportunity to retreat. "I shall now . . . face about with such Troops as are here fit for service, and march back to Princeton and there govern myself by circumstances and the movements of Genl Lee." He was halfway to Princeton when the British lion stirred.

It was December 7, 1776, a day that should have marked the end of Washington and his little army. The American rear guard fled on first notice of the renewed British advance, but Washington did not learn of it until he was already several miles east of Trenton. He ordered his column back, but for several critical hours it straggled across miles of open country, easy pickings for a determined pursuer. But the British advanced languidly. "The rebels were always barely ahead of us," Howe's aide wrote in his diary. "Since General Howe was with the vanguard, we advanced very slowly, and the rebels had time to withdraw step by step without being engaged." The retreat across the Delaware began that night.

Howe entered Trenton at 2:00 P.M. on December 8th. "Some inhabitants came running toward us," his aide recalled, "urging us to march through the town in a hurry so we could capture many of the enemy who were just embarking in boats and were about to cross." Howe refrained from giving Washington one last kick. Fearing a trap—at least, that is what he told his aide—Howe halted his troops on the outskirts of Trenton while the last American boats pushed off shore. "Here we remained in the woods," an American lieutenant wrote dismally from the west bank of the Delaware, "having neither blankets nor tents." By all appearances the campaign of 1776 was over.

REDEMPTION

Trenton; December 1776

ON DECEMBER 11, 1776, a nervous Congress assembled at the State House in Philadelphia. The delegates began work by considering a proposal to declare a day of prayer and fasting and urge "repentance and reformation" on the officers of the Continental Army, who would be told to refrain from all "profane swearing" and other immorality at this trying time. The proposal was piously approved and published. The delegates then turned their attention to "a false and malicious report . . . spread by the enemies of America that the Congress was about to disperse." Outraged, they ordered Washington "to contradict the said scandalous report in general orders, this Congress having a better opinion of the spirit and vigour of the army and the good people of these states than to suppose it can be necessary to disperse." Adjourning, they then scurried off to their respective lodgings, where many of them had already packed their belongings in readiness for a quick departure. The next day, after solemnly granting Washington "full power" to carry on the war, Congress abandoned Philadelphia for Baltimore. As the delegates' carriages rattled southward, the previous morning's resolution denying their intention to disperse was quietly struck from the records.

The crisis of December 1776 was less military than psychological. Rather, it was military *because* it was psychological. In material terms, the Americans were not so bad off as they seemed. New York was lost, and on December 7th a British force occupied Newport, Rhode Island. But Boston was free, and the upper Hudson remained closed to British shipping. Good clothes, muskets, and cannon were hard to come by, but young men remained plentiful enough to fill the gaps left by Long Island and Fort Washington. The problem was getting them away from their firesides and into uniform. For, ultimately, the significance of the military defeats of 1776 lay not in blood, territory, and treasure, but in their effect on the Americans' belief in ultimate victory.

These were halcyon days for the loyalists. Theirs now looked like the faster horse in the race, and thousands of pragmatic farmers and tradesmen in the middle states bet on it when Howe offered pardon in exchange for allegiance to the king. Howe informed Germain on December 20th that New Jersey was in "almost general submission." All the state governments in the mid-Atlantic region were losing popularity and finding it difficult to garner enough financial and political support to stay afloat.

Patriotic writers and speakers tried their best to stem the tide of disaffection. Thomas Paine declared in his famous first installment of *The American Crisis* that "these are the times that try men's souls" and tried to convince the people not to despair. Congress, talking a good fight, issued a parting "why we fight" manifesto "to the People in general, and particularly to the Inhabitants of Pennsylvania and the adjacent States" over its shoulder as it left Philadelphia. Exploiting the reputation of Howe's "foreign mercenaries, who, without feeling, indulge themselves in rapine and bloodshed," the fleeing delegates publicized German and British atrocities against civilians in New Jersey. Newspapers went further, inflating genuine episodes of cruelty and misconduct into lurid, improbable crimes, especially against women and children.

Defections continued despite efforts to rally the public and the troops, and even the most optimistic patriots began speaking of their cause with an air of finality. "I do not regret the Part I have taken in a Cause so just and interesting to Mankind," Sam Adams wrote to his wife on December 9th, "[but] I must confess it chagrins me greatly to find it so illy supported by the People of Pennsylvania and the Jerseys. They seem to me to be determined to give it up—but I trust that my dear New England will maintain it at the Expence of every thing dear to them in this Life." Other patriots admitted that they "looked upon the contest as near its close, and considered ourselves a vanquished people." Washington warned cousin Lund that "matters to my view, but this I say in confidence to you, as a friend, wears so unfavourable an aspect (not that I apprehend half so much danger from Howes Army, as from the disaffection of the three States of New York, Jersey & Pensylvania) that I would look forward to unfavorable Events, & prepare Accordingly in such a manner however as to give no alarm or suspicion to any one." As a discreet preliminary, he had all of his private papers removed from Mount Vernon and sent into the mountains of western Virginia.

—

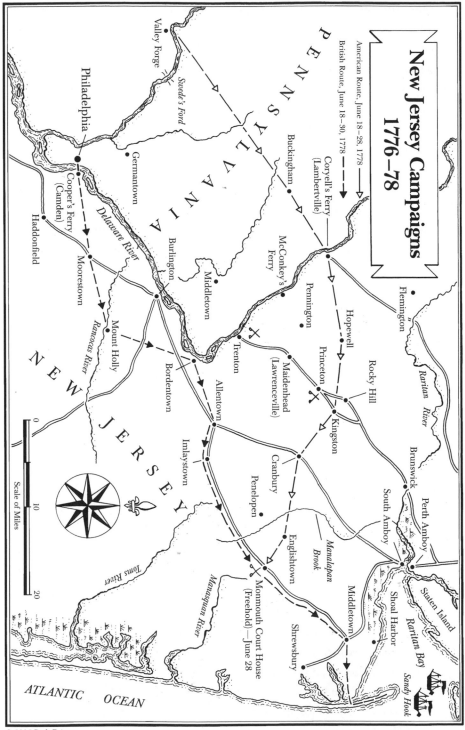

New Jersey Campaigns 1776–78

American Route, June 18–28, 1778
British Route, June 18–30, 1778

PENNSYLVANIA

Valley Forge

Swede's Ford

Philadelphia

Germantown

Cooper's Ferry (Camden)

Haddonfield

Delaware River

Moorestown

Rancocas River

Mount Holly

Burlington

Middletown

Buckingham

Coryell's Ferry (Lambertville)

McConkey's Ferry

Pennington

Hopewell

Flemington

Trenton

Maidenhead (Lawrenceville)

Princeton

Rocky Hill

Raritan River

Bordentown

Allentown

Kingston

Cranbury

Penelopen

Brunswick

South Amboy

Perth Amboy

NEW JERSEY

Imlaystown

Englishtown

Manalapan Brook

Staten Island

Scale of Miles

0

10

20

Toms River

Manasquan River

Monmouth Court House (Freehold) — June 28

Shrewsbury

Middletown

Shoal Harbor

Raritan Bay

Sandy Hook

ATLANTIC OCEAN

© 2005 Rick Britton

"We find Sir," Washington wrote Hancock on December 20th from his headquarters at Trenton Falls, "that the Enemy are daily gathering strength from the disaffected; This strength, like a Snowball by rolling, will increase, unless some means can be devised to check effectually, the progress of the Enemy's Arms." Only a military victory, in other words, would convince the timid that the war was winnable. Thanks to Congress, however, that rather obvious point was well on the way to becoming moot. In less than two weeks, most of the army again was due to evaporate.

One of the most fundamental lessons of the winter of 1775–76 concerned the system of yearly Continental enlistments, which threatened to leave the country undefended every time a new army had to be recruited. Washington learned the lesson immediately and spent a year trying to convince the politicians to enlist troops for the duration of the war. Still expecting a short war and fearful of creating a standing army, the delegates refused to reconsider. The Continentals recruited for 1776 agreed to serve for a term of no longer than one year. Most of them would quit the army on New Year's Day 1777.

In September 1776 Congress finally resolved to recruit a new army of eighty-eight regiments, consisting of men now enlisted "to serve during the present war" instead of for just a year. In theory, this force would appear as soon as the old one disbanded; but, as Washington had frequently warned, recruiting was a difficult process, complicated by factors that the politicians failed to consider. A single call would not bring recruits to the colors. They needed convincing. Congress dreamed of an army of idealists, but offered such pathetic salaries that prospective volunteers spurned Continental recruiters in favor of the militia.

For the average farmer or town-dweller, the militia offered a good deal. For a state bounty comparable to that offered by Congress he could join the militia for six weeks, and be home for planting or the harvest. Besides, Continental soldiers tended to end up in the front lines; militia service was considered safer. So long as Congress refused to offer a better choice, therefore, the regular army would remain a mere shell. Washington's precious columns of Continentals might even disappear altogether, to be replaced by seething throngs of militia—an unhappy prospect indeed! They "come in," he complained, "you can not tell how—go, you cannot tell when—and act, you cannot tell where—consume your provisions—exhaust your Stores, and leave you at last at a critical moment." How could he fight with such creatures?

Washington warned and instructed Congress, but all his letters seemed to disappear into a bottomless pit of shady, short-lived committees and windy politicians. Although he trusted John Hancock, the president of Congress, Washington had little confidence in the delegates' ability to act swiftly and in concert. In the final calculation, he alone could act decisively. In representing his concerns about Congress to Hancock, of course, Washington had to explain himself diplomatically. The distance from camp to Baltimore offered a reliable hook. If "we have to provide in this short interval and make these great & arduous preparations," he wrote, and "every matter that in its nature is self evident, is to be referred to Congress, at the distance of 130 or 40 miles, so much time must necessarily elapse as to defeat the end in view." He therefore asked for temporary freedom from political oversight, displacing Congress as the supreme arbiter of both military and civilian affairs within his army's zone of operations.

On December 12th, Congress gave him "full power to order and direct all things relative to the department, and to the operations of war" until the delegates revoked it. It was a useful resolution, and he employed it to offer incentives for reenlistment and Continental recruiting that normally lay outside his province. But Washington—backed by Greene, who wrote a vociferous letter to Congress on his behalf—also hoped for something more specific. He wanted the right to negotiate with departing soldiers on his own accord, offering them any money he thought necessary to keep them in uniform after New Years' Day. He asked to raise new infantry regiments in addition to cavalry, artillery, and engineers, appointing the officers and determining their rates of pay. Washington furthermore wished to appoint, promote, demote, or relieve every officer under the rank of brigadier general in the entire army. Nor did he limit himself to a military mandate. Authority to imprison suspected loyalists or anyone who refused to supply the army, he hinted, would be most welcome.

Washington insisted that he had "no lust after power"; but to a patriot, his suggestions verged on the blasphemous. Greene backed up the commander-in-chief by pledging to Hancock that "I can see no Evil nor Danger to the States in delagating such Powers to the General, reserving to yourselves the Right of Confirming or repealing the Measures . . . and I can assure you that the General will not exceed his Powers altho' he may sacrifice the Cause. There never was a man who might be more safely trusted nor a Time when there was a louder Call." Yet suspicions remained that Washington was taking the first steps toward dictatorship.

Washington's proposals seemed to put him within easy reach of absolute power. The suggestion that he appoint most of his officers appeared especially dangerous, since Congress would thereby lose much of its control over the army. Officers indebted to the commander-in-chief for their pay and position might obey him before anyone else. What Greene called "a discretionary Power to punish the disaffected" was risky, too. Loosely interpreted, it could give Washington dominion over every man in America. As Congress deliberated his request, the Revolution seemed nearing an end in spirit if not in fact.

General James Grant's spies sent him regular reports on the problems plaguing the American army. One report indicated, accurately, that the Americans were "scarce of Provisions—particularly Flour—not above six thousand Bushells of Wheat—about three Days Salt Provisions—ill clothed—in want of Shoes & Stockings & Blankets[.] Part of Washingtons Life Guards gone the rest to follow when their time is out—Lees Army determined not to serve after the later end of this Month when their time is expired." Washington's army was shriveling in numbers, equipment, and the will to fight.

The Americans also had lost what the British believed to be their only good general. On December 13th, a detachment of seventy British cavalry swooped upon Charles Lee at an isolated tavern near Basking Ridge, New Jersey. For weeks he had disobeyed Washington's orders to follow him across the Delaware, waiting instead for an opportunity to gain glory and possibly even displace his chief by attacking the British in New Jersey. Now, as Lee continued to dally, he became separated from the main body of his troops. He had just finished writing Gates that he thought "a certain great man is most damnably deficient" when he looked out the window to see the redcoats galloping to his door. Easily subduing Lee's small guard detachment, the horsemen captured the general and spirited him off to New York City.

"Victoria! We have captured General Lee, the only rebel general whom we had cause to fear," Howe's aide crowed in his diary. A leader of Lee's military experience seemed irreplaceable, and Howe's more aggressive officers wanted to take advantage of Lee's capture to press the offensive, take Philadelphia, and end the war by Christmas. The Delaware River barrier would disappear when the river became solid with ice, which had already started spreading. Alternately, a few dozen boats might enable the British to cross the river before it froze.

But Howe once again declined to administer the *coup de grâce*. Why risk his dying quarry's claws, he may have thought, when he could await the spring's melting snow to reveal its corpse? The day after Lee's capture, Howe declared an official end to the campaign of 1776 and sent the army into winter quarters. He retired to Manhattan, Cornwallis prepared to sail for England to tend to his ill wife, and General James Grant, based at New Brunswick, took command of New Jersey. The troops settled into a ninety-mile chain of cantonments, or fortified camps, at Staten Island, Amboy, New Brunswick, Princeton, Bordentown, and Trenton. Posting them so close to the American army was slightly unorthodox, and would have been deemed too risky against a European adversary; but Howe, who had chosen the posts upon Cornwallis's advice, saw nothing to fear from his presumably broken adversary. The cantonments, he assured Germain, "will be in perfect security."

The Americans did not dare dream of another respite. Many civilians had already evacuated Philadelphia along with Congress. Others, feeling their backs to the wall, wanted to deal one last blow to the enemy. "We are all of Opinion my dear General," now Adjutant General Joseph Reed prodded Washington, "that something must be attempted to revive our expiring Credit. . . . [E]ven a Failure cannot be more fatal than to remain in our present Situation in short some Enterprize must be undertaken in our present Circumstances or we must give up the Cause."

Washington actually had considered an attack as early as December 14th, when he wrote Connecticut governor Jonathan Trumbull, Sr., that he hoped to "attempt a stroke upon the Forces of the Enemy, who lay a good deal scattered, and to all appearance, in a state of security. A lucky blow in this Quarter would be fatal to them, and would most certainly raise the spirits of the People, which are quite sunk by our late misfortunes." Unfortunately, his army was just too small for a major assault, but by pushing some small detachments of militia across the river north and south of Trenton he was able to contest control of some parts of the countryside and keep the enemy from assuming control of the river crossings.

A larger offensive became possible only after the 20th, when General John Sullivan, exchanged since his capture on Long Island, herded Lee's remnant of 2,000 men through a snowstorm and into camp. Washington watched them stumble past and disgustedly pronounced them fit only for the hospital. But with other reinforcements, including 600 Continentals brought from the north by Horatio Gates on the 22nd, 1,000 Philadelphia militia, and a regiment of German settlers from Maryland and Pennsylvania, they brought his army's total strength to 6,000 men.

For a brief period, then—less than two weeks—Washington would command a wretched but usable military force. His self-proclaimed defensive strategy dictated that he use it with caution. If it were destroyed, the British could walk nearly unopposed over every part of America south of the Hudson and prevent the rebellion from ever getting back on its feet. On the other hand, a victory might set Howe back on his heels before his troops could burst across the Delaware's ice into Pennsylvania, and thus gain time for Washington and Congress to build a new army—or so it seemed to the Americans, who refused to believe that Howe had entered winter quarters.

On December 22nd, Washington's senior generals and their aides slogged through deep snow to a top-secret council of war at headquarters. One of them, apparently an aide, was a British spy; and he listened carefully as the commander-in-chief spoke to the assembled officers. The enemy looked temptingly weak in New Jersey, Washington declared. On the extreme left at Bordentown, Colonel Carl von Donop commanded a brigade of 1,500 of the hated Germans and a crack regiment of Scottish Highlanders. To his right at Trenton, Colonel Johann Rall led another brigade of about equal size, composed of the Rall, Lossburg, and Knyphausen regiments. Twelve miles farther north—a long way over snowy ground—General Alexander Leslie led two battalions of British light infantry and three troops of dragoons at Princeton. Leslie's closest support was another fifteen miles northeast at Grant's headquarters, New Brunswick.

Each enemy post was unusually isolated and lacked logistical support from the countryside. The militias so far held the upper hand in the war of patrols, keeping the Germans bottled up in their garrisons, intercepting couriers, and screening the Delaware River ferries from enemy scouts. The Continental Army therefore might cross the Delaware and move through New Jersey undetected, surrounding the German and British cantonments and defeating them in detail. Before Grant had a chance to react, the Americans would be safely back in Pennsylvania.

Washington finished speaking, and the British spy waited for the officers to respond. If they came to a decision, he could report it to General Grant. But although Stirling spoke in favor of the proposal, the rest of the officers equivocated and the meeting broke up without resolution. The spy then scurried off to New Brunswick with an inconclusive report, unaware that the council's final decision would be made in more secure surroundings later that night. And there the attack was approved. "Christmas day at Night, one hour before day," Washington confided to Joseph Reed on the 23rd, "is the time fixed upon for our Attempt upon Trenton. For heaven's sake keep this to yourself, as the discovery of it may prove fatal to us."

Formed in haste, the attack plan showed surprising subtlety; such subtlety, in fact, that it would have tested the abilities of rested, well-equipped, and professional troops. Washington proposed advancing in four columns, with Trenton as the first target. The largest column, comprising 2,400 troops and eighteen artillery pieces, would march under his personal command, crossing the Delaware eight miles north of Trenton, at McConkey's Ferry. It would then turn right and surround the Germans to the north and east. At Trenton itself, Brigadier General James Ewing was ordered to take 600 militiamen across the river and seize the Assunpink Bridge, on the southern edge of town, thus denying Rall his last route of escape. Colonel John Cadwalader would cross with 1,500 Pennsylvania militiamen and a weak brigade of 900 New England Continentals at Bristol, attacking Donop and preventing him from giving support to Colonel Rall. Finally, Washington asked General Israel Putnam—whose responsibilities had declined since his glory days at Bunker Hill—to lead a body of militia that he had been trying to gather in Philadelphia into New Jersey behind Cadwalader. Putnam's men would function either as a reserve or, if possible, an independent striking force.

Washington may have suspected that this dangerous plan would end in disaster. Never, as Benjamin Rush saw when he visited headquarters on the morning of Christmas Eve, had his nerves troubled him more. "He appeared much depressed," Rush later remembered, "and lamented the ragged and dissolving state of his army in affecting terms. I gave him assurance of the disposition of Congress to support him, under his present difficulties and distresses. While I was talking to him, I observed him to play with his pen and ink upon several pieces of paper. One of them by accident fell upon the floor near my feet. I was struck with the inscription upon it. It was 'Victory or Death.' " In keeping with the desperate nature of the coming attack, Washington had selected the words as the sentinels' passwords for Christmas night.

—

Christmas morning dawned clear and cold, with temperatures hovering just below freezing. Pennsylvania's dirt roads, kept brown and slushy by the passage of wagons and troops, dissected snow-covered fields and woods. No Christmas tree decorated the American camp—that tradition had yet to cross the Atlantic from Germany. Nor was there much time for celebration of any sort. The troops were too busy cleaning weapons, packing new issues of flints and cartridges, wrapping bare feet in tattered cloth, and cooking three days' provisions of salt pork. For enemy cannon that needed to be destroyed in a hurry, the men brought spikes to apply to the guns' touch holes and hammers to drive them in; they also coiled drag ropes in case there was time to carry them off, and brought torches to burn any houses the Germans tried to fortify. At the riverside, boatmen spent the day readying their vessels for the crossing.

Adam Stephen, Washington's tempestuous old comrade from the French and Indian War, had recently been appointed brigadier general and would lead the first brigade of the main attack force. His brigade left McConkey's Ferry early that morning, then joined two more brigades under Stirling and General Hugh Mercer to form Greene's second division, the "left wing of the Army." On the right, Sullivan commanded the first division, consisting of three brigades under Generals Arthur St. Clair, Paul Dudley Sargent, and John Glover. Another brigade under the Frenchman Matthias-Alexis la Rochefermoy marched independently, and Stirling's and St. Clair's brigades were designated reserves. Colonel Henry Knox led the artillery and was given command of the embarkation. The troops paraded one mile from the ferry at 4:00 P.M. and then headed for the boats.

Their march had hardly commenced before cold wind started blowing in gusts from the northeast. Lashes of icy rain followed, and eventually sleet and snow that soaked through the soldiers' rags and buried their bloody footprints. "It is fearfully cold and raw and a snow-storm setting in," an officer wrote in his diary at 6:00 P.M. "The wind is northeast and beats in the faces of the men. It will be a terrible night for the soldiers who have no shoes. Some of them have tied old rags around their feet; others are barefoot, but I have not heard a man complain." Washington had warned them to maintain "a profound silence" and promised any man who broke ranks to expect instant death. There was no point in complaining, anyway, Massachusetts fifer John Greenwood recollected, "for it was all the same owing to the impossibility of being in a worse situation than their present one, and therefore the men always liked to be kept moving in expectation of bettering themselves."

At the Delaware riverside, the embarkation quickly ran into difficulties. "Troops began to cross about sunset," St. Clair's aide James Wilkinson remembered, "but the force of the current, the sharpness of the frost, the darkness of the night, the ice . . . and a high wind rendered the passage of the river extremely difficult." Ice floes slammed into the bulky, sixty-foot-long Durham boats as the oarsmen—Marblehead natives from Glover's Fourteenth Continental Regiment—struggled to paddle them across the water. From shore, Knox directed operations in "a deep bass heard above the crash of the ice which filled the river," fretting lest the overloaded transports carrying his artillery capsize. Washington, who crossed on one of the first boats and stood "wrapped in his cloak . . . calm and collected, but very determined," watched each man step ashore. The last soldiers debarked at about 3:00 A.M., about three hours behind schedule.

The pincers on Trenton, meanwhile, had lost a prong. Putnam had sent word late the previous evening that "the shortness of time and the unprovided state of the militia" would not permit him to leave Philadelphia. Cadwalader, who was supposed to cross around Bristol, found the passage too dangerous, and moved six miles away to Dunk's Ferry. There he succeeded in getting 600 men across by ordering them to debark on the ice that spread over a hundred yards from the Jersey shore, but because of his inability to support them with artillery he pulled them back at 4:00 A.M. "I imagine the badness of the night must have prevented you from passing as you intended," he wrote Washington as he marched his "wet and very cold" men back to Bristol. And at Trenton, Ewing struggled all night to cross the river with his 600 militiamen before admitting failure.

Washington permitted his troops to warm themselves in front of bonfires, presumably on the assumption that no enemy scouts could see the light they cast in the storm. At 4:00 A.M. his troops formed into column and began marching down the Bear Tavern Road. A scouting party of forty men under two captains, one of them the commander-in-chief's cousin William Washington, led the way with orders to capture anyone they saw, soldier and civilian alike. Greene's division came next, with Stephen's brigade in the lead. Rochefermoy's brigade marched between Greene and Sullivan's first division, which took up the rear.

The weather continued to be horrendous, and torches that the troops had wedged into wagon harnesses and field pieces "sparkled & blazed in the Storm all night." The soldiers groped ahead in mute urgency. There were nine miles to Trenton, which they had been scheduled to reach at dawn. Halfway there, the two divisions split and continued to Trenton on parallel roads. Sullivan took the right along River Road, and Washington accompanied Greene and Knox's artillery on Pennington Road to the left. Just outside Trenton, Rochefermoy's brigade filed off from Greene's column to the left, cutting Princeton Road. Together, Sullivan, Greene, and Rochefermoy thus blocked every road leading out of town to the north.

"About day light [7:20 A.M.] a halt was made at which time his Excellency & Aids came near to front on the Side of the path where the Soldiers Stood," Connecticut soldier Elisha Bostwick remembered. "I heard his Excellency as he was comeing on Speaking to & Encourageing the Soldiers. The words he Spoke as he pass'd by where I stood & in my hearing were these [']Soldiers keep by your officers for Gods Sake keep by your officers[,'] Spoke in a deep & Solemn voice[.]" Tall, grave, and erect in the saddle, Washington maintained an inspiring dignity amid the storm's shrieking wind; but his bearing faltered when "passing a Slanting Slippery bank his excellencys horse['s] hind feet both slip'd from under him." The soldiers gasped as their leader lurched in the saddle, nearly pitching headlong into the mud; but Washington quickly "Siez'd his horses Mane & the horse recovered."

A mixture of anger and fear gripped the Americans as they prepared to face "the damn Hessians." Colonel Rall's troops, who had shown such bravery under fire at White Plains and Fort Washington, made imposing adversaries. With their brass hats, white or straw-colored breeches, and blue coats with red, black, or orange trim, the Germans looked more intimidating than foolish to eighteenth-century eyes. They also treated prisoners and civilians with conspicuous cruelty. The Americans all looked to them like "black Negroes and yellow dogs," and they often failed to distinguish between loyalists and rebels. Contemptible as they may have seemed to Rall's men, however, the militiamen had conducted pinprick raids for several nights running, leaving the Germans sleepless, tense, and grumbling as they endured an exhausting cycle of guard duty, picket duty, and patrols.

The Germans at Trenton also had little affection for or confidence in their commander, Colonel Johann Rall, who lacked the ruthlessness that they prized. He was simply too nice, his men thought, to be a good military leader.

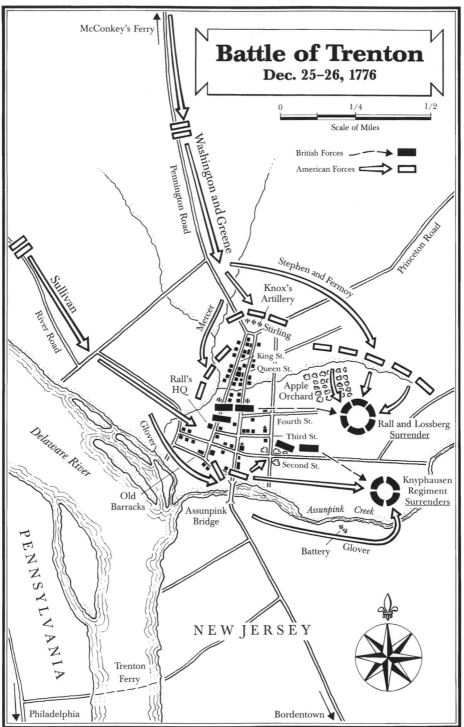

"His love of life was too great," one of his officers complained. "A thought came to him, then another, so that he could not settle on a firm decision. . . . He was generous, magnanimous, hospitable, and polite to everyone; never groveling before his superiors but indulgent with his subordinates. To his servants he was more a friend than a master." Unlike Washington, he avoided hard work and showed no concern for his troops' lodging, clothing, or ammunition. He preferred to spend his days relaxing, often following his regimental band in musical processions around Trenton's sleepy streets.

Rall responded to word of an impending attack on his post in the same casual manner. On the 24th, at 11:00 P.M., the British spy who had attended the American council of war two days earlier reported to Grant that Washington was mulling an attack on Trenton and Princeton. "I own I did not think them equal to the attempt," Grant later wrote. "However I was determined not to fall into the Error of dispising the Enemy and therefore sent a Light Dragoon immediatly to Genl Leslie & Col. Donop to inform them of the Rebells intention." Grant wrote Leslie that "I do not believe he will attempt it, but be assured that my information is undoubtedly true, so I need not advise you to be upon your guard." Leslie then forwarded the letter to Donop, and Rall received a copy at 5:00 P.M. on Christmas Day. But Rall dismissed the warning and responded to a suggestion that he call yet another alarm with a profane oath. "Let them come," he cried. "Why defenses? We will go at them with the bayonet."

The German troops probably regarded those as the most sensible words they had heard from their commander in days. Unfortunately, their hopes for a restful evening were promptly dashed. That evening, some American scouts fired at Rall's sentries and then fled, forcing the enraged Germans to drag cannon through woods and snowdrifts in fruitless pursuit. The troops plodded back into Trenton cranky and cold, grumbling about endless false alarms and privately resolving not to respond so quickly next time. Patrols sent that night to reconnoiter along the roads from Trenton did their work halfheartedly. The storm that began that night made them yearn for their bunks, and a sympathetic officer cancelled the usual predawn patrols. Rall retired to drink and play cards. Surely even the Americans would not be so obtuse as to venture out in such weather!

The Battle of Trenton began at about 8:00 A.M. on December 26th, under leaden skies dropping steady sleet and rain. Greene's division began the attack from a position 500 yards from the German outposts, and Sullivan ordered his troops to advance a few minutes later. The two divisions showed remarkable coordination as they chased away the surprised sentries and then descended on Trenton.

Lieutenant Andreas Wiederhold of the Knyphausen Regiment commanded an outpost of seventeen men who faced the first assault down Pennington Road. An hour after sunrise, long after his morning patrols had returned and reported everything quiet, he was suddenly attacked by Americans emerging from nearby woods. "If I had not stepped out of the picket hut and seen the enemy," he recalled, "they would possibly have been upon me before I could take up arms because my guards were not alert enough because it was a holiday." Startled but assuming that the attacking force was just a skirmishing party, Wiederhold and his seventeen men "awaited the enemy with fortitude." But as battalion after battalion of Americans debouched from the woods, he realized that this was no militia raid and ordered a hasty withdrawal.

The Germans were dazed and tired, but there is no truth to the legend claiming that they were helplessly drunk. They "behaved very well," Washington told Congress, "keeping up a constant retreating fire from behind houses." Had their commanders not failed them by refusing to order a proper watch, they might well have repulsed Washington's ragtag soldiers, who had trouble keeping formation as they advanced.

Virginia major George Johnston saw the attack begin from the other side of the lines, and remembered Washington's conduct with pride. "Our noble countryman . . . at the head of the Virginia Brigades, exposed to the utmost danger, bid us follow," he wrote. "We cheerfully did so in a long trot, till he ordered us to form, that the cannon might play. [We] pursued to the very middle of the Town, where the whole Body of the Enemy, drawn up in a solid column, kept up a heavy fire with Cannon and Muskets, till our Cannon"—which Knox brought forward with brilliant alacrity—"threw them in confusion."

"We forc'd & enter'd the Town with them pell-mell," Knox wrote his wife two days later, "& here succeeded a scene of war of Which I had often Conceived but never saw before." Knox's cannon scattered the Germans "in the twinkling of an eye" when they tried to form in the streets, and their subsequent terror and confusion reminded him of "that which Will be when the last Trump shall sound." Jaegers took cover behind houses, wagons, and anything else they could find; but the Continentals easily outflanked and dislodged them. Within minutes, Germans had begun streaming out of Trenton and into open fields to the south and east.

Rall was overwhelmed and became lost in the confusion. His adjutant had waked him with difficulty, calling at his door three times. Hurriedly buttoning his uniform and plunging into the street, Rall tried to form his groggy troops in the center of town. The Americans fell upon them quickly. Two German artillery pieces fired a few shots and then had to be abandoned; two more became inoperable because of burnt-out touch pans. Rall then assembled the remains of his own and the Lossburg Regiment, and ordered them to follow the fugitives who had fled east into a field and apple orchard outside of town. There he finally formed them successfully to the accompaniment of his military band, while the Knyphausen Regiment pulled itself together southeast of the town. Rall considered retreating down the Princeton Road, but Washington's prescience in sending Rochefermoy in that direction paid off when the German commander found himself blocked.

By this time, Sullivan's division had come into Trenton from the west. Glover's and Sargent's brigades took the bridge that Ewing's militia force had been unable to reach, faced north, and cut off the last obvious route of retreat. The Germans were surrounded, leaving Rall at a loss. Unwilling to surrender, he could think of nothing to do except try to retake Trenton. "He called to his regiment then," Wiederhold later wrote, "before mounting his horse. 'Forward march! Advance! Advance!' and staggered back and forth without knowing what he was doing."

Wiederhold looked on incredulously as Rall attempted to lead his troops, without artillery support, against an entrenched force five times their number. Washington had not let his victorious troops relax their vigilance, and as soon as he saw the enemy preparations he ordered them into positions from where they could fire on the German front and flank. Rall's soldiers showed the same mute courage that they had demonstrated at Fort Washington, marching to the steady beat of their drummers, but the sleet ruined their cartridges and prevented their guns from firing properly. As they struggled forward, Rall, who was conspicuously mounted on his horse, shuddered and pitched forward, his body pierced by two musket balls. His regiment, which had been leading the attack, then turned and fled through the following Lossburgers "like a swarm of bees." The officers tried to lead their men back to the apple orchard, only to find Rochefermoy's brigade marching toward them from that direction, shouting in German and English for the panicked Germans to surrender.

The wholesale capitulation of the German brigade followed within minutes. The Rall and Lossburg regiments threw up their hands first, and seeing it, the Knyphausen Regiment surrendered, too. They had lost twenty-two men killed—including Rall, to whom Washington offered consolation before he died—and eighty-four wounded. Over 650 Germans escaped through the loose American perimeter by darting into woods or braving the icy waters of Assunpink Creek, but 893 officers and enlisted men were taken captive. American losses were two killed and four slightly wounded, among the latter Captain William Washington.

Many of the prisoners were the same men who had roughed up Fort Washington's captured garrison. The American soldiers had also heard plenty of tales about German looting, murder, and rapes in New Jersey. But Washington, implored by the dying Rall to treat his men well, permitted no reprisals. The prisoners were gathered up and divested of watches and other trinkets. Washington then sent them back across the Delaware River to what one angry prisoner complained was a "rotten prison" near Philadelphia, where they lived on bread "shaken down out of a basket from above into the bare courtyard and onto the snow." Many Americans thought that was better than the Germans deserved.

Washington invited several German prisoners to dinner before they departed for prison or parole. He "received us very politely," one officer wrote, "but we understood very little of what he said because he spoke nothing but English—a language which at that time none of us handled well." They regarded the American commander-in-chief curiously. "In the face of this man nothing of the great man showed for which he would be noted," a German remembered. "His eyes have no fire, but a slight smile in his expression when he spoke inspired love and respect." Another officer recalled Washington as "a polite and refined man, [who] seldom speaks, and has a cunning physiognomy. He is not especially tall"—the Germans prided themselves on their height—"but also not short, but rather of middle height with a good body."

In American eyes he looked taller than that, having grown overnight to something like seven feet tall. His army's size had likewise doubled by reputation alone. Nor did the redcoats seem as frightening as they had a few weeks before. "I now think that Britain will make a contemptible figure in

America & Europe," Samuel Adams wrote to a friend. Yesterday's defeatists complacently predicted a campaign to "drive the Enemy back to New York" and spoke of winning the war. Patriots dreamed again of the day when they could say "farewell the glory of England."

The day after Trenton, though before receiving news of the battle, Congress invested Washington with broad civil authority. For a period of six months, or "unless sooner determined by Congress," he could fix bounties, appoint and discharge officers below the rank of brigadier general, determine systems of promotion, fix rates of pay, and raise sixteen additional regiments of infantry, three regiments of artillery, three thousand cavalry, and a "Corps of Engineers." Washington was also given the right "to take where-ever he may be, whatever he may want for the Use of the Army, if the Inhabitants will not sell it, allowing a reasonable Price for the same; [and] to arrest and Confine Persons who refuse to take the Continental Currency, or are otherwise disaffected to the American Cause," for trial by civilian courts.

Congress made clear that it still ran the country, and even as it granted these powers to Washington it imposed restrictions that would have made it difficult for him to usurp control. Yet although historians downplay Washington's authority in retrospect, to contemporaries his position looked powerful indeed. "Genl. Washington," Captain Thomas Rodney of Delaware wrote in his diary, "is Dictator." For patriots rebelling against despotism and tyranny, the decision to award what *looked* like supreme authority to one man was psychologically difficult, in the extreme. They would not have done it for anyone else. Washington had earned their trust.

The dedication and brilliance that Washington had showed at Trenton, and his modest response to the praise subsequently lavished upon him, reinforced faith in his character and raised him in the public esteem. Even ardent patriots like Benjamin Rush and Sam Adams, naturally suspicious men and uncompromising defenders of individual liberty, now supported his augmented powers. "Happy it is for this Country," a congressional committee told Washington, "that the General of their Forces can safely be entrusted with the most unlimited Power & neither personal security, liberty or Property be in the least degree endangered nearby." To which he replied: "I shall constantly bear in Mind, that as the Sword was the last Resort for the preservation of our Liberties, so it ought to be the first thing laid aside, when those Liberties are firmly established."

Washington had gained the good opinion of his soldiers, and his popularity showed signs of encouraging recruitment for the new army. Yet December 1776 was nearly over, and the victors of Trenton yearned for home. Nothing, they swore, could make them stay. Asked by his commanding officer to reenlist for six weeks in exchange for twenty-six dollars and a promotion, fifer John Greenwood saucily responded that "I would not stay to be a colonel." He was sick of army life. Like many of his comrades, he "had the itch then so bad that my breeches stuck to my thighs, all the skin being off, and there were hundreds of vermin upon me, owing to a whole month's march and having been obliged, for the sake of keeping warm, to lie down at night among the soldiers who were huddled close together like hogs."

Washington knew that his men were miserable, but he also knew that without a follow-up victory, Trenton would have no strategic consequences whatsoever. He was not interested in symbolic victories. He wanted to drive the British out of New Jersey and completely change the terms on which the campaign of 1777 would be fought. To do that, he needed men. On December 27th, Washington assembled his tired, cold, and dirty troops for one last parade, stood before them, and asked them to stay and fight. He was approaching one of the most decisive moments of his military career.

11

PRINCETON

December 1776 – January 1777

IN THE DREARY light of dawn on December 26th, two companies of German jaegers foraged in the vicinity of Mount Holly, New Jersey. Months of practice had made their work routine, and Captain Johann Ewald habitually ignored the cries of the civilians whose property his soldiers plundered. "Both parties were occupied with driving off several hundred oxen, cows, pigs, and sheep," he wrote, "amidst the fervent wailings of the inhabitants, who followed us constantly, when a messenger appeared who delivered us orders to come back immediately and leave all the animals behind." The civilians who recovered their livestock after Ewald's hurried retreat were among the first beneficiaries of Washington's victory at Trenton.

Ewald's commander, Colonel Donop, was responsible for the cantonment at Bordentown, which included a brigade of Germans and the Scottish Black Watch Regiment. Being "extremely devoted to the fair sex," he had taken a few hundred of his troops twelve miles south to Mount Holly, where he courted an American widow while his men foraged. News of Trenton disrupted his amours and threw him into panic. If Washington followed up his victory by marching eight miles southeast to Crosswicks, he would cut Bordentown off. Donop reacted by sending orders for that town's garrison to withdraw southeast, and he galloped north with his own detachment for Princeton, "with the firm resolve to cut his way through at all costs." Ewald and 150 terrified soldiers were left alone at Mount Holly, where they hunkered down and threatened to burn the town if any vengeful civilians molested them.

From his headquarters at New Brunswick, General James Grant urged Colonel Donop to remain calm. "If I was with you [and] your Grenadiers and Jagers," Grant wrote, "I should not be afraid of an attack from Washington's army, Which is almost naked and do[es] not exceed eight thousand men." Yet although some of his officers refused to believe that Washington—who had recrossed the Delaware River and withdrawn to Newtown, Pennsylvania—would risk another attack, Grant expected the Americans to come back and "renew the Attack upon Prince Town in two or three Days." Grant knew that his enemies had both supply and recruitment problems—"they are pressed in time, as their Men absolutely refuse to inlist again notwithstanding their late Success," spies told him—but to him their strike on Trenton looked like much more than a raid. "They expect," he wrote on the bottom of an intelligence report, "to make us quit the Jerseys before the Winter is *over.*"

At Princeton, too, the mood was far from calm. Donop reached there on the afternoon of December 28th to find General Leslie almost as jumpy as himself, expecting "to be attacked by enemy forces from different sides at any hour." Leslie directed the Black Watch and some British dragoons to take an advanced post at Maidenhead (now Lawrenceville) and found shelter for Donop's Germans—whose numbers had been swelled by 600 escapees from Rall's brigade—between Princeton and Kingston, across the Millstone River to the east. All the while his scouts prowled the roads to Trenton for news of Washington's return.

The shocking news of Washington's victory at Trenton did not penetrate the festive atmosphere of British-ruled New York so quickly. "Here we have balls, concerts, and meetings, which I am already weary of," Howe's aide Friedrich von Muenchhausen griped to his diary. Howe, deep into the first rounds of his beloved winter banqueting, observed Washington's military antics like an overfed cat watching a mouse scurrying across the kitchen floor. Something so "highly malapropos" as Trenton roused him, but just a little.

Writing the nervous Grant, Howe approved the abandonment of Bordentown but permitted the withdrawal to proceed no farther east than Princeton. Cornwallis was preparing to leave for England, but since his ship had not yet sailed, Howe sent him back to New Brunswick to consult with Grant on the rearrangement of living quarters in the now overcrowded cantonments. With those rather obvious measures taken, Howe detected no cause for further alarm. "Merry Christmas to you notwithstanding all our disasters," he wrote to Grant in commiseration. He then returned to his celebrations and feasts.

On December 27th, Washington's little army retreated across McConkey's Ferry to the west bank of the Delaware, where the Continentals left their

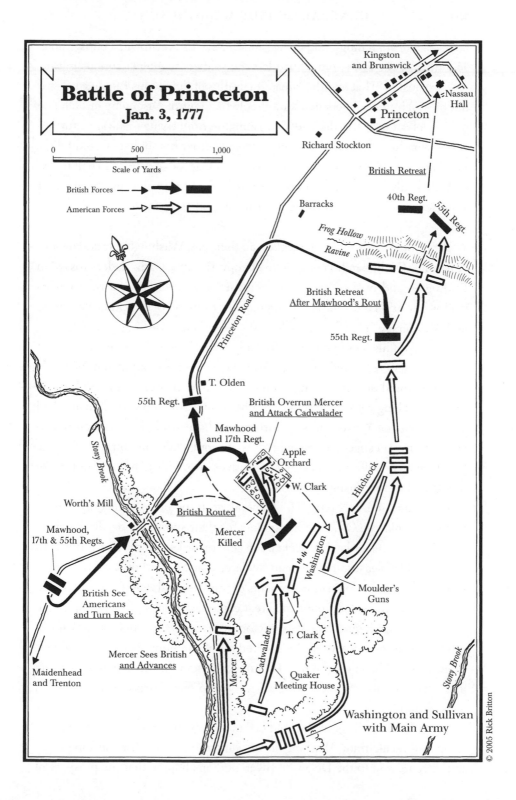

Battle of Princeton
Jan. 3, 1777

0   500   1,000
Scale of Yards

British Forces ———▶ ◼
American Forces ⇒ ⇨ ▭

Kingston and Brunswick

Nassau Hall

Princeton

Richard Stockton

British Retreat

40th Regt.

55th Regt.

Barracks

Frog Hollow Ravine

British Retreat After Mawhood's Rout

55th Regt.

T. Olden

55th Regt.

British Overrun Mercer and Attack Cadwalader

Mawhood and 17th Regt.

Apple Orchard

W. Clark

Hitchcock

Story Brook

Worth's Mill

British Routed

Mercer Killed

Mawhood, 17th & 55th Regts.

British See Americans and Turn Back

Washington

Moulder's Guns

Maidenhead and Trenton

Mercer Sees British and Advances

Mercer

Cadwalader

T. Clark

Quaker Meeting House

Stony Brook

Washington and Sullivan with Main Army

© 2005 Rick Britton

boats before marching another five miles west to Newtown, Pennsylvania. The trials of the last two days had left the soldiers feeling victorious but utterly exhausted. That and the "great Quantities of Spirituous Liquors at Trenton of which the Soldiers drank too freely to admit of Discipline or Defence in Case of Attack," had dissuaded Washington from trying to advance further and exploit his advantage. He had no idea whether his soldiers would follow him back into New Jersey but wrote Colonel Cadwalader that "I shall be extremely ready, and it is my most earnest wish, to pursue every means that shall seem probable to distress the Enemy and to promise success on our part."

While the troops rested and collected their pay, Washington ordered General James Ewing's militia brigade to occupy Trenton. Cadwalader crossed to Burlington and pushed on to Bordentown, now deserted, and then Crosswicks; but expected militia reinforcements from New England, New York, and New Jersey failed to materialize. Without them, Washington would have to depend on his Continentals to fuel any drive through New Jersey. But not many regulars remained in camp. After December 31st all of the New Englanders would depart, leaving behind 1,400 men in twelve tattered Virginia regiments along with some scraps of other units. Somehow, Washington had to convince the Yankees to stay with him a little while longer. Victory had added to his prestige and enhanced his authority, allowing him to offer the troops almost unlimited material incentives to reenlist, but it would take drama and showmanship to tip the scales.

First came some flattery. "The General, with the utmost sincerity and affection, thanks the Officers and soldiers for their spirited and gallant behavior at Trenton yesterday," he declared in general orders on the 27th. "It is with inexpressible pleasure that he can declare, that he did not see a single instance of bad behavior in either officers or privates; and that if any fault could be found, it proceeded from a too great eagerness to push forward upon the Enemy." Never before had Washington addressed such praise to them in public. As an added reward, he ordered all of the guns, horses, and equipment that had been captured at Trenton to be sold for the benefit of officers and men. He also "strictly ordered" the camp commissary to ladle out an issue of rum.

Tentative soundings of the soldiers' mood on the 27th and 28th showed them still recalcitrant. Washington responded on the 29th by leading them out of camp and to the Delaware River, perhaps hoping that the prospect of action would change their minds. The weather conspired against him, however, suddenly turning bitterly cold. Greene's division made it across the river below Trenton by stepping gingerly over freshly frozen ice, but at McConkey's Ferry the river was not passable on foot or by boat. Sullivan's troops stood there for a day, shivering amid drifting snow flurries, before the boatmen figured out a way to ferry them through the floes to the solid shelves of ice. By the evening of the 30th most of them had found shelter in Trenton.

Now, with the Delaware behind him and time running out, Washington made his final bid for the army's allegiance. He paraded them on New Year's Eve, in streets and fields covered by six inches of snow, to hear the offer of ten dollars' bounty in addition to the usual pay in return for another six weeks' service. Thomas Mifflin, Washington's former aide who was now a brigadier general in command of a force of Pennsylvania militiamen, rode into Trenton to offer his oratory services. He had convinced the few New England regiments serving with Cadwalader to stay, and now harangued Washington's Continentals with all his might. The obese but charismatic Knox, "mounted on a noble-looking horse and clothed in an overcoat made up of a large rose blanket and a large fur cap on his head," gave his best, too. But the real drama commenced only when Washington rode forward to address the troops.

The men to whom Washington appealed, arranged in regiments ranging from a third to a tenth of their original size, were veterans of campaigns more bloody and grueling than any of them had anticipated. Some had hauled Colonel Rufus Putnam's chandeliers up Dorchester Heights and watched the last British transports sail out of Boston Harbor in March 1776. Others had fought on Long Island and Manhattan, followed Washington in the humiliating retreat across New Jersey, or marched hundreds of miles from the frontiers of Canada. One regiment, the Fourteenth Continentals, was made up of fishermen and sailors from Marblehead, Massachusetts, and had earned the general's special affection after ferrying him and his troops across the Delaware on Christmas night. Without exception, all of the troops were cold, hungry, ragged, and eager to go home.

Years later, an American sergeant remembered Washington's speech, perhaps embellishing a little for the benefit of his listeners: "He alluded to our recent victory at Trenton; told us that our services were greatly needed, and that we could now do more for our country than we ever could at any future period; and in the most affectionate manner entreated us to stay." Washington paused. Those who accepted the offer were asked to poise their firelocks. Yet "the drums beat for volunteers, but not a man turned out."

Washington never showed much flair as an orator, and it may be that his prepared speech fell as flatly as it had been delivered. It took a spontaneous gesture to win his listeners' affection. The sergeant described it: "the General wheeled his horse about, rode in front of the regiment, and addressing us again said, 'My brave fellows, you have done all I asked you to do, and more than could be reasonably expected; but your country is at stake, your wives, your houses, and all that you hold dear. You have worn yourselves out with fatigue and hardships, but we know not how to spare you. If you will consent to stay only one month longer, you will render that service to the cause of liberty, and to your country, which you probably never can do under any other circumstances. The present is emphatically the crisis, which is to decide our destiny.' "

The words were nothing special; one can only imagine that the force with which Washington delivered them determined what happened next. "The soldiers felt the force of the appeal," the sergeant remembered. "One said to another, 'I will remain if you will.' Others remarked 'We cannot go home under such circumstances.' A few stepped forth, and their example was immediately followed by nearly all who were fit for duty. . . . An officer enquired of the General if these men should be enrolled. He replied,—'No! Men who will volunteer in such a case as this, need no enrolment to keep them to their duty.' "

If Washington said these last words, the soldiers must have gasped. Being trusted was all very well, but without enrolling how would they get paid? Some demanded their bounty money immediately and departed when their officers confessed they did not have the cash in hand. Luckily, two canvas bags containing over 400 Spanish silver dollars, some English shillings and a French half-crown arrived in camp from Philadelphia on New Year's Day, providing the necessary currency to pay the troops' bounty. Hundreds of men refused the bounty and tramped homeward, but after they left Washington still had 3,335 Continentals in his army. At Crosswicks, Cadwalader and Mifflin commanded a combined force of about 3,500, mostly militia but including a few old New England regiments and four freshly raised regiments of Pennsylvania Continentals. Taken as a whole, this army of 6,500 really existed only on a shoestring; but it sufficed for Washington's purposes. With it he intended to reverse almost all the defeats of the past three months.

—

Not all of the action on New Year's Eve took place in Trenton. All through central New Jersey parties of regular and irregular cavalry galloped to and fro, crossing the footpaths of infantry or militia scouts. Farmers found themselves caught in between, pressed by each side to spy on the other, and getting punished by both. Skirmishes went on incessantly and spattered the snow-covered countryside with British, German, and American blood. The victors of these forgotten encounters dragged their battered captives back to camp for interrogation. Washington and his adversaries were trying to feel one another out.

Washington was the beneficiary of some of the earliest and best intelligence. On New Year's Day, an American patrol surprised and captured a foraging party of twelve British dragoons. The Americans brought their prisoners back to Trenton that day, where after separate questioning they provided useful information on General Leslie's and Colonel Donop's dispositions at Princeton. Cornwallis, the dragoons claimed, had just reached Princeton "with a Body of pickd Troops & well appointed." With this reinforcement there were between seven and eight thousand British and German troops at Princeton, all in good spirits and preparing to march on Trenton.

At about the same time, Washington received what can only be described as an intelligence bombshell. On December 31st, Colonel Cadwalader wrote that he had found "a very intelligent young Gentleman" willing to risk his life by entering Princeton, spying on the British, feeding them misinformation, and then slipping out again. The young man returned safely after adventures worthy of a novel, but the result was what mattered. If everything the amateur spy told was true—and of course he might be a double agent—Princeton could be captured.

"From the best information he could get" (gathered before the arrival of Cornwallis's detachment, which the spy did not mention), Cadwalader thought the town held about five thousand British and German troops. Most of them were camped on Princeton's western approaches, in preparation for an American attack from that direction. "They parade every Morng an hour before day—and some Nights lie on their Arms," he wrote. The spy reported, however, that he had seen "no Sentries on the back or East Side of the Town." A dirt road, used by farmers' wagons only rarely and thus not well known, passed to that side of town; Cadwalader marked it on the sketch map he enclosed to Washington as leading through fields and fences "to the back part of Prince Town which may be entered any where on this Side." Leslie and Donop neglected to patrol this area carefully, making it possible for a stealthy march to catch them unawares.

The dragoons had warned of Cornwallis's blade; now the spy pointed out a chink in his armor. Unwilling to decide by himself whether to parry or thrust, Washington called a council of war. The officers met on the evening of January 1st in the commander-in-chief's headquarters, a large two-story house on Queen Street in Trenton. Some of the officers apparently proposed retreating to Pennsylvania, but Washington insisted on remaining in New Jersey. To retreat, he mused, would destroy "every dawn of hope which had begun to revive in the breasts" of his soldiers and the people of New Jersey. Agreement on how to meet the British threat proved difficult, however, and the house lamps burned for hours as sentries watched in the street outside. Finally, at around 10:00 P.M., Dr. Benjamin Rush ran out the front door with a note that Washington had asked him to carry to Cadwalader at Crosswicks.

The note was pointed and terse. "Some pieces of Intelligence renders it necessary for you to March your Troops immediately to this place," Washington wrote. "I expect your Brigade [with his and Mifflin's troops] will be here by five O'clock in the Morning without fail. At any rate do not exceed 6." Rush later recalled that "the weather was damp and cold, the roads muddy, and the night extremely dark" as he plunged into it. A brief thaw had begun, accompanied by rain, and turned the dirt roads into glutinous streams of mud. A mile outside Crosswicks an alert patrol held a cocked pistol to Rush's chest before finally admitting him to see Cadwalader, who roused his troops and set them on the road to Trenton.

Rush rode with Cadwalader and arrived with him in Trenton at 7:00 A.M. He had spent a sleepless night and "begged" a bed at General St. Clair's quarters in town. The prospect of rest proved illusory. "Just as I began to sleep," Rush remembered, "an alarm gun was fired at the General's door. I started up, and the first creature I saw was a black woman crying and wringing her hands in my room. She was followed by Genl. St. Clair"—a tall, dignified, handsome Scot—"with a composed countenance. I asked him what was the matter. He said the enemy were advancing, and 'what do you intend to do?' said I. 'Why, fight them,' said he with a smile. He then took down his sword, and girdled it upon his thigh with a calmness such as I thought seldom took place at the expectation of a battle."

Events, it seemed, had overtaken Washington.

—

Lord Cornwallis's refined manners and rather soft contours belied a nature far more vigorous than Howe's. As ordered, he had postponed his leave to England and ridden to New Brunswick for what he expected to be little more than a morale-booster for General Grant. On arriving at New Brunswick on New Year's Eve, however, Cornwallis discovered that Grant had left with 1,000 troops to reinforce Princeton in the face of Washington's reported return to New Jersey. Distrusting his subordinate's judgment, Cornwallis promptly remounted his horse and galloped off in pursuit. He covered fifty miles before catching up to Grant on the evening of January 1st, around the same time that Washington was meeting with his council of war.

Cornwallis found Grant and Donop in a more aggressive mood than he had anticipated. With their combined force they no longer felt vulnerable and may even have felt a little ashamed of their earlier alarm. Eager "to give the enemy a beating," they asked Cornwallis for permission to attack Trenton the next morning. Caught on the wrong side of the Delaware, the Americans would be destroyed before they could navigate their way back across the ice-filled river. Donop, slavering for the opportunity to avenge Rall, begged Cornwallis not to hold him back; and Grant, rediscovering his long-standing contempt for the Yankee "saints," promised an easy victory. The absence of Howe's restraining hand made them especially enthusiastic, like mischievous children temporarily freed from parental supervision. Catching their spirit, Cornwallis endorsed the plan.

Donop's brigade, reinforced by British light infantry and dragoons, drew brandy and hard biscuits from the commissaries and led the way southwest toward Maidenhead at daybreak. Cornwallis rode next to Donop in the vanguard. The rest of the army, commanded by Grant, formed sloppily in sodden fields and proceeded in brigades down Princeton Road—now a churned-up mass of mud. Gaps formed between units, and the troops marched in fits and starts as officers struggled to close them up.

Cornwallis reached Maidenhead, six miles from Trenton, before the rear of the army had left Princeton. He waited there for a couple of hours before ordering the advance to resume at about noon. Just as the troops got into motion, some Americans appeared, emptied several saddles with a volley of musketry, and withdrew into the woods before Cornwallis's surprised troops could pursue. The Americans were part of a force of one thousand Continentals in two brigades under Colonels Charles Scott of Virginia and

Edward Hand of Pennsylvania, who Washington had ordered "to skirmish with the enemy during their march and retreat to Trenton, as occasion should require . . . by which means [the British] march was [to be] so much retarded as to give ample time for our forces to form and prepare them a warm reception upon their arrival." They fulfilled that mission admirably, wrecking bridges, staging periodic ambushes that forced Germans and British to halt and form in battle order, and disappearing before they could fall victim to Cornwallis's bayonets. Washington rode to encourage them personally, urging them to keep the enemy away from Trenton until dark—ostensibly so that the rest of the army could withdraw to Pennsylvania.

The skillful American withdrawal astonished the British—"their rearguard behaved better than usual," Grant grudgingly admitted. By late afternoon the skirmishing had reached Assunpink Creek, a mile and a half northeast of Trenton. Here, British engineer Archibald Robertson wrote in his diary, "in order to amuse us they Manoeuvre'd 2 or 3,000 men on their Right very well making a Demonstration of Passing the Creek at two Different places in their Possession where it was fordable, so that by that means to turn our left Flank if we advanced towards Trenton." More precious time was wasted as Cornwallis hesitated at the sight of these detachments, which Washington had placed to defend two fords over the creek northeast of town. Finally deciding that these Americans could do him no harm, Cornwallis cautiously pushed his troops southwest into Trenton. By now it was after 5:00 P.M., and the sun had set.

From the fords where Washington had stationed troops northeast of Trenton, Assunpink Creek flowed southwest and then west before entering the Delaware River just south of the town. Action now centered on the stone bridge that crossed the creek at this place, which now formed the only escape route out of Trenton. Rall had ignored this route on December 26th, but Washington did not. He and most of his army had crossed the bridge earlier that day to high ground south of town, leaving a covering force on the creek's north bank to hold the way open for Scott and Hand. Other American soldiers had stayed in Trenton, lurking behind fences and in houses and barns, and as the British marched through town in the darkening twilight several fell victim to snipers' bullets. Shrugging off these losses, Cornwallis's men continued forward until they emerged into an open area facing the north end of the stone bridge. Ahead they saw the American rear guard drawn up, shielding several hundred Continentals who had yet to make their way across the bridge. Forming quickly, the German troops fixed bayonets and charged the Americans while British light infantry gave supporting fire from the flanks. Washington's thin rear guard nearly collapsed under the onslaught. Another few moments, and the Germans would begin slashing into the mass of retreating troops jostling and struggling over the bridge to the creek's south bank.

Sensing a crisis, Washington promptly plunged into its center. Riding toward the bridge, he pushed his horse through the crowd of men streaming across it and shouted to the rear guard to pull back a short distance and regroup under cover of Knox's artillery, which lined the creek's south bank. The hard-pressed Continentals obeyed, and opened lanes for the cannon to fire into the dense enemy formations. The Germans fell back and the American line held. Subsequent German and British attempts to storm across the bridge or ford the creek near it were thwarted, and within minutes the last of Scott's and Hand's troops had withdrawn safely to the south. By 6:00 P.M., well after dark, the day's fighting drew to a close—"except," as Knox contentedly told his wife, "a few shells we now & then chuck'd into Town to prevent their enjoying their new quarters securely."

Cornwallis chose not to leave his troops to endure the American bombardment, but pulled them back through town to the south bank of Shabakunk Creek. This was a precaution against an American night attack, but Cornwallis's prime reason for withdrawing was that he intended to resume the attack in the morning by driving southeast across a ford over Assunpink Creek at Philip's Mill, three miles from Trenton. From there his troops would wheel to the southwest, pin Washington against the Delaware, and destroy him. Another day, he hoped, would avenge Rall and crush the Continental Army.

Washington chose this crucial moment to display a genuine—though fleeting—flash of brilliance. On the night of January 2nd–3rd, the temperature dropped almost twenty degrees, to well below freezing. While the soldiers tried to sleep—which Lieutenant James McMichael and his company of Pennsylvanians "very commodiously did upon a number of rails for bed"— Washington called his officers into another council of war. The previous night's council had been inconclusive, but this one was not.

Knox undoubtedly attended, and provided a sketchy record of the deliberations in a letter he wrote to his wife five days later. The army's position "was strong to be sure," he wrote, "but hazardous on this account that had our right wing been defeated the defeat of the left would almost have been an inevitable consequence, & the whole thrown into Confusion or push'd into the Delaware." Cornwallis blocked the road north, and retreating south would serve no purpose except to expose the army on less defensible terrain. As Grant had foreseen, floating ice made the Delaware "impassable by boats." That left east.

"From these circumstances," Knox told his wife, "the General thought it was best to attack Princeton 12 miles in the rear of the enemys Grand army." The campfires on the Assunpink would be left burning, tended by a special detachment of 500 men who would alternately stoke the flames and noisily hack entrenchments in the frozen ground. Two cannon would also remain to lob the occasional shell into Trenton. Meanwhile, the main body of Washington's army—6,000 men and thirty or forty cannon—would leave their positions under cover of darkness, marching up the Quaker Road, approach Princeton via its lightly guarded eastern outskirts, and attack after sunrise. Leaving the fires burning at Trenton "would avoid the appearance of a retreat," Washington later explained, preventing "the hazard of the whole Army being cut off." Meanwhile, at Princeton "I knew they could not have much force left and might have Stores . . . whilst we might by a fortunate stroke withdraw Genl Howe from Trenton and give some reputation to our Arms."

Captain Thomas Rodney recorded the night march in his diary. "At two o'clock in the morning the ground having been frozen firm by a keen N. West wind secret orders were issued to each department and the whole army was at once put in motion, but no one knew what the Gen. meant to do. Some thought that we were going to attack the enemy in the rear; some that we were going to Princeton." The troops had learned to move silently, and they suppressed their grumbles at the bitter cold. Wagon and cannon wheels were wrapped in thick cloth, and torches stayed unlit. Men's and horses' feet made little noise, since they were largely unshod, but the animals "when passing over the ice would slide in every direction." The exhausted soldiers had a hard time keeping themselves and their horses standing.

The vanguard—minus a Pennsylvania militia regiment that had fled back to Philadelphia after a false alarm—reached Stony Brook, three miles from Princeton, just before sunrise. The bridge there had been weakened or destroyed, and they hastily built a replacement strong enough to bear the artillery. The sun came up at 7:30 A.M. as the troops started marching across. Reaching a fork in the road ten minutes later, they paused to re-form while

Washington consulted with Sullivan and Greene, his two divisional commanders. While they waited, a captain in Sullivan's division passed around a
bucket containing an unusual mixture of gunpowder and rum. He ordered
each man to drink a shot of the concoction to build courage for the coming
encounter.

Sensing that Cornwallis still remained at Trenton, Washington divided his
army. Sullivan's division, composed of three brigades of New England Continentals and a hodgepodge of other units, would turn northeast, marching
up Saw Mill Road to the area labeled most vulnerable by Cadwalader's
spy. Greene's division formed the other column, which continued north on
Quaker Road in the direction of the main thoroughfare that Cornwallis had
used to march from Princeton to Trenton. Brigadier General Hugh Mercer's
brigade, mostly Pennsylvanians with a smattering of Virginians and Marylanders, led Greene's column with orders to seize another bridge, where the main
road passed over Stony Brook, "for the double purpose of intercepting fugitives from Princeton, and to cover our rear against Lord Cornwallis from
Trenton." The plan was similar to the one Washington had tried to execute at
Trenton on December 26th.

The orders given, Washington drew his aides aside and watched his troops
march by on their respective missions. He had been there only a short time
when an officer spotted a few British light horse on a hill to the left. "General
Washington happened to be near," a witness remembered, "and with the
glass descryed a body of infantry, but intervening trees &c made it impossible
to form any judgement about their numbers." Washington assumed that the
British were "a detachment sent out of Princeton to reconnoitre," and sent a
messenger forward to Mercer with orders to attack it. He then joined Sullivan's column, the spearhead of his coming attack.

Washington was wrong about the enemy force. It was not—as the presence of infantry should have warned him—a patrol from Princeton, but two
whole British regiments, the Seventeenth and Fifty-fifth, and a troop of dragoons. These units, totaling 392 men under the command of Lieutenant
Colonel Charles Mawhood, had left town before dawn as escorts for a convoy of supplies and convalescents to Trenton. The Fortieth Foot, an infantry
regiment mustering about 450 men, stayed behind to protect Princeton.

Mercer, a Virginia pharmacist who had bought Washington's boyhood
home, Ferry Farm, in 1774, moved his brigade of 325 men forward through
shin-deep snow topped by a crust of ice. Assuming that the enemy force was

small, he veered uphill to the east in order to prevent it from retreating to Princeton. Passing a group of farm buildings, his troops climbed over a fence and then, seeking another victory, pushed rashly ahead into an orchard. They marched a short distance through the trees and then halted at the edge of a clearing. A British regiment and two cannon were waiting for them behind a fence fifty yards away.

Mawhood had withdrawn toward Princeton immediately after his flankers detected the American movement. Dispatching the supply convoy back to Princeton, he sent the Fortieth and Fifty-fifth regiments to block Sullivan. Mawhood himself remained with the Seventeenth and the dragoons, who faced west and formed up behind the fence a mile outside of town. Mercer thus confronted a force about equal in size to his own, but with one major difference—the British had bayonets.

Mercer "immediately formed his men, with great courage," Captain Rodney wrote, "and poured a heavy fire in upon the enemy." The British fired back with greater accuracy and devastating effect, shooting Mercer and his officers from their saddles and slaughtering the Continentals as they stood without cover in the snowy field. An American who witnessed the tragedy never forgot the rivulets of blood that ran over the ice, or the agony on the face of an officer shot from his horse who lay "rolling and writhing in his blood, unconscious of anything around him." Shivering and by now mostly officerless, the Americans milled confusedly and then reeled backward as Mawhood's troops charged into their midst, bayoneting wounded men as they lay shrieking on the ground. Mercer's second in command, Delaware Colonel John Haslet, tried to rally them only to fall dead with a bullet through the brain.

Cadwalader's brigade of 1,100 men, mostly Pennsylvania militia, was next in line. His troops had left the road and marched east a few hundred yards to Mercer's right. They encountered the other brigade fleeing in confusion with the redcoats in pursuit. Greene ordered Cadwalader to deploy in line on a hill about 300 yards away from the enemy. Cadwalader did so, and advanced downhill "under a shower of grape shot" and musketry as the British took cover behind another convenient fence. Weaker but better disciplined, the British again won the ensuing duel. The Americans first fired from too far away, and then advanced only to find their muskets unable to shoot through the fence. Backed by the two cannon, Mawhood's regiment fired to much greater effect, and the American brigade began to splinter and break.

Washington now appeared, seemingly out of nowhere, at the hottest place on the battlefield. Leaving Sullivan after hearing the noise from Mercer's attack, the commander-in-chief rode frantically back to the crossroads and then up Quaker Road, cresting the hill behind Cadwalader's brigade just as it started to break. Washington took one look at the dangerous situation and then charged down the slope. Bellowing furiously, he and Cadwalader tried to herd the skittish troops back toward the enemy. Washington quickly reached the front line and then passed beyond it. Insensible to being thus "exposed to both firings," he continued to rage amid flying grapeshot and bullets. Colonel John Fitzgerald, one of the general's aides and a close personal friend, covered his eyes with his hat lest he witness the commander-in-chief's bloody demise. Washington survived, providing just enough moral glue to keep Cadwalader's brigade from falling apart as it withdrew a hundred yards in reasonably good order.

The battle's momentum now shifted, quickly and decisively. Some participants later painted the moment in heroic colors. "Parade with us, my brave fellows! There is but a handful of the enemy, and we will have them directly," a sergeant claimed to remember Washington shouting; Fitzgerald put him down as declaring "away, my dear Colonel, and bring up the troops!" before leading a dashing charge at the enemy. Yet whatever Washington said, his presence meant less than the fact that the Seventeenth was badly outnumbered. Washington, Greene, and Cadwalader had only to bring up reinforcements and file the troops off to the left and right around Mawhood's flanks. This they did, with predictably disastrous results for the British.

At Washington's orders, Cadwalader gathered what he could of his brigade and led it to the right. Most of his troops climbed over a fence and continued toward the British flank, but two small detachments turned slightly left and "bravely pushed up in the face of a heavy fire." Mawhood's men stubbornly refused to retreat, inclining left and firing several volleys that killed and wounded many of the Americans. Absorbing these casualties, Cadwalader moved the rest of his troops into position and then sent them crashing into Mawhood's left. The redcoats could take no more, and they dropped their packs and scattered in all directions before the cheering Americans. Unable to contain his jubilation, the usually tight-lipped Washington cried, "It's a fine fox chase, my boys!" and joined the pursuit.

As the shattered remnants of the Seventeenth Regiment fled north and west, Mawhood bolted for Princeton, "mounted on a brown poney, with 10 or

12 file of infantry, and a pair of springing spaniels playing before him." American snipers picked off two of his party before he decided to change direction and follow his retreating troops. Sullivan meanwhile cautiously advanced on Princeton from the east, exerting no real pressure on the Fortieth and Fifty-fifth regiments but making clear to them that they had no chance of holding the town. Soon, either on Mawhood's orders or on their own initiative, the British regiments pulled out and withdrew toward New Brunswick. An officer with a white handkerchief on his sword then formally notified the Americans that Princeton belonged to Washington.

"After we had been about two hours at Princeton," Henry Knox informed his wife a few days later, "word was brought that the enemy were advancing from Trenton—this they did as we have since been inform'd in a most infernal Sweat, running puffing & blowing & swearing at being so outwitted." General Leslie, in fact, had been posted only three miles away at Maidenhead when the battle began. Leslie moved his brigade toward the firing as soon as he heard it, but he reached Stony Brook at about 10:00 A.M., only to find the bridge destroyed. He paused, ordered his troops to ford the creek, and then halted them on the other side. Too weak to attack, he decided to await reinforcements. But Cornwallis had not discovered Washington's ruse until 8:00 A.M., and it would take hours for him to get back to Princeton.

Washington thus gained a valuable respite, but much of it was wasted. As soon as his troops entered Princeton, they began looting the abandoned British supply wagons and the town itself. The wagons held flour, blankets, and other items that the Americans desperately needed, while buildings like Nassau Hall contained treasures calculated to delight the soldiers: elegant dining sets, pictures of the king, women's clothing, and uneaten breakfasts. The army became badly disorganized in the process of the ensuing celebration.

Troops unable or unwilling to slip away from their officers meanwhile found themselves detailed to guarding prisoners or to gathering weapons from the field, picking their way among "pale, mangled corpses lying in the mud and blood." Some found comrades who had dropped out of the fighting with only light wounds now lying dead in pools of blood, their skulls crushed and their bodies hacked to pieces by murderous redcoats. Yet when vengeful Continentals started stripping wounded British soldiers of their uniforms and provisions Washington put a stop to it at once. He himself escorted two agonized redcoats, one "shot in at his hip and the bullet lodged in his groin," and another "shot through his body just below his short ribs" to beds in a civilian home. Other non-ambulatory British wounded were placed in wagons and escorted into the countryside under the care of civilians or surgeons like Rush, who amputated the legs of four soldiers.

A Princeton resident who saw Washington's entourage as it moved about town remembered that "though they were both hungry and thirsty some of them were laughing outright, others smiling, and not a man among them but showed joy in his countenance." But with Cornwallis bearing down on them they could not afford to enjoy themselves for long. After an hour, Washington ordered a stop to the looting, dispatching Sullivan, Greene, and their officers to gather their troops and put them in marching order. By noon the army had left Princeton, taking as many supplies as they could carry and leaving the rest in flames. Leslie entered town on their heels, Cornwallis arrived by mid-afternoon, and the looting of Princeton, this time by the British, began anew.

Washington's route of retreat led fifteen miles north to Somerset Court House. Most of the soldiers, almost too tired to stand, made it there by 8:00 P.M. They flung themselves down to sleep anywhere—even, Lieutenant Charles Willson Peale noticed in surprise, "amongst a fine heap of straw, where some Hessians had lain." Though at other times the Americans would have refused to use German bedding "for fear of their vermin—now they were glad to lie down, and were asleep in a few moments." The next morning, January 4th, Washington roused his stiff and miserable men and pushed them northeast to Bound Brook.

Now came the last, and perhaps most critical decision of the campaign: should the Americans attack New Brunswick, less than ten miles down the Raritan River to the southeast? Washington was all for the attempt. "In my Judgement Six or Eight hundred fresh Troops upon a forced march would have destroyed all their Stores and Magazines," he wrote Hancock the next day, "taken as we have since learnt their Military Chest containing 70,000£ and put an end to the War." His officers overruled him, pointing out the extreme fatigue of the troops; and this was to his extreme luck, because Cornwallis had led his men on a forced march overnight to arrive in New Brunswick early that morning. They were ready, and might have shattered Washington's army if he had chosen to attack.

Instead Washington turned his troops northwest and marched them uphill into the rugged country around the town of Pluckemin, ten miles from Somerset Court House. There he halted for two nights, waiting for over 1,000 stragglers to come up while his men were "obliged to encamp on the bleak mountains whose tops were covered with snow, without even blankets to cover them." Lieutenant James McMichael noted with satisfaction that he and his men were "very well supplied with large stones, which served us instead of pillows." Those who had looted items like cloth and flour from Princeton instead of trinkets and baubles were better off. One of the wounded British prisoners died in Pluckemin and was buried with full honors. He was Captain William Leslie of the Seventeenth Regiment, son of General Alexander Leslie. Fitzgerald carried a flag of truce to New Brunswick to inform the father of his loss.

On January 6th Washington's army left Pluckemin and marched twelve miles to a more secure location at Morristown, arriving at around 5:00 P.M. The soldiers camped at first "in the woods, the snow covering the ground," but moved into more comfortable lodgings in town over the next few days. "Morristown is devoid of beauty, both in its form and location," Lieutenant James McMichael wrote; but with roofs finally over his head, and enjoying the company of "young ladies" who were "very fond of the soldiers, but much more so of officers," he was not disposed to complain. Morristown and its environs would be the army's home for the next four months. The winter campaign had finally come to an end.

The bloody skirmishing in and around Trenton on January 2nd had left about two dozen casualties on each side. Official British casualties for the Battle of Princeton on January 3rd were 276, with 200 of those being prisoners from Mawhood's three regiments. American losses were less exactly calculated at about twenty-five killed and forty wounded. Washington as usual overestimated British casualties, setting them to at least twice their actual number; but the death of his old friend, the "brave and worthy" Hugh Mercer, dealt him a serious personal loss.

Washington had won two major victories, but the better known and most dramatic of the two encounters was not really the most impressive. In crossing the Delaware and attacking Trenton on December 26th, he had carried out a bold maneuver that destroyed an entire brigade of seasoned German troops. But this success owed a great deal to luck and to the incompetence of his opponent. Washington's victory at Princeton was by contrast almost entirely his own. On December 31st, he preserved the army as it was about to disband. On January 2nd, with a river at his back, he held off a vigorous attack by Cornwallis that came within a hairsbreadth of routing him from Trenton. And on January 3rd—one of the most remarkable days of his military career—Washington marched his entire army out from under Cornwallis's nose, marched around his rear, and shattered three regular British regiments at Princeton before slipping once again out of the enemy's grasp.

Trenton and Princeton effectively quashed, at least for the present, every question as to Washington's military skill. Contrary to what has sometimes been said, though, these victories did not save his job—that was already safe, if only because there was no alternative to his leadership. Congress voted to grant him extraordinary powers before receiving word of the victory at Trenton and would not have withdrawn those powers had he chosen to remain on the Pennsylvania side of the Delaware.

The fruits of victory were intangible. Although it is impossible to measure exactly how far opinions changed after the battles, it is clear that patriots felt more confident and loyalists more discouraged than they had before. The most significant shift in opinion, however, seems to have occurred among the soldiers themselves. They had not just defeated German mercenaries, as at Trenton; nor had they slaughtered redcoats advancing upon fixed positions, as at Bunker Hill. The Americans had attacked three regular British regiments, routed them, and driven them from the field!

Friendly disputes erupted concerning who had whipped the enemy most badly. Some said the Virginians had won Trenton and Princeton; others claimed it was the New Englanders. New Hampshire General John Sullivan had no doubts on that score. "I have been much pleased to See a Day approaching to try the Difference between yankee Cowardice & Southern valor," he declared. "The Day has or Rather the Days have arrived and all The General officers allowed & do allow that the yankee Cowardice assumes the shape of True valor in the field & The Southern valor appears to be a Composition of Boasting & Conceit."

Of course everyone—north and south, Continentals and militia—shared the credit; but the degree to which Washington, a Virginian who always showed a partiality for troops from his state, had won the trust of the New Englanders is significant. A claim to the commander-in-chief's favor had become a cause for pride. "General Washington made no Scruple to say publickly that the Remains of the Eastern Regiments were the strength of his army though their numbers were Comparatively Speaking but Small," Sullivan continued. "He calls them in front when the Enemy are there—he Sends them to the Rear when the Enemy Threaten that way."

Perhaps the most telling measure of Washington's success was the way in which it left his enemies fuming. Writing to a friend in England on January 15th, Grant griped that "Washington has since taken post at Morris Town—where We can not get at Him—And as He can move a Force from thence to any given Point we have been obliged to Contract our Cantonments to Brunswick Amboy and the Communication between those two places . . . in short it is the most unpleasing situation I ever was in." Cornwallis also remembered this as perhaps his most frustrating military campaign. "You have nothing to accuse yourself of," Howe consoled him. "Had one deserter given you intelligence of the night march from Trentown, you would have finish'd the war, I have no doubt, by the entire defeat of Washington's army—Better luck another time."

Howe was one of the only British officers to regard the American victories with complacence. The more he considered it, the more Washington's canniness even began to look like stupidity. "I heartily agree with you in Washingtons wretch'd behavior in not either following up his advantage over [Mawhood's] 4th brigade or waiting to receive you at Princeton," he wrote Grant on the 9th. "It plainly indicates the inability of his ever standing against us when we are in force & what kind of figure would he make in the attack of a post properly occupied?"

To most British officers and soldiers, however, the Trenton-Princeton campaign enkindled a new respect for their opponents. "Though they seem to be ignorant of the precision, order, and even of the principles, by which large bodies are moved," British Lieutenant Colonel William Harcourt observed, "yet they possess some of the requisites for making good troops, such as extreme cunning, great industry in moving ground and felling wood, activity and a spirit of enterprise upon any advantage. Having said thus much, I have no occasion to add that, though it was once the fashion of this army to treat them in the most contemptible light, they are now become a formidable enemy." Washington's long-suffering soldiers certainly deserved the tribute.

12

PHILADELPHIA

December 1776 – September 1777

THE HUDSON RIVER dominated British strategic thinking in 1776. Both Lord Germain and William Howe thought that by controlling it Britain could end the rebellion. Their plan for the river's conquest envisaged two armies thrusting along it from New York City and Canada. When the prongs of this pincer met near Albany, they would sever New England from the middle colonies. The Hudson would open to British navigation, and royal influence would extend not only through the colonies but to Native American tribes as well. The rebellion could then be crushed at leisure. Howe's landing at New York City and the subsequent ejection of the rebels from Manhattan and New Jersey marked a preliminary stage in this strategy, and once an army could be assembled in Canada he intended to advance upriver to meet it.

But the Hudson River strategy was never fully carried out, thanks to Howe's desire to court American public opinion. As of December 1776, the British commander's spies told him, King George III was one of the most popular men in America. This was true especially among the farmers of Delaware, New Jersey, and eastern Pennsylvania. Howe wanted to solidify this sentiment, but if his army left New Jersey and marched for Albany he feared alienating the loyalists of that region; and without their support, he might lose any chance of ending the war in the middle colonies. If he occupied Philadelphia, on the other hand, Howe could cheer the loyalists, demonstrate Washington's inability to protect his capital, and discourage the French from supporting America. In any case, the rebellion looked so weak after Washington's retreat across the Delaware that Howe thought sending two armies to Albany might prove unnecessary.

On December 20th, Howe wrote to London asking permission to postpone the Hudson offensive in favor of a land or sea assault on Philadelphia;

but his request had no sooner reached Whitehall than news arrived of Washington's victories at Trenton and Princeton. Germain viewed reports of royalist sentiment in America more skeptically than did his general, and he was amazed that Howe could think of abandoning the Hudson in light of the "extremely mortifying" events at Trenton. Washington's exploits had reinvigorated the rebels, and the loyalist opinion that Howe hoped to court by capturing Philadelphia looked like a will-o'-the-wisp.

Howe's proposed southern offensive also posed potential military problems, not just for himself but also for the army slated to invade the Hudson Valley from Canada. Without support from the south, this army would have to face the New Englanders alone, and in dense terrain well suited for ambush. Fearful of disaster, Germain prepared to quash Howe's plans; but at the last moment General John Burgoyne, who would lead the Canadian army of 8,000 British troops, 2,000 Canadians, and 1,000 Indians, intervened to dispel his doubts. A brash, boastful, but experienced officer, Burgoyne assured Germain that he could advance safely from Lake Champlain to around Albany even if Howe went to Philadelphia. From there, Burgoyne could clear the whole river at leisure, push east to link up with the garrison at Rhode Island, or settle down for the winter at Albany. He anticipated no serious opposition from the Americans.

Burgoyne's reasoning convinced a reluctant Germain to revise his strategic objectives for 1777. Instead of forming pincers on the Hudson, two British armies reinforced by thousands of troops from Europe would operate independently against Philadelphia and Albany. Their movements would be uncoordinated, and they would have no way of giving each other support. Yet this weaker, *ad hoc* British strategy nevertheless almost succeeded. Moving in two different directions, the British summer offensives would beguile Washington and inflict multiple severe defeats on his army. Ironically, they also set the stage for American independence.

While the British carved up the map of America, Washington scrambled to keep his army alive. The positive aftereffects of the victories at Trenton and Princeton had proved transitory. Troops who had enlisted for an extra six weeks to fight the Battle of Princeton took their bounty money and went home, leaving gaps that would remain unfilled for months. Recruiters continued to have trouble finding volunteers. States still tempted away recruits to the militia or home guard units by offering inflated bounties. Then smallpox

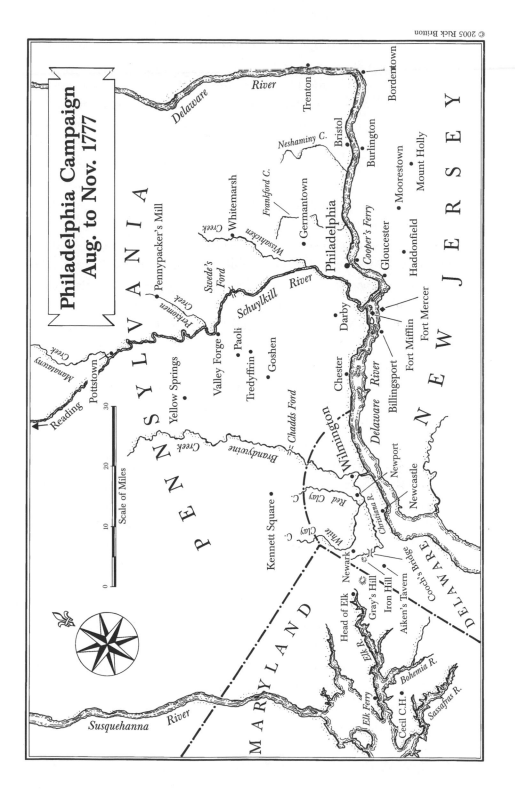

Philadelphia Campaign
Aug. to Nov. 1777

© 2003 Rick Britton

appeared at Morristown, spurring desertions and providing men another reason to avoid their local recruiters.

The spring weather brought some improvement in the army's situation. In May recruits finally began taking their places in line, filling in the creases on the army's gaunt hide. Formations that once existed only on paper could now boast of 25 percent of their allotted strength. By the end of the month nearly 9,000 troops were fit for duty and ready to begin the new campaign, and hundreds more recruits joined the army every week. Almost all of them, Washington noted without surprise, were appallingly inexperienced and undisciplined.

The troops were arranged in five divisions under the command of Major Generals Greene, Stephen, Stirling, Sullivan, and Benjamin Lincoln, who stood at the top of a revamped officer corps. Everywhere Washington looked he saw new faces, some of whom he had taken a role in promoting. Some were Americans who had risen through the ranks. Three of the new brigadier generals were: William Maxwell of New Jersey, an ugly, stubborn, hard-drinking but resourceful Scotsman; "Mad" Anthony Wayne of Pennsylvania, a rash, handsome martinet with a florid tongue; and the refined and well-educated William Smallwood of Maryland. Other officers, most notably a cranky Irishman named Thomas Conway, whom Washington appointed a brigadier general, emerged from a crop of overseas volunteers. Dozens of French volunteers, fresh off their ships and arrogantly self-assured, added desperately needed artillery and engineering experience to the army but also infuriated Americans with their demands for promotion.

The new army functioned more like a professional force than anything Washington had ever led. He had contributed to its development by using the authority that Congress had given him in December to appoint commissaries and other officials. Congress, which returned to Philadelphia from Baltimore on March 12th, belatedly adopted most of the recommendations for army reform that Washington had made the previous autumn. Cumulatively, the changes organized the Continental Army and made it much more efficient. They also had a profound effect upon how the troops lived and fought.

For the first time, a comprehensive set of regulations was adopted to govern the quartermaster department, which now contained separate offices for the management of materiel, such as wagons and forage. The commissariat was rearranged as well and staffed by specialists whose only function was to procure and distribute provisions. A new official, the "clothier general," took

Portrait of George Washington's half brother Lawrence Washington (1718–1752), oil on canvas, attributed to John Wollaston, c. 1741. *Courtesy of the Mount Vernon Ladies' Association*

Page from George Washington's school exercises, August 1745. *Library of Congress*

The burial of General Edward Braddock, July 1755. *Library of Congress*

Washington watches the British evacuation of Boston in March 1775.
Library of Congress

Portrait by Gilbert Stuart of Major General Henry Knox. *Library of Congress*

A Picturesque View of the State of the Nation for February 1778.

Above: English cartoon showing a befeathered American cutting the horns off a cow representing British commerce. A Dutchman milks the cow while a Frenchman and a Spaniard gleefully await their turns. The Howe brothers loll drunkenly in Philadelphia, where their flagship has run aground; meanwhile a dog urinates on the British lion.
Library of Congress

Fanciful nineteenth-century engraving of Major General Israel Putnam escaping from British dragoons.
Library of Congress

GENL ISRAEL PUTNAM.
THE IRON SON OF "76"
Effecting his escape from the British Dragoons

English cartoon showing British politicians responding to General Henry Clinton's evacuation of Philadelphia in June 1778. Maps in the background compare British holdings in America in 1762 and 1778. *Library of Congress*

Portrait of Washington by Charles Willson Peale. *Library of Congress*

Continental soldiers.
Library of Congress

Lord Richard Howe, brother of General
William Howe and commander of the
British fleet. *Library of Congress*

General William Howe, Washington's
nemesis from 1775 through the
beginning of 1778. *Library of Congress*

The evacuation of Long Island, August 1776. *Library of Congress*

Painting by George Trumbell of Washington at the Battle of Princeton,
January 1777. *Library of Congress*

Brigadier General "Mad" Anthony Wayne and his horse. *Library of Congress*

The Battle of Brandywine, September 11, 1777. *Library of Congress*

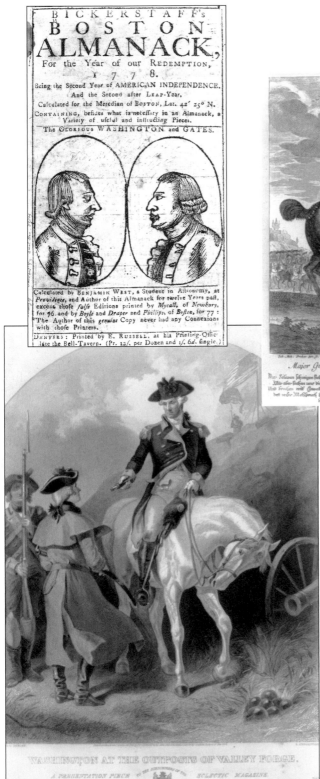

BICKERSTAFF's
BOSTON
ALMANACK,
For the Year of our REDEMPTION,
1 7 7 8.
Being the Second Year of AMERICAN INDEPENDENCE,
And the Second after LEAP-Year,
Calculated for the Meredian of BOSTON, Lat. 42° 25° N.
CONTAINING, besides what is necessary in an Almanack, a
Variety of useful and instructing Pieces.
The GLORIOUS WASHINGTON and GATES.

Calculated by BENJAMIN WEST, a Student in Astronomy, at
Providence, and Author of this Almanack for twelve Years past,
except those false Editions printed by Mycall, of Newbury,
for 76, and by Boyle and Draper and Phillips, of Boston, for 77:
The Author of this genuine Copy never had any Connexions
with those Printers.

DANVERS: Printed by E. RUSSELL, at his Printing-Office,
late the Bell-Tavern. (Pr. 12/. per Dozen and 1/. 6d. single.)

Charles Lee, Esqr.
Major General of the Continental · Army in America.

WASHINGTON AT THE OUTPOSTS OF VALLEY FORGE.

A PRESENTATION PIECE OF THE SUBSCRIBERS TO THE ECLECTIC MAGAZINE.

Above left: Unflattering portraits of Washington and Horatio Gates. *Library of Congress*

Above right: Fanciful European rendition of Major General Charles Lee. *Library of Congress*

Left: Nineteenth-century engraving of Washington at Valley Forge. *Library of Congress*

Nineteenth-century engraving
of Washington standing with his
foreign officers, including Steuben,
Lafayette, Kalb, Pulaski, and
Kosciuszko. *Library of Congress*

Washington and Lafayette at
Valley Forge. *Library of Congress*

Heroic painting of Washington at the Battle of
Monmouth, June 1778. *Library of Congress*

General Henry Clinton, Washington's
opponent at Monmouth. *Library of Congress*

Detail of an eighteenth-century painting showing Washington reviewing
the troops at Fort Cumberland, Maryland. *Library of Congress*

Painting by John Trumbull of the surrender of
Lord Cornwallis at Yorktown, October 1781.
Library of Congress

charge of supplying the army with uniforms, blankets, and shoes. A Washington appointee headed the ordnance department as "commissary of military stores," establishing ammunition magazines at strategic points and manufacturing guns and artillery. The reestablished Hospital Department organized "flying hospitals" to attend each detachment of the Continental Army. Finally, Washington chose a "commissary general of prisoners" to tend to American prisoners in British hands and help organize exchanges.

Washington's own position at the head of the army had also become more secure, and more flexible, than ever before. The congressional resolution of December 27th that increased his authority expired after six months without his becoming a military dictator, as some had feared. By then his respect for civilian government was taken for granted, and no one thought to congratulate him on his restraint. But formal authority had in some respects become unnecessary. In the summer of 1777 Washington could get almost anything he wanted simply by asking for it. The coming campaign would raise questions about his ability to use this freedom judiciously.

Washington regarded Philadelphia as Howe's most likely objective for 1777, but he could not afford to base all his decisions on that assumption. "The designs of the Enemy are not, as yet, clearly unfolded," he wrote Edmund Pendleton, speaker of the Virginia House of Delegates, on April 12th, "but I believe that Philadelphia is the object in view—this however may, or may not be the case, as the [Hudson] River must also be a capitol concern of theirs, whilst they keep an army in Canada—Circumstances therefore will govern their movements." He also had to consider that the British could move by land or sea. In truth, their options were almost limitless. If they chose to attack Philadelphia, they could march through New Jersey, sail up the Delaware River, or enter the Chesapeake Bay for a landing near Head of Elk and an advance across Maryland and southeastern Pennsylvania. A British advance up the Hudson could take place by land, sea, or some combination of the two. Howe even had the option of sailing to Charleston, South Carolina, for a campaign in the south.

Several forces existed to counter these threats. Horatio Gates took control of the northern department in April, and he could call on thousands of New England militiamen as well as Continentals detached from Washington's army. General Arthur St. Clair commanded 3,500 troops at Ticonderoga. A ragged collection of Continentals and militia at Peekskill under Putnam blocked any potential thrust from New York to the Hudson Highlands. But Washington's army was the largest, so he had to stay in a position to support the other forces or march south to protect Philadelphia.

Washington nevertheless chose to make the first move rather than let Howe set the tone for the summer campaign. On May 29th, he shifted his army from Morristown about twenty miles south to Middlebrook and detached Sullivan to Princeton with a brigade of Continentals. Lying on the edge of the Watchung Mountains, Middlebrook had the advantage of being both secure and in a good position from which Washington could intercept any British move on Philadelphia. Howe, who had assembled 18,000 troops at Amboy, responded on June 12th by marching to New Brunswick and then pushing on to Somerset Court House.

Almost immediately Washington noted a peculiarity in the British movement. Howe's advance seemed consistent with the expected attack on Philadelphia, but American spies reported that the British had left all of their heavy baggage, boats, and bridging materials at New Brunswick. Without those supplies a crossing of the Delaware would be impossible. Suspecting a trap, Washington ordered Sullivan to a safer position at Flemington and kept his main force at Middlebrook. The British reacted on June 19th by retreating toward New Brunswick, burning and ravaging the country as they went. Washington confessed himself utterly baffled at such "dark and mysterious" behavior, but he moved his army cautiously east in Howe's wake. Elements of Greene's division skirmished with the enemy's rear guard at New Brunswick, but the British continued their withdrawal all the way to Amboy. Washington took up new positions at Quibbletown and detached Stirling's division to a point near Metuchen.

Howe spent a week in Amboy. Then, suddenly, he came back again, leading two columns in a determined sally to the northwest on June 26th. His intention became apparent almost immediately: to isolate Stirling and "to bring on a General Engagement upon disadvantageous Terms" by cutting Washington off from Middlebrook. The British moved quickly, driving Stirling toward Westfield and capturing three small cannon in the process, but the Americans reacted even faster. The Continental Army rushed back to Middlebrook before the trap could close, and Howe withdrew again to Amboy. The approaching campaign, it was now clear, would be more complicated than Washington had anticipated.

—

While Washington and Howe sparred inconclusively in New Jersey, important events were going on elsewhere. One was Burgoyne's arrival at Quebec, heralding an offensive toward Albany that the British made no attempt to hide from the Americans. Another was the assembly of a massive British fleet off Sandy Hook in Raritan Bay. Ships had been gathering there for months, but Washington remained in doubt about their purpose until the troops at Amboy began embarking on July 8th. That narrowed down the summer's prospects somewhat. Howe clearly intended an amphibious movement, but Washington still did not know where. To guard against every possibility north and south, he camped his army at Morristown and sent Sullivan north to a place called the Clove in the Ramapo Mountains, a gateway to the Hudson Highlands.

Two weeks later, shortly after sunrise on the morning of July 23rd, the American scouts who had been watching the British armada off Sandy Hook heard signal guns echo across the bay. Through their field glasses they could see sailors begin crawling over the rigging, unfurling sails and weighing anchors. Within a few hours, after tacking to and fro to the befuddlement of the Americans, most of the approximately 270 ships headed out to sea.

News of the British departure, and reports from coast watchers who had seen the ships heading south, reached Washington the next day. Presuming that this meant an eventual landing near Philadelphia, he ordered all his divisions—including Sullivan's—to march in that direction. Almost immediately, however, Washington reconsidered. The British move seemed almost too obvious. St. Clair, he learned, had evacuated Ticonderoga without a fight; and with Burgoyne driving relentlessly on for Albany, it seemed likely that Howe would want to join him. But he could not be sure.

Continuing toward Philadelphia, Washington's army arrived at the Delaware near Coryell's Ferry on the evening of the 28th. The soldiers had endured an exhausting forced march, interrupted by frequent halts as wagons broke down or horses died in the July heat. As usual many of the men walked barefoot, and the paucity of wheeled transport forced some to carry kettles, pans, and other cooking utensils in their hands. As soon as they glimpsed the muddy, cool waters of the Delaware, the tired and dusty men broke ranks and plunged in. They spent the balance of the next two days shouting and splashing about while the commander-in-chief fretted through

hours of "constant perplexity and the most anxious conjecture." He refused
to order his troops across the river, just in case they needed to reverse course
to the Hudson.

On the morning of July 31st Washington received a report from the
Delaware militia. The British fleet had appeared off the Delaware Capes on
the 29th, and seemed set to enter the mouth of the Delaware River. In response the commander-in-chief instructed his troops to ford the Delaware
"with all possible dispatch" and make for Philadelphia. In their haste many
men drowned or lost valuable supplies in the river current, but they ignored
their losses and pressed south.

Washington did not stay to watch the crossing. Instead he raced ahead
with his aides and an escort of 200 light horse, and galloped to Philadelphia.
From there, in the comfort of the City Tavern he issued "peremptory orders"
that no soldiers were to set foot in the city during their march south, lest they
relax their discipline in bawdiness and drunken carousing. He then rode to
Chester, where he looked over the river fortifications and selected ground for
an encampment. He had just immersed himself in this business when another express rider arrived and broke his concentration. The horseman
brought a most "provoking account" from a coast watcher at Cape May. Instead of entering the Delaware as expected, the British fleet had unaccountably disappeared. Nobody, as Washington might have guessed, knew in what
direction the ships had gone.

Howe's original plan for the 1777 campaign had involved a naval approach
to Philadelphia by way of the Chesapeake Bay. After landing at Head of Elk,
Maryland, the army would march northeast and threaten the rebel capital.
Presumably Washington would fight in Maryland or Pennsylvania to defend
Philadelphia, and expose his army to defeat and destruction. Yet when Sullivan went to the Clove in mid-July, the British commander saw it as an indication that the Americans might abandon Philadelphia and march north
against Burgoyne instead. To forestall that move, Howe decided to enter the
Delaware River and put his army to Washington's rear with a landing at or
near Philadelphia.

The British fleet reached the Delaware Capes after six days of stormy
weather and adverse winds. After passing the Cape Henlopen lighthouse on
the morning of July 30th, the fleet encountered the warship HMS *Roebuck,*

which had been anchored there for several days. The *Roebuck's* captain reported to Howe that the Delaware bristled with shore batteries and underwater obstructions. Reaching Philadelphia through these American defenses would take weeks, the captain claimed, giving Washington plenty of time either to attack Burgoyne or entrench his forces in southeast Pennsylvania. Disappointed with this report but unwilling to check if it was accurate, Howe returned to his original plan of landing in the Chesapeake and sent his armada back out to sea. Not until months later did he learn that the Americans had left the Delaware River practically defenseless.

The fleet's change of direction augured three weeks of misery for the troops and horses on board its transports. Washington spent the same three-week period in a state of continuous nervous tension. He believed at first that the British fleet's disappearance proved the whole maneuver from Sandy Hook to the Delaware to have been a ruse designed to draw him away from a "sudden stroke" on the Hudson. The Continental Army, he declared in a state of the "greatest anxiety," must therefore immediately reverse course and march for the Hudson.

Two days later, with the main army at Germantown and detachments scattered across New Jersey, Washington reconsidered. Each report he received contradicted the last. Why should Howe have sacrificed weeks of the campaigning season and exposed his troops to the ocean's hardships just to bewilder the Americans? Could the British be moving south to the Chesapeake after all? Or was it a feint? Approaching despair, Washington ordered his columns to halt. During the days and weeks that followed, Washington stewed in "a very irksome state of Suspence." The enemy's movements, he lamented, were "distressing beyond measure, and past our comprehension." All the marching and countermarching had left him baffled, embarrassed, and fearful of the effect that it would have on his soldiers and their confidence in his leadership.

The only diversion in this trying period came in the form of a young French officer, the Marquis de Lafayette, who appeared in camp on July 31st. As a rule, Washington did not like Frenchmen. "I am haunted and teazed to death by the importunity of some & dissatisfaction of others," he complained, and he found the "pompous narrative[s] of their services" both laughable and intolerable. But Washington detected something that set Lafayette apart from the other Frenchmen. The thin, pale, nineteen-year-old aristocrat had charm, money, and energy, and used them all to squeeze a major general's commission out of a skeptical American Congress. Lafayette also yearned for battlefield glory, and flattered Washington with his admiration for the older man's military wisdom.

"He has said that he is young, & inexperienced," Washington wrote to his friend Benjamin Harrison, "but at the same time has always accompanied it with a hint, that so soon as *I* shall think *him* fit for the Command of a division, he shall be ready to enter upon the duties of it; & in the meantime, has offer'd his service for a smaller Command." He promised to oblige this wish once a position opened and in the meantime allowed Lafayette to accompany his staff. As they got to know each other the two men developed a sincere and lasting friendship. Washington became a mentor to the young man, and Lafayette became a loyal friend who eventually earned his commander's trust as an active, resourceful, and reliable general. Washington would need such an officer during the coming year.

As the first days of August 1777 passed with no news of the British fleet, Washington grew increasingly convinced that the enemy's destination was the Hudson. On August 6th, he shifted his army north toward Coryell's Ferry. Four days later, while the commander-in-chief rode up and down the ferry road while supervising his marching troops, an express rider reported that scouts had sighted the British fleet heading south off Sinepuxent Inlet, a scant thirty miles south of Cape Henlopen, off Delaware. The sighting proved that Howe was still in motion toward the Chesapeake but—incredibly—Washington still suspected a ruse. Instead of marching directly for Maryland to confront a British landing, he ordered his army to Neshaminy Creek, twenty miles north of Philadelphia. Once there he intended to await further intelligence.

Weeks of uncertainty had only reinforced Washington's innate stubbornness—what Jefferson later called his slowness of mind. The new information notwithstanding, he wrote to Artemas Ward that "I am now as much puzzled about their designs as I was before, being unable to account upon any plausible plan, for Genl Howe's conduct in this instance or why he should go to the Southward rather than cooperate with Mr Burgoyne." He could not bring himself to give up the idea of British pincers on the Hudson, which "appeared to me so probable and of such importance and still does, that I shall with difficulty give into a contrary belief, till I am obliged by some unequivocal event." Accordingly, Washington kept his army on the Neshaminy for almost two more weeks while he waited for further confirmation of British intentions.

Washington still might have made wise use of the time by conducting a vigorous reconnaissance of the region between Philadelphia and the Chesapeake Bay. He could not deny the possibility of a British offensive in the area even if he denied its probability. He could have chosen potential ground for attack or defense, or at least have familiarized himself with a part of the country about which he knew next to nothing. The governments of Maryland and Delaware would also certainly have complied with a request to call the militia. But Washington did none of these things, instead allowing his army to lapse into inactivity. The effect would be crippling to the army's efforts to defend Philadelphia.

Washington's officers showed no greater prescience, but their imaginations were just as healthy—or overactive. On August 21st, still lacking conclusive information about the enemy, the commander-in-chief called a council of war. While the officers disregarded the idea of an elaborate naval feint, they also refused to believe that Howe would enter the Chesapeake. Instead, they decided unanimously that the British were bound for Charleston. With no hope of marching all the way to South Carolina, they suggested leaving the south to its own devices and attacking Burgoyne instead. Washington readily agreed and issued orders for the army to march north the next morning.

A few hours later he learned that the British fleet had entered the Chesapeake Bay.

As Washington lingered on the Neshaminy, the British troops on board Lord Howe's fleet endured a trying three weeks in the August heat. Forced to choose between the suffocating atmosphere of the holds and the sunscorched decks, men stripped to the skin and wandered back and forth in wretched lethargy. Nights offered little relief. The weather cooled only during the frequent storms, which in combination with adverse currents and occasional dead calms reduced the armada's pace to a crawl. Some days the fleet made no progress at all. Stocks of fresh provisions dwindled away to nothing, and the water supply on some transports became contaminated. Officers heard the groans of their men and rowed from ship to ship to beg supplies from those better off. Troops who did not fall ill were detailed to drag dead horses from the holds and fling them overboard.

Cape Charles finally came into view on August 14th, and the fleet entered Chesapeake Bay. Four days later the ships passed the mouth of the Rappahannock River, sighting American vessels and even exchanging shots with some Virginia militiamen on shore. On the evening of the 22nd, just as Washington learned they had entered the Chesapeake, the British dropped anchor four miles from the mouth of the Elk River. Two days of preparations followed, as loyalists and escaped slaves rowed out to greet their liberators.

The landing began at dawn on August 25th, thirty-two days after the fleet left Sandy Hook. Flatboats left the transports and made their way to Turkey Point on the west bank of the Elk River. Confident that he would encounter little opposition, William Howe accompanied his brother, Lord Richard Howe, in the lead boat and stepped ashore at 10:00 A.M. His troops cheered and then came ashore in their turn to establish a landing perimeter. The surrounding woods were "filled with snakes and toads" and insects (cicadas and katydids) so loud that "two men could not speak to each other." A few American militia companies fired their cannons at the invaders from long range and then scattered into the countryside.

British and German troops continued to stumble ashore on the next day, their spirits boosted by an issue of rum but dampened by wilting heat and devastating thunderstorms. The Germans' soggy, itchy, heavy uniforms caused them terrible misery. Dragoons coaxed and yanked their skeletal horses only to find in many instances a dead weight at the end of their ropes. Hundreds of the animals had already died during the voyage, and others dropped dead shortly after setting foot on land. Almost none remained in condition for work or riding, and to revive them on the Maryland grass would take time. The British army would remain immobile for days to come.

The British fleet's appearance in the Chesapeake forced Washington to countermand his order for a march to the Hudson soon after he had issued it. Timely news of Burgoyne's defeat at the hands of a New England army at Bennington, Vermont, convinced him that the northern army under Gates and Arnold could do well on its own. Washington now became wildly optimistic, and his attitude was not wholly unjustified. "As there is not now the least danger of General Howes going to New England," he wrote Putnam on the 22nd, "I hope the whole Force of that Country will turn out, and by following the great stroke struck by Genl Stark near Bennington intirely crush Genl Burgoine."

The main American army paraded through Philadelphia on the way to Head of Elk. Washington issued strict marching orders and demanded that his officers prevent straggling. Taverns were strictly off-limits to the troops. Led by Washington, his aides, and general officers, the Continentals marched twelve deep in heavy rain down Chestnut Street and through the Commons. Crowds of delegates and citizens watched the soldiers, their hats festooned with green branches, march "with a lively smart Step" to the sound of drums and fifes; the morning's general orders had been quite explicit that the music was to be played "with such moderation, that the men may step to it with ease; and without *dancing* along, or totally disregarding the music, as too often has been the case." Pleased with the spectacle, Washington and his entourage celebrated with punch and grog at the City Tavern while the troops crossed the Schuylkill and camped on the other side.

While his divisions marched toward Wilmington, Delaware, on the 25th, Washington convened a tense council of war. Some officers insisted on an immediate, full-scale attack before the British landing force could organize. Others urged patience, preferring to observe Howe before he advanced. Eventually, they said, he would expose himself to a surprise attack. The commander-in-chief agreed with the more cautious, wait-and-see approach, but still planned to fight in defense of Philadelphia.

The morning after the council of war, Washington set out with Greene, Lafayette, and a strong cavalry guard to scout the British positions and their probable route of advance. He and his officers knew little of the country. Riding from place to place, interrogating locals, and eluding enemy patrols took them the better part of the day. After sunset the commander-in-chief found himself just fifteen minutes' ride from Howe's lines, in the pitch dark and pouring rain. Despite the warnings of his officers he decided to take shelter in an empty farmhouse—owned by a Tory, he later learned—rather than risk stumbling into an enemy patrol in the dark. Luckily no informers told the British of his presence, and the night passed without incident.

Washington wanted to harass the enemy advance with militia and light troops while his main army waited for the right moment to make a stand, but the American farmers again disappointed him. Militia companies formed slowly and then droned across Maryland like sluggish bumblebees, occasionally snatching enemy stragglers and patrols. The cavalry, under the overall command of the dashing but ineffective Polish volunteer general Casimir Pulaski and the dapper American colonel Theodorick Bland, provided next to no useful intelligence. Washington yearned for Daniel Morgan's riflemen, the best scouts and light troops in the army; but they had gone north to reinforce Gates. In their absence Washington decided to form a light infantry corps of about 500 men under Brigadier General William Maxwell "to be constantly near the Enemy and to give 'em every possible annoyance." This *ad hoc* formation guarded the roads leading north from Head of Elk.

By now, recruits and reinforcements had brought the Continental Army to about 16,000 troops, with the greatest number of them camped in the vicinity of Wilmington. Greene's division lay at White Clay Creek, six miles to the southwest, and some Pennsylvania militiamen idled at Christiana Bridge. Not content with the observations of others, and undeterred by previous close calls, Washington spent most of his days on horseback, examining the terrain. Thanks to his earlier neglect of reconnaissance, he had a lot to see and learn.

The commander-in-chief regarded the coming contest as an opportunity rather than a dire necessity. With his rebuilt army he intended not just to block the enemy advance, but to deliver a crushing blow and perhaps end the war. The young men staffing his new officer corps were full of fight, too, and even the canny Greene expected to inflict a "deadly wound" on the British. So much for Washington's heralded Fabian strategy. The Continental Army was eager and overconfident, just as it had been on Long Island a year before.

Howe, who had allowed his troops to rest for three days, finally moved them forward in hot, dry weather on the morning of August 28th. The vanguard halted just beyond the attractive little town Head of Elk and waited as British engineers repaired a damaged bridge across the Elk River. Infantry meanwhile waded in water up to their knees and clambered up the opposite bank. As Howe and his staff tarried nearby they scanned Grays Hill, about two miles away, from which a party of what appeared to be American officers and cavalry was watching. One of the Americans stood out among the brightly attired group in his plain gray coat. The British studied the figure for some time before deciding that he was the enemy commander-in-chief. Washington and his entourage eluded the cavalry that Howe threw in pursuit.

After chasing Washington away and occupying Grays Hill, Howe ordered a pause of several days to rest the sickly horses. He resumed the advance at dawn on September 3rd and split his force into two divisions. Knyphausen headed one, which had crossed the Elk River to Cecil Court House on the last day of August to gather forage and protect the right flank. Howe accompanied the other division under Cornwallis as it marched from Head of Elk. Cornwallis arrived first at the rendezvous at Glasgow, Delaware, and took the lead on the road north at 9:00 A.M.

Captain Johann Ewald rode at the head of Cornwallis's column with a group of six German dragoons. Seeking to find the best route to Christiana Bridge, they passed through mixed terrain of fields, woods, and hedgerows. Before Ewald had gone far, a group of William Maxwell's American marksmen rose from behind a hedge and discharged a volley that blasted all six of the dragoons from their saddles. Ewald, who was the only one unhurt, turned and rode back on his wounded horse, yelling for the foot jaegers to advance on the double. They responded quickly and drove the Americans from one tree or hedge to another. Maxwell's men fired sporadic volleys but inflicted light casualties.

This skirmishing continued for about two miles before the Americans attempted to make a stand in some woods at Cooch's Bridge. When the British light infantry came up, Cornwallis attempted a double envelopment of the American position. The light infantry gamely attempted to get around Maxwell's right, but bogged down in the underbrush and muck of the aptly named Purgatory Swamp. German grenadiers had more success in gaining the American left, which they wrecked with a bayonet charge preceded by a cannonade from some small guns called "amusettes." Maxwell's troops then fled in disorder to White Clay Creek. The Americans had taken about sixty casualties, the British slightly fewer. Howe did not pursue but camped his troops and their large herd of confiscated cattle in the vicinity of the Cooch's Bridge battlefield. They remained there for four days.

The defeat at Cooch's Bridge—painted as a victory by some Americans— did not discourage Washington's Continentals, who eagerly anticipated the coming battle. For several days they had watched civilian refugees, women and children on foot driving cows or seated atop carts piled high with furniture, crowding the roads to Lancaster or Philadelphia. Some sobbed out accounts of robbery and rape. Despite Howe's best efforts—which included execution for marauders—his soldiers plundered without mercy. The Americans yearned to punish them. News of Burgoyne's defeat at Bennington passed from tent to tent and made the Continentals even more certain they would succeed.

Washington sensed his troops' determination and delivered a prebattle exhortation. The "last effort" of the enemy to take Philadelphia approached, he declared. "The critical, the important moment is at hand." If they faced it well, the Continentals would win the decisive battle for the city and the Revolution itself. They must not falter but deliver "one bold stroke" that would leave the enemy "utterly undone." Not trusting wholly in the troops' patriotic instincts, however, he warned that deserters and malingerers would be "instantly shot down."

Washington decided to make his first stand on Red Clay Creek, even though that shallow, easily fordable waterway offered no real protection against attack. He placed his army behind it on September 6th and sent Maxwell's corps a few miles southwest to form a screen at White Clay Creek. The next day Washington learned that the British had left behind all of their heavy baggage in readiness for rapid movement, and he ordered his troops to shed their packs and prepare for battle. In the early morning of September 8th, the enemy stirred. The Continentals waited for them under the lights of a bizarre, unseasonable aurora borealis.

Howe did not oblige Washington with a frontal assault. Instead, while a small detachment demonstrated in front of the Americans, he sent the rest of his troops around Washington's right. The redcoats set out just before dawn and marched for several hours through the early morning chill. They passed close enough to the Americans to hear their alarm guns firing and camped for the night about five miles northwest of Newport. The move threatened to cut Washington off from Lancaster and possibly Philadelphia itself.

Washington waited all day for Howe to attack. The British detachment demonstrating to his front kept him guessing until nightfall. Then, in the early morning of the 9th—several hours after the enemy army had settled down on his right—Washington ordered his troops to retreat to Chadds Ford. Awakened after a few hours' rest, they stumbled off through the darkness, splashed across Brandywine Creek, and dropped in exhaustion at the ford later that afternoon. By the time the camp settled down for the night, Greene wrote his wife that he had been on horseback for thirty hours and without sleep for forty.

The last three months had been one long nightmare of marching and countermarching. That time was now over. The year's bloodiest battle was about to begin.

On the 9th, while the Americans retreated to Chadds Ford, Howe pushed his army forward to the vicinity of Kennett Square. As his soldiers made camp that evening the British commander set out to reconnoiter the American positions. Physically just as fearless as Washington, Howe probed the Continental outposts closely and nearly got killed in the dark by one of his own patrols before he finished tracing the American positions along the east bank of Brandywine Creek overlooking Chadds Ford. Their left, he saw, was well anchored in rugged terrain south of the ford. Their right flank extended a few miles to the north before fading away into a series of low hills and defiles. Outflanking these positions looked difficult—all the main crossing places appeared to be covered—but Howe nevertheless returned to camp determined to attack as soon as possible. He would do it frontally if he had to.

The next evening, while Howe drew up plans for his attack, a British spy padded past redcoats savoring the day's rum issue and entered headquarters. The Americans, the spy told Howe, would not have to be assaulted frontally. They could be outflanked. On Washington's right, about a mile north of the farthest Continental outpost, at Buffington's Ford, the Brandywine forked northeast and northwest. Just above the forks a road crossed both branches of the creek over Trimble's and Jeffries' fords, and continued east and south into the American rear. Amazingly, the fords and road were unguarded; but getting to them would not be easy. The British army would have to march a dozen miles northeast of Kennett Square on a road through the long limestone ditch known as the Great Valley, to a point just above the forks of the Brandywine. From there Howe could turn east, cross the two fords, and continue through a defile around the American right. If Washington knew about the defile—and Howe could not be certain that he did not—just a few hundred militiamen posted there could delay and stifle the attack. But if the defile was unguarded and the British passed through it quickly, they could roll up Washington's right and win the battle.

Howe promptly revised his attack plans, deciding to split his army into two

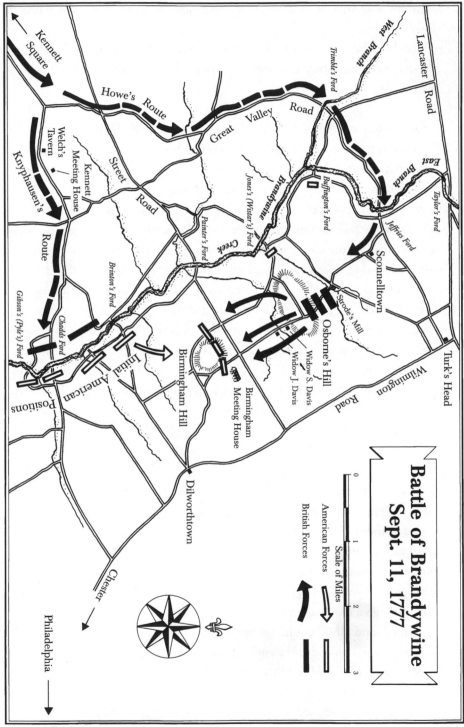

Battle of Brandywine
Sept. 11, 1777

Scale of Miles

British Forces
American Forces

0   1   2   3

Kennett Square

Howe's Route

Great Valley Road

Trimble's Ford

West Branch

Lancaster Road

East Branch

Taylor's Ford

Jeffries Ford

Sconnelltown

Buffington's Ford

Strode's Mill

Osborne's Hill

Widow S. Davis

Widow J. Davis

Birmingham Meeting House

Birmingham Hill

Dilworthtown

Chester

Philadelphia

Initial American Positions

Chadds Ford

Britton's Ford

Gibson's (Pyle's) Ford

Painter's Ford

Jones' (Wistar's) Ford

Brandywine Creek

Street Road

Kennett Meeting House

Welch's Tavern

Knyphausen's Route

Wilmington Road

Turk's Head

© 2005 Rick Britton

columns. The first, led by himself and General Cornwallis, would take the route pointed out by the spy and march around Washington's right flank. The second, led by Knyphausen, would advance directly from Kennett Square on Chadds Ford. Knyphausen's orders were to take the heights on the west side of the ford and then fire a cannonade to signal that he had taken his objective. He would then wait until firing to the north announced the arrival of Howe's column on Washington's right before pushing straight across the Brandywine and on toward Chester. If Howe and Knyphausen coordinated properly and had enough daylight, their two forces would catch Washington in a vise and cut off his retreat.

Howe scheduled the attack to begin in the early morning of September 11th. If all worked as planned, it could result in the long-awaited decisive battle that would destroy the Continental Army. Washington would never be in greater danger of losing the war.

Washington believed that he had chosen his position wisely. To all appearances, Brandywine Creek formed a strong natural obstacle to the British advance on Philadelphia. From its mouth on the Delaware at Wilmington, where marshy land and deep water hindered any potential crossing, the creek ran in a generally northern direction through steep ravines flanked by wooded granite hills. This beautiful but rugged country faded into a region of heavily cultivated rolling hills just across the Pennsylvania-Maryland border. Two miles north of the border, Chadds Ford was the first major crossing place on the road from Head of Elk, and Howe's most direct route to the American capital.

Chadds Ford consisted of a ferry and a ford, the former about three hundred yards downstream from the latter. The water at the ferry flowed only waist deep, so civilians often forded the creek there, too. On the east bank of the creek stood a ferry house and tavern. Steep wooded bluffs rose south of these buildings, but open hills of about two to three hundred feet dominated the ford itself. Upstream, the Brandywine meandered through more hilly farmland, but it still ran swiftly enough to hinder crossing at anywhere other than a series of fords. These, from south to north respectively, were Brinton's, Painter's, Jones's, and Buffington's fords, the last being at the forks of the creek, about six miles above Chadds Ford. Scouts told Washington that there were no usable crossing places within twelve miles above Buffington's Ford.

Two American divisions defended Chadds Ford. Greene's division, comprising two brigades of Virginians under Brigadier Generals Weedon and Muhlenberg, guarded the ferry. To Greene's right, Lincoln's division (under the temporary command of Anthony Wayne since Lincoln had joined the northern army in July) defended the heights over the ford, which the Americans had clogged with fallen trees. Wayne had two brigades of Pennsylvanians and four guns of the Continental artillery under Colonel Thomas Proctor. Stephen's division with two brigades of Virginians waited in reserve behind Wayne. Sullivan's division of Maryland Continentals stood about a mile north of Wayne, at Brinton's Ford. In reserve to Sullivan's left rear was Stirling's division, made up of Conway's brigade of Pennsylvanians and another brigade of New Jersey troops. Finally, Washington posted Maxwell's light infantry to the west, along the Nottingham Road, with orders to slow a direct advance along that route.

Given the rugged terrain to the south, Howe's troops could launch only a frontal assault or march around the American right. It seems clear, however—despite some later interpretations of the battle—that Washington did not expect a direct attack on Chadds Ford. Instead, he predicted correctly that the enemy would try to maneuver, or turn his right flank. Yet Washington did not explore that flank personally but left the responsibility for reconnoitering and defending it to General Sullivan and Colonel Bland. Sullivan detached Colonel Josias Hall's Delaware Regiment to cover Painter's Ford, and ordered Colonel Moses Hazen's mixed "Canadian" Regiment to guard Jones's and Buffington's Ford. Bland roamed freely north to the forks of the Brandywine and reported to headquarters only rarely.

Why did Washington not make a better effort to scout and secure his right? One reason is that he put too much trust in Sullivan, Bland, and their scouts. Another is that he planned either to withdraw without fighting, or to attack before his right was turned. On his march from Head of Elk, Howe had taken his time, ordering halts with a frequency that suggested the British horses and soldiers had not yet recovered from their ordeal at sea. Expecting the British to continue moving slowly, even if Howe marched his entire force around the American right, Washington anticipated having plenty of time to react by shifting reserves or, if necessary, withdrawing to Chester.

Another possibility was that Howe would repeat his earlier performance on Red Clay Creek and divide his army, sending a portion to demonstrate at Chadds Ford while the rest crossed the Brandywine somewhere to the

British left. If that happened, Washington planned to attack and defeat the enemy detachment to his front before the flanking force returned to its support or crossed the Brandywine. Success nevertheless would depend either on a glacial British flank march or the absence of any suitable crossing places less than ten or fifteen miles above Buffington's Ford.

Washington feared only that Howe, without dividing his force, would lure him into an attack and trap the Continental Army on the left bank of the Brandywine. The commander-in-chief apparently did not consider that even if Howe *did* divide his army, any Americans who crossed the creek would have to fight with water to their backs while large enemy forces remained to the west and north. That invited disaster. To avoid it, the Continentals would have to cross the Brandywine, massacre the detachment facing them, and return—all in a matter of a few hours. The lightning successes at Trenton and Princeton apparently led Washington to underestimate the enemy, and to overestimate his own and his troops' ability to perform miracles on the battlefield. Fortunately, even if his tactical sense deserted him, his luck did not.

The British army marched before dawn on the 11th. Fog lay dense on the ground, but the day promised to be warm and fair. Howe left camp first with Cornwallis and a mixed British-German column of about 8,200 men at 5:00 A.M., following the Nottingham Road east for a short distance before turning north on the Great Valley Road. Knyphausen marched an hour later with 6,800 British, Germans, and loyalist provincials, marching directly down the Nottingham Road toward Chadds Ford.

Green-coated loyalist units—the Queen's Rangers and Ferguson's sharpshooters—led Knyphausen's column. They marched through forested country interspersed by occasional clearings, hills, and marshes for about an hour before encountering the first American sentinels, who fired a few volleys and fled into the woods. Every ten or fifteen minutes they repeated the process. Light skirmishing continued for another five miles until 8:00 A.M., when the loyalists passed a house in a clearing to their right. Across the clearing on the other side of the house trickled a small stream. Beyond that stood a fence and a line of trees at the foot of a wooded slope leading up to the heights above Chadds Ford, only a musket shot away.

Expecting little opposition, the loyalists started across the clearing without taking any precautions. Suddenly a rattle of musketry from behind the fence left several greencoats writhing on the ground. Behind the powder smoke emerged a well-formed line of Maxwell's light infantry, who yelped excitedly at the sight of the hated provincials falling before their ambuscade. The loyalists fell back, dragging their wounded, before woods that now seemed full of enemy troops. Ferguson's sharpshooters, bearing breech-loading rifles that their commander had partly designed, dodged behind the house and its surrounding walls on the right while the Queen's Rangers filed off into the woods to the left of the road. Knyphausen arrived quickly on the scene, but the provincials rallied only when redcoats came trotting forward with artillery. Two regiments of British infantry then moved to Ferguson's support along with four pieces of artillery. These they posted on an eminence behind the house. Another regiment of British foot moved to support the Queen's Rangers on the left.

Some of Greene's troops heard the firing and waded across the creek to support Maxwell's main body. Observing enemy preparations for a renewed attack, Maxwell's infantry slapped together a breastwork on the left and placed a few pieces of light artillery behind it. Greene's men supported them while other infantry filtered into the woods along the road and to the right. But Knyphausen moved quickly, and the British fieldpieces pummeled the breastwork before the Americans had finished erecting it. At about the same time the British and provincial soldiers started forward with their bayonets. They took some casualties but succeeded in clearing the woods on the American right, outflanking and then capturing the breastwork.

Proctor's artillery on the other side of the Brandywine attempted to support Maxwell as Knyphausen's troops reached the heights, but, incredibly, the poorly sited guns only shredded the branches above their adversaries' heads. Maxwell nevertheless withdrew his infantry across the ford in good order. Knyphausen rested most of his troops in the woods, but he placed a corps of about 500 picked marksmen with fieldpieces on the heights. They announced their arrival to the Americans—and to Howe—with desultory firing across the creek, but otherwise made no move to cross. It was 10:30 A.M.

Washington had moved from his headquarters at the Benjamin Ring house that morning to watch the commotion from the heights overlooking Chadds Ford. Posted nearby, Proctor's artillery merrily defoliated the trees across the Brandywine while British counterfire knocked the head off an artilleryman not far from where Washington stood. Maxwell rode up to the commander-in-chief and exulted that he had inflicted some three hundred enemy casualties to only fifty of his own. The British seemed disinclined to advance farther, presumably out of horror at their ghastly losses, and Washington decided that he need not expect a direct attack across the ford. Yet he still could only guess the size of the force facing him. It did not seem very large. Where was the rest of the British army?

Washington suspected that Howe had divided his command, and reiterated his demand for prompt intelligence of any British activity on his right flank lest a force try to cross the Brandywine farther north. A rider from Hazen arrived before 11:00 A.M. with news that increased his worries. A British column, the horseman said, had been seen marching north up the Great Valley Road to the west of the creek. Yet Bland, who was supposed to be patrolling that area, had sent no word of such a movement. Washington complained bitterly of this renewed sign of the ineffectiveness of his cavalry. The cheers that his troops gave him as he rode up and down the line offered slight recompense for the uncertainty that pricked his mind.

About noon a rider handed Washington news from an unlikely source. Lieutenant Colonel James Ross of the Eighth Pennsylvania Regiment, scouting across the Brandywine with about seventy men, reported that he had skirmished about an hour earlier with a column of about 5,000 British infantry and artillery somewhere on the Great Valley Road. Ross insisted that he had seen Howe himself at the head of the British force. Unfortunately Ross did not specify *where* he had skirmished, but he did write that the road led to two hitherto unknown fords over the Brandywine, Taylor's and Jeffries'. What impression this news made on Washington, or whether anyone told him the location of the two fords, is unclear. Neither he nor Sullivan made any move to confirm their existence and location.

Just in case, though, Washington ordered Stephen's and Stirling's small reserve divisions to Birmingham Hill, just behind Sullivan's right. These two divisions would not be able to halt a major British attack on their own, but they might delay a late-afternoon attack until sundown. Washington discounted the possibility of an attack from that direction any sooner than the early evening. Instead, he set his mind on the opportunity offered by the divided state of Howe's army and ordered a general assault across the Brandywine.

At about noon Washington instructed Sullivan to cross with his division and attack Knyphausen's left, while the rest of the army assaulted the enemy's right. Continentals on both wings began crossing the Brandywine within the hour. At Chadds Ford Maxwell and Greene pushed forward with about 2,000 men, and Sullivan sent the Third Maryland Regiment across

Brinton's Ford. They quickly made contact with the enemy and awaited reinforcements.

As Sullivan watched the Marylanders cross Brinton's Ford and formed the rest of his division to follow them, however, Major Joseph Spear of the Chester County Militia reined in at divisional headquarters with some surprising intelligence. All that morning, Spear claimed, he had ridden the Great Valley Road from Martin's Tavern in the forks of the Brandywine to Welch's Tavern east of Kennett Square and back again, without seeing a single redcoat.

This puzzling report contradicted the intelligence given earlier by Hazen's scouts, and Sullivan, who probably knew nothing of Ross's skirmish with Howe, hesitated before sending it on to the commander-in-chief. Spear claimed to be acting under the orders of Washington himself, but Hazen's report had also been specific and believable. If false, Spear's information might spoil a rare opportunity for victory by forcing Washington to cancel his attack. If correct, it could mean that the Americans would end up facing the whole British army with the Brandywine at their back. In such a case Sullivan would find his own head on the chopping block for withholding information. On that thought he scribbled a hasty summary of the major's report and sent him along with it to the commander-in-chief.

Washington's interrogation of Spear must have made both men uneasy. If no British were on the Great Valley Road, with whom had Ross skirmished? Who had Hazen's scouts seen? Unfortunately, neither Ross nor Hazen had specified where on the road they had made contact with the enemy. If their sightings had in fact been far to the south, and *before* Spear rode to Welch's Tavern, Howe's column might have countermarched to Chadds Ford. If so, the American troops crossing the Brandywine might find themselves in a trap.

The evidence, weak and contradictory as it was, apparently convinced Washington that this was the case. It accounted both for the intelligence he had received, and that which he had not received. Bland, who presumably still reconnoitered the northern reaches of the Great Valley Road, would have reported if Howe had continued marching for the forks of the Brandywine. If the British column had, on the other hand, left the road by turning east for Jones's or Painter's fords, it surely would have run into Sullivan's advanced parties by that time. Howe must therefore have gone to all that trouble to deceive the American scouts and draw Washington into battle on the wrong side of the creek. As it had in August, when he had imagined an elaborate British feint to draw him away from the Hudson, Washington's imagination led him astray.

In this instance, however, the results were not all bad. Washington countermanded his orders for an attack on Knyphausen, thereby averting the disaster that would have occurred if Howe's flank attack had caught the Americans halfway across the creek. Washington's next order, withdrawing Stephen and Stirling from Birmingham Hill to their original positions behind Chadds Ford, was less prudent; for in obeying that order they left the right flank practically undefended.

Howe's column spent the morning of September 11th in a tiring but largely uneventful march. There were no countermarches or other subterfuges. A heavy fog lay in the valley until mid-morning, concealing the British, and it may have caused Major Spear and his party to miss them by taking a wrong road. Captain Ewald commanded the advance guard of jaegers and Scottish light infantry, throwing out a screen on either side of the road. Americans, probably part of the force commanded by Ross, skirmished with them from time to time, and Ewald advanced with caution to avoid ambuscades. A loyalist guide with an intimate knowledge of the defiles and woods along the road accompanied the advance guard, preparing Ewald for every new American position and preventing Ross's men from inflicting the kind of casualties that the loyalists had suffered before Chadds Ford.

Howe's column marched much faster than Washington had expected, crossing the forks of the Brandywine around midday after a trek of about twelve miles. By this time Ross's men had disappeared, and the men and horses waded through three feet of water without opposition. As the head of the column reached the other side of Jeffries' Ford, Ewald paused. Ahead the road ran through a short but steep defile, terrain in which any competent enemy would stage an ambush. A regiment or two of Continental infantry posted there with a few field guns could delay the advance for hours. "My hair stood on end as we crammed into the defile," Ewald recalled, "and I imagined nothing more certain than an unexpected attack at the moment when we would have barely stuck our nose out of the defile." But he led his troops forward.

The troops labored up the steep road in the midday heat, in no condition to face a determined enemy; but as the advance continued and no musket or cannon fire rang out from the hills, Ewald's fear gave way to amazement. The Americans had left the pass undefended! After several minutes the advance guard passed the defile and the road turned south through less rugged country. They continued for almost another mile, until 2:30 P.M., when Cornwallis ordered a halt.

At his direction the lead infantry formed up into lines by brigade on the barren heights of Osborne's Hill, and then toppled over to rest after a march of seventeen miles. Troops from the middle and rear of the column continued to file in during the next hour, disposing of their packs as they arrived. Howe invited Cornwallis and the others to lunch with him on the grass as they listened to the sound of Knyphausen's cannonade and scanned the country ahead. Howe laughed and joked with his officers as they watched American troops and flags begin appearing on the crest of Birmingham Hill, a mile to the south.

The British crossing had been unopposed, but it did not go undetected. At 1:15 P.M., Bland, who hitherto had ridden about the country to little purpose, discovered a group of British scouts near a widow's house at the foot of Osborne's Hill and dutifully sent a note off to Washington. He waited almost another hour before sending word to Sullivan that the British had appeared in force on the road north of Osborne's Hill, and added that he had placidly watched dust rise from the advancing British column since well before 1:00 P.M.—without mentioning it to anybody.

This new information sent Washington's camp into a frenzy. On receipt of Bland's first note Washington ordered Stephen and Stirling to retrace their steps to Birmingham Hill, some four or five miles from the reserve positions to which they had recently returned. While this movement was under way, at 2:00 P.M. Sullivan received Bland's second letter and immediately forwarded it to the commander-in-chief. Washington replied within half an hour, but told Sullivan only to withdraw from Brinton's Ford, march in the direction of the enemy, and form a junction with the other two divisions. Sullivan threw his troops in the general direction of Osborne's Hill without knowing exactly what position he would have to defend, for Washington had not specified. And although he urged Stephen and Stirling to drive their troops on to Birmingham Hill at a trot, he had not told them how to coordinate their movement with Sullivan, who would take command of all three divisions.

Sullivan led his troops north until Birmingham Hill loomed to their right and rear. Along the way he ran into Hazen, whose regiment had fled before what they judged to be the bulk of the British army. Sullivan's officers then directed his attention to the redcoats sprawled on Osborne's Hill and to Stephen and Stirling's divisions drawing up on Birmingham Hill. Sullivan immediately ordered his division to file off toward Birmingham Hill while Hazen's regiment covered the movement.

At first, Howe allowed the American line to form in peace. Stephen and Stirling, with an hour's head start on Sullivan, formed their troops into line among well-sited three- and four-pounder cannon that the men had dragged with tremendous effort across the country and up the partially wooded hill. Stephen placed his Virginians behind a wall surrounding the Quaker church across the Birmingham Road to the east, among the small buildings lining the road, and on the eastern slopes of Birmingham Hill. Stirling held the rest of the hill with his own division. Delayed by poor terrain and the inexperience of officers who had not learned to maneuver infantry on the battlefield, Sullivan's division took a long time to arrive on the left.

At 3:30 P.M., as Sullivan struggled to move his division into position, the officers of Howe's advance guard moved their troops forward. Ewald formed his foot jaegers into line and advanced, followed by mounted jaegers and light infantry, across some farmland toward the cluster of buildings around the church. The Germans moved cautiously across the field, but before they reached the houses a line of Americans appeared among the trees of an orchard and delivered a volley that sent them scurrying for cover behind a split-rail fence that crossed their path. Here the Germans remained, returning fire as well as they could for the next thirty minutes.

Anticipating Howe's main attack, Ewald left his jaegers and with three companions scouted the slopes of Birmingham Hill. Racing across the road and emerging from cover at the foot of the hill, he was astonished to find Stirling's well-formed line just a few hundred feet away. The Americans saw him and waved their hats in mockery, but allowed the small party to escape. Ewald sent a note to Cornwallis and then returned to his original position, where he brandished his sword and forced some nearby civilians to help dismantle the fence so that it would not obstruct the coming advance.

Howe began the attack at 4:00 P.M., sending his troops forward in three columns and then deploying them into two lines. British light infantry and the rest of the jaegers moved to the left behind Ewald; the British and German grenadiers advanced directly on Birmingham Hill in the center; and the Guards marched toward Sullivan's straggling lines on the right. The music of the Grenadier March accompanied the advance, followed by a marching cadence on the drums. Despite Ewald's work, the soldiers had to pause from time to time to remove fences and other obstructions.

Stephen's and Stirling's Continentals waited until the enemy lines came within easy musket shot; then they opened fire with everything they had. The artillery began with solid shot, switching to canister and grape as the enemy neared the hill. On the British center and left the American fire tore gaps in the advancing lines and forced the infantry to take cover. Despite the aid of some light fieldpieces brought up to support them, the British infantry could advance no farther. But on the right, the Guards continued their advance past Birmingham Hill out of sight of the American artillery. The German grenadiers in the second line of the center also moved in this direction, but approached the hill from the west rather than bypassing it as the Guards had done.

The advance on the west side of Birmingham Hill caught Sullivan's division in a difficult situation. Sullivan, who had ridden to the crest of the hill to confer with Stephen and Stirling, no longer accompanied his division, which was commanded in his absence by the impetuous—or cowardly—French brigadier general Preudhomme de Borré. The division might as well have been leaderless, for its officers proved unable to get their troops into position. They were still marching and countermarching through a narrow lane and some gates when the German grenadiers gained the lower slope of Birmingham Hill and began picking off the exposed Continentals. The Guards meanwhile plowed straight ahead, driving the ineffective Hazen aside and crashing into Sullivan's division, which quickly broke. De Borré fled with his troops through the underbrush. He later tried to convince his skeptical American comrades that the briar scratches on his face had been inflicted by English muskets loaded with fish hooks.

As Sullivan tried to rally his shattered division, the British redoubled their assault on Birmingham Hill. Some companies of British light infantry gained a blind spot on the east slope of the hill, though not without sustaining severe casualties. With them on the east slope and the German grenadiers on the left slope, Cornwallis, who had taken cover with his troops in the center, ordered the grenadiers to renew their advance. The half hour that followed was one of the hardest-fought in the war. As the British and Germans moved forward in rushes, taking advantage of cover when they could, the crest of the hill surged in point-blank musket fire and hand-to-hand fighting. Sullivan, Stirling, and Conway rallied their men for counterattacks, and the crest changed possession five times—"till," Sullivan claimed, "we had almost Covered the Ground . . . with The Dead Bodies of the Enemy."

Finally, sheer numbers and the British bayonet told on Stirling's division, which left several fieldpieces behind and withdrew to the south along with the remnants of Hazen's regiment. Stephen's division followed not far behind. The whole contest had taken over an hour and a half, and left scores of American and British dead and wounded lying on the hill and in the area around the church. Surgeons tore off the doors of the church and set to work there on the wounded.

The Americans had already lost the battle; the question now was whether Washington would be able to get his army off the battlefield. As the fighting on Birmingham Hill began, Washington had ordered Greene to withdraw his division from Chadds Ford and move into a position from which he could either support the right flank or cover a retreat. Maxwell, Proctor, and Wayne remained facing Knyphausen. Washington then rode furiously for Birmingham Hill, arriving just in time to watch his line collapse.

As the Continentals streamed south, the three divisional commanders tried to rally fragments of their commands and form a rear guard. The only intact formation was Conway's Pennsylvania Brigade, which he formed on a small hill a short distance to the southeast. Washington remained long enough to understand the seriousness of the situation, then rode back to join Greene. Lafayette, eager to see some of the fighting, remained behind with Conway.

On this occasion, Howe's energy did not fail. The fight on Birmingham Hill had been severe and the casualties heavy, but at Howe's direction Cornwallis urged his troops to pursue the fleeing Americans. Plunging ahead, they savaged the rear of Stephen's column and then smashed into Conway's brigade. The tired Pennsylvanians resisted stoutly at first, but crumbled abruptly before a British bayonet charge. Lafayette received a musket ball in the leg and had to be carried off the field while Conway's shattered brigade retreated east toward Dilworthtown behind the rest of the army.

Washington's left flank caved in at the same time that his right disintegrated. As planned, Knyphausen had waited until firing began around Birmingham Hill before beginning his own attack on Chadds Ford. Artillery

supported this prepared position, but after Greene's withdrawal the only infantry were from Wayne's and Maxwell's formations. Knyphausen's troops
thus outnumbered the force facing them by about two thousand men.

The British guns began pounding the American lines at Chadds Ford at
4:00 P.M. After waiting a short time for the bombardment to take effect,
Knyphausen's troops started across the ferry, regiment by regiment. The men
moved slowly in the log-strewn, waist-deep water, but by crossing at that
point instead of at the better-defended ford upstream they avoided the worst
of Proctor's artillery fire and suffered fewer casualties. On reaching the other
side, they formed and then drove forward with the bayonet against the American positions, which collapsed almost at once. The infantry tried to make a
stand in a buckwheat field farther back, but they broke before a bayonet
charge and fled down the road to Chester. Proctor's men abandoned all four
of their guns and followed them.

By 6:00 P.M. the only unbroken American troops remaining on the field belonged to Greene's division. Since withdrawing from Chadds Ford they had
marched almost four miles in forty-five minutes, an impressive feat that left
them aching but gave time for preparing defensive positions. At Dilworthtown, Greene found the three American divisions that had been posted on
the right flank "routed and retreating precipitately, and in the most broken
and confused manner." He also met Washington and Sullivan and discussed
with them the urgent question of where to place his two brigades of Virginians. They eventually decided to place Muhlenberg's brigade and some artillery on a slight rise to the front of Cornwallis's rapidly approaching line,
while Weedon's brigade halted a short distance away in a plowed field to take
the enemy in the flank.

Two battalions of English and German grenadiers led the advance on Dilworthtown. The Germans approached the village about 6:00 P.M., probably
expecting no further serious opposition from the Americans, but they ran
into a powerful barrage of musket fire and grapeshot from Muhlenberg's men
and their fieldpieces. The grenadiers at first broke, but with support from
their English comrades they re-formed and renewed the attack. Meanwhile
two regiments of English infantry moved into position on a small hill to their
left. When they reached the top they encountered vigorous musket fire from
Weedon's brigade, which had intended to take the grenadiers in the flank but
turned in time to meet this new threat. Half of the British infantry, and almost all of their officers, pitched to the ground dead or wounded. Some field-

pieces rushed to their support, but the Virginians held their ground in the field under intense fire. The rest of the American army used the opportunity to escape.

Greene's troops had little ammunition remaining when darkness finally fell at Dilworthtown an hour later, and they withdrew to the southeast. After a few miles the road they followed converged with the Nottingham Road leading east from Chadds Ford. The army then merged into one weary column, marching for several hours before the Continentals collapsed in fields around Chester. All that night men staggered into camp in twos and threes, while wagons full of wounded creaked toward Philadelphia.

Howe, fortunately for the Americans, decided not to pursue. The bravery of Greene's division had already allowed the bulk of Washington's army to slip out of the British vise, and while a close pursuit might have netted a few hundred more prisoners, there was no longer any chance of bagging the entire Continental Army. And the redcoats were exhausted. They had been marching and fighting since early morning, and the stubborn resistance of the Americans on Birmingham Hill and elsewhere had taken a steep toll in killed and wounded. The British commander told his troops to rest.

Washington and his staff, drooping weakly in their saddles, arrived in Chester just before midnight and established headquarters in a private home. The aides wanted to go to bed, but Washington asked his aide Robert Hanson Harrison to prepare an account of the day's action for dispatch to Congress. Harrison had already written to Hancock early that morning and again at 5:00 P.M., so he begged off. Washington then turned to his aide Timothy Pickering, who grudgingly went to another room and drew up the desired document. Washington scanned Pickering's gloomy lines. They would do, he said, along with some "words of encouragement" that he dictated. "Notwithstanding the misfortune of the day," Washington said, "I am happy to find the troops in good spirits; and I hope another time we shall compensate for the losses now sustained."

The toll of men dead, wounded, and captured on September 11, 1777, has never been precisely determined. Howe reported 89 killed and 488 wounded, probably only a slight underestimation. Washington's army suffered something like 200 killed, 500 wounded and 400 captured, with their greater number of fatalities probably attributable to the British bayonet. Most of those captured were taken at the end of the day. The Americans also lost ten artillery pieces. It was a notable victory for the British army, one of Howe's finest moments, and probably Washington's worst battlefield performance of the war.

Washington, and indeed most Americans, assumed that the final casualty count tallied much more in his favor than was the case. Yet few had any illusions that the Continental Army had been defeated. Recriminations began almost immediately after the battle, yet no one pointed a finger at the commander-in-chief. Instead, Major General John Sullivan, who had already fallen into trouble after a failed raid on Long Island earlier that summer and oversaw the collapse of Washington's right flank on the Brandywine, became the popular scapegoat. Thomas Burke reflected the gossip in Philadelphia when he wrote a friend that "the Glory of a Compleat Victory . . . was certainly in our Power if Sullivan had not by his Folly and misconduct ruined the Fortune of the Day." Washington did not encourage this kind of talk and even wrote a letter in Sullivan's favor; but although he would not apportion blame, he also refused to accept it.

He also refused to admit defeat. The decisive battle had arrived, and the Continental Army had lost. But the road to Philadelphia still remained closed to the British, and Washington was prepared to risk everything in order to keep it that way.

13

GERMANTOWN

September – October 1777

WASHINGTON SHOWED NO public signs of discouragement in the aftermath of his defeat on the Brandywine. "A Spirited Effort by the people," he assured Brigadier General William Smallwood on September 12th, could still "put a happy & speedy end to the present contest." Americans, he maintained, had no choice but to offer "another Appeal to Heaven," fight on, and hope that "we shall prove successful." What he might have felt privately is more difficult to determine, for by this time Washington had become an expert at hiding his inner thoughts from contemporaries and from posterity. There can be little doubt, however, that he felt the sting of his recent drubbing and longed to even the score.

The tired Continentals had only a few hours of rest at Chester on September 12th before Washington marched them east to Darby and then north across the Schuylkill River to a point near Germantown, an old Quaker settlement six miles northwest of Philadelphia. Here they halted on the morning of the 13th. After pitching their tents, which they had not used in over a week, the Continentals assembled on parade to hear the commander-in-chief tell them that, although the results of the 11th had been "not so favorable as could be wished," they had inflicted heavy losses on the enemy. Congress thanked the troops in a way they could better understand—by voting to give them thirty hogsheads of rum.

Encouraged by Howe's apparent disinclination to pursue, Washington decided to risk another encounter in hopes of saving Philadelphia. Early on the morning of the 14th he marched his army seven miles northwest to Swede's Ford on the Schuylkill. Not wanting to getting their clothes wet, the officers borrowed horses or boats to cross to the river's west bank. The common soldiers had to strip off their shoes and stockings before fording the river over sharp rocks that slashed their feet. They then trudged several miles farther west along the Lancaster Road before Washington let them stop, "denied [of] every desirable refreshment," in a field near two taverns. Many of them had lost or thrown away their blankets, and the remaining shreds of their uniforms could not keep out the cold northern wind that began blowing the day after the battle. They remained willing to fight, but men had their limits.

The next morning the Continental Army proceeded another few miles southwest to the loyalist-owned Admiral Warren Tavern near Paoli. This position protected Swede's Ford, the best crossing place on the Schuylkill northwest of Philadelphia, and threatened the flank of the British advance on the city. As Washington wryly told Hancock, it also prevented the enemy "from turning our right flank, which they seem to have a violent inclination to effect by all their movements."

On September 16th the weather caused the troops more suffering. It had rained heavily all the previous night, and although it tapered off in the morning a blustery wind drove moisture down the men's necks and through their coats. They could not spend the day under cover, though, for at 9:00 A.M. a report of an enemy advance forced them to tumble out of their tents and stand under arms while the quartermasters carried off their baggage. Casimir Pulaski galloped out of camp to scout with a few hundred cavalry and infantry, but within minutes his men came stumbling back to camp. They had seen the enemy and fled without firing a shot.

The British army encamped on the Brandywine for four days after the battle at Chadds Ford. The redcoats spent that time resting while surgeons tended the wounded from both sides. In response to a request from Howe, Washington dispatched Benjamin Rush and a delegation of American surgeons to help. After passing Howe's checkpoints, the Americans scattered over the battlefield in search of untended casualties. They found plenty. Everywhere they looked the doctors discovered wounded Continentals, languishing in ditches, behind woodpiles or in empty rooms, wearing uniforms caked with dried blood. Many of them had suffered without medical aid for two or three days and were past help.

Howe kept the American doctors occupied elsewhere as his army moved forward at 5:00 A.M. on the 16th. Scouts had informed him of Washington's camp near Paoli, and despite the nasty weather he decided to probe the American positions. After chasing away Pulaski's party, Howe's force ran into Wayne's and Maxwell's forward posts at 2:00 P.M., near a tavern called the

Sign of the Boot. The Americans pretended to flee into the woods, only to turn around and engulf a pursuit party of jaegers under Colonel Donop. Enraged at this "partisan trick," the Germans cut their way out and linked up with the rest of the army before continuing the advance. Wayne and Maxwell then slowly pulled back to the main American camp, skirmishing all the way as the rain resumed and intensified.

Washington waited for Wayne and Maxwell to return and then faced his army south. The maneuver was barely complete when he discovered that he had made a terrible mistake by placing his men at the bottom of a waterlogged valley, where they would have been unable to resist a British attack. The American officers frantically herded their troops back to higher ground. Howe, who had reorganized the Germans and pushed them forward, patiently waited for the Americans to finish their movement before assembling his own army on a hilltop opposite. The rain now came down in torrents. The Continentals had protected their paper cartridges all morning, but once in the open they stood at the mercy of the heavens. Water soon ruined all of their ammunition, leaving them—as they had no bayonets—helpless. But the British and German soldiers had problems of their own, sinking "in mud up to our calves" with the north wind driving rain into their faces, and Howe chose not to attack.

Washington sensibly ordered a retreat, and his Continentals slogged eleven miserable miles north to Yellow Springs. Artillery and wagons sank up to their hubs in the mud as the rain continued to pour. The troops arrived in camp that night and struggled to light campfires and take shelter. At parade the next morning, the 17th, they discovered that water had soaked all of their ammunition past recovery. With no choice but to find another supply, Washington drove his army overnight to Reading Furnace, several miles to the northwest. There, on the morning of the 18th, quartermasters started issuing fresh cartridges.

As the Continentals replaced their supplies, the British left the waterlogged fields where they had fought what became known as the "Battle of the Clouds" and marched slowly east toward the Schuylkill. Howe sent a light column to Valley Forge on the 18th, devastating a large American supply depot there, and the rest of his troops camped the same day at Tredyffrin. There, about ten miles west of Swede's Ford and seven miles south of another potential crossing at Fatland Ford, they waited for the rain-gorged waters of the Schuylkill to fall sufficiently to allow a crossing. Many of Howe's soldiers had sickened in the bad weather, so he let them rest. Philadelphia could wait.

Washington saw Howe's slow march as an opportunity to delay or prevent the occupation of the capital, and ordered Wayne, who had halted near Yellow Springs, to move south and place himself to the British army's rear. With help from Maxwell's corps and the Pennsylvania and Maryland militias, Wayne was to "Harrass & Distress" the enemy's march and even raid Howe's baggage train while avoiding any "disagreeable situation." Meanwhile, Washington would march his "jaded men" east across the Schuylkill and then turn south to block the crossing places at Swede's Ford and Fatland Ford, half a mile below Valley Forge. "I yet hope," he wrote Hancock, "from the present State of the River, that I shall be down in time to give them a meeting, and if unfortunately they should gain Philadelphia, that it will not be without loss."

Overstepping his instructions, Wayne declined to wait for support and continued to the vicinity of Paoli. He encamped with 1,500 men on the afternoon of the 18th just a few miles from the main body of the enemy and two miles from his own home. He spent the next day near the British lines, close enough to observe that they appeared "very quiet, washing & Cooking." He led his men forward early on the morning of the 19th to within half a mile of the British camp, but finding them "too Compact to admit of an Attack with prudence," he withdrew to his own camp and waited for a better opportunity. Most of the following day passed in the same manner. Even after two days in the same camp just a few miles from the British camp, Wayne remained confident that the enemy knew nothing of his whereabouts.

Howe actually had learned of Wayne's exposed position on the 19th, but an attempt to surprise the Americans that evening failed when some drunken redcoats set off the alarm in the American division's camp by firing at a picket. This should have alerted Wayne to his danger, but to Howe's surprise the Americans complacently remained in the same position on the following day. He decided to try surprising them again.

On the night of the 20th, five British infantry regiments under Major General Charles Grey left camp by two different roads on a night march of about three miles. Most of the troops marched with fixed bayonets but unloaded muskets, and in many cases without flints as well. They detained every civilian unfortunate enough to cross their path in order to prevent them from warning the Continentals. The British columns converged before midnight

at the foot of the wooded hill on which Wayne's Pennsylvanians were encamped. At a nearby forge they captured a blacksmith, forcing him to divulge
the location of the American sentries and pickets. Reluctantly, the man accompanied his captors as they moved silently up the hill.

The pickets managed to fire a few shots to warn their fellows, but they had
taken posts too close to camp. Calling "Dash on, light infantry," Grey led his
cheering soldiers in a sudden rush that ended among the American campfires. Several minutes of butchery followed. The shouts of the attackers and
screams of the wounded that echoed through the dark woods terrorized the
Pennsylvanians, and sent them scrambling in all directions. Few of them
even fired their muskets before they fled. Wayne rallied some of his troops a
few miles away, but they were in no condition to mount a counterattack and
he ordered a withdrawal. The sunlight that filtered through the leaves at
dawn revealed two to three hundred Americans dead by the sword or bayonet, with dozens captured and wounded. Even the British who walked
among the corpses found the sight unsettling, and one officer remembered
the affair as being "more expressive of Horror than all the Thunder of the Artillery &c on the Day of action." It would be some time before Wayne's remaining men were fit to take the field.

The main American army, meanwhile, endured a trying two days but
achieved a significant tactical victory. Leaving Reading Furnace at dawn on
the 19th, Washington's men trudged eastward to Parker's Ford on the
Schuylkill, which they reached in the early afternoon. The Continentals hesitated at their first sight of the river. Rapid and muddy, the waters carried logs
and other debris that promised to pummel them during the crossing; but
after being admonished by their officers, the men dutifully stripped and
toiled through water up to their chests. Grumbling intensified to sullen cursing as the soldiers emerged, surprisingly without significant loss, on the other
side of the river and untied the bundles containing their saturated uniforms
and other belongings.

Despite their ill temper they fell into line and pushed on without rest
through the mud, cold, and fog. From time to time the commander-in-chief
appeared, riding along the drooping column and encouraging the men, who
responded with a final effort that brought them opposite Fatland Ford by
midday on the 20th. Their bedraggled presence on hills within easy sight of
Howe's camp and blocking his passage of the Schuylkill both there and at
Swede's Ford made a mockery of the leisurely British advance. Howe and his

aides could not imagine how Washington had managed to get past them and place his army in such a strong position.

Howe's superb tactical skill is evident in his reaction to this turn of events, which he did not allow to delay him. At first light on the 21st he sent one of his trumpeters across Fatland Ford to carry a message for the American commander-in-chief while surreptitiously testing the river's depth. Writing with his usual mix of politeness and subtle sarcasm, Howe informed Washington that some Continentals had just been wounded and captured near Paoli, and that their numbers were so great that some of the overworked American surgeons might again prove themselves useful. The news, which of course left Washington to wonder at the magnitude of the defeat, was particularly galling because it came well before Wayne's own account of the affair.

Even as Washington waited to receive the communication from the British trumpeter, American scouts detected activity in the enemy camp. Scanning the other side of the river through drizzle and mist, they could see cavalry and infantry fall into formation and proceed north. It was another of Howe's "perplexing Maneuvres." Once again he seemed to be pursuing his "unvaried Object" of turning the American right. As Washington thought about it further and studied his maps, he came to another unsettling realization. If the British army continued on their present route, within a couple of days they would reach the town of Reading, which held a crucial American arsenal. Its loss could stifle the war effort for months to come.

At this vital moment Washington's intelligence network failed him once again. Local civilians—"to a man disaffected," he concluded—could not or would not tell him the whereabouts of Howe's army. Bland's cavalry and the Pennsylvania militia were supposed to be scouting but remained out of contact. Doubtless they found raiding farms more amusing. As Washington waited for them to report, Howe could march once again around his right and possibly put Reading to the torch. Forced to make a quick decision whether to protect Reading or Philadelphia, the commander-in-chief had to fall back on his intuition. That failed him, too. He chose Reading.

At three in the afternoon the Continentals, many of them shivering or coughing with pneumonia, turned against the weather and marched north toward Pottstown. Harassed farmers and innkeepers at Trappe thought they had seen the last of the soldiers until they opened their doors that night to find miserable, ragged men begging for food, fire, and dry wood to cheer their dreary camp. Despite orders for strict march discipline, stragglers fell out of column all that day and the next, causing trouble in an already unfriendly countryside, while those who remained in formation marched without shelter from the "uncommonly cold and biting" wind.

As the Americans marched to defend Reading on the evening of the 22nd, the British army began crossing the Schuylkill River behind them at Fatland Ford. The patrols that Washington had left there were quickly driven off, and by the next morning most of the British army had made it to the east bank of the Schuylkill. Philadelphia lay helpless. Congress fled the city, abandoning buildings and sites precious to the Revolution, including the assembly room where Washington had accepted his commission as commander-in-chief. Patriots, some of whom Howe had driven from New York the year before, followed the delegates into exile in the Pennsylvania backcountry. As if to celebrate the occasion, the wind, clouds, and rain miraculously disappeared.

On September 23rd the sunshine mocked a gloomy American camp as Washington assembled his council of war. Howe's supposed move to the north, he now realized, had been a feint—the British army had inserted itself neatly between the American army and Philadelphia, and it only took a glance at the limp and wasted soldiers lying about camp to see that the Continentals had reached the end of their endurance. The council unanimously decided to halt the army and wait for reinforcements from New England, where Gates seemed to be faring rather better than Washington.

Three days later, on September 26th, a conquering army under Lord Cornwallis marched into Philadelphia "amidst the acclamation of some thousands of inhabitants mostly women and children." The Continental Army rested over forty miles away, powerless to intervene.

Neither Howe nor Washington believed that the capture of Philadelphia would end the year's campaign. For one thing, Burgoyne's northern offensive had not turned into the parade down the Hudson that many people had expected. His advance had stirred up the New England militia like a nest of hornets, and the reports that reached Pennsylvania indicated that he might be in severe trouble indeed. For another, the British did not yet have a secure grip on Philadelphia itself. Over the past couple of months the Americans had worked feverishly to block the Delaware River below the city, and by late September they had succeeded in constructing a series of underwater obstacles. To support these obstacles (chevaux-de-frise) they built a few ramshackle forts: at Billingsport and Red Bank, both in New Jersey, and Fort

Mifflin on Mud Island, in the middle of the river itself. The Royal Navy could not supply Howe's army until the forts and chevaux-de-frise were cleared; in the meantime he would have to depend on a vulnerable overland supply line across Pennsylvania and Maryland to Head of Elk. Nor did Howe imagine Washington's army to be out of the picture.

Howe detailed Cornwallis for the occupation of Philadelphia with the British and German grenadiers and two squadrons of light dragoons, and on September 29th he detached two more regiments to attack the puny American fort at Billingsport. That left about seven or eight thousand soldiers in the main British army, which Howe placed northwest of Philadelphia on the Germantown Road. He did not expect a serious American attack, but kept his troops alert in case Washington tried to stage another Trenton.

The Continental Army camped from September 23rd to 26th on the Schuylkill River at Pottsgrove, Pennsylvania. Most of it did, anyway; for bands of Continentals and militia roamed without orders through the countryside, committing atrocities that made Washington furious and would have made a redcoat blush. The Reverend Henry Muhlenburg went to bury a child at a church near Valley Forge, for example, only to find it overflowing with a regiment of Pennsylvania militia. "The church was crowded with officers and privates with their guns," he wrote sadly in his journal that evening. "The organ loft was filled, and one man was playing the organ while others sang to his accompaniment. Down below lay straw and manure, and several had placed the objects of their gluttony, etc., on the altar. In short, I saw, in miniature, the abomination of desolation in the temple." As he entered, the militia officers mocked the reverend—a German settler—and called for the organist to play a German march.

Though not atypical of militiamen even at the best of times, such behavior reflected the declining morale of Washington's army. Over two months of incessant marching and countermarching punctuated with days of defeat and withdrawal had worn the men out and made them cynical. The only thing keeping them from complete collapse at this point may have been the commander-in-chief himself, for Washington had not given up. At Trenton and Princeton he had led the shattered, beaten remnants of an American army to stunning victories against their rested and confident foes. Why not try to repeat last winter's performance?

Even before hearing that the British had occupied Philadelphia, Washington inched his army closer to the city, marching it southeast on the morning of the 26th and camping at Pennypacker's Mill, in modern-day Schwenksville, Pennsylvania. There he tried to procure supplies and restore some discipline to the troops while keeping an eye on Howe's dispositions. He noticed the British commander's growing concern for the Delaware and encouraged it by detaching troops and artillery to garrison Fort Mifflin, Red Bank, and Billingsport.

The commander-in-chief called a council of war on September 28th, and informed his officers that reinforcements of 900 Continentals from Peekskill and 1,700 Maryland and New Jersey militiamen had brought the army's strength to about 8,000 Continentals and 3,000 militia. He estimated the size of Howe's force in and around Philadelphia at 8,000 men. The Americans thus outnumbered the British, but the advantage might not last long. Would it be better, Washington asked, to let the opportunity pass by waiting for yet more reinforcements, or to seize it by making a "general & vigorous attack upon the Enemy"? The council hemmed, hawed, and finally compromised. The army should move toward the northernmost British outposts at German-town, but not attack just yet.

The next day the Continental Army slid a little farther down the Schuylkill to Skippack Creek. On October 2nd it moved another five miles to Peter Wentz's farmhouse in Worcester township, fifteen miles northwest of the British lines at Germantown. There Washington learned that Howe had detached about 1,300 troops from his army on the 29th, sending them to attack Billingsport as a preliminary to an offensive on the Delaware. The British seemed to have turned their backs on the Continental Army, leaving their own camp at Germantown weak and distracted. Washington "thought it was time to remind the English that an American army still existed." His officers agreed.

Speaking to his troops through general orders on the morning of the 3rd, the commander-in-chief announced Horatio Gates's victory against Burgoyne at Freeman's Farm, New York, on September 19th. "This surely must animate every man," he declared. "This army—the main American Army—will certainly not allow itself to be outdone by their northern Brethren—they will never endure such disgrace; but with an ambition becoming freemen, contending in the most righteous cause, rival the heroic spirit which swelled their bosoms, and which so nobly exerted, has procured them deathless renown. *Covet!* My Countrymen, and fellow soldiers! Covet! A share of the glory due to heroic deeds! Let it never be said, that in a day of action, you

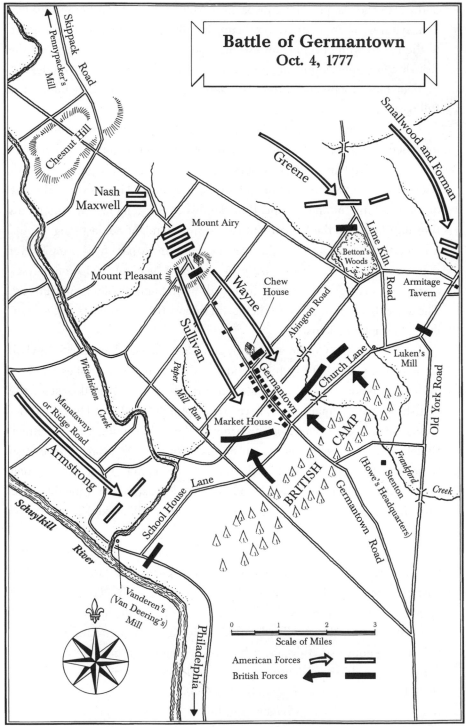

Battle of Germantown
Oct. 4, 1777

turned your backs on the foe." And so on for several more minutes, until it became obvious how the men could expect to spend the next day. "A sudden attack is intended," Lieutenant James McMichael wrote in his diary.

Washington devised a complicated blueprint for the coming battle. He ordered the army to advance in four columns, two made up of Continentals under Sullivan and Greene, and two composed of Armstrong's Pennsylvanians and Smallwood's New Jersey and Maryland militiamen. Washington would accompany Sullivan and his 3,000 men as they marched southeast down the Germantown Road, confronting Howe to his front and left. Greene would simultaneously advance down a modest thoroughfare known as the Lime Kiln Road and attack Howe's right with a larger column of 5,000 troops. Washington told Armstrong to march his 2,000 Pennsylvania militiamen southeast along the Schuylkill on Sullivan's right, and entrusted Smallwood's force of about 1,000 militia with a confusing route of advance among the maze of woods and roads that crisscrossed the region to Greene's left. With these forces, the commander-in-chief hoped to pin Howe against the Schuylkill and destroy him—an immodest but not entirely hopeless plan of attack.

The troops assembled at 6:00 P.M. on October 3rd, their pockets and haversacks bulging with provisions and ammunition. To increase their mobility, Washington ordered them to leave their packs behind. He also directed each soldier to stick a piece of white paper in his hat, partly to distinguish him at night and partly to keep his comrades from firing on him. The Continental Army still lacked uniform clothing and appeared in a variety of costumes. To complicate matters yet further, the troops of Colonel David Forman's New Jersey regiment wore captured British uniforms, and were known as the "redcoats."

The left wing under Greene and Smallwood had the longest march and departed first; Washington followed at around 8:00 P.M. with Sullivan and Armstrong. The Continentals marched all night, stopping frequently as scouts felt their way forward through darkness and thickening fog to the British pickets. Sullivan's vanguard reached a rise known as Chestnut Hill a short time before daybreak. Three miles farther down the Germantown Road to the southeast lay the first British outpost, on a small hilltop estate known as Mount Airy. A drunken British dragoon captured by Washington's scouts said that his comrades slept unaware of the American advance. But he also claimed that the detachment sent to Billingsport had just returned to camp, reducing the numerical advantage the Americans had expected to enjoy. With Greene and Smallwood out of contact, Washington decided to go ahead and attack anyway. He sent two regiments ahead to Mount Airy and followed behind with the rest of Sullivan's column.

Coincidentally, the 300 men of the Second Light Infantry Regiment posted at Mount Airy had participated in the slaughter at Paoli two weeks before. Upon hearing the sound of musketry that accompanied the rout of their pickets, they assumed that Wayne had come to seek revenge. After jumping out of bed and hastily donning his uniform, British lieutenant Martin Hunter saw two American regiments advancing out of the fog as his regiment formed in a small orchard. "We heard a loud cry of 'Have at the bloodhounds! Revenge Wayne's affair!' and they immediately fired a volley," he remembered. "We gave them one in return, cheered, and charged." Pressed by a force perhaps half their number, the Americans gave way.

Seeing the disorganization of his leading regiments, Sullivan ordered Conway's brigade, following immediately behind, to support the attack. The British "maintained their ground with great Resolution," Sullivan admitted. Incredibly, the light infantry then sidestepped to the right, seeking to outflank the entire American brigade! Musket and cannon fire—the British had a few light pieces—took a heavy toll on both sides. A major in Conway's brigade later regretted this as the moment one of his best soldiers "had his leg shot off just below the knee." Another Continental "who was alongside, had his pantaloons covered with the poor fellow's blood," but carried his wounded comrade to the rear. The British lost heavily, too, but not until Sullivan brought up Wayne's division did they halt their attack. The British light infantry's bugler then called the retreat, and they began a fighting withdrawal before overwhelmingly superior numbers. "This was the first time we had retreated from the Americans," Lieutenant Hunter remembered, "and it was with great difficulty we could get our men to obey our orders."

Sullivan's troops pushed the British back through fog, which did not lift but settled more densely with every minute. Poor visibility and broken terrain disorganized their advance. Officers lost contact with their men or fell victim to accidents. Colonel Josias Carvil Hall of the Second Maryland Regiment galloped about, trying to keep his men in formation until, "riding one way and looking another, the horse run him under a cider-press, and he was so hurt he was taken from the field." Several dirt lanes flanked by walls made of logs or loose stones bisected the Germantown Road, offering cover for British rear guards and forcing the Americans to dismantle them under fire.

The retreating British soldiers also grew disoriented in the fog. Small groups of reinforcements came up to their support, but instead of stiffening the light infantry they only confused the situation further. The redcoats continued their retreat into Germantown proper, passing several stone houses, pausing to fire volleys, and pulling back southeast toward Philadelphia. As they did so, British and American gunfire increased from every direction. "The crackling of thorns under a pot, and incessant peals of thunder only can convey the idea of their cannon and musketry," an American officer wrote, and "the smoke of the fire of cannon and musketry, the smoke of several fields of stubble, hay and other combustibles, which the enemy fired combined, made such a midnight darkness that great part of the time there was no discovering friend from foe but by the direction of the shot, and no other object but the flash of the gun."

A mounted figure emerged from the fog behind the retreating light infantry and cursed them roundly. General Howe had finally arrived. "For shame, Light Infantry!" he cried. "I never saw you retreat before. Form! form! it's only a scouting party." American artillery promptly silenced Howe's protests by firing grapeshot at him and his entourage as they stood under a chestnut tree. "I think I never saw people enjoy a discharge of grape before," Lieutenant Hunter recalled, "but we really all felt pleased to see the enemy make such an appearance, and to hear the grape rattle about the commander-in-chief's ears, after he had accused the battalion of having run away from a scouting party. He rode off immediately, full speed."

Washington, who had exposed himself "to the hottest fire of the enemy" until Sullivan begged him to retire, meanwhile rode through the fog and smoke just to the rear of the advancing Continentals. A swarming coterie of messengers, hangers-on, and aides surrounded him, including Timothy Pickering. "General Sullivan's divisions, it was evident, were warmly engaged with the enemy," Pickering remembered, "but neither was in sight. This fire, brisk and heavy, continuing, General Washington said to me; 'I am afraid General Sullivan is throwing away his ammunition; ride forward and tell him to preserve it.'" Pickering galloped a few hundred yards forward and delivered the commander-in-chief's orders to Sullivan. Returning, he noticed a stone house that he had ignored on his way to the front. "The first notice I received of it was from the whizzing of musket balls, across the road, before, behind, and above me," he remembered. "Instantly turning my eye to the right, I saw the blaze of the muskets, whose shot were still aimed at me, from the windows of a large stone house, standing back about a hundred yards from the road. This was Chew's house."

The Benjamin Chew estate, also known as Cliveden, consisted of outbuildings and a "strong stone house" of two and a half stories. The routed British Second Light Infantry had retreated directly past it without pausing, but Lieutenant Colonel Thomas Musgrave of the Fortieth Regiment took one look at the house's imposing bulk and decided it would make an ideal fortress. He ordered his detachment of one hundred men, which had reinforced the light infantry's lines a short time earlier, to break off and enter it. Some of Sullivan's troops tried to harry them as they did so, but the redcoats turned, fired a volley at point-blank range, and then took advantage of the resulting confusion to enter the house and shut its heavy wooden doors. The British then stacked furniture against every entrance and began sniping from the windows. Resolved to give or take no quarter, they offered a serious obstacle to Sullivan's advance.

Pickering galloped a short way past Musgrave's bastion to find the commander-in-chief in front of another house with a group of officers, earnestly debating "whether the whole of our troops then behind should immediately advance, regardless of the enemy in Chew's house, or first summon them to surrender?" Pickering and one of the commander-in-chief's other aides—a young man named Alexander Hamilton—both urged Washington to bypass the house, and a French engineer quietly remarked that he "remembered such a thing occurring in Italy, [where] the Army passed on & gained the Victory, & the Cassino full of soldiers fell into their hands." But Knox, no doubt looming in the fog like a shadowy behemoth, argued that "it would be unmilitary to leave a castle in our rear." Knox was a good officer, and Washington listened. The British would be summoned to surrender; and if they did not, Knox's artillery would pummel them into submission.

Washington's decision had immediate and tragic results. He asked for a volunteer to carry the flag of truce to the Chew house, and Caleb Gibbs, one of his aides, offered but was refused. A French officer then stepped forward only to retire after admitting that he spoke hardly any English. The commander-in-chief finally settled on a young officer from Virginia, "who being preceded by a drum, and displaying a white handkerchief, it was imagined, would not incur the smallest risk; but the English replied to this officer only with musket fire, and killed him on the spot." Washington saw him die, and then ordered the attack to begin.

The Americans had four small field guns available—three- and six-pounders—and used them to pummel the British bastion. Cannonballs and grapeshot shattered doors and windows, and sent stone splinters ripping into the flesh of several British soldiers; but the house's solid outer walls resisted everything the cannoneers could throw at them. Washington then ordered three regiments of Continentals from Pennsylvania and New Jersey to try and take the house. Advancing apparently without bayonets, they sacrificed their lives in a hopeless slaughter.

"To do them justice, they attacked with great intrepidity," a British officer who lived through the assault later recalled, "but [they] were received with no less firmness; the fire from the upper windows was well directed and continued; the rebels nevertheless advanced, and several of them were killed with bayonets getting in at the windows and upon the steps, attempting to force their way in at the door." Some Americans flattened themselves by the house's outer walls and tried to set fire to the shutters; but British marksmen shot the attackers down through the cellar windows.

Washington finally called off the attack after Benjamin Chew's yard became saturated with American blood. Meandering over the estate the next day, German captain Johann Ewald "counted seventy-five dead Americans, some of whom lay stretched in the doorways, under the tables and chairs, and under the windows, among whom were seven officers. The rooms of the house were riddled by cannonballs, and looked like a slaughter house because of the blood splattered around." Musgrave lost only four men killed and twenty-nine wounded, yet shattered three American regiments.

Fog lay thick over the battlefield as the attack on the Chew house died down. Powder flashes burst like miniature bolts of lightning in every direction, while the muskets and cannon crackled and boomed like thunder. For the troops who lived through it, the experience must have been horrifying. Friend and foe looked the same until they faced each other at point-blank range; a shadow might be another scared Continental or a redcoat with a bloodied bayonet. Men easily became separated from their fellows, and on finding themselves alone they fled in panic. As if on signal, Sullivan's advancing troops stopped, hesitated, and then started drifting back the way they came. Officers could not see the troops they had to rally and became caught up in the flood of retreating troops. Some stayed to fight and ended up firing on other Americans.

Washington tried to stem the retreat, but failed despite the help of his cavalry, which had not yet engaged the enemy. "I threw my squadron of horse across the road, by order of Gen. Washington, repeatedly to prevent the retreat of the infantry," remembered Major Benjamin Tallmadge of the Second Continental Dragoons, but the fleeing Continentals simply bypassed the horses or crawled under their bellies. Superior British training paid off, however, as Howe carefully arrayed his troops and sent them tramping forward in tight formation. The American infantry melted before them.

On Sullivan's left, meanwhile, Greene's troops floundered helplessly through the fog in Germantown's maze of back alleys and lanes. They had experienced serious problems from the beginning of their march. A guide had led them astray early that morning, costing them to lose an hour before they made contact with the enemy—some regiments of loyalists and British light infantry—where the Lime Kiln Road forked at Betton Woods. The contact occurred about forty-five minutes after Sullivan attacked Mount Airy. Greene's column had then divided into three divisions under himself, Stephen, and Alexander McDougall, and advanced, driving the British outposts back for a distance of two or three miles over extremely difficult terrain. The Ninth Virginia Regiment, a part of Greene's column, pushed ahead so fast that it reached a market square in central Germantown, which Sullivan's troops had occupied for a short time before they fled.

Sullivan's retreat now left Greene's force exposed to counterattack. Grant had rallied his regiments, and he sent them to envelop both American flanks. "When their main body attacked our left," Continental lieutenant James McMichael wrote in his diary, "we advanced into a field and put every party to retreat that attacked us in front; but by this time we sustained a fire from front, left and part to the rear." Some American units nevertheless continued to stand and fight, most notably Colonel Forman's New Jersey "redcoats." "Forman's Red Coats stood firm and advanced upon the British Red Coats, who were at least three times our number," an officer proudly wrote. Their bravery was useless, though—other fleeing Continental units broke their lines and forced them to scatter as well. Greene saw his force collapse and ordered a retreat.

Most of Greene's men made it away through the dense fog—all except the Ninth Virginia, which was surrounded and captured—while Sullivan's troops "made a Safe retreat Though not a Regular one." They received no support from the Maryland and Pennsylvania militiamen. Smallwood's column wandered hopelessly lost northeast of Germantown, while Armstrong's force fled from Sullivan's right after engaging in some light skirmishing. Although Cornwallis arrived with reinforcements just as the retreat began, the British did not press the Americans very hard. By 9:00 P.M. the bulk of Washington's army had straggled into camp at Pennypacker's Mill. The Americans had marched thirty-five miles in one day and lost a battle.

The Battle of Germantown cost the Continental Army 152 men killed, 521 wounded, and about 400 captured. Among their losses were Brigadier General Francis Nash of North Carolina and Major James Witherspoon of New Jersey, whose thigh and head were respectively "both taken away by one & the same Cannon Ball." The British lost 70 killed, including a general and a lieutenant colonel, 450 wounded, and 14 taken prisoner. The Ninth Virginia troops had taken perhaps a hundred British prisoners during their advance into Germantown, only to release them when they were themselves captured. One of Howe's dogs, which had broken free during the noise and fog of battle only to be taken prisoner by the Americans, also gained early release when Washington chivalrously sent it back to the British lines.

The attack on Germantown never came close to ending in an American victory. Although they had driven—with extreme difficulty—a few regiments of British light infantry into retreat, the Continentals fled even before the bulk of Howe's forces became engaged. The fog caused confusion on both sides, but even under clear skies Washington's overly complicated battle plan was unlikely to succeed. At Trenton, even when some of their columns had failed to arrive on the battlefield, the Americans had easily defeated a small German force. At Germantown, success against a large force of British regulars absolutely depended on bringing every man to bear. Washington nevertheless divided his force into widely separated columns and squandered Smallwood's and Armstrong's 3,000 militiamen by relegating them to the periphery.

The commander-in-chief's apparent ignorance of Germantown's topography—although he had camped there two months before—further contributed to the defeat. The fences, ditches, and narrow lanes that crossed the American route of advance down the Germantown Road at right angles made the town ideally suited for defense. Conceivably Washington could have negated this advantage by exploiting these lanes to enter Germantown at multiple points. Even disregarding that possibility, he had to foresee the danger that such broken terrain would pose to keeping his army in formation. Finally, the affair at the Chew house shows Washington at his most indecisive. Granted, the defeat of the American attack there probably had little impact on the battle's final outcome; but it wasted dozens of lives. Instead of calling an *ad hoc* council, Washington undoubtedly ordered a reserve regiment to surround the house and continued the advance with the rest of his troops.

Washington blamed his failure at Germantown on two factors: bad luck caused by the foggy weather, and the weakness of his troops. "Every account confirms the Opinion, I at first entertained, that our Troops retreated at the Instant, when Victory was declaring herself in our favor," he informed Hancock. "The tumult, disorder, & even despair, which it seems had taken place in the British Army were scarcely to be paralleled; And it is said, so strongly did the Ideas of a retreat prevail, that Chester was fixed on as their Rendezvous. I can discover no other cause for not improving this happy Opportunity, than the extreme haziness of the Weather." He did not, of course, accept any blame in public; but it is worth noting that after Germantown, Washington never attempted another large-scale surprise attack on the British army.

Other officers also blamed the fog for the defeat. The most common story was that it had made Sullivan's troops mistake one another for the enemy and imagine that they had been outflanked. "I attribute the loss . . . principally to the thickness of the Fog which did not permit us to see immediately when the enemy retreated," one wrote. Otherwise, they thought they would have won. "We fled from victory," claimed Armstrong. Fog made a remarkably ephemeral scapegoat, however, and some men tried to find more tangible victims. The luckless Sullivan came in for yet more criticism, and after bearing it for a few months he fled to take a peripheral military post in Rhode Island. William Maxwell, who had commanded part of Sullivan's reserve, rode out charges of intoxication and barely preserved his commission. Henry Knox was blasted for his bad advice at the Chew house. Greene fought accusations of dithering. And Washington's old friend Adam Stephen, who had marched under Greene, was accused of drunkenness and dismissed in favor of Lafayette, who took over his division.

The commander-in-chief eluded the fiery bolts of criticism that charred

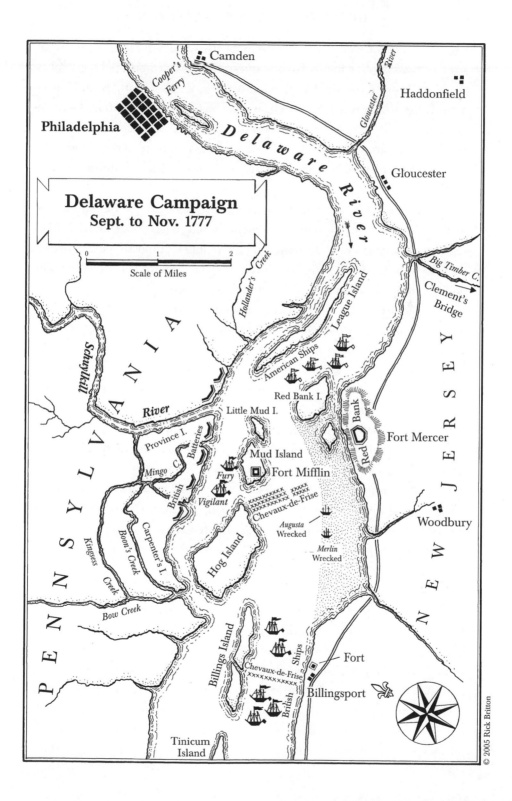

Camden

Haddonfield

Cooper's Ferry

Philadelphia

Delaware River

Gloucester River

Gloucester

Delaware Campaign
Sept. to Nov. 1777

0   1   2

Scale of Miles

Hollander's Creek

Big Timber C.

Clement's Bridge

PENNSYLVANIA

League Island

Schuylkill

River

American Ships

Red Bank I.

Little Mud I.

Province I.

Mingo C.

British Batteries

Fury

Mud Island

Red Bank

Fort Mercer

Fort Mifflin

Vigilant

xxxxxxxxx xxxxx
xxxxxxxxxx xxxxx
Chevaux-de-Frise

Augusta Wrecked

Woodbury

Merlin Wrecked

NEW JERSEY

Carpenter's I.

Boon's Creek

Kingsess Creek

Hog Island

Bow Creek

Billings Island

Ships

Fort

Chevaux-de-Frise
xxxxxxxxxxxxx

Billingsport

British

Tinicum Island

© 2005 Rick Britton

many of his subordinates. Congress publicly thanked him for his bravery and struck a medal in his honor. No one questioned his complicated battle plan or his decision to risk the Continental Army in an all-out attack on Howe's main force, which was inconsistent with a Fabian war of attrition. German Captain Ewald sneered at the decision of "the usually so-called 'Clever Washington'" to attack the Chew house; but American soldiers and politicians either blamed that fiasco on Knox or minimized its impact on the battle.

Among the common soldiers, Germantown was perhaps the only defeat of the war that actually *improved* morale. Continentals had faced British regulars—though admittedly only in lightly manned outposts—and defeated them. Surely, the Continentals believed, they could have defeated the main body of Howe's army as well. Exhausted though they were, this time—unlike after Brandywine—the Continentals looked forward to fighting again. "We most certainly were drubbed," an American doctor admitted, but the troops remained in "exceedingly good spirits."

Captain William Beatty of the Seventh Maryland Regiment summed up his fellow soldiers' attitudes in a letter that he wrote to his father on October 6th: "I was in the action the Whole time and in the hottest of the fire, I Received a Dead Ball On my thigh the Very first fire the Enemy made. But did me no harm Only made the place a little Red, I Know no Body fell Except Unkle Michael and he fell Dead on the Spot. . . . I Expect We Shall Soon have another touch With [the British] Which Will Soon lessen their numbers." The next week he wrote his father again, claiming that the British had lost 2,000 men killed and wounded at Germantown. He punctuated this good news with an appeal for "the Breeches [which] I hope you Will procure for I Want them Verry Bad."

The remainder of the campaign of 1777 now focused on the Delaware River. The British needed to clear that waterway of obstructions in order to keep Philadelphia supplied over the winter, and went about it methodically. Billingsport, a small, practically indefensible fort, fell on October 2nd; but it took almost three more weeks to remove the chevaux-de-frise that obstructed the river there. Lord Howe's warships then proceeded upriver to Hog Island, which anchored an even stronger network of chevaux-de-frise. Before these obstacles could be removed, either Fort Mifflin (on Mud Island, just to their rear) or Fort Mercer (at Red Bank, behind the obstacles and just upriver on the New Jersey coast) needed to be neutralized.

Washington has been accused of neglecting the Delaware River defenses, and to some extent the accusation is just. He paid little attention to the river until early August of 1777, when he inspected it personally and found it passable to enemy shipping. At that time he had vigorously recommended the fortification of the Delaware to Congress and the Pennsylvania government, but the politicians had found little time for the job, and only minimal progress was made in sinking underwater obstructions and shoring up Fort Mifflin's crumbling walls. That fort's garrison consisted of only sixty invalids and sixty militia artillerymen until September 23rd, when Washington sent two hundred Continentals and some sailors from the Pennsylvania navy to reinforce it.

Washington slowly moved his army north in the latter half of October, taking it from Pennypacker's Mill to a camp near Whitemarsh. By the time the British approached Hog Island, the main American army was too far away to offer the river forts direct support. Lord Howe's warships bombarded Fort Mifflin with the help of artillery batteries on the Pennsylvania shore. The American guns could not effectively respond, but small groups of Continentals rowed out to Mud Island overnight to reinforce Fort Mifflin while other boats carried the wounded to New Jersey. With this help the garrison continued to hold out—just barely.

A German detachment under Colonel Donop attacked Fort Mercer on October 22nd, but Colonel Christopher Greene of Rhode Island and his garrison repulsed them, causing over four hundred casualties, including Donop himself, who fell mortally wounded. Commodore John Hazelwood's ramshackle Pennsylvania navy—consisting almost entirely of row galleys—supported both American forts and harassed Lord Howe, who lost two warships that ran aground on the New Jersey shore. Thanks to the heroism of these little groups of American soldiers and sailors, Washington grew hopeful of blocking the Delaware permanently and forcing Howe into an ignominious winter retreat back to Head of Elk.

On October 18th Washington learned of Burgoyne's defeat at Saratoga, and several days later a courier told him that the Articles of Capitulation had been signed on the 17th. While this "glorious termination" of the northern campaign of course left him extremely happy, it also caused bitter reflections. Gates, he heard, had been supported by over 12,000 New England militiamen, "who shut the only door by which Burgoyne could Retreat, and cut off all his supplies." But "how different our case!" he wrote his friend Landon Carter. "The disaffection of [a] great part of the Inhabitants of this State— the languor of others, & internal distraction of the whole, have been among the great and insuperable difficulties I have met with, and have contributed not a little to my embarrassments this Campaign."

Washington sensed that the Saratoga victory made his own repeated failures look even worse, and began to fear that some would now question his leadership. Gates sparked this feeling by reporting his victory to Congress and a host of friends and junior officers long before he told Washington what had occurred. Then, on the evening of November 4th, Washington received a letter from General Stirling. That general wrote that his aide-de-camp had recently spoken with Gates's aide, who slyly supplied him with an extract of a letter from General Thomas Conway to Gates. Stirling now quoted that extract for Washington: "Heaven has been determind to save your Country; or a weak General and bad Councellors would have ruind it." A weak general! The reference to the commander-in-chief was obvious. Angrily, he forwarded the extract to Conway, without comment, commencing a bitter dispute that would only burn itself out in the mud and snow of Valley Forge.

The Delaware River campaign, meanwhile, ended as Washington might have expected. Fort Mifflin's garrison held bravely, but the British finally found a way to squeeze past the chevaux-de-frise, allowing them to further concentrate their fire on the hapless defenders. Further resistance served no purpose. With Washington's approval, the Americans evacuated Fort Mifflin on the night of November 15th–16th. Five days later they abandoned Fort Mercer as well; and on November 21st the British cleared a route on the Delaware that allowed them access to Philadelphia. The city entered firmly and indefinitely into British possession.

As 1777—a year that began on a happy note with an improbable victory at Princeton—approached its end, Philadelphia was occupied, Congress was in exile at York (a hundred miles to the west), and the Continental Army was reeling after a string of defeats. The optimism the troops had felt following their phantom success at Germantown dissipated as the Delaware forts fell, and their mood declined further as the weather worsened. By contrast, loyalism revived. Civilians in the middle states sold supplies to Howe's troops and once more flirted with the idea of royal government. The only hopeful lights for America burned far away at Saratoga and in Paris, where diplomats lobbied for French intervention. One decision remained, however, before the commander-in-chief could draw this miserable campaign year to a close. In making it, Washington would inaugurate the gravest crisis of his life and set the stage for his greatest victory—a victory won not against enemy soldiers but against the pitiless forces of nature.

14

VALLEY FORGE

December 1777 – May 1778

WHITEMARSH, PENNSYLVANIA, WAS no place for a winter encampment. The Continental Army could neither defend southeastern Pennsylvania from there nor secure itself from British attack. Washington needed to find another location before the winter weather arrived, and asked his officers for suggestions. Nathanael Greene, referring to Hannibal's winter quarters at Capua in the Carthaginian War, warned that "men are naturally apt to sink into negligence without there is something constantly to rouse their attention," and advised staying within striking distance of Howe's army. Henry Knox, citing Frederick the Great's admonition that "the first object in Winter quarters is Tranquility," argued that the Continentals should take safer quarters at Lancaster and Reading. Other officers discussed military history and suggested various options but agreed on nothing.

Congress had convened at York and the Pennsylvania Assembly at Lancaster, both within reach of the British army in Philadelphia. The delegates of both bodies urged Washington to interpose his army between them and Philadelphia, both to guarantee their safety and to intimidate the loyalists. It was "a melancholly truth," the Pennsylvanians admitted, "that too many of our People are so disafected already that nothing but the neighbourhood of the army keeps them subject to Government." They promised Washington that the barns of southeastern Pennsylvania bulged with provisions. Could he afford to abandon them to the British?

These considerations convinced Washington to move his army west of Philadelphia, but he was still unsure of his destination when he evacuated Whitemarsh on December 10th. The troops marched west, reached Swede's Ford on the 12th and crossed the Schuylkill over a bridge of wagons and rails. Then they marched another three miles west to a place called the Gulph. Here, "on a high uncultivated hill, in huts & tents laying on the Cold

Ground," the men lived miserably for several days. Morale plummeted. "I am Sick—discontented—and out of humour," Connecticut surgeon Albigence Waldo wrote in his diary on the 14th. "Poor food—hard lodging—Cold Weather—fatigue—Nasty Cloaths—nasty Cookery—Vomit half my time—smoak'd out of my senses—the Devil's in't—I can't Endure it—Why are we sent here to starve and Freeze."

On the 19th, drums and bugles roused the soldiers from their frosted tents. Officers told them that the commander-in-chief had chosen a permanent winter encampment and sent them marching northwest over frozen roads. After seven miles they reached a place most of them had probably never heard of: Valley Forge. It was a typical corner of rural Pennsylvania, about 2,000 acres of mostly wooded hills broken by occasional clearings surrounding farm buildings. The Schuylkill River formed its northern border. To the west, Valley Creek flowed north through a deep gorge, which faded into rolling hills where the creek entered the river. A series of ridges, sloping downward in the direction of well-cultivated farmland in the plains below, completed Valley Forge's natural boundaries to the south and east.

Valley Creek had supplied water for an iron forge and gristmill since the 1750s; thus the name Valley Forge. This small industrial complex, owned by the Potts family, stretched along the lower reaches of the creek, and included a stone mill house built by Isaac Potts on the east side of the creek's mouth. After 1775 the forge and mill supplied munitions and flour to the Continental Army. Military authorities also established a supply depot there. The British put an end to this brief heyday in September 1777 by destroying the depot and forge—but not the gristmill—in a raid. The ruins they left behind offered a cheerless welcome to the Continental Army as it filed into Valley Forge on December 19th.

Washington had settled on this unlikely spot for several reasons. Twenty miles from Philadelphia, it provided a base from which to intercept British foraging parties, punish loyalists, encourage patriots, and protect the Pennsylvania Assembly and the Congress. Valley Forge also was easily defensible. Open country to the south and east made it impossible for Howe to approach the camp undetected, and the ridges bordering the camp in that direction could be fortified. To the rear, Fatland Ford—which Washington improved with a bridge—offered a secure line of retreat. Furthermore, wood and water existed in abundance. "With activity and diligence," Washington told the troops, "Huts may be erected that will be warm and dry."

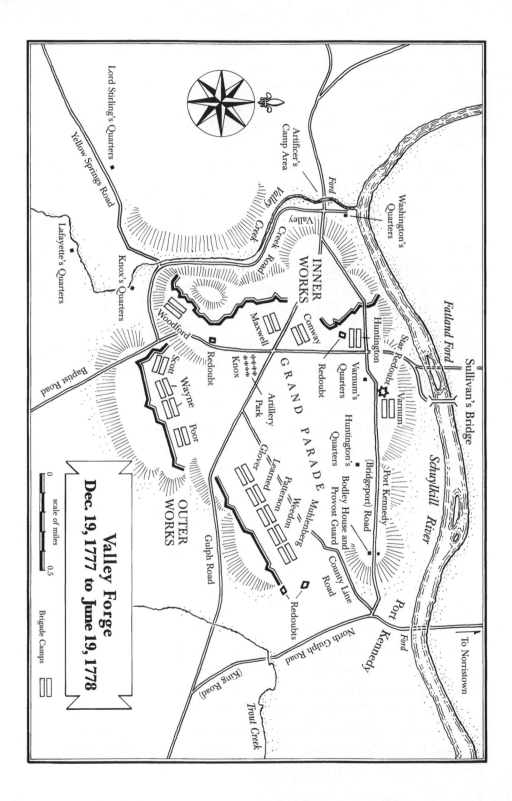

Valley Forge
Dec. 19, 1777 to June 19, 1778

To them, Valley Forge's frozen woods and fields seemed to show that America's leaders did not care if common soldiers lived or died. Patriotic propagandists described the Continental soldier laboring through mud and cold "with a song in his mouth extolling War & Washington." The reality, soldiers knew, was different. Surgeon Waldo pictured "a Soldier, his bare feet are seen thro' his worn out Shoes, his legs nearly naked from the tatter'd remains of an only pair of stockings, his Breeches not sufficient to cover his nakedness, his Shirt hanging in Strings, his hair dishevell'd, his face meager . . . He comes, and crys with an air of wretchedness & despair, I am Sick, my feet lame, my legs are sore, my body cover'd with this tormenting Itch—my Cloaths are worn out, my Constitution is broken, my former Activity is exhausted by fatigue, hunger & Cold, I fail fast I shall soon be no more! and all the reward I shall get will be—'Poor Will is dead.' " What did Valley Forge's supposed military advantages matter to Will if he died of malnutrition or exposure?

The troops spent just two days at Valley Forge before serving notice that they would not suffer indefinitely in silence. For weeks the commissaries had issued them rotten pulp—or bones with a few scraps of stringy flesh—and called it salt beef. On December 20th a committee of officers declared it "unwholesome & destructive to nature for any person to make use of Such fude." The next evening "a general cry" rose through the camp. "No Meat! No Meat!" the soldiers howled. "The Distant vales Echo'd back the melancholy sound—'No Meat! No Meat!' " They hooted and cawed in imitation of owls and crows, refusing to stop until officers promised that their "confused Musick" had reached headquarters.

The next day a British foraging party ventured near Valley Forge. Washington prepared to intercept it. "I ordered the Troops to be in readiness, that I might give every Opposition in my power," he wrote Henry Laurens, president of the Continental Congress, "when behold! To my great mortification, I was not only informed, but convinced, that the Men were unable to stir on account of provision, and that a dangerous mutiny, begun the night before and which with difficulty was suppressed by the spirited exertions of some Officers, was still much to be apprehended for want of this article." Unless adequate supplies arrived immediately, he asserted, "this Army must inevitably be reduced to one or other of these three things. Starve—dissolve—or disperse."

—

For Washington, Valley Forge was about makeshift measures, improvisation, and, more than anything, hard work. The simultaneous emergencies that arose during that winter of crisis made quick solutions impossible. One day, provision shortages demanded immediate attention; the next, poor clothing, typhus, desertion, loyalist sedition, British raids, Continental marauding, bad weather, inadequate transport, depreciated currency, officer resignations, prisoner exchanges, recruiting shortages, rank disputes, or any of a hundred other problems appeared. Each patch to the army's tattered fabric lasted only weeks or days before coming unraveled.

The provision crisis of December 1777 was like that. Washington addressed it by "declaring the danger of an immediate Mutiny in the Army" and sending detachments from each brigade to scour the country for food. The foragers found only "a very trifle" at first, but after repeated efforts they scrounged enough flour and meat to feed the soldiers for a few days. They had to repeat the process almost every week, keeping the army alive in a hand-to-mouth existence. Washington knew that his supply system was failing, but could not get at the administrative source of the problem right away. There were just too many other things to do.

Most important, he had to get the army under shelter. He established his own headquarters in the Isaac Potts house at the mouth of Valley Creek. His general officers sequestered rooms in the area's other farmhouses. There was no preexisting shelter for the troops, however, so Washington directed them to build huts. His strict regulations on size and form were ignored. Some men cut down trees for logs; others, lacking axes or other tools, dismantled farmers' fences or barns. Roofs were made of logs, bark shingles, or turf; uneven planks, tent strips or blankets served as doors; and split wood or mud covered the floors. Sometimes a dozen men shared a single filthy room, while next door a few officers reclined in multiple rooms with stone chimneys. But at least the troops were "tolerably well covered." The endless problems confronting Washington prevented him from paying the huts further attention.

His army was sick. Poor living conditions, wretched sanitation, and the aftereffects of a difficult campaign wore down the men until they became vulnerable to disease. But the military hospitals, scattered at various locations through Pennsylvania and New Jersey, were unequipped to handle the growing sick list. "We now have upwards of 5000 Sick in our hospitals," Benjamin Rush informed Washington on December 26th, and the men were packed to overflowing in small buildings. "I have seen 20 sick men in One room ill with fevers & fluxes, large eno' to contain only 6, or 8 well men without danger to their health." Typhus and other diseases flourished in such crowded conditions and killed soldiers and hospital staff alike. Medical supplies of all kinds were scarce. Inadequate stocks of blankets or sheets forced patients to shiver in tattered, lice-infested summer uniforms. Men tottered outside their hospitals and begged from door to door, offering to trade their muskets, hospital rations—usually rancid beef or bread—or other items to farmers in exchange for blankets, milk, or vegetables. Entering a hospital, in short, was at best risky and at worst suicidal. Many sick soldiers chose instead to remain in their huts and spread their diseases through camp.

Death also courted soldiers who fell into captivity. The British had captured many thousands of Americans since 1775. They confined some of them to horrific prison ships off New York and herded others into foul, icy barracks on Long Island or in Philadelphia. Rations of food and clothing were poor, so the prisoners relied on Continental aid shipments to stay alive. But bureaucratic incompetence and miscommunications kept these shipments intermittent. British and German prisoners also suffered from bad treatment, partly because of Congress's decision to retaliate for reputed atrocities against prisoners in New York and Philadelphia. Prisoner exchanges were infrequent, and as a result many men stayed captive for three or more years—if they survived.

Prisoners, hospital inmates, and soldiers in camp shared one thing—their rags. "Our sick naked—Our well naked—Our unfortunate men in captivity naked!" Washington wailed. An inventory taken on December 23rd showed that about 3,000 of the approximately 12,000 troops at Valley Forge were "unfit for duty by reason of their being bare foot and otherwise naked," but even the so-called "fit" were thinly clad. Most wore their home clothes or the remnants of cloth that their states had issued at the beginning of 1777. Overcoats and blankets were rare, shoes a luxury, and shirts and trousers prizes worth fighting for. "Hundreds of our poor worthy fellows have not a single ragg of a shirt," Anthony Wayne wrote to the Pennsylvania government in February, "but are obliged to wear their waistcoats next their skins & to sleep in them at nights . . . for the want of which our men are falling sick in numbers every day—contracting vermin and dying in Hospitals, in a condition shocking to Humanity, & horrid in Idea." The emotional Wayne exhorted the politicians to make up the shortage by any means possible: "for God sake," he begged, "procure a Quantity for me if you strip the [Pennsylvania] Dutchmen for them."

Supplies of clothing, food, weapons, ammunition, camp equipment, tools, wagons, horses, and fodder all were scarce; but they existed outside camp, sometimes in great quantity. Forges and cottage workshops manufactured huge numbers of weapons, tools, and equipment. Farmers in the mid-Atlantic states possessed food, livestock, and wagons in plenty. Mills produced tons of flour. Why did only a trickle of this reservoir of supplies reach the army?

Weather was partly to blame. Temperatures at Valley Forge in the winter of 1777–78 were not colder than usual for that time of year. If anything, they were slightly higher than normal. But that, ironically, contributed to the army's hardships. Clouds produced more rain than snow, turning dirt roads into muddy sloughs and transforming streams and rivers into impassable torrents. Supply convoys that tried to get through the mess broke down and reached camp late, if at all. One wagon train carrying precious cloth literally fell into a rain-swollen river.

Loyalists snatched other shipments of food and clothing. They attacked convoys, massacred small bands of militia, and abducted patriots from their homes. Continental cavalry, including an independent detachment under captain Henry "Lighthorse Harry" Lee, fought the raiders, but with only moderate success. Washington failed to achieve the dominance over the countryside that he had enjoyed in New Jersey during the previous winter. The army at Valley Forge was even somewhat isolated from the civilian population that surrounded it. Southeastern Pennsylvania's farmers, mostly Quakers or recent German settlers, hid their livestock and provisions when Continental agents sought to purchase supplies with bills of credit. Defying Congressional pronouncements making them subject to military justice and even death, the farmers often traded instead with the British. Howe's agents offered hard money—typically pounds sterling—far more valuable than the unreliable Continental currency.

Poor military administration was a bigger problem at Valley Forge than bad weather or unsympathetic civilians. Externally, the Continental Army of 1777 resembled the professional force that Washington cherished; but it was plagued by incompetent staff, poorly defined departmental responsibilities, and intersecting chains of command. Many officials, like Clothier General James Mease and Commissary General of Purchases William Buchanan, were lazy or corrupt. Others, like acting Quartermaster General Henry Emanuel Lutterloh, could not cope with their duties. State and national agents competed for the same supplies. Commissaries took bribes, pilfered, or went home for the winter; and their superiors lacked the authority to coerce them. Supplies rotted in depots or disappeared in transit to Valley Forge.

Such inefficiency cost lives and infuriated Washington. "In conversation with his Excellency to day on the Subject of Supplies," a commissary wrote to William Buchanan on December 28th, "he expressed himself as follows— Dam it what is that reason Mr. Buchanan is not here does he think to indulge himself at home whilst we are distressed and suffering for want of provision. This is Language that his Excellency is by no means accustom'd to use and you may Judge of the provocation when he is oblig'd to adopt." But Washington could not convince Buchanan, Mease, or any of his other supply deputies to do their duty. Appointed by Congress and lacking direct oversight by higher officials, they did as they pleased.

So did many of Washington's field officers. "Longing, & hankering after their respective homes," they demanded furloughs in unprecedented numbers. Some went home on furlough and never came back. Others simply resigned, leaving behind regiments commanded by majors, and brigades led by colonels. Washington lost the support network of junior officers that he needed to run the army. "It is matter of no small grief to me, to find such an unconquerable desire in the Officers of this Army to be absent from Camp, as every day exhibits," he complained. "I must attempt (for it can be no more than an attempt) to do all these duties myself, and perform the part of a Brigadier—a Colonel—&c. (because in the absence of these every thing relative to their business comes directly to me) or, I must incur displeasure by the denial."

He was not totally alone. Henry Knox stayed at Valley Forge, and so did Nathanael Greene, who took over the Quartermaster department in March. A few dedicated junior officers and officials composed reports and provided advice on specialized subjects where Washington's knowledge fell short. Aides wrote letters and conducted mundane business. And Martha came in early February to encourage her husband and share his trials. The commander-in-chief accepted all forms of aid gladly, but ultimately he considered the burden of administering the army to be his alone. Today he might be called a micromanager.

Almost every day he rode through camp, directing repairs or modifications to the huts and pointing out instances of poor sanitation such as "dead horses in and about the camp" and unburied offal. He inspected hospitals and wrote meticulous instructions on their management, supply, discipline, and reform. He thwarted smallpox epidemics—the *bête noire* of all army encampments—by enforcing widespread inoculation. (This painful procedure, which required an uninfected person's arm to be cut open and infused with smallpox-infested pus, was new to the eighteenth century and quite controversial; Washington promoted it against considerable opposition.) He remonstrated with Howe on the treatment of individual American prisoners, intervened on behalf of British and German captives, and attempted to secure regular exchanges and aid shipments. He mediated officer disputes, and helped settle controversies over promotion and pay. And in the scraps of time left over from more important duties, the commander-in-chief issued orders about things like cutting cloth efficiently, and preparing soap from beef tallow.

Minutiae nevertheless did not distract Washington from fundamental needs like food and clothing. These were always his prime concern. He monitored the supply situation daily, for experience had taught him not to leave this duty to subordinates. He told commissaries where to look for cloth or provisions, directed quartermasters to procure horses and wagons, determined the routes individual convoys took to camp, traced their progress through the country, and made sure they were not diverted.

Short-term measures kept the army intact through the winter, but Washington understood that endemic administrative weaknesses required a comprehensive and permanent fix. What kind of force would take the field in June? Would it be a pathetic remnant of survivors, or a reinvigorated army capable of defeating the enemy? Moreover, what if the war lasted for several more years? Would next year's encampment be like this one, a struggle to stay alive? To Washington, the answer was clear. If America stood any chance of winning the war, the Continental Army would have to be rebuilt.

A heavy rain drenched Valley Forge on the morning of January 28, 1778, dissolving the snow-covered ground into a morass of mud and slush. Soldiers not on duty huddled in their smoky huts, swapping complaints and cooking small cakes or gruel. The commander-in-chief took his own simple breakfast at headquarters, and then mounted his horse and rode to the nearby estate of

Moore Hall, where a congressional committee that had convened to consider the future of the Continental Army awaited him.

A month earlier, Washington had announced his intention of re-forming the army and asked every general officer to submit written statements on the subject. Alexander Hamilton took dictation as the commander-in-chief condensed the officers' views and his own into a comprehensive proposal for the committee at Moore Hall. It took two drafts—about eighty pages of paper covered with Hamilton's notes and emendations—before Washington pronounced himself satisfied. The resulting thirty-eight-page letter was one of the longest of his career and a minor masterpiece of military administration. It occupied the committee for six weeks, and ultimately laid the basis for victory at Monmouth and Yorktown. In some respects, Washington's ideas also influenced the form and administrative structure of the modern American army.

Washington's advice was founded on principles that he had learned from hard experience. He had explained them to Congress before, with varying degrees of success, and now put them as simply and directly as he could. "A small knowlege of human nature will convince us, that, with far the greatest part of mankind, interest is the governing principle; and that, almost, every man is more or less, under its influence," Washington observed. "Motives of public virtue may for a time, or in particular instances, actuate men to the observance of a conduct purely disinterested; but they are not of themselves sufficient to produce a persevering conformity to the refined dictates and obligations of social duty. Few men are capable of making a continual sacrifice of all views of private interest, or advantage, to the common good. It is in vain to exclaim against the depravity of human nature on this account—the fact is so, the experience of every age and nation has proved it, and we must, in a great measure, change the constitution of man, before we can make it otherwise. No institution, not built on the presumptive truth of these maxims, can succeed."

No corner of the army escaped Washington's gaze. His appraisal encompassed the large and small, the short and long term; his solutions were creative, reasoned, and explicit. Under the current establishment, America's thirteen states fielded ninety-seven Continental regiments, none of them full strength. Washington proposed amalgamating the weaker units to create eighty complete regiments. To make up for weak recruiting, he suggested drafting men from the militia. Resignations and corruption would be reduced by better pay, new systems of rank and promotion, and pensions for officers, and their widows and orphans. To reduce indiscipline, Washington designed a "provost-marshalcy," or military police, going so far as to determine the number of executioners and their rate of pay. He also offered advice on re-forming hospitals; redesigning the commissary, clothing, and quartermaster departments; importing supplies from France; Indian alliances; drill and training; camp sanitation; distributing liquor; and even conscripting slaves as wagon drivers.

Taken as a whole, these measures dispensed with the present military system—an accretion of stopgap measures enacted over the preceding three years—and created a new army, conceived and built as a single unit. The committee refined the plan, elaborating points, where possible, in greater de-tail and making improvements. But the framework remained Washington's own. He shepherded his proposals through the committee at Moore Hall, oversaw their presentation to Congress, and lobbied them toward legisla-tion. Not all of them made it. Delegates diluted some and delayed others for years. A few of Washington's suggestions passed from hand to hand until someone filed them away and they disappeared. But by the spring of 1778, the most important recommendations had been adopted into law. On May 27th, Congress enacted a new "establishment of the American Army"—essentially as Washington had envisioned it.

Washington's success in getting his new army adopted is a tribute to his industry and political savvy. Congress was no rubber-stamp assembly for the commander-in-chief. For a time, it looked like it was becoming his adversary. In the winter of 1777–78 some observers detected a "Strong Faction" develop-ing among delegates from New England and the far south. It was said that these men wanted to depose Washington in favor of Horatio Gates. Lafayette called them "stupid men who without knowing a Single word about war un-dertake to judge You, to make Ridiculous Comparisons; they are infatuated with Gates without thinking of the different Circumstances, and Believe that attaking is the only thing Necessary to Conquer." President of Congress Henry Laurens wrote his son, Washington's aide John Laurens, that he had seen the commander-in-chief's "opinions treated [in Congress] with so much indiscreet freedom & Levity as affected me exceedingly & convinced me that your suspicions of a baneful influence are not Ill founded."

Nor were the commander-in-chief's detractors limited to members of

Congress. Washington's public aura had faded, too. Over the past year his army had endured repeated defeats, losing Philadelphia and surrendering much of the mid-Atlantic countryside to British control. The only bright spot of 1777 had come in a battle with which Washington had had nothing to do. The victory at Saratoga, proclaimed Dr. Benjamin Rush in an anonymous letter to Patrick Henry, "has Shewn us what Americans are capable of doing with a *General* at their head. . . . A Gates—a [Charles] Lee, or a Conway would, in a few weeks render them an irresistible body of men." An unknown person left a written tirade on the steps of Congress, prophesying "that the people of America have been guilty of idolatry by making a man [Washington] their god—and that the God of Heaven and Earth will convince them by wofull experience that he is only a man." One official even reported to headquarters that he had overheard people in a Lancaster inn complaining that Washington "was not the man people Imagined nor yet the General, & that he was unpardonable for Missing the Many Oppertunities he had over the Enemy."

Enemies were also appearing among Washington's own officer corps. General Thomas Conway was openly contemptuous toward the commander-in-chief, and Washington assumed that he inspired every attempt to unseat him. Calling Conway his "enemy," he told Congress—which had just named the Irish mercenary the army's inspector general—that it would have to decide between the two of them. Conway's insolent behavior "affects the Genl very sensibly," John Laurens told his father. "It is such an Affront as Conway would never have dared to offer if the General's Situation had not assured him of the impossibility of it's being revenged in a private way." Washington would "lay the whole matter before Congress [and] they will determine whether Genl W. is to be sacrificed to Gnl C. for the former can never consent to be concern'd in any transactions with the latter from whom he has received such unpardonable Insults." Congress declined to support Conway, whose erratic temper won him few friends, and he eventually resigned and returned to Europe. But Washington did not stop there. Convinced that Conway had been only one member of a "malignant faction" determined to overthrow him, he sought out the rest. His friends became like undercover agents, or moles, burrowing for enemies through layers of rumor into regions of fancy.

Several men now found themselves in uncomfortable positions. The victor of Saratoga, Horatio Gates, disavowed Conway but was nevertheless ostracized by Washington's allies, including Generals Greene and Knox. His standing in Congress and the army gradually declined. Thomas Mifflin and Congressman Richard Henry Lee were forced to deny publicly any opposition to the commander-in-chief. Even John Adams, who had introduced Washington to Congress in 1775, now found himself subject to scrutiny. Henry Knox visited Adams at Braintree (south of Boston) in February. "The design of his Visit was As I soon perceived to sound me in relation to General Washington," Adams recalled. "He asked me what my Opinion of him was. I answered with the Utmost Frankness, that I thought him a perfectly honest Man, with an amiable and excellent heart, and the most important Character at that time among Us, for he was the Center of our Union." Rumors of his disaffection nevertheless persisted until he left for France later that month.

Washington did have opponents. Some, like Conway and Benjamin Rush, may even have wanted to depose him. But there was no conspiracy—no, as some historians have called it, "Conway cabal." The critics instead reflected a generalized discontent with the course of the war, and a reaction against the high hopes that had followed Trenton and Princeton. Since then, everything seemed to have gone wrong. All of Washington's major battles had ended in defeat. His soldiers were demoralized, and his camp a shambles—one visitor to Valley Forge labeled the main army an "unformed mob." It was not unreasonable to speculate, as one detractor put it, "that the Head cant posobly be sound when the whole body is disordered."

Washington was right to complain that his critics failed to see how hard he had worked to keep the army together, but reaction was disproportionate. He had always been sensitive to criticism, but on this occasion his sensitivity verged on paranoia. Perhaps Washington's anger was not completely uncalculated. Left alone, his critics might have eventually posed a threat to his leadership, or at least undercut his relations with Congress and the state governments, with potentially disastrous results for the army. In publicly confronting his critics, he served notice that opposition carried a political price.

What Washington called Valley Forge's "fatal crisis" came in February 1778. Since December, Washington's efforts to plug holes in the decrepit supply system had kept barely adequate quantities of food flowing into camp. Then, suddenly, even the trickle ran dry. First the troops ran out of meat. Then they had no bread. Inventories of storehouses throughout southeastern

Pennsylvania turned up only odd barrels of salt fish or peas. Commissaries swore there was no more to be found. Even hay and oats had disappeared from army storehouses; and destitute of fodder, horses died. The wagons they had once pulled now lay empty and idle.

Washington's officers predicted disaster. "The Camp is in a melancholy Condition for Want of Provisions," Brigadier General Jedediah Huntington wrote Lord Stirling on February 12th. "There is great Danger that the Famine will break up the Army." Brigadier General James Mitchell Varnum told Nathanael Greene on the same day that "the Situation of the Camp is such, that in all human probability the Army must soon dissolve—Many of the Troops are destitute of Meat, & are Several Days in Arrear—The Horses are dying for want of Forage." Stirling concluded that "the Complaints of the want of provisions and forage are become universal and Violent, every officer speaks of it with dread of the probable Consequences."

These were not idle worries. As he rode through camp on the 15th, Francis Dana, chair of the committee at Moore Hall, witnessed the first signs of "mutiny in the army." That morning a Massachusetts regiment "rose in a body and proceeded to general Patterson's quarters, in whose brigade they are, laid before him their complaints, and threatened to quit the army. By a prudent conduct he quieted them, but was under a necessity of permitting them to go out of camp to purchase meat as far as their money would answer." Patterson promised to pay personally for anything they could not afford. "The same spirit was rising in other regiments," Dana reported, "but has been happily suppressed for the present by the prudence of some of their officers." "An American Army in the Bosom of America," delegate Gouverneur Morris declared, "is about to Disband for the Want of something to eat."

"Naked and starving as they are," Washington maintained, "we cannot enough admire the incomparable patience and fidelity of the soldiery, that they have not been, ere this, excited by their sufferings, to a general mutiny and dispersion." The popular image of Valley Forge depicts him riding among the huts, hunched with care but aglow with determination, and spurring the troops to new feats of endurance. But Washington was a realist. The soldiers did not seek heroic gestures. They wanted to see their leaders taking practical measures to bring food into camp. Practicality was the key to his influence over them. He did not waste time in banqueting, socializing, or making speeches. He worked. Even on days when Washington never stepped out of headquarters, the sight of aides and express riders riding to and from his front door showed he was toiling to keep the troops fed. Never was that perception more important than now.

Washington devoted much of his time in February to "indulging his penchant for graphic embellishment" in letters to Congress, governors, local officials, generals, and commissaries. His complaints became almost artistic in their refinement. He did not threaten or cajole. He exaggerated—but cautiously, almost delicately, without the kind of lurid language that would have made others scoff. He praised subtly, so that his correspondents did not notice they were being flattered. Provisions in New Jersey, Pennsylvania, and Maryland were "nearly exhausted," he assured Connecticut governor Jonathan Trumbull, Sr., and "any relief that can be obtained from the more Southern States will be but partial, trifling and of a day." In fact, as he wrote other officials, he hoped for a great deal from these states; but in asking Trumbull for aid he appealed to the New Englander's regional pride. "We must turn our views to [New England] and lay our account of support from thence," he wrote. "Without it we cannot but disband—I must therefore, Sir, intreat you, in the most earnest terms, and by that zeal which has so eminently distinguished your character in the present arduous struggle," to send supplies to Valley Forge "and thereby prevent such a melancholy and alarming Catastrophre." And he got results. By the end of the month, herds of cattle and wagon trains of all sizes had begun wending their way from Pennsylvania, New Jersey, Maryland, Virginia, North Carolina, and New England to Valley Forge.

The food that these convoys brought to Valley Forge tasted the sweeter because it had been purchased rather than confiscated. For Washington, this was of fundamental importance. He could not win the war without popular support. And he could not command that support unless the army remained a defender and not an oppressor of the people. Otherwise the American soldiers would be indistinguishable from the redcoats, and the cause of liberty would be lost. "The people at large are governed by custom," Washington observed. "To acts of Legislation or Civil authority, they have ever been taught to yeild a willing obedience without reasoning about their propriety. On those of Military power, whether immediate or derived originally from another Source, they have ever looked with a jealous & Suspicious Eye."

When Congress directed him "to order every kind of stock and provisions . . . to be taken from all persons without distinction, leaving such quantities only as he shall judge necessary for the maintenance of their families," he hesitated to obey. Even a few "small seizures" of food and clothing "excited the greatest alarm & uneasiness imaginable, even among some of Our Best & Warmest Friends," and convinced Washington that further confiscations would be counterproductive. Besides enraging civilians, they raised "in the Soldiery a disposition to licentiousness—plunder and Robbery, which has ever been found exceedingly difficult to suppress and which has not only proved ruinous to the Inhabitants, but in many instances to Armies themselves."

Washington's unwillingness to confiscate supplies of course did not preclude other active measures. On February 12th he ordered large Continental detachments under Nathanael Greene, Anthony Wayne, and Henry Lee to scour the surrounding states for food. They spent a month purchasing grain and cattle from farmers, uncovering hoards of provisions overlooked by negligent commissaries, and evading redcoats. By the beginning of March the Americans had ridden the complete circuit of Philadelphia and gathered respectable quantities of supplies, enough to preserve the army in the short term. "The little collections I had made and some others," Greene wrote proudly, "prevented the army from disbanding." With food in camp, more on the way, and a thorough administrative reform in the offing, Washington could now devote his attention to preparing the army for the summer campaign.

Friedrich Wilhelm von Steuben, who came ashore at Portsmouth, New Hampshire, on December 1, 1777, was a former captain in the Prussian army and styled himself—spuriously—a baron. Liberty meant nothing to him. For "glory" and "great possessions," however, he would go to great lengths, including crossing the Atlantic Ocean to join a rebel army fighting against the British empire. He was a mercenary, an opportunist. But he knew about armies. In the 1760s he had served in the headquarters of Frederick the Great, learning the harsh but effective Prussian philosophy of training and drill. That was why, in March 1778, Washington tapped Steuben to become inspector general in Conway's place and train the Continental Army.

Steuben did not attempt to impose Prussian-style discipline on the American soldiers. He "seems to understand what our Soldiers are capable of," John Laurens wrote his father, "and is not so starch a Systematist as to be averse from adapting established forms to stubborn Circumstances—he will not give us the perfect instructions absolutely speaking, but the best which we are in condition to receive." Instead he focused on fundamentals. First he formed 150 men into a model company, who drilled as the others watched. He made them march in step, without music, and stand at attention. When he was satisfied that these basic movements had taken hold, he extended training to the other troops. Shouting his few words of English and lapsing occasionally into German, he taught simple maneuvers before proceeding to more complicated steps. Soon Steuben's staff of assistants began drilling troops on their own.

Prussian officers routinely maltreated their men with floggings and beatings; but Steuben told his officers to "explain with mildness what the soldiers are to do; they are not to use them ill, neither by abusive words or otherwise, but to point out their Faults patiently. There will be no other punishment for the soldier, who neglects his duty or is inattentive, than to make him exercise an whole hour after the others have done." His sensitivity to American attitudes ensured that the intensive training regimen caused no resentment. Drilling twice a day in platoons, companies, and finally in regiments, the Continentals gradually got the hang of the new system.

Steuben's ministrations instilled confidence. The more they drilled, the more the men began to feel like soldiers. At the same time rations grew heartier, and clothing, weapons, and all kinds of supplies became more plentiful; and the weather grew warmer. At the end of April, the troops received stunning news. Two months earlier the American representatives in Paris, who had spent months trying to convince France to enter the war against Britain, had signed treaties of alliance, amity, and commerce with King Louis XVI. By these treaties the king allied himself with the states and acknowledged their independence. War between Britain and France had to follow. America was no longer alone!

Washington announced the French alliance to his army on May 5th. "It having pleased the Almighty ruler of the Universe propitiously to defend the Cause of the United American-States and finally by raising us up a powerful Friend among the Princes of the Earth to establish our liberty and Independence upon lasting foundations," he proclaimed, "it becomes us to set apart a day for gratefully acknowledging the divine Goodness & celebrating the important Event which we owe to his benign Interposition." The next morning the troops paraded under arms before their chaplains, who led them in prayer and thanksgiving. Steuben's inspectors examined their uniforms and equipment, and then formed them into regiments. They loaded and grounded their muskets.

A cannon fired. Each regiment then wheeled right by platoon and formed into two lines. A signal was given, and thirteen cannon discharged at once. The front line of infantry replied with a running fire, from right to left. The second line followed, from left to right. Then a moment of silence, as powder smoke wafted across the parade grounds.

"Huzza!" the troops shouted suddenly. "Long Live the King of France!" Thirteen cannon fired again, and the muskets crackled in another running fire. Silence.

"Huzza! And long live the friendly European Powers!" Cannon, musketry, and again silence.

"Huzza! To the American States!"

A short time later the troops were dismissed, and with an issue of rum in their cups they began to celebrate. The provost opened its doors, so that even prisoners "might taste the Pleasur of the Day." Tables were erected into a "grand harber" in the center of camp, where all the officers were invited to sample a "profusion of fat meat, strong wine and other liquors" with the commander-in-chief. "Several remarkable toasts were drunk," and Washington joined with the men in an afternoon of "mirth and rejoicing." Among the many subjects that they could joke about was a picture that soldiers had painted four days earlier in mock celebration of Saint George's Day. It showed "the King of England kneeling on one knee with the latest compromise proposal in his hand. Next to him was the figure of George Washington, standing upright with his sword in his hand, uttering the following words to the King: 'My dear King, if you wish to beg for something, bend your knee, then let me speak.' "

Over two thousand Continentals had died of disease or privation during the previous three months. But the bitter winter at last had ended.

15

MONMOUTH

May – June 1778

THE WAR WITH America wreaked havoc on Lord North's nerves. Unsteady at the best of times, he seemed to melt a little with every passing year; and by 1778 it was only King George III's stubbornness that kept him in office as prime minister. Then, in March 1778, came news of the French alliance with America. With a new world war on his hands and his political enemies baying for his blood, North accused himself of incompetence and begged to be relieved. "Capital punishment itself," he wailed despairingly to his king, was "preferable to that constant anguish of mind which he feels from the consideration that his continuance in office is ruining his Majesty's affairs without resource." But the king would have none of it. North was his prime minister; no one else would do.

The French alliance with America fragmented the British administration. Hawks and doves savaged one another while moderates kept their heads down and cursed the degrading effects of political parties. The hawks, who included Lord Germain and his allies, insisted on thrashing the Americans into submission. Abandoning the colonies, they swore, would destroy Great Britain's economy. The doves, led by the Whig politicians Lord Rockingham and Charles James Fox, countered that the real threat to Britain lay in trying to fight America and France—and eventually Spain and the Netherlands, who each dreamed of snatching slices of the British imperial pie—simultaneously. They claimed, furthermore, that granting independence to America would not sever her bonds with the mother country but restore Atlantic commerce and revitalize the British economy.

The roads to peace and war were both treacherous, and required a firm step. A peace offer was useless if it did not present acceptable terms, while war demanded bold and creative direction. But the king and his ministers were irresolute. Looking neither to the right nor left at this policy crossroads, they stomped stolidly forward into a ditch. Peace commissioners went to America in June 1778. But independence was not a part of their negotiating package, and Congress refused to listen to any other terms. The war continued, and in the same old way. There were no new leaders, no fresh ideas; no one like William Pitt, who had revolutionized Britain's conduct of the Seven Years' War but died before he could do the same with this one. Fearing to embolden the Whigs by sacking his ministers, George III figuratively tied the dejected prime minister to the mast. He also retained Germain as supreme warlord. The men who had failed to subdue America on its own thus became responsible for fighting a global conflict.

British naval dominance had been one of the defining factors of the war's first years. Now the old formula no longer applied. Stretched to cover a vast and sprawling empire, the British navy could not respond to every possible threat. By concentrating to gain local superiority, the smaller French navy could successfully attack British supply convoys and possessions. Britain's West Indian sugar islands were especially vulnerable. They were isolated, thinly garrisoned—and rich with booty. So were the coastal garrisons in North America. The British could not protect them, crush the Americans, hold Canada, and shield the home islands all at the same time. Something had to give.

The first thing to give was the leadership of the British army in North America. Sir William Howe had beaten Washington almost every time he met him in the field but, nevertheless, had failed to win the war. He fell out of political favor in London and was recalled, though he would not leave America until May 1778. In the meantime his successor, Sir Henry Clinton, received Germain's instructions for the new campaign: "The war must be prosecuted upon a different plan from that upon which it has hitherto been carried on." He had decided to send no more reinforcements to the army in North America, and to "relinquish the idea of carrying on offensive operations against the rebels within land." Instead of pursuing Washington, Clinton would detach 8,000 troops for service in Florida and the Caribbean. Then, Germain ordered, "it is our will and pleasure that you do evacuate Philadelphia." Clinton was told to abandon the loyalists that Howe had spent the winter cultivating, gather his forces in Pennsylvania and New Jersey, and "proceed with the whole to New York."

Germain's decision to abandon Philadelphia may have been necessary under the circumstances. The city's garrison was isolated, and obviously failing in its efforts to extend control over the surrounding country. Yet abandoning Philadelphia rendered the sacrifices of 1777 irrelevant. The storms and squalid heat on the voyage from Sandy Hook to Head of Elk; the arduous march over the Brandywine; the bloody encounter at Birmingham Hill; the "massacre" at Paoli; the heroic stand at Chew's house in Germantown; the grueling effort to open the Delaware; all, from the British point of view, now seemed to count for nothing. British influence would recede to the immediate vicinity of New York and Rhode Island. The Continental Army was intact, and the Hudson Valley—scene of three years of fighting—remained out of King George III's reach. It seemed that all Washington needed to do now was await French help and hold on for victory. A lot of blood would be spilled along the way.

On the evening of Sunday, May 17th, a group of bedraggled American prisoners completed an escape tunnel under the walls of their Philadelphia jail. "Skillfully and laboriously dug," the tunnel served them well. Seven officers and forty-nine men fled through it that night, dodged through the dark city streets, tiptoed past sleepy pickets, and scattered into the countryside. The next day the British discovered the tunnel and assessed the cost of the breakout. They did not mind losing the prisoners. The officers' paroles had been taken, so by the rules of war they could not serve again until officially exchanged, and the enlisted men no longer needed to be fed. But Washington habitually interviewed escapees. Would these tell him about the evacuation of Philadelphia?

William Howe no longer worried about such matters. Today was his farewell banquet, the so-called Mischianza—a made-up word derived from the Italian words *mescere* (to mix) and *mischiare* (to mingle)—that would mark the last public celebration of empire in Britain's wayward colonies. It began at 3:00 P.M., when galleys bearing the Howe brothers, fashionably dressed ladies, and other guests floated down the Delaware past Philadelphia. Flatboats packed with 108 oboists playing in unison led the majestic procession, which continued until the vessels landed at the city's marketplace. Musicians played "God Save the King" and warships boomed a salute while the Howes and their guests stepped ashore. The chattering partygoers then sauntered between lines of flag-bearing troops to "a square where two contingents of knights with their armor-bearers fought with lances and swords in the style of Don Quixot and Sanchopancha, their Dulcineas, sitting on elevated thrones, watching the knights who fought for them." The tournament "surpassed the most sanguine expectations of the beholders," British lieutenant colonel Francis Downman chortled, "for they did not expect to see anything so ridiculous."

The revelers then capered gleefully behind the Howes and their ladies through a specially constructed triumphal arch. "At the top stood Master Neptune with his trident," Downman observed, "but, poor fellow, he had got his arm broke by the tail of a fish I suppose." Beyond lay a "an avenue of 500 yards in length and 40 in breadth, lined with troops and decorated with the colours of the different regiments placed at proper distances," a second arch decorated by "Miss Fame with her trumpet," and finally a festive country house, where girls and silk-clad pages presented 1,030 plates of food in a "very large luxurious hall" festooned with thousands of candles. Fireworks, gambling, dancing, and other acts of elegant dissipation continued till dawn. The total cost of the extravaganza, according to Howe's aide, was "somewhat more than 4,000 guineas, that is about 25,000 dollars."

George Washington dined that night on the relatively humble contents of his larder: veal, eggs, butter, salad, and potatoes. He drank an after-dinner glass or two of Madeira wine, and then his work resumed. Recent reports, some of them from escaped prisoners, indicated that the British would soon leave Philadelphia. To find out for certain he ordered Lafayette to march 2,200 men close to the city. The force was too large for a scouting expedition and too small to face a major attack, but Washington hoped that Lafayette might use it to harass the enemy. "A variety of concurring accounts make it probable the enemy are preparing to evacuate Philadelphia," Washington told the eager young Frenchman. "This is a point, which it is of the utmost importance to ascertain; and if possible the place of their future destination. Should you be able to gain certain intelligence of the time of intended embarkation; so that you may be able to take advantage of it, and fall upon the rear of the enemy in the act of withdrawing, it will be a very desireable event. . . . You will remember that your detachment is a very valuable one, and that any accident happening to it would be a severe blow to this army. You will therefore use every possible precaution for its security, and to guard against a surprise. No attempt should be made nor any thing risked without the greatest prospect of success, and with every reasonable advantage on your side."

Lafayette marched his force to Barren Hill, just northwest of Germantown. Twelve miles from Valley Forge and eleven miles from Philadelphia, the position was both isolated and vulnerable. The Schuylkill River flowed to the right, the left hung in the air, and Germantown's buildings masked any advance to the front. Lafayette's only line of retreat over the river at Matson's Ford lay over two miles to the rear. He dispatched patrols of militiamen and Oneida Indians to watch for an enemy advance, but if it came it could not be delayed for long. In short, the American positions at Barren Hill invited surprise. Informed by a spy of the movement, Howe accepted the invitation and made plans for another sumptuous dinner. This time, he intended to entertain Lafayette.

Three columns of British troops left Philadelphia on the evening of May 19th. Howe and Clinton accompanied the main force, which marched directly up the Ridge Road toward Germantown. Major General Charles Grey meanwhile took 2,000 troops toward Lafayette's left, and Major General James Grant led 5,000 more in a wide circuit to the east and north with the intention of blocking the road to Matson's Ford. None of the routes were heavily guarded; it was simply a matter of completing them before Lafayette had time to react. Once the British columns reached their final positions, the Americans would be trapped against the river with no option but surrender.

Grant and Grey faced minimal opposition from Lafayette's militiamen, who scurried away without bothering to inform anyone of the British advance. Fortunately, a patrol of Delaware Continentals in Germantown took their duties more seriously, and after capturing a couple of scouts from Howe's column they sounded the alarm. It was around dawn when Lafayette, who had been "chatting with a young lady," suddenly "heard the cry that they were surrounded, and he had to smile at the sad news." Much as he yearned for glory, the ambitious French aristocrat realized that this was no time for bravado. Though he had been at Barren Hill for less than two days he was minutely familiar with the terrain. Grant had blocked the main road to Matson's Ford, but Lafayette knew another route of retreat. It was a low, obscure trail that led north along the riverbank, through concealing underbrush and past the British positions.

Gathering his troops, who were showing signs of panic, Lafayette led them down the river trail. In doing so he discovered that Steuben's drilling had paid off. A year before, the Continentals would have bunched in jostling crowds or strung out in single file, but now they formed in compact platoon columns. Only during the crossing at Matson's Ford did their fear get the better of them. "The warter was up to our middle," private Elijah Fisher attested, "and run very swift so that we were obliged to hold each other to keep the Corrent from sweeping us away and all in a fluster expecting the Enemy to fire in upon us for we could see them Plain." They made it safely across thanks to Lafayette, who directed feints that deceived the British into thinking he intended to assault and break through their lines. His choice of position at Barren Hill had been dubious; his retreat, masterful. Only a few stragglers were lost.

The British detected Lafayette's escape only when Grant's scouts advanced south to meet Howe's vanguard on the now aptly named Barren Hill. Their officers promptly began arguing. The plan "would have been effected," griped Lieutenant Colonel Francis Downman, "but, d——— your buts, but the officer who had the honour to command this detachment of the finest part of our army, after making a further detour than was necessary, made also a halt. Now, sir, you can see why I d———d the buts. General Grant made his *halt* very critically for it happened to be at the very time he ought to have advanced with all his speed. How fortunate is our most gracious sovereign to be blessed with such truly intrepid soldiers, and such consummate generals. D——— the buts, I wish he were drowned in a butt of Yankee cider." Howe had missed his chance at a parting gift before leaving for England on May 24th. In recompense, he left Washington with General Charles Lee.

The story of Lee's imprisonment in New York is reminiscent of the O. Henry story "The Ransom of Red Chief," in which a rambunctious boy makes his kidnapers willing to pay to get rid of him. When the British captured Lee in November 1776 they thought he was the only competent American general, but Washington promptly defeated them at Trenton and Princeton. Lee's captors then sounded him out as a turncoat or a go-between for negotiations with Congress. Seeking his goodwill, they provided him with a large bed "into which he tumbled jovially mellow every night" and even relented when he begged "that My Dogs should be brought as I never stood in greater need of their Company." Lee cooperated with his captors and even fawningly gave them suggestions on how to win the war; but Congress rejected his offer to mediate peace talks. The British then tried to exchange him for an officer of equal rank, only to find the Americans were in no hurry to get him back. Negotiations dragged on for months before he was finally traded for a British general.

Washington welcomed Lee to headquarters at Valley Forge immediately after his release on April 5, 1778. The commander-in-chief and several officers treated him to dinner. After the final toasts, Lee flopped down, apparently exhausted, in a den behind Martha's sitting room. He rose late next morning and arrived at breakfast looking seedier than ever. "When he came out he looked as dirty as if he had been in the street all night," remembered Elias Boudinot, who despised him. Lee had brought "a miserable dirty hussy with him from Philadelphia (a British sergeants wife)," claimed Boudinot, "and had actually taken her into his room by a back door and she had slept with him that night." If true, Washington was remarkably tolerant; but when the scraggy Lee mounted a bony old nag for his journey to Congress that morning he could not help chuckling at the sight. When Lee returned, Washington teased, hopefully it would not be on "quite so limping a jade as the one you set out to york on."

Lee's exchange allowed Washington to fill one hole in the army's arrangement for the summer campaign. By the end of May, he had roughly 12,000 soldiers fit for duty, loosely arranged in five divisions of three brigades each. Lee, Stirling, and Lafayette led three of the divisions. Sickness and politics removed the commanders of the other two, which were informally led by Inspector General Steuben and Quartermaster General Nathanael Greene when the army took the field in June. Further down the chain of command, the hemorrhaging of field officers that marked the winter months had slowed. After replacements, the complement of officers for each regiment and brigade was, finally, something near normal.

Greene's brilliant performance as quartermaster general was one of the factors contributing to the army's remarkably quick recovery from the winter. Gradually, most of the men responsible for the supply catastrophe of February were replaced. Bit by bit, Congress enacted Washington's proposed reforms. Supply bottlenecks cleared, and an influx of French imports and domestic products made up for shortfalls in clothing and munitions. And, as Barren Hill showed, Steuben's continuing training and drill was making a difference.

Redcoats remained formidable opponents even in retreat, so this revitalized Continental Army had to proceed carefully. Intelligence received after Barren Hill confirmed rumors of the impending evacuation of Philadelphia. Washington correctly attributed this move to French intervention and expected the British to retreat to New York. But he had no inkling of whether the British would leave the city by sea or land. If by sea, he figured on marching to Newburgh on the Hudson River and awaiting developments. If by land, he intended to follow and seek opportunities to attack. Yet the British were sure to move carefully, with strong flank and rear guards. They might even turn on their pursuers in open country. Defeating them would require meticulous planning and faultless execution.

There were two possible routes for a land evacuation across New Jersey. The most obvious led northeast through Haddonfield, Mount Holly, Allentown, Cranbury, and New Brunswick to Staten Island. In this case, Washington could shadow Clinton from the west and, if the Continentals marched quickly enough, cut him off at Cranbury. But Clinton might also advance to Mount Holly or Allentown, veer east toward Monmouth Court House (now Freehold), and board Royal Navy transports at Sandy Hook. Blocking such a movement would be impossible, although Washington could still snap at Clinton's rear guard. But either way, it behooved the Americans not to venture too close. At a council of war on June 17th the commander-in-chief asked his officers how the Continental Army should react to the impending evacuation. Most of them—with the exception of Anthony Wayne, who dreamed of "*Burgoyning* Clinton," voted to follow the British at an ample distance, and not to attack under almost any circumstances. They also insisted on keeping the American army whole. "I would not detach from this Army," Greene advised, "for in doing that we hazard both parts, & if it's dangerous for the whole army to go into the neighbourhood of the Enemy it must be still more so for a part."

The evacuation of Philadelphia began at four o'clock that morning as several regiments of Germans and provincials under Knyphausen boarded flatboats and floated across the Delaware to New Jersey. The dawn was sultry, and presaged "terrible" daytime heat. On the opposite shore, Knyphausen joined a detachment of redcoats and provincials who had filtered across in the preceding days and deployed to protect the bridgehead. Clinton led the remainder of his ten-thousand-man army out of the city the following morning. In his wake came 1,500 wagons laden with vast amounts of plunder and baggage, guards, loyalist refugees, and a rambling flock of camp followers and cattle.

Most of the British army departed Philadelphia by that afternoon, June 18th. Captain Allen McLane's company of Delaware light infantry slipped into the city just as the last British patrols were leaving and captured a few officers who had dallied too long with their "tender acquaintances." Otherwise the Americans found "positively nothing but empty redoubts and houses." Military supplies had been removed or destroyed, dwellings looted, and merchant ships burned at the wharves. Washington appointed Benedict Arnold city commandant.

Now 12,000 strong, the Continentals broke camp and marched by divisions northeast. They grumbled, as was their right, but maintained discipline. Quartermaster General Greene kept them happy by ordering regular rest halts, and shooed stragglers back into formation. The leading divisions of the army reached the Delaware at Coryell's Ferry on June 20th. The river crossing was leisurely, and the last troops did not enter New Jersey until the morning of the 22nd. On the 23rd, leaving "all our tents standing & our heavy baggage behind us," the army marched about ten miles east to Hopewell, New Jersey. The soldiers camped that night in the open, and awoke the next morning well-rested and in fighting trim.

The British did not have it so easy, thanks in part to Washington's adeptness in irregular warfare. Before the evacuation of Philadelphia he had instructed Major General Philemon Dickinson of the militia "that the way to annoy, distress, and really injure the Enemy on their march (after obstructing the roads as much as possible) with Militia, is to suffer them to act in very light Bodies . . . as the Enemy's Guards in front flank and Rear must be exposed and may be greatly injured by the concealed and well directed fire of Men in Ambush. This kind of Annoyance ought to be incessant day and Night and would I think be very effectual." He was right. As the British tramped northeast in two divisions, under Clinton and Knyphausen, they swatted at clouds of American light infantry and militia, who gave "resistance at every defile, woods, or bridge, and tore up every bridge." This forced them to stop and start repeatedly as they cleared obstacles or skirmished with elusive enemy bands; and hot, stormy weather intensified their misery. Sunstroke, straggling, and desertion became alarmingly common by the time the British reached Allentown, only fifteen miles away from the American positions at Hopewell, on the 24th.

Clinton now decided that it was too dangerous to continue northeast through the broken and swampy terrain that began past Cranbury. Doing so would expose his long flank to attack while allowing the Americans the luxury of remaining near the mountainous safety of northwestern New Jersey. Instead, on the morning of the 25th he turned his troops away from Washington's baleful gaze and drove them east through Monmouth County toward Sandy Hook. The roads were narrower in that direction and the ground sandy, but with fewer obstructions. By moving east Clinton also "had hopes Mr. Washington might possibly be induced to commit himself" in the open. For that reason, as the march began he shifted his best troops, "the Guards, Grenadiers & Light Infantry," from the front to the rear of the column.

Washington had convened another council of war at Hopewell on the morning of the 24th. Not many days were left for an attack, for whichever direction the British marched they would soon be out of reach. He therefore asked the officers present—Lee, Greene, Stirling, Lafayette, Steuben, Knox, and Wayne, among others—whether the time had come for the army to "hazard a general action." They answered succinctly that it had not. The most they would accept was that Washington should detach only 1,500 men "to act as occasion may serve, on the enemy's left flank and rear, in conjunction with the other Continental troops and militia, which are already hanging about them; and the main body to preserve a relative position, so as to be able to act as circumstances may require." Alexander Hamilton left the council in disgust, grumbling that it "would have done honor to the most honorab[le] society of midwives, and to them only."

The council's decision was a bitter disappointment for Washington, but almost immediately he received letters from Greene and Lafayette suggesting that not all the officers felt so cautious. Apologizing that "the delicate situation I am in prevents my speaking in councels of war with that openness I should if I was to take a part in the command," Greene proposed attacking the British with light troops while the rest of the army remained in supporting distance. "If we suffer the enemy to pass through the Jerseys without attempting any thing upon them," he wrote, "I think we shall ever regret it." Lafayette revealed that he, Greene, Steuben, Wayne, and two brigadier generals took the same point of view, and suggested sending 2,500, not 1,500 men toward Clinton—"not to Scout as Some Say, but to attak any part of the english army or of theyr baggage as will furnish a proper opportunity." He even chided Washington for having called a council at all. "Such a council is a school of logic," he wrote, but "it will never be a mean of doing what is consistent with the good of the Service, the advantage of the occasion, and indeed the authority of the commander-in-chief."

Perhaps shamed by the admonishments of the twenty-two-year-old Lafayette, Washington for once decided to overrule the decision of his council. The advance contingent would be not 1,500, not 2,500, but 4,000 strong; and it would follow Clinton aggressively. Washington offered the command to General Lee, but he rejected it as "a more proper busyness of a Young Volunteering General than of the Second in command in the Army." Washington then turned to Lafayette, who accepted with obvious delight. After watching him prance out of camp on the morning of June 25th, aide James McHenry recorded in his diary that "the young Frenchman in raptures with his command and burning to distinguish himself moves toward the enemy who are in motion."

Determined to stay close to Clinton's left rear, Lafayette moved east rapidly, entering Cranbury on the evening of the 25th and leaving at dawn the next day. Washington marched with the rest of the army in Lafayette's wake and arrived at Cranbury later on the 26th. Now, as the Continental Army closed on the enemy, General Lee decided he had misunderstood the size and importance of Lafayette's command. What had once seemed an insignificant detachment now seemed "undoubtedly the most honourable command next to the Commander in Chief." He wanted to lead it after all; and warned that if Lafayette did not step down he would consider himself "disgrac'd"— in other words, he would resign.

Some have argued that Lee's superior experience justified this untimely demand, and that Washington had been foolish to entrust such an important command to the youthful Lafayette. Even Alexander Hamilton saw some disquieting signs of carelessness in the Frenchman's impetuous advance. Yet a look at the two generals' past battlefield performances reveals some profound differences. Lee's slothful, self-serving conduct in the 1776 New Jersey campaign contrasted starkly with the nimbleness Lafayette displayed at Barren Hill. There were other considerations. Lafayette, though occasionally rash, was the commander on the spot and knew his situation better than anyone else. Replacing him just as his force was about to make contact with the enemy invited confusion, delay, or worse. Furthermore, as Baron Henri Jomini wrote in 1815 in his *Précis de l'Art de la Guerre,* "To commit the execution of a purpose to one who disapproves of the plan of it, is to employ but one-third of the man; his heart and his head are against you; you have command only of his hands." Lee regarded offensive operations against Clinton as unwise, so letting him lead the attack was folly.

Washington nevertheless relented, feeling he had little choice. Based on seniority, Lee had a right to supersede Lafayette. To mask the blow to his French friend, Washington sent Lee forward with another 1,000 men, bringing the detachment up to a total strength of 5,000—almost half the army. When Lee caught up with Lafayette at Englishtown on the 27th, he also took command of Daniel Morgan's 600 riflemen and Philemon Dickinson's 1,000 militiamen, operating respectively on the right and left flanks of the British column. Lee quipped that he hardly knew any of the officers who would serve under him, and would have little time to get acquainted. The British were less than five miles away.

Clinton's army had endured two nightmarish days after leaving Allentown on the 25th. The troops, encased in thick wool uniforms and lugging packs that weighed up to sixty pounds, slogged toward Sandy Hook through temperatures passing 100 degrees. No march in the war was more terrible. There was no rain or shade. Drinking water became scarce because of clogged or poisoned wells. Snipers laid ambushes, killed randomly and then fled through the underbrush. On one day, the 26th, Captain Johann Ewald lost sixty casualties or a third of his command. Twenty had "dropped dead from the great heat and fatigue." Forty fell to American bullets.

Desertion became common, so much so that stories entered local folklore of soldiers who abandoned the march to become settlers or frontiersmen. Thomas Sullivan, a twenty-three-year-old private in the Forty-ninth Regiment of Foot, had served in America for three years, but now he decided he could endure no more. Goaded by the American wife he had married the previous winter in Philadelphia, he joined thirteen others in slipping away as the column passed a small stand of woods on June 25th. Three days later, "after a tedious and troublesome march, through woods and marshes," he reached Philadelphia, where he found 800 other recent deserters. Some of them enlisted in the Continental Army.

Late on the 26th, the British army halted in limp exhaustion around Monmouth Court House, with the baggage train and 4,000 men under Knyphausen east of the building and 6,000 troops under Cornwallis to the west. Middletown, a safe position on high ground about ten miles from Sandy Hook, was just a day's march away; but Clinton declared the 27th a day of rest. His troops needed it. Moreover, he still hoped that "Mr. Washington might yet afford me an opportunity of having a brush with him." The 27th passed uneventfully, however, and as evening approached, Clinton decided that an

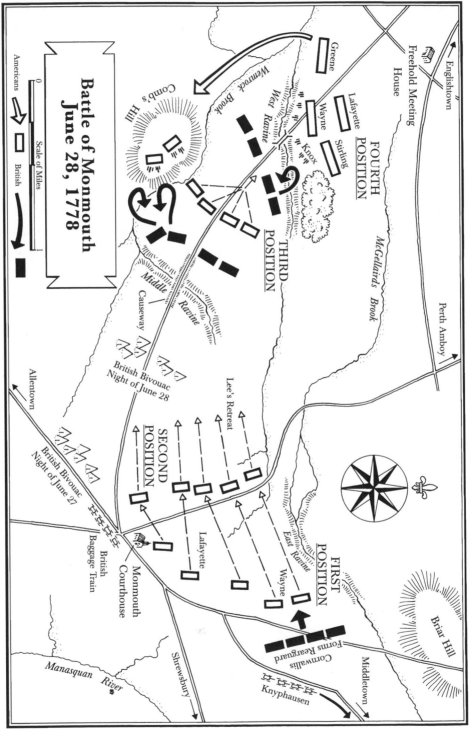

**Battle of Monmouth
June 28, 1778**

Scale of Miles

0

Americans

British

Englishtown

Freehold Meeting
House

Greene

Wenrock Brook

Comb's Hill

Wayne

Lafayette

Stirling

Knox

West Ravine

FOURTH
POSITION

McGellaird's Brook

Perth Amboy

THIRD
POSITION

Middle
Ravine

Causeway

British Bivouac
Night of June 28

Lee's Retreat

SECOND
POSITION

Allentown

British Bivouac
Night of June 27

British
Baggage Train

Monmouth
Courthouse

Lafayette

Wayne

East Ravine

FIRST
POSITION

Briar Hill

Manasquan   River

Shrewsbury

Cornwallis
Forms Rearguard

Knyphausen

Middletown

© 2005 Rick Britton

American attack was unlikely. Disappointedly relinquishing "every idea of a decisive action," he ordered the retreat to resume on the morning of the 28th. Another day would put his pursuers out of reach.

Washington, too, sensed the last chance for a battle slipping away, but at this crucial moment his army was divided. Three days' accretion had transformed Lee's detachment from a small harassing force into half the army. It was now much larger than even Greene or Lafayette had envisaged, and in truth an awkward size; too large to risk losing, and too small to prevail in a general action. But by the afternoon of the 27th the two halves were not too far apart, with Lee's 5,000 soldiers at Englishtown, and the rest at Penolopon Bridge, three miles to the southwest. Five miles southeast of Lee was Monmouth Court House, where the British soldiers sprawled in the wilting heat. Washington called a meeting of his officers. Tomorrow, he declared, the Continental Army would attack.

Monmouth Court House, later called Freehold, was a village of some forty houses named after its most prominent building. It stood at a crossroads. One road ran south into open country; a second southwest to Allentown; a third west to Englishtown; a fourth north to Amboy; and a fifth northeast to Middletown and Sandy Hook. The "V" formed by these last two roads was bisected a mile north of the courthouse by boggy bottomland known as the East Ravine. An army advancing from the west, on the road from Englishtown, would not have an easy march. Three miles from Monmouth the road sloped down into a marshy bottom, crossing a branch of Wemrock Brook over a small bridge before rising back to drier land on the other side. This was the West Ravine. Continuing southeast through a mile of briery woods and hedged fields, the road then narrowed to a causeway as it crossed another branch of Wemrock Brook in the Middle Ravine. From there it passed through partially cultivated land, and on into Monmouth Court House. "I could not entertain so bad an opinion of Mr. Washington's military abilities," Clinton recalled, as to suppose he would attack through "such a country."

Washington offered no battle plan when he met with Lee and his officers—Lafayette, Wayne, Maxwell, and Charles Scott—on the afternoon of June 27th. He simply directed them to attack when the British began marching in the morning, and promised to bring the rest of the army within supporting range. His orders left several crucial questions unanswered. Was Lee's corps supposed to probe the British, harass their retreat, or bring on a general engagement? How far should the attack proceed before breaking off? Should Lee push toward Monmouth? Should he try to seize Clinton's baggage train? By failing to provide explicit answers on these points, whether because he was careless or overworked, Washington left his subordinates uncertain of what he expected from them, and abdicated much of his responsibility as commander-in-chief.

Lee was not the man to fill the gap left by Washington's neglect. Lee saw no purpose in devising a plan of attack over ground of which he was ignorant, against an enemy who was posted he knew not where. Instead, Lee told his generals to rouse the troops before dawn, advance cautiously toward the courthouse, and let circumstances guide what they did next. He asked Dickinson and Morgan to act as scouts, and told them to join the attack whenever they chose to do so. The only amendment to this nonplan came just after midnight, when Washington sent a message ordering Lee to advance 600 men toward Monmouth as scouts and skirmishers. He complied—four hours after the message arrived—but otherwise made no attempt to learn about local topography and enemy dispositions before morning. In short, the Continental Army was about to advance into unknown terrain against unknown positions, and without specific orders.

The British withdrew from Monmouth in two divisions. Knyphausen's division moved out sometime between 3:00 and 4:00 A.M. and escorted the artillery baggage train northeast on the road to Middletown. Cornwallis marched in the same direction at 5:00 A.M. Knyphausen's leading troops had advanced about five miles at 9:00 A.M., when they were surprised by the appearance of Americans on their left toward the East Ravine. Excited by the sight of the lumbering baggage train, the Americans sprinted forward; and some of them "got between the wagons and maltreated the drivers and some patrols alongside them" before the British forced their withdrawal. The attackers were either militiamen or members of the 600-man advance guard, which Lee had placed under Colonel William Grayson. The rest of Lee's troops, who had decamped about 7:00 A.M. and struggled through the broken country northwest of Monmouth across the west and middle ravines, panted close behind.

By mid-morning the Americans were arrayed in a haphazard line running roughly north-south, with the courthouse to their right rear and the East Ravine to their left rear. Clinton quickly assembled a force of three British brigades to cover the baggage train's escape, and over the next few hours Lee toyed with various methods of dislodging them. Continental regiments—

sometimes acting on their colonels' independent initiative—moved forward, skirmished, withdrew, repositioned, advanced again, and got themselves into a deepening muddle. Dickinson's militia filtered in and confused the situation still further. Finally Lee determined on a complicated pincers movement to cut off the British rear guard, but his tired and disoriented troops advanced so hesitantly that the attack promptly broke down. Clinton meanwhile hurried Knyphausen's troops and the baggage out of range and prepared Cornwallis's entire division for a counterattack. With fourteen mostly British battalions, a couple of German and loyalist units, and the Sixteenth Light Dragoons, Cornwallis had about six thousand men, roughly equal to Lee's and Dickinson's combined forces.

It was now near 1:00 P.M., and after maneuvering and countermaneuvering for hours in the increasingly brutal heat, the American units were not only tired but also hopelessly mixed up. Stymied in his attempt to destroy Clinton's rear guard, and observing attack preparations from a British force that was much larger than he had expected, Lee ordered Lafayette to lead three regiments and some artillery to a position from which they could anchor his right flank. Lafayette complied, but found the position unsuitable, so he moved to another. Officers from other units saw this shift and, as it took place just as the British began a general advance, mistook it for retreat. Not wanting to be left behind, they "made Tracks Quick Step towards English Town." The same thing happened simultaneously on other parts of the battlefield. Regiments that had scattered hither and thither in the course of the morning now discovered that they were isolated, without flank support, and out of contact with one another. They fled, too. Soon the entire force was streaming to the west, with the bewildered Lee in its wake.

The retreat did not become a rout, partly—as Lee and his defenders insisted—because he kept his force "more or less intact, offering effective resistance all the way." He attempted a number of delaying actions as he withdrew southwest through the village of Monmouth Court House and then west along the Englishtown Road. Yet since many units retreated on their own initiative, equal credit may be due to officers like Lafayette, Wayne, and Scott, who stayed with their men and shepherded them back to safety. Wayne and Scott were both furious at what they saw as Lee's incompetence, and directed their troops without regard to his orders. Wayne was so angry that he refused to speak with Lee.

At first Clinton did not press the Americans very hard. The weather was less generous, but at least it tortured both sides equally. By mid-afternoon the heat was infernal. Soldiers, many of whom had emptied their canteens in the sultry morning, now gasped helplessly as they stumbled through briars or over roads shrouded by powder smoke and choked with dust. Along the way they passed prostrate men who had "fainted and given out with the heat"; dozens of British, Germans, and Americans simply dropped dead.

Washington and his entourage approached the battlefield after noon, leading 6,000 troops of Stirling's and Greene's divisions down the Englishtown Road. Hearing of a possible flanking movement to his right, the commander-in-chief ordered Greene to file off in that direction and then continued east. Just then a young fifer came staggering down the road from the West Ravine. An aide collared the trembling boy and dragged him before Washington, who demanded to know where he was going. The fifer stammered "that he was a soldier, and that the Continental troops that had been advanced were retreating." The general then wrathfully threatened the unfortunate lad that "if he mentioned a thing of the sort, he would have him whipped," and spurred his horse forward. He had gone less than fifty yards when he met two soldiers, then small groups, and finally whole units in retreat. Two of his aides rode ahead past the West Ravine to find out what was happening and found more of the same. None of the officers they interviewed knew why the troops were retreating. "By God!" swore one colonel, "they are flying from a shadow."

Eventually the aides found Lee, who asked where he could find the commander-in-chief. He might better have sought a place to hide. The two men met on the road a few hundred feet past the West Ravine, and within a few minutes Lee was wilting like a plant in the summer sun—whether from Washington's words or just his blistering gaze is open to question. Scott said the commander-in-chief "swore that day till the leaves shook on the trees. Charming! Delightful! Never have I enjoyed such swearing before or since. Sir, on that memorable day he swore like an angel from heaven!" Others claim Washington hurled epithets at Lee and ended by calling him a "damned poltroon." Yet Lee himself never accused the general of cursing. According to more trustworthy accounts, Washington demanded the meaning of the retreat and Lee dazedly stammered, "Sir. Sir." When he had recovered enough to speak coherently, Lee insisted "that from a variety of contradictory intelligence, and that from his orders not being obeyed, matters were thrown into confusion, and that he did not chuse to beard the British army with troops in such a situation. He said besides, the thing was against his own opinion. General Washington answered, whatever his opinion might have been, he expected his orders would have been obeyed, and then rode on towards the rear of the retreating troops."

Washington crossed the West Ravine to a copse bordering the road on the east side. He stayed there for a short time, watching the retreating troops, and learned that the British were less than fifteen minutes behind them. He then "looked about and said that it appeared to be an advantageous spot to give the enemy the first check." Wayne appeared at that moment. Washington told him to take command of the nearest regiments—Colonel Walter Stewart's Third Pennsylvania and Lieutenant Colonel Patrick Ramsay's Third Maryland—turn them about, and hold off the British until the rest of the army had a chance to form behind the ravine. The commander-in-chief "encouraged the men—he took the officers by the hand—he told them how much depended on a moments resistance, and he said he was satisfied every thing would be attempted." Washington then turned to the troops and asked if they could fight, and they responded with three hearty cheers. "We shall check them," Ramsay promised.

Returning across the ravine, Washington asked Lee to take command of Wayne's rear guard. Lee suppressed the memory of his earlier humiliation and agreed, promising to be among the last men to leave the field. Washington then turned away, and Lee rode forward to join Wayne. Hamilton galloped along beside him, flourishing his sword and prattling words of encouragement. "That's right, my dear General," Hamilton blurted out, "and I will stay, and we will all die here on this spot." Noticing the young aide "much flustered and in a sort of frenzy of valour," Lee acidly asked him "to observe me well and to tell me if I did not appear tranquil and master of my faculties." Hamilton abashedly responded that he was. Well, then, Lee snapped, "you must allow me to be a proper judge of what I ought to do." Pointing out where he would post his troops, Lee continued, "When I have taken proper measures to get the main body of them in a good position, I will die with you on this spot, if you please."

Lee barely had time to station a few New England regiments and about ten guns behind a hedgerow on Wayne's right before the advancing British came plowing into the thin American line. The impact of their assault at first sent the Continentals scattering backward, but they came back to grapple with and even charge the bayonet-wielding redcoats. The ensuing carnage claimed many victims on both sides. Clinton raced madly back and forth "like a Newmarket jockey," brandishing his sword and screaming at his overheated men not to stop until the Continental line was broken. He was almost killed when an American officer fired at him before falling to a guard's bayonet. Stewart was wounded and taken off the field. Ramsay lost his horse to enemy gunfire and was then almost trampled by a charging British dragoon. The dragoon fired his pistol, missed, and then drew his saber. Ramsay stood his ground, skewered the dragoon with his sword, and hopped into the empty saddle; but he was promptly set upon and captured by a party of enemy cavalry. The second in command of a Rhode Island regiment lost an eye to a cannonball that whizzed past, brushing his face. Hamilton was hurt and nearly crushed when his horse fell, slain, beneath him. And somewhere, so the story goes, a foul-mouthed, tobacco-chewing young woman named Molly Pitcher manned a cannon left untended by her wounded husband.

The Continentals fought for an hour before falling back across the bridge that spanned the ravine. Lee had kept some fresh units in reserve, and used them to cover the retreat. His troops remembered Steuben's drill, and marched across the bridge in good order instead of swarming in panic. There was no rout. On the other side, Washington greeted the retreating soldiers and told Lee to shepherd them back toward Englishtown. Lee hesitated and started complaining of his treatment during their earlier encounter. Washington curtly informed him that he had no time for explanations, and trotted away to his troops. The battle, he knew, was far from over.

Lee later claimed that by withdrawing from Monmouth Court House he delivered Clinton into Washington's hands. In a sense this was true, for the Americans now occupied an extremely strong position. Stirling's division and Knox's artillery, which had advanced straight down the Englishtown Road, were posted along a ridge overlooking the West Ravine. To their right lay Greene's division, the forward elements of which occupied Comb's Hill only 700 yards from Clinton's left. Surrounded by swamps on three sides, this hill was almost impregnable. Cannon that Greene had astutely placed there now enfiladed the redcoats lining the Englishtown Road. Knox's artillery joined the bombardment, and the British returned fire from their lower elevation. Lieutenant Colonel Henry Dearborn of the Third New Hampshire Regiment remarked of the cannonade that "if any thing Can be Call'd Musical where their is so much Danger, I think that was the finest musick, I Ever heared.

[H]owever the agreeableness of the musick was very often Lessen'd by the balls Coming too near."

This artillery duel lasted for perhaps two hours, during which time Washington recalled portions of Lee's command to buttress Stirling's line. Then, as the sun finally passed its zenith in the late afternoon, Clinton attacked. He apparently tried to dislodge Stirling first by using light infantry, grenadiers, and the Scottish Black Watch to infiltrate the American left in conjunction with a frontal assault across the West Ravine. Advancing through heavy artillery fire and suffering casualties, the British crossed the ravine and occupied an orchard that threatened Washington's entire position. Brutal fighting followed as Stirling's Continentals tried to push them back. Muskets and artillery fired at such close range that they blew some soldiers to pieces, and the sweltering heat claimed dozens of new victims.

Washington exposed himself to heavy fire while riding back and forth along the line. He had taken the same risk many times before. At Monmouth, however, the impact of his appearance was greater than it had ever been. Troops now rallied to his encouragement as they had not at Kip's Bay or Germantown. Perhaps he had finally won their confidence during the long winter at Valley Forge. "The commander in Chief was every where," Nathanael Greene remembered. "His Presence gave Spirit and Confidence and his command and authority soon brought every thing into Order and Regularity." "America owes a great deal to General Washington for this day's work," Hamilton reported. "By his own presence, he brought order out of confusion, animated his troops and led them to success." Lafayette thought that "General Washington seemed to arrest fate with a single glance. His nobility, grace, and presence of mind were never displayed to better advantage."

After an hour of combat, Washington ordered three regiments of New Hampshire and Virginia Continentals to wade through the smoke-clogged woods and attack the British right. With shouldered arms, the well-drilled Americans advanced relentlessly until they were about sixty feet from the enemy. Then, behaving "very Coolly" despite a constant barrage of British musketry and grapeshot, the Continentals opened fire. The redcoats abandoned the orchard and retreated across the ravine. Lieutenant Colonel Aaron Burr subsequently led his Continental regiment and three others across the bridge in an impetuous counterattack, but the British inflicted heavy casualties and forced the Americans to retreat. At around the same time a column of grenadiers and Coldstream Guards under Cornwallis tried to attack Greene, but it withdrew after being pulverized by the artillery on Comb's Hill.

It was now 6:00 P.M., and the soldiers on both sides were half dead with heat, thirst, and exhaustion. Convinced that his troops had "repulsed very superior numbers with honor to themselves and no small disgrace to the enemy," Clinton withdrew half a mile toward Monmouth, out of range of the American artillery. Washington thought of pursuing but dropped the idea—his troops were unfit for further action. He spent the night lying next to Lafayette under a single cloak, talking about Lee and planning for the morning's advance. But now it was time for Clinton to follow an example that Washington had set several times before. Leaving their campfires burning, the British rose around midnight and retreated through Monmouth to the Middletown Road. The Americans did not detect the withdrawal until daylight, by which time Clinton was well on the way to Sandy Hook. The Battle of Monmouth was over.

The Continentals, some still tottering from the effects of yesterday's fatigue, assembled on June 29th to hear compliments from their general. "The Commander in Chief congratulates the Army on the Victory obtained over the Arms of his Britanick Majesty yesterday and thanks most sincerely the gallant officers and men who distinguished themselves upon the occasion," they were told. The next evening Washington assembled the troops again to "publickly unite in thanksgivings to the supreme Disposer of human Events for the Victory which was obtained on sunday over the Flower of the British Troops." In his mind there was no doubt. The best of the British army had been engaged, vanquished, and driven from the field. But was that really the case? And if so, who deserved the credit?

"Nothing, surely, can be more ridiculous than the claim to advantage which both Mr. Washington and Mr. Lee have set up in their respective accounts of this day's action," wrote Sir Henry Clinton in his memoir. The British army's casualties were probably slightly higher, perhaps 500, as compared to 350 Americans, including victims of sunstroke—but not including the several hundred redcoats and Germans who had deserted during the retreat from Philadelphia. Yet, as Clinton argued, the rear guard had done its duty and more. It had protected the army's baggage train, driven back the attackers, and withdrawn without being cut off. Washington made much of being left in possession of the field, but that had not been either side's objective. The Continental Army in fact started the day with no objective except to attack the enemy. The results might best be called a draw.

Even so, there were heroes on the American side. The Continentals showed incredible fortitude under hellish conditions—as did the British. Steuben had taught them well; and on the battlefield he led by example, accompanying the commander-in-chief on his rounds and helping to embolden the troops. Stirling, Wayne, Knox, Lafayette, and especially Greene behaved with coolness and valor. So did Washington, who rallied Lee's retreating forces, formed a strong line of defense, and helped to hold it against determined enemy attack. Yet some claim that Washington's laurels came at the expense of another. Was Charles Lee "Washington's scapegoat"?

On the morning of June 28th Lee advanced, attacked—sort of—and withdrew before superior enemy forces. Washington had not specifically told him to do anything more. Yet when the two men met in the afternoon the commander-in-chief publicly accused Lee of disobeying orders. Two days later, after Lee complained of Washington's "very singular expressions" during their exchange and demanded the right to justify his conduct "to the Congress, to America, and to the world in general," he was placed under arrest prior to facing a court-martial on charges of disobedience and insubordination. Lee claimed his treatment was undeserved. After all, as he asserted (and as Clinton would later agree), if he had not retreated from the territory adjoining the East Ravine, his force might have been destroyed. And by pulling back to the West Ravine, he enticed the British into a disadvantageous position.

Washington's angry outburst about Lee's disobeying orders was unfair, if only because he had not given him specific instructions in the first place. But if Lee accomplished anything positive at Monmouth, it was by accident. He had advanced that morning without making any serious attempt to gather intelligence on terrain or enemy dispositions. He let his units drift out of contact with one another, confused them further with complex and uncoordinated maneuvers, and finally lost control of them altogether in the face of Clinton's advance. He failed to use Dickinson's militia effectively and wrote an incoherent and misdated note to Colonel Daniel Morgan that caused that officer's elite riflemen to sit idle and miss the day's action entirely. Perhaps most damning, Lee lost the confidence of his three senior commanders—Lafayette, Scott, and Wayne—long before Washington expressed his displeasure. Lee's

court-martial found him guilty of disobeying orders, treating Washington disrespectfully, and conducting an unnecessary, disorderly, and shameful retreat. It might as well have simply declared him incompetent, which he was.
In any case, Congress suspended Lee in December 1778 and permanently
dismissed him in 1780. He did not live to see the end of the war, suddenly
falling ill and dying in Philadelphia in 1782, at the age of fifty-one.

Washington's army celebrated July 4, 1778, at New Brunswick, New Jersey.
"The Anniversary of the Declaration of Independence," the previous evening's
general orders had decreed, "will be celebrated by the firing thirteen Pieces
of Cannon and a *feu de joie* of the whole line. . . . The Soldiers are to adorn
their Hats with *Green-Boughs* and to make the best appearance possible. . . .
Double allowance of rum will be served out." The festivities ended with three
cheers and the roaring cry of "Perpetual and undisturbed Independence to
the United States of America." The next day Sir Henry Clinton's army embarked at Sandy Hook and sailed for New York.

On July 8th, Major General Benedict Arnold, commandant of Philadelphia, sent Washington a letter of congratulations for his accomplishments in
New Jersey. "[I] am very happy to hear the Enemy have suffered so very considerably in their march thro' the Jerseys," he wrote. "I make no doubt this
Campaign will be crown'd with success, & that your Excellency will soon
enjoy in peace the Laurels you have with so much perseverence, toil & hazard reaped in the Iron field of War." As Arnold wrote, Admiral Charles Hec-
tor Théodat, Comte d'Estaing, arrived off the Eastern Shore of Virginia with
sixteen warships bearing 4,000 French soldiers. "The talents and great actions of General Washington have insured him in the eyes of all Europe, the
title, truly sublime of deliverer of America," the Frenchman declared. "I have
the honor of imparting to Your Excelly the arrival of the King's fleet; charged
by his Majesty with the glorious task of giving his allies the United States of
America the most striking proofs of his affection." Washington and his army
would no longer bear the brunt of British military might alone.

16

THE DARK BEFORE THE DAWN

1778 – 1781

WASHINGTON WAS NEVER very good at waiting, but that is how he spent the years between 1778 and 1781. The war continued in New England, on the frontiers, in the South, and even on the shores of Great Britain. Armies and armed bands crisscrossed the continent. There were skirmishes, raids, and major battles on land and at sea. There was bloody civil conflict, complete with gruesome atrocities against both soldiers and civilians. Washington hungered to share in the action. He still sought that climactic battle. But so long as the main British army in America camped in New York, he felt constrained to hover nearby. And so, for three years, he had to do without leading troops in the field.

The Comte d'Estaing's arrival off Virginia's Eastern Shore in July 1778 portended the end of Great Britain's monopoly on the seas. But many months passed before the promise became reality. D'Estaing was a land general, and his attempts to engage the British navy only demonstrated his ineptitude at sea. He missed intercepting Clinton's fleet at Sandy Hook by three days and then sailed for New York, where he failed to penetrate the harbor. The French admiral next sailed to British-occupied Newport, Rhode Island, which he reached at the end of the month. Washington, camped with his army at White Plains, sent Greene, Lafayette, and thousands of reinforcements to help d'Estaing take Newport; but the admiral quarreled with John Sullivan, who commanded the American army. After a storm and the arrival of a smaller British fleet, the French fled to Boston and then sailed for the West Indies. Left exposed, the American land forces barely evaded a British entrapment before disengaging.

The failure of the Newport expedition concluded the brief Franco-American honeymoon. The Americans had expected immediate and fabulous results from the alliance, and their disappointment was profound.

Lafayette noticed that when the French left Newport the American officers and soldiers "turn'd mad at theyr departure, and wishing them all the evils in the world did treat them as a generous one would be asham'd to treat the most inveterate ennemys—you ca'nt have any idea of the horrors which were to be heard in that occasion." Even Lafayette himself was not safe from their rage. "Frenchmen of the highest characters have been expos'd to the most disagreable Circumstances," he complained, "and me, yes, myself the friend of america, the friend of general washington, I am more upon a warlike footing in the american lines, than when I come near the british lines at newport." Other Frenchmen also threatened to rethink their commitment to aid America.

Washington was no Francophile, despite his friendship with Lafayette. The foppishness and excitability that he perceived in many French officers made him wince. Unlike many of his countrymen, however, Washington understood the necessity of tolerating, if not pandering to, French idiosyncrasies. "The disagreement between the army under your command and the fleet has given me very singular uneasiness," he wrote Sullivan. "The Continent at large is concerned in our cordiality, and it should be kept up by all possible means that are consistent with our honor and policy. First impressions, you know, are generally longest remembered, and will serve to fix in a great degree our national character among the French. In our conduct towards them we should remember that they are a people old in war, very strict in military etiquette, and apt to take fire when others scarcely seem warmed—Permit me to recommend in the most particular manner, the cultivation of harmony and good agreement, and your endeavours to destroy that ill humour which may have got into the officers. It is of the greatest importance also that the minds of the soldiers and the people should know nothing of the misunderstanding." In time, the commander-in-chief's good offices helped to restore faith in the alliance on both sides.

Washington valued the French alliance for many reasons, but he especially looked forward to the impact that the French navy would have on the war at sea. This theater had interested him since the fall of 1775, when he commissioned a fleet of eight schooners, crewed them with soldiers from his army, and sent them to attack enemy shipping at Boston. He administered this tiny flotilla himself, handling purchase, fitting, and provision, setting rules of engagement, and helping to determine the legal status of prizes. The schooners captured thirty-one enemy vessels before the siege ended, and their operations were instructive for the Naval Committee that built the Continental Navy in 1776. Washington also invested in a twelve-gun privateer, the *General Washington,* and shared in the profits from its prizes.

The Continental Navy never became strong enough to challenge British naval superiority. Washington did not expect it to. Instead he assisted its development into a respectable regional force, providing advice on constructing and fitting ships, recruiting crews, winter docks, and active operations. At times he overreached himself, giving unwanted directions on problems outside his landlubber's expertise; but he also promoted cooperation between army and navy at a time when most of his fellow officers considered the two services incompatible. This was especially true during the 1777 campaign for control of the Delaware River forts. When the commanders of the army garrisons at Fort Mifflin and Red Bank began bickering with Commodore John Hazelwood of the Pennsylvania navy, Washington refused to take sides, expressing instead his "ardent desire that harmony and a good understanding between the fleet and the garrisons, may be mutually cultivated. On this everything depends, nothing but disappointment and disgrace can attend the want of it." His understanding of this principle would play a significant role in the victory at Yorktown in 1781.

The naval war also provided Washington with opportunities to express his quixotic side. His imagination became particularly fertile as he pondered ways of destroying British vessels docked at Philadelphia during the winter of 1777–78. On one occasion he encouraged a French officer's plot to "Creep upon the ice" on the Delaware, and "set on fire one or two of the enemys ships, by means of two sulphured shirts." Washington personally conceived a bizarre plan to attack British shipping with an armada of explosive barrels in January 1778. The barrels were prepared in secrecy, but unfortunately one of them broke loose prematurely, blowing up two boys who pursued it on a raft. Thus alerted, the British turned all of their weapons against the rest of the kegs that came tumbling downriver. "The shipping in the harbor, and all the wharves in the city were fully manned," an American journalist reported. "The battle began, and it was surprising to behold the incessant blaze that was kept up against the enemy, the kegs. Both officers and men exhibited the most unparalleled skill and bravery on the occasion; whilst the citizens stood gazing as solemn witnesses of their prowess. . . . [N]ot a wandering ship, stick, or drift log, but felt the vigor of the British arms. . . . The kegs were either totally demolished or obliged to fly, as none of them have shown their *heads* since." A British observer noted the deaths of the two boys, and less humorously observed that "the fellow who invented the mischief may quit his conscience of the murder or injury done the lads, as well as he can."

The appearance of the French navy off American shores in the summer of 1778 substantially altered the balance of naval power, allowing Washington to dispense with schooners and "sulphured shirts" and play for larger stakes. From the moment he learned of the French alliance, the commander-in-chief understood that the outcome of the war would depend on how well the American land forces and French naval forces could coordinate their efforts. With this in mind, he refused to leave liaison to others and communicated with French admirals directly. His informed and thoughtful letters impressed the Frenchmen, as did his respectful tone. They responded by consulting him on most of their important decisions. The allies' strategic objectives did not, of course, always converge; but thanks to Washington's careful diplomacy and the intervention of Lafayette and others their disagreements were settled without ill will. Three years would pass before these efforts bore fruit, but Cornwallis's surrender at Yorktown was worth the wait.

Washington had little experience of life at sea, but the frontier was different. He understood what it meant to travel and fight there and sensed its value to the country's future. It was a region of wonderful opportunity and incredible cruelty, where vast expanses of virgin wilderness separated tiny armed outposts. Between the outposts, British and American agents contended for influence with the Indians—who slaughtered, and were slaughtered. But the frontier was no backwater. It was rather the domain of the individual, a place where single or small groups of chiefs, warriors, traders, and soldiers could decide the fate of areas the size of France. George Rogers Clark, a twenty-five-year-old surveyor, seized the entire Illinois Territory in 1778–79 with less than two hundred men.

The frontier represented both prizes to be won and threats to be faced. Despite Clark's success, British agents typically were more successful than their American rivals in gaining Indian support. Indian raids that plagued the western reaches of Virginia, Pennsylvania, and New York from 1776 to 1778 caused militia units and Continental regiments from these areas to insist on being posted close to home. Congress, focused on events in the East, offered little help and left frontier defense to the states, which in turn delegated re-

sponsibility to the settlers themselves. Nor could Washington offer any substantial assistance so long as British armies were in the field against him. He
permitted frontier units to remain at home rather than join the main army,
but refused to weaken his force by sending Continental regiments to the settlers' aid.

By the winter of 1778–79, Iroquois and loyalist activity in the Mohawk Valley of western New York State threatened to destroy American influence
throughout the entire region. Mohawk chief Joseph Brant was particularly
notorious, burning settlements, devastating farmland, and annihilating companies of militiamen and Continentals sent to intercept him. Brant treated
his captives well, but reputed Indian atrocities and property damage caused
such outrage that even Congress had to pay attention. On February 25, 1779,
the delegates directed Washington to organize a military expedition for the
"chastisement of the savages."

Washington welcomed the order. Normally he did not care if Indians were
friendly or not so long as they remained quiet, but when they became warlike
he favored swift and ruthless punishment. The strategic situation in the
spring of 1779 offered him an opportunity to mete such punishment out with
crushing force. After an inactive winter the British seemed disinclined to
venture out of New York, and the French were too distracted by the ongoing
war over the sugar islands of the West Indies to cooperate in any attack in
North America. Uncommitted to any major operations in the East and with
some disposable military assets, Washington could afford to detach a significant number of Continentals to the frontier for the first time.

The commander-in-chief entrusted the expedition to Major General John
Sullivan, whose lost battles since 1776 had earned him countless enemies in
Congress and the army. Only Washington, it seems, had not lost faith in the
gruff New Hampshire lawyer. He gave Sullivan a whole division—three
brigades totaling about 2,300 Continental troops—and instructed him to link
up with another division of 1,400 under Brigadier General James Clinton at
Tioga, where the Susquehanna crossed the Pennsylvania–New York border.
The two generals were then to drive north together through Indian country.
Washington stated "the immediate objects" of the incursion to be "the total
destruction and devastation of their settlements and the capture of as many
prisoners of every age and sex as possible." Captives would make valuable
hostages, but the Indians' land, he emphasized, must "not be merely *overrun,*
but *destroyed.*" No compromises would be permitted. "You will not by any

means," he admonished, "listen to any overture of peace before the total ruin of their settlements is effected."

Washington respected Indians as warriors and warned Sullivan to advance with an "extraordinary degree of vigilance and caution" lest there be a repeat of Braddock's defeat in 1755. Success, he declared, depended on sound discipline, reconnaissance, and supply. It also required what Washington claimed to possess: an understanding of the Indian way of thinking. In 1754 Washington had advised Governor Dinwiddie to frighten the natives by outfitting his soldiers in bloodred uniforms, but by now he had come to believe that a ruthless attitude projected ferocity better than a brightly colored wardrobe. "I beg leave to suggest," he wrote Sullivan, "as general rules that ought to govern your operations—to make rather than receive attacks, attended with as much impetuosity, shouting and noise as possible, and to make the troops acts in as loose and dispersed a way as is consistent with a proper degree of government concert and mutual support—It should be previously impressed upon the minds of the men, wherever they have an opportunity, to rush on with the war [w]hoop and fixed bayonet—Nothing will disconcert and terrify the indians more than this."

Whether the advice was sound or not, it proved unnecessary. Sullivan encountered no serious combat. His troops left Easton, Pennsylvania, in June and efficiently ravaged the prosperous Iroquois settlements before returning in October. The weak Indian war parties they encountered were dispersed after causing only a couple of dozen casualties, including some soldiers whom the Indians captured and hideously tortured to death. For their part the Americans took no hostages, although they managed to butcher a few elderly squaws. Facing starvation from the destruction of their crops, the Iroquois withdrew from the Mohawk Valley to the shelter of British forts at Niagara.

In some respects the expedition was a disastrous failure for the Americans. With their homes and crops irretrievably ruined, the Iroquois itched for vengeance; and they swooped on the frontier in 1780 and 1781 to inflict worse damage on white settlements than ever before. The punitive raids that Washington authorized against Indians in western Pennsylvania in 1779 had similar results. But in the long run the Indians would be the losers. After Sullivan's expedition, the Iroquois Confederacy was so gravely weakened that it would never again seriously contest the fate of North America as it had during the French and Indian War. Washington's war against the Indians—a precursor to the total wars of the twentieth century—had thus resulted in a brutal victory.

For all the trouble they caused on the frontier, Indians might have helped Washington to solve the army's chronic manpower shortage. Several tribes were willing to fight alongside the Continental Army as auxiliary troops. Another potential source of manpower lay in America's half a million free blacks and slaves, thousands of whom expressed their eagerness to enlist. The few who succeeded in doing so made exceptional soldiers. Yet politics and prejudice can make cowards of the best of men, and Washington proved too cautious to make effective use of either resource.

"The enemy have set every engine at work, against us, and have actually called savages and even our own slaves to their assistance," Washington told Congress in January 1778; "would it not be well to employ two or three hundred Indians against General Howe's army [in] the ensuing campaign? . . . Such a body of indians, joined by some of our woodsmen would probably strike no small terror into the British and foreign troops, particularly the new comers." Congress agreed, and for a time there was talk of forming a mixed corps of Indians and light infantry to fight loyalists and British foraging parties. Nevertheless, the stigma against sending "savages" to fight fellow whites—even in retaliation for like behavior by the other side—was too great for Washington to consider employing Indians in large numbers, and he used them only for symbolic purposes. At Valley Forge he dispatched a force of "fictitious Indians," apparently white men in native costume, to romp around the country intimidating loyalists; but when a group of Oneida warriors offered their services that spring he used them only as scouts.

Social considerations—or, to put it more acutely, prejudice—also prevented Washington from welcoming blacks into the Continental Army; but his attitudes on this subject shifted over time. In July 1775 at Cambridge, Massachusetts, he had expressed consternation at the number of "Boys, Deserters, & Negroes" in the ranks. At his instigation the adjutant general promptly directed recruiting officers not to enlist "any deserter from the Ministerial army, nor any stroller, negro, or vagabond." Three months later, when Washington asked his officers whether blacks already in the army should be reenlisted, they "agreed unanimously to reject all Slaves, & by a great Majority to reject Negroes altogether." The commander-in-chief agreed, and on November 12th he ordered that "neither Negroes, Boys unable to bare Arms, nor old men unfit to endure the fatigues of the campaign, are to be inlisted." Blacks, the directive implied, were just as "unfit" to serve as boys or old men.

Washington issued these orders unaware that days before, on November 7th, royal governor Lord Dunmore of Virginia had declared his willingness to grant freedom to slaves and indentured servants who joined the British standard. This socially subversive proclamation outraged Virginia slaveholders. Writing to Virginia delegate Richard Henry Lee on December 26th, Washington denounced Dunmore's "diabolical schemes" and rumbled that "if My Dear Sir that Man is not crushed before Spring, he will become the most formidable Enemy America has—his strength will Increase as a Snow ball by Rolling; and faster, if some expedient cannot be hit upon to convince the Slaves and Servants of the Impotency of His designs." Washington's feeble "expedient" amounted to allowing recruiting officers to enroll new volunteers who were free blacks, but not slaves. Congress promptly undercut him by resolving only to reenlist "the free negroes who have served faithfully in the army at Cambridge," but not to accept any new applicants.

After Dunmore and his supporters abandoned their last Virginia stronghold in July 1776 and fled to England, Washington did not renew his suggestion to enlist freedmen. Two years later, on January 2, 1778, Washington received a letter from Brigadier General James Mitchell Varnum of Rhode Island. The army was in the midst of a recruiting crisis, and Varnum had a number of ideas about how to strengthen the regiments from his state. One was to raise "a Battalion of Negroes." "Should that Measure be adopted, or recruits obtained upon any other Principle," Varnum wrote, "the Service will be advanced."

Some historians have assumed that Washington enthusiastically approved this idea. He did not. What he *did* do was forward Varnum's suggestions to the governor of Rhode Island, under cover of a letter stating that recruiting officers should be assisted in carrying out their duties. He appended no comment, approving or disapproving, on the proposal to enlist a black regiment, which suggests that while Washington was willing to entertain any measure that would strengthen his army, he stopped short of endorsing the recruitment of freed slaves. The Rhode Island Assembly made the final decision— under protest from some of its delegates—by voting in February 1778 to enlist black, mulatto, and Indian freedmen into segregated companies of the First

Rhode Island Regiment. The order was rescinded four months later, after which no more nonwhites were permitted to enlist.

The First Rhode Island Regiment remained in New England until 1781, by all accounts performing with exemplary discipline and bravery. It was then consolidated with the Second Rhode Island Regiment and sent to join Washington's army. In July 1781 a French observer, Ludwig von Closen, claimed that "Three-quarters" of the troops in the consolidated Rhode Island battalion were black. Closen's estimate is often cited, but he probably exaggerated. Only half of the consolidated battalion came from the First Rhode Island; the Second, which made up the other half, remained primarily white. In any case, the First Rhode Island Regiment would be the only unit above company size into which blacks were recruited systematically, although some states—Connecticut, Maryland, Massachusetts, New Hampshire, New Jersey, and New York—would pass laws that permitted freedmen and slaves to join the Continental Army in certain circumstances.

Another proposal to enlist a black regiment came from one of the commander-in-chief's aides, John Laurens. Born in 1754 in Charleston, South Carolina, he was the son of president of Congress Henry Laurens and a handsome, dashing, well-educated, and intractable idealist. John Laurens joined headquarters as a volunteer aide in 1777 and served faithfully as Washington's scribe, translator, and liaison to the French. He also wounded Charles Lee in a duel in December 1778 after taking offense at some of Lee's remarks about the commander-in-chief. But Washington and his aide did not agree on everything; particularly slavery, which Laurens hated with a passion alien to the Virginian. Laurens insisted that slaveholding was incompatible with the ideals of the Revolution, and he denounced it despite the ire of its powerful supporters. By contrast, Washington—perhaps because his public responsibilities were much greater—refused to campaign openly against the practice despite his careful criticism of the institution. Whatever his private intentions may or may not have been, the slaves at Mount Vernon did not become free until after his death.

Laurens seethed with enthusiasm when he heard of Rhode Island's decision to enlist blacks. Why not, he declared, create a new Continental regiment made up entirely of freed slaves from South Carolina? "Cede me a number of your able bodied men Slaves, instead of leaving me a fortune," he begged his father. "I would bring about a twofold good, first I would advance those who are unjustly deprived of the Rights of Mankind to a State which would be a proper Gradation between abject Slavery and perfect Liberty—and besides I would reinforce the Defenders of Liberty with a number of gallant Soldiers." A conversation with the commander-in-chief left Laurens imagining he had Washington's unqualified support. "You ask what is the General's opinion upon this subject," he confided to his father in February 1778. "He is convinced that the numerous tribes of blacks in the Southern parts of the Continent offer a resource to us that should not be neglected—with respect to my particular Plan, he only objects to it with the arguments of Pity, for a man who would be less rich than he might be."

There is a touch of gentle sarcasm in these words that suggests the commander-in-chief was humoring his romantic young aide. In any event, Washington offered no public support for the proposal. And a year later, as Laurens still struggled to make his dream reality, Washington dismissed it as infeasible. The idea "has never employed much of my thoughts," he admitted in a March 20, 1779, letter to Henry Laurens, but "the policy of arming Slaves is in my opinion a moot point, unless the enemy set the example, for should we begin to form Battalions of them I have not the smallest doubt . . . of their following in it, and justifying the measure upon our own ground. The upshot then must be who can Arm fastest—and where are our Arms?" The last thing America needed was for the British to put muskets in the hands of thousands of ex-slaves. "Besides," Washington continued, "I am not clear that a descrimination will not render Slavery more Irksome to those who remain in it—Most of the good and evil things of this life are judged of by comparison, and I fear Comparison in this case will be productive of Much discontent in those who are held in servitude." In short, he seems to have feared that arming blacks on a large scale would spur an exodus from the plantations that might destroy the institution of slavery altogether. And *that* was something he feared to contemplate.

John Laurens pursued his plan for the remainder of 1779. He even won the support of his father and a cautious endorsement from Congress. But he failed to overcome entrenched opposition in his native state. "We are much disgusted here at the Congress recommending us to arm our Slaves," South Carolina politician Christopher Gadsden complained; "it was received with great resentment, as a very dangerous and impolitic Step." The commander-in-chief's authority might have convinced them, but Laurens could go no further without such support. Disappointed, he left Washington's staff to seek glory on the battlefield and was killed in an insignificant skirmish in South

Carolina in August 1782. There were no further efforts to form a black regiment before the end of the war.

It has been stated that the Continental Army was better integrated than any American army before Vietnam. Ludwig von Closen, the same French officer who reported that the Rhode Island battalion was 75 percent black, believed that "a quarter" of the American troops at White Plains in July 1781 "were negroes, merry, confident, and sturdy." But none of Closen's contemporaries corroborated this claim, and there is no reliable evidence to substantiate it. A "Return of Negroes in the Army," prepared at Washington's request in August 1778, lists 755 black soldiers exclusive of the First Rhode Island Regiment, or about 4.85 percent of the army's total strength at that time. Adding the 175 or so blacks of the First Rhode Island brings this figure close to 6 percent—not a negligible percentage by any means, but probably closer to the truth for most of the war than Closen's 25 percent. The most common estimate of the number of black troops who served in the Continental Army during the entire war is 5,000. If true, it strains credibility to suggest that half of them (a quarter of Washington's army in July 1781 would have numbered about 2,500 men) were in uniform at White Plains as Closen suggested.

One historian seeks to circumvent the absence of evidence for more widespread black enlistment by insisting that "there were so many black soldiers in the Revolutionary army that their presence had ceased to be remarkable to contemporary observers and therefore was underreported." Such speculation fails to explain why none of Closen's fellow Europeans remarked on the supposed presence of thousands of black soldiers. It also implies a degree of racial harmony that seems, to put it mildly, far-fetched. Why, if indeed there were so many black soldiers in an army run in part by slaveholders, are there no recorded instances of significant racial tension?

If somewhere between 5 and 6 percent of the army was black, as seems likely, Washington had nothing to do with it. The only occasion when he advocated enlisting black soldiers was as a ploy to counteract Lord Dunmore's proclamation. That some blacks nonetheless *did* join Continental regiments from various states is certain, but they did so by taking advantage of the frequently *ad hoc,* informal recruiting methods used throughout the army. The credit for the Continental Army's diversity—that is, if it *was* diverse—belongs not to Washington or his officers, but to the blacks (and Indians, deserters, indentured servants, boys, vagabonds, and old men) who enlisted and fought despite the prejudice that prevailed throughout the army. That blacks did not serve in the proportions sometimes claimed does not imply that they were unwilling to fight, or reduce their contribution to history; but it does help to indicate the depth and extent of the racism they faced.

On June 1, 1779, while Sullivan assembled his frontier expedition at Easton, Pennsylvania, a force of 6,000 British and German troops marched up the Hudson River and seized two small American forts at Stony Point and Verplanck's Point without opposition. These installations guarded a busy river crossing at King's Ferry; but, more significant, they were only twelve miles south of the crucial fortifications at West Point. Washington reacted with alarm, moving his army from its winter quarters at Middlebrook, New Jersey, to New Windsor, New York, from which it could block any further British advance up the Hudson. He then reconnoitered the captured forts in person while Delaware captain Allen McLane slipped into and out of Stony Point in disguise. Apprised that the British were not planning a major offensive, and that they had left the captured forts lightly garrisoned, Washington ordered Brigadier General Anthony Wayne to lead a night attack against Stony Point with his brigade of 1,200 men. Carried out on July 16th, the attack was a brilliant success. Wayne captured the fort and took 472 prisoners, after which Washington prudently razed the indefensible fortifications and withdrew his army upriver to West Point.

The success at Stony Point inspired Washington to seek another easy victory. He decided that Paulus Hook, a tiny peninsula on the west bank of the Hudson, opposite Manhattan, was the place. This small fortification, originally built by Americans to protect New York in 1776, enclosed a weak, isolated garrison that had reportedly grown lazy with inactivity. Washington entrusted the attack to one of his favorite officers, the dashing young Major Henry Lee, Jr., and the equally redoubtable Captain Allen McLane. With a force of 300 men, the officers stormed the fort on August 19th, put 50 men to the bayonet—a weapon that had gradually become more common in American arsenals—took 158 prisoners, and retreated without significant loss.

The Paulus Hook raid concluded the 1779 field campaign. The British accepted their losses and did not strike back. D'Estaing was occupied with the war in the West Indies and evinced no desire to return to North America anytime soon. That left Washington with the decision of where his army should spend the winter. By the time he chose Morristown, New Jersey, in November, the weather had already grown unseasonably chilly. Then, during the weeklong trek from West Point to the new camp, it became cold like nothing anybody had ever experienced before. The sun fled and freezing rain, sleet, and snow fell seemingly without end while Washington's 8,500 Continentals plodded south. The combination would prove fatal for many soldiers before the army reached Morristown in early December. Yet worse was to come.

Morristown, site of a previous winter encampment from January to May 1777, was familiar ground for Washington and some of the soldiers. But that was the best that could be said about it. The village itself offered little shelter, so the troops had to build huts as they had at Valley Forge. The land was alternately rough and swampy, and the woods dense, while the hardscrabble farms of the region bore no comparison to the rich German settlements of southeastern Pennsylvania. This winter the New Jersey farmers' larders were even emptier than usual, for a poor harvest in 1779 had caused a severe grain shortage throughout the mid-Atlantic region. Their livestock were scrawny, too. The only things that existed in abundance were trees, snow, and loyalists.

And then there was the weather. The winter of 1779–80 remains one of the longest and most ferocious in recorded American history. From December to April, the entire East Coast was blanketed with snow, and ice blocked every major harbor. Streams and rivers froze several feet thick. People rode sleighs on New York Harbor from Manhattan to Staten Island. Even the Chesapeake Bay froze. At Morristown an incessant north wind blew snowdrifts so massive that movement became next to impossible. Soldiers braved frostbite as they worked to clear the roads for supply wagons, and repeated the job every day because of fresh snowfall and drifts. The temperature almost never rose above freezing, averaging twenty-two degrees Fahrenheit for most of the winter. In February, Nathanael Greene reported that "almost all the wild beasts of the field, and the birds of the Air, have perished with the cold."

The commissariat was better organized and staffed than it had been at Valley Forge, but even an efficient, well-intentioned commissary could not force a rickety supply wagon through the four to six feet of snow that often covered the roads. Another dangerous problem was the collapse of the nation's finances. Continental dollars depreciated in a mad spiral, and continued to do so even after Congress scrapped the old paper in favor of a new currency. Before long, a new hat cost $400, and a horse $20,000! Wads of money thick enough to bed a stable of horses was not enough to buy a sack of grain. Farmers refused to sell their provisions to supply agents, military pay became worthless, and soldiers starved.

"Those who have only been in Valley Forge and Middlebrook during the last two winters, but have not tasted the cruelties of this one, know not what it is to suffer," lamented Major General Johann Kalb. Provisions became scarcer than at Valley Forge, and remained so for week upon week. For much of January there was no food in camp at all, and the troops resorted to desperate measures to stay alive. "We were absolutely literally starved," wrote the soldier Joseph Plumb Martin. "I do solemnly declare that I did not put a single morsel of victuals into my mouth for four days and as many nights, except a little black birch bark, which I knawed off a stick of wood, if that can be called victuals. I saw several . . . men roast their old shoes and eat them, and I was afterwards informed by one of the officers' waiters that some of the officers killed and ate a favorite little dog that belonged to one of them." Packs of marauding soldiers sacked nearby farms for their pittance of food.

Washington had no choice but to tolerate the plundering. "The distress has in some instances prompted the men to commit depredations on the property of the inhabitants," he wrote on January 8th, and although "at any other period [such behavior] would be punished with exemplary severity, [it] can now only be lamented as the effect of an unfortunate necessity." Once again he had to look to short-term measures to save the army. With the state governors unable or unwilling to lend any significant aid, in January Washington requisitioned food through the local magistrates, designating a quota to be provided from each county. This brought relief, but only for a time. By February the troops were starving and plundering again, and it was only by desperate appeals to various civilian officials that the commander-in-chief could manage to keep them alive. His skill as an administrator, honed at Valley Forge, went only so far in the face of monetary and meteorological factors beyond his control.

The arrival of spring brought no improvement in the army's plight. Snowfall continued into April, and the stubbornly anemic currency prolonged the food shortage. Once again, the soldiers were starving. On May 25, 1780, the troops of a Connecticut brigade assembled "with the Beating of Drums." They had subsisted for several days on crusts of stale bread and had gone five months without pay. They would take no more. "Growling like soreheaded dogs," they roughed up their officers, bayoneted a colonel, and threatened to quit the army and return home. It took a brigade of loyal Pennsylvania troops to coax the mutineers back into their huts. Fortunately a supply of food arrived in camp shortly thereafter, and the Connecticut troops submitted to their officers' authority.

A tribunal sentenced the mutiny's ringleaders to death, but Washington sympathized with their misery and pardoned them all. "The men have borne their distress with a firmness and patience never exceeded," he told Connecticut governor Jonathan Trumbull, Sr., "and every possible praise is due the Officers for encouraging them to it, by precept—by exhortation—by example. But there are certain bounds, beyond which it is impossible for Human nature to go. We are arrived at those." It was a low point. "This matter I confess . . . has given me infinitely more concern than any thing that has ever happened," he lamented. But Washington was mistaken if he imagined it could get no worse. A week after the mutiny, news arrived at Morristown that the British had captured an entire American army at Charleston, South Carolina.

The southern campaign began in December 1778, when a British expeditionary force captured Savannah, Georgia. A Continental force under Major General Benjamin Lincoln blocked the redcoats from marching overland to Charleston, but in the ensuing months southern loyalists became increasingly militant and strengthened their grip on the interior. A botched Franco-American attempt to retake Savannah in October 1779 especially encouraged them, and in its aftermath they inflicted a succession of small-scale defeats on the patriots and succeeded in throwing the rural South into anarchy. Their victories were "indubitable proof of the indisposition of the inhabitants to support the rebel government," Lord Germain declared ecstatically, and he encouraged Clinton to support them by sending an expedition to Charleston. "The possession of Charleston would . . . be attended with the recovery of the whole of that province," Germain asserted. "Probably North Carolina would soon follow."

Clinton agreed. In December, just before the harbor froze, he sailed from New York with a fleet bearing 8,700 troops. He landed near Charleston in February and promptly surrounded the city. On May 12th, Charleston capitulated to the British, and Lincoln's 2,500 Continentals, including the whole of Washington's beloved Virginia line, entered captivity. Loyalists exploited the catastrophe by dismantling the state governments of Georgia and South Carolina and chasing dejected patriots into the woods. North Carolina showed signs of crumbling in the wake of its southern neighbors.

"The loss of Charlestown . . . will no doubt give spirit to our Enemies, and have a temporary effect upon our affairs," Washington observed in June 1780, "but if extensively considered and rightly improved, it may be attended in the end by happy consequences. The enemy, by attempting to hold conquests so remote, must dissipate their force, and of course afford opportunities of striking one or the other extremity." The capture of Lincoln's army left almost nothing between Charleston and Virginia, but Washington balked at weakening his own army to reinforce the South. Enemy raids in New Jersey were alarmingly vigorous, and Clinton's return in June to command the New York garrison made Washington suspect an imminent British offensive up the Hudson toward West Point.

Congress nevertheless charged Major General Horatio Gates with the reconstitution of the southern army, allocating him a cadre of 1,400 Maryland and Delaware Continentals Washington would have preferred to keep at Morristown. Gates rode to North Carolina in July and gathered enough militiamen and Continental detachments to form the semblance of an army. But then he squandered it by advancing south through barren, mosquito-infested country to the British supply depot at Camden, South Carolina, where Cornwallis caught him on August 16th. The Battle of Camden left Gates in disgrace—he disposed his troops incompetently and fled the field as they broke—thus demolishing yet another American army. The defeat also opened the road for a British invasion of North Carolina, and Cornwallis lost no time in exploiting the opportunity. Within weeks he was marching north through the same difficult region that Gates had traversed, touching off battles between loyalists and patriots that left much of the South engulfed in civil war.

Washington could do nothing about the deteriorating strategic situation. Battered by the Morristown winter and continually weakened by supply shortages, his army was in no condition to march, let alone fight. The treason of Major General Benedict Arnold nearly put it in a hopeless strategic situation as well. Arnold was a brilliant general whose incredible march to Quebec in 1775 and contribution to the victory at Saratoga gave him just claim to his country's gratitude. He was also an exceedingly vain man, and by 1779 he seethed with bitterness at the lack of respect Congress and Washington had supposedly shown him. His collaboration with the British began in May of that year, while he commanded the garrison at Philadelphia, and culminated in September 1780 with a plot to betray West Point. His reward for this perfidy was to be £6,000, a commission in the king's army, and—he hoped—respect. If the plot had been successful, almost the entire Hudson River would have fallen under Clinton's control.

Military history is full of wars and battles won or lost through treason. Arnold's betrayal of West Point might well have ended the American Revolution, but the plot failed when Major John André, a pleasant and cultivated young man who served as Arnold's main British contact and collaborator, was captured by three alert militiamen on September 23, 1780. Searching André's civilian clothes, the astonished Americans discovered papers detailing Arnold's treasonous plan to turn West Point over to the British. Reinforcements were rushed to the Hudson, and although Arnold escaped to a British ship, West Point remained in American hands.

The episode left Washington—who was forced to execute the courageous André as a spy despite a personal appeal from General Henry Clinton to spare his life—severely shaken. John Laurens promised him that Arnold would "undergo a punishment . . . in the permanent increasing torment of a mental hell," but Washington doubted it. He took Arnold's betrayal personally, and struggled to understand what had motivated it. "I am mistaken if at *this time,*" he replied, "Arnold is undergoing the torments of a mental Hell. He wants feeling!" The American public also had trouble understanding Arnold, and resorted to describing him with bloodthirsty invective. A correspondent to the *Pennsylvania Packet* dubbed Arnold "a gigantick overgrown monster, of such a variety of shapes, all over ulcerated, that it is in vain to attempt to describe them."

Victors write the history books, and only time could determine how Arnold would be remembered. From the British perspective, he was a virtuous American who had courageously repented of an unnatural rebellion and returned to the mother country's embrace. In the autumn of 1780, as America—her finances ruined, her army mutinous, and much of her land occupied—trembled on the verge of collapse, Arnold looked very much like a visionary; or perhaps like a rat with the sense to abandon a sinking ship.

17

VICTORY

September 1780 – December 1783

TWO WEEKS AFTER the Battle of Camden, Horatio Gates wrote to the commander-in-chief from Hillsborough, North Carolina. "Anxious for the public Good, I shall continue my unwearied Endeavors, to stop the Progress of the Enemy; to reinstate our Affairs, to recommence an Offensive War, and recover all our Losses in the Southern States," he squeaked defiantly amid the remnants of his pulverized army. "But if being unfortunate, is solely Reason sufficient for removing me from Command, I shall most chearfully submit to the Orders of Congress, and resign an Office few Generals would be anxious to possess." Congress took Gates at his word, ordering his removal from office pending a court of inquiry into his conduct. Washington's choice to replace him was Nathanael Greene.

"I only lament that my abilities are not more competent to the duties that will be required of me," Greene wrote in response to his appointment, "and that it will not be in my power, on that account, to be as extensively useful as my inclination leads me to wish. But as far as zeal and attention can supply the defect, I flatter myself my Country will have little cause to complain." Such modesty obscured the delight with which he tossed aside the quartermaster general's pen and unsheathed his sword. He would not have much to start with—a few shattered Continental regiments, some giddy militia units, an assortment of partisan bands—but no matter. It was an independent command, and a mark of the commander-in-chief's esteem. Washington found quickly that his trust was not misplaced.

The military situation improved even before Greene traveled south. Cornwallis's capture of Charlotte, North Carolina, on September 26th was not the first step of the triumphant procession through the South that the British expected to take place. Loyalist depredations real and reputed—especially those of Lieutenant Colonel Banastre Tarleton's Tory Legion—incensed southern patriots, who joined guerrilla fighters like Thomas Sumter and Francis Marion in butchering British detachments and menacing Cornwallis's supply lines. Their resistance culminated on October 7th in the Battle of King's Mountain, South Carolina, where a remarkable assembly of "over-the-mountain men" from eastern Tennessee cornered and destroyed a force of a thousand loyalists under Major Patrick Ferguson. Cornwallis responded by withdrawing his force to Camden.

Greene took formal command of the 2,000-man southern army at Charlotte on December 2nd. Uncomfortably conscious that he had never before ventured south of the Potomac River, he commissioned detachments to survey the roads, settlements, and especially the rivers of Virginia and the Carolinas. Unlike Washington, who was ignorant of the land on which he fought and lost the 1777 campaign, Greene acquired superb knowledge of the southern geography. He also cultivated the southern guerrilla leaders, who found his deferential demeanor a welcome contrast to that of the arrogant Gates. But his most momentous decision was also a most unorthodox one. Instead of waiting at Charlotte to collect a larger army, Greene split his force, leading half southeast to Cheraw, South Carolina, while the canny Virginia frontiersman Daniel Morgan took the other half southwest toward the Catawba River. Doing so violated the ageless principle of not dividing one's force before the enemy; but Greene argued that "it makes the most of my inferior force, for it compels my adversary to divide his, and holds him in doubt as to his own line of conduct. He cannot leave Morgan behind him to come at me . . . and he cannot chase Morgan far . . . while I am here with the whole country open before me."

Cornwallis reacted as Greene had hoped, splitting his 4,000-man army into three parts, one of which shielded Camden while the others went after Morgan. Tarleton, who led one division of 1,100 men in direct pursuit while Cornwallis took a similar force north across Morgan's presumed line of retreat, bounded off like a frenzied hound; but the canny Virginian withdrew until he reached the hamlet of Cowpens on January 16, 1781. Morgan then rounded on Tarleton, and in a classic double envelopment killed or captured over 800 of his men. Shocked at the defeat but unwilling to concede the campaign, Cornwallis combined the remaining two-thirds of his army, burned his heavy baggage, and hurried after Morgan, who discreetly fled. Greene followed, and on February 9th he linked up with Morgan at Guilford Courthouse, near the Virginia border.

Rain-swollen rivers delayed the British advance and gave Greene time to prepare for battle. By March he had accumulated over 4,000 men, more than half of them militiamen from Virginia and North Carolina. Cornwallis had only half that number, and although his troops were almost all regulars, they were tired and suffering privations from the loss of their baggage. Greene was also close to the waterways that carried arms and provisions from Virginia, while Cornwallis's supply line stretched hundreds of miles across contested country to Charleston, South Carolina. Only the timidity of Greene's militiamen and his own caution prevented the March 15th Battle of Guilford Courthouse from becoming a decisive American victory. As it was he inflicted over 500 casualties on Cornwallis's already weak army to only 250 of his own before relinquishing the field. Battered and incapable of further combat, the British army limped east toward Wilmington while Greene trailed cautiously behind. He had won the first act of the southern campaign.

Washington's army spent the winter of 1780–81 in grim cantonments from Morristown to West Point. Food and clothing remained in short supply despite mild weather. Inflation continued unchecked. A horse that sold for $40,000 in the spring of 1780 now cost $150,000. Salaries were seldom paid, and bought little anyway. Farms and businesses withered and collapsed, impoverishing soldiers' families. Politicians talked and promised relief, but the troops were skeptical. The whole country seemed to have become corrupt. How else could merchants and other stay-at-homes flourish while servicemen's families starved? Soldiers cursed "the populace that had deserted the defenders of the cause." Civilians reciprocated by complaining of the army's apparent preference for plundering farms over fighting the British. The gap between soldiers and citizens yawned wider every day.

The mutiny of General Anthony Wayne's Pennsylvania brigade at Morristown on New Year's Day 1781 exposed the situation to public view. It was the first time that Continentals rebelled against the government instead of just defying their officers. Over a thousand armed soldiers assembled at 9:00 P.M. and solemnly declared their intention of marching on Philadelphia (to which Congress had returned after the British evacuated it in the summer of 1778) to confront Congress. Officers who tried to intervene were shoved aside and told that the soldiers' quarrel was with the civil authorities and not with them. The Pennsylvanians then marched southwest, occupying Princeton on

January 3rd and electing a Board of Sergeants that opened negotiations with Congress. Placed under a guard of rebel soldiers but allowed to write letters, the wretched Wayne advised the delegates to flee Philadelphia. They refused.

Washington was ensconced with the largest portion of the army at New Windsor, New York, when he learned of the mutiny in a letter of the 2nd from Wayne. "The most general and unhappy mutiny suddenly took place in the Pennsa Line about 9. OClock last Night," Mad Anthony whimpered. "It yet subists . . . how long it will last God knows." Resisting a first impulse to ride south and stamp out the fire in person, the commander-in-chief decided to stay put. His own soldiers sympathized with the mutiny and might join it if he departed. Washington watched from a distance, sick with fear that Clinton would exploit the revolt.

The situation remained volatile for several days. The mutineers indignantly imprisoned two emissaries that Clinton sent to win their defection, but also refused to surrender them to Congress. Their negotiators were civil but tough. At last, on January 10th, the soldiers agreed to terms granting them amnesty and release from service. By the end of the month 1,300 Pennsylvania Continentals had been honorably discharged; another 1,200 accepted extended furloughs. The mutineers turned Clinton's emissaries over to the army, and they were executed.

The Pennsylvanian mutineers were mostly German immigrants, and Washington hoped that his American-born troops would not be jealous at the deal they had received. "The rest of our Army (the Jersey Troops excepted) being cheifly composed of Natives, I would flatter myself, will continue to struggle under the same difficulties, they have hitherto endured, which I cannot help remarking, seem[s] to reach the bounds of human patience," he wrote on January 20th. As if on cue, two hundred men of the New Jersey brigade at Pompton—again, largely Germans—revolted that day and marched for Trenton. Washington was determined to prevent them from winning the same bargain. "Unless this dangerous spirit can be suppressed by force," he declared, "there is an end to all subordination in the Army, and indeed to the Army itself. The infection will no doubt shortly pervade the whole mass." Washington detailed General Robert Howe to surround them with 500 picked troops, and the mutineers capitulated. Twelve of them were forced to execute two of the ringleaders. The army stayed quiet, but the tension did not subside. Some of the troops had been bought off; that was all. The rest nursed their grievances and waited for the day when they could make Congress feel their collective wrath.

Ironically, the mutinies of January 1781 coincided with the beginning of the last campaign of the war. On December 20, 1780, Benedict Arnold, now a brigadier general in the British army, sailed from New York at the head of an expeditionary force of about 1,500 troops. His eventual destination was Portsmouth, a small but important port in southeast Virginia. The expedition's "primary object" was to establish a base at Portsmouth that would function as a rallying point for loyalists and divert pressure from Cornwallis. But on the way there Arnold had liberty to raid along the Virginia coast. This he did, sacking Richmond on January 5th–7th and gleefully stamping on the hapless parties of militia that came running to defend Governor Thomas Jefferson's Virginia anthill. He then retreated to Portsmouth and awaited new opportunities to humiliate his former comrades.

While Jefferson raged impotently at the "parricide Arnold," there were others who saw an opportunity for revenge. Portsmouth could be invested by land. Might it also be attacked by sea? For once the idea of a land-sea expedition was not just a fantasy. D'Estaing had finally returned to France. In his place now came Admiral Destouches, who entered Newport, Rhode Island (which the British had abandoned) with a fleet bearing 5,500 French soldiers under the Comte de Rochambeau on July 10, 1780. For several months a British blockade prevented the French ships from leaving Newport, but in January 1781 a winter storm scattered the British fleet. John Brown, a sea captain who had been landlocked at Providence since the loss of his privateer ship *General Washington*—"a Very beautifull, Valuable and Favorite Ship with a Striking of the Person whose Name She bore, affixed to her Head"— begged Washington to order the French to sail south to Portsmouth. If they arrived there in conjunction with an attack by land, he insisted, "the Infamous Arnold with all the Enemys Fleet and Armey may fall in to our Hands, and that State Rescued from their present Distresses."

Washington and Rochambeau had the same idea. Rochambeau encouraged Destouches to sail for the Chesapeake with all his ships and the entire French army. Washington urged the same course of action. "It is in my opinion essential," he wrote Rochambeau, "that there should be a cooperation of land and naval Forces, and that Mr des Touche should protect the expedition with his whole fleet." Assuming that Destouches would feel the same, he sent Lafayette south with 1,200 men and orders to invest Portsmouth. But the admiral wavered. First assuming that the Virginia militia was "sufficient to destroy the 1600 men that Arnold has with him, if We can but destroy his ships," he dispatched just a few vessels from Newport; but they returned without having been able to harm Arnold's well-sheltered fleet. Then, on March 8th, Destouches sailed from Newport with a larger force of eleven warships and 1,200 troops. But he had waited too long. Long since recovered from the storm, the British fleet defeated Destouches at the mouth of the Chesapeake on the 16th and sent him scampering back to Newport.

The initiative now shifted to the British. On March 26th, Arnold was reinforced at Portsmouth by 2,600 troops under Major General William Phillips, who superseded him in command. With an ample garrison and no need to fear the French fleet or Lafayette's small force—which was presumably still trudging toward the Potomac—Phillips ordered Arnold to resume his raiding further inland. Arnold sallied forth with 2,500 soldiers on April 18th, crushed a force of militiamen under Brigadier General Peter Muhlenburg, and burned warehouses full of tobacco at Petersburg on the 25th. He was about to repeat the act in Richmond on the 29th when Lafayette, who had pushed his Continentals across Virginia at an amazing speed, entered the city. Unwilling to engage in a major fight, the British withdrew to Petersburg, reentering it on May 10th.

Ten days later, Cornwallis appeared at Petersburg with 1,500 troops, remnants of the army that had staggered to Wilmington after the Battle of Guilford Courthouse. Clinton had not sanctioned this march. He wanted to finish subduing the Carolinas without abandoning the southern loyalists. But Cornwallis was fed up with North Carolina's sultry swamps and pine barrens. Virginia seemed greener—richer—easier to conquer. "I cannot help expressing my wishes that the Chesapeake may become the seat of war even (if necessary) at the expense of abandoning New York," Cornwallis explained to Clinton. "Until Virginia is in a manner subdued our hold of the Carolinas must be difficult if not precarious. The rivers of Virginia are advantageous to an invading army, but North Carolina is of all the provinces in America the most difficult to attack . . . on account of its great extent, of the numberless rivers and creeks, and the total want of interior navigation." Clinton prophetically replied that he thought large-scale campaigning in Virginia a "great risk unless we are sure of a permanent superiority at sea." But he lacked the will to overrule his subordinate, who had recently found favor with the politicians in London, and at Clinton's expense.

The linkage of Cornwallis, Arnold, and Phillips, whose force had been augmented by more reinforcements from New York, brought to 7,200 the number of British troops in southeastern Virginia. The only organized American army in the region belonged to Lafayette, who mustered 3,000 men after an infusion of Virginia militiamen. Greene was no longer in the picture, having taken his army south to expunge the isolated royalist bastions in western South Carolina. That left the British, in Arnold's words, "in force to operate as we please in Virginia or Maryland." Cornwallis's first objective was fairly simple. "I shall now," he informed Clinton on May 26th, "proceed to dislodge La Fayette from Richmond and with my light troops to destroy any magazines or stores in the neighbourhood. . . . From thence I purpose to move to the neck at Williamsburgh, which is represented as healthy and where some subsistence may be procured." The next stage was to find "a proper harbour and place of arms," or base of operations from which he could be supplied by sea. "At present," he mused, "I am inclined to think well of York."

Yorktown was a tiny settlement, with only sixty houses and a few public buildings. Its importance lay not in size but location. It was situated on a bluff overlooking the York River, opposite a peninsula called Gloucester Point where the river narrowed to about half a mile across. Easily defensible by land if properly fortified, Yorktown also provided anchorage for supply vessels or warships operating in the Chesapeake. Clinton had considered it for a base even before Cornwallis showed up in Petersburg. "I know of no place so proper as York Town if it could be taken possession of, fortified, and garrisoned with 1000 men," Clinton wrote to Germain in April. From there, in connection with another post at or near Portsmouth, "our cruisers might command the waters of the Chesapeak."

Cornwallis kept Yorktown in the back of his mind as he left Petersburg on May 24th to squash Lafayette. "The boy cannot escape me," legend has him boasting. But the Frenchman was too nimble. Relinquishing Richmond and withdrawing quickly westward, Lafayette linked up with small reinforcements of Continentals under Steuben and Wayne. Cornwallis did not pursue. Instead he sent cavalry and loyalist raiders into central Virginia, wrecking depots, smashing supply convoys, and even flushing Jefferson and the Virginia Legislature out of their refuge in Charlottesville. Cornwallis then recalled his raiders and withdrew, leaving Richmond on June 20th and marching southeast to Williamsburg. Lafayette, his army reinforced to 4,500 men, followed close behind. The adversaries fought two skirmishes, one at Spencer's Tavern on June 26th and another at Green Spring on July 6th, before Cornwallis—whom Clinton baffled with a series of contradictory orders before finally letting him do what he thought best—entered Yorktown and began building fortifications. Reasoning that "a superiority in the field will not only be necessary to enable us to draw forage and other supplies from the country but likewise to carry on our works without interruption," he ordered all the British troops in southeastern Virginia to be concentrated at that place. It was where most of them would end the war.

Washington observed the fighting in Virginia from his distant aerie at New Windsor on the western bank of the Hudson. From there he received inklings of a promising shift in the strategic situation. The balance of British military strength was shifting gradually from Manhattan to Virginia. By mid-May his spies estimated that Clinton had only 4,500 redcoats and 3,000 loyalist volunteers at New York, compared to 8,250 Continentals in the region. With the addition of the 4,500 French soldiers from Newport, the British would be outnumbered almost two to one. There was good news from Europe, too. On May 13th, Washington learned that another French admiral, the Comte de Barras, was about to replace the ineffective Destouches at Newport. Word also came of the departure from France of a powerful fleet under Admiral de Grasse. De Grasse's first destination was the West Indies; but after that he might sail north if some use could be found for his ships there. Excited by these developments, Rochambeau invited Washington to a conference at Wethersfield, Connecticut, to make joint plans for the coming campaign.

The Wethersfield Conference of May 22nd included Washington, Rochambeau, Major General the Chevalier de Chastellux, and a collection of aides. The mood was serious but friendly. Chastellux acted as interpreter, since Rochambeau spoke no English, but both were meticulously polite and deferential to the commander-in-chief. All agreed that the French and American armies should conduct joint operations. The question was, where? Virginia seemed an obvious possibility, but Barras had earlier ruled out transporting the army by sea, and Washington thought that logistical difficulties made an overland march impracticable. The best way to protect the Old Dominion, Washington suggested, was to attack New York. "In the present reduced State of the Garrison," he argued, the city "would fall, unless relieved"; and even if it did not fall, the pressure thus exerted on Clinton would "enfeeble their Southern operations, and in either case be productive of capital advantages."

Rochambeau consented to this plan, and asked a final question. What should the Franco-American army do if de Grasse's fleet finished its tour of the West Indies in time to operate on the American coast? The prospect raised all sorts of possibilities, but Washington refused to consider any of them. So far he had seen none of the miracles promised from French naval power, and he was not about to count on them now. Nor would he speculate. All he would say was that "Should the West India Fleet arrive upon the Coast; the force thus combined may either proceed in the operation against New Yk. Or may be directed against the enemy in some other quarter, as circumstances shall dictate." With that noncommittal reply the conference concluded, and the participants separated to prepare their forces for the drive on Manhattan.

As the French and American armies marched slowly toward their junction at Peekskill, New York, their commanders debated what to do if de Grasse arrived early. On June 10th Rochambeau informed Washington that the admiral had promised to reach America by the end of the summer. Where should he be told to sail? The commander-in-chief favored New York. "Your Excellency will be pleased to recollect that *New York* was looked upon by us as the only practicable object under present circumstances," he reminded Rochambeau; "but should we be able to secure a naval superiority, we may perhaps find others more practicable and equally advisable." He did not specify which "others" might be "equally advisable," but the French general had no doubts. Diplomatically, he told Washington "that I submitted, as I ought, my opinion to yours" by writing to de Grasse in favor of New York. But what he actually did was urge the admiral to make way for the Chesapeake. Rochambeau, sensibly, had little confidence in Washington's assault on New York. It was in Virginia, he was convinced, that the allied forces would have the greatest impact.

The American and French armies linked near White Plains, New York, on July 6th. Three days later they paraded jointly for Washington's inspection, giving the Europeans a chance to gawk at their allies. Opinions were mixed. For Rochambeau's aide Baron Ludwig von Closen, "the whole effect was rather good." He found them well drilled, and marveled particularly at the partly black Rhode Island Battalion, which was "the most neatly dressed, the best under arms, and the most precise in its maneuvers." Another officer was less impressed. "In beholding this army I was struck, not by its smart appearance, but by its destitution," he sneered. "The men were without uniforms and covered with rags; most of them were barefoot. They were of all sizes, down to children who could not have been over fourteen." If Rochambeau thought likewise, he kept his opinions to himself.

He also kept his doubts about Manhattan from Washington. At the beginning of July the commander-in-chief had attempted to launch a surprise attack on the northern part of the island; but his officers took one look at the British positions and withdrew. Rochambeau considered that a wise choice. Who could think of taking a city that the British had spent three years in fortifying? Washington nevertheless insisted that New York remain "our primary Object," and the Frenchman obediently went along, assisting in the grueling firsthand reconnaissance and surveying expeditions that the Virginian practiced so well. On July 23rd they went with a party of engineers to a small peninsula opposite Long Island. The engineers surveyed while the two generals "slept, worn out by fatigue, at the foot of a hedge, under fire from the cannon of the enemy's ships, who wished to hinder the work." Rochambeau woke first, looked about in surprise, and immediately jostled Washington. They had forgotten the tide! Hurrying back, they found that the causeway by which they had come was underwater, leaving them cut off from the mainland. A single longboat full of redcoats could have captured them in minutes. Luckily some American dragoons saw the generals' predicament and found two boats to bring them ashore.

The probing still continued on August 14th, when Washington opened a packet from Barras to find a letter that de Grasse had written from Haiti two and a half weeks before. With twenty-nine warships and 3,200 troops, the admiral was on his way—to Virginia! Warning that he could not remain on the coast any later than mid-October, de Grasse went on to express his anxiety that Washington and Rochambeau should "have every thing in the most perfect readiness to commence our operations in the moment of his arrival." That left only two months for the army to march from New York to Yorktown, a distance of over four hundred miles. Washington would have to make an immediate choice either to cooperate with de Grasse or stay where he was, awaiting another chance to bring the British to battle.

No decision that Washington made in his long military career was more

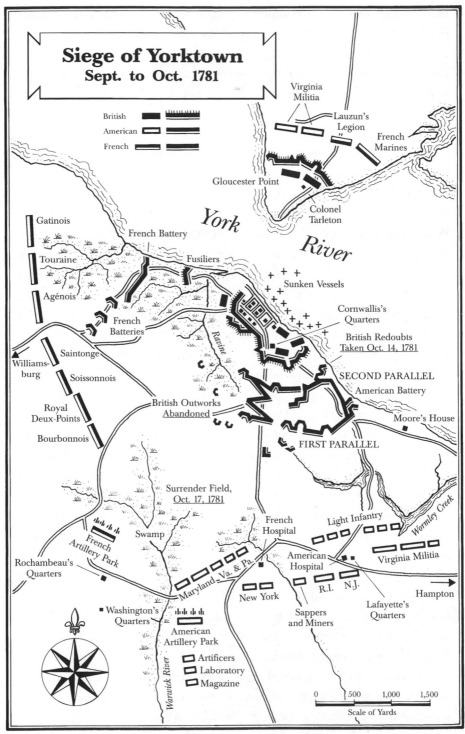

Siege of Yorktown
Sept. to Oct. 1781

British
American
French

Virginia Militia

Lauzun's Legion

French Marines

Gloucester Point

Colonel Tarleton

York River

Gatinois

French Battery

Touraine

Fusiliers

Sunken Vessels

Agénois

French Batteries

Ravine

Cornwallis's Quarters

British Redoubts Taken Oct. 14, 1781

Saintonge

Williamsburg

Soissonnois

SECOND PARALLEL

American Battery

Royal Deux-Points

British Outworks Abandoned

Moore's House

Bourbonnois

FIRST PARALLEL

Surrender Field, Oct. 17, 1781

Wormley Creek

French Hospital

Light Infantry

Swamp

French Artillery Park

American Hospital

Virginia Militia

Rochambeau's Quarters

Maryland, Va. & Pa.

New York

R.I. N.J.

Hampton

Washington's Quarters

Sappers and Miners

Lafayette's Quarters

American Artillery Park

Artificers

Laboratory

Magazine

Warwick River

0   500   1,000   1,500
Scale of Yards

important than this one. Marching south would exhaust his army and leave the Hudson Valley open to British attack—all for the sake of a promise of French aid that might or might not be kept. He might have remembered his predicament exactly four years before in August 1777, when he marched his troops up and down Maryland and Pennsylvania in search of the British fleet only to leave his Continentals tired, demoralized, and unprepared to fight the Battle of Brandywine. He also might have recalled how his enemies had accused him of hesitancy and indecision. But his military instinct told him only one thing: go where the enemy is, and seek battle. There was never really any doubt what Washington would do. "Matters having now come to a crisis and a decisive plan to be determined on," he wrote in his diary, "I was obliged . . . to give up all idea of attacking New York; & instead thereof to remove the French Troops & a detachment from the American Army to Head of Elk to be transported [on ships] to Virginia for the purpose of cooperating with the force from the West Indies against the Troops in that State." He had resumed the diary three months before, as if suspecting the approach of his final military campaign.

The trek to Yorktown began on August 19th. About 4,000 French soldiers and 3,000 Continentals—the rest stayed behind to shield the Hudson Valley—marched south in three columns, entering Princeton on the 30th and parading through Philadelphia from the 2nd through the 4th of September. Their passage attracted the usual crowds of civilians, some of them clutching newspaper reports that three French ships had arrived in Boston with tons of supplies and 2.5 million livres in hard currency. Word of the windfall passed through the ranks, and as the soldiers tramped on toward Head of Elk they pondered those chests full of gold and their own empty purses. The reaction was inevitable. Unless Congress gave them a month's pay in coin, the troops proclaimed, they would not leave Maryland. And with Philadelphia nearby, they might choose to sack the capital itself. The delegates complied and granted the pay.

On September 5th, Washington learned of the arrival of de Grasse's fleet off the Virginia Capes. After his French troops debarked and joined Lafayette, the admiral planned to send his empty transports to pick up the northern army. Their return, and the arrival of Barras's squadron bearing Rochambeau's siege guns, would complete the combination against Yorktown. Of course Washington would never submit to watching the grand assembly from afar. And at last, six years after taking up his commission as commander-in-chief—six years filled with tedium and work, interspersed with brief moments of victory and defeat—Mount Vernon was within reach. He left Head of Elk on the 7th, riding with Rochambeau and his aides through Baltimore and the farms and small towns of southern Maryland. Everywhere citizens turned out to welcome him. Washington spent four days at Mount Vernon, from September 9th through 12th. The respite must have been bittersweet despite the "princely entertainment" with which he regaled his guests. The house was dilapidated, the farms sadly run wild; the only real warmth came from Martha, who had shared over fifty of the war's hardest months in camp with her husband.

Events at sea, meanwhile, were bringing the war nearer to its conclusion. In New York, Henry Clinton had watched Washington's march for Virginia with equanimity. He knew of the approach of de Grasse's fleet but underestimated its size. In late August a British fleet of nineteen warships had assembled at New York under the command of Admiral Thomas Graves. Clinton assumed that the fleet could handle the threat to Yorktown, and Cornwallis, who felt the same way, made no attempt to drive for the interior before escape by land became impossible. Both men were disastrously wrong. Sailing from New York on August 31st, Graves arrived at the mouth of the Chesapeake on September 5th and promptly stumbled upon de Grasse and his twenty-nine warships. The battle that followed left Graves's ships severely mauled; and as the British contingent drifted south, stunned, toward Cape Hatteras, Barras slipped into the Chesapeake undetected. On the 14th, seeing that his weakened force was incapable of facing the reinforced French fleet, Graves sailed for New York.

Washington stepped onstage as the British navy departed, entering Williamsburg in the afternoon of September 14th. His arrival was unexpected but welcome. "He had passed our camp which is now in the rear of the whole army, before we had time to parade the militia," one of Lafayette's officers observed. "The French line had just time to form. The Continentals had more leisure. He approached without any pomp or parade attended only by a few horsemen and his own servants. . . . [Lafayette] rode up with precipitation, clasped the General in his arms and embraced him with an ardor not easily described. The whole army and all the town were presently in motion. The General . . . rode through the French lines. The troops were paraded for the purpose and cut a most splendid figure. Then he visited the Continental line." That evening the commander-in-chief dined on an "elegant supper" while "an elegant band played an introductive part of a French Opera."

There was good cause for celebration. For perhaps the first time in Washington's military career, everything had fallen into place at the right time. With the arrival on September 26th of the transports from Head of Elk, he commanded the most powerful army he would ever assemble: 7,800 French soldiers, 3,100 militiamen, and 8,000 Continentals. Trapped before him lay a hitherto inconceivable prize: Cornwallis, an army of nearly 9,000 men, and—he hoped—the arch-traitor Benedict Arnold. The only enemy was time. In conference with de Grasse, Washington was unable to convince him to stay past November 1st. British supply ships and transports could reach Yorktown after that, so Washington could not starve the redcoats into submission. He would have to find a way to pry them out of their fortifications.

On September 28th, Washington marched the whole of his army, the French on the left and the Americans on the right, to positions forming a six-mile arc around the British entrenchments. The siege had begun. Cornwallis had erected a chain of seven redoubts and batteries linked by earthworks, and a battery of heavy guns dominating the narrows of the York River at Gloucester Point. Yorktown was no fortress. But it was too strong to fall before unsupported infantry, who would have to attack across hundreds of yards of open ground under punishing fire before reaching the British entrenchments. The only way to close on the enemy would be by regular approaches, which meant digging zigzagging trenches, or "parallels," with redoubts to shelter infantry and artillery. Time-consuming, but it was the only way.

Cornwallis shortened the process by presenting Washington with an unexpected gift. On the night of September 29th–30th, the redcoats abandoned all of their outlying entrenchments (except for the so-called Fusilier's Redoubt on the west of town and redoubts 9 and 10 on the east) and withdrew into earthworks immediately surrounding the town. False intelligence precipitated the move. A recent letter from Clinton had promised relief within a week, and Cornwallis decided to anticipate it by tightening his lines. But there was no help on the way—Graves would put to sea from New York only on October 19th, the day of the British surrender—and the abandonment of the outworks at Yorktown only hastened the end. The Americans and French gladly occupied the empty fortifications with their own batteries.

Washington's ignorance of siege warfare did not dissuade him from taking characteristically minute interest in its progress at Yorktown. He reconnoitered the ground in person and directed the assembly of the tools and equipment necessary for digging the approaches. On the evening of October 6th the work parties were ready, and the commander-in-chief "struck a few blows with a pickaxe, a mere ceremony, that it might be said, 'General Washington with his own hands broke first ground at the siege of Yorktown.' " The main effort was on the right, where American soldiers under the expert direction of French engineers dug trenches toward redoubts 9 and 10, while on the left the French infantry launched diversionary attacks against Fusilier's Redoubt. By the 9th the French and American artillery were securely emplaced in old British and newly constructed redoubts, and the bombardment of Yorktown—promptly answered by a British counterbombardment—began. "His Excellency General Washington put the match to the first gun," a young Massachusetts doctor named James Thacher wrote in his diary on that date, "and a furious discharge of cannon and mortars immediately followed."

As the works inched forward, Washington issued fifty-five directives on everything from the dimensions of the trenches and other earthworks to the timing of relief parties. He made sure to prohibit smoking near powder kegs, and threatened to bring officers who employed escaped slaves as personal servants to the "severest account." But even such micromanagement did not prevent things from getting a little lackadaisical as the works progressed. On October 9th, Washington felt compelled to order that "Persons whose duty does not call them to the Trenches and who Assemble there merely to indulge Curiosity are to walk on the Reverse of the Trenches that they may not interrupt the works." The Continentals, feeling optimistic as they sensed approaching victory, even found cause for amusement in the British bombardment of their trenches. Sergeant Joseph Plumb Martin wrote that the British "had a large bulldog and every time they fired he would follow their shots across our trenches. Our officers wished to catch him and oblige him to carry a message from them into the town to his masters, but he looked too formidable for any of us to encounter."

By October 14th, the trenches had advanced to within 150 yards of redoubts 9 and 10. These small earthworks were a quarter of a mile apart. Redoubt 10, nearer the river, held just forty-five men; redoubt 9 held 120 British and Germans. They were heavily fortified. Rows of abatis—razor-sharp logs and branches—surrounded them at a distance of about twenty-five yards, and muddy ditches encircled the steep central earthworks. Behind the thick wooden palisades that rimmed the walls, the well-armed defenders waited with their muskets and upturned bayonets. Artillery fire had been directed against the redoubts for days, causing little damage but alerting the British and Hessian garrisons to the coming assault.

Washington's plan relied on surprise. Shortly after dusk on the 14th the French would launch a diversionary assault against Fusilier's Redoubt. The attacks on the two eastern redoubts would commence half an hour later. Redoubt 9, presumably the tougher because of its large garrison, was made the responsibility of 400 French regular soldiers under Colonel Guillaume Deux-Ponts. Redoubt 10 would be assaulted by 400 troops under Alexander Hamilton, who demanded and secured the command on grounds of seniority. Hamilton's command consisted of Continentals from Connecticut and Massachusetts, along with a single company of forty Rhode Island light infantry under the command of Captain Stephen Olney.

Olney's company, which Hamilton chose to lead the assault, was composed of former members of the Second Rhode Island Regiment. Rolls show that some of them had earlier served with the First Regiment, and a few may have been black. But Olney's company was probably largely white. This is worth mentioning in light of erroneous recent assertions that the First Rhode Island Regiment, which for four months in 1778 had accepted black recruits, led the assault. That regiment, numbering perhaps 200 men and consolidated since early 1781 into the Rhode Island Battalion, was part of Colonel Elias Dayton's brigade of Benjamin Lincoln's division. It spent October 14th and 15th in a different part of the lines. That the First Rhode Island did not participate in the assault on redoubt 10 does not, of course, in any way detract from the bravery or dedication of its members.

Fired with anticipation of a glorious role in the war's consummation, Hamilton wrote his wife: "Five days more the enemy must capitulate or abandon their present position . . . and then I fly to you. Prepare to receive me decked in all your beauty, fondness, and goodness." Washington's own sense of anticipation was mixed with dread at what would happen if the attacks went wrong. Olney remembered him visiting the troops just before they took up their attack positions, when he "made a short address or harangue, admonishing us to act the part of firm and brave soldiers, showing the necessity of accomplishing the object, as the attack on both redoubts depended on our success. I thought then that his Excellency's knees rather shook, but I have since doubted whether it was not mine."

Gunfire announced the diversion against Fusilier's Redoubt at 6:30 P.M., and at other places in the line demonstrations were made as if in preparation for a general assault on Yorktown. A German private in Cornwallis's army remembered hearing shouts in his own language: " 'The entire column or brigade, forward march! Halt! Cannons to the front!' And that, two or three times. Also, a few rifle balls flew over the wall and into the middle of our line. By this means they created a false alarm and we believed that they would attack us in the middle." Opposite redoubts 9 and 10, meanwhile, the assault troops waited for half an hour in their shadowy trenches. At 7:00 P.M. they advanced, bearing muskets without charges and fixed bayonets, and silently approached the prickly outlines of the redoubts that loomed in the darkness ahead. They were nearly upon the abatis when a sentry at redoubt 9 detected movement and bawled a challenge. The French rushed forward, and the fight was on.

"During this attack they made such a terrible screaming and loud hurrah shouting that there was nothing otherwise to believe than that all hell had broken loose," a German soldier remembered. At redoubt 9, French pioneers, or engineers, delayed the attack as they cleared lanes through the abatis, while the defenders fired into them with severe effect. The French infantry then filed through the gaps in the abatis, leapt into the ditches, tore down the palisades, and scrambled over the earthen walls. By this time they had lost fifteen men dead and seventy-seven wounded, but still outnumbered their opponents three to one. The garrison surrendered. At redoubt 10, Hamilton decided to avoid the "delay and loss" that would have attended "the removal of the abatis and palisades." His troops first surrounded the redoubt and then rushed it simultaneously from all sides. They took only light casualties before the enemy capitulated. The captives were evacuated, and by dawn on the 15th the redoubts had been incorporated in the American lines.

The capture of redoubts 9 and 10 had enormous tactical repercussions. It completed the entrapment of Cornwallis's army and allowed Washington's artillery to bring Yorktown under fire from three directions. But there was also a lesson to be learned, one that the commander-in-chief wasted no time in passing on to his troops. "The General reflects with the highest degree of pleasure on the Confidence which the Troops of the two Nations must hereafter have in each other," he announced in general orders on October 15th. "Assured of mutual support he is convinced there is no danger which they will not chearfully encounter. No difficulty which they will not bravely overcome." He might in justice have added that the cooperation was in large measure a result of his own and Rochambeau's efforts.

The Franco-American alliance was tested in battle for one last time at dawn on the 16th, when a picked force of 350 redcoats under Lieutenant Colonel Robert Abercromby sortied out of Yorktown to spike the French and American artillery in the captured redoubts. The British commander was determined—"Push on, my brave boys, and skin the bastards," he supposedly shouted—but so were the defenders, who drove the redcoats back after taking only minor losses. Resuming their bombardment that day, the French and American gunners engaged in a friendly competition to see who could do the most damage. Hits elicited cheers from both contestants, especially when French shots ricocheted over the enemy defenses. For the British, "there was nothing to be seen but bombs and cannonballs raining down on our entire line."

Five years earlier Cornwallis had ridden with the vanguard of the British army as it chased Washington's tattered Continentals through New Jersey into Pennsylvania. Now he lay helpless before his old foe. His infantry and artillery suffered under constant and effective enemy fire. "There was no part of the whole front attacked in which we show a single gun and our shells were nearly expended," he complained, and with his fortifications "going to ruin" it looked increasingly likely that the Americans would carry them by storm. A French officer who toured Yorktown immediately after its surrender found the scene "frightful and disturbing. . . . One could not take three steps without running into some great holes made by bombs, some splinters, some balls, some half covered trenches, with scattered white or negro arms or legs, [and] some bits of uniforms. Most of the houses [were] riddled by cannon fire, and [there were] almost no window-panes in the houses." The shortage of provisions led the British to expel from Yorktown all of the escaped slaves who had taken shelter there, and when German captain Johann Ewald led a nighttime patrol on October 14th he found dozens of blacks huddled miserably in ditches in no-man's land, afraid to enter the American lines. "We had used them to good advantage and set them free," he noted bitterly, "and now, with fear and trembling, they had to face the reward of their cruel masters."

For the British and German troops there could be no breaking out, and Clinton offered no hope of relief. In desperation, on the night of October 16th–17th Cornwallis attempted to evacuate his troops across the York River to Gloucester Point; but a "violent storm of wind and rain" sank many of his boats and carried the rest downriver. Their loss, and the continuing devastation wrought by Washington's guns, convinced Cornwallis that it would be "wanton and inhuman to the last degree to sacrifice the lives of this small body of gallant soldiers, who had ever behaved with so much fidelity and courage, by exposing them to an assault which from the numbers and precautions of the enemy could not fail to succeed. I therefore proposed to capitulate."

On the morning of October 17th an American soldier saw "a drummer mount the enemy's parapet and beat a parley, and immediately an officer, holding a white handkerchief, made his appearance outside their works. The drummer accompanied him, beating. Our batteries ceased." The British officer was led blindfolded behind the American lines and divested of a letter from Cornwallis requesting a cease-fire of twenty-four hours to discuss terms of surrender. The letter was then presented to the commander-in-chief. "An Ardent Desire to spare the further Effusion of Blood," Washington replied to Cornwallis, "will readily incline me to listen to such Terms for the Surrender of your Post & Garrisons at York & Gloucester, as are admissible."

Negotiations began the next morning as two British officers met with Colonel John Laurens, who spoke on behalf of the Americans, and the Marquis de Noailles, who represented the French. Washington was not going to permit any last-minute falling out between the allies and insisted that the French be given an equal share in every step of the surrender process. To de Grasse he wrote: "I should be anxious to have the honor of your Excellencys personal participation in the treaty which will according to present appearances shortly take place—I need not add how happy it will make me to welcome Your Excellency in the name of America on this shore, and embrace you upon an occasion so advantageous to the interests of the common cause—and on which it is so much indebted to you."

The Articles of Capitulation were signed on the morning of October 19, 1781. They were standard for the times, declaring all of Cornwallis's men prisoners of war, promising them good treatment in American camps, and permitting officers to return home after taking their parole. At 2:00 P.M. the allied army entered British positions and then lined up with the French on the left and the Americans on the right. The captives then marched between them, "their Drums in front beating a slow March"—reputedly the tune of "The World Turned Upside Down"—with "Their Colours furl'd and

Cased. . . . Having passed thro' our whole Army they grounded their Arms & march'd back again thro' the Army a second Time into the Town—The sight was too pleasing to an American to admit of Description."

The British nevertheless "showed the greatest scorn for the Americans," Rochambeau's aide observed, "who, to tell the truth, were eclipsed by our army in splendor of appearance and dress, for most of these unfortunate persons were clad in small jackets of white cloth, dirty and ragged, and a number of them were almost barefoot. The English had given them the *nickname* of *Yankee-Doodle*. What does it matter! An intelligent man would say. These people are much more praise-worthy and brave to fight as they do, when they are so poorly supplied *with everything*." Captain Ewald also became a reluctant admirer of his tatterdemalion captors. "I have seen many soldiers of this army without shoes, with tattered breeches and uniforms patched with all sorts of colored cloth, without neckband and only the lid of a hat, who marched and stood their guard as proudly as the best uniformed soldier in the world. With what soldiers in the world," he asked, "could one do what was done by these men, who go about nearly naked and in the greatest privation? Deny the best-disciplined soldiers of Europe what is due them and they will run away in droves. . . . But from this one can perceive what an enthusiasm—which these poor fellows call 'Liberty'—can do!"

Cornwallis refused to meet formally with Washington. He did not surrender his sword, but delegated that duty to Brigadier General Charles O'Hara, who presented it to Benjamin Lincoln. O'Hara also took Cornwallis's place at a dinner that Washington had offered in his honor. Nor would there be the satisfaction of watching Arnold swing from the end of a rope, for the arch-traitor had fled. But the cake still tasted good, even without the icing. Eight thousand British and German soldiers and seamen were now prisoners, along with 214 artillery pieces, thousands of muskets, two dozen transport ships, wagons, horses, £2,113 in specie, and over twenty battle standards. On hearing the figures Prime Minister Lord North is supposed to have "opened his arms, exclaiming wildly, as he paced up and down the apartment during a few minutes, 'Oh God! It is all over!' "

American officers and men meanwhile "could scarcely talk for laughing, and they could scarcely walk for jumping and dancing and singing as they went about." Determined to retain his self-control even at the moment of his greatest military victory, Washington was more restrained. But he could not altogether avoid the general hilarity. On October 21st, he boarded de Grasse's flagship and had cause to repent his careless earlier proposal of an "embrace" as de Grasse delightedly kissed him "first on one cheek, then the other, & thirdly on the lips." According to a witness, he received the salutation "like a coy damsel." Congress voted Washington thanks and resolved to erect a victory column at the site of the surrender.

Cornwallis's surrender at Yorktown threw the nation into a frenzy of sometimes rowdy celebration. In Brookfield, Massachusetts, the local militia "assembled under arms in the morning" of November 14th. "An elegant oration was delivered on the occasion, to a crouded audience, by the Rev. Mr. Fiske; after which the company dined upon a beef, which was barbecued for that purpose. The military companies, fired several vollies of small arms. In the evening the houses were illuminated, and a number of toasts were drank by a company of gentlemen assembled on this joyful occasion. The business of the day was conducted with the greatest decorum and good order, to the satisfaction of every individual present." At another place a party prepared to burn an effigy of Benedict Arnold; but "just as they were going to commit the effigy to the flames, one of the company observed, that one of Arnold's legs was wounded when he was fighting bravely for America, that this leg ought not to be burnt, but amputated; in which the whole company agreed; and this leg was taken off, and safely laid by."

Yet the war was not yet over, a fact many people seemed to have forgotten. Washington feared that his countrymen's happiness would cause them to overlook how much work remained to be done. He wrote a friend that "my only apprehension (which I wish may be groundless) is lest the late important success, instead of exciting our exertions, as it ought to do, should produce such a relaxation in the prosecution of the War, as will prolong the calamities of it." Leaving Rochambeau and the French army at Yorktown and detaching a large force of Continentals to help Greene in the south, he sent the remainder of his army to winter quarters at Newburgh, New York. He himself spent much of the winter in Philadelphia, lobbying Congress for further army reforms and nervously watching the economy, which continued to struggle despite French loans. Washington rejoined his troops at Newburgh in March 1782 and then recommenced the weary but essential routine of supplying and administering the army.

The summer of 1782 brought new hopes and worries. Lord North resigned, taking Clinton with him; and a new general, Sir Guy Carleton, took command of the British forces in North America. On August 4th Carleton informed Washington, whose intelligence came more slowly, of the beginning of peace negotiations in Paris between American and British representatives. He also declared an end to active hostilities and evacuated Savannah in July, followed by Charleston in December. The remainder of the British army lay inert in New York. But even as George III's minions became quiescent, a new and dangerous enemy to American liberties appeared from within the ranks of the Continental Army. Washington's practically single-handed defeat of this threat marked one of his most signal accomplishments of the war.

In January 1783 Washington was fifty years old, and had spent nearly eight years serving his country as commander-in-chief. He had lived most of that time not in the saddle, but in his headquarters office, reading tens of thousands of letters, reports, maps, and returns—many of them semiliterate or indecipherable scrawls—and composing an equally vast number of letters to others. His aides took the majority of his outgoing correspondence by dictation, but he proofread their drafts, noting corrections before ordering them to write the final copies that he signed. Working like this without interruption for some three thousand days had taken a toll, not just on his energy, but also on his eyes. He found partial relief in a new pair of spectacles that arrived at headquarters in February. "The Spectacles suit my Eyes extremely well," he wrote to his supplier, "as I am perswaded the reading glasses also will when I get more accustomed to the use of them—At present I find some difficulty in coming at the proper Focus—but when I do obtain it they magnify properly & shew those objects very distinctly which at first appear like a mist blended together & confused." Within a month, those spectacles would help end the war's final crisis.

On January 6th, four days before Washington ordered his spectacles, Congress assembled at Philadelphia to consider a petition from the officers of the Continental Army. For four years their pay had been almost continually in arrears. By some accounts, the government owed them a cumulative total of between four and five million dollars. Their families were pauperized. Promises of half pay and other forms of compensation had not been kept. Furthermore, although costs of rations and clothing had been deducted from their salaries, the goods had never arrived. Their patience was wearing thin. "Our distresses are now brought to a point," the officers declared. "We have borne all that men can bear—our property is expended—our private resources are at an end." They asked for money, rations, clothes—some "just recompense for several years of hard service, in which the health and fortunes of the officers have been worn down and exhausted."

Their language was moderate, but they warned that further delay in granting relief for the officers might throw the already bitter enlisted soldiers "blindly into extremities." This implied threat of a general mutiny, Virginia delegate James Madison noted, provoked "much loose conversation" in Congress "on the critical state of things . . . & the consequences to be apprehended from a disappointment of the mission from the army." Yet the delegates could not agree on a solution. They were full of sympathy—and overflowing with words—but short on guarantees. Another state's policies or corrupt representatives were always to blame. Some had never supported pensions, and continued to balk at paying them now. No one had enough funds. The officers were sent back to camp at Newburgh, essentially empty-handed.

While the army stewed during February, Washington experimented with his new spectacles and tended to routine administration. But he could sense an explosion approaching. "The predicament in which I stand as Citizen & Soldier," he wrote Alexander Hamilton on March 4th, "is as critical and delicate as can well be conceived. It has been the subject of many contemplative hours. The sufferings of a complaining Army on one hand, and the inability of Congress and tardiness of the States on the other, are the forebodings of evil." Lacking the power to rectify the situation, all he could do was wait and hope that his fears did not come true, pursuing "the same steady line of conduct which has governed me hitherto; fully convinced that the sensible, and discerning part of the army, cannot be unacquainted (although I never took pains to inform them) of the services I have rendered it, on more occasions than one." Six days later the pressure cooker blew.

On March 10th, somebody handed Washington a note calling all of the army's officers to a general meeting the next day. Included was an exhortation to the troops from an anonymous "fellow soldier." It was later dubbed the First Newburgh Address. The unknown author's tone was extremely provocative. America, he declared, had become "a country that tramples upon your rights, disdains your cries and insults your distresses." Congress had already shown its lack of concern. Yet "in any political event," he insisted, "the army has its alternative." If Britain and America made peace, the soldiers should refuse to disarm—presumably as a preliminary to imposing their demands on the nation by force. And if the war resumed, then "courting the auspices, and inviting the direction of your illustrious leader [Washington], you will retire to some unsettled country, smile in your turn, and 'mock when their fear cometh on.' " In other words, the army would withdraw from the field, leaving America's civilian government at the mercy of the armed forces of Great Britain.

Horrified, Washington immediately issued general orders condemning such an "irregular invitation" and such "disorderly proceedings." But he also realized that setting himself directly against the officers was no solution and might even get him deposed. He therefore preempted the leaders of this incipient rebellion by calling another meeting for March 15th. Representatives from the staff and each army company would confer on the officers' demands and, after "mature deliberation," determine what "further measures ought to be adopted as most rational and best calculated to attain the just and important object in view." He reported developments to Congress.

The crafty author of the First Newburgh Address—whoever he was—responded to Washington's announcement with an outflanking maneuver of his own. On March 12th he issued the so-called Second Newburgh Address in flyers that passed from hand to hand. "The general orders of yesterday," he explained, "which the weak may mistake for disapprobation, and the designing dare to represent as such, wears, in my opinion, a very different complexion, and carries with it a very opposite tendency." The commander-in-chief's agreement to a meeting indicated his assent in its purpose; and his "private opinion has sanctified your claims." The insinuation that Washington supported the rebellion was outrageous cheek—and ominous. Sensing that he might be placed in a situation where he would have to repudiate either Congress or the army, he urged the delegates to assist him by granting relief. If they refused, he warned, "they must be answerable for all the ineffable horrors which may be occasioned thereby."

At noon on March 15th, Washington entered a large wooden building that his soldiers had recently built for dual service as a chapel and dance hall. "Visibly agitated," he walked to a lectern, faced the attendees, and began to speak. He had no intention, he said, to dictate to the assembly, or force the pace or content of deliberations. But the wide distribution of the two anonymous addresses made it necessary to present his own point of view, which was that their author, despite "the goodness of his Pen," had "the most insidious purposes . . . to impress the Mind, with an idea of premeditated injustice in the Sovereign power of the United States, and rouse all those resentments which must unavoidably flow from such a belief." The man had forwarded this end by calling a hasty meeting, in order to "take advantage of the passions, while they were warmed by the recollection of past distresses, without giving time for cool, deliberative thinking, & that composure of Mind which is so necessary to give dignity & stability." Washington appealed to the officers' reason, and to their trust in himself as their leader. Had he not been a "faithful friend to the Army"? Was he not "among the first who embarked in the cause of our common Country"? "I have been the constant companion & witness of your Distresses," he declared, "and not among the last to feel, & acknowledge your Merits." He shared in their misery.

But the "dreadful alternative" offered in the First Newburgh Address— that of refusing to disarm or retreating into the country—had "something so shocking in it, that humanity revolts at the idea. My God! What can this Writer have in view, by recommending such measures? Can he be a friend to the Army? Can he be a friend to this Country? Rather, is he not an insidous Foe? Some Emissary, perhaps, from New York, plotting the ruin of both, by sowing the seeds of discord & seperation between the Civil & Military powers of the Continent?" Congress had so far failed to win the officers' confidence. But Washington begged them not to give up. He felt convinced that the delegates would do them "compleat Justice: That their endeavors, to discover & establish funds for this purpose, have been unwearied, and will not cease, till they have succeeded, I have not a doubt. But, like all other large Bodies, where there is a variety of different Interests to reconcile, their deliberations are slow." They must be given time.

Washington concluded with some of the most moving phrases he ever composed. "Let me conjure you," he urged, "in the name of our common Country, as you value your own sacred honor—as you respect the rights of humanity, & as you regard the Military & national character of America, to express your utmost horror & detestation of the Man who wishes, under any specious pretences, to overturn the liberties of our Country, & who wickedly attempts to open the flood Gates of Civil discord, & deluge our rising Empire in Blood. By thus determining & thus acting, you will pursue the plain & direct road to the attainment of your wishes. You will defeat the insidious designs of our Enemies, who are compelled to resort from open force to secret Artifice. You will give one more distinguished proof of unexampled patriotism & patient virtue, rising superior to the pressure of the most complicated sufferings; And you will, by the dignity of your Conduct, afford occasion for Posterity to say, when speaking of the glorious example you have exhibited to man kind, 'had this day been wanting, the World had never seen the last stage of perfection to which human nature is capable of attaining.' " With that he concluded his speech, and gauged its effect.

He was unsatisfied. Perhaps his audience was too quiet; he may even have heard a grumble or two. Fearing that he had failed and fumbling for one last weapon, he began reading a letter from Joseph Jones describing Congress's fiscal difficulties. This move could have backfired. The letter was dull, clumsily penned, and densely composed. Washington had read many like it, but his hearers had not; and one imagines them shifting in their seats and even becoming a trifle bored. Then he remembered his spectacles, and, probably without premeditation, withdrew them from his pocket and put them on. Glancing at his audience, he said, "Gentlemen, you must pardon me. I have grown gray in your service and now find myself growing blind."

It is hard to say which had more effect: Washington's magnificent speech, or his humble, almost pathetic remark about growing blind in the army's service. Either way, he completely changed the officers' mood. After finishing the letter from Jones, he strode out of the building and returned to headquarters. The meeting then formally convened, and under the chairmanship of Horatio Gates—Washington's sometime enemy—the officers passed a vote of thanks to the commander-in-chief. They then rejected the Newburgh Addresses, endorsed the moderate proposals that had been presented in January, avowed their confidence in Congress, and requested Washington to mediate future negotiations with the delegates. Not a single voice was raised in dissent. The meeting adjourned and the officers returned to their quarters. None of the victories that Washington had won in the field—not even Trenton or Yorktown—was more complete than this.

The conclusion of the so-called Newburgh Conspiracy coincided with the arrival of news that a preliminary peace agreement had been signed in Paris. Britain was prepared to recognize American independence and accept it as a nation. Within six months, the war would be over.

On September 5, 1783, Washington invited the president and members of Congress to dinner in a captured British marquee tent. No one had seen him so cheerful since the war began. Rhode Island delegate David Howell "observed with much pleasure that the Generals front was uncommonly open & pleasant—the contracted, pensive Air betokening deep thought & much care, which I noticed on Prospect Hill in 1775 is done away: & a pleasant smile sparkling vivacity of wit & humour succeeds." Jokes dropped from his lips almost nonstop. Some fell flat; but the fact that he was joking at all was worthy of remark. Congress's recent vote to erect an equestrian statue of the commander-in-chief added to the bonhomie. "No honor short of those, which the Deity vindicates to himself," Howell avowed, "can be too great for Gen. Washington."

The Treaty of Paris that officially ended the Revolutionary War was signed on September 3, 1783. Word of it reached America at the end of October, along with news of British preparations for the evacuation of New York. In response, Congress began the long process of discharging the troops of the Continental Army. The time had come for goodbyes. On November 2nd, from his headquarters at Rocky Hill near Princeton, New Jersey, Washington issued his farewell orders "to the Armies of the United States of America." It was a ponderous document but not without its highlights, particularly as the commander-in-chief recalled the process by which the rabble he had encountered before Boston in 1775 evolved into a victorious army. "Who," he asked, "has before seen a disciplined Army formed at once from such raw materials? Who that was not a witness could imagine, that the most violent local prejudices would cease so soon, and that Men who came from the different parts of the Continent, strongly disposed by the habits of education, to despise and quarrel with each other, would instantly become but one patriotic band of Brothers?"

Washington also emphasized to his soldiers the importance of their returning home as citizens and productive members of society. Not all of their grievances had been addressed. The national economy was still a shambles. But by working with instead of against their government, they could help to inaugurate a new era of prosperity. "It is earnestly recommended to all the Troops that with strong attachments to the Union, they should carry with them into civil Society the most conciliating dispositions; and that they should prove themselves not less virtuous and usefull as Citizens, than they have been persevering and victorious as Soldiers. . . . [T]he private virtues of economy, prudence and industry, will not be less amiable in civil life, than the more splendid qualities of valour, perseverence and enterprise, were in the Field: Every one may rest assured that much, very much of the future happiness of the Officers and Men, will depend upon the wise and manly conduct which shall be adopted by these, when they are mingled with the great body of the Community."

The officers of the army responded to Washington's address on November 15th. "Relieved at length from long suspense, our warmest wish is to return to the bosom of our Country, to resume the character of citizens," they promised; "and it will be our highest ambition to become useful ones." For themselves they sought peace, prosperity, and justice. And for Washington, "we sincerely pray *GOD* [that] this happiness may long be yours—and that when you quit the stage of human life, you may receive from the *Unerring Judge* the rewards of valor exerted to save the oppressed, of patriotism and disinterested virtue."

On November 25, 1783, the last redcoat disappeared from Manhattan. Washington entered the city that afternoon, riding beneath a blue sky next to New York governor George Clinton. There were crowds, speeches, and elaborate ceremonies; and during the following week the commander-in-chief was regaled with banquets, sermons, public addresses, and fireworks. He sailed through all of these formalities in his usual sober and erect style. But at the final leave-taking on December 4th, his self-control unraveled. At noon, he entered Fraunces Tavern for a last meeting with his officers. A small crowd filled the tavern, but only Steuben and Knox remained to represent his closest compatriots. Their presence was symbolic of the rest—some gone home, some dead, some disgraced. The memory of their comradeship was still sharp in Washington's mind.

"With a heart full of love and gratitude, I now take leave of you," he said tearfully after the company's cups had been filled with wine. "I most devoutly wish that your later days may be as prosperous and happy as your former ones have been glorious and honorable." They drained their cups and approached to bid farewell. In front, his burly form blotting out the others, Knox extended his hand. Washington could not take it. Instead, crying freely, he embraced his old friend and kissed him on the cheek. Each man received the same. Finally, "the General walked across the room, raised his arm in an all-inclusive silent farewell and passed through the door, out of the tavern, between the open ranks of a guard of honor, and then along the street to Whitehall." A few minutes later he was on a barge that would take him on the first leg of his journey home.

The last days were almost anticlimactic. Washington rode into Philadelphia on December 8th, and the round of dinners and speeches began again. He settled his accounts with Congress—accepting perhaps a bit more money than his expenses merited but not more than he deserved—and then departed on the 15th. Hurrying to complete his final duties in time to reach Mount Vernon and Martha for Christmas, he entered Baltimore on the 17th and waited for Congress, which had convened at Annapolis, to send word that it was ready to accept his resignation. The invitation finally came; and on the 23rd, Washington stood before them to give his Farewell Address.

This famous address was delivered through tears. Washington read the passage thanking his officers while clutching the paper with two trembling hands: "I should do injustice to my own feelings not to acknowledge in this place the peculiar services and distinguished merits of the Gentlemen who have been attached to my person during the War. It was impossible the choice of confidential Officers to compose my family should have been more fortunate." By the time he reached the final words, his unsteady voice had recovered, clear and strong: "Having now finished the work assigned me, I retire from the great theatre of action; and bidding an Affectionate farewell to this August body under whose orders I have so long acted, I here offer my commission, and take my leave of all the employments of public life." Washington then handed his commission and address to his erstwhile enemy Thomas Mifflin, who held the chair. There was no applause. Mifflin read a brief note of thanks, the delegates removed their hats, and Washington, now a private citizen, left the room.

The next morning he galloped homeward. Douglas Southall Freeman picturesquely described the last stages of his journey: "At last the cold, clear waters of the Potomac came in sight, then the ferry and after that the blusterous passage, the last swift stage of the ride, the beloved trees, the yard, the doorway, Martha's embrace and the shrill, excited voices [of Martha's grandchildren]—all this a richer reward than the addresses of cities, the salute of cannon and the approving words of the President of Congress." It was December 24th, and Washington had achieved every soldier's fondest dream. He was home for Christmas.

18

OLD SOLDIER

1784 – 1799

LIKE ALL VETERANS, Washington had some difficulty readjusting to civilian life. "I am just beginning to experience that ease, and freedom from public cares which, however desireable, takes some time to realize," Washington wrote to Henry Knox in February 1784. "For strange as it may tell, it is nevertheless true, that it was not 'till lately I could get the better of my usual custom of ruminating as soon as I waked in the Morning, on the business of the ensuing day; and of my surprise, after having revolved many things in my mind, to find that I was no longer a public Man, or had any thing to do with public transactions." Declaim though he might on the happiness of remaining aloof from national affairs, Washington kept involved in politics. He observed the struggles of the Confederation with growing worry; and when he went to the Constitutional Convention in Philadelphia in May 1787 it was with a conviction that the American system of government needed an overhaul. Elected unanimously as president of the Convention, he played a central role in the creation of the Constitution and its signing on September 17th.

In military affairs Washington found less to do. In May 1783, before the formal end of the war with Great Britain, he had encouraged the Continental Congress to maintain a small peacetime establishment of about three thousand Continental troops. Congress, reverting to the traditional American suspicion of standing armies, refused. The Continental Army was dissolved, and by June 1784 less than a hundred soldiers remained in service, in garrisons at Fort Pitt and West Point. Over the next few years the American armed forces consisted merely of militia and temporary formations of regular troops. They could barely hold off Indian raiders, let alone chase the British from the frontier forts that they continued to hold in violation of the Treaty of Paris. So wary were Americans of a standing army that no effort was made to strengthen the nation's defenses. Even the Society of the Cincinnati, an organization of former Continental Army and Navy officers, was viewed in some quarters—by Thomas Jefferson, for example—as a royalist cadre plotting to take over the government. Nor did Washington's position as the head of the Society reassure its opponents, who suspected a plot to make him king.

The same restraints applied after Washington was inaugurated president of the United States on April 30, 1789. Thanks to him and Alexander Hamilton, the Constitution had not specifically prohibited the creation of a standing army. But it also failed to mandate one. In 1790, Secretary of War Henry Knox had a force of only 1,200 men with which to defend thousands of miles of territory on the frontier. Popular opposition dissuaded the president from raising more despite the increasingly dangerous situation on the frontier. Since the end of the war, settlers—many of them former soldiers laying claim to bounty land given as a reward for their Revolutionary War services—had been invading regions Indians had traditionally claimed as their own. The army could not restrain the settlers, and Indian anger grew as they continued to seize tribal lands and flaunt treaties. Soon the Indians and settlers were engaged in a vicious frontier war, committing countless outrages on each other in the name of justice or revenge.

"The *basis* of our proceedings with the Indian Nations has been, and shall be *justice,* during the period in which I may have any thing to do in the administration of this government," Washington promised Lafayette in August 1790. When the Wabash Indians on the northwest frontier violently resisted settler incursions, he "observed forcibly that a War with the Wabash Indians ought to be avoided by all means consistently with the security of the frontier inhabitants, the security of the troops and the national dignity," and directed his negotiators to prove "to the Indians the dispositions of the general government for the preservation of peace." He probably also feared the impact of war on his pathetic little army. But no one cared to address the real causes of the conflict, and Congress, settlers, and the military all demanded that the Indians be punished. In the autumn of 1790, following the collapse of half-hearted negotiations with the Wabash, Knox dispatched Brigadier General Josiah Harmar and 1,400 troops, mostly Kentucky militiamen, to "extirpate" Indian "banditti" along the Miami River in what is now southwestern Ohio.

"My forebodings with respect to the Expedition against the Wabash Indians are of disappointment; and a disgraceful termination under the conduct of B. Genl Harmer," Washington warned Knox in November. Led by Harmar, a drunk, and beset by carelessness and indiscipline, the expedition was thrashed by the Indians and barely returned intact. The Indians subsequently grew bolder, torching one settlement after another and dismissing offers of negotiation. In March 1791, Congress authorized another expedition, this time under Major General Arthur St. Clair, a respected officer who had served under Washington during the Revolutionary War. St. Clair commanded a substantial force of 1,000 regular infantry and 2,000 militiamen, but the results of his expedition were worse than the one that had preceded it. In November, as St. Clair's little army straggled through the woods near the upper Wabash River in western Ohio, it was set upon and slaughtered by a large force of Indians. Nearly 650 soldiers were killed and hundreds wounded before the rest of the army could escape. It was Braddock's defeat all over again.

In March 1792, Congress authorized the president to raise a new expeditionary force consisting of over 5,000 troops in five infantry regiments with artillery. The political fallout from the failure of the previous expeditions had been severe, and Washington anticipated more trouble if this one did not succeed. But who would lead it? There was no obvious choice, but he came up with a list of sixteen possibilities. Steuben, he noted, was "Sensible, Sober & brave," but a "foreigner." George Weedon, like many others, was "no enemy it is said to the bottle." Daniel Morgan was "intemperate" and "troubled with a palpitation which often lays him up. And it is not denied that he is illiterate." Then there was Anthony Wayne, Washington's faithful, though erratic, comrade through much of the Revolution. Mad Anthony was "more active & enterprising than judicious and cautious," the president informed his cabinet. "[He was] no œconomist it is feared. Open to flattery—vain— easily imposed upon—and liable to be drawn into scrapes. Too indulgent . . . to his Officers & men. Whether sober—or a little addicted to the bottle, I know not." It was not much of an endorsement, but Wayne got the command.

Wayne began assembling his force that summer, but because of continuing peace negotiations with the Indians, some two years passed before he marched to the frontier. In the interim Washington encouraged Wayne to impose tight discipline on his troops and sent regular instructions on administration, training, and tactics. The president also tended to the expedition's equipment and supply, and intervened personally to break administrative bottlenecks. When Wayne finally set out to fight in the summer of 1794, Washington dogged him with constant letters of military advice. Wayne bore the oversight, and the implied distrust of his abilities, patiently. After all, it was the president's personal interest that kept the army supplied. In August 1794, Wayne won the Battle of Fallen Timbers against a half-starved force of about five hundred Indians. Exhausted by years of war and discouraged by the refusal of the British to support them, the northwestern tribes would fight no longer. In August 1795, they formally ceded most of modern-day Ohio and part of Indiana to the United States.

The only other significant military event of the Washington presidency also took place on the frontier. This event, the Whiskey Rebellion, came about because of an excise tax on distilled spirits that Congress had imposed in 1791. Many settlers opposed the tax because it reduced profits on their grain shipments to the East Coast, and they clamored for its repeal. Resistance became particularly violent in western Pennsylvania, where attempts of revenue officers to halt illegal distilling provoked an insurrection in the summer of 1794. Washington strove to find a peaceful solution, but when the rebellion threatened to spread into Maryland and Virginia he was forced to act. The moment having come when "Government is set at defiance, the contest being whether a small portion of the United States shall dictate to the whole union, and at the expence of those, who desire peace, indulge a desperate ambition," he called for the militias to put the insurgents down. Sensing that his personal presence might become necessary, he rode to join his troops at Carlisle, Pennsylvania. Whether because of his presence or the size of his force, the rebels dispersed.

With the foregoing exceptions, Washington's presidency was a time of military, if not political, peace. The situation in Europe was very different. In 1789, the French Revolution overturned the old absolutist government and created a constitutional monarchy, and over the next three years the Revolution grew increasingly radical. The king was executed in January 1793, and the Terror that followed in 1793–94 killed thousands, both royalists and revolutionaries, in an orgy of destruction. The Thermidorian Reaction of July 1794 ended the Terror, but was followed by a brief White Terror that victimized the radicals. A five-man Directory, despised by both radicals and royalists, and dangerously dependent on the military to maintain control, ruled France from October 1795 until November 1799, when Napoleon seized the government in a *coup d'état*.

In April 1792, France declared war on Austria and inaugurated the War of the First Coalition, the first in a series of brutal European wars that lasted until 1815. Prussia, Spain, Holland, several German states, and Great Britain joined Austria, but at Valmy in September 1792, French troops repulsed a combined Prussian-Austrian-Hessian army and forced its retreat from France. The Revolution then burst outward, following the armies of generals like Napoleon into the Low Countries, Germany, and Italy. In the process the French overthrew governments, crippled the old political order, and transformed the map of Continental Europe. Only Great Britain, protected by the Royal Navy, remained impervious to the revolutionary tidal wave; and by 1798 it seemed clear that the outcome of the conflict between that nation and France would determine the fate of Europe, and possibly the world.

The New World could not afford to ignore the European conflict, nor was it allowed to do so. Both France and Great Britain alternately threatened America and sought her support. Washington, who had at first welcomed the French Revolution, recoiled as it grew bloodthirsty, and tried to steer a neutral course between France and Britain. His policy was deeply unpopular in the United States. French sympathizers like Thomas Jefferson bitterly condemned the president's refusal to support his old allies and denounced the Jay Treaty of November 1794. This treaty settled several disputes between America and Great Britain, for which it served as a kind of nonaggression pact; but it also angered the French and polarized American politics by spawning debates on foreign policy and government. Pro-British "Federalists" like Secretary of the Treasury Alexander Hamilton—and, by association, Washington—were accused of incipient monarchism; while pro-French "Republicans" like Jefferson and James Madison were dubbed ravenous incendiaries. The bile spread until scurrilous personal attacks were directed against the president himself. One Republican newspaper even tried to defame Washington by resurrecting some forged letters, purportedly from him, that the British had circulated during the Revolutionary War.

Provoked and embittered, Washington yearned to leave public life behind and retire to his beloved farms at Mount Vernon. He welcomed the end of his second term in March 1797. Yet his relief at leaving office was mixed with dread that political passions would soon engulf America in the European war. Few knew better than he what a disaster that would mean. The nation was worse than unprepared—it was defenseless. Washington had overseen the creation of a tiny U.S. Navy, and established some dockyards and arsenals.

But he had never been able to create a genuine, professional army. When he delivered his farewell address in September 1796, the American armed forces consisted of a few warships—barely a flotilla—and three to four thousand soldiers scattered in isolated frontier posts. This knowledge helped to inspire his injunction for America to pursue neutrality, "maintain inviolate the relations of Peace and amity towards other Nations," and "steer clear of permanent Alliances, with any portion of the foreign World." If he had heeded his own advice, the final years of his life might have been more peaceful.

Thomas Jefferson remarked in 1814 that in his sixties Washington's "memory was already sensibly impaired by age, the firm tone of mind for which he had been remarkable, was beginning to relax, its energy was abated; a listlessness of labor, a desire for tranquillity had crept on him, and a willingness to let others act, and even think for him." In fact, Washington lost no mental acuity in retirement. The care and energy with which he refurbished the mansion at Mount Vernon and tended its farms showed that he was as sharp as he had ever been. Yet he *had* changed. It may have been the absence of that desire to shine that had fired him in his youth. Perhaps the years had made him cynical, or bitter. Whatever the cause, by 1797, Washington had lost some of the qualities—stoicism, self-control, or the certainty that he, as an individual, could make a difference in the fate of an army or a nation— that had inspired him twenty years earlier. The change would not have mattered if he had been allowed to enjoy the well-deserved shade of his vine and fig tree. But the American people were not yet through with Washington. In 1798, just a year after he renounced public life, they called on the old soldier at Mount Vernon to save them once again.

Washington's retirement—at least, that is what he hoped it would be— began with the inauguration of John Adams as the second president of the United States on March 4, 1797. Adams had suggested Washington as commander-in-chief in 1775 and served for eight years as his vice president. The two men had much in common, including their political outlook— Adams considered Washington's to be "exactly like mine"—but the two men never really understood each other. During the war, Adams had refused to join in the public adulation of the commander-in-chief, and as vice president he had chafed at the insignificance of his office and the president's apparent indifference to his counsel. For his part, Washington tended to underestimate the squat, pudgy Massachusetts lawyer, never detecting the broad intelligence and astuteness of his mind. Poisoned by misunderstanding, their friendship did not survive the strains of the so-called Quasi-War between America and France.

The 1794 Jay Treaty between America and Great Britain provoked the French into an undeclared war against American merchant shipping. In one year, from June 1796 to June 1797, they captured over three hundred vessels and put severe pressure on American commerce. Washington stoked the tension further in the summer of 1796 by recalling his minister to France, Republican James Monroe, who had become cozy with the Directory that had controlled the French government since 1795. The Directory refused to recognize Monroe's replacement, the South Carolina Federalist Charles Cotesworth Pinckney, and threatened him with arrest until he fled to Holland. When Adams became president in March 1797, relations between America and France had become so strained that there was open talk of war.

Sensibly wanting to avoid a war that America could not hope to win, Adams formed a commission of Pinckney, Federalist John Marshall, and Republican Elbridge Gerry and sent them to mend relations with the Directory in Paris. The French foreign minister Talleyrand received the commissioners coldly and kept them waiting for permission to meet with the Directory. In the meantime an American and two Swiss merchants with connections in the French government contacted the commissioners and offered to admit them to the Directory in return for a bribe of $250,000, an apology for the Jay Treaty, and a hefty loan from the United States to France. "No! No! Not a sixpence!" Pinckney exclaimed; and when their counterproposal to grant France a pact similar to the Jay Treaty was rejected in January 1798, they ended negotiations. In March, Adams reported to Congress how the French government had insulted his envoys, referring to the trio who had solicited their bribe as X, Y, and Z.

Washington shared wholeheartedly in the indignation that Adams's report created among the American public. "Whether we consider the injuries and plunder which our commerce is suffering or the affront to our national independence and dignity in the rejection of our envoys," he ranted to some visitors at Mount Vernon, "everywhere we recognize the need to arm ourselves with a strength and zeal equal to the dangers with which we are threatened. . . . Yea, rather than allowing herself to be insulted to this degree, rather than having her freedom and independence trodden under foot, America, every American, I, though old, will pour out the last drop of blood which is in my veins." Washington applauded Congress as it canceled the alliance of 1778 and invited American privateers to attack French merchant ships, even though he expected these measures to result in a French invasion. He also implicitly endorsed the Alien and Sedition Acts of July 1798, which muzzled Republican orators and newspapers by placing limits on the right to free speech.

The next step was more difficult for Washington because it was personal. On July 11, 1798, Secretary of War James McHenry—a former Revolutionary War aide—arrived at Mount Vernon with a letter from Adams and a commission for Washington as "Lieutenant General and Commander in Chief of all the Armies raised or to be raised for the service of the United States." The ex-president could not feign surprise. He was still the most respected military leader in America, and his own public fury at the conduct of "intoxicated," "rapacious," and "lawless" France made him a leading instigator of the war. Still, he regretted losing the consolations of his "peaceful abode" for "the boundless field of public action—incessant trouble—and high responsibility." Washington accepted the commission on one condition: he would not leave Mount Vernon "until the Army is in a Situation to require my presence, or it becomes indispensable by the urgency of circumstances." He narrowed this proviso later by stipulating that he would not take the field unless the French had invaded or were about to do so.

This was a ridiculous condition in military terms, but Adams had no time to argue. There was an army to build. In July, Congress voted to augment the already existing national army of 3,000 soldiers with twelve infantry regiments plus cavalry, thus establishing a modest so-called New Army that could face the first wave of any French invasion. These troops would be recruited immediately. And in the event of war yet another force, a "provisional army" of 10,000 men, would be formed; bringing the total size of the American army to about 20,000. This was a mammoth undertaking, but before it could begin Washington had to decide who would serve on his general staff. Heading the staff would be three major generals, ranked in order of seniority, with the highest acting also as inspector general of the army. In practical terms, Washington's refusal to leave Mount Vernon meant that the inspector general would be charged with the actual business of building and arranging the New Army in the field.

Washington's nominees were Alexander Hamilton, Charles Cotesworth

Pinckney, and Henry Knox, ranked in that order. Although Hamilton had served during the Revolution as Washington's aide and had led the assault on redoubt 10 at Yorktown, he still was more a politician than a soldier. So was Pinckney, despite his wartime service at Brandywine, Germantown, and Charleston as a colonel. Of the three, only Knox was all soldier. During the war he had served loyally as Washington's artillery commander, riding at the commander-in-chief's side in every battle from Trenton to Yorktown. From 1785 to 1794 he had served as secretary of war. And in 1798 he was only forty-eight years old, his ungainly three-hundred-pound bulk concealing an active mind overflowing with military knowledge. Washington's decision to put Knox at the bottom of the three major generals, beneath two men whom he had outranked during the last war, was both unusual and deeply hurtful to the genial man who had considered Washington his friend.

In explaining the ranking to Knox, Washington made little effort to be tactful. Hamilton was inspector general because "I know not where a more competent choice could be made." Pinckney, the South Carolinian, was second because Washington believed "that if the French intend an Invasion of this Country in Force, their operations will commence South of Maryland; probably Virginia." Pinckney would thus inspire the southerners to a "unity of sentiment" they might otherwise lack. But that still did not explain why the Bostonian Knox was rated last under both Pinckney and Hamilton, who had made his political career from New York. Not surprisingly, Knox was upset, and he made his feelings known to the president. Adams responded by overturning Washington's ranking—which he had every authority to do—and placing Knox at the top and Hamilton at the bottom.

Washington responded to this revision with anger and petulance that had not been seen since his days as a provincial colonel in the 1750s. Adams, he thought, had breached an informal understanding that the army's commander would have the final say on the choice of his deputies. The affront to his authority would not be tolerated. "The matter is, or very soon will be brought, to the alternative of submitting to the Presidents forgetfulness of what *I* considered a compact, or condition of acceptance of the Appointment with which he was pleased to honor me, or, to return him my Commission," he warned McHenry. Before resigning, however, he intended to seek redress— even if it meant immersing himself in political intrigue. Working secretly, Washington enlisted three prominent members of Adams's cabinet, Secretary of State (and arch-intriguer) Timothy Pickering, Secretary of War James McHenry, and Secretary of the Treasury Oliver Wolcott, Jr., in a campaign to persuade or force Adams to change his mind.

In October, Washington succeeded. Under constant pressure on this subject, and overwhelmed by the needs of his gravely ill wife, Adams backed down. Hamilton would rank first and Knox last. But in the process Washington had undermined the president's relations with his cabinet and sown disunity among the Federalists. More poignantly, he lost Knox, who declined his commission. On November 4th, Knox wrote Washington "in the presence of almighty God, that there is not a creature upon the surface of this globe, who was, is, and will remain, more your sincere friend." But if the friendship remained, all warmth had departed from it. Knox never wrote Washington again.

The intrigue did not end with Adams's capitulation on the major generals. Washington continued corresponding with the cabinet behind his back, accepting their reports on economics, politics, and diplomacy and offering his own recommendations on national policy. He entered internal feuds, sided with some ministers against others, and even wrote a letter to McHenry expressing doubts on his competence as secretary of war. The affable McHenry took the criticism in good part. But Washington went further. When Adams bravely risked his political reputation in February 1799 by appointing William Vans Murray a new minister to France, with instructions to resume negotiations for peace, Washington barely contained his contempt. His suspicion that the mission would involve the United States in further humiliation was expressed, thinly veiled, in letter after letter to friends and members of the cabinet; and in an astonishing epistle to Pickering he even laid out the more cautious "course I should have pursued" in Adams's place.

There were some who saw Washington's continued interest in politics as indicative of a willingness to return to public office, and they urged him to run for president in 1800. He swiftly quashed the idea. "It would be a matter of sore regret to me, if I could believe that a serious thot was turned towards me as [Adams's] successor," he wrote in July 1799, particularly because it would make him once again "a mark for the shafts of envenomed malice, and the basest calumny to fire at; when I should be charged not only with irresolution, but with concealed ambition, which wants only an occasion to blaze out; and, in short, with dotage and imbecility." Washington's intrigues with

the Adams cabinet probably were driven less by ambition than by an instinctive sense—which many retirees have shared—that no one could run the
country as well as he. Washington had, after all, spent most of his life in positions of power. But the vitriol in his letters, fueled in part by lingering resentment at the Republican abuse he had endured during his second term in
office, was new; and it is well that it did not last for much longer.

Though he doubted its propriety, the Murray mission set America and
France on the road to reconciliation and granted Washington a welcome
respite from the task of building the army. At the beginning he had put substantial effort into the work, meeting with Hamilton and Pinckney in Philadelphia and hammering out a long list of potential officers, from ensigns to
generals. In doing so he paid particular attention to each man's political relia-
bility. As months passed and the signs of war faded, however, he increasingly
turned over responsibility for the army to Hamilton. By the summer and fall
of 1799, as Hamilton drilled the New Army's recruits and placed them in
their winter quarters, Washington's heart had left the battlefield and returned
to his farms.

Washington spent the last months of his life riding around Mount Vernon,
relaxing with Martha, reading newspapers, lamenting politics, compiling a
list of his slaves, writing a will, and sketching a long, incredibly detailed plan
for crops and farm renovation in 1800. He also pursued plans to erect a building to house his massive collection of private and public documents and letters, most of them relating to his military career. In 1781, referring to his
military correspondence "as a species of Public property, sacred in my
hands," he had directed all of his papers to be copied and bound into twenty-
eight volumes by a team of copyists directed by his secretary Richard Varick.
All of these had since been hauled to Mount Vernon, where in 1799 he kept
a young clerk named Albin Rawlins busy cataloguing and arranging them.

On December 12, 1799, Washington spent several hours in a snow and
hailstorm, riding through his farms. He returned to his mansion wet, but
went to dinner without changing his clothes. The next morning he had developed a sore throat, and although he stayed inside he refused medication, observing of his cold that he intended to "let it go as it came." It did not go. That
night his throat became more and more swollen, and in his distress he finally
consented to call his doctor, James Craik, who had accompanied him to Fort
Necessity forty-five years before. At Washington's insistence Craik bled him,

probably hastening his end. On the afternoon of December 14th, Washington whispered some final instructions. "Do you arrange & record all my late Military letters & papers," he told his friend and secretary, Tobias Lear. It was his last gift to posterity. He died just after 10:00 P.M., a commissioned officer still technically on active duty.

19

FIRST IN WAR?

TWO MILITARY HISTORIANS, R. Ernest Dupuy and Trevor N. Dupuy, argued in 1970 that Washington "merits comparison" with leaders like Frederick the Great of Prussia, Napoleon, and Lord Nelson. In recent years the attitudes of military historians and Washington scholars have become more ambiguous. Many studies of the young Washington now portray him as a vain, obsessively ambitious fumbler who carefully concealed his errors and defeats, while others examine his youth for hints of future greatness. As Revolutionary War commander-in-chief he appears in many guises: charismatic hero, master of guerrilla warfare, incompetent or infallible battlefield commander, strategic genius, nationalist visionary, fanatical micromanager, and lucky dog—or beneficiary of British mistakes. There is some truth in all of these labels; but as historians are finding out, there is much more to Washington than can be conveyed in a few words.

So, what kind of a soldier—what kind of a man—was George Washington? It may be best to begin with what he was not.

He was not a great tactician. In his defeats at Fort Necessity, New York, Fort Washington, Brandywine, and Germantown he bungled badly. On some occasions, especially during the retreat across New Jersey in the autumn of 1776, he escaped destruction only by the grace of an overcautious enemy. He regularly neglected reconnaissance, overestimated his own troops, and underestimated the enemy. His planning could be careless, as at Monmouth, or overprecise, as at Germantown. In defending positions he often disposed his troops amateurishly, and in attack he could be dangerously rash. During battles he sometimes endangered his army by sending vague or contradictory orders to subordinates, losing contact with his officers and their units, misconceiving his enemy's intentions, and failing to maintain authority over his troops.

Even in victory Washington was less than perfect, and he often owed his successes to others. The credit for occupying Dorchester Heights and forcing Howe out of Boston in March 1776 belongs not to him but to his officers, who resisted his urge for a frontal attack on the British entrenchments. At Trenton in December 1776 he took a gamble that paid off. If the German commander had been competent it might have ended badly for the Americans. Washington followed that victory up with a brilliant performance in the Princeton campaign. But the performance was not repeated, at least in battle. At Monmouth in June 1778 he turned a defeat that would have been partly his fault into a draw. And at Yorktown in 1781 he could not have won without a series of coincidences with which he had nothing to do—most notably the appearance of de Grasse's French fleet, which Washington had wanted to sail to New York.

Much has been made of Washington's supposedly "Fabian" view of warfare. It has also been called a war of position, or of posts. He sought, it is said, to defeat the British by isolating them in their urban bastions and wearing them down until they tired of the war. This meant avoiding major battles and engaging only in supply interdiction and small-scale raids. But in practice, he scrapped policy and acted by instinct. From Jumonville's Glen to Yorktown, he could never resist a chance at fighting the decisive battle. At Trenton, Princeton, and Yorktown the urge paid off; but more often it did not. At Boston in the winter of 1775–76 his officers barely restrained him from a suicidal frontal attack; and on Long Island and at Fort Washington he left portions of his army exposed. At Brandywine, Germantown, and Monmouth he risked his army where nothing of vital importance was at stake. And in early 1781 he pursued a quixotic assault on New York until dragged away by his French allies. Any of these impulses might have ended in disaster, and some of them nearly did.

Washington was not a creative military thinker. He made no contributions to military theory, and fought largely by the book. That is not to say that he was unimaginative. On rare occasions he surprised his enemy with bold maneuvers. He made reasonably good use of militia troops against British supply lines, encouraged espionage, and conceived bold and sometimes wacky raids on enemy shipping and land installations. But although he pondered using militias on a larger scale, he never called them up *en masse,* or pursued a well-defined system of irregular warfare. He also was unwilling to use Indians or blacks in significant numbers, although he passively accepted their presence in his army from time to time.

Washington was not a professional soldier. Though well read in military history and theory, he had no practical training in handling troops in the field. This was a particular disadvantage in the eighteenth century, when good generalship depended on knowing how to maneuver efficiently in precise formation, both in and out of battle. Some of Washington's enemies criticized him for allowing his army to degenerate into a mob, and with good reason. But it was not all, or even mostly, his fault. His officers were amateurs, too. Some of them actively resisted regimentation as inconsistent with the American Way of Warfare, and others were simply incompetent. The enlisted Continentals were fractious and often intractable. Even a thoroughly professional commander would have had difficulty controlling them; and in the end it took the Prussian Steuben to turn them into regular soldiers.

Steuben was one of Washington's more capable general officers. The commander-in-chief's other assets included Nathanael Greene, Henry Knox, Lord Stirling, Lafayette, Colonel Daniel Morgan, and Captains Allen McLane and Henry Lee, Jr. On the whole, however, Washington was not well served by his subordinates. Men like Israel Putnam, John Sullivan, Anthony Wayne, Adam Stephen, and William Maxwell were mediocre commanders. Others, like Thomas Conway, Horatio Gates, and Charles Lee, were dangerous liabilities. Unlike Napoleon, Robert E. Lee, and Ulysses S. Grant, Washington had no Prince Eugene, Davout, Stonewall Jackson, James Longstreet, Phil Sheridan, or William T. Sherman to back him up. The closest he had was Nathanael Greene, who spent much of his time as quartermaster general or in command of armies elsewhere.

For all of their differences, Washington and his officers were profoundly loyal to one another. No commander, especially one who served as long as he did, can avoid making enemies. Yet Thomas Conway, Horatio Gates, and Charles Lee were exceptional. On most occasions Washington avoided public criticism of his subordinates even when they deserved censure. In the autumn of 1777, when he came under heavy scrutiny after enduring a series of defeats, it would have been easy for him to shift the blame to John Sullivan or Anthony Wayne, who were unpopular. But Washington did not do so, and consistently defended them against their civilian and military enemies even when their conduct was questionable.

His officers usually showed the same restraint. Those who did not and openly questioned his authority faced Washington's vindictiveness. He brooked no gossip or backbiting directed at him or anyone else. But he accepted respectful dissent in good part. In mid-June 1778, Charles Lee set down his opposition to some of the commander-in-chief's military decisions in a frank letter to headquarters. Washington disagreed with his arguments, but assured Lee that "I shall be always happy in a free communication of your Sentiments upon any important subject relative to the Service, & only beg that they may come directly to myself—the custom which many Officers have of speaking freely of things & reprobating measures which upon investigation may be found to be unavoidable is never productive of good, & often of very mischievous consequences."

On occasion, Washington's regard for his officers' judgment got him into trouble. Before battles or during periods of maneuver he liked to convene his council of war. This tendency—whether it arose from lack of confidence, democratic scruples, or fear of being blamed for defeat—flattered his officers but led some people to call him indecisive. Sometimes he deserved the label. In the autumn of 1776, rosy reports from Nathanael Greene convinced him to keep troops in Fort Washington against his own inclinations. In the summer of 1777, conflicting intelligence reports and councils of war led him astray when he would have done better to hunt the British fleet according to his own instincts. But there was an antidote to his indecision. On hearing gunfire and experiencing the adrenaline surge that came with it, Washington typically ceased equivocating and acted with aplomb. Poise in battle was one of his most obvious merits.

Washington's courage thrilled his men. But he was not an enlisted man's general. He did not interact personally with them, and would not let his officers do so either. Officers under his command who supped or slept in enlisted men's quarters were routinely punished. To Washington's mind, discipline and hierarchy were central to maintaining unit cohesion and integrity. "No warm, outgoing person," notes one historian, Washington "bound men to him by his own sense of justice and dedication." Yet how his troops viewed him, and in what ways their opinions may have changed over time, is uncertain. Although nineteenth-century history books and old soldiers' memoirs resonate with references to the commander-in-chief's inspirational presence, diaries and other accounts written in wartime rarely mention him.

Judging from their behavior in battle, it appears that the soldiers' attitudes toward Washington went through three phases. Before December 1776, it is probably safe to say that the majority of them neither liked nor trusted him. At Fort Necessity in 1754 and at Boston and New York in 1775–76, his hold on his men was often tenuous and sometimes, as at Kip's Bay, failed altogether. Attitudes improved after the victories at Trenton and Princeton, and his men learned to trust if not exactly like him. Yet only after the Valley Forge winter of 1777–78 were the Continentals ready to follow Washington anywhere. Monmouth was the first time his personal presence on the battlefield had a palpable impact on the course of a battle; and during the hard winters of 1779–80 and 1780–81 his influence was crucial in putting down dangerous mutinies. How had he earned their trust and admiration? To some extent it may have been that Steuben's training had taught the soldiers greater discipline and respect for authority. But probably the most critical factor was the sight of Washington spending his days and nights at Valley Forge, working for the benefit of his men while many of his officers went home.

That image is a good place to begin in assessing the qualities that made Washington great. He had tremendous dedication. No one in the army showed greater concern for the private soldier, not just at Valley Forge or Morristown, but every day of the war. No detail was too small for his attention if it affected the troops' comfort. The same dedication inspired his patriotism. In the war's darkest moments, when everything seemed lost, he never doubted the cause for which he fought. Washington's dedication to his country did not emerge from jingoism or hatred of the British, but from passionate belief in the ideals on which the new country had been founded. This ideological devotion fed his deep and enduring respect for civilian authority.

Yet Washington's dedication would have meant little had it not been for his strengths as an administrator and politician. These qualities were mutually supportive. In managing the day-to-day affairs of the army, Washington was indefatigable. He worked with almost superhuman stamina, organizational ability, and regard for detail. He was a micromanager in the best sense of the word. But he never allowed his work to isolate him. Washington understood that running an army efficiently depended not just on soldiers but civilians. That is where his ability as a politician becomes obvious. His relations with the national and state governments were almost wholly good. Among the many presidents of Congress, governors, and delegates, he counted few enemies and many close friends. They trusted him, and he them. As a result he could count on them to give him the supplies and other support he needed to keep his troops in the field. Probably no other man alive at the time could have done the same.

Washington was uncommonly, though not uniquely, brave. The sound of gunfire drew him like a magnet. This put him in positions where he could make quick decisions and encourage his troops. In some instances it also nearly got him killed. Fortunately, Washington's gift of courage coincided with remarkable luck. Legend says of Washington that after Braddock's defeat some Indians prophesied that bullets would never harm him. And his luck worked other ways, too. It is the key, for example, to what some have called his brilliance in retreat. Washington's withdrawals from places like Brooklyn Heights and Brandywine were prudent and well-conducted. But they were also incredibly lucky. Had it not been for Howe's inexplicable lethargy on these and other occasions, the Continental Army might have been defeated and destroyed many times over. No better example exists of the old maxim that to be good, a commander only has to be better than his opponent. That Washington was.

Yet perhaps Washington's most remarkable quality was his strategic, national, and continental vision. Don Higginbotham argues persuasively that Washington outpaced his contemporaries in seeing America not as a collection of disparate peoples forced together by interest and circumstances, but as a nation of free men and women with a collective destiny. This vision emerged from his travels on the frontier and his experience leading the "Continental" and heterogeneous American army, and manifested itself in a variety of ways. He fathomed the strategic implications of American settlements and topography, and had a sound sense of the importance of sea power and the potential for cooperation between army and navy. He also learned something of his country's place in the world, and if he later grew to fear the dangers of foreign entanglements, he also knew how important it was to have good friends in times of national crisis.

Washington was imperfect. In strictly military terms, he does not merit the comparisons that have sometimes been made between him and generals like Marlborough, Frederick the Great, Napoleon, or Robert E. Lee. Yet he remains a remarkable man, one of those Tolstoyan figures whose acts determine the course of history. James Thomas Flexner has called him "the indispensable man." Nobody—not Nathanael Greene or Henry Knox, and certainly not Thomas Jefferson, Benjamin Franklin, or John Adams—united the military, political, and personal skills that made Washington unique.

True, the country's future did not rest on him alone. He shared that burden with many others, from militia privates, tradesmen, and farmers to generals, diplomats, and statesmen. But without George Washington there could have been no victory in the Revolutionary War, no United States. As a soldier, he was erratic but competent. As a man he was impulsive, vindictive, brave, hardworking, intelligent, and virtuous. And as a leader, he was great. Those who mourned Washington's passing in 1799 were right to regard him, for all his flaws, as the savior of his country.

NOTES

Prologue

VII "The good opinion of honest men" GW to Edward Pemberton, June 20, 1788 (*Papers, Confederation Series*, 6:170).

VII "the death of its beloved Chief" *Pennsylvania Gazette* (Philadelphia), December 24, 1799.

VII "desirous that the Navy and Marines" Ibid.

VIII "Where shall I begin in opening to your view" Quoted in George Washington Parke Custis, *Recollections and Private Memoirs of Washington* (New York: Derby & Jackson, 1860), 615–23.

IX "the mournful cadence of the muffled drums" Gerald Edward Kahler, "Washington in Glory, America in Tears: The Nation Mourns the Death of George Washington, 1799–1800" (Ph.D. diss., College of William and Mary, 2003), 91.

IX "something charming" GW to John Augustine Washington, May 31, 1754 (*Papers, Colonial Series*, 1:118).

X "a series of judicious measures" John Marshall, *The Life of George Washington, Commander in Chief of the American Forces, during the War which Established the Independence of His Country, and First President of the United States* (5 vols., Philadelphia: C. P. Wayne, 1804–7), 5:774.

X "bland miracle-worker" Rupert Hughes, *George Washington: The Savior of the States* (New York: William Morrow, 1930), 693.

X "important scamp" John R. Alden, *George Washington: A Biography* (Baton Rouge: Louisiana State University Press, 1984), 1.

XI "cardinal characteristics" Douglas Southall Freeman, *George Washington: A Biography* (7 vols., New York: Charles Scribner's Sons, 1948–57), 5:488–90.

XI "unreconstructed civilian" James Thomas Flexner, *George Washington in the American Revolution (1775–1783)* (Boston: Little, Brown and Company, 1968), 533.

XI "military glory was *not* the source" Gordon Wood, "The Greatness of

George Washington," in Don Higginbotham, ed., *George Washington Reconsidered* (Charlottesville: University Press of Virginia, 2001), 313.

1. Young Frontiersman

The best source for information on Washington's early life remains Douglas Southall Freeman's monumental *George Washington: A Biography* (1948–57); see also Donald Jackson and Dorothy Twohig, eds., *The Diaries of George Washington* (6 vols., 1976–79; hereafter cited as *Diaries*) and W. W. Abbot and Dorothy Twohig, eds. *The Papers of George Washington, Colonial Series* (10 vols., 1983–95; hereafter cited as *Papers, Colonial Series*). Thomas A. Lewis's *For King and Country: The Maturing of George Washington, 1748–1760* (1993) somewhat overestimates the role ambition played in GW's character.

4   "Blacksmiths, Tailors, Barbers, Shoemakers"   quoted in Richard Harding, *Amphibious Warfare in the Eighteenth Century: The British Expedition to the West Indies, 1740–1742* (London: Boydell Press, 1991), 70.

6   "Our Regiment has not recd that treatment we expected"   Lawrence Washington to Augustine Washington, May 30, 1741 (New York Public Library).

8   "I might perhaps form some pleasures"   GW to John Washington, c.1749–50 (*Papers, Colonial Series*, 1:42).

8   "as straight as an Indian"   Quoted in Freeman, *George Washington*, 3:6.

8   "he never met any man"   David Humphreys, *David Humphreys' "Life of General Washington": with George Washington's "Remarks."* Edited by Rosemarie Zagarri (Athens: University of Georgia Press, 1991), 7.

9   "the graceful accomplishments"   Ibid.

10   "when called on for a sudden opinion"   Quoted in Frank E. Grizzard, Jr., *George Washington: A Biographical Companion* (Santa Barbara, California: ABC-CLIO, 2002), 81–82.

11   "his mental acquisitions"   Humphreys, *Life of General Washington*, 7.

11   "it was rather the wish of my eldest brother"   Ibid.

11   "I was ten times more afraid"   George Washington Parke Custis, *Recollections*, 131.

12   "be steady and thankfully follow your Advice"   William Fairfax to Lawrence Washington, September 9–10, 1746. Moncure D. Conway, *Barons of the Potomack and the Rappahannock* (New York: Grolier Club, 1892), 238.

12   "several trifling objections"   Robert Jackson to Lawrence Washington, September 18, 1746 (Washington Headquarters Library, Morristown, New Jersey).

12 "aprentice to a Tinker" Joseph Ball to Mary Washington, May 19, 1747 (Library of Congress: Joseph Ball Letterbook).

14 "A Journal of my Journey over the Mountains" For this and subsequent quotes from that source, Donald Jackson and Dorothy Twohig, eds., *The Diaries of George Washington* (Charlottesville: University Press of Virginia, 1976–79), 1:6–23.

15 "much mended since I saw you last" GW to Lawrence Washington, May 5, 1749 (*Papers, Colonial Series*, 1:6).

16 "clear & pleasant Weather" *Diaries*, 1:51.

16 "We soon tire of the same prospect" Jared Sparks, ed., *The Writings of George Washington: Being His Correspondence, Addresses, Messages, and Other Papers, Official and Private, Selected and Published from the Original Manuscripts.* (12 vols., Boston: John B. Russell, 1833–37), 2:422.

16 "the utmost confusion" GW to Robert Orme, April 2, 1755 (*Papers, Colonial Series*, 1:247).

17 "In case Colo. Fitzhugh does not" GW to Robert Dinwiddie, June 10, 1752 (*Papers, Colonial Series*, 1:50).

18 "both strongly recommended" William Nelson to GW, February 22, 1753 (*Papers, Colonial Series*, 1:55).

2. The Ohio

The sources for this chapter include volume 1 of *Papers, Colonial Series*; volume 1 of Washington's *Diaries*; *Christopher Gist's Journals with Historical, Geographical and Ethnological Notes and Biographies of His Contemporaries*, edited by William Darlington (1893); Hugh Cleland's *George Washington in the Ohio Valley* (1955); and Charles H. Ambler's *George Washington and the West* (1936).

20 "offered himself to go" H. R. McIlwaine, Wilmer L. Hall, and Benjamin Hillman, eds., *Executive Journals of the Council of Colonial Virginia* (6 vols., Richmond: Virginia State Library, 1925–66), 5:444–45.

20 "with all convenient & possible Dispatch" Commission from Robert Dinwiddie, October 30, 1753 (*Papers, Colonial Series*, 1:58).

20 "Sachems of the Six Nations" Instructions from Robert Dinwiddie, October 30, 1753 (*Papers, Colonial Series*, 1:60–61).

22 "extreamly well situated" *Diaries*, 1:132.

23 "majestic, easy current" Christopher Gist, *Christopher Gist's Journals with Historical, Geographical and Ethnological Notes and Biographies of His Contemporaries,* ed. William Darlington (Pittsburgh: J.R. Weldin, 1893), 99.

23 "Flies or Musquito's" *Diaries*, 1:137.

24 "by Order of your Brother" Ibid., 1:139.

24 "French Speech Belt" Ibid., 1:140.

24 "consented to stay" Ibid.

24 "A greater Number" Ibid., 1:142.

25 "The Wine" Ibid.

25 "great Perswasion" Ibid., 1:147.

25 "many Mires & Swamps" Ibid.

26 "much the air of a Soldier" Ibid., 1:148.

26 "extreamly complaisant" Ibid., 1:151.

26 "ploting every Scheme" Ibid.

26 "I can't say," he wrote Ibid., 1:152.

26 "Power of Liquor" Ibid.

27 "seeing the French overset" Christopher Gist, *Journal*, 83.

27 to guard against Joncaire's "Flattery" *Diaries*, 1:154.

27 "an Indian walking Dress" Ibid.

27 "I took my necessary Papers" Ibid., 1:155.

27 Gist . . . "unwilling" Christopher Gist, *Journal*, 84.

27 "That night," Gist wrote Ibid.

28 "Are you shot?" Ibid., 85.

28 "one poor Hatchet" *Diaries*, 1:155.

28 "expected every Moment" Ibid.

29 "stop'd one Day to . . . rest" Ibid., 1:158.

3. Fort Necessity

The best modern history of the French and Indian War and Washington's part in it is Fred Anderson's *Crucible of War: The Seven Years' War and the Fate of Empire in British North America, 1754–1766* (2000). Other sources for this chapter include volume 1 of *Papers, Colonial Series*; volume 1 of *Diaries*; David Humphreys' *"Life of General Washington": with George Washington's "Remarks,"* ed. Rosemarie Zagarri (1991); and a manuscript "autobiography" by Adam Stephen in the Library Company of Philadelphia: Rush Papers.

30 "notoriously known to be the Property" Quoted in *Diaries*, 1:127.

30 "As to the summons you send" Quoted in Ibid., 1:151.

31 "The command of the whole forces" GW to Richard Corbin, February– March 1754 (*Papers, Colonial Series*, 1:70).

31 "loose, Idle Persons" GW to Robert Dinwiddie, March 9, 1754 (*Papers, Colonial Series*, 1:73).

31 "selfwill'd" and "ungovernable" GW to Robert Dinwiddie, March 20, 1754 (*Papers, Colonial Series*, 1:78).

32 "It is the nature of Indians"   GW to Robert Dinwiddie, March 7, 1754 (*Papers, Colonial Series,* 1:72).

32 "You have not Time to get them made"   Robert Dinwiddie to GW, March 15, 1754 (*Papers, Colonial Series,* 1:75).

33 "Connotaucarious"   GW to Robert Dinwiddie, April 25, 1754 (*Papers, Colonial Series,* 1:88).

33 "raise a Fortification"   *Diaries,* 1:180.

33 "this interesting cause"   GW to Horatio Sharpe, April 24, 1754 (*Papers, Colonial Series,* 1:86).

34 "Upon the whole"   GW to Robert Dinwiddie, May 18, 1754 (*Papers, Colonial Series,* 1:99–100).

34 "ill timed Complaints"   Robert Dinwiddie to GW, May 25, 1754 (*Papers, Colonial Series,* 1:102–3).

35 "an acct of a french armey"   GW to Robert Dinwiddie, May 27, 1754 (*Papers, Colonial Series,* 1:105).

35 "made a good Intrenchment"   Ibid.

35 "every Thing in the House"   *Diaries,* 1:193.

35 Captain Hog "in pursuit"   GW to Robert Dinwiddie, May 27, 1754 (*Papers, Colonial Series,* 1:105).

35 "act on the Difensive"   Robert Dinwiddie to GW, January 1754 (*Papers, Colonial Series,* 1:65).

36 "its desired Effect"   *Diaries,* 1:194.

36 "low obscure Place"   Ibid., 1:195.

36 "that very Moment"   Ibid.

37 "a Night as dark as Pitch"   Ibid.

37 "fall on them together"   Ibid.

38 "servd to knock the poor unhappy wounded"   GW to Robert Dinwiddie, June 3, 1754 (*Papers, Colonial Series,* 1:124).

38 "sculking place"   This and subsequent quotes in this paragraph: GW to Robert Dinwiddie, May 29, 1754 (*Papers, Colonial Series,* 1:110–11); *Diaries,* 1:198.

38 "we had but 40 Men"   GW to Robert Dinwiddie, June 3, 1754 (*Papers, Colonial Series,* 1:124).

39 "I fortunately escaped without a wound"   GW to John Augustine Washington, May 31, 1754 (*Papers, Colonial Series,* 1:118).

39 "He would not say so"   Horace Walpole, *Memoirs of the Reign of King George the Second* (3 vols., London: H. Colburn, 1847), 1:400.

39 "I shall expect every hour"   GW to Robert Dinwiddie, May 29, 1754 (*Papers, Colonial Series,* 1:112).

39 "with all imaginable dispatch"   Ibid.

39 "many smooth Story's"   GW to Robert Dinwiddie, May 29, 1754 (*Papers, Colonial Series,* 1:116).

39   "a small palisadod Fort"   GW to Robert Dinwiddie, June 3, 1754 (*Papers, Colonial Series*, 1:124).

40   "highly pleasing" defeat of the French   Robert Dinwiddie to GW, June 2, 1754 (*Papers, Colonial Series*, 1:121).

41   "treacherous Devils"   *Diaries*, 1:207.

42   "Point of Woods"   Account by George Washington and James Mackay of the Capitulation of Fort Necessity, July 19, 1754 (*Papers, Colonial Series*, 1:159).

43   charged . . . with a "great Cry"   *A Memorial Containing a Summary View of Facts, with Their Authorities. In Answer to the Observations Sent by the English Ministry to the Courts of Europe.* Trans. from the French (New York: H. Gaine, 1757), 99–100.

43   "from every little rising"   Humphreys, *Life of General Washington*, 12–13.

43   "the most tremendous rain"   Ibid., 13.

43   "a few . . . Bayonets"   Ibid.

43   "even to the very Dogs"   Account by George Washington and James Mackay of the Capitulation of Fort Necessity, July 19, 1754 (*Papers, Colonial Series*, 1:160).

44   to treat the Americans and British as "friends"   *A Memorial Containing a Summary View of Facts*, 100–101.

44   "venger L'assasin"   Articles of Capitulation, July 3, 1754 (*Papers, Colonial Series*, 1:165–66).

45   "kicked the fellows back side"   Adam Stephen Autobiography, Library Company of Philadelphia: Rush Papers.

46   "There is nothing more unworthy"   Quoted in *Diaries*, 1:172.

48   "I have the consolation itself"   GW to William Fitzhugh, November 15, 1754 (*Papers, Colonial Series*, 1:226).

4. Braddock

Sources for this chapter include Fred Anderson's *Crucible of War;* volume 1 of *Papers, Colonial Series;* Winthrop Sargent's *The History of an Expedition against Fort Du Quesne, in 1755* (1855); *Military Affairs in North America 1748–1765: Selected Documents from the Cumberland Papers in Windsor Castle,* ed. Stanley Pargellis; Paul E. Kopperman's *Braddock at the Monongahela* (1977); *Braddock's Defeat,* ed. Charles Hamilton (1959); and Paul K. Longmore's wonderful book, *The Invention of George Washington* (1988).

49   "small Engagement, conducted with Judgment"   R. A. Brock, ed. *The Official Records of Robert Dinwiddie, Lieutenant-Governor of the Colony of Virginia, 1751–1758, Now First Printed from the manuscript in the Collections of the Virginia Historical Society* (2 vols., Richmond: Virginia Historical Society, 1883–84), 1:242.

50 "a very Iroquois in disposition" Walpole, *Memoirs,* 3:337.

51 "be very glad of your Company": Robert Orme to GW, March 2, 1755 (*Papers, Colonial Series,* 1:241).

51 "I am thereby freed from all command" GW to John Augustine Washington, May 14, 1755 (*Papers, Colonial Series,* 1:278).

51 "I wish for nothing more earnestly" GW to Robert Orme, March 15, 1755 (*Papers, Colonial Series,* 1:243).

51 "a good oppertunity" GW to John Augustine Washington, May 14, 1755 (*Papers, Colonial Series,* 1:278).

51 "my attending your Fortunes" GW to Robert Orme, April 2, 1755 (*Papers, Colonial Series,* 1:246).

52 "a man, whose good & bad qualities" Humphreys, *Life of General Washington,* 19.

52 "that instead of marching to the Ohio" Winthrop Sargent, *The History of an Expedition Against Fort Du Quesne, in 1755* (Philadelphia: Lippincott, Grambo & Co., 1855), 159.

53 "Our march must be regulated" GW to William Fairfax, April 23, 1755 (*Papers, Colonial Series,* 1:258).

53 "retard me considerably" Stanley Pargellis, ed. *Military Affairs in North America 1748–1765: Selected Documents from the Cumberland Papers in Windsor Castle* (Hamden, Connecticut: Archon Books, 1969; reprint of 1936 edition), 82.

53 what . . . "cou'd induce People ever to think" Ibid., 62.

53 "languid, spiritless, and unsoldierlike" Sargent, *The History of an Expedition,* 312.

53 Braddock made "use of every argument" Ibid., 309.

53 "behaved as kindly to them" Quoted in Paul E. Kopperman, *Braddock at the Monongahela* (Pittsburgh: University of Pittsburgh Press, 1977), 101.

54 "I shall spend my time" GW to Augustine Washington, May 14, 1755 (*Papers, Colonial Series,* 1:272).

54 French opposition would be "trifling" GW to John Augustine Washington, May 14, 1755 (*Papers, Colonial Series,* 1:277).

54 "we shall not take possession" GW to John Carlyle, June 7, 1755 (*Papers, Colonial Series,* 1:306).

54 over trails of "perpendicular rock" Sargent, *The History of an Expedition,* 323.

55 Feeling "infinite delight" This and subsequent quotes in this paragraph: GW to John Augustine Washington, June 28–July 2, 1755 (*Papers, Colonial Series,* 1:319–22).

55 "many threats and bravados" Sargent, *The History of an Expedition,* 341.

59 "by one common consent"   Ibid., 356.

59 "The shocking scenes which presented themselves"   Humphreys, *Life of General Washington,* 18.

60 "The dastardly behaviour of those they call regular's"   GW to Mary Ball Washington, July 18, 1755 (*Papers, Colonial Series,* 1:336).

60 "the wild Bears of the Mountains"   GW to Robert Dinwiddie, July 18, 1755 (ibid., 1:339–40).

60 "my dear Blue's"   John A. Schutz, ed. "A Private Report of General Braddock's Defeat" (*Pennsylvania Magazine of History and Biography,* 79 [1955], 376–77).

62 "that heroic Youth"   Quoted in Paul K. Longmore, *The Invention of George Washington* (Charlottesville: University Press of Virginia, 1999; reprint of 1988 edition), 30.

62 "Heroick Virtue"   William Fairfax to GW, July 26, 1755 (*Papers, Colonial Series,* 1:345).

62 "gallant Behavior"   Robert Dinwiddie to GW, July 26, 1755 (ibid., 1:344).

62 "thought he deserved every thing"   Philip Ludwell to GW, August 8, 1755 (ibid., 1:356).

62 "the People in these Parts"   Charles Lewis to GW, August 9, 1755 (ibid., 1:358).

5. The Virginia Regiment

Sources for this chapter include volumes 1–6 of *Papers, Colonial Series; Writings of General John Forbes Relating to His Service in North America* (1971); Fred Anderson's *Crucible of War;* and Paul Longmore's *The Invention of George Washington.*

63 "I am so little dispirited"   GW to Augustine Washington, August 2, 1755 (*Papers, Colonial Series,* 1:352).

63 "Honoured Madam"   GW to Mary Ball Washington, August 14, 1755 (ibid., 1:359).

63 "small Military Chest"   GW to Warner Lewis, August 14, 1755 (ibid., 1:362).

64 "Remember" . . . "that it is the actions"   GW, Address, January 8, 1756 (ibid., 2:257).

64 "if it shou'd be said"   GW to Robert Dinwiddie, March 10, 1757 (ibid., 4:113).

65 "to blow out my brains"   GW to Robert Dinwiddie, October 11, 1755 (ibid., 2:102).

65 "Chimney Corner Politicians" GW to John Campbell, Earl of Loudoun, January 10, 1757 (ibid., 4:83).

66 "Dogworthy" Adam Stephen to GW, October 4, 1755 (ibid., 2:72).

66 "never submit to the command" GW to Robert Dinwiddie, December 5, 1755 (ibid., 2:200).

66 "determined to resign a Commission" GW to Robert Dinwiddie, January 14, 1756 (ibid., 2:284).

68 "My Constitution I believe" GW to John Stanwix, March 4, 1758 (ibid., 5:102).

68 "I am much concern'd to hear" John Stanwix to GW, March 10, 1758 (ibid., 5:104).

68 "now in a fair way of regaining my health" GW to Richard Washington, March 18, 1758 (ibid., 5:106).

69 "motley herd" This and the following quote: GW to John Stanwix, April 10, 1758 (ibid., 5:117).

70 "a good and knowing Officer" John Forbes to John Blair, March 20, 1758 (quoted in ibid., 5:139).

70 "to assure you, that to merit" GW to John Forbes, April 23, 1758 (ibid., 5:138).

70 "a fine body of men" quoted in Freeman, *George Washington*, 2:309.

70 "the only Troops fit to Cope" GW to John Forbes, June 19, 1758 (*Papers, Colonial Series*, 5:224).

71 "altho' I advance but gradually" John Forbes, *Writings of General John Forbes Relating to His Service in North America* (New York: Arno Press, 1971), 117–18.

71 "seemd to forebode our manifest Ruin" GW to Francis Fauquier, August 5, 1758 (*Papers, Colonial Series*, 5:370).

71 "Making it over such monstrous Mountains" This and the following quote: GW to Henry Bouquet, August 2, 1758 (ibid., 5:354).

72 "If Colo. Bouquet succeeds" GW to Francis Halkett, August 2, 1758 (ibid., 5:361).

72 "unguarded" . . . "I am now at the bottom" Forbes, *Writings*, 171.

72 "very roundly know" Ibid., 173.

72 "all is lost" GW to John Robinson, September 1, 1758 (ibid., 5:432–33).

72 Forbes's "fatal Resolution" GW to Francis Fauquier, August 5, 1758 (*Papers, Colonial Series*, 5:370).

73 "rather than receive any Orders" Sylvester K. Stevens and Donald H. Kent, eds. *The Papers of Henry Bouquet* (25 vols., Harrisburg: Pennsylvania Historical Commission, 1940–43), 2:434–35.

74 "Had it not been for the Virginians" quoted in Freeman, *George Washington*, 2:349.

74   Grant's "rash attempt"   This and the quotes in this and the following paragraph: Forbes, *Writings*, 215, 218–19.

75   "imminent danger by being between two fires"   Humphreys, *Life of General Washington*, 22.

75   "gave rise to a resentment"   Thomas W. Bullitt, *My Life at Oxmoor: Life on a Farm in Kentucky Before the War* (Louisville, Ky.: John P. Morton, 1911), 3–4.

76   "General Braddocks road"   GW to John Forbes, November 16, 1758 (*Papers, Colonial Series*, 6:131).

76   "great merit"   GW to Francis Fauquier, November 28, 1758 (ibid., 6:159–60).

77   "disagreeable News"   Address from the Officers of the Virginia Regiment, December 31, 1758 (ibid., 6:178–81).

77   "your approbation of my conduct"   GW to the Officers of the Virginia Regiment, January 10, 1759 (ibid., 6:186).

78   "Do not forget," Washington exhorted   GW, Address, January 8, 1756 (ibid., 2:257).

6. Call to Arms

The best work on Washington's political consciousness and career in the years leading up to the Revolutionary War is Paul Longmore's *The Invention of George Washington*; see also Freeman's *George Washington*; volumes 6–10 of *Papers, Colonial Series*; and volume 1 of *Papers, Revolutionary War Series*. An excellent source for political and military letters and documents of the period is Paul H. Smith, et al., eds., *Letters of Delegates to Congress, 1774–1789* (1976–98). Don Higginbotham's *The War of American Independence: Military Attitudes, Policies, and Practice, 1763–1789* (1971) and *George Washington and the American Military Tradition* (1995) provide good background on the American side of the war; Piers Mackesy's *The War for America: 1775–1783* (1964) and Robert Harvey's *A Few Bloody Noses: The American War of Independence* (2001) do equally well for the British side.

81   Stamp Act . . . "ill judgd"   GW to Francis Dandridge, September 20, 1765 (*Papers, Colonial Series*, 7:395).

82   "our lordly Masters in Great Britain"   This and subsequent quotes in the next paragraph: GW to George Mason, April 5, 1769 (ibid., 8:178).

82   "Tyrannical System"   GW to Bryan Fairfax, July 20, 1774 (ibid., 10:129).

84   "farthest of anything"   Tench Tilghman, *Memoir of Lieut. Col. Tench Tilghman, Secretary and Aid to Washington, Together with an Appendix, Contain-*

ing Revolutionary Journals and Letters, Hitherto Unpublished (New York: Arno Press, 1971; reprint of 1876 edition), 167.

84 "use every Means"   This and subsequent quotes in this paragraph: Fairfax County Resolves, July 18, 1774 (*Papers, Colonial Series,* 10:119–28).

85 "boys, who are still quite small"   Henry Melchior Muhlenberg, *The Journals of Henry Melchior Muhlenberg.* Trans. and edited by Theodore G. Tappert and John W. Doberstein (3 vols., Philadelphia: Muhlenberg Press, 1942–58), 2:701.

85 "Firing at Marks"   Paul H. Smith, et al., eds., *Letters of Delegates to Congress, 1774–1789* (25 vols., Washington, D.C.: Library of Congress, 1976–98), 1:437.

85 North's "despotick Measures"   GW to George William Fairfax, June 10–15, 1774 (*Papers, Colonial Series,* 10:96).

85 "He seems discret & Virtuous"   Smith, *Letters of Delegates,* 1:499–500.

87 "So far from seeking this appointment"   GW to Martha Washington, June 18, 1775 (*Papers, Revolutionary War Series,* 1:3).

87 "take Advantage of our delays"   L. H. Butterfield, et al., eds., *Diary and Autobiography of John Adams* (4 vols., Cambridge, Massachusetts: Harvard University Press, 1961), 3:322–23.

88 a little bit "too modest"   Smith, *Letters of Delegates,* 1:499.

88 "I am truly sensible"   GW, Address to the Continental Congress, June 16, 1775 (*Papers, Revolutionary War Series,* 1:1).

88 "that he was unequal to the station"   Benjamin Rush, *The Autobiography of Benjamin Rush: His "Travels Through Life" Together with His Commonplace Book for 1789–1813,* edited by George W. Corner (Princeton: Princeton University Press, 1948), 113.

88 "from a consciousness"   GW to Martha Washington, June 18, 1775 (*Papers, Revolutionary War Series,* 1:3).

89 "Unhappy it is"   GW to George William Fairfax, May 31, 1775 (*Papers, Colonial Series,* 10:368).

89 "political motives"   GW to Burwell Bassett, June 19, 1775 (*Papers, Revolutionary War Series,* 1:13).

90 "May God grant"   Ibid.

90 "exposing my Character"   GW to Martha Washington, June 18, 1775 (ibid., 1:4).

90 "As it has been a kind of destiny"   Ibid.

90 "I can answer but for three things"   GW to Burwell Bassett, June 19, 1775 (ibid., 1:13).

90 "have the consolation of knowing"   GW to John Augustine Washington, June 20, 1775 (ibid., 1:19).

91 "Cash paid a beggar" Account for August 10, 1777 in GW's household account book, April 11, 1776–November 21, 1780 (Library of Congress: George Washington Papers, series 5, vol. 28).

91 "I am now to bid adieu" GW to John Augustine Washington, June 20, 1775 (*Papers, Revolutionary War Series,* 1:19).

91 "return safe to you in the fall" GW to Martha Washington, June 18, 1775 (ibid., 1:4).

93 "the Troops of the United Provinces" General Orders, July 4, 1775 (ibid., 1:54).

95 "take every method in your power" This and subsequent quotes in this and following paragraph: Instructions from the Continental Congress, June 22, 1775 (ibid., 1:21–22).

95 "To compel them to remain there" GW to Samuel Washington, July 20, 1775 (ibid., 1:136).

100 "a cowardly and cruel manner" Quoted in Jeremy Black, *War for America: The Fight for Independence, 1775–1783* (New York: St. Martin's Press, 1991), 64.

101 "the re establishment of Peace & Harmony" GW, Address to the New York Provincial Congress, June 26, 1775 (*Papers, Revolutionary War Series,* 1:41).

7. Boston

This chapter is based largely on volumes 1–3 of Papers, *Revolutionary War Series;* other primary source material comes from Richard K. Showman et al., eds., *The Papers of General Nathanael Greene* (1976–); *Archibald Robertson, Lieutenant General Royal Engineers: His Diaries and Sketches in America, 1762–1780,* ed. Harry Miller Lydenberg (1930); William Heath's *Memoirs of the American War* (1798); and the priceless *Documents of the American Revolution, 1770–1783* (*Colonial Office Series*), ed. K.G. Davies. Christopher Ward's beautifully written but outdated *The War of the Revolution* (1952) remains one of the best military histories of the war and provides a good outline of the Boston campaign.

102 "the Commander in Chief of the American armies" This quote and the following paragraph: Rush, *Autobiography,* 112–13.

102 "I shall feel no pain" GW to Martha Washington, June 18, 1775 (*Papers, Revolutionary War Series,* 1:4).

103 "I go fully trusting" GW to Martha Washington, June 23, 1775 (ibid., 1:27).

103 "poor creature, worn out" L. H. Butterfield, et al., eds., *Adams Family Correspondence* (6 vols. to date, Cambridge, Massachusetts: Harvard University Press, 1963–), 1:226.

103 "the repeated shouts and huzzas" Thomas Jones, *History of New York During the Revolutionary War, and of the Leading Events in the Other Colonies at That Period,* ed. Edward F. DeLancey (2 vols., New York: New-York Historical Society, 1879), 1:55.

105 "Joy was visible on every countenance" Richard K. Showman et al., eds., *The Papers of General Nathanael Greene* (11 vols. to date, Chapel Hill: University of North Carolina Press, 1976–), 1:99.

106 "nothing remarkable" Charles Martyn, *The Life of Artemas Ward: The First Commander-in-Chief of the American Revolution* (New York: Artemas Ward, 1921), 153.

106 "the Youth in the Army" Address from the Massachusetts Provincial Congress, July 3, 1775 (*Papers, Revolutionary War Series,* 1:53).

106 "curiously wrought with doors and windows" Allen French, *The First Year of the American Revolution* (New York: Houghton Mifflin, 1934), 300.

106 "a numerous army of Provencials" GW to Samuel Washington, July 20, 1775 (*Papers, Revolutionary War Series,* 1:135).

106 "very equivocal" Joseph Hawley to GW, July 5, 1775 (ibid., 1:65).

106 "It requires no military Skill" GW to John Hancock, July 10–11, 1775 (ibid., 1:90–91).

107 "Be strict in your discipline" GW to William Woodford, November 10, 1775 (ibid., 2:346–47).

107 "bauble" . . . "spew" Charles Lee, *The Lee Papers* (4 vols., *Collections of the New-York Historical Society,* vols. 4–7. New York: New-York Historical Society, 1872–75), 1:207.

107 "Disobedience of orders" General Orders, August 25, 1775 (*Papers, Revolutionary War Series,* 1:360).

107 "Smiles" . . . "kind of stupidity" GW to Richard Henry Lee, August 29, 1775 (ibid., 1:372).

108 "it is unmanly" General Orders, July 5, 1775 (ibid., 1:63).

108 "profane cursing" General Orders, July 4, 1775 (ibid., 1:55).

108 "Toss-up, pitch & hustle" General Orders, October 3, 1775 (ibid., 2:81).

108 "running about naked" General Orders, August 22, 1775 (ibid., 1:346).

108 "utmost severity" General Orders, July 15, 1775 (ibid., 1:119).

108 "strictly required and commanded" General Orders, July 4, 1775 (ibid., 1:55).

108 "one continued round" GW to Richard Henry Lee, August 29, 1775 (ibid., 1:375).

108 "an exceeding dirty & nasty people" GW to Lund Washington, August 20, 1775 (ibid., 1:336).

109 "speedy and exact" General Orders, July 5, 1775 (ibid., 1:63).

109 "all the Provisions" General Orders, July 4, 1775 (ibid., 1:54).

109 "not being sufficiently acquainted"   GW to John Hancock, August 4–5, 1775 (ibid., 1:227).

109 "threatning means"   GW to Richard Henry Lee, July 10, 1775 (ibid., 1:98).

110 "The Cause"   This and the following quotes in this sentence: GW to Nicholas Cooke, August 4, 1775 (ibid., 1:221); GW to John Hancock, August 4–5, 1775 (ibid., 1:227); GW to the New Hampshire Committee of Safety, August 4, 1775 (ibid., 1:242).

110 "peremptory requisition"   Jonathan Trumbull, Jr., to GW, September 15, 1775 (ibid., 1:468).

111 "Under the Generals"   Showman, *Greene Papers,* 1:99.

112 "exceeding dangerous" nature   GW to Richard Henry Lee, July 10, 1775 (*Papers, Revolutionary War Series,* 1:99).

112 "The publick Service"   Council of War, July 9, 1775 (ibid., 1:80).

113 "go and do as they pleased"   Samuel Bixby, "Diary of Samuel Bixby," (*Proceedings of the Massachusetts Historical Society,* 1st series, 14 [1875–76]), 291.

113 "general Action"   GW to John Augustine Washington, September 10, 1775 (*Papers, Revolutionary War Series,* 1:447).

113 "An Expedition"   GW to Philip Schuyler, August 20, 1775 (ibid., 1:332).

113 "not to plunder, but to protect"   GW, Address to the Inhabitants of Canada, c. September 14, 1775 (ibid., 1:462).

114 "The inactive state"   GW to John Augustine Washington, September 10, 1775 (ibid., 1:447).

114 "the Country to desolation"   GW, Circular to the General Officers, September 8, 1775 (ibid., 1:433).

114 "These things are not unknown"   Ibid.

115 "Bombarding, & Firing the Town"   Council of War, November 2, 1775 (ibid., 2:282).

116 "the Town must of Consequence"   Proceedings of the Committee of Conference, October 18–24, 1775 (ibid., 2:186).

116 "if General Washington"   Worthington Chauncey Ford et al., eds., *Journals of the Continental Congress* (34 vols., Washington, D.C.: Government Printing Office, 1904–37), 3:344–45.

116 "destroy the little subordination"   GW to Joseph Reed, November 28, 1775 (*Papers, Revolutionary War Series,* 2:449).

116 "not only fix eternal disgrace"   General Orders, December 28, 1775 (ibid., 2:614).

116 "dirty, mercenary Spirit"   GW to Joseph Reed, November 28, 1775 (ibid., 2:449).

117 "Such a dearth of Publick Spirit"   Ibid.

117 "the vast volumes of history"   GW to Joseph Reed, January 4, 1776 (ibid., 3:24).

117 "I have often thought" GW to Joseph Reed, January 14, 1776 (ibid., 3:89).

118 "obliged to use art" GW to Joseph Reed, February 10, 1776 (ibid., 3:287).

118 "All the Generals upon Earth" GW to Joseph Reed, January 14, 1776 (ibid., 3:90).

118 "indispensable necessity" Council of War, January 16, 1776 (ibid., 3:103).

119 "A Bombardment might probably" This and following quotes: Council of War, February 16, 1776 (ibid., 3:321).

119 "glad to see the attempt made" Showman, *Greene Papers*, 1:194.

119 "Perhaps a greater Question" This and following quotes: Council of War, February 16, 1776 (*Papers, Revolutionary War Series*, 3:322–24).

120 "golden opportunity" to attack GW to Jonathan Trumbull, Sr., February 19, 1776 (ibid., 3:345).

120 "Perhaps the irksomeness" GW to Joseph Reed, February 26–March 9, 1776 (ibid., 3:370).

121 "ready waterd & their Sails bent" GW to Charles Lee, February 26, 1776 (ibid., 3:367).

121 "the Eyes of the whole Continent" GW to John Hancock, February 18–21, 1776 (ibid., 3:336).

121 "I am determined" GW to Philip Schuyler, February 27, 1776 (ibid., 3:383–84).

121 "be so kind as to come out" GW to Joseph Reed, February 26–March 9, 1776 (ibid., 3:370).

122 "to throw, without delay" GW to Jonathan Trumbull, Sr., February 19, 1776 (ibid., 3:346).

122 "small parcells" GW to John Hancock, February 26, 1776 (ibid., 3:365).

123 "for fractured limbs" James Thacher, *Military Journal of the American Revolution, from the Commencement to the Disbanding of the American Army: Comprising a Detailed Account of the Principal Events and Battles of the Revolution, with Their Exact Dates, and a Biographical Sketch of the most Prominent Generals* (Hartford, Connecticut: Hurlbut, Williams, & Co., 1862), 37.

123 "without hurting any Body" Archibald Robertson, *Archibald Robertson, Lieutenant General Royal Engineers: His Diaries and Sketches in America, 1762–1780,* ed. Harry Miller Lydenberg (New York: New York Public Library, 1930), 73.

123 "two for one" Quoted in *Papers, Revolutionary War Series*, 3:404.

123 "the Moon shining" GW to Joseph Reed, February 26–March 9, 1776 (ibid., 3:373).

124 "incessant roar" William Heath, *Heath's Memoirs of the American War,* ed. Rufus Rockwell Wilson (New York: A. Wessels Company, 1904; reprint of 1978 edition), 49.

124 "answerd our expectation"   GW to Joseph Reed, February 26–March 9, 1776 (*Papers, Revolutionary War Series*, 3:373).

124 "Perhaps there never was"   Heath, *Memoirs*, 49.

124 "The Materials for the whole Works"   Robertson, *Diaries*, 73–74.

124 "the rebels have done more in one night"   William Gordon, *The History of the Rise, Progress, and Establishment, of the Independence of the United States of America: Including an Account of the Late War; and of the Thirteen Colonies, from Their Origin to That Period* (4 vols., London: Charles Dilly and James Buckland, 1788), 2:193.

124 "great activity and Industry"   GW to John Hancock, March 7–9, 1776 (*Papers, Revolutionary War Series*, 3:420).

125 "a day never to be forgotten"   GW to Joseph Reed, February 26–March 9, 1776 (ibid., 3:374).

125 "In a situation so critical"   K. G. Davies, ed., *Documents of the American Revolution, 1770–1783 (Colonial Office Series)* (21 vols., Shannon, Ireland: Irish University Press, 1972–81), 12:81–84.

125 "the most serious step"   Robertson, *Diaries*, 74.

125 "But" . . . "kind Heaven"   Heath, *Memoirs*, 50.

125 "agreed immediately to Embark"   Robertson, *Diaries*, 74.

125 "the utmost precipitation"   GW to John Hancock, March 7–9, 1776 (*Papers, Revolutionary War Series*, 3:424).

125 "Intire destruction"   Boston Selectmen to GW, March 8, 1776 (ibid., 3:434).

125 "shameful retreat"   GW to Jonathan Trumbull, Sr., March 14, 1776 (ibid., 3:471).

126 "Images dressed in the Soldiers Habit"   Quoted in Christopher Ward, *The War of the Revolution*, ed. John Richard Alden (2 vols., New York: Macmillan, 1952), 1:132.

126 "hidden treasures"   Quoted in *Papers, Revolutionary War Series*, 3:482.

126 "joy inexpressible"   Heath, *Memoirs*, 52.

126 "Genl Gages chariot"   Inventory of British Stores left in Boston, March 20, 1776 (*Papers, Revolutionary War Series*, 3:525).

126 "made with so little Effusion"   Address from the Boston Selectmen, March 1776, (ibid., 3:571).

126 "scarce forbear lamenting"   GW to Landon Carter, March 27, 1776 (ibid., 3:545).

126 "an Event which will render"   George Mason to GW, April 2, 1776 (ibid., 4:17).

127 "This Success of our Arms"   John Hancock to GW, March 25, 1776 (ibid., 3:533).

127 "To obtain the applause"   GW to Josiah Quincy, March 24, 1776 (ibid., 3:528–29).

8. New York

Primary sources for this chapter include volumes 4–6 of *Papers, Revolutionary War Series*; Bruce E. Burgoyne, ed., *Enemy Views: The American Revolutionary War as Recorded by the Hessian Participants* (1996); Edward H. Tatum, Jr., ed., *The American Journal of Ambrose Serle, Secretary to Lord Howe, 1776–1778* (1940); and Joseph Plumb Martin's *Private Yankee Doodle: Being a Narrative of Some of the Adventures, Dangers and Sufferings of a Revolutionary Soldier* (1962). The best secondary accounts of the Revolution in New York include Barnet Schecter's *The Battle for New York: The City at the Heart of the American Revolution* (2002); Eric I. Manders's *The Battle of Long Island* (1978); and Richard Ketchum's *Divided Loyalties: How the American Revolution Came to New York* (2002). See also Thomas Jones's *History of New York During the Revolutionary War, and of the Leading Events in the Other Colonies at That Period* (1879).

128 "the total stagnation of business"   quoted in Freeman, *George Washington*, 4:78.

129 "Should they get that town"   GW to Lord Stirling, March 14, 1776 (*Papers, Revolutionary War Series*, 3:470).

129 "of the last importance to us"   GW to Jonathan Trumbull, Sr., June 10, 1776 (ibid., 4:496).

129 "What to do with the City"   Charles Lee to GW, February 19, 1776 (ibid., 3:340).

131 "almost impossible," Lee believed   Ibid.

131 "I am much pleas'd"   GW to Charles Lee, March 14, 1776 (ibid., 3:468).

132 "Several of them ware handeld"   Henry B. Dawson, ed., *New York City During the American Revolution: Being a Collection of Original Papers (Now First Published) from the Manuscripts in the Possession of the Mercantile Library Association, of New York City* (New York: Mercantile Library Association of the City of New-York, 1861), 97.

132 "as deep as Hell"   King's District Committee of Correspondence to GW, May 13, 1776 (*Papers, Revolutionary War Series*, 4:290).

132 "it would have been happy"   GW to Joseph Reed, April 1, 1776 (ibid., 4:11).

133 "snapping their pieces"   General Orders, May 21, 1776 (ibid., 4:349).

133 "the most shocking situation"   General Orders, May 19, 1776 (ibid., 4:339).

133 "The clothing of the enemy is bad"   Bruce E. Burgoyne, ed., *Enemy Views: The American Revolutionary War as Recorded by the Hessian Participants* (Bowie, Maryland: Heritage Books, 1996), 71–72.

133 "We expect a very bloody Summer"   GW to John Augustine Washington, May 31–June 4, 1776 (*Papers, Revolutionary War Series*, 4:413).

133 "every possible dispatch"   General Orders, April 16, 1776 (ibid., 4:73).

133 abandoned the project as "useless"   GW to Israel Putnam, May 21, 1776 (ibid., 4:355).

135 "fell into great Confusion"   Robertson, *Diaries*, 86.

136 "The General hopes this important Event"   General Orders, July 9, 1776 (*Papers, Revolutionary War Series*, 5:246).

136 "In Congress, July 4, 1776"   Ford, *Journals of the Continental Congress*, 5:510–15.

136 "seemed to have . . . hearty assent"   GW to John Hancock, July 10, 1776 (*Papers, Revolutionary War Series*, 5:258).

136 "It is certain that It is not"   Ibid.

137 "will have to wade through much blood"   GW to John Hancock, July 10, 1776 (ibid., 5:260).

137 "A finer Scene"   Edward H. Tatum, Jr., ed., *The American Journal of Ambrose Serle, Secretary to Lord Howe, 1776–1778* (San Marino, California: Huntington Library, 1940), 30.

137 "proves to me beyond doubt"   Henry Knox to Lucy Knox, July 15, 1776 (Massachusetts Historical Society, Boston).

138 "I have a letter sir from Lord Howe"   Ibid.

138 "Genl Washington &ca &ca"   William Howe to GW, August 1, 1776 (*Papers, Revolutionary War Series*, 5:538).

139 "left behind burned-out houses"   Burgoyne, *Enemy Views*, 69–70.

139 "Remember" . . . "that you are Freemen"   General Orders, August 23, 1776 (*Papers, Revolutionary War Series*, 6:109–10).

140 "disagreable Ideas" his men   GW to John Hancock, August 13, 1775 (ibid., 6:5).

140 "The most of the Troops"   Showman, *Greene Papers*, 1:287.

140 "raging Fever"   Ibid., 1:288.

140 "The brave old man"   William Bradford Reed, *Life and Correspondence of Joseph Reed* (2 vols., Philadelphia: Lindsay and Blakiston, 1847), 1:220.

141 "to land the Main Body"   GW to John Hancock, August 26, 1776 (*Papers, Revolutionary War Series*, 6:129).

141 "Your best men should"   GW to Israel Putnam, August 25, 1776 (ibid., 6:128).

142 "advanced party" that could inflict   Council of War, August 29, 1776 (ibid., 6:153).

142 "A few days more"   GW to Lund Washington, August 26, 1776 (ibid., 6:136–37).

142 "prevent or at least weaken them"   GW to Artemas Ward, August 26, 1776 (ibid., 6:135).

143 "There was no ground"   Tatum, *Journal of Ambrose Serle*, 124.

144 called himself a "shy bitch"   Henry Clinton, *The American Rebellion: Sir*

Henry Clinton's Narrative of His Campaigns, 1775–1782, with an Appendix of Original Documents, ed. William B. Willcox (New Haven: Yale University Press, 1954), xvii.

145 "surrendered and dropped their weapons" Burgoyne, *Enemy Views,* 69.

146 "When they came out of the water" Joseph Plumb Martin, *Private Yankee Doodle: Being a Narrative of Some of the Adventures, Dangers and Sufferings of a Revolutionary Soldier,* ed. George F. Scheer (Boston: Little, Brown, 1962), 26.

146 "I will not ask any man" This and the following quote: quoted in Eric I. Manders, *The Battle of Long Island* (Monmouth Beach, New Jersey: Philip Freneau Press, 1978), 46.

146 "if we succeeded" Henry Clinton, *The American Rebellion: Sir Henry Clinton's Narrative of His Campaigns, 1775–1782, with an Appendix of Original Documents,* ed. William B. Willcox (New Haven: Yale University Press, 1954), 44.

146 "It is my opinion" Davies, *Documents of the American Revolution,* 12:217–18.

146 "would not have stopped a foxhunter" Piers Mackesy, *The War for America: 1775–1783* (Lincoln: University of Nebraska Press, 1992; reprint of 1964 edition), 88.

147 "It must be allowed" Frederick Mackenzie, *Diary of Frederick Mackenzie, Giving a Daily Narrative of His Military Service as an Officer of the Regiment of Royal Welch Fusiliers During the Years 1775–1781 in Massachusetts, Rhode Island and New York* (2 vols., Cambridge, Massachusetts: Harvard University Press, 1930), 1:89.

147 "Good God!" Quoted in Manders, *The Battle of Long Island,* 46.

147 "a pretty considerable loss" Robert Hanson Harrison to John Hancock, August 27, 1776 (*Papers, Revolutionary War Series,* 6:142).

147 "some with broken arms" Martin, *Private Yankee Doodle,* 24.

147 "With the deepest concern" This and following quotes: GW to John Hancock, September 2, 1776 (*Papers, Revolutionary War Series,* 6:199–200).

148 "still, the water quiet" Charles Francis Adams, *Studies Military and Diplomatic, 1775–1865* (New York: Macmillan, 1911), 47.

148 "In the history of warfare" Benjamin Tallmadge, *Memoir of Col. Benjamin Tallmadge, Prepared by Himself at the Request of His Children* (New York: Arno Press, 1968; reprint of 1858 edition), 11.

148 "If a good Bleeding" James Grant to Edward Harvey, September 2, 1776 (Library of Congress: James Grant Papers, reel 29).

9. Retreat

Sources for this chapter include volumes 6–7 of *Papers, Revolutionary War Series;* William Bell Clark, et al., eds., *Naval Documents of the American Revolution* (1964–); John Montresor's *The Montresor Journals* (1882); Carl Leopold Baurmeister, *Revolution in America: Confidential Letters and Journals, 1776–1784, of Adjutant General Major Baurmeister of the Hessian Forces* (1957); and Friedrich von Muenchhausen, *At General Howe's Side, 1776–1778: The Diary of General William Howe's Aide de Camp, Captain Friedrich von Muenchhausen* (1974); see also Barnet Schecter's *Battle for New York.*

149 "It is now extremely obvious"   This and following quotes: GW to John Hancock, September 8, 1776 (*Papers, Revolutionary War Series,* 6:248–52).

150 "wade through much blood"   GW to John Hancock, July 10, 1776 (ibid., 5:260).

150 "the Arguments on which"   GW to John Hancock, September 8, 1776 (ibid., 6:249).

150 "a while longer"   Ibid., 6:251.

150 "a Moment longer than . . . proper"   Ford, *Journals of the Continental Congress,* 5:749.

152 "necessary tho' unfortunate resource"   Quoted in *Papers, Revolutionary War Series,* 6:228.

152 "All is well"   Martin, *Private Yankee Doodle,* 33.

152 "generous, merciful, forbearing"   Quoted in Schecter, *Battle for New York,* 175.

153 "like a large clover field"   Martin, *Private Yankee Doodle,* 33.

153 "It is hardly possible to conceive"   William Bell Clark, et al., eds., *Naval Documents of the American Revolution* (10 vols. to date, Washington, D.C.: Naval Historical Center, Department of the Navy, 1964–), 6:841.

153 "I Lay myself on the Right wing"   William Douglas, "Letters Written During the Revolutionary War by Colonel William Douglas to His Wife Covering the Period July 19, 1775, to December 5, 1776" (*New-York Historical Society Quarterly Bulletin,* 12–14 [1929–30]), 13:122.

153 "Take the walls!"   Charles Samuel Hall, *Life and Letters of General Samuel Holden Parsons, Major General in the Continental Army and Chief Judge of the Northwestern Territory, 1737–1789* (Binghamton, New York: Otseningo Publishing, 1905), 67.

153 "surprize and Mortification"   GW to John Hancock, September 16, 1776 (*Papers, Revolutionary War Series,* 6:313).

154 "I used every means in my power"   Ibid.

154 "He laid his Cane over many"   Tilghman, *Memoir,* 137.

154 "snapped his pistols" This and following quotes about GW's behavior: quoted in *Papers, Revolutionary War Series,* 6:316; and Schecter, *Battle for New York,* 185–86.

154 "The dastardly Behaviour" Tatum, *Journal of Ambrose Serle,* 104.

154 "curious trifles" Clark, *Naval Documents,* 6:841–42.

154 "quaffing and laughing" Washington Irving, *Life of George Washington* (5 vols., New York: G.P. Putnam, 1855–59), 2:355.

154 "flying, on his horse" Quoted in Schecter, *Battle for New York,* 188.

155 "rabble on the walls" Clark, *Naval Documents,* 6:846.

155 "like overjoyed Bedlamites" Ibid., 6:843.

155 "in order to convince them" John Montresor, *The Montresor Journals,* ed. G. D. Scull (*Collections of the New-York Historical Society,* vol. 14., New York: New-York Historical Society, 1882), 123.

155 "excessively fatigued" Quoted in Schecter, *Battle for New York,* 193.

156 "the Enemy appeared in open view" Reed, *Life and Correspondence of Joseph Reed,* 1:237.

156 "as If to attack them in front" This and the following quote: GW to John Hancock, September 18, 1776 (*Papers, Revolutionary War Series,* 6:331).

157 "gave a Hurra" Tilghman, *Memoir,* 138–39.

157 "every visage was seen" Quoted in Schecter, *Battle for New York,* 201.

157 "Had I been left to the dictates" GW to Lund Washington, October 6, 1776 (*Papers, Revolutionary War Series,* 6:494).

157 "It will be next to impossible" Ibid.

157 "devilish purpose" Davies, *Documents of the American Revolution,* 12:231.

158 "picked incendiaries" Carl Leopold Baurmeister, *Revolution in America: Confidential Letters and Journals, 1776–1784, of Adjutant General Major Baurmeister of the Hessian Forces,* trans. and ann. Bernhard A. Uhlendorf (New Brunswick, New Jersey: Rutgers University Press, 1957), 51.

158 "with faggots dipp'd in Brimstone" Robertson, *Diaries,* 99.

158 "one fanatical rebel" Baurmeister, *Revolution in America,* 51.

158 "such a Spirit has gone forth" GW to John Hancock, September 22, 1776 (*Papers, Revolutionary War Series,* 6:368–69).

159 "Being subject to no controul" GW to John Augustine Washington, September 22, 1776 (ibid., 6:374).

159 "If I were to wish the bitterest curse" GW to Lund Washington, September 30, 1776 (ibid., 6:442).

159 "from the hours allotted to Sleep" This and the following quotes from this letter: GW to John Hancock, September 25, 1776 (ibid., 6:393–401).

160 "amazing strong tide" Clark, *Naval Documents,* 6:1221.

160 "as defensible as they can be wished" Quoted in *Papers, Revolutionary War Series,* 6:536.

161 "that of getting in our rear" GW to Artemas Ward, October 13, 1776 (ibid., 6:562).

161 "urged the absolute necessity" Robert Hanson Harrison to John Hancock, October 14–17, 1776 (ibid., 6:565).

161 "to maintain it if possible" Ibid.

161 "Humours & intolerable Caprices" GW to Philip Schuyler, October 22, 1776 (ibid., 7:15).

161 "Yonder" . . . "is the ground we ought to occupy" This and following quotes: Heath, *Memoirs,* 87–88.

162 "withstood an even hotter fire" Baurmeister, *Revolution in America,* 64–65.

162 "As we were on the declivity" William S. Powell, "A Connecticut Soldier Under Washington: Elisha Bostwick's Memoirs of the First Years of the Revolution" (*William and Mary Quarterly,* 3rd series, 6 [1949]), 101.

163 "In this affair" William Hand Browne, ed. *Journal and Correspondence of the Maryland Council of Safety. Archives of Maryland* (vol. 12, Baltimore: Maryland Historical Society, 1882), 488–89.

163 "all matters are as quiet" Peter Force, ed. *American Archives.* (5th series, 9 vols., Washington, D.C., 1837–53), 3:486.

163 "enduring almost a Weeks" Benjamin Trumbull, "Journal of the Campaign at New York, 1776–7" (*Collections of the Connecticut Historical Society,* 7 [1899]), 206.

163 "did not think the driving" Davies, *Documents of the American Revolution,* 12:258–64.

164 "advising with your council" Instructions from the Continental Congress, June 22, 1755, (ibid., 1:21–22).

165 "every art and whatever expence" Ford, *Journals of the Continental Congress,* 6:866.

165 "when I considered that our policy" GW to Joseph Reed, August 22, 1779 (Library of Congress: Washington Papers).

165 "whose judgment & candor" Ibid.

165 "The late passage of the 3 Vessells" GW to Nathanael Greene, November 8, 1776 (*Papers, Revolutionary War Series,* 7:115–16).

165 "prodigiously shatterd from . . . Cannon" Showman, *Greene Papers,* 1:337–38.

165 "I cannot help thinking" Ibid., 1:344.

166 "A flag of truce" Quoted in *Papers, Revolutionary War Series,* 7:162.

166 "The Troops were in high Spirits" GW to John Hancock, November 16, 1776 (ibid., 7:163).

166 "great Hopes the Enemy" Ibid.

166 "Before us, beside, and behind us" Burgoyne, *Enemy Views,* 94.

167 "many dead and wounded"   Ibid., 97.

167 "There we all stood"   Showman, *Greene Papers*, 1: 352.

167 "The Rebel prisoners"   Mackenzie, *Diary,* 1:111–12.

167 "Despite the strictest orders"   Burgoyne, *Enemy Views,* 97.

168 "The Hessians were roused"   James Grant to Edward Harvey, November 22, 1776 (Library of Congress: James Grant Papers, reel 29).

168 "This is a most unfortunate affair"   GW to John Augustine Washington, November 6–19, 1776 (*Papers, Revolutionary War Series,* 7:103).

168 "Oh General"   Charles Lee to GW, November 19, 1776 (ibid., 7:187).

168 "[I] lament with you"   Quoted in ibid., 7:237–38.

168 "General Washington's own Judgment"   Quoted in ibid., 7:238.

169 "of no importance"   GW to John Hancock, November 19–21, 1776 (ibid., 7:180).

169 "broken & dispirited"   GW to Charles Lee, November 21, 1776 (ibid., 7:193).

169 "The people here"   Clark, *Naval Documents,* 7:188.

170 "Should we retreat"   William Gordon, *The History of the Rise, Progress, and Establishment, of the Independence of the United States of America: Including an Account of the Late War; and of the Thirteen Colonies, from Their Origin to That Period* (4 vols., London: Charles Dilly and James Buckland, 1788), 2:354.

170 "for the purpose of Carrying over"   GW to Richard Humpton, December 1, 1776 (*Papers, Revolutionary War Series,* 7:248).

170 "standing quietly"   Friedrich von Muenchhausen, *At General Howe's Side, 1776–1778: The Diary of General William Howe's Aide de Camp, Captain Friedrich von Muenchhausen.* Trans. Ernst Kipping, ann. Samuel Smith (Monmouth Beach, New Jersey: Philip Freneau Press, 1974), 6.

170 "Nothing but necessity"   GW to John Hancock, December 5, 1776 (*Papers, Revolutionary War Series,* 7:262).

171 "The rebels were always"   Muenchhausen, *At General Howe's Side,* 6.

171 "Some inhabitants"   Ibid.

171 "Here we remained"   James McMichael, "Diary of Lieutenant James McMichael of the Pennsylvania Line, 1776–1778" (*Pennsylvania Magazine of History and Biography,* 16 [1892]), 139.

10. Redemption

David Hackett Fischer's *Washington's Crossing* (2004) will remain the best book on the Trenton and Princeton campaigns for many years to come; see also William M. Dwyer, *The Day Is Ours! November 1776–January 1777: An Inside View of the Battles of Trenton and Princeton* (1983); Samuel Smith, *The Battle of*

Trenton (1965); and William S. Stryker, *The Battles of Trenton and Princeton* (1898), which contains many primary documents on the battles unavailable elsewhere. Other primary sources include volume 7 of *Papers, Revolutionary War Series,* and the microfilm edition of the James Grant Papers in the Library of Congress.

172   "repentance and reformation"   This and following quotes: Ford, *Journals of the Continental Congress,* 6:1022–27.

173   "almost general submission"   Davies, *Documents of the American Revolution,* 12:267.

173   "to the People in general"   Ford, *Journals of the Continental Congress,* 6:1018–19.

173   "I do not regret the Part"   Smith, *Letters of Delegates,* 5:590–91.

173   "looked upon the contest"   Quoted in William S. Stryker, *The Battles of Trenton and Princeton* (Spartenburg, South Carolina: Reprint Co., 1967; reprint 1898 edition), 80.

173   "matters to my view"   GW to Lund Washington, December 10–17, 1776 (*Papers, Revolutionary War Series,* 7:291).

175   "We find Sir"   GW to John Hancock, December 20, 1776 (ibid., 7:382).

175   "to serve during the present war"   Ford, *Journals of the Continental Congress,* 5:762.

175   "come in," . . . "you can not tell how"   GW to John Hancock, December 20, 1776 (*Papers, Revolutionary War Series,* 7:382).

176   If "we have to provide"   Ibid.

176   "full power to order"   Ford, *Journals of the Continental Congress,* 6:1027.

176   "no lust after power"   GW to John Hancock, December 20, 1776 (*Papers, Revolutionary War Series,* 7:382–83).

176   "I can see no Evil"   Showman, *Greene Papers,* 1:372–74.

177   "a discretionary Power"   Ibid.

177   "scarce of Provisions"   Undated intelligence memorandum, Library of Congress: James Grant Papers, reel 37.

177   "a certain great man"   Henry Steele Commager and Richard B. Morris, eds., *The Spirit of 'Seventy-Six: The Story of the American Revolution as Told by Participants* (New York: Harper and Row, 1967; reprint of 1958 edition), 500.

177   "Victoria!"   Muenchhausen, *At General Howe's Side,* 7.

178   "will be in perfect security"   Davies, *Documents of the American Revolution,* 12:267.

178   "We are all of Opinion"   Joseph Reed to GW, December 22, 1776 (*Papers, Revolutionary War Series,* 7:415).

178   "attempt a stroke"   GW to Jonathan Trumbull, Sr., December 14, 1776 (ibid., 7:340).

180 "Christmas day at Night" GW to Joseph Reed, December 23, 1776 (ibid., 7:423).

180 "He appeared much depressed" Rush, *Autobiography,* 124.

181 "left wing of the Army" Ibid.

181 "It is fearfully cold" Stryker, *Battles of Trenton and Princeton,* 362.

181 "a profound silence" General Orders, December 25, 1776 (*Papers, Revolutionary War Series,* 7:436).

181 "for it was all the same" Isaac J. Greenwood, ed., *The Revolutionary Services of John Greenwood of Boston and New York, 1775–1783* (New York: De Vinne Press, 1922), 82.

182 "Troops began to cross" Quoted in William M. Dwyer, *The Day Is Ours! November 1776–January 1777: An Inside View of the Battles of Trenton and Princeton* (New York: Viking Press, 1983), 232.

182 "a deep bass heard" Ibid.

182 "wrapped in his cloak" Stryker, *Battles of Trenton and Princeton,* 362.

182 "the shortness of time" Joseph Reed, "General Joseph Reed's Narrative of the Movements of the American Army in the Neighborhood of Trenton in the Winter of 1776–77" (*Pennsylvania Magazine of History and Biography,* 8 [1884]), 393.

182 "I imagine the badness of the night" John Cadwalader to GW, December 26, 1776 (*Papers, Revolutionary War Series,* 7:442).

183 "sparkled & blazed in the Storm" Powell, "A Connecticut Soldier Under Washington," 102.

183 "About day light" Ibid.

183 "the damn Hessians" Jared C. Lobdell, ed. "The Revolutionary War Journal of Sergeant Thomas McCarty" (*Proceedings of the New Jersey Historical Society,* 82 [1964]), 41.

183 "black Negroes and yellow dogs" Burgoyne, *Enemy Views,* 114.

185 "His love of life" Ibid., 116–17.

185 "I own I did not think" James Grant to Edward Harvey, December 27, 1776 (Library of Congress: James Grant Papers, reel 29).

185 "I do not believe" Quoted in Samuel Smith, *The Battle of Trenton* (Monmouth Beach, New Jersey: Philip Freneau Press, 1965), 17.

185 "Let them come" Burgoyne, *Enemy Views,* 118.

186 "If I had not stepped out" Ibid., 119.

186 They "behaved very well" GW to John Hancock, December 27, 1776 (*Papers, Revolutionary War Series,* 7:454).

186 "Our noble countryman" Robert C. Powell, ed., *A Biographical Sketch of Col. Leven Powell* (Alexandria, Virginia: G.H. Ramey & Son, 1877), 41–43.

186 "We forc'd & enter'd" Quoted in *Papers, Revolutionary War Series,* 7:458.

187 "He called to his regiment then" Burgoyne, *Enemy Views,* 120.

187 "like a swarm of bees"   Quoted in Smith, *Battle of Trenton,* 24.

188 "rotten prison" near Philadelphia   Burgoyne, *Enemy Views,* 115.

188 He "received us very politely"   Ibid., 124–25.

188 "I now think that Britain"   Smith, *Letters of Delegates,* 6:3.

189 "drive the Enemy back"   Ibid., 6:8.

189 "farewell the glory of England"   Ibid., 6:10.

189 "unless sooner determined"   Ford, *Journals of the Continental Congress,* 6:1043–46.

189 "Genl. Washington" . . . "is Dictator"   Caesar A. Rodney, ed., *Diary of Captain Thomas Rodney, 1776–1777* (Wilmington: Historical Society of Delaware, 1888), 53.

189 "Happy it is"   Executive Committee of the Continental Congress to GW, December 31, 1776 (*Papers, Revolutionary War Series,* 7:495).

189 "I shall constantly bear in Mind"   GW to the Executive Committee of the Continental Congress, January 1, 1777 (ibid, 7:500).

190 "I would not stay"   Greenwood, *Revolutionary Services,* 86.

11. Princeton

See Johann Ewald, *Diary of the American War: A Hessian Journal* (1979); Samuel Smith, *The Battle of Princeton* (1967); volume 8 of *Papers, Revolutionary War Series;* and sources cited in the notes for chapter 10.

191 "Both parties were occupied"   This and following quotes: Johann Ewald, *Diary of the American War: A Hessian Journal,* trans. and ed. Joseph P. Tustin (New Haven: Yale University Press, 1979), 42.

191 "If I was with you"   This and the following quote: quoted in Paul David Nelson, *General James Grant: Scottish Soldier and Royal Governor of East Florida* (Gainesville: University Press of Florida, 1993), 110.

192 "they are pressed in time"   This and the following quote: undated intelligence report, Library of Congress: James Grant Papers, reel 37.

192 "to be attacked by enemy forces"   Quoted in Dwyer, *The Day Is Ours!,* 299.

192 "Here we have balls, concerts"   Muenchhausen, *At General Howe's Side,* 8.

192 "Merry Christmas to you"   William Howe to James Grant, December 28, 1776 (Library of Congress: James Grant Papers, reel 37).

194 "great Quantities of Spiritous Liquors"   Reed, "General Joseph Reed's Narrative," 391.

194 "I shall be extremely ready"   GW to John Cadwalader, December 27, 1776 (*Papers, Revolutionary War Series,* 7:450).

194 "The General, with the utmost sincerity"   General Orders, December 27, 1776 (ibid., 7:448–49).

195 "mounted on a noble-looking horse" Stryker, *Battles of Trenton and Princeton,* 254.

195 "He alluded to our recent victory" This and following quotes: Sergeant R., "The Battle of Princeton" (*Pennsylvania Magazine of History and Biography,* 20 [1896]), 515–16.

197 "with a Body of pickd Troops" Reed, "General Joseph Reed's Narrative," 400.

197 "a very intelligent young Gentleman" This and following quotes: John Cadwalader to GW, December 31, 1776 (*Papers, Revolutionary War Series,* 7:491–93).

198 "every dawn of hope" GW to John Hancock, January 5, 1777 (ibid., 7:521).

198 "Some pieces of Intelligence" GW to John Cadwalader or Thomas Mifflin, January 1, 1777 (ibid., 7:510).

198 "the weather was damp and cold" This and following quotes: Rush, *Autobiography,* 127.

199 "to give the enemy a beating" Ewald, *Diary,* 45.

199 Yankee "saints" James Grant to Edward Harvey, September 2, 1776 (Library of Congress: James Grant Papers, reel 29).

200 "to skirmish with the enemy" Stryker, *Battles of Trenton and Princeton,* 466–68.

200 "their rearguard behaved better" James Grant to Edward Harvey, January 15, 1777 (Library of Congress: James Grant Papers, reel 29).

200 "in order to amuse us" Robertson, *Diaries,* 199.

201 "except" . . . "a few shells" Quoted in *Papers, Revolutionary War Series,* 7:526.

201 "very commodiously did" McMichael, "Diary," 140.

201 "was strong to be sure" Quoted in *Papers, Revolutionary War Series,* 7:526.

202 "impassable by boats" This and the following quote: ibid.

202 "would avoid the appearance" GW to John Hancock, January 5, 1777 (ibid., 7:521).

202 "At two o'clock in the morning" Rodney, *Diary,* 32.

202 "when passing over the ice" Quoted in Samuel Smith, *The Battle of Princeton* (Monmouth Beach, New Jersey: Philip Freneau Press, 1967), 19.

203 "for the double purpose" James Wilkinson, *Memoirs of My Own Times* (3 vols., Philadelphia: Abraham Small, 1816), 1:141.

203 "General Washington happened to be near" quoted in Smith, *The Battle of Princeton,* 20.

203 "a detachment sent out of Princeton" Ibid.

204 Mercer "immediately formed his men" Rodney, *Diary,* 33–34.

204 "rolling and writhing" Sergeant R., "Battle of Princeton," 518.

204 "under a shower of grape shot" Stryker, *Battles of Trenton and Princeton,* 447.

205 "exposed to both firings"   quoted in Smith, *The Battle of Princeton*, 25.

205 "Parade with us"   Sergeant R., "Battle of Princeton," 517.

205 "away, my dear Colonel"   quoted in Dwyer, *The Day is Ours!*, 347–48.

205 "bravely pushed up"   Stryker, *Battles of Trenton and Princeton*, 447.

205 "It's a fine fox chase"   quoted in Dwyer, *The Day is Ours!*, 351.

205 "mounted on a brown poney"   Quoted in Smith, *The Battle of Princeton*, 27.

206 "After we had been about two hours"   Quoted in *Papers, Revolutionary War Series*, 7:529.

206 "pale, mangled corpses"   This and following quotes: quoted in Dwyer, *The Day Is Ours!*, 352.

207 "though they were both hungry and thirsty"   Quoted in Smith, *The Battle of Princeton*, 27.

207 "amongst a fine heap of straw"   Lillian Miller, ed., *The Selected Papers of Charles Willson Peale and His Family* (4 vols., New Haven, Connecticut: Yale University Press, 1983–96), 1:282.

207 "In my Judgement"   GW to John Hancock, January 5, 1777 (*Papers, Revolutionary War Series*, 7:523).

208 "obliged to encamp"   Rodney, *Diary*, 38.

208 "very well supplied with large stones"   McMichael, "Diary," 141.

208 "in the woods, the snow"   This and following quotes: ibid.

208 "brave and worthy" Hugh Mercer   GW to John Hancock, January 5, 1777 (*Papers, Revolutionary War Series*, 7:521).

209 "I have been much pleased"   This and the following quote: John Sullivan, *Letters and Papers of Major-General John Sullivan, Continental Army*, ed. Otis G. Hammond (3 vols., Concord: New Hampshire Historical Society, 1930–1939), 1:319–20.

210 "Washington has since taken post"   James Grant to Edward Harvey, January 15, 1777 (Library of Congress: James Grant Papers, reel 29).

210 "You have nothing to accuse yourself of"   William Howe to Lord Cornwallis, January 13, 1777 (Library of Congress: James Grant Papers, reel 38).

210 "I heartily agree with you"   William Howe to James Grant, January 9, 1777 (Library of Congress: James Grant Papers, reel 38).

210 "Though they seem to be ignorant"   Quoted in Don Higginbotham, *The War of American Independence: Military Attitudes, Policies, and Practice, 1763–1789* (New York: Macmillan, 1971), 170.

12. Philadelphia

The main source for this chapter is volumes 9–11 of *Papers, Revolutionary War Series;* for additional primary sources on the Philadelphia campaign see the bibliography to volume 11 of that series. Among the secondary sources, see especially Stephen R. Taaffe's *The Philadelphia Campaign, 1777–1778* (2003), which fills an important gap in Revolutionary War scholarship; John F. Reed's *Campaign to Valley Forge, July 1, 1777–December 19, 1777* (1965); and Samuel Smith's *The Battle of Brandywine* (1976).

212 "extremely mortifying" events   Davies, *Documents of the American Revolution,* 14:46–47.

215 "The designs of the Enemy"   GW to Edmund Pendleton, April 12, 1777 (*Papers, Revolutionary War Series,* 9:140).

216 "dark and mysterious" behavior   GW to John Hancock, June 20, 1777 (ibid., 10:85).

216 "to bring on a General Engagement"   GW to John Hancock, June 28, 1777 (ibid., 10:137).

218 "constant perplexity and . . . conjecture"   GW to John Hancock, July 25, 1777 (ibid., 10:410–12).

218 "with all possible dispatch"   General Orders, July 31, 1777 (ibid., 10:465).

218 "peremptory orders"   GW to Nathanael Greene, August 1, 1777 (ibid., 10:473).

218 a most "provoking account"   GW to George Clinton, August 1, 1777 (ibid., 10:475).

219 "sudden stroke" on the Hudson   Ibid.

219 "greatest anxiety"   GW to Israel Putnam, August 1, 1777 (ibid., 10:481).

219 "very irksome state of Suspence"   GW to John Augustine Washington, August 5–9, 1777 (ibid., 10:515).

219 "distressing beyond measure"   GW to Jonathan Trumbull, Sr., August 4, 1777 (ibid., 10:506–7).

219 "I am haunted and teazed"   GW to Richard Henry Lee, May 17, 1777 (ibid., 9:454).

220 "He has said that he is young"   GW to Benjamin Harrison, August 19, 1777 (ibid., 11:4).

220 "I am now as much puzzled"   GW to Artemas Ward, August 11, 1777 (ibid., 10:589).

222 "filled with snakes and toads"   Ewald, *Diary,* 74–75.

222 "As there is not now"   GW to Israel Putnam, August 22, 1777 (*Papers, Revolutionary War Series,* 11:46).

223 "with a lively smart Step"   Smith, *Letters of Delegates,* 7:540–42.

223 "with such moderation"   General Orders, August 23, 1777 (*Papers, Revolutionary War Series,* 11:51).

224 "to be constantly near the Enemy"   GW to John Hancock, August 30, 1777 (ibid., 11:93).

224 "deadly wound" on the British   Showman, *Greene Papers*, 2:149.

226 "last effort" of the enemy   This and following quotes: General Orders, September 5, 1777 (*Papers, Revolutionary War Series*, 11:147–48).

226 "instantly shot down"   General Orders, September 6, 1777 (ibid., 11:157).

235 "My hair stood on end"   Ewald, *Diary*, 80.

239 "till we had almost Covered the Ground"   Sullivan, *Letters and Papers*, 1:465.

240 "routed and retreating precipitately"   Showman, *Greene Papers*, 2:471.

241 "words of encouragement"   Octavius Pickering and Charles W. Upham, *The Life of Timothy Pickering* (4 vols., Boston: Little, Brown, 1867–73), 1:156.

241 "Notwithstanding the misfortune"   GW to John Hancock, September 11, 1777 (*Papers, Revolutionary War Series*, 11:200).

242 "the Glory of a Compleat Victory"   Smith, *Letters of Delegates*, 7:680–81.

13. Germantown

Aside from a few minor works such as Thomas G. McGuire's *The Surprise of Germantown, or, The Battle of Cliveden* (1994), there remains no serious study of the Battle of Germantown; this chapter relies almost exclusively on volume 11 of *Papers, Revolutionary War Series*, and the primary sources cited therein. See also Taaffe, Reed, and other works cited in chapter 12.

243 "A Spirited Effort"   GW to William Smallwood, September 12, 1777 (*Papers, Revolutionary War Series*, 11:210).

243 "another Appeal to Heaven"   General Orders, September 13, 1777 (ibid., 11:211–12).

243 "not so favorable"   Ibid., 11:211.

244 "denied [of] every desirable refreshment"   McMichael, "Diary," 151.

244 "from turning our right flank"   GW to John Hancock, September 15, 1777 (*Papers, Revolutionary War Series*, 11:237).

245 "partisan trick"   Ewald, *Diary*, 89.

245 "in mud up to our calves"   Baurmeister, *Revolution in America*, 114.

246 "Harrass & Distress"   Quoted in *Papers, Revolutionary War Series*, 11:266.

246 "jaded men"   GW to Anthony Wayne, September 18, 1777 (ibid.).

246 "I yet hope"   GW to John Hancock, September 19, 1777 (ibid., 11:269).

246 "very quiet, washing & Cooking"   Anthony Wayne to GW, September 19, 1777 (ibid., 11:273).

246 "too Compact"   Ibid.

247 "Dash on, light infantry"   "Massacre at Paoli" (*Historical Magazine*, 4 [November 1860]), 346.

247 "more expressive of Horror"   Henry Pleasants, "The Battle of Paoli" (*Pennsylvania Magazine of History and Biography,* 72 [1948]), 46.

248 Howe's "perplexing Maneuvres"   GW to John Hancock, September 23, 1777 (*Papers, Revolutionary War Series,* 11:301).

248 "unvaried Object"   GW to Alexander McDougall, September 22, 1777 (ibid., 11:292).

248 "to a man disaffected"   GW to John Hancock, September 23, 1777 (ibid., 11:301).

249 "uncommonly cold and biting"   Muhlenberg, *Journals,* 3:79.

249 "amidst the acclamation"   Montresor, *Journals,* 458.

250 "The church was crowded"   Muhlenberg, *Journals,* 3:80.

251 "general & vigorous attack"   Council of War, September 28, 1777 (*Papers, Revolutionary War Series,* 11:339).

251 Washington "thought it was time"   Howard C. Rice, Jr., ed., *Travels in North America in the Years 1780, 1781, and 1782 by the Marquis de Chastellux* (2 vols., Chapel Hill: University of North Carolina Press, 1963), 1:137.

251 "This surely must animate every man"   General Orders, October 3, 1777 (*Papers, Revolutionary War Series,* 11:373).

253 "A sudden attack is intended"   McMichael, "Diary," 152.

254 "We heard a loud cry"   Commager and Morris, *Spirit of 'Seventy-Six,* 625.

254 The British "maintained their ground"   Sullivan, *Letters and Papers,* 1:544.

254 "had his leg shot off"   "Revolutionary Services of Captain John Markland," (*Pennsylvania Magazine of History and Biography,* 9 [1885]), 107.

254 "This was the first time"   Commager and Morris, *Spirit of 'Seventy-Six,* 625.

254 "riding one way and looking another"   John Eager Howard, "Col. John Eager Howard's Account of the Battle of Germantown," (*Maryland Historical Magazine,* 4 [1909]), 315.

255 "The crackling of thorns"   Hamilton B. Tompkins, "Contemporary Account of the Battle of Germantown" (*Pennsylvania Magazine of History and Biography,* 11 [1887]), 330.

255 "For shame, Light Infantry"   Commager and Morris, *Spirit of 'Seventy-Six,* 625–26.

255 "I think I never saw people"   Ibid.

255 "to the hottest fire"   Sullivan, *Letters and Papers,* 1:547.

255 "General Sullivan's divisions"   Timothy Pickering, letter of August 23, 1826, in *North American Review,* new series, 23 (October 1826), 427–28.

256 "strong stone house"   Commager and Morris, *Spirit of 'Seventy-Six,* 629.

256 "whether the whole of our troops"   Pickering, letter in *North American Review,* 428.

256 "remembered such a thing"   Charles Cotesworth Pinckney, "The Battles of

Brandywine and Germantown," (*Historical Magazine*, 10 [July 1866]), 203–4.

256   "who being preceded by a drum"   Rice, *Travels in North America*, 1:140.

257   "To do them justice"   William J. Potts, "Battle of Germantown from a British Account," (*Pennsylvania Magazine of History and Biography*, 11 [1887]), 114.

257   Ewald "counted seventy-five dead"   Ewald, *Diary*, 96.

258   "I threw my squadron of horse"   Tallmadge, *Memoir*, 23.

258   "When their main body attacked"   McMichael, "Diary," 153.

258   "Forman's Red Coats"   Asher Holmes, "Letter Concerning the Battle at Germantown, 1777 (*New Jersey Historical Society Proceedings*, 7 [1922]), 34.

259   "made a Safe retreat"   Sullivan, *Letters and Papers*, 1:547.

259   "both taken away"   Samuel Hazard, et al., eds., *Pennsylvania Archives* (9 series, 138 vols., Philadelphia and Harrisburg: various publishers, 1852–1949), 1st series, 5:646.

260   "Every account confirms"   GW to John Hancock, October 7, 1777 (*Papers, Revolutionary War Series*, 11:417).

260   "I attribute the loss"   Pinckney, "Battles of Brandywine and Germantown," 204.

260   "We fled from victory"   Hazard, *Pennsylvania Archives*, 1st series, 5:646.

262   "the usually so-called 'Clever Washington' "   Ewald, *Diary*, 93.

262   "We most certainly"   Lyon G. Tyler, "The Old Virginia Line in the Middle States During the American Revolution," (*Tyler's Quarterly Historical and Genealogical Magazine*, 12 [1930–31]), 134.

262   "I was in the action"   William Beatty, "Captain William Beatty's Correspondence, 1776–1781," (*Historical Magazine and Notes and Queries Concerning the Antiquities, History, and Biography of America*, 2nd series, 1 [February 1867]), 148.

263   "glorious termination"   GW to Benjamin Lincoln, October 26, 1777 (*Papers, Revolutionary War Series*, 12:19).

264   "who shut the only door"   GW to Landon Carter, October 27, 1777 (ibid., 12:27).

264   "Heaven has been determin'd"   Stirling to GW, November 3, 1777 (ibid., 12:111).

14. Valley Forge

Wayne Bodle's *The Valley Forge Winter: Civilians and Soldiers in War* (2002), based on his three-volume *Valley Forge Historical Research Project* (1980), provides a thorough and insightful account of the Valley Forge winter; a detailed study of the logistical and administrative problems facing Washington is in Erna

Risch's *Supplying Washington's Army* (1981). On Steuben, see Philander Dean Chase, "Baron von Steuben in the War of Independence" (1972). For primary documents about Valley Forge, see volume 13 of *Papers, Revolutionary War Series*, edited by myself, and volumes 12 and 14 of the same series.

266 "men are naturally apt"   Nathanael Greene to GW, December 1, 1777 (*Papers, Revolutionary War Series*, 12:461).

266 "the first object in Winter quarters"   Henry Knox to GW, December 1, 1777 (ibid., 12:465).

266 "melancholly truth"   Hazard, *Pennsylvania Archives*, 1st series, 6:105.

266 "on a high uncultivated hill"   Lloyd A. Brown and Howard H. Peckham, eds., *Revolutionary War Journals of Henry Dearborn, 1775–1783* (New York: Da Capo Press, 1971; reprint of 1939 edition), 118.

267 "I am Sick"   Albigence Waldo, "Diary of Albigence Waldo, of the Connecticut Line," (*Pennsylvania Magazine of History and Biography*, 21 [1897]), 306.

267 "With activity and diligence"   General Orders, December 17, 1777 (*Papers, Revolutionary War Series*, 12:620).

269 "with a song in his mouth"   Waldo, "Diary," 307.

269 "a Soldier, his bare feet"   Ibid.

269 "unwholesome & destructive"   Committee to Inspect Beef to GW, December 20, 1777 (*Papers, Revolutionary War Series*, 12:648).

269 "a general cry"   Waldo, "Diary," 309.

269 "I ordered the Troops"   GW to Henry Laurens, December 23, 1777 (*Papers, Revolutionary War Series*, 12:683).

270 "declaring the danger"   Quoted in ibid., 12:664.

270 "a very trifle"   Hazard, *Pennsylvania Archives*, 1st series, 6:130.

270 "tolerably well covered"   GW to Benedict Arnold, January 20, 1778 (*Papers, Revolutionary War Series*, 13:288).

270 "We now have upwards"   Benjamin Rush to GW, December 26, 1777 (ibid., 13:6–9).

271 "Our sick naked"   GW to William Livingston, December 31, 1777 (ibid., 13:86).

271 "unfit for duty"   Circular to the States, December 29, 1777 (ibid., 13:37).

271 "Hundreds of our poor worthy fellows"   Hazard, *Pennsylvania Archives*, 1st series, 6:251.

273 "In conversation with his Excellency"   Quoted in *Papers, Revolutionary War Series*, 13:30.

273 "Longing, & hankering"   GW to George Weedon, February 10, 1778 (ibid., 13:506).

273 "It is matter of no small grief"   Ibid.

274 "dead horses"   General Orders, January 7, 1778 (ibid., 13:165–66).

275 "A small knowlege of human nature"   GW to a Continental Congress Camp Committee, January 29, 1778 (ibid., 13:377).

276 "establishment of the American Army"   Ford, *Journals of the Continental Congress,* 11:538.

276 "Strong Faction"   James Craik to GW, January 6, 1778 (*Papers, Revolutionary War Series,* 13:160).

276 "stupid men"   Lafayette to GW, December 30, 1777 (ibid., 13:68).

276 "opinions treated [in Congress]"   Smith, *Letters of Delegates,* 8:549.

277 "has Shewn us what Americans"   Quoted in *Papers, Revolutionary War Series,* 13:610.

277 "that the people of America"   Quoted in ibid., 13:366.

277 "was not the man people Imagined"   Quoted in ibid., 13:146.

277 Calling Conway his "enemy"   GW to Lafayette, December 31, 1777 (ibid., 13:83).

277 "affects the Genl very sensibly"   Philip M. Hamer, George C. Rogers, Jr., David R. Chesnutt, et al., eds., *The Papers of Henry Laurens* (16 vols. to date, Columbia: University of South Carolina Press, 1968–), 12:246.

277 "malignant faction"   GW to Henry Laurens, January 31, 1778 (*Papers, Revolutionary War Series,* 13:420).

278 "The design of his Visit": Butterfield, *Diary and Autobiography of John Adams,* 4:5.

278 "unformed mob"   Quoted in *Papers, Revolutionary War Series,* 13:366.

278 Valley Forge's "fatal crisis"   GW to William Buchanan, February 7, 1778 (ibid., 13:465).

279 "The Camp is in a melancholy"   Quoted in ibid., 13:516.

279 "the Situation of the Camp"   Ibid.

279 "the Complaints of the want of provisions"   Ibid.

279 "mutiny in the army"   Smith, *Letters of Delegates,* 9:108–9.

279 "An American Army"   Ibid., 9:117.

279 "Naked and starving"   GW to George Clinton, February 16, 1778 (ibid., 13:553).

280 "indulging his penchant"   Wayne K. Bodle and Jacqueline Thibaut, *Valley Forge Historical Research Project* (3 vols., Valley Forge, Pennsylvania: U.S. Department of the Interior, National Park Service, 1980), 1:268.

280 Provisions . . . were "nearly exhausted"   GW to Jonathan Trumbull, Sr., February 6, 1778 (*Papers, Revolutionary War Series,* 13:464–65).

280 "The people at large"   GW to Henry Laurens, December 14–15, 1777 (ibid., 12:606).

280 "to order every kind of stock"   Ford, *Journals of the Continental Congress,* 9:1013–15.

281   Even a few "small seizures"   GW to the Board of War, January 2–3, 1778 (*Papers, Revolutionary War Series,* 13:112).

281   "The little collections I had made"   Showman, *Greene Papers,* 2:293.

281   For "glory" and "great possessions"   Quoted in Philander Dean Chase, "Baron von Steuben in the War of Independence" (Ph.D. diss., Duke University, 1972), 38.

281   He "seems to understand"   Hamer, et al., *Papers of Henry Laurens,* 12:483.

282   "explain with mildness"   Quoted in Chase, "Baron von Steuben," 65.

282   "It having pleased the Almighty"   General Orders, May 5, 1778 (Library of Congress: Washington Papers).

283   "Huzza!"   Ibid.

283   "might taste the Pleasur"   Carlos E. Godfrey, *The Commander-in-Chief's Guard, Revolutionary War* (Washington, D.C.: Stevenson-Smith, 1904), 7–8.

283   "profusion of fat meat"   quoted in Freeman, *George Washington,* 5:2.

283   "Several remarkable toasts"   Joseph Clark, "Diary of Joseph Clark, Attached to the Continental Army from May, 1778, to November, 1779" (*New Jersey Historical Society, Proceedings,* 7:3 [1854]), 105.

283   "the King of England kneeling"   Ewald, *Diary,* 128.

15. Monmouth

Amazingly, no in-depth military history of the Battle of Monmouth has appeared in print since William S. Stryker's *The Battle of Monmouth* (1927); Samuel Smith's *The Battle of Monmouth* (1965) is brief and frequently inaccurate. On Charles Lee, see John R. Alden, *General Charles Lee: Traitor or Patriot?* (1951), and Theodore Thayer, *The Making of a Scapegoat: Washington and Lee at Monmouth* (1976). For primary documents, see volume 15 of *Papers, Revolutionary War Series,* edited by myself, and the sources cited therein; and Charles Lee's invaluable *Lee Papers* (1872–75), which contains a complete record of Lee's court-martial and numerous firsthand accounts of the battle. An official British account is in Henry Clinton's *The American Rebellion* (1951).

284   "Capital punishment itself"   John William Fortescue, ed., *The Correspondence of King George the Third from 1760 to December 1783, Printed from the Original Papers in the Royal Archives at Windsor Castle* (6 vols., London: Macmillan, 1927–28), 4:63.

285   "The war must be prosecuted"   Davies, *Documents of the American Revolution,* 15:58–59.

285   "it is our will and pleasure"   Ibid., 15:75.

286   "Skillfully and laboriously dug"   Muenchhausen, *At General Howe's Side,* 52.

286 "a square where two contingents" Ibid.

287 "surpassed the most sanguine expectations" Francis Downman, *The Services of Lieut.-Colonel Francis Downman, R.A. in France, North America, and the West Indies, between the Years 1758 and 1784,* ed. F. A. Whinyates (Woolwich: Royal Artillery Institution, 1898), 60–61.

287 "somewhat more than 4,000 guineas" Muenchhausen, *At General Howe's Side,* 52.

287 "A variety of concurring accounts" GW to Lafayette, May 18, 1778 (Library of Congress: Washington Papers).

288 "chatting with a young lady" Stanley J. Idzerda, et al., eds., *Lafayette in the Age of the American Revolution: Selected Letters and Papers, 1776–1790* (5 vols. to date, Ithaca, New York: Cornell University Press, 1977–), 2:6–7.

289 "The warter was up to our middle" Godfrey, *Commander-in-Chief's Guard,* 8.

289 The plan "would have been effected" Downman, *Services,* 59.

289 "into which he tumbled" Quoted in John R. Alden, *General Charles Lee: Traitor or Patriot?* (Baton Rouge: Louisiana State University Press, 1951), 167.

289 "that My Dogs should be brought" Charles Lee to GW, February 9, 1777 (*Papers, Revolutionary War Series,* 8:289).

290 "When he came out" Quoted in Alden, *General Charles Lee,* 190.

290 "quite so limping" GW to Charles Lee, April 22, 1778 (*Papers, Revolutionary War Series,* 14:585).

291 "*Burgoyning* Clinton" Anthony Wayne to GW, June 18, 1778 (Library of Congress: Washington Papers).

291 "I would not detach" Nathanael Greene to GW, June 18, 1778 (Library of Congress: Washington Papers).

291 "terrible" daytime heat Burgoyne, *Enemy Views,* 266.

292 "tender acquaintances" Baurmeister, *Revolution in America,* 182.

292 "positively nothing" Ibid.

292 leaving "all our tents standing" Ebenezer Wild, "The Journal of Ebenezer Wild (1776–1781), Who Served as Corporal, Sergeant, Ensign, and Lieutenant of the American Army of the Revolution" (*Proceedings of the Massachusetts Historical Society,* 2nd series, 6 [1890–91]), 109.

292 "that the way to annoy" GW to Philemon Dickinson, June 5–7, 1778 (Library of Congress: Washington Papers).

292 "resistance at every defile" Burgoyne, *Enemy Views,* 264.

293 "had hopes Mr. Washington" Clinton, *American Rebellion,* 91.

293 "the Guards, Grenadiers & Light Infantry" James Pattison, "A New York Diary of the Revolutionary War," ed. Carson I. A. Ritchie (*New-York Historical Society Quarterly,* 50 [July 1966]), 259.

293 "hazard a general action" Council of War, June 24, 1778 (Library of Congress: Washington Papers).

293 "would have done honor" Harold C. Syrett, et al., eds., *The Papers of Alexander Hamilton* (27 vols., New York: Columbia University Press, 1961–87), 1:510.

293 "the delicate situation" Nathanael Greene to GW, June 24, 1778 (Library of Congress: Washington Papers).

293 "not to Scout as Some Say" Lafayette to GW, June 24, 1778 (Library of Congress: Washington Papers).

294 "a more proper busyness" Charles Lee to GW, June 25, 1778 (Library of Congress: Washington Papers).

294 "the young Frenchman" James McHenry, *Journal of a March, a Battle, and a Waterfall: Being the Version Elaborated by James McHenry from his Diary of the Year 1778, begun at Valley Forge, & Containing Accounts of the British, the Indians, and the Battle of Monmouth* (Greenwich, Connecticut: privately printed, 1945), 4.

294 "undoubtedly the most honourable command" Charles Lee to GW, June 25, 1778 (Library of Congress: Washington Papers).

294 "To commit the execution" Quoted in William S. Stryker, *The Battle of Monmouth* (Princeton: Princeton University Press, 1927), 102.

295 Twenty had "dropped dead from the great heat" Ewald, *Diary*, 135.

295 "after a tedious and troublesome march" Joseph Lee Boyle, ed., *From Redcoat to Rebel: The Thomas Sullivan Journal* (Bowie, Maryland: Heritage Books, 1997), 223–24.

295 "Mr. Washington might yet afford" Clinton, *American Rebellion*, 91.

297 "every idea of a decisive action" Ibid.

297 "I could not entertain" Ibid.

298 "got between the wagons" Baurmeister, *Revolution in America*, 186.

299 "made Tracks Quick Step" Brown and Peckham, *Journals of Henry Dearborn*, 126.

299 "more or less intact" Showman, *Greene Papers*, 2:454.

300 "fainted and given out with the heat" Wild, "Journal," 110.

300 "that he was a soldier" Lee, *Papers*, 3:73.

300 "By God!" Ibid.

300 "swore that day" Quoted in Grizzard, *George Washington*, 222.

300 "damned poltroon" Quoted in Stryker, *Battle of Monmouth*, 180.

300 "Sir. Sir." Lee, *Papers*, 3:78.

300 "that from a variety of contradictory intelligence" Ibid., 3:81.

301 "looked about and said" Ibid., 3:75.

301 "encouraged the men" McHenry, *Journal of a March*, 6.

301 "We shall check them" Quoted in Stryker, *Battle of Monmouth*, 183.

301 "That's right, my dear General" Lee, *Papers,* 3:201.

302 "like a Newmarket jockey" Quoted in Theodore Thayer, *The Making of a Scapegoat: Washington and Lee at Monmouth* (Port Washington, New York: Kennikat Press, 1976), 55.

302 "if any thing Can be Call'd Musical" Brown and Peckham, *Journals of Henry Dearborn,* 127.

303 "The commander in Chief was every where" Showman, *Greene Papers,* 2:451.

303 "America owes a great deal" Syrett, *Papers of Alexander Hamilton,* 1:512.

303 "General Washington seemed to arrest" Idzerda, *Lafayette in the Age of the American Revolution,* 2:11.

303 behaving "very Coolly" Brown and Peckham, *Journals of Henry Dearborn,* 128.

304 "repulsed very superior numbers" Clinton, *American Rebellion,* 97.

304 "The Commander in Chief congratulates" General Orders, June 29, 1778 (Library of Congress: Washington Papers).

304 "publickly unite" General Orders, June 30, 1778 (Library of Congress: Washington Papers).

304 "Nothing, surely" Clinton, *American Rebellion,* 97.

305 "Washington's scapegoat" Thayer, *Making of a Scapegoat,* 104.

305 "very singular expressions" Charles Lee to GW, c. June 30, 1778 (Library of Congress: Washington Papers).

306 "The Anniversary of the Declaration" General Orders, July 3, 1778 (Library of Congress: Washington Papers).

306 "Perpetual and undisturbed Independence" General Orders, July 4, 1778 (Library of Congress: Washington Papers).

306 "[I] am very happy to hear" Benedict Arnold to GW, July 8, 1778 (Library of Congress: Washington Papers).

306 "The talents and great actions" D'Estaing to GW, July 8, 1778 (Library of Congress: Washington Papers).

16. The Dark Before the Dawn

Primary sources for this chapter were taken from various published volumes of *Papers, Revolutionary War Series,* and copies of unpublished documents in the library of the Papers of George Washington documentary editing project. Secondary sources include Chester G. Hearn, *George Washington's Schooners: The First American Navy* (1995); Dale Van Every, *A Company of Heroes: The American Frontier, 1775–1783* (1962); Samuel Smith, *Winter at Morristown, 1779–1780: The Darkest Hour* (1979); John Buchanan, *The Road to Guilford Courthouse: The American Revolution in the Carolinas* (1997); and Benjamin Quarles, *The Negro in the American Revolution* (1961). Despite its many merits, Henry Wiencek's *An Imperfect God: George Washington, His Slaves, and the Creation of America* (2003) contains a number of significant misconceptions about Washington's attitudes toward black troops and their role in the Continental Army during the war.

308 "turn'd mad at theyr departure" Lafayette to GW, August 25, 1778 (Lafayette College, Easton, Pennsylvania).

308 "The disagreement between the army" GW to John Sullivan, September 1, 1778 (New Hampshire Historical Society: Sullivan Papers).

309 "ardent desire" GW to John Hazelwood, October 21, 1777 (*Papers, Revolutionary War Series,* 11:569).

309 "Creep upon the ice" Quoted in ibid., 13:270.

309 "The shipping in the harbor" Frank Moore, *Diary of the American Revolution from Newspapers and Original Documents* (2 vols., New York: Charles Scribner, 1859), 2:6–7.

310 "the fellow who invented" Ibid., 7.

311 "chastisement of the savages" Ford, *Journals of the Continental Congress,* 13:252.

311 "the immediate objects" GW to John Sullivan, May 31, 1779 (Library of Congress: Washington Papers).

312 "I beg leave to suggest" Ibid.

313 "The enemy have set" GW to a Continental Congress Camp Committee, January 29, 1778 (*Papers, Revolutionary War Series,* 13:402).

313 "fictitious Indians" Quoted in ibid., 13:408.

313 "Boys, Deserters, & Negroes" GW to John Hancock, July 10–11, 1775 (ibid., 1:90).

313 "any deserter from the Ministerial army" Quoted in Pete Maslowski, "National Policy Toward the Use of Black Troops in the Revolution" (*South Carolina Historical Magazine,* 73 [January 1972]), 2.

313 "agreed unanimously to reject" Council of War, October 8, 1775 (*Papers, Revolutionary War Series,* 2:125).

314 "neither Negroes" General Orders, November 12, 1775 (ibid., 2:354).

314 Dunmore's "diabolical schemes" GW to Richard Henry Lee, December 26, 1775 (ibid., 2:611).

314 "the free negroes who have served" Ford, *Journals of the Continental Congress,* 4:60.

314 "a Battalion of Negroes" James Mitchell Varnum to GW, January 2, 1778 (*Papers, Revolutionary War Series,* 13:125).

315 "Three-quarters" of the troops Ludwig von Closen, *The Revolutionary Journal of Baron Ludwig von Closen, 1780–1783,* trans. and ed. Evelyn M. Acomb (Chapel Hill: University of North Carolina Press, 1958), 92.

315 "Cede me a number of . . . Slaves" Hamer, *Papers of Henry Laurens,* 12:305.

316 "You ask what is the General's opinion" Ibid., 12:392.

316 "has never employed much" GW to Henry Laurens, March 20, 1779 (Library of Congress: Washington Papers).

316 "We are much disgusted here" Quoted in Maslowski, "Black Troops in the Revolution," 12.

317 "a quarter" of the American troops Closen, *Journal,* 89.

317 "Return of Negroes in the Army" Return or chart, dated August 24, 1778 (Library of Congress: Washington Papers); Charles H. Lesser, ed., *The Sinews of Independence: Monthly Strength Reports of the Continental Army* (Chicago: University of Chicago Press, 1976). Of the blacks listed in the return, 399 were serving with regiments from Connecticut, Massachusetts, and New Hampshire; 315 with regiments from Delaware, Maryland, North Carolina, and Virginia; 39 with regiments from New York, and only 2 with regiments from Pennsylvania.

317 "there were so many black soldiers" Henry Wiencek, *An Imperfect God: George Washington, His Slaves, and the Creation of America* (New York: Farrar, Straus and Giroux, 2003), 243.

319 "almost all the wild beasts" Showman, *Greene Papers,* 5:365.

320 "Those who have only been" Quoted in A. E. Zucker, *General De Kalb, Lafayette's Mentor* (Chapel Hill: University of North Carolina Press, 1966), 190.

320 "We were absolutely" Martin, *Private Yankee Doodle,* 124.

320 "The distress has in some instances" GW to the Magistrates of New Jersey, January 8, 1780 (Library of Congress: Washington Papers).

320 "with the Beating of Drums" Return Jonathan Meigs to GW, May 26, 1780 (Library of Congress: Washington Papers).

320 "Growling like soreheaded dogs" Martin, *Private Yankee Doodle,* 132.

321 "The men have borne their distress" GW to Jonathan Trumbull, Sr., May 26, 1780 (Connecticut State Library: Trumbull Papers).

321 "This matter I confess" GW to Jedediah Huntington, May 27–28, 1780 (National Archives: Papers of the Continental Congress, item 152).

321 "indubitable proof" Davies, *Documents of the American Revolution,* 17:224.

322 "The loss of Charlestown" GW to Jonathan Trumbull, Sr., June 11, 1780 (Library of Congress: Washington Papers).

323 "undergo a punishment" John Laurens to GW, October 4, 1780 (Library of Congress: Washington Papers).

323 "I am mistaken" GW to John Laurens, October 13, 1780 (Historical Society of Pennsylvania: Conarroe Collection).

323 "a gigantick overgrown monster"   Quoted in Charles Royster, *A Revolutionary People at War: The Continental Army and American Character, 1775–1783* (Chapel Hill: University of North Carolina Press, 1979), 291.

17. Victory

Another important gap in Revolutionary War scholarship was filled with the recent publication of Richard Ketchum's *Victory at Yorktown: The Campaign That Won the Revolution* (2004); see also Henry Phelps Johnston, *The Yorktown Campaign and the Surrender of Cornwallis, 1781* (1881); Burke Davis, *The Campaign That Won America: The Story of Yorktown* (1970); and Thomas J. Fleming, *Beat the Last Drum: The Siege of Yorktown, 1781* (1963). Primary documents are from volume 3 of the *Diaries;* Davies, *Documents of the American Revolution;* and unpublished manuscripts in the library of the Papers of George Washington. The best account of the last months of the war, including a beautifully moving description of Washington's journey home, is in Douglas Southall Freeman's *George Washington.*

324 "Anxious for the public good"   Horatio Gates to GW, August 30, 1780 (Library of Congress: Washington Papers).

324 "I only lament"   Showman, *Greene Papers,* 6:396.

325 "it makes the most"   Ibid., 6:588.

326 "the populace that had deserted"   Royster, *A Revolutionary People at War,* 295.

327 "The most general and unhappy mutiny"   Anthony Wayne to GW, January 2, 1781 (Library of Congress: Washington Papers).

327 "The rest of our Army"   GW to Rochambeau, January 20, 1781 (privately owned manuscript, copy in library of Papers of George Washington).

327 "Unless this dangerous spirit"   GW to Samuel Huntington, January 23, 1781 (National Archives: Papers of the Continental Congress, item 152).

328 "primary object"   Davies, *Documents of the American Revolution,* 18:256.

328 "parricide Arnold"   Thomas Jefferson to GW, January 10, 1781 (Library of Congress: Washington Papers).

328 "a Very beautifull . . . Ship"   John Brown to GW, February 4, 1781 (Library of Congress: Washington Papers).

328 "It is in my opinion essential"   GW to Rochambeau, February 15, 1781 (privately owned manuscript, copy in library of Papers of George Washington).

329 "sufficient to destroy"   Rochambeau to GW, February 12, 1781 (Library of Congress: Washington Papers).

329 "I cannot help expressing"   Davies, *Documents of the American Revolution,* 20:108.

329 "great risk unless"   Ibid., 20:114.

330 "in force to operate as we please"   Ibid., 20:145.

330 "I shall now proceed"   Ibid., 20:148.

330 "I know of no place so proper"   Ibid., 20:120.

330 "The boy cannot escape me"   quoted in Ward, *War of the Revolution,* 2:873.

331 "a superiority in the field"   Davies, *Documents of the American Revolution,* 20:198.

331 "In the present reduced State"   *Diaries,* 3:369.

332 "Should the West India fleet"   Conference with Rochambeau, May 23, 1781 (privately owned manuscript, copy in library of the Papers of George Washington).

332 "Your Excellency will be pleased"   GW to Rochambeau, June 13, 1781 (privately owned manuscript, copy in library of the Papers of George Washington).

332 "that I submitted, as I ought"   Quoted in *Diaries,* 3:385.

332 "the whole effect was rather good"   Closen, *Journal,* 91–2.

333 "In beholding this army"   Quoted in *Diaries,* 3:390.

333 "our primary Object"   Conference with Rochambeau, July 19, 1781 (privately owned manuscript, copy in library of the Papers of George Washington).

333 "slept, worn out by fatigue"   Quoted in *Diaries,* 3:401–2.

333 "have every thing in the most perfect readiness"   *Diaries,* 3:409.

335 "Matters having now come to a crisis"   *Diaries,* 3:410.

336 "princely entertainment"   Jonathan Trumbull, Jr., "Minutes of Occurrences Respecting the Siege and Capture of York in Virginia, Extracted from the Journal of Colonel Jonathan Trumbull, Secretary to the General, 1781" (*Proceedings of the Massachusetts Historical Society,* 1st series, 14 [1876]), 333.

336 "He had passed our camp"   Mary Haldane Coleman, *St. George Tucker, Citizen of No Mean City* (Richmond, Virginia: Dietz Press, 1938), 70–71.

337 "elegant supper"   Richard Butler, "General Richard Butler's Journal of the Siege of Yorktown," (*Historical Magazine,* 8 [1864]), 106.

338 "struck a few blows"   Martin, *Private Yankee Doodle,* 168.

338 "His Excellency General Washington"   Thacher, *Military Journal,* 283.

338 "severest account"   General Orders, October 9, 1781 (Library of Congress: Washington Papers).

338 "Persons whose duty"   Ibid.

338 "had a large bulldog"   Martin, *Private Yankee Doodle,* 168.

339 "Five days more"   Syrett, *Hamilton Papers,* 2:678.

339 "made a short address or harangue"   Catherine R. A. Williams, *Biography of Revolutionary Heroes: Containing the Life of Brigadier Gen. William Bar-*

ton, and also, of Captain Stephen Olney (Providence, Rhode Island: privately printed, 1839), 276.

340 "The entire column or brigade" Johann Conrad Döhla, *A Hessian Diary of the American Revolution,* trans. and ed. Bruce E. Burgoyne (Norman: University of Oklahoma Press, 1990), 171.

340 "During this attack" Ibid., 170.

340 "delay and loss" Syrett, *Hamilton Papers,* 2:681.

340 "The General reflects" General Orders, October 15, 1781 (Library of Congress: Washington Papers).

341 "Push on, my brave boys" quoted in Freeman, *George Washington,* 5:373.

341 "there was nothing to be seen" Döhla, *Hessian Diary,* 172.

341 "There was no part" Davies, *Documents of the American Revolution,* 20:246.

341 "frightful and disturbing" Closen, *Journal,* 155.

341 "We had used them" Ewald, *Diary,* 335.

341 "violent storm of wind and rain" Davies, *Documents of the American Revolution,* 20:246–47.

342 "wanton and inhuman to the last degree" Ibid.

342 "a drummer mount the enemy's parapet" Ebenezer Denny, *Military Journal of Ebenezer Denny, an Officer in the Revolutionary and Indian Wars* (Philadelphia: Historical Society of Pennsylvania, 1859), 44.

342 "An Ardent Desire" GW to Cornwallis, October 17, 1781 (Public Record Office, London, 30/11/74: Cornwallis Papers).

342 "I should be anxious" GW to de Grasse, October 17, 1781 (Library of Congress: Washington Papers).

342 "their Drums in front" Edward M. Riley, ed., "St. George Tucker Journal of the Siege of Yorktown, 1781" (*William and Mary Quarterly,* 3rd series, 5 [1948]), 392–93.

343 "showed the greatest scorn" Closen, *Journal,* 153.

343 "I have seen many soldiers" Ewald, *Diary,* 340–41.

343 "opened his arms, exclaiming wildly" George F. Scheer and Hugh Rankin, *Rebels and Redcoats* (Cleveland: World Publishing, 1957), 497.

343 "could scarcely talk for laughing" Ibid., 495.

344 "first on one cheek, then the other" Anne Fontaine Maury, ed., *Intimate Virginiana: A Century of Maury Travels by Land and Sea* (Richmond, Virginia: Dietz Press, 1941), 3.

344 "assembled under arms" *Pennsylvania Gazette* (Philadelphia), November 22, 1781.

344 "just as they were going" Heath, *Memoirs,* 337.

344 "my only apprehension" GW to Thomas Nelson, Jr., October 27, 1781 (Henry E. Huntington Library, San Marino, California).

345 "The Spectacles suit my Eyes"   GW to David Rittenhouse, February 16, 1783 (Library of Congress: Washington Papers).

345 "Our distresses are now brought"   Ford, *Journals of the Continental Congress,* 24:291–93.

346 "blindly into extremities"   Smith, *Letters of Delegates,* 19:580.

346 "much loose conversation"   Ibid., 19:557.

346 "The predicament in which I stand"   GW to Alexander Hamilton, March 4, 1783 (Library of Congress: Washington Papers).

346 an anonymous "fellow soldier"   Ford, *Journals of the Continental Congress,* 24:295–97.

347 "irregular invitation"   General Orders, March 11, 1783 (Library of Congress: Washington Papers).

347 "The general orders of yesterday"   Ford, *Journals of the Continental Congress,* 24:298–99.

347 "they must be answerable"   GW to Alexander Hamilton, March 12, 1783 (Library of Congress: Hamilton Papers).

347 "Visibly agitated"   Freeman, *George Washington,* 5:434.

347 "the goodness of his Pen"   GW to the Officers, March 15, 1783 (Massachusetts Historical Society, Boston).

349 "Gentlemen, you must pardon me"   Quoted in Freeman, *George Washington,* 5:435.

349 "observed with much pleasure"   Smith, *Letters of Delegates,* 20:646.

350 "No honor short of those"   Ibid., 20:647.

350 "to the Armies of the United States"   Address to the Officers, November 2, 1783 (Library of Congress: Washington Papers).

351 "Relieved at length"   Officers to GW, November 15, 1783 (Library of Congress: Washington Papers).

351 "With a heart full of love": Tallmadge, *Memoir,* 63.

351 "the General walked across the room"   Freeman, *George Washington,* 5:468.

352 "I should do injustice"   Grizzard, *George Washington,* 382–83.

352 "At last the cold, clear waters"   Freeman, *George Washington,* 5:477–78.

18. Old Soldier

This chapter is based on various volumes of *Papers, Confederation Series; Papers, Presidential Series;* and especially *Papers: Retirement Series.* A useful study of the Quasi-War is Alexander De Conde's *The Quasi-War: The Politics and Diplomacy of the Undeclared War with France, 1797–1801* (1966).

353 "I am just beginning"   GW to Henry Knox, February 20, 1784 (*Papers, Confederation Series,* 1:137–38).

354 "The *basis* of our proceedings" GW to Lafayette, August 11, 1790 (*Papers, Presidential Series*, 6:234).

354 "observed forcibly" GW to Arthur St. Clair, October 6, 1789 (ibid., 4:141).

354 "extirpate" Indian "banditti" Walter Lowrie, et al., eds., *American State Papers: Documents, Legislative and Executive, of the Congress of the United States* (38 vols., Washington, D.C.: Gales & Seaton, 1832–61), class II: *Indian Affairs*, 1:97.

354 "My forebodings" GW to Henry Knox, November 19, 1790 (*Papers, Presidential Series*, 6:668).

355 "Sensible, Sober & brave" Memorandum on General Officers, March 9, 1792 (ibid., 10:74–75).

356 "Government is set at defiance" Quoted in Grizzard, *George Washington*, 350.

358 "maintain inviolate the relations" Quoted in ibid., 395–96.

358 Washington's "memory was already sensibly" Thomas Jefferson, *Writings*, ed. Merrill Peterson (New York: Literary Classics, 1984), 673.

358 "exactly like mine" quoted in Grizzard, *George Washington*, 2.

359 "No! No!" Quoted in Alexander De Conde, *The Quasi-War: The Politics and Diplomacy of the Undeclared War with France, 1797–1801* (New York: Scribner, 1966), 49.

359 "Whether we consider the injuries" Julian Ursyn Niemcewicz, *Under Their Vine and Fig Tree: Travels Through America in 1797–1799, 1805, with Some Further Account of Life in New Jersey*, trans. and ed. Metchie J. E. Budka (Elizabeth, New Jersey: Grassmann, 1965), 107.

360 "Lieutenant General and Commander in Chief" Commission, July 4, 1798 (*Papers, Retirement Series*, 2:404).

360 "intoxicated," "rapacious" GW to Henry Hill, July 15, 1798 (ibid., 2:373).

360 "peaceful abode" GW to John Adams, July 13, 1798 (ibid., 2:403).

361 "I know not where" GW to Henry Knox, July 16, 1798 (ibid., 2:424).

361 "The matter is" GW to James McHenry, September 16, 1798 (ibid., 3:4).

362 "in the presence of almighty God" Henry Knox to GW, November 4, 1798 (ibid., 3:178).

362 "course I should have pursued" GW to Timothy Pickering, March 3, 1799 (ibid., 3:406).

362 "It would be a matter" GW to Jonathan Trumbull, Jr., July 21, 1799 (ibid., 4:202–3).

363 "as a species of Public property" quoted in ibid, 4:500.

363 "let it go as it came" Tobias Lear Account of GW's Death, December 14, 1799 (ibid, 4:548).

364 "Do you arrange & record" Ibid., 5:549.

19. First in War?

365 Washington "merits comparison"   R. Ernest Dupuy and Trevor N. Dupuy, *The Encyclopedia of Military History, from 3500 B.C. to the Present* (New York: Harper & Row, 1970), 663.

368 "I shall be always happy"   GW to Charles Lee, June 15, 1778 (Library of Congress: Washington Papers).

368 "No warm, outgoing person"   Higginbotham, *War of American Independence,* 413.

BIBLIOGRAPHY

My position as an associate editor with the Papers of George Washington documentary editing project in Charlottesville, Virginia, gives me access to the largest collection of Washington-related research materials in existence. This collection includes copies of 135,000 manuscript documents, mostly letters to and from Washington, gathered from public and private repositories all over the world. It also includes a massive array of books, articles, pamphlets, newspapers, and other printed materials about Washington and related aspects of eighteenth-century America used by the editors of the project in preparing annotation for its print publication *The Papers of George Washington*. The project's library was my main resource for the primary and secondary materials used in writing this book. As such, a complete bibliography for *General George Washington* would run hundreds of pages and largely replicate the bibliographies that appear at the beginning of each volume of *The Papers of George Washington*. I have, accordingly, listed below only quoted sources and those to which I referred frequently in the course of my research. Readers interested in a complete list are referred to individual volumes of *The Papers of George Washington,* or are invited to visit the project in person.

Manuscript Sources and Newspapers

Most of the manuscripts cited are taken from photocopies in the library of the Papers of George Washington documentary editing project in Charlottesville, Virginia, with the original repository noted in the citation. The only exceptions to this are documents in the James Grant Papers, which were consulted from microfilm at the Library of Congress in Washington, D.C. Newspapers, including the *Pennsylvania Gazette* (Philadelphia and York) and the *Virginia Gazette* (Williamsburg), were consulted from electronic editions and microfilms at the University of Virginia.

Published Sources

Abbot, W. W., Dorothy Twohig, Philander D. Chase, et al., eds. *The Papers of George Washington.* 5 series, 45 vols. to date. Charlottesville: University of Virginia Press, 1983–.

Adams, Charles Francis. *Studies Military and Diplomatic, 1775–1865.* New York: Macmillan, 1911.

Alberts, Robert C. *The Most Extraordinary Adventures of Major Robert Stobo.* Boston: Houghton Mifflin, 1965.

Alden, John R. *General Charles Lee: Traitor or Patriot?* Baton Rouge: Louisiana State University Press, 1951.

———. *George Washington: A Biography.* Baton Rouge: Louisiana State University Press, 1984.

Ambler, Charles H. *George Washington and the West.* Chapel Hill: University of North Carolina Press, 1936.

Anderson, Fred. *Crucible of War: The Seven Years' War and the Fate of Empire in British North America, 1754–1766.* New York: Alfred A. Knopf, 2000.

André, John. *Major John André's Journal: Operations of the British Army under Lieutenant Generals Sir William Howe and Sir Henry Clinton, June 1777 to November 1778.* New York: Arno Press, 1968 (reprint of 1930 edition).

Atwood, Rodney. *The Hessians: Mercenaries from Hessen-Kassel in the American Revolution.* New York: Cambridge University Press, 1980.

Baurmeister, Carl Leopold. *Revolution in America: Confidential Letters and Journals, 1776–1784, of Adjutant General Major Baurmeister of the Hessian Forces.* Translated by Bernhard A. Uhlendorf. New Brunswick, New Jersey: Rutgers University Press, 1957.

Beatty, William. "Captain William Beatty's Correspondence, 1776–1781." *Historical Magazine and Notes and Queries Concerning the Antiquities, History, and Biography of America,* 2nd series, 1 (Feb. 1867), 147–50.

Bixby, Samuel. "Diary of Samuel Bixby." *Proceedings of the Massachusetts Historical Society,* 1st series, 14 (1875–76), 285–98.

Black, Jeremy. *War for America: The Fight for Independence, 1775–1783.* New York: St. Martin's Press, 1991.

Bland, Theodorick. *The Bland Papers: Being a Selection from the Manuscripts of Colonel Theodorick Bland, Jr., of Prince George County, Virginia.* Edited by Charles Campbell. 2 vols. Petersburg, Virginia: E. and J. C. Ruffin, 1840.

Boatner, Mark Mayo. *Encyclopedia of the American Revolution.* New York: D. McKay, 1966.

Bodle, Wayne K. *The Valley Forge Winter: Civilians and Soldiers in War.* University Park: Pennsylvania State University Press, 2002.

Bodle, Wayne K., and Jacqueline Thibaut. *Valley Forge Historical Research Proj-*

ect. 3 vols. Valley Forge, Pennsylvania: U.S. Department of the Interior, National Park Service, 1980.

Bowler, R. Arthur. *Logistics and the Failure of the British Army in America, 1775–1783.* Princeton, New Jersey: Princeton University Press, 1975.

Boyd, Julian P., et al., eds. *The Papers of Thomas Jefferson.* 29 vols. to date. Princeton, New Jersey: Princeton University Press, 1950–.

Boyd, Thomas. *Mad Anthony Wayne.* New York: Charles Scribner's Sons, 1929.

Boyle, Joseph Lee. "From Saratoga to Valley Forge: The Diary of Lt. Samuel Armstrong." *Pennsylvania Magazine of History and Biography,* 121 (1997), 237–70.

———. "The Israel Angell Diary, 1 October 1777–28 February 1778." *Rhode Island History* 58 (2000), 107–38.

Bradford, S. Sydney, ed. "A British Officer's Revolutionary War Journal, 1776–1778." *Maryland Historical Magazine,* 56 (1961), 150–75.

Brock, R. A., ed. *The Official Records of Robert Dinwiddie, Lieutenant-Governor of the Colony of Virginia, 1751–1758.* 2 vols. Richmond: Virginia Historical Society, 1883–84.

Browne, William Hand, ed. *Journal and Correspondence of the Maryland Council of Safety. Archives of Maryland.* vol. 12. Baltimore: *Maryland Historical Society,* 1882.

Buchanan, John. *The Road to Guilford Courthouse: The American Revolution in the Carolinas.* New York: John Wiley & Sons, 1997.

Bullitt, Thomas W. *My Life at Oxmoor: Life on a Farm in Kentucky Before the War.* Louisville, Kentucky: John P. Morton, 1911.

Burgoyne, Bruce E., ed. and trans. *Diaries of Two Anspach Jaegers, Lt. Heinrich Carl Phillipp von Feilitzsch and Lt. Christian Friedrich Bartholomai.* Bowie, Maryland: Heritage Books, 1997.

Burgoyne, Bruce E., ed. *Enemy Views: The American Revolutionary War as Recorded by the Hessian Participants.* Bowie, Maryland: Heritage Books, 1996.

Butler, Richard. "General Richard Butler's Journal of the Siege of Yorktown." *Historical Magazine,* 8 (1864), 102–12.

Butterfield, L. H., et al., eds. *Adams Family Correspondence.* 6 vols. to date. Cambridge, Massachusetts: Harvard University Press, 1963–.

———. *Diary and Autobiography of John Adams.* 4 vols. Cambridge, Massachusetts: Harvard University Press, 1961.

Callahan, North. *Henry Knox: General Washington's General.* New York: Rinehart, 1958.

Carp, E. Wayne. *To Starve the Army at Pleasure: Continental Army Administration and American Political Culture, 1775–1783.* Chapel Hill: University of North Carolina Press, 1984.

Champagne, Roger J. *Alexander McDougall and the American Revolution in New York.* Schenectady, New York: Union College Press, 1975.

Chase, Philander Dean. "Baron von Steuben in the War of Independence." Ph.D. diss., Duke University, 1972.

Clark, Joseph. "Diary of Joseph Clark, Attached to the Continental Army from May, 1778, to November, 1779." *Proceedings of the New Jersey Historical Society,* 7:3 (1854), 93–110.

Clark, William Bell, et al., eds. *Naval Documents of the American Revolution.* 10 vols. to date. Washington, D.C.: Naval Historical Center, Department of the Navy, 1964–.

Cleland, Hugh. *George Washington in the Ohio Valley.* Pittsburgh, Pennsylvania: University of Pittsburgh Press, 1955.

Clinton, Henry. *The American Rebellion: Sir Henry Clinton's Narrative of His Campaigns, 1775–1782, with an Appendix of Original Documents.* Edited by William B. Willcox. New Haven, Connecticut: Yale University Press, 1954.

Closen, Ludwig von. *The Revolutionary Journal of Baron Ludwig von Closen, 1780–1783.* Translated and edited by Evelyn M. Acomb. Chapel Hill: University of North Carolina Press, 1958.

Coleman, Mary Haldane. *St. George Tucker, Citizen of No Mean City.* Richmond, Virginia: Dietz Press, 1938.

Commager, Henry Steele, and Richard B. Morris, eds. *The Spirit of 'Seventy-Six: The Story of the American Revolution as Told by Participants.* New York: Harper and Row, 1967 (reprint of the 1958 edition).

Conway, Moncure D. *Barons of the Potomack and the Rappahannock.* New York: Grolier Club, 1892.

Cooch, Edward W. *The Battle of Cooch's Bridge, Delaware: September 3, 1777.* Cooch's Bridge, Delaware: privately printed, 1940.

Crane, Elaine Forman, ed. *The Diary of Elizabeth Drinker.* 3 vols. Boston: Northeastern University Press, 1994.

Custis, George Washington Parke. *Recollections and Private Memoirs of Washington.* New York: Derby and Jackson, 1860.

Darlington, Mary Carson, ed. *History of Colonel Henry Bouquet and the Western Frontiers of Pennsylvania, 1747–1764.* Privately printed, 1920.

Davies, K. G., ed. *Documents of the American Revolution, 1770–1783 (Colonial Office Series).* 21 vols. Shannon, Ireland: Irish University Press, 1972–81.

Davis, Burke. *The Campaign That Won America: The Story of Yorktown.* New York: Dial Press, 1970.

Dawson, Henry B., ed. *New York City During the American Revolution: Being a Collection of Original Papers (Now First Published) from the Manuscripts in the Possession of the Mercantile Library Association, of New York City.* New York: Mercantile Library Association of the City of New York, 1861.

Dayton, Elias. "Papers of General Elias Dayton Received from His Grandson,

Aaron Ogden Dayton, Esq." *Proceedings of the New Jersey Historical Society*, 9 (1857), 175–94.

De Conde, Alexander. *The Quasi-War: The Politics and Diplomacy of the Undeclared War with France, 1797–1801.* New York: Scribner, 1966.

Denny, Ebenezer. *Military Journal of Ebenezer Denny, an Officer in the Revolutionary and Indian Wars.* Philadelphia: Historical Society of Pennsylvania, 1859.

Döhla, Johann Conrad. *A Hessian Diary of the American Revolution.* Translated and edited by Bruce E. Burgoyne. Norman: University of Oklahoma Press, 1990.

Douglas, William. "Letters Written During the Revolutionary War by Colonel William Douglas to His Wife Covering the Period July 19, 1775, to December 5, 1776." *New-York Historical Society Quarterly Bulletin*, 12 (1929), 145–54; 13 (1929–30), 37–40, 79–82, 118–22, 157–62; 14 (1930), 38–42.

Downman, Francis. *The Services of Lieut.-Colonel Francis Downman, R.A. in France, North America, and the West Indies, Between the Years 1758 and 1784.* Edited by F. A. Whinyates. Woolwich: Royal Artillery Institution, 1898.

Drake, Francis Samuel. *Life and Correspondence of Henry Knox, Major-General in the American Revolutionary Army.* Boston: S. G. Drake, 1873.

Duane, William, ed. *Extracts from the Diary of Christopher Marshall, Kept in Philadelphia and Lancaster, During the American Revolution, 1774–1781.* New York: New York Times, 1969 (reprint of the 1877 edition).

Duncan, Henry. "Journals of Henry Duncan, Captain, Royal Navy, 1776–1782." Edited by John Knox Laughton. *The Naval Miscellany*, vol. 1. *Publications of the Navy Records Society*, 20 (1902), 105–219.

Dupuy, R. Ernest, and Trevor N. Dupuy. *The Encyclopedia of Military History, from 3500 B.C. to the Present.* New York: Harper & Row, 1970.

Dwyer, William M. *The Day Is Ours! November 1776–January 1777: An Inside View of the Battles of Trenton and Princeton.* New York: Viking Press, 1983.

Ewald, Johann. *Diary of the American War: A Hessian Journal.* Translated and edited by Joseph P. Tustin. New Haven: Yale University Press, 1979.

Fields, Joseph E., ed. *"Worthy Partner": The Papers of Martha Washington.* Westport, Connecticut: Greenwood Press, 1994.

Fischer, David Hackett. *Washington's Crossing.* New York: Oxford University Press, 2004.

Fischer, Joseph R. *A Well-Executed Failure: The Sullivan Campaign Against the Iroquois, July–September 1779.* Columbia: University of South Carolina Press, 1997.

Fitzpatrick, John C., ed. *The Writings of George Washington.* 39 vols. Washington, D.C.: U.S. Government Printing Office, 1931–44.

Fleming, Thomas J. *Beat the Last Drum: The Siege of Yorktown, 1781*. New York: St. Martin's Press, 1963.

Flexner, James Thomas. *George Washington in the American Revolution (1775–1783)*. Boston: Little, Brown and Company, 1968.

Forbes, John. *Writings of General John Forbes Relating to His Service in North America*. New York: Arno Press, 1971.

Force, Peter, ed. *American Archives*. 9 vols. Washington, D.C., 1837–53.

Ford, Paul Leicester. *The True George Washington*. Philadelphia: J. B. Lippincott Company, 1904.

Ford, Worthington Chauncey. *The Spurious Letters Attributed to Washington*. Brooklyn, New York: privately printed, 1889.

Ford, Worthington Chauncey, et al., eds. *Journals of the Continental Congress*. 34 vols. Washington, D.C.: Government Printing Office, 1904–37.

Fortescue, John William, ed. *The Correspondence of King George the Third from 1760 to December 1783, Printed from the Original Papers in the Royal Archives at Windsor Castle*. 6 vols. London: Macmillan, 1927–28.

Freeman, Douglas Southall. *George Washington: A Biography*. 7 vols. New York: Charles Scribner's Sons, 1948–57.

French, Allen. *The First Year of the American Revolution*. New York: Houghton Mifflin, 1934.

Frey, Sylvia R. *The British Soldier in America: A Social History of Military Life in the Revolutionary Period*. Austin: University of Texas Press, 1981.

Gerlach, Don R. *Philip Schuyler and the American Revolution in New York, 1733–1777*. Lincoln: University of Nebraska Press, 1964.

Gifford, Edward S. *The American Revolution in the Delaware Valley*. Philadelphia: Pennsylvania Society of Sons of the Revolution, 1976.

Gist, Christopher. *Christopher Gist's Journals with Historical, Geographical and Ethnological Notes and Biographies of His Contemporaries*. Edited by William Darlington. Pittsburgh: J. R. Weldin, 1893.

Godfrey, Carlos E. *The Commander-in-Chief's Guard, Revolutionary War*. Washington, D.C.: Stevenson-Smith, 1904.

Gordon, William. *The History of the Rise, Progress, and Establishment, of the Independence of the United States of America: Including an Account of the Late War; and of the Thirteen Colonies, from their Origin to that Period*. 4 vols. London: Charles Dilly and James Buckland, 1788.

Graydon, Alexander. *Memoirs of His Own Time. With Reminiscences of the Men and Events of the Revolution*. Edited by John Stockton Littell. Philadelphia: Lindsay and Blakiston, 1846.

Greenman, Jeremiah. *Diary of a Common Soldier in the American Revolution, 1775–1783: An Annotated Edition of the Military Journal of Jeremiah Green-*

man. Edited by Robert C. Bray and Paul E. Bushnell. DeKalb: Northern Illinois University Press, 1978.

Greenwood, Isaac J., ed. *The Revolutionary Services of John Greenwood of Boston and New York, 1775–1783.* New York: De Vinne Press, 1922.

Grizzard, Frank E., Jr. *George Washington: A Biographical Companion.* Santa Barbara, California: ABC-CLIO, 2002.

Gruber, Ira D. *The Howe Brothers and the American Revolution.* New York: Athenaeum, 1972.

Hall, Charles Samuel. *Life and Letters of General Samuel Holden Parsons, Major General in the Continental Army and Chief Judge of the Northwestern Territory, 1737–1789.* Binghamton, New York: Otseningo Publishing, 1905.

Hamer, Philip M., George C. Rogers, Jr., David R. Chesnutt, et al., eds. *The Papers of Henry Laurens.* 16 vols. to date. Columbia: University of South Carolina Press, 1968–.

Hamilton, Charles, ed. *Braddock's Defeat.* Norman: University of Oklahoma Press, 1959.

Harding, Richard. *Amphibious Warfare in the Eighteenth Century: The British Expedition to the West Indies 1740–1742.* Woodbridge, Suffolk: The Royal Historical Society/Boydell Press, 1991.

Harrington, J. C. "The Metamorphosis of Fort Necessity." *Western Pennsylvania Historical Magazine,* 37 (1954–55), 181–88.

Harvey, Robert. *A Few Bloody Noses: The American War of Independence.* London: John Murray, 2001.

Hastings, Hugh, and J. A. Holden, eds. *The Public Papers of George Clinton, First Governor of New York, 1777–1795, 1801–1804.* 10 vols. New York: AMS Press, 1973 (reprint of 1899–1914 editions).

Hazard, Samuel, et al., eds. *Pennsylvania Archives.* 9 series, 138 vols. Philadelphia and Harrisburg: various publishers, 1852–1949.

Hearn, Chester G. *George Washington's Schooners: The First American Navy.* Annapolis, Maryland: Naval Institute Press, 1995.

Heath, William. *Heath's Memoirs of the American War.* Edited by Rufus Rockwell Wilson. New York: A. Wessels Company, 1904 (reprint of the 1798 edition).

Higginbotham, Don. *The War of American Independence: Military Attitudes, Policies, and Practice, 1763–1789.* New York: Macmillan, 1971.

———. *George Washington and the American Military Tradition.* Athens: University of Georgia Press, 1985.

———. *George Washington: Uniting a Nation.* Lanham, Maryland: Rowman and Littlefield, 2002.

Higginbotham, Don, ed. *George Washington Reconsidered.* Charlottesville: University Press of Virginia, 2001.

Holmes, Asher. "Letter Concerning the Battle at Germantown, 1777." *New Jersey Historical Society Proceedings,* 7 (1922), 34–35.

Howard, John Eager. "Col. John Eager Howard's Account of the Battle of Germantown." *Maryland Historical Magazine,* 4 (1909), 314–20.

Hughes, Rupert. *George Washington: The Savior of the States.* New York: William Morrow, 1930.

Humphreys, David. *David Humphreys' "Life of General Washington": with George Washington's "Remarks."* Edited by Rosemarie Zagarri. Athens: University of Georgia Press, 1991.

Idzerda, Stanley J., et al., eds. *Lafayette in the Age of the American Revolution: Selected Letters and Papers, 1776–1790.* 5 vols. to date. Ithaca, New York: Cornell University Press, 1977–.

Irving, Washington. *Life of George Washington.* 5 vols. New York: G. P. Putnam, 1855–59.

Jackson, Donald, and Dorothy Twohig, eds. *The Diaries of George Washington.* 6 vols. Charlottesville: University Press of Virginia, 1976–79.

Jackson, John W. *The Pennsylvania Navy, 1775–1781: The Defense of the Delaware.* New Brunswick, New Jersey: Rutgers University Press, 1974.

———. *With the British Army in Philadelphia, 1777–1778.* San Rafael, California: Presidio Press, 1979.

Jefferson, Thomas. *Writings.* Edited by Merrill Peterson. New York: Literary Classics, 1984.

Johnston, Henry Phelps. *The Battle of Harlem Heights, September 16, 1776.* New York: AMS Press, 1970 (reprint of 1897 edition).

———. *The Yorktown Campaign and the Surrender of Cornwallis.* 1881. Reprint. Spartanburg, S.C.: The Reprint Co., 1973.

Jones, Thomas. *History of New York During the Revolutionary War, and of the Leading Events in the Other Colonies at That Period.* Edited by Edward F. De-Lancey. 2 vols. New York: New-York Historical Society, 1879.

Kahler, Gerald Edward. "Washington in Glory, America in Tears: The Nation Mourns the Death of George Washington, 1799–1800." Ph.D. diss., College of William and Mary, 2003.

Kemble, Stephen. *The Kemble Papers.* 2 vols. Collections of the New-York Historical Society, vols. 16–17. New York: New-York Historical Society, 1884–85.

Ketchum, Richard M. *Divided Loyalties: How the American Revolution Came to New York.* New York: Henry Holt, 2002.

———. *Victory at Yorktown: The Campaign That Won the Revolution.* New York: Henry Holt, 2004.

Knollenberg, Bernhard. *Washington and the Revolution, a Reappraisal; Gates, Conway, and the Continental Congress.* New York: Macmillan, 1940.

Koontz, Louis Knott, ed. *Robert Dinwiddie Correspondence*. Berkeley: University of California Press, 1951.

Kopperman, Paul E. *Braddock at the Monongahela*. Pittsburgh: University of Pittsburgh Press, 1977.

Krafft, John Charles Philip von. *Journal of Lieutenant John Charles Philip von Krafft*. New York: Arno Press, 1968 (reprint of 1882 edition).

Kwasny, Mark V. *Washington's Partisan War, 1775–1783*. Kent, Ohio: Kent State University Press, 1996.

Labaree, Leonard Woods, et al., eds. *The Papers of Benjamin Franklin*. 37 vols. to date. New Haven: Yale University Press, 1959–.

Lacey, John, Jr. "Memoirs of Brigadier-General John Lacey, of Pennsylvania." *Pennsylvania Magazine of History and Biography*, 25 (1901), 1–13, 191–207, 341–54, 498–515; 26 (1902), 101–11, 265–70.

Leduc, Gilbert Francis. *Washington and "the Murder of Jumonville."* Boston: La Société Historique Franco-Américaine, 1943.

Lee, Charles. *The Lee Papers*. 4 vols. *Collections of the New-York Historical Society*, vols. 4–7. New York: New-York Historical Society, 1872–75.

Lee, Henry. *Memoirs of the War in the Southern Department of the United States*. 2 vols. Philadelphia: Bradford and Inskeep, 1812.

Lesser, Charles H. *The Sinews of Independence: Monthly Strength Reports of the Continental Army*. Chicago: University of Chicago Press, 1976.

Lobdell, Jared C., ed. "The Revolutionary War Journal of Sergeant Thomas McCarty." *Proceedings of the New Jersey Historical Society*, 82 (1964), 29–46.

Longmore, Paul K. *The Invention of George Washington*. Charlottesville: University Press of Virginia, 1999 (reprint of 1988 edition).

Lowell, Edward J. *The Hessians and the Other German Auxiliaries of Great Britain in the Revolutionary War*. Williamstown, Massachusetts: Corner House, 1970 (reprint of 1884 edition).

Lowrie, Walter, et al., eds. *American State Papers: Documents, Legislative and Executive, of the Congress of the United States*. 38 vols. Washington, D.C.: Gales & Seaton, 1832–61.

Lundin, Leonard. *Cockpit of the Revolution: The War for Independence in New Jersey*. New York: Octagon Books, 1972 (reprint of 1940 edition).

McDowell, Jr., William, ed. "Affidavit of John Shaw." *Colonial Records of South Carolina: Documents Relating to Indian Affairs, 1754–1757*. 2nd series, vol. 2, pp. 3–7. Columbia: University of South Carolina Press, 1970.

McGuire, Thomas G. *The Surprise of Germantown, or, The Battle of Cliveden*. Gettysburg, Pennsylvania: Thomas Publications, 1994.

McHenry, James. *Journal of a March, a Battle, and a Waterfall: Being the Version Elaborated by James McHenry from His Diary of the Year 1778, Begun at Valley*

Forge, & Containing Accounts of the British, the Indians, and the Battle of Monmouth. Greenwich, Connecticut: privately printed, 1945.

McIlwaine, H. R., ed. *Official Letters of the Governors of the State of Virginia.* 3 vols. Richmond: Virginia State Library, 1926–29.

McIlwaine, H. R., Wilmer L. Hall, and Benjamin Hillman, eds. *Executive Journals of the Council of Colonial Virginia.* 6 vols. Richmond: Virginia State Library, 1925–66.

MacKenzie, Frederick. *Diary of Frederick Mackenzie, Giving a Daily Narrative of His Military Service as an Officer of the Regiment of Royal Welch Fusiliers During the Years 1775–1781 in Massachusetts Rhode Island and New York.* 2 vols. Cambridge, Massachusetts: Harvard University Press, 1930.

Mackesy, Piers. *The War for America: 1775–1783.* Lincoln: University of Nebraska Press, 1992 (reprint of 1964 edition).

McMichael, James. "Diary of Lieutenant James McMichael of the Pennsylvania Line, 1776–1778." *Pennsylvania Magazine of History and Biography,* 16 (1892), 129–59.

Manders, Eric I. *The Battle of Long Island.* Monmouth Beach, New Jersey: Philip Freneau Press, 1978.

Markland, John. "Revolutionary Services of Captain John Markland." *Pennsylvania Magazine of History and Biography,* 9 (1885), 102–12.

Marshall, John. *The Life of George Washington, Commander in Chief of the American Forces, During the War Which Established the Independence of His Country, and First President of the United States.* 5 vols. Philadelphia: C. P. Wayne, 1804–7.

Martin, Joseph Plumb. *Private Yankee Doodle: Being a Narrative of Some of the Adventures, Dangers and Sufferings of a Revolutionary Soldier.* Edited by George F. Scheer. Boston: Little, Brown, 1962.

Martyn, Charles. *The Life of Artemas Ward: The First Commander-in-Chief of the American Revolution.* New York: Artemas Ward, 1921.

Maslowski, Pete. "National Policy Toward the Use of Black Troops in the Revolution," *South Carolina Historical Magazine,* 73 (January 1972), 1–17.

"Massacre at Paoli." *Historical Magazine,* 4 (November 1860), 346–47.

Mattern, David B. *Benjamin Lincoln and the American Revolution.* Columbia: University of South Carolina Press, 1995.

Maury, Anne Fontaine, ed. *Intimate Virginiana: A Century of Maury Travels by Land and Sea.* Richmond, Virginia: Dietz Press, 1941.

A Memorial Containing a Summary View of Facts, with Their Authorities. In Answer to the Observations Sent by the English Ministry to the Courts of Europe. Translated from the French. New York: H. Guine, 1757.

Miller, Lillian, ed. *The Selected Papers of Charles Willson Peale and His Family.* 4 vols. New Haven, Connecticut: Yale University Press, 1983–96.

Montresor, John. *The Montresor Journals.* Edited by G. D. Scull. Collections of the New-York Historical Society, vol. 14. New York. New-York Historical Society, 1882.

Moore, Frank. *Diary of the American Revolution from Newspapers and Original Documents.* 2 vols. New York: Charles Scribner, 1859.

Muenchhausen, Friedrich von. *At General Howe's Side, 1776–1778: The Diary of General William Howe's Aide de Camp, Captain Friedrich von Muenchhausen.* Translated by Ernst Kipping and annotated by Samuel Smith. Monmouth Beach, New Jersey: Philip Freneau Press, 1974.

Muhlenberg, Henry Melchior. *The Journals of Henry Melchior Muhlenberg.* Translated and edited by Theodore G. Tappert and John W. Doberstein. 3 vols. Philadelphia: Muhlenberg Press, 1942–58.

Muir, Dorothy Troth. *General Washington's Headquarters, 1775–1783.* Troy, Alabama: Troy State University Press, 1977.

"Narrative of George Fisher." *William and Mary Quarterly,* 1st series, 17 (1908–9), 100–39, 147–76.

Nelson, Paul David. *General Horatio Gates: A Biography.* Baton Rouge: Louisiana State University Press, 1976.

———. *Anthony Wayne, Soldier of the Early Republic.* Bloomington: Indiana University Press, 1985.

———. *William Alexander, Lord Stirling.* Tuscaloosa: University of Alabama Press, 1987.

———. *General James Grant: Scottish Soldier and Royal Governor of East Florida.* Gainesville: University Press of Florida, 1993.

Niemcewicz, Julian Ursyn. *Under Their Vine and Fig Tree: Travels Through America in 1797–1799, 1805, with Some Further Account of Life in New Jersey.* Translated and edited by Metchie J. E. Budka. Elizabeth, New Jersey: Grassmann, 1965.

Papers. See Abbot, W. W., et al., eds. *The Papers of George Washington.*

Pargellis, Stanley, ed. *Military Affairs in North America 1748–1765: Selected Documents from the Cumberland Papers in Windsor Castle.* Hamden, Connecticut: Archon Books, 1969 (reprint of 1936 edition).

Pattison, James. "A New York Diary of the Revolutionary War," edited by Carson I. A. Ritchie. *New-York Historical Society Quarterly,* 50 (July 1966), 221–80, 401–46.

Peckham, Howard Henry. *The Toll of Independence: Engagements and Battle Casualties of the American Revolution.* Chicago: University of Chicago Press, 1974.

Pennypacker, Morton. *General Washington's Spies on Long Island and in New York.* Brooklyn, New York: Long Island Historical Society, 1939.

Pickering, Octavius, and Charles W. Upham. *The Life of Timothy Pickering.* 4 vols. Boston: Little, Brown, 1867–73.

Pickering, Timothy. Letter of August 23, 1826. *North American Review,* new series, 23 (October 1826), 425–30.

Pinckney, Charles Cotesworth. "The Battles of Brandywine and Germantown." *Historical Magazine,* 10 (July 1866), 202–4.

Pleasants, Henry. "The Battle of Paoli." *Pennsylvania Magazine of History and Biography,* 72 (1948), 44–53.

Potts, William J. "Battle of Germantown from a British Account." *Pennsylvania Magazine of History and Biography,* 11 (1887), 112–14.

Powell, Robert C., ed. *A Biographical Sketch of Col. Leven Powell.* Alexandria, Virginia: G. H. Ramey & Son, 1877.

Powell, William S. "A Connecticut Soldier Under Washington: Elisha Bostwick's Memoirs of the First Years of the Revolution." *William and Mary Quarterly,* 3rd series, 6 (1949), 94–107.

Prechtel, Johann Ernst. *A Hessian Officer's Diary of the American Revolution.* Translated and edited by Bruce E. Burgoyne. Bowie, Maryland: Heritage Publishers, 1994.

Quarles, Benjamin. *The Negro in the American Revolution.* New York: Norton, 1961.

R., Sergeant. "The Battle of Princeton." *Pennsylvania Magazine of History and Biography,* 20 (1896), 515–19.

Reed, John F. *Campaign to Valley Forge: July 1, 1777–December 19, 1777.* Philadelphia: University of Pennsylvania Press, 1965.

Reed, Joseph. "General Joseph Reed's Narrative of the Movements of the American Army in the Neighborhood of Trenton in the Winter of 1776–77." *Pennsylvania Magazine of History and Biography,* 8 (1884), 391–402.

Reed, William Bradford. *Life and Correspondence of Joseph Reed: Military Secretary of Washington, at Cambridge, Adjutant-General of the Continental Army, Member of the Congress of the United States, and President of the Executive Council of the State of Pennsylvania.* 2 vols. Philadelphia: Lindsay and Blackiston, 1847.

"Revolutionary Services of Captain John Markland." *Pennsylvania Magazine of History and Biography,* 9 (1885), 102–12.

Rice, Howard C., Jr., ed. *Travels in North America in the Years 1780, 1781, and 1782 by the Marquis de Chastellux.* 2 vols. Chapel Hill: University of North Carolina Press, 1963.

Riley, Edward M., ed. "St. George Tucker Journal of the Siege of Yorktown, 1781." *William and Mary Quarterly,* 3rd series, 5 (1948), 375–95.

Risch, Erna. *Quartermaster Support of the Army: A History of the Corps, 1775–1939.* Washington, D.C.: Quartermaster Historian's Office, Office of the Quartermaster General, 1962.

———. *Supplying Washington's Army.* Washington, D.C.: U.S. Army Center of Military History, 1981.

Robertson, Archibald. *Archibald Robertson, Lieutenant General Royal Engineers: His Diaries and Sketches in America, 1762–1780.* Edited by Harry Miller Lydenberg. New York: New York Public Library, 1930.

Rodney, Caesar A., ed. *Diary of Captain Thomas Rodney, 1776–1777.* Wilmington: Historical Society of Delaware, 1888.

Royster, Charles. *A Revolutionary People at War: The Continental Army and American Character, 1775–1783.* Chapel Hill: University of North Carolina Press, 1979.

———. *Light-Horse Harry Lee and the Legacy of the American Revolution.* New York: Alfred A. Knopf, 1981.

Rush, Benjamin. *The Autobiography of Benjamin Rush: His "Travels Through Life" Together with His Commonplace Book for 1789–1813.* Edited by George W. Corner. Princeton: Princeton University Press, 1948.

———. *Letters.* Edited by L. H. Butterfield. 2 vols. Princeton: Princeton University Press, 1951.

Rutland, Robert A., ed. *The Papers of George Mason, 1725–1792.* 3 vols. Chapel Hill: University of North Carolina Press, 1970.

Ryden, George Herbert, ed. *Letters to and from Caesar Rodney, 1756–1784.* Philadelphia: University of Pennsylvania Press, 1933.

Sargent, Winthrop. *The History of an Expedition Against Fort Du Quesne, in 1755.* Philadelphia: Lippincott, Grambo & Co., 1855.

Schecter, Barnet. *The Battle for New York: The City at the Heart of the American Revolution.* New York: Walker, 2002.

Scheer, George F., and Hugh Rankin. *Rebels and Redcoats.* Cleveland: World Publishing, 1957.

Schutz, John A., ed. "A Private Report of General Braddock's Defeat." *Pennsylvania Magazine of History and Biography,* 79 (1955), 374–77.

Seybolt, Robert Francis, ed. "A Contemporary British Account of General Sir William Howe's Military Operations in 1777." *Proceedings of the American Antiquarian Society,* new series, 40 (1931), 69–92.

Showman, Richard K., et al., eds. *The Papers of General Nathanael Greene.* 11 vols. to date. Chapel Hill: University of North Carolina Press, 1976–.

Slaughter, Thomas P. *The Whiskey Rebellion: Frontier Epilogue to the American Revolution.* New York: Oxford University Press, 1986.

Smith, Paul H., et al., eds. *Letters of Delegates to Congress, 1774–1789.* 25 vols. Washington, D.C.: Library of Congress, 1976–98.

Smith, Samuel. "The Papers of General Samuel Smith." *Historical Magazine and Notes and Queries concerning the Antiquities, History, and Biography of America,* 2nd series, 7 (1870), 81–92.

Smith, Samuel Stelle. *The Battle of Monmouth.* Monmouth Beach, New Jersey: Philip Freneau Press, 1964.

———. *The Battle of Trenton.* Monmouth Beach, New Jersey: Philip Freneau Press, 1965.

———. *The Battle of Princeton.* Monmouth Beach, New Jersey: Philip Freneau Press, 1967.

———. *Fight for the Delaware, 1777.* Monmouth Beach, New Jersey: Philip Freneau Press, 1970.

———. *The Battle for Brandywine.* Monmouth Beach, New Jersey: Philip Freneau Press, 1976.

———. *Winter at Morristown, 1779–1780: The Darkest Hour.* Monmouth Beach, New Jersey: Philip Freneau Press, 1979.

Sparks, Jared, ed. *The Writings of George Washington: Being His Correspondence, Addresses, Messages, and Other Papers, Official and Private, Selected and Published from the Original Manuscripts.* 12 vols. Boston: John B. Russell, 1833–37.

Stevens, Sylvester K., and Donald H. Kent, eds. *The Papers of Henry Bouquet.* 25 vols. Harrisburg: Pennsylvania Historical Commission, 1940–43.

Stryker, William S. *The Battle of Monmouth.* Princeton: Princeton University Press, 1927.

———. *The Battles of Trenton and Princeton.* Spartanburg, South Carolina: Reprint Co., 1967 (reprint of 1898 edition).

Sullivan, John. *Letters and Papers of Major-General John Sullivan, Continental Army.* Edited by Otis G. Hammond. 3 vols. Concord: New Hampshire Historical Society, 1930–39.

Sullivan, Thomas. "Before and after the Battle of Brandywine: Extracts from the Journal of Sergeant Thomas Sullivan of H.M. Forty-Ninth Regiment of Foot." *Pennsylvania Magazine of History and Biography,* 31 (1907), 406–18.

Syrett, Harold C., et al., eds. *The Papers of Alexander Hamilton.* 27 vols. New York: Columbia University Press, 1961–87.

Szymanski, Leszek. *Casimir Pulaski: A Hero of the American Revolution.* New York: Hippocrene Books, 1994.

Taaffe, Stephen R. *The Philadelphia Campaign, 1777–1778.* Lawrence: University Press of Kansas, 2003.

Tallmadge, Benjamin. *Memoir of Col. Benjamin Tallmadge, Prepared by Himself at the Request of His Children.* New York: Arno Press, 1968 (reprint of 1858 edition).

Tatum, Edward H., Jr., ed. *The American Journal of Ambrose Serle, Secretary to Lord Howe, 1776–1778.* San Marino, California: Huntington Library, 1940.

Thacher, James. *Military Journal of the American Revolution, from the Commencement to the Disbanding of the American Army: Comprising a Detailed Account of the Principal Events and Battles of the Revolution, with their Exact*

Dates, and a Biographical Sketch of the Most Prominent Generals. Hartford, Connecticut: Hurlbut, Williams, & Co., 1862.

Thayer, Theodore. *The Making of a Scapegoat: Washington and Lee at Monmouth.* Port Washington, New York: Kennikat Press, 1976.

Tilghman, Tench. *Memoir of Lieut. Col. Tench Tilghman, Secretary and Aid to Washington, Together with an Appendix, Containing Revolutionary Journals and Letters, Hitherto Unpublished.* New York: Arno Press, 1971 (reprint of 1876 edition).

Tompkins, Hamilton B. "Contemporary Account of the Battle of Germantown." *Pennsylvania Magazine of History and Biography,* 11 (1887), 330–32.

Trumbull, Benjamin. "Journal of the Campaign at New York, 1776–7." *Collections of the Connecticut Historical Society,* 7 (1899), 175–218.

Trumbull, Jonathan, Jr. "Minutes of Occurrences Respecting the Siege and Capture of York in Virginia, Extracted from the Journal of Colonel Jonathan Trumbull, Secretary to the General, 1781." *Proceedings of the Massachusetts Historical Society,* 1st series, 14 (1876), 331–38.

Tyler, Lyon G. "The Old Virginia Line in the Middle States During the American Revolution." *Tyler's Quarterly Historical and Genealogical Magazine,* 12 (1930–31), 1–43, 90–141, 198–203, 283–89.

Van Doren, Carl. *Secret History of the American Revolution.* New York: Viking Press, 1941.

Van Every, Dale. *A Company of Heroes: The American Frontier, 1775–1783.* New York: William Morrow, 1962.

Waldo, Albigence. "Diary of Albigence Waldo, of the Connecticut Line." *Pennsylvania Magazine of History and Biography,* 21 (1897), 299–323.

Walpole, Horace. *Memoirs of the Reign of King George the Second.* 3 vols. London: H. Colburn, 1847.

Ward, Christopher L. *The Delaware Continentals, 1776–1783.* Wilmington: Historical Society of Delaware, 1941.

———. *The War of the Revolution.* Edited by John Richard Alden. 2 vols. New York: Macmillan, 1952.

Ward, Harry M. *Major General Adam Stephen and the Cause of American Liberty.* Charlottesville: University Press of Virginia, 1989.

Webb, Samuel Blachley. *Correspondence and Journals of Samuel Blachley Webb.* Edited by Worthington Chauncey Ford. 3 vols. Lancaster, Pennsylvania: Wickersham Press, 1893.

Whittemore, Charles Park. *A General of the Revolution: John Sullivan of New Hampshire.* New York: Columbia University Press, 1961.

Wiencek, Henry. *An Imperfect God: George Washington, His Slaves, and the Creation of America.* New York: Farrar, Straus and Giroux, 2003.

Wild, Ebenezer. "The Journal of Ebenezer Wild (1776–1781), Who Served as Corporal, Sergeant, Ensign, and Lieutenant of the American Army of the Revolution." *Proceedings of the Massachusetts Historical Society,* 2nd series, 6 (1890–91), 79–160.

Wilkinson, James. *Memoirs of My Own Times.* 3 vols. Philadelphia: Abraham Small, 1816.

Williams, Catherine R. A. *Biography of Revolutionary Heroes: Containing the Life of Brigadier Gen. William Barton, and also, of Captain Stephen Olney.* Providence, Rhode Island: privately printed, 1839.

Wright, Robert K., Jr. *The Continental Army.* Washington, D.C.: U.S. Army Center of Military History, 1986.

Zucker, A. E. *General De Kalb, Lafayette's Mentor.* Chapel Hill: University of North Carolina Press, 1966.

INDEX

About the Author

EDWARD G. LENGEL is an associate professor at the University of Virginia, where he works as an associate editor and military history specialist on the Papers of George Washington documentary editing project. An omnivorous historian whose interests include the personal experiences of soldiers at war and World War I, he is the author of *The Irish Through British Eyes: Perceptions of Ireland in the Famine Era* and *World War I Memories: An Annotated Bibliography of Personal Accounts Published in English Since 1919*. He lives in Charlottesville, Virginia, with his wife and three children.

About the Type

This book was set in Fairfield, the first typeface from the hand of the distinguished American artist and engraver Rudolph Ruzicka (1883–1978). In its structure Fairfield displays the sober and sane qualities of the master craftsman whose talent has long been dedicated to clarity. It is this trait that accounts for the trim grace and vigor, the spirited design and sensitive balance, of this original typeface.

Rudolph Ruzicka was born in Bohemia and came to America in 1894. He set up his own shop, devoted to wood engraving and printing, in New York in 1913 after a varied career working as a wood engraver, in photoengraving and banknote printing plants, and as an art director and freelance artist. He designed and illustrated many books, and was the creator of a considerable list of individual prints—wood engravings, line engravings on copper, and aquatints.